P9-CNC-397

COMPUTER ORGANIZATION
A Top-Down Approach

COMPUTER ORGANIZATION
A Top-Down Approach

Greg W. Scragg
Computer Science Department
SUNY Geneseo

McGraw-Hill, Inc.
New York St. Louis San Francisco Auckland Bogotá
Caracas Lisbon London Madrid Mexico City Milan
Montreal New Delhi San Juan Singapore
Sydney Tokyo Toronto

This book was set in Times Roman by Publication Services.
The editor was Eric M. Munson;
the production supervisor was Kathryn Porzio.
The cover was designed by Joseph Gillians.
Project supervision was done by Publication Services.

COMPUTER ORGANIZATION
A TOP-DOWN APPROACH

6 7 8 9 10 11 12 13 14 BKMBKM 9 9 8 7

ISBN 0-07-055843-4

Library of Congress Cataloging-in-Publication Data

Scragg, Greg W.
Computer organization: a top-down approach / Greg W. Scragg.
p. cm.
Includes bibliographical references and index.
ISBN 0-07-055843-4
1. Computer organization. I. Title
QA76.9.C643S37 1992
004—dc20 91-39733

This book is printed on recycled paper containing a minimum of 50% total recycled fiber with 10% postconsumer de-inked fiber.

ABOUT THE AUTHOR

Greg W. Scragg is currently Professor and Chair of Computer Science at the State University of New York at Geneseo. He received his bachelor's degree with high honors in mathematics from the University of California at Riverside (1969), where he was also elected to the Phi Beta Kappa and Pi Mu Epsilon honor societies. He obtained his Masters (1972) and his Ph.D. in Computer Science (1974) from the University of California at San Diego, where he specialized in artificial intelligence, studying the field from the perspectives of both computer science and psychology and writing his dissertation in the area of natural language processing. Prior to accepting his present position, Dr. Scragg has served to the faculties of both engineering and liberal arts institutions in the United States and Europe. He has consulted for major computer vendors in both artificial intelligence and computer science education. He has served on several curriculum-planning groups, including the Liberal Arts Computer Science Consortium. He is also a member of the ACM subcommittee on student chapters, currently serving on the editorial board of the *ACM Student Journal*. He has published articles in the areas of artificial intelligence, human factors, and computer science education.

ABOUT THE AUTHOR

To Jamie Leigh

CONTENTS

PREFACE

THE INTENDED AUDIENCE

An unfortunate conundrum for authors of texts such as this follows from the inconsistent use of the terms "computer architecture" and "computer organization" within the computer science education community. While the two terms are distinguished conceptually in the research literature, when it come to course names and book titles, the terms are not used at all consistently. Some departments use "organization" to refer to the lower-level or introductory material and "architecture" to refer to the higher-level or advanced course. Some use exactly the reverse. Textbook titles reflect this dichotomy, with some authors subscribing to each of the two conventions. In this text, I use "computer organization" to refer to the first hardware-oriented course, usually aimed at sophomore computer science majors, with a background provided by the conventional "CS1" and "CS2" courses. This text corresponds very closely to the computer science organization courses described in the appendix to the new ACM/IEEE-CS Curricula 1991 report [ACM/IEEE], most closely to *C_J203: Computer organization*. In terms of more established or traditional curricula, the text closely corresponds to the course *CO1: Principles of computer organization*, of the Liberal Arts Computer Science Curriculum [Gibbs/Tucker], and could also be used for the course *CS3: Introduction to Computer Systems*, of the ACM Curriculum '78 (and parts of *CS4: Introduction to computer organization*) [ACM78]; or the course *CSIS3: Machine organization and assembly programming*, of the small college model [Biedler].

The typical student background for an introductory organization course includes a year of programming experience using a higher-level procedural language. That introduction includes a year of progamming experience using a block-structured higher-level language. That introduction includes modern concepts of programming, such as modularity, data abstraction, top-down design, etc. The student usually has also taken a year of college-level mathematics (calculus and/or discrete mathematics). *Computer Organization: A Top-Down Approach* assumes—and uses—that background. Typically, the organization course serves as a prerequisite for many of the advanced courses in a curriculum, ceratinly including the undergraduate offerings in operating systems, compilers, and advanced architecture. This text provides the background needed by students who take those courses.

RELATIONSHIP TO COMPUTING CURRICULA 1991

In 1991, the ACM/IEEE-CS Joint Task Force released its new curricular guidelines. These new guidelines, which represent the first major revisions by the ACM in over 10 years and in almost as long for the IEEE, will certainly have a significant impact on all computer science curricula during the next few years. The guidelines represent significant departures from earlier curricula in at least three important dimensions.

First, the task force explicitly recognizes that although the material needed by various subgroups of the computing community has a significant common core, the subgroups also have individual needs with respect to both the specific aspects which should be emphasized and the approach that should be taken to their presentation. The task force, therefore, created 10 sample curricula, each aimed at a slightly different audiences. This text embraces that spirit, with a distinct computer science emphasis; it does not attempt to serve all audiences. *Computer Organization: A Top-Down Approach* very closely resembles the course *C_J203: Computer organization*, of implementation J: A liberal arts program in computer science, but it could also be applicable for other courses and implementations such as *C_f203: Computer architecture* (F: A program in computer science (theoretical emphasis)); *C_d301: Computer organization and assembly language programming* (D: Program in computer science); *C_e203: Levels of architecture, Language and applications* (E: Program in computer science (breadth first)); *C_H203: Levels of architecture, Language and applications* (H: Liberal arts program in computer science (breadth first)); or even a combined *C_F203: Computer architecture/C_F305: Computer System and Interfaces* (F: A program in computer science (theoretical emphasis)); or *C_C301: Computer organization and assembly language programming* (C: A program in computer engineering).

Second, the Task Force embraced the three-process concept, as articulated in the Denning report [Denning]. These processes—theory, abstraction, and design—are each found in every one of the subject areas of computing. In earlier curricula, individual courses often emphasized one process, sometimes to the exclusion of others. Computer organization courses—both the assembly language-based and the digital logic-based versions—were often heavily weighted toward the design process. This text weaves all three processes into a single whole. It includes formal *theory* as embodied in binary arithmetic and Boolean algebra, *abstraction* and modeling at several levels, and the *design* of programs and circuits.

Finally, the new curricula follow the Denning report's suggestion that the early stages of computing education should be broad-based, providing overviews of all nine subject areas (e.g., algorithms, architecture, artificial intelligence, etc.) and introducing students to the recurring themes of the discipline (e.g., binding, complexity, formal models, etc.). Again, this text approaches the subject matter in the same spirit. Many themes recur throughout the text, and aspects of many subject areas are included wherever appropriate. For example, Boolean algebra, logical assembly language commands, and digital logic are addressed as an integrated package. Themes of the ACM/IEEE report such as conceptual models, level of abstraction, reuse and tradeoffs, recur throughout the text.

WHY ANOTHER TEXT?

While many excellent texts exist for teaching assembly language and for computer organization, none seems to be exactly right for the course as I see it. Each time I taught the course using one of these texts, I discovered that I provided increasing quantities of class notes to bridge the difference between material as presented in the text and the material I wanted to present. The pedagogical problems raised by other texts include:

TOP-DOWN VERSUS BOTTOM-UP APPROACH. Most computer organization texts are "bottom-up." They start with low-level details of binary arithmetic and logic gates, and work upward through progressively larger components toward assembly language. Unfortunately, this starting point is far removed from the principles most familiar from the student's previous experience in CS1 and CS2. Although CS1 and CS2 emphasize procedural and data abstraction, the typical third course begins with logic and circuits which are at the low end of the abstraction hierarchy. This shift breaks the student's natural learning sequence. Although, introductory courses present their material in terms of higher-level languages or abstract models, computer organization courses often postpone the most closely related topic, assembly language, until after machine language, which in turn may follow microprogramming. Students know that computer arithmetic is binary, but they may have no experience with this aspect of the machine. In their experience, numeric input has always been decimal. The coverage of number systems and binary arithmetic at the beginning of most computer organization courses may encounter students who cannot see how or why this fits into their experience. Similarly, the introduction of `nand` and `nor` gates is distant from any concept previously covered by sophomores. Starting with gate-level hardware thus can leave students overwhelmed by the task of "putting it all together."

Model comprehension is a top-down process. Student's need the framework of a general model to provide the structure needed for understanding a lower-level model. If concepts such as digital circuitry are introduced later in the course, they fit naturally into the student's hierarchical view of computation. The student must understand the general approach before addressing the details. The beginning computer organization student already has a model of computation—explicit or implicit—based on a conceptual machine that responds to procedural language commands. The student's understanding of problem solving and computation is at a high level of abstraction. This text builds on the existing understanding, beginning with a review of the higher-level language model, ensuring that the instructor and student both use the same terminology, and that the terminology is conceptual rather than language-specific (e.g., "iteration" rather than "For-loops"). It then explores successively lower-level (finer grained) models of the computation process. Each new level of abstraction investigates details ignored in the previous level. Each new model is a refinement of the previous model—never an apparently unrelated topic. Thus, when students arrive at a digital logic model, it helps expand existing knowledge rather than initiating an unrelated topic. The overall direction is from higher to lower levels of abstraction; from previously familiar concepts to newer related concepts.

ROLE OF ASSEMBLY LANGUAGE IN COMPUTER ORGANIZATION. Historically, the "computer organization" course evolved from courses with titles such as "assembly language programming," which became "assembly language programming and computer organization," and finally just "computer organization." As the field evolved, I found myself asking the introspective question: "Why do we continue to teach assembly language at all?" Certainly it is no longer to provide a language tool that students will use throughout their careers. No, the primary reason for teaching assembly language to computer scientists is as a tool for reaching a better understanding of the underlying hardware than can be provided by the higher-level language model. Assembly language serves as a vehicle for learning about computer organization—it is not an end unto itself. Yet, most texts that teach assembly language address the topic as if the details of specific languages were the primary concern. Few teach it as a vehicle for learning about machines in general, or push beyond the language as a programming tool.

COMPUTER SCIENCE AND COMPUTER ENGINEERING. Often the first computer organization course also serves other disciplines such as electrical engineering (or, conversely, the EE course serves the CS students). As observed by the Computing Curricula 1991 Task Force, the appropriate approach may well be quite different for each discipline. Other disciplines have designed courses that meet their specific objectives, but these do not necessarily provide the background that computer scientists need. A computer scientist needs to understand computer organization as support for a general understanding of computing systems; an electrical engineer may need to understand circuitry as a fundamental object of study; the natural scientist may need to understand low-level hardware details in order to interface a laboratory device. No single text can be best for all disciplines. For computer science students, digital electronics provides the support rather than the focus of study. In contrast with the pure assembly language texts, many engineering texts assume a background well beyond that of the average computer science sophomore students (indeed, many assume previous experience with assembly language programming). Some architecture texts list "advanced undergraduate or beginning graduate students" as their target audience. Some even assume a working knowledge of basic physics or engineering concepts.

A course aimed at a target audience of computer scientists should emphasize principles and concepts rather than engineering design details. The typical attitude of computer scientists toward hardware is largely summed up by the old saw:

Q: How many computer scientists does it take to screw in a light bulb?
A: None. That's a hardware problem.

Yet, a basic understanding of hardware is essential. *Computer Organization: A Top-Down Approach* attempts to provide that understanding for computer science students. The computer science student needs more exposure to computers as integrated systems, but less exposure to practical implementation issues than does the electrical engineer. Hardware details will change, but the underlying principles remain the same. The computer science student needs to view hardware as another example of the recurring themes of the field. This text pays greater attention to principles by relating specific hardware constructs to their software analogues.

MACHINE-SPECIFIC TERMINOLOGY. Tying a course too closely to a specific machine or assembler can hide important general principles. Vendor-specific terminology or details (e.g., order of operands or legal addressing modes) may overshadow important concepts of the model (e.g., the logical foundation for operations). A book devoted to a single processor necessarily devotes a major portion of its text to details of that specific machine.

A student should leave a computer organization course with an understanding of the important general concepts—one that is transferable to other machine models, other vendors, and other hardware. Therefore, this text uses machine-independent terminology throughout. Students should be expected to translate from generic concepts to the terminology of their specific hardware and vice versa. For example, in our department we use the *M68000 Programmers' Reference Manual* to provide the machine specific details for the 68000-based Macintoshes the students use in the laboratory. The separation of general principles from machine-dependent details serves three important pedagogical functions. First, it helps the student understand that there are important concepts that are truly independent of a particular machine. These ideas will recur throughout the discipline of computer science. Second, the use of a programmer's reference manual as a supplementary text provides an ideal introduction to the problems (and joys?) of reading a reference manual. Finally, the book is designed primarily to teach rather than as a reference volume. Therefore, *this text is intended to be used in conjunction with a programmers' reference manual for the appropriate hardware*. When concrete examples are needed, a simple generic language is used. The generic language used in this text is a simplified version of the more complex real languages, yet it includes most of their essential principles, with a minimum of low-level details. The actual language used by students serves as an instantiation of those principles.

COMPARTMENTALIZATION. Many texts over-compartmentalize material. For example, some cover all of number representation in a single chapter. Even though positive integers are needed early in the course, real numbers often cannot be examined on many machines until near the end of a course (after traps and/or co-processors are discussed). Most computer science educators have recognized the need to integrate the many aspects of program and data structure throughout CS1 and CS2, but for the most part, they have not yet applied that principle to computer organization. The Denning report [Denning] emphasizes the importance of such integration, by suggesting a three-semester introductory overview.

ADDITIONAL PHILOSOPHIES OF THIS TEXT

While no approach is problem-free, *Computer Organization: A Top-Down Approach* does address the above problems. The approach creates a course that fits the computer science curriculum and relieves student frustration. Certainly, if student reaction is an appropriate gage, it has helped considerably. In addition, the text subscribes to several additional pedagogical philosophies, which smooth and integrate the material.

MODELS. The formation of models is a central theme in all of the sciences. This text presents its material as a series of abstractions or models of computation, starting with a very general but already familiar "higher-level language machine," and progressing through assembly and machine language models, down to a digital circuit model. Each new model presents a coherent view of computation that brings significant new insights, while remaining consistent with previous models. The concept of model is used here as it is in the natural sciences. Each new abstraction represents the description of "real" computers, but with a different set of properties emphasized. The implementation of each model will vary from machine to machine, but the fundamental concepts will always be present.

RECURRING THEMES. In the spirit of the ACM/IEEE report, this text uses several consistent themes to provide connections between models. For example, the assembly language model incorporates the same control and data structures as were used by the higher-level language model. After students understand the assembly language model, the corresponding machine language can be introduced, again using the same structures. Still later, lower-level models such as microprogrammed and bit-level operations can be shown to address the same issues. These recurring concepts reinforce the coherence of the discipline.

MOTIVATION AND THE SEQUENCING OF TOPICS. Motivation should precede detail. The student should see the rationale for each new concept or model. Digital logic is important, but bits and gates may seem useless for computers that process a higher-level language, but not so useless when described as the explanation of how a computer holds or transfers a single byte of data. Ideally, each new topic should be introduced at just about the time the student asks "Yes, but what about . . . ?" The presentation also attempts to introduce new theoretical or mathematical tools at points where they are needed to explore the next organization topic. For example, binary and hexadecimal arithmetic are introduced only when students start to use debuggers.

The progression of topics should encourage exploration of ideas. In addition to motivating student questions through the order of presentation, I have included a number of "Start the wheels turning" questions. These questions [marked: "(▷)"] are inserted at various points in the text to prod students into thinking about issues that are yet to come. These questions are not usually answerable at the time they are asked, but the thinking they initiate can provide motivation for future topics.

When the student independently discovers a concept, it will usually be understood better than if it were simply read from the text. Where possible, I lead the reader toward solutions, rather than simply presenting those solutions. For example, introduction using an "almost correct" solution can often lead a student to grasp the necessity for an alternative approach even before that alternative is presented.

ROLE OF LABORATORIES WITHIN COMPUTER ORGANIZATION. True learning requires hands-on experience and practice. Assembly language serves a computer organization course as a vehicle for understanding. To be useful as such a tool, assembly language should be presented early in the course. The principles learned in CS1 and CS2 should provide the starting point for a study of computer organization, which students can apply directly to assembly language. My intent is that students should be programming in assembly language from the first week or two of the course, devoting most of the semester to learning about organization, but using the language as a tool for understanding. Although couched in terms of language, the purpose of assignments should be the exploration of the machine. The term projects included help illustrate this focus.

ROLE OF COMPUTER ORGANIZATION WITHIN THE CS CURRICULUM. Specific material should be relevant beyond the scope of a single course, to previous and later courses. The content of the computer organization course should be governed by the needs of later courses in the curriculum such as operating systems, compilers, programming languages, networking, and even the theory of computation. This text attempts to incorporate material already known by students, serving both as a base point for new material, and as a reiteration of previous experience. Similarly, advanced courses depend on student exposure to computer organization. This text places greater emphasis on those topics that students will need as foundation material for later computer science courses.

ORGANIZATION OF THE TEXT

The organization of the text provides a smooth flow from the initial review of higher-level language model through the integration of a classic von Neumann machine into a working system, complete with I/O and interrupts. Each section of the text presents a single model of computation, based on the previous and leading to the next. Material that may be tangential or otherwise inappropriate for some offerings, is isolated in the last section. These topics do not depend extensively on earlier units, reducing the problems commonly created when an instructor prefers to vary the order of presentation.

PART I: THE HIGHER-LEVEL LANGUAGE MODEL (CHAPTER 1). The first chapter sets the stage and terminology for the rest of the course. It presents a generic model similar to the "Pascal machine" model used in some texts, and includes a review of the general terminology of the higher-level language model: data types, variables, constants and declarations, control statements, and modularity. It thus provides a review of earlier material and ensures that students are using the appropriate technical terms (e.g., iteration and conditional) rather than the colloquial or language-dependent names for the same concepts (e.g., for-loop, or if-then). The review focuses attention on the concepts that will be important later.

PART II: THE ASSEMBLY LANGUAGE MODEL (CHAPTERS 2–5). Chapter 2 plunges students immediately into assembly language programming, viewing it as a variant of higher-level languages. It includes a minimal architectural overview of memory, central processing unit, arithmetic logic unit, and control unit. Students can be writing assembly language programs by the end of Chapter 2. After covering numeric representations (Chapter 4), the model is completed with more advanced control and data structures (Chapter 5). The supplementary material in Chapter 13 on debuggers can provide support for the process.

PART III: THE MACHINE LANGUAGE MODEL (CHAPTERS 6–7). The machine language model parallels Part II, expanding the model to include the fetch/execute cycle. Description of the cycle introduces the internal aspects such as program counter, instruction register, and bus. The model of computation is thus expanded from one that was really based on the higher-level language model into one that reflects the internal structure of a computer. Chapter 7 then introduces assemblers and related software as the bridge between these two models.

PART IV: THE DIGITAL LOGIC MODEL (CHAPTERS 8–10). Chapter 8 reviews or introduces Boolean algebra as the logical foundation for digital circuits, and builds correlations between that logical foundation and assembly language. (Much of this chapter may easily be skipped by students who have had a course in discrete mathematics.) Chapter 9 then models the principal digital constructs: flip-flops, decoders, adders, etc., as a supporting structure for previous models, and as tools needed by Chapter 10 for a meaningful discussion of memory.

PART V: THE INTEGRATED SYSTEM MODEL (CHAPTERS 11–12). Part V completes the model series by embedding a processor into a working machine, filling in details that are external chronologically (e.g., the bootstrapping process) or physically (e.g., interrupts and external devices) to the processor as modeled in earlier parts.

PART VI: EXTENSIONS (CHAPTERS 13–16). The final part includes several topics that extend the coverage to fill in the gaps in areas covered by some courses but not others. Individual courses are influenced by available hardware, preceding and following courses in the curriculum, faculty needs, etc. The chapters of this part may be included or skipped according to the needs of a specific course. Some chapters of Part VI are essential to an organization course, but may not be applicable to a specific environment (e.g., debuggers, and real arithmetic). Others are useful for students who will not be taking an advanced architecture course later in their career (e.g., microcode, RISC architectures, parallel processing).

TEACHING AIDS AND INSTRUCTOR'S MANUAL

Two tools for integrating the material are included as appendices to this text. A third is available in the instructor's guide and in machine readable form.

INSTRUCTOR'S MANUAL. Any new pedagogical approach brings new problems. The supplementary instructor's manual is designed to address just such issues. For example, it contains translations of the generic examples used in the text into two common assembly languages: M680x0 and i80x86. The translations not only illustrate principles using a language in which the students themselves must program, but also provide evidence of the transferability of concepts to new domains. The manual also includes discussion of alternative orders of presentation, omitted material, creation of macros for student use, and test data for term projects.

TERM PROJECTS. Larger projects are essential for every student. Term projects represent much more comprehensive learning experiences than smaller exercises. In addition to the usual short exercises found at the end of chapters, Appendix 2 includes five sample term projects. These projects emphasize the conceptual material covered by the text, but require the student to address the material in the context of a local "real" machine. The first project (machine emulation) demonstrates the universality of the models by bridging two distinct instantiations of the machine-language model. The third (assembler) project helps bridge the model hierarchy. The second project (calculator), is not a traditional term project (due at the end of the term), but is a term-long series of smaller projects. A sequence of assignments allows the student to build a significant project by incorporating new concepts into an existing project. I believe that such term projects, even for sophomores, are probably the best approach to providing the hands-on experience that has become an integral part of computer science education.

STYLE AND STRUCTURE GUIDE. The free-form nature of assembly language code often entices students to ignore the structured approach they learned in previous courses. Appendix 1 provides a rather dogmatic "structure and style" guide to help students develop consistent coding habits for a new environment. This style guide emphasizes more universal "safe programming practices," perhaps at the expense of "fast assembly language techniques."

MACROS AND DATA. When I teach our organization course, I use a set of macros, which transform the assembly language of our 68000-based machines into the generic language, GAL, used in the text. Plunging students directly into assembly language in week two of a course can be traumatic. These macros greatly simplify the introductory portion of an organization course, hiding many of the low-level details of assembly language until the students have the necessary background to understand them. Also available is test data for the emulation term project listed in Appendix 2. These are included in the instructor's manual, and I will also be happy to provide machine readable copies of macros and labs to anyone who requests one from me at:

Scragg@cs.Geneseo.edu

ACKNOWLEDGMENTS

Finally, I wish to thank all the people who helped me complete this task. First and foremost, thanks to all the students in CSc 241, Computer Organization, who put up with draft versions of this text. Extra special thanks go to those who went the extra mile, providing me with an endless stream of corrections and suggestions. My deepest appreciation and condolences go to my colleagues in the SUNY Geneseo Computer Science Department who tolerated endless months of an irritable chair-in-hiding. Thanks also to the members of the Liberal Arts Computer Science Consortium, who encouraged me to follow through on the project (even to those who have previously written texts and therefore knew better), especially to Allen Tucker, Michael Schneider, and Charles Kelemen who provided valuable feedback on specific aspects of the project. Reviews acquired by McGraw-Hill proved to be very helpful and came from James Archer, Texas Technological University; David Garnick, Bowdoin College; Karen Lemone, Worcester Polytechnic Institute; David Magagnosc, Drexel University; and Donald Miller, Arizona State University. Amy Gravitz provided help in more ways than I can even understand, including (but not limited) proof reading, figure and cover ideas, and just being there when the going got tough. Finally, I could not have kept my sanity (note underlying assumption) throughout the task without the diversions provided by the Country Dancers of Rochester, the Flower City Dulcimer Club, the Canadice String Band, and the Hemlock Lake Regatta and Music Festival.

Greg W. Scragg

REFERENCES

[ACM78] ACM Curriculum Committee on Computer Science, Curriculum 78. *Communications of the Association for Computing Machinery*, V 22.3, pp. 147–156 (March 1979).

[ACM/IEEE] ACM/IEEE-CS Joint Curriculum Task Force, Computing Curricula 1991. New York: ACM Press, 1991.

[Biedler] Biedler, J., R. Cassal, and L. Austing, Computing programs in small colleges. *Communications of the Association for Computing Machinery*, V 28.6, pp. 605–611 (June 1985).

[Denning] Denning, P., et al. Computing as a discipline. *Communications of the Association for Computing Machinery*, V 32.1, pp. 9–23 (January 1989).

[Gibbs/Tucker] Gibbs, N. and A. Tucker: A model curriculum for a liberal arts Degree in computer Science. *Communications of the Association for Computing Machinery*, V 29.3, pp. 202–210 (March 1986).

[M68000] *M68000 Programmers Reference Manual*. Englewood Cliffs: Prentice-Hall, 1991.

COMPUTER ORGANIZATION
A Top-Down Approach

PART I

THE HIGHER-LEVEL LANGUAGE MODEL

You already know everything in this section! Part I consists of a single chapter describing a generic higher-level language. It assumes that every student in a computer organization course has approximately one year of programming experience using a higher-level language such as Pascal or Modula. The purpose of Chapter 1 is as follows:

- It provides a very quick review of common terminology,
- It provides a forum for questions about the nature of computation,
- It establishes a standard vocabulary for describing the concepts common to most higher-level languages, and by extension a notation for describing later models,
- It describes the model of computation implicit in a higher-level language—the first of several models that you will see in this book.

You probably have experience with at least two models of computation already. In the higher-level language model, a computer is described as an entity that can obey instructions stated in a higher-level language. In the system model, a computer is simply a black box, capable of performing high-level tasks such as word processing or perhaps executing a program (although it may not even be clear exactly what a program is). You may have additional views based on specific applications such as spreadsheets, data bases, and word processors. One of the goals of this book is to demonstrate that no one view is absolute; each represents a conceptually correct model for understanding certain aspects of computation. The primary difference between the views is in the level of detail. People maintain such multileveled models of many topics. For example, you may view a telephone as part of a large network of communications equipment. On another occasion you may view it as a 1-pound plastic object that holds down the papers on your desk. Which of these two models is preferable depends on your current task: the former is clearly preferable if you need to communicate with a friend and the latter if you are cleaning the house.

For comprehension purposes, the best model to begin with is one with which you are already familiar. Perhaps you are not even aware of some of the concepts that you have incorporated into your own conceptual model of computation. Reviewing the model will help elucidate these concepts. Many formally defined concepts are often called by colloquial names. Such use can be very pervasive, sometimes obscuring the relationship between analogous concepts in distinct situations. As an analogy, consider a stewardess on a large airline who actually has a nametag identifying her by her colloquial name, "Oh Miss." I assume she does have a more formal name, such as Mary Jones, but apparently no one addresses her by that name on the job. A more relevant computer science example is the frequent use of "loop" for the concept "iterate." Chapter 1 identifies many of these formal names for structures. Much of the material in later chapters uses this terminology to describe subsequent models.

CHAPTER 1

THE HIGHER-LEVEL LANGUAGE MODEL

THE HIGHER-LEVEL LANGUAGE MACHINE

Most programming today is performed in a family of languages collectively known as *higher-level languages* (or *hll*'s). Most introductory computer science courses reflect this by incorporating a higher-level language into their presentation. These courses either explicitly or implicitly describe computation as if computers directly accepted instructions written in a higher-level language. That is, they are based on a higher-level language *model* of computation. The most common such model is often called the Pascal machine. With such a model or abstraction, the programmer need not know the actual internal details but can think of a computer as a machine that supports exactly those concepts supported by the language. Therefore, most students have established some mental model of the organization of a computer based heavily on their understanding of a higher-level language. Although the later chapters of the text will describe several new models of computation, it is important to note that the higher-level language model is not incorrect—just more abstract. This class of languages makes an excellent starting point in the study of computer organization because any student in a course such as Computer Organization is certainly familiar with at least one of these languages. More important, such languages reflect to a significant degree the model of computation currently held by those students. This chapter describes a particular class of higher-level languages known as *procedural* or *block-structured* languages. This class includes Pascal, Modula, Ada, C, and even newer versions of Basic and Fortran. Other classes of languages include functional (e.g., Lisp), logic (Prolog), and object oriented (C++, Smalltalk). Procedural languages provide the best starting point for the study of computer organization for three reasons: they are popular and well-known; historically, they are the most significant; and they are most closely related to the underlying structures characteristic of additional models discussed later.

A remarkably constant set of structures underlies all higher-level procedural languages. Chapter 1 describes many of these, illustrating the principles where needed with a generic hll called Hill (HIgher Level Language). Hill looks much like Pascal or Modula but may be thought of as describing a "Hill machine," a machine that obeys Hill instructions. Most hll's have a fairly specific set of common features. In each language, the nomenclature and syntax of these features may vary, but the concepts are nearly identical and can all be summarized fairly quickly by example. The following generic description is intended to be a summary only. It is neither exhaustive nor sufficiently extensive to serve as a full introduction to higher-level languages. It is intended for review purposes: to provide buzz words that remind you of material from previous studies and to set the stage for the material covered in the remainder of the text. If any of the concepts are unfamiliar, you should look them up in any up-to-date "Introduction to Computer Science" text that uses Pascal, Modula, or a similar language (a few suggestions are provided at the end of the chapter). Much of this review is presented in a slightly skewed, nonstandard manner designed to emphasize those concepts that will be important in dealing with computer organization.

One can view a hll as a set of tools for describing algorithms or step-by-step solutions to problems. Many of these tools are provided explicitly in constructs that are realized directly at the syntax of the language. A hll machine is therefore an engine that executes these tools. Other tools are not explicitly represented in the language but are implicit in the relationships between other aspects of the language. The first part of the chapter focuses primarily on those concepts explicitly supported by typical higher-level languages. The last section attempts to draw your attention to the implicit, or hidden, aspects of hlls. Its intent is not to answer questions but to raise them.

DATA TYPES

Simple Types

Programs are divided into two explicit sections: one containing the steps of the algorithm and the other describing the data upon which that algorithm will operate. Most hlls provide the user with a built-in set of primitive *data types,* which the user can use in building a program. Most data types have an associated set of operations that can be used to manipulate data of the given type (e.g., arithmetic operations for manipulating numeric data types). The programmer may create as many *variables* as needed from any of the available types.

Integer. A cell of type integer can hold any integer value, within limits. The most common limits are approximately $\pm 33,000$ or $\pm 2,000,000,000$.

▷ *Why these specific values?*[1]

Real. A variable of type *real* can hold any numeric value, within a magnitude limit and to some precision. Some languages provide a form of the real data type known as *double precision,* which provides about 16 decimal digits of accuracy and may allow even larger numbers.

▷ *Typically, the largest real number is around* 10^{35} *or so, with an accuracy of about 7 decimal digits. Why these particular limits?*

Character. A cell of type *character* holds a single character. Usually the documentation specifies that the character is an ASCII character (unfortunately, just as usually, there is no explanation of what ASCII means). Characters include not only the characters of the alphabet but the digits 0 through 9, the punctuation marks (".", ",", "/", etc.), and even the characters " " (space), and *return* (also called <cr>[2]), and *eol* (the end-of-line character).

▷ *What does ASCII mean? What does it mean for a number to be a character? How can a return be a character?*

Boolean. A variable of type *Boolean* can contain only the values `true` and `false`. Sometimes Boolean data is called *logical data* because its dominant use is for logical expressions.

String. A variable *string* is like a character but is composed of several (i.e., a string) of them. Strings inherit the concept of alphabetical order from characters. Hill also supports the concepts of *position* within the string (the first character of the string, the next, etc.), and *length* of the string. Most languages distinguish between a character and a string of length 1.

▷ *Why distinguish between a character and a string of length 1?*

Structured Data Types

Hlls contain grouping mechanisms for creating compound structures from simpler variable data. A compound data structure is created from two or more data cells or elements of any existing data type. There are four primary tools for combining data elements.

---

[1] The notation: ▷ . . . ? will be used to focus your attention on "future questions," questions that will be answered in later chapters. These questions should serve to start you thinking about "Why is it done this way anyway?"

[2] "cr" for *carriage return,* a holdover from the days when all typewriters had a carriage which moved across the page.

Arrays are fixed-size collections of simpler data types, in which subscripts distinguish the members of the collection from each other. An array may be composed of any data type. The subscript may be of any enumerated data type (integer, character, Boolean, or user-defined) independent of the type of the array. Arrays are useful in situations requiring several storage items that are both logically and representationally the same. For example, an array can contain all of the (integer) test grades for your computer organization class. Typically, a simple variable is used for the *subscript*. By varying the subscript, a single expression may be made to reference any individual *element* of the array.

Records, like arrays, are collections of simpler data types; but a record may be composed of individual *fields* that are not all of the same type. The fields are distinguished by name rather than number. Records are useful when the associated data is all logically related, such as the name, address, and phone number of an individual. There is usually no mechanism for systematically accessing all the subparts of the structure.

Files are similar to arrays in that all of the elements are of the same type, but the size need not be fixed. Often access to files is restricted to sequential passes through the elements of the file.

Pointers are technically a simple data type, but they are meaningful only in the presence of other data and are most useful as part of a compound data type. Pointers are not so much data, as indicators of how to find data. A pointer "points to" an item of data and provides access to the data elements that they point to. Such accesses are said to be *indirect,* because data elements are not referenced directly but are pointed to indirectly by the pointer. They are especially useful for creating more complicated data structures than those normally provided by the host hlls, such as linked lists, trees, rings, stacks and queues.

Variables, Constants, and Declarations

For any simple data type, Hill allows data to be represented as

- *literals,* which explicitly mention the data value within the code—for example, `5`, `true`, or `'B'` are all literal values;
- *constants,* which will not change in value for the duration of the program; and
- *variables,* which are allowed to change under direction of the programmer.

Both variables and constants provide mnemonic tools for representing the concept as well as the value of a data item. Declaration statements enable the programmer to specify an *identifier* that will serve as the name of a variable or constant. The general form of the constant declaration is

```
constants
  <constant_name> = <value>;
       . . .
  <constant_name> = <value>;
```

which should be interpreted as "`constant_1` will always have the value `value_1`," "`constant_n` will have the value `value_n`," and so on.

Note that throughout this text the following relatively standard conventions will be used whenever syntactic examples are provided for any example language:

- Items enclosed in angle brackets (< >) may be replaced with arbitrary identifiers or expressions of the appropriate type.
- Items enclosed in square brackets ([ ]) are optional.
- Items enclosed in curly brackets ({ }) or preceded by a single semi-colon (";") are comments.
- Items listed with no brackets should appear verbatim "as is."

In addition, any word that is used as a reserved word of a language, a variable name, a language statement or expression, or other than as a conventional English language word will be written in a different `font` to help clarify the special use.

All identifiers in Hill, including those naming constants, may be composed of any string of alphanumeric characters (including the underscore "_") as long as the first character is alphabetic. Each constant will maintain its given value for the life of the program segment. It is illegal for the programmer to attempt to change the constant by any of the means described below. It is not necessary to specify the type of each constant, since the value assigned to the constant makes the type explicit.

The general form for the variable declaration is

```
variables
      <variable_name>:<type>;
               . . .
      <variable_name>:<type>;
```

The declaration does not give an initial value to the variables; it only specifies the type. Later commands in the body of the program may give values to a variable. It is sometimes helpful to view these declarations as a sort of contract between programmer and language compiler:[3] the compiler agrees to maintain and keep track of the variable; the programmer agrees to use the variable only for storage of the designated type.

The pointer variable has a slightly different appearance. Since pointers have meaning only insofar as they point to another variable, it must be possible to distinguish between reference to the pointer itself and reference to the item to which the pointer points. The indirect syntax can be read as follows:

---

[3] Although the term *compiler* is certainly familiar, exactly what it does may not be. One of the goals of computer organization is to provide an understanding of what programs like compilers actually do. For the moment assume that it is a program that processes your hll program, getting it ready to execute. Apparently from the current context, it must be the entity that checks the legality of your code.

`pointer` is the name of a pointer to some item,

`pointer↑` refers to the item to which `pointer` points.

Although very similar in syntax, the meanings are quite distinct. The mnemonic of reading the "↑" as "points to" helps in the interpretation.

EXECUTABLE STATEMENTS OR ACTIONS

The statements of a higher-level language can be broadly categorized into three groups:

- Those that *move* data
- Those that *manipulate* or change data
- Those that *control* the execution of the program

Data Movement

Before thinking about data movement, first consider the computer as an entity. Data may be internal to the computer, such as the data contained in a variable (or a literal or a constant), or data may be external to the computer, such as information that the human knows but that has not yet been communicated to the computer. Note that data held on disks or tape is treated in most hlls as if it is external to the computer. On microcomputers with external disk drives, the clear physical separation helps provide visual support for this distinction.

If data can be thought of as residing in two sorts of locations, data movement can be thought of as having $2^2 = 4$ possible forms:

- internal to internal
- external to internal
- internal to external
- external to external

The last of these corresponds to people talking to people and obviously has little significance for this categorization of computer data movement. (Copying one disk file to another might be considered an external to external data movement. But this operation is normally accomplished by copying the data from one file into the computer and then copying it back out to the second.) The first three, however, provide an important insight into the nature of computer languages.

INTERNAL TO INTERNAL. There is only one mechanism in most higher-level languages for moving data from one place to another internally: the simple *assignment* statement

```
assign <destination>⇐<value>
```

This is sometimes surprising. It is worth the mental exercise to reflect on the lack of any other mechanism for moving data. At first it may seem as if other mechanisms, such as procedure calls involving `var` parameters, must certainly exist. However, deeper reflection will reveal that the subprocedure must have either used an assignment statement, obtained the value from external sources, or called a second subprocedure (to which these same comments would apply recursively). Ultimately an assignment statement must be involved in any internal data movement. The value to be copied into a variable can be represented as a literal, a constant, another variable, or (as will be seen) an expression. A second useful observation about the assignment statement is that it might be more aptly named "copy," since the values held in the source (which are "copied" into the destination) are never destroyed. The use of the left-arrow, "$\Leftarrow$", in Hill is intended to reduce the confusion sometimes caused by the more comon assignment operators "=" or ":=". Use of a simple assignment will always result (perhaps only temporarily) in two locations having the same value, one an original and one a copy.

> ▷ *Is it possible that the assignment operator ":=" used in many hlls was designed to look like a left arrow?*

EXTERNAL TO INTERNAL. For all practical purposes, there is only a single mechanism for moving data from the external world into the computer: the *input* statement `read`, although many languages provide variations such as `read-line` and support functions such as `eoln` and `eof`.

Read. `Read` moves values from the external world (keyboard, disk, tape, or even—perish the thought—keypunch). The common form

```
read (<item1>, <item2>, . . .)
```

inputs as many items from the external world as are specified in the parameter list and places them sequentially in the corresponding locations: first value into `<item1>`, second into `<item2>`, and so on. A little reflection will also reveal that `Read` is an incredibly powerful statement that can read any number of items, each of which can be of any data type.

> ▷ *Yes,* `read` *is a procedure, so "parameter list" is the correct name for the list of variables to be read. What do the use and syntax of* `read` *imply about this observation?*

Variations. Most hlls provide a simple variation in the `read` syntax, which also specifies the input stream to be read, allowing for input from disks, etc. `Readln` is a variation on `read` that not only reads values into the specified locations but also finds the end-of-line character in the input stream. It is especially valuable for dealing with string input.

End_of_line is a function enabling the program to "peek ahead" at the next character without actually transferring its value into a variable. In particular, end_of_line seeks the "end of line" character. It is most useful when the number of input items is not known.

▷ *But how can it look ahead if the data has not yet been read? What is the end of line character?*

End_of_file is similar but looks for the "end of file" character.

▷ *Is the end of file character distinct from the physical end of the file?*

All of the input functions use the function `get`, which always obtains the next *character* in the input stream. This is true even if the variable to be read is an integer or a real, which suggests that the `read` procedure has the ability to translate a string of characters into a single number.

▷ *Why read a number as a character?*

INTERNAL TO EXTERNAL. As was the case with input, there is a single mechanism for moving data from internal to external locations: the *output* statement, `write`. Syntax of the output statement mirrors that of the `read`:

```
write (<item1>, <item2>, . . .)
```

which moves the values from the given variable to the output stream. `Write` is also a powerful statement, taking any number of arguments, each of any type, and the output stream may optionally be specified. An additional variant, `writeln`, is analogous to `readln`, which always terminates the output line after writing the specified value(s) by placing the `eoln` character `<cr>` in the output stream. All output involves the low-level procedure `put`. Again, this suggests that the output procedures are capable of translating numeric and other forms of data into characters.

Data Manipulation

The computer can manipulate internally held data. The particular operations allowed depend on the data itself. Usually, the result of any manipulation is immediately moved or copied to a more permanent location. For example, the statement

```
assign  A⇐(B + C)
```

performs the manipulation "add B and C together," and then copies the result into the location A. An *expression* is any operation together with its operands. Because each expression has a value, more complicated expressions can be built from simpler ones:

```
assign  A⇐(B + C) * D ;
```

ARITHMETIC MANIPULATION. Most Hlls contain a reasonably predictable set of arithmetic operators: addition, subtraction, multiplication, and division. They can also find remainders when dealing with integer division and may manipulate either real or integer numbers. Usually there are at least a few of the more powerful operations, such as exponentiation, modular arithmetic, square roots, and logarithms. Most arithmetic operations are binary, requiring two numeric operands and yielding a numeric result.

> ▷ *Why are some operations provided in almost all hlls, but others are only provided by some? What is the relationship between the hll concept of operator and the mathematical concept* function*?*

CHARACTER AND STRING MANIPULATION. Characters and strings have their own set of operations that can be performed upon them: *concatenation* and *substring* combine strings and break them apart, respectively.

LOGICAL MANIPULATION. Boolean values can also be manipulated using the *Boolean operators* `and`, `or`, and `not`. The first two are binary—operations on two Boolean operands—and yield a Boolean result. The last is unary. Boolean values have a second interesting property: they can be created using *relational operators* or comparisons ($=$, $<>$, $<$, $\leq$, $>$, and $\geq$) between values in most data types. Thus the comparison "$3 < 4$" creates the value `true`, which can then be stored in a Boolean variable. For example,

```
assign  bool_var⇐(3 < 4)
```

places `true` into `bool_var`, which can then be used as the operand of a Boolean operation:

```
(bool_var or false)
```

which yields the value `true`. Mathematically, we say that a Boolean operator is a binary function $O : B^2 \Rightarrow B$ that maps two Boolean values into a single Boolean value, but that a relational operator is a function $R : N^2 \Rightarrow B$ that maps two numeric values into a Boolean value.

Although Boolean values can be copied into Boolean variables in exactly the same way that arithmetic values are saved, the results of logical operations are more frequently used in control statements and not actually stored in a variable.

DATA CONVERSION. Many languages provide a mechanism, called *type transfer*, for creating data of one type from data of another type. Because these languages insist that all operations must only be performed upon data of appropriate types, these type-transfer functions enable the programmer to accomplish data operations that would otherwise be impossible.

> ▷ *Why do languages make such rigid restrictions? Would it ever make sense to perform operations on data of an "incorrect" type?*

CONTROL STRUCTURES AND PROGRAM FLOW

The third and final important aspect of every higher-level language is control structure. In general, each language provides a set of control structures that are (or were believed to be at the time the language was created) useful for the type of applications the language was intended to address. The almost universally accepted control structures are the following.

Sequential (or Default)

Each program statement normally follows the one sequentially preceding (above) it in the listing. No statement is ever executed unless the statement immediately preceding it is executed first (with the obvious exception of the first statement). The default can be over-ridden with any of several well-formed exception mechanisms. That is, actions proceed as: the first, then the syntactically next, and the next, and so on.

▷ *This observation is actually true in most modern languages, even in the context of the control structures described below. Can you convince yourself of the validity of this statement?*

Conditional Structures

Conditional structures contain two segments, a *test* and an *action* (*consequent*). As with any simple statement, the conditional is executed when sequential execution of the program reaches the statement. The test is always executed, but execution of the action described in the statement body depends upon the logical condition specified in the test. That is, a conditional structure enables a statement body to be executed conditionally. There are three principal variations of the conditional statement.

IF-THEN. The simple conditional takes the form

```
if <test>
  then <body>
```

and can be paraphrased as "the `<body>` will be executed (only) if the `<test>` yields a true result." That is, the test is evaluated whenever the conditional statement is reached, but the body will be executed only if the test is true. Simple `if-thens` are useful whenever an all-or-nothing situation exists, in which the programmer wants an action either to be executed or not executed but will not know which until the entire program is executed. The body of a conditional may be a simple action or a compound (block) statement.

IF-THEN-ELSE. The alternative if-then-else has the form

```
if <test>
  then <then-body>
  else <else-body>
```

As with the if-then, the <test> is always evaluated, but exactly one of the <then-body> or the <else-body> will be executed (never both, never neither). It is useful for situations in which one of exactly two things must be done, such as writing the gender of a client. The if-then statement can be thought of as a special case of the if-then-else statement in which the <else-body> is null (has no steps).

> ▷ *You have probably seen other situations in which computer scientists make use of the concept of null entities. Why do you suppose the concept of "null" seems to recur frequently?*

CASE. The case statement takes the form

```
case <selection criteria> of
  <val_1>:<body_1>;
  <val_2>:<body_2>;
  . . .
  <val_n>:<body_n>;
  otherwise:<escape body>
```

Again, the <selection criteria> is always evaluated, but rather than producing a logical true-false value as in the if-then and if-then-else, it produces an index into the following blocks of code. Generally, the <selection criteria> should point to a single <val_i> and the corresponding body is executed. If no <val_i> corresponds to <selection criteria>, the "otherwise" <escape body> will be executed (perhaps a message saying "no value found"). The if-then-else can be thought of as a special form of the case statement in which only two values (true and false) are possible. Conversely, the case statement can be thought of as a series of nested if-then-elses of the form

```
if (<selection_criteria> = val_1)
  then <body_1>
else if (<selection criteria> = val_2)
  then <body_2>
  . . .
else <escape body>.
```

As with the simple conditionals, the entire case statement should be viewed as a single statement. That is, the default (sequential) organization of the program applies to the entire conditional statement—when viewed with respect to the preceding and following statements in the program. The `case` statement itself is executed after the preceding statement and prior to the following statement. The body (or body segment) may or may not be executed as part of that step.

Iteration Constructs

Iterate means "perform repeatedly." In most higher-level languages, iteration takes the form of loops. Such loop constructs provide the programmer with a mechanism to indicate that a statement (including a compound statement) may be executed several times. This is useful in any situation in which the same calculation will be needed repeatedly. There are three common forms of the loop structure.

PRETEST LOOP (`WHILE`). Generally a pretest loop takes the form

```
while <test> do
      <body>
```

A pretest loop tests for a continuation condition *prior* to the execution of each iteration of the loop body. Since the test is made prior to entering the loop body, pretest loops are well-suited for conditions in which it is not certain that the loop should be executed *at all*. For example, in processing strings, the loop may not be executed even once in the case of the null string.

POST-TEST LOOP (`UNTIL`). Post-test iteration usually takes the form

```
repeat
        <body>
until   <test>
```

A post-test loop tests for the terminating condition at the end of the loop. This implies that every post-test loop will be executed at least once, because the test is not reached until the end of the loop body. Thus, post-test loops are useful for situations in which at least one iteration is essential for successful execution, such as when the continuation/termination conditions cannot be known until the loop has begun. In addition, sometimes a post-test loop is preferable to a pretest loop, because a pretest may create misunderstanding. For example, consider the situation in which the user must provide explicit input to indicate whether or not the loop should be executed additional times. A pretest loop can create the awkward situation in which the user is asked, "More tests?" even though there have not yet been *any* tests.

Note that in many languages, the condition is a "termination" condition, unlike the pretest loop that used a "continuation" condition of each loop. That is, in the pretest loop the body *continues* to be executed as long as `<test>` is true, but the body of a post-test loop *ceases* to be executed when `<test>` becomes true.

COUNTER-CONTROLLED LOOP (`FOR LOOP`). The form of a counter-controlled loop is

```
for <counter>⇐<start> to <stop> do
    <body>
```

The counter-controlled loop can be thought of as a special case of the pretest loop, in which the test involves a counter:

```
initialize <counter>⇐<start>
while (<counter> ≤ <stop>) do
      <body>
      increment (<counter>)
```

The counter-controlled loop is useful when it is desirable to repeat an action a specified number of times. A counter is incremented each pass through the loop, and the terminating condition is that the counter has reached a predetermined value. Note that the counter-controlled loop is a special case of the more general pretest loop, not the other way around. Some programmers habitually use counter-controlled loops even though their purpose would be better served with a pre- or post-test loop.

PROPERTIES OF LOOP STRUCTURES. In most hlls, it is not possible to perform a fractional number of passes (e.g., three and a half) through a loop. Loops can only be entered at the top and exited at the top or bottom—never the middle. In this manner, one can never leave a task "half done." Either a loop is executed or it is not; thus, it can never happen that some statements of the `<body>` were executed, but some were not. This is very helpful in eliminating the so-called *fence post* errors.[4] There do exist exceptional situations in which it is desirable to exit in the middle of a loop. For example, in a program that handles customer transactions (such as a bank ATM), the user may enter a command to abort the transaction in the middle (perhaps after a sudden realization that there was not enough money in the account). The program will need to reflect that change and get out of the current control structure. Some languages, such as Ada, acknowledge that such situations exist and include explicit constructs (e.g., `break`, `exit`) that enable exits from the middle of loops. As their names seem to imply, these constructs are designed for the exceptional circumstance.

▷ *In a fence post error, one inadvertently counts the number of fence posts, when what was needed was the number of rails. If these are unfamiliar, can you complete an example such as Exercise 1.6 at the end of the chapter?*

---

[4]In addition, for practitioners of formal verification, such a restriction makes the specification of loop invariants and post-conditions considerably more straightforward.

After completion of a loop, control is always left at the syntactically next statement. This is a property of all control structures in hlls. That is, each iteration construct is treated as a single statement within the (default) sequential organization of the language. After completion of an integral number of iterations, control is always left at the (syntactically) following statement. No matter which form of loop is used, the terminating condition at the completion of a loop is always known. For debugging, this is an important fact to know. If control reached the statement following the loop, the terminating condition is available for debugging.

The loop can be treated as a single (powerful) statement. As with the conditional statements, iteration constructs can be viewed globally as single statements and simultaneously as locally control structures.

READ LOOP. Finally, Hill contains one additional loop structure that, although it would be very useful, is not explicitly provided in most hlls, namely the *read loop,* which takes the form

```
while (<new input> ≠ <val>) do
      <body>
```

or

```
while (<new input> exists) do
      <body>
```

The `eoln` and `eof` functions of Pascal provide some ability to do the latter of these, as in the Pascal loop

```
while (not eoln) do
      <body>.
```

There is no direct construct provided in Pascal for the former. Such a structure would be very useful for situations in which a user is asked to provide additional input or indicate that there is no more. The read loop can be used with "flag data" indicating that the end has been reached. Often data may be organized so that multiple data items must be read in each pass through a loop. Unfortunately, it may not be determined that the last item has been found until the first input item for the next program segment has been found. Consider a situation in which every set of data has two data elements except the very last one, which has only one data element. For example, the user is entering pairs of numbers to be added. With a read-loop, a single zero value could be used as the termination condition. Assuming that the last data set can be recognized, the program should end immediately. But all of the generally available constructs prove very awkward in this situation.

▷ *Why don't most languages have a read-loop construct?*

MODULARITY CONSTRUCTS

It can be demonstrated that the set of constructs just discussed is sufficient to write any program that can be written in any procedural language. In fact, the set can easily be reduced even further. Staying within a relatively limited set of constructs reduces errors due to interaction between the data structures. Additional structures can be built up from the individual simple elements. Complicated structures of statements can be built up by nesting conditional and iterative constructs. Complicated data types can be built up from combinations of the structured data types. This concept of building up complicated structures from simple ones is a theme that permeates all of computer science. The final set of structures, *modularity constructs,* is valuable for this sort of structured build-up.

▷ *Why was the particular set of control structures chosen?*

Perhaps the single most important contribution of modern higher-level languages is modularity: division of a program into syntactic sections that reflect the logical structure of the program. Modularity helps insulate the programmer from the "bowl of Jell-O" phenomenon, in which a program is said to "wiggle all over" if you touch it anywhere. The frequently voiced problem of "it used to work, but now it doesn't and I didn't change anything" is usually more correctly stated as: ". . . but I didn't change anything that I thought should have an impact on this section of my program." In a highly modular program, changes in one section of the code will have little or no impact on changes in other sections. In addition, the programmer is free to think of the program at multiple levels of abstraction or sophistication. This enables the programmer to address general concepts without getting bogged down with all of the details. Most higher-level languages provide several specific tools to enhance modularity of code.

Blocks (`begin-end`)

Any group of statements can be logically associated by bracketing them with a `begin–end` pair

```
begin
    <statement 1>;
    <statement 2>;
    . . .
    <statement n>;
end {of block}
```

The group can then be treated as a single statement and used in any way in which a single statement can be used. This enables the programmer to think in terms of the accomplishments of the entire block rather than the sum of the accomplishments of the individual statements. Viewing the important collective properties of the block is called *abstraction*. The documentation structure may reflect this "block approach."

Subprograms

Subprograms expand the block structure concept further by providing a mechanism for naming the block:

```
Procedure <name>;
begin
    <statement 1>;
    <statement 2>;
    . . .
    <statement n>;
end {of procedure }
```

The block can then be referred from many places within the program simply by calling the procedure by name:

```
    <statement before>;
    {call } <procedure name>;
    <statement after>
```

Such a named block of statements is called a *procedure*. In general, procedures (and other subprograms) behave in exactly the same manner as programs. They can contain all of the same types of statements and types of data. The only distinction is that they are "called" from another "main" or "calling" program.

PARAMETERS. An additional advantage of procedures is that the calling and called programs can communicate through *parameters,* enabling the procedure to work with a specific limited set of data. This set can be specified at the time the procedure is called or referenced. Typically, the list is provided through *formal* or *dummy* parameters defined within the procedure header

```
Procedure <name> (<param_1>, <param_2> ...)
```

and passed to the procedure through actual parameters specified in the calling statement in the program body

```
<statement before>;
<procedure name> (<actual_1>, <actual_2>, . . .);
<statement after>
```

The formal parameters must match the *actual* parameters on a position-by-position basis. They must match exactly in type, number, and size. Most hlls are not capable of performing transformations between types. The parameters provide the mechanism to separate the information needed by this procedure from the information needed by the program as a whole. Generally, the body of a procedure should contain no variable identifiers other than those designating the formal parameters and any variables declared locally within the procedure. Such localization of data helps prevent errors by ensuring that the procedure alters no values other than those specifically indicated. The similarity in the syntax of procedure calls to that of the input/output commands `read` and `write` is no accident. By definition I/O involves events and objects external to the computer. It should not be surprising that this creates a fairly complex situation. The details of the input or output are hidden within the bodies of built-in procedures of Hill.

▷ *Why don't most hlls allow operations on mixed types?*

FUNCTIONS. A *function* is a special form of procedure that returns a single value as the result of executing the function. This value can then be used in exactly the same manner as any other expression (of the same type). Thus, while procedures are used as complete statements, functions can be used as part of expressions. Typical definitions take the form

```
function <name> (<param_1>, <param_2>...)⇒<result-type>
    begin
          <body>
          assign      <result>⇐<value>
    end
```

The typical use of a function takes the form

```
assign <variable>⇐<name> (<actual_1>, <actual_2>,...)
```

As with procedures, function bodies should normally contain no global variables.

COMMUNICATION. Parameters to subprograms take two forms, depending on whether the subprogram should be allowed to alter the data passed to it. If the program should not be allowed to alter the data, a copy of the data is passed to the subprogram. Any changes to the data within the subprogram are actually changes to the copy, and the actual parameter remains unaltered. Such parameters are said to be *value* (or `val`) parameters because only the value of the data is passed. They are also referred to as *call-by-value* parameters, or *input* parameters (since information can be passed into, but not back out of, the subprogram). This is the most common case, and the default case in most hlls since it protects the program from accidental changes in value.

The second form allows the subprogram to alter the value of parameters. In this case, the calling program passes the location of the actual parameter to the subprogram, thereby informing it of the internal location (or *address*) of that variable. The subprogram makes its alterations directly to the actual parameter itself. Such parameters are said to be *variable* (or `var`) parameters (since the actual parameter must be capable of changing, i.e., a variable), or *call-by-address* parameters (since the physical address of the parameter is what is passed), or *output* parameters (since the subprogram can output information to the calling program through this mechanism). A call-by-address parameter is closely related to the "pointer" data type. The address serves as a pointer to the data itself in much the same manner as pointer variables serve as pointers to data. Only the address, not the data itself, is passed. Therefore, a second benefit of this form of parameter is that complex data structures can be passed with a single address (pointer).

> ▷ *Are there other parallels between call-by-value parameters and pointers in most hlls?*

RECURSION. A minor (minor in form, not importance) variant of procedures and functions is *recursion*. Procedures and functions may call themselves simply by referencing their own names within their bodies. Simple recursion is useful in many of the same situations as iteration. For many people this provides an alternative way of thinking about such problems. The factorial of n is easily conceived as

$$\text{factorial}(n) = \begin{cases} 1 & \text{if } n \leq 1 \\ n * \text{[the factorial of } (n-1)] & \text{otherwise} \end{cases}$$

rather than

> "you start with one and
> successively multiply all of the numbers up to n, and
> the result is the factorial."

The former is closely related to the definition, while the latter is really a description of how to calculate the factorial. Since the art of programming can be thought of as the art of converting descriptions of desired results into descriptions of processes that create those results, the use of recursion as a control structure often results in conceptually easier code. Recursion is even more useful in more complex situations such as tree searches in which a procedure will call itself from more than one location within its body. Corresponding procedures become extraordinarily complex when the programmer is restricted to iteration as a control structure.

Documentation

Even the means of documentation provided by most hlls encourage hierarchical structure. The simple fact that all hlls provide a method of documentation is testimony to its importance. The tools provided can all be thought of as encouraging a hierarchical program. Comments can be provided at any level to describe the program itself, its types and variables, its procedures and functions, and its statements. They can occur in subprograms, blocks, single lines, and parts of lines. They can provide visual separation between sections of the code. Even blanks provide very simple means of enforcing structure.

This completes the discussion of all of the distinct forms of operation that computers can perform when viewed as higher-level language machines. While this may seem incredibly simplistic, you should consider any additional construct that you know of and attempt to describe it within the above set of classifications. Surprisingly, there are few—if any—statements that do not fit this simple classification. One of the advantages of higher-level languages is precisely that there are relatively few distinct classes of command.

THE HIGHER-LEVEL LANGUAGE AS PROTECTOR

The whole is not always the sum of the parts. No description of the higher-level language model of computation would be complete without some general observations about the capabilities of the language and intent of the designers. Beyond the specific statements provided, all hlls include additional features that are useful to the programmer. However, the remaining features are more abstract and often do not have direct representations in the surface syntax of the language. In fact, these features are often demonstrated as much by what is not allowed as by what is allowed. Unlike the constructs discussed in the previous section, you may not have thought of many of the following observations about higher-level languages.

Abstraction

Perhaps the single most important feature of all higher-level languages is that they provide an abstraction mechanism. The language itself provides a default level of abstraction with which the programmer views the machine and the program running on the machine. Furthermore, the language provides a mechanism for altering the level of abstraction. All aspects of hlls can be hierarchical structures:

- Statements are grouped into blocks.
- Statements are grouped using the control structures.
- Statements or blocks can be grouped into procedures.
- Procedures can be grouped to form programs.
- Groups of statements can be grouped to form larger groups.
- Data elements can be grouped into arrays and records.
- Data items and operations can be grouped into modules.

This abstraction capability frees the programmer first from the details of lower-level machine-oriented models and later from details of the programmer's own implementation. The most common examples of such abstraction capabilities are abstract data types and procedures. Thus, important concepts such as stack, queues, and trees can be created in any hll, even though the abstract data types themselves are not present in the language.

Label and Naming Conventions

Naming identifiers is an important power provided by all hlls. Programming would be almost impossible if the programmer were required to make all references by description: the first variable declared; the tenth procedure declared; the item in the second array described by the contents of the third variable, and so on. To alleviate the problem, Hill provides a set of naming rules or conventions for identifiers (e.g., must start with a letter; can be composed of any letter or digit) for variables, procedures, and so on. Since hlls restrict the form but not the content of names, they provide an important mechanism for the programmer to help ensure the quality of work. For example, `status_of_the_users_account` can be a self-descriptive variable name.

UNIFORMITY. With a single set of naming conventions, the programmer may name any portion of the program: a variable, a type for variables, a procedure, a function, or even a statement. Primitive languages had one mechanism for referencing variables, a second for referencing statements, and so on.

LOCALITY. The same mechanisms provide the ability to localize names. The contents of a location can be protected against inadvertent alteration or use by other segments of the program. Early languages not only allowed such accidents but encouraged them, by allowing two locations to be equivalent to each other or by allowing large blocks of storage to be commonly addressable by multiple routines. *Local variables* provide an additional conceptual tool to help the programmer think in terms of a hierarchical program.

Hierarchical Nature

Many of the constructs of hlls are designed expressly to provide a hierarchical approach to programming. They allow the programmer to think only of the details needed for the current level of abstraction, while hiding those that are irrelevant. Such features enable the programmer to think top-down in the development process. Subprograms and blocks are the most obvious examples of this concept. While the use of blocks, procedures, and functions provides obvious examples of such capabilities, most hlls provide a number of less-obvious tools.

EXPRESSIONS. Like programs, expressions can be viewed as hierarchically organized. In fact, most classes of expressions can be defined recursively by a set of rules such as STOPPED

```
expression  :==  <constant> | <variable>
expression  :==  <expression> <operator> <expression>
```

(read as "an expression can be a constant or a variable; it can also be two expressions connected by an operator"). For example, in the case of arithmetic expressions, `<operator>` might be "+" or "−". In any situation calling for an expression, a more complicated expression can always be used in place of a simple one. Thus, wherever one can say `x+y`, one can say `x`, and (almost) vice versa.[5] The definition may be recursively applied, allowing these constructs to be built up: 2 + 3 + 3 + 4 can be used wherever 2 + 3 or just 2 can be used. Parentheses provide a visual mechanism for organizing the expression. The hierarchical definitions of most expressions enable the programmer to visualize complex series of operations as a single operation. Similarly, after the user has created a function, that function can be used in place of a value of the corresponding type, again providing the ability to think of more complex computations in the same manner as simpler ones. The same is true of expressions of other data types such as Boolean or character.

STRICT TYPING. Most hlls restrict most expressions to involve only variables of a single type, thereby further reducing confusions that may exist. For situations in which the user indeed wants to convert data from one type to another type, explicit *type-transfer* operations are provided. Common examples of these include

`ord:`	character to integer
`char:`	integer to character
`float:`	integer to real
`round:`	real to integer

Strict typing virtually eliminates accidental use of an inappropriate operand by an operator because the programmer must explicitly indicate that the type transfer is to take place.

TYPE (AND RANGE) CHECKING. There is no obvious logical meaning for the addition of two characters or the `and`ing of two integers. Fortunately most hlls prohibit us from attempting such operations. In the case of clearly distinct types, this protection is obvious. But many hlls go much further. For example, placing an integer value into an integer variable is a legal operation, but if an integer value is too large for the location to hold, the attempt may be intercepted and an error message generated. Similarly many hlls protect the programmer from

---

[5]The "almost" reflects that fact that the equivalence only holds in those situations in which the expression will be evaluated, such as the right-hand side of an assignment statement or an output statement. The syntax of most hlls specifies that identifiers—not expressions—appear on the left-hand side of assignments or in `read` statements.

inadvertently exceeding the length of a string, the bounds of an array, or the limits of any enumerated type.

> ▷ *Under what circumstances would you want to treat a value as if it were a different type?*

UNIVERSALITY. In most hlls, the syntax is almost constant across the various data types, which saves the programmer problems induced by confusion about the current context.

INTEGRATION. Hlls provide statements that naturally form single units, sets of frequently occurring operations. For example, the assignment statement can group a series of arithmetic operations (of any complexity) with an internal data movement; conditional statements group an arbitrary set of Boolean operations with a selection of control. Thus, hlls are "pre-structured" into a hierarchy even at the single statement level.

LOGICAL, HUMAN-ORIENTED STEPS. Hlls treat a set of actions, specified in terms of machine capabilities, into terms better-suited to humans; that is the compiler for a hll translates a process stated in terms that are useful to humans into the internal form needed by a computer. Items that are complex for a machine are often very simple conceptually for humans. Occasionally, inconvenient constructs have also been introduced. Early languages, designed more for the convenience of the computer, contained such antediluvian constructs as the "arithmetic if" or the "computed go to," which encouraged very error-prone programming practices. Modern constructs such as the `if-then-else` or the `while` loop were invented later as the result of experience and practice with higher-level languages. Yet few languages have taken the extra step of allowing arbitrary mathematical expressions, such as

```
1 < x < 10
```

> ▷ *Why not allow such abbreviated relational constructs?*

COMPLEX STATEMENTS. Individual statements may specify multiple actions. For example,

```
readln (item1, item2, item3)
```

or

```
assign root⇐((-b) + sqrt((b^2) - (4 * a * c))) / (2 * a)
```

both specify actions that require extensive processing by a machine. In the second case, the individual steps are clear (although the complexity of the substep `sqrt` is not clear). In the first example, however, many events must occur, about which the higher-level language programmer may never have thought. Beyond the fact that this `read` statement asks for three items, the computer needs to perform several other operations:

- it must determine if any input has been received at the device (if not, wait);
- it must convert the input stream into the appropriate data type; and
- it may even require that instructions be sent to the device.

All these and more are hidden from the user by the higher-level language.

SEPARATION OF DECLARATIONS FROM PROGRAM. Most hlls distinctly separate the description of the data from the description of the operations on that data. This not only increases the abstraction and modularity available but actually protects the program from itself.

> ▷ *We will see later that some programmer errors can destroy not only data but part of the program body, causing catastrophic errors. How could this be?*

ORDER INDEPENDENCE. Most of us think of programming as a very ordered process and are keenly aware of the fact that we must provide sequential operations, Hlls often protect us from even these common details. For example, if we wish to execute the conditional statement

```
if (A < B) and (B < C)
  then <body>
```

the programmer need not worry about whether the first or second comparison is performed first. Similarly, if for associative operations such as

```
assign  A⇐B + C + D
```

the programmer need not specify whether B and C are added and then D added to that sum, or if D and C are first added (or even if B and D might be added first). For nonassociative operations in which the order does matter, such as

```
assign  A⇐B - (C - D)
```

parentheses can provide the necessary grouping. The important observation is that once the programmer identifies a situation in which the order of operations does not matter, the order can be ignored. Additionally, although we must worry about which argument to a procedure is specified first, we need not worry about the order in which they are delivered to the subroutine.

COORDINATION. Internal and external events—such as user input and program execution of an input statement—must be coordinated. The higher-level language takes care of this coordination for the programmer. Otherwise the user would have to enter data at precisely the moment that a program reached the input statement—a virtual impossibility. The computing system uses interrupts for this coordination as well as for additional tasks, such as running a clock. Fortunately, the hll programmer can be completely oblivious to the existence of interrupts.

▷ *How can a computer possibly stop executing a program, do something else, and return to the program without ever losing its place?*

MACHINE CORRESPONDENCE. The human need not deal with any internal details of a machine: the compiler performs all needed translation. This not only means that the programmer saves much effort by working at a higher level of abstraction, but also that a program that works on one machine should work with little or no modification on almost any other machine.

PREVIEW

The higher-level language model of computation can provide a coherent view of the computing process. Yet few machines (exceptions include Lisp machines and the Boroughs 6500, an Algol-based machine) provide direct implementations of such a model. Instead, a *compiler* translates a hll program into an appropriate internal representation. This internal representation can be thought of as another model of computation and will be the subject of the next few chapters.

Understanding the various models provides the foundation for understanding the function of major software systems such as compilers. Understanding the nature of compilation helps one understand the errors that can occur in any program. One important classification of errors is by the point of detection.

- Compile time: the compiler could not understand the syntax of some statement of your program,
- Run time: the compiler translated your program into an internal format, but the computer still could not run it, and
- Logical: the program ran but produced incorrect results.

The same breakdown exists within each of the other models.

Following are several questions that will be answered in later sections. You may have wondered about some of these at the time that you first learned about higher-level languages. Others may have occurred to you while reading the summary provided in this chapter. Still others may be totally new to you. Some you may be able to answer and, to some you may say, "so what?" As we "crank up the microscope" to look at computing systems with successively more powerful lenses, these questions and more will be answered.

Why are integers and real numbers distinct?

Why is a string of length 1 different from a character?

Why these specific control structures and not others?

What is a pointer, really?

Why does the largest possible integer (`maxint`) have the value that it does?

Why do real numbers sometimes yield strange results (like .999 for 1.0)?

Why does "pure" Pascal have `mod` but not exponentiation?

Why did early languages have only uppercase characters?

Why do modern languages have the set of characters that they have?

Why are strings typically restricted to 256 characters?

How do `ord` and `char` work?

Why did many early microcomputers have 64k? (For that matter, what is a "k"?)

What is a one-megabyte machine?

Why did we choose the term *k* as our primary measure of size?

Why are programs compiled?

What is the distinction between compilation and interpretation?

Why did early hlls restrict variable names to six characters?

How can we implement recursion?

Are some operations more efficient than others?

Are there actions that can be accomplished by computers—but not in hlls?

Why do people say "computers can only deal in numbers"?

We never use it, so what's all the talk about binary arithmetic?

SUMMARY

This chapter itself was a summary of general ideas present in most higher-level languages. Its purpose was to provide you with a starting point for languages that cannot be called higher-level. You are urged to create a summary for yourself!

SUGGESTED READING

You are urged to review any aspects of higher-level languages that were somehow missed. The following references may be helpful.

Abelson, H., and J. Sussman. *Structure and Interpretation of Computer Programs*. New York: McGraw-Hill, 1985.

Brookshear, J. G. *Computer Science; An Overview*. Reading, MA: Addison-Wesley, 1991.

Cooper, D., and M. Clancy. *Oh Pascal*. New York: Norton, 1985.

Garland, S. *Introduction to Computer Science with Applications in Pascal*. Reading, MA: Addison-Wesley, 1986.

Goldschlager, L. and A. Lister. *Computer Science; A Modern Introduction*. Englewood Cliffs, N.J.: Prentice Hall, 1988.

Pratt, T. *Pascal: A New Introduction to Computer Science*. Englewood Cliffs, N.J.: Prentice Hall, 1990.

Schneider, G. M., and S. Bruell. *Advanced Concepts in Data Representation and Software Development*. Chicago: West, 1991.

Tucker, A. *Computer Science, A Second Course Using Modula*. New York: McGraw-Hill, 1988.

Tucker, A., J. Bradley, R. Cupper, and D. Garnick. *Fundamentals of Computing, Volume I*. New York: McGraw-Hill, 1991.

Walker, H. *Computer Science 2*. Glenview, IL: Scott, Foresman, 1989.

EXERCISES[6]

1.1. Identify at least one feature of your favorite higher-level language that is not present in Hill.

1.2. Identify at least one feature of Hill that is not present in your favorite higher-level language.

1.3. Convert any simple program that you have written in a higher-level language into Hill.

1.4. What would be the result if the Hill or Pascal read statement were restricted to a given data type or a given number of input items?

1.5. Select any programming problem from the middle of any hll text and write the program. Think about each feature that you use and reflect on its role within the language.

1.6. Assume that when dropped on a hard floor, a rubber ball will return to 90% of the height from which it was dropped. Write a program that counts the number of times that a ball dropped from a height of 2 m will bounce back up to a height of greater than 0.1 m. Try this using a pretest loop and again using a post-test loop. Try it counting the bounces and try it counting the peaks. This problem is typical of ones that can generate fence post errors.

1.7. Given the pretest loop

```
while (test) do
      <action>;
```

What steps are necessary to convert it to a post-test loop?

1.8. Consider the Hill `begin` and `end` statements. What errors or confusions would exist if they were not included in the language? What alternatives are possible?

1.9. Earlier hlls did not have pretest or post-test constructs. How can one construct an indefinite loop without those constructs?

1.10. How does strict typing protect the programmer? Give three examples of errors that are possible without strict typing.

1.11. Most languages require that procedures have a single entry point and single exit point. For each, give one example of a situation that could cause an error if this rule were relaxed.

1.12. Suppose an array is defined with bounds [1..10]. What might happen if a program referred to location [0]? The language you are used to may or may not detect the problem. Answer the question assuming each condition.

---

[6]In addition to these exercises, Appendix 2 includes several larger exercises presented in the form of term projects or continuing projects.

1.13. Write a code segment that prints out all of the uppercase and then all of the lowercase letters.

1.14. Modify the program from Exercise 1.13 so that it prints the uppercase and lowercase versions of each letter sequentially: AaBbCc. . . .

1.15. Write a program that prints out the series: 1, 2, 4, 8, 16,. . . . Experiment with the upper bound. How high can you make the bound? What happens beyond that point? Does it make a difference if you use a pre-test loop or a counter controlled loop?

1.16. The Fibonacci sequence,

```
1, 1, 2, 3, 5, 8, 13,. . .
```

is defined as

$$\text{Fib}(n) = \begin{cases} 1 & \text{if } n \leq 2 \\ \text{Fib}(n-1) + \text{Fib}(n-2) & \text{otherwise} \end{cases}$$

Write two versions of subroutine to calculate the nth Fibonacci number, one recursive and one not recursive. Compare the two procedures for complexity. Then time each version for 1000 calls. Describe the tradeoff that results.

PART II

THE ASSEMBLY LANGUAGE MODEL

Higher-level languages derive their name from the fact that they represent a higher level than do assembly or machine languages. Higher-level languages do present a "higher level" of power in the constructs supported by the languages, but the term actually refers more to the greater level of abstraction that they provide. The next logical question is "Higher than what?" The comparison is to the assembly and machine languages that dominated the programming field in an earlier time. The price the programmer pays for the power of this abstraction is further removal from the details of the machine: the model of the machine employed is more abstract. Examination of the lower-level model embodied in an assembly language can reveal additional details of the internal structure of a machine. In order to program in an assembly language, the user must specify more details when writing a program and keep track of more information when debugging it. On the other hand, the assembly language user gains a level of control and degree of freedom not enjoyed by hll programmers. In this section, we begin the study of assembly language as the underlying support structure for all higher-level languages. More important, we begin the exploration of the machine at this lower level of abstraction. In Chapter 2, we will view assembly language as a reflection of hlls. But it is a two-way reflection: we will also see that many of the features of hlls are reflections of the essential capabilities of assembly languages and that these features exist because of the nature of the machine. Later we will view assembly language more as a reflection of its own underlying machine language. As we continue to view computing from differing perspectives, the terminology we employ will evolve in an orderly manner.

After the initial overview, Chapter 3 discusses practical guidelines for assembly language programmers. Chapter 4 then introduces binary arithmetic, which underlies all computer mathematics. Armed with this foundation, you are then equipped to investigate structures such as arrays and lists in Chapter 5 or to use debuggers, as described in Chapter 13.

Keep in mind the purpose of this study: an understanding of the underlying machine. As new concepts are introduced, reasonably concrete examples will be needed. The generic language, GAL, and the machine on which it runs, GAM, are abstractions designed for such illustrations. They embody the conceptual features common to essentially all (or at least most) assembly languages—but, therefore, look like no existing language.

CHAPTER 2

OVERVIEW OF THE ASSEMBLY LANGUAGE MODEL: A HIGHER-LEVEL LANGUAGE PERSPECTIVE

The assembly language model or view of the internal structure of a machine is a more detailed version (lower level of abstraction) of that used by hll programmers. The higher-level language model and the remaining models presented in this text are all variations on one general model: the von Neumann Machine.[1] The concepts

[1]Named after the Hungarian-American mathematician John von Neumann (1903–57), who is generally credited with the invention of the "stored program digital electronic computer." This credit seems to be almost universally ascribed to von Neumann, even though a number of other persons almost simultaneously contributed many of the same ideas. Notable among these were British mathematician Alan Turing, and American physicists John Atanasoff, John Eckert, and John Mauchly. Although some of the others actually had working machines at an earlier date, only Turing and von Neumann incorporated the concept of stored programs, and only von Neumann actually built such a machine.

described in this chapter are universal and can be applied generally to any *assembly language* (AL) running on any modern machine. However, the concepts are illustrated by use of the hypothetical assembly language GAL (Generic Assembly Language) designed to run on the equally hypothetical machine GAM (Generic Assembly Machine). Both GAL and GAM are "moving targets," designed for illustration. The exact syntax of the languages will vary and become more specific in subsequent chapters. Do not worry so much about the details of the language as the principles they embody.

ARCHITECTURAL OVERVIEW

The higher-level language model distinguished between data declarations and executable code. In an analogous manner, an assembly language machine can be thought of as having two primary components:

> *memory,* which holds the data and the running program, and
>
> *the central processing unit* (CPU), which executes that program.

Figure 2-1*a* schematically illustrates the conceptual model thus far. As each of these is further broken down, this ridiculously simple model will slowly become more complex and, therefore, more interesting.

MEMORY

Memory consists of storage locations into which data can be placed and from which that data can later be retrieved. In hlls, each variable declaration reserves a memory storage location. Values were placed in that location (usually by an assignment or a `read` statement) and could be retrieved later (using an assignment, write, or other statement). Many analogies to memory exist outside the computer realm, including human memory, notes on scraps of papers, phonograph records,

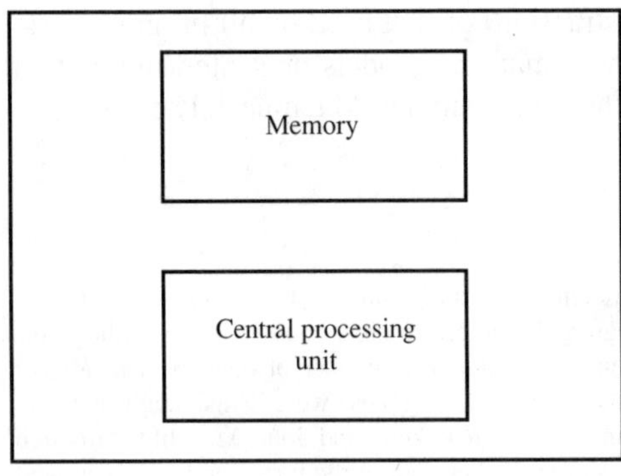

FIGURE 2-1(*a*)
The simplest conceptual view of a computer.

and photographs. As indicated in Figure 2-1*b*,[2] memory can be categorized into two subclasses:

register memory and
main memory

Registers

The first form of memory is the register. In general, a computer has relatively few registers, typically between one and 32. In GAM there are eight registers, named `reg0`, `reg1`, `reg2`, and so on, up to `reg7`. Since there are so few registers, they generally have standard names such as those used above. Note that these names are sufficiently descriptive to identify the registers, but they are not at all useful in identifying their function as are the more general variable names of most hlls. Eight registers cannot hold nearly enough data for even the simplest of programs. In fact we will see that some of the registers are often reserved for special purposes. Registers are working storage; they are not intended for holding large quantities of data, or for holding a value for an extended period of time. Their principal advantage is their speed, which is much faster than that of main memory.

[2]This somewhat pedantic or repetitious diagram is included at this point, in part, to preview a technique that will be used repeatedly within the text: a topic is first explained at one level of detail. When the discussion seems complete, the level of detail will be increased, revealing a new world underneath.

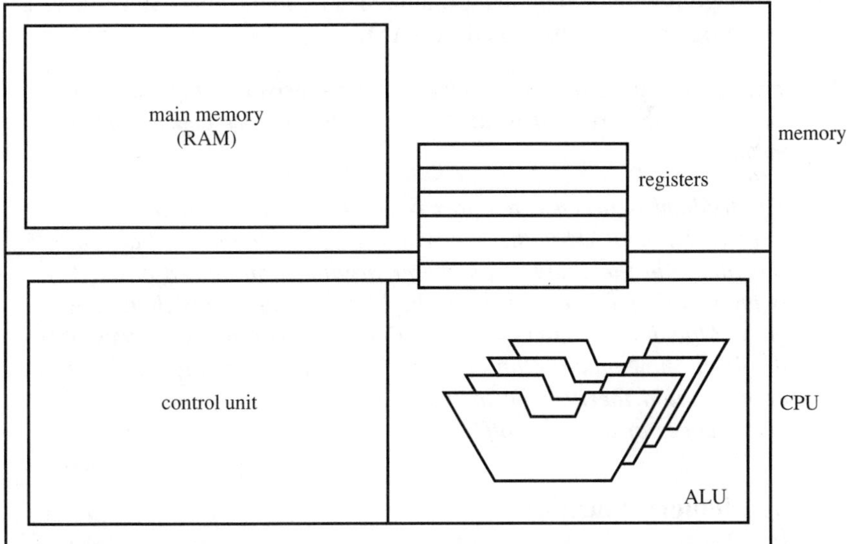

FIGURE 2-1(*b*)
Slight magnification of (*a*).

▷ *These naming conventions suggest several questions: Why do computer scientists prefer to start counting at zero rather than one? Can we create more descriptive names than* `reg0`*? If some of the registers are reserved for special purposes, who reserved them?*

Main Memory

The second form of memory is called *main memory* or *random access memory* (*RAM*) because any location in RAM can be accessed at any time—not because access is actually a random process. It is by far the dominant form and comprises the greatest portion of memory. Modern computers have millions of storage locations in main memory. Thus, main memory can hold the large quantities of data used in most programs. Unfortunately, access to main memory is not nearly as fast as it is to the registers, a fact that occasionally restricts the use of RAM. It is usually up to the programmer to decide which locations must be accessed very quickly (and therefore should be in registers) and which need not be accessed quite so quickly (and can be kept in main memory). Generally, data that will be accessed often or in the immediate future is stored in fast registers, while data that will not be used often, that will not be accessed again for a long time, or that requires large amounts of storage (e.g., arrays) will be kept in main memory.

In all modern computers, the running program itself is stored in memory. Each of the statements that comprise a program must be stored in memory while a program is running. Generally, each assembly language instruction occupies one (or more) memory location. Programs obviously are relatively large; even simple assembly language programs may require hundreds of statements. Since there are few registers, programs must be stored in RAM.

▷ *Yes, "stored program" is a defining characteristic of the von Neumann architecture, but what does it mean to store a program in memory?*

▷ *The tradeoff between a few fast registers and large quantities of relatively slow RAM is the first instance of a rule that will appear repeatedly in the study of computer organization: speed costs. It is financially more expensive to build fast components than slow ones. Machine designers must continually make tough choices of the form "how much of an expensive item should be included" or even "should the item be included at all." Watch for additional occurrences of this tradeoff.*

Identifying Memory Locations

VARIABLES. Because there are thousands or even millions of locations in main memory, a mechanism is needed for naming individual cells. Statements called *directives* are used to name RAM locations in assembly language. These are not unlike the `variable` or `constant` declarations of hlls. A typical GAL memory directive looks like

```
my_loc   variable:character
```

or

```
my_loc   variable:char                ;(for short)
```

which can be read as "reserve RAM memory storage, to be called `my_loc`, sufficient to hold one character." This interpretation is roughly equivalent to the Hill declaration:

```
    variable
        my_loc:char;
```

`My_loc` now identifies the storage location declared, enabling reference by any of the statements described later. Data can be placed into `my_loc` or retrieved from it, just as in Hill. The general syntax of the `variable` storage directive is

```
    <identifier>     variable:<type>     [;<comment>]
```
[3]

Storage for other forms of data such as integers can be similarly requested:

```
An_int     variable:integer
```

or

```
An_int     variable:int               ;(for short)
```

A significant difference follows from the protection provided by higher-level languages. The rules of most hlls, such as Pascal or Hill, insist that the user declare the type (integer, real, character, etc.) for every storage location. The compiler then protects the user by rejecting any use of a variable that does not conform to the declaration. Assembly languages, however, provide little such protection. Each statement is interpreted locally. There is little checking against other uses of the term, including its declaration. The declaration does not imply any binding agreement between assembler and programmer. Once

---

[3]The notation used to describe GAL statements is essentially the same as that used in Chapter 1 to describe Hill:

- Items shown without any bracketing should appear exactly as in the specification.
- Items enclosed in angle brackets (<. . .>) should be replaced with specific values.
- Items enclosed in square brackets ([. . .]) are optional.
- White space may be of any size.
- Semi-colons set off comments.

Rules for identifiers are exactly the same as for identifiers in Hill or Pascal: a string composed of an alphabetic character, followed by any number of alphanumeric characters, including the underscore "___".

storage has been reserved, further statements are not compared with the declared type of the variable. The declaration ensures only that the reserved storage is appropriate for the type of variable requested. GAL will reserve the appropriate type and quantity of storage but will provide no further checking to assure that the programmer follows the established convention. It is up to the programmer to remember the declaration and to guarantee consistency. If the programmer declares a storage location to be a character and then uses it as if it were an integer, most assemblers will not object and the results may be unpredictable. This is the first of many instances of "naked programming": the AL programmer must work without the protection provided by higher level languages.

CONSTANTS. Storage locations containing an explicit value can also be created in most assembly languages. In GAL, they are created using the `constant` data directive, a declaration very similar to the `variable` directive, in both syntax and interpretation:

```
<identifier>  constant:<type>   <value> [<comment>]
```

allocates a single storage location of type `<type>` called `<identifier>`, and places `<value>` into that location. Thus

```
my_int  constant:integer      5
```

and

```
my_char constant:character    'x'
```

request storage locations with the initial values 5 and "x", roughly equivalent to the Hill declarations

```
        constant     my_int = 5;
                     my_char = 'x';
```

The `variable` and `constant` data directives both reserve named storage locations for use by the program. For the `variable` directive, that is all that it does—no value is saved. The `constant` directive additionally places the value specified by `<value>` into the newly reserved location. The obvious intent of the constant directive is for the creation of constants. However, there is nothing to prevent the programmer from altering the value later—it behaves more like an "initialized variable."

▷ *Contrast other similarities and the differences between the GAL* `variable` *and* `constant` *directives on the one hand with those of the* `variable` *and* `constant` *declarations of Hill on the other. For example, Hill is "smart" enough to figure out the type of constants from the value provided, but GAL is not. The type should always be provided. Why might this be?*

Both main memory and register memory serve many of the same purposes. Both can hold any form of data. The contents of each can be changed via program instructions. Most instructions can access either registers or main memory, but there will be some restrictions, especially with respect to main memory access.

LITERALS. The AL language programmer may use literal data in manners analogous to those of Hill. A literal numeric or character value may be assigned directly to a constant, as seen in the examples above. Many GAL statements also allow the use of a literal directly in the statement. However, unlike Hill, GAL requires that any use of a literal within a statement be explicitly marked with the *immediate sign*, called #, to indicate the presence of a literal. For example,

```
    add         #5⇒reg2
```

is a GAL instruction equivalent to the Hill

```
    assign      loc⇐5 + loc
```

In addition, the *equals* operator can be used to establish symbolic names for literals:

```
my_val    equals  5
```

establishes `my_val` as a symbolic name for the value 5, which can later be used wherever the literal 5 may be used. For example,

```
    add         #my_val⇒reg2
```

▷ *Why should the immediate sign be necessary? What else could a literal symbol possibly mean?*

Organization of Data

A second protection provided by most hlls is the complete separation of data from code by means of several structuring commands, such as `begin`, `end`, and `procedure`. Variables and constants are declared in a designated area prior to the `begin–end` block to which they apply. Technically in GAL, data may legally be declared anywhere in the program: beginning, ending, or middle. It is up to the programmer to separate variables from code. GAL provides two formating directives designed to help structure data declarations: `begin_data` and `end_data`. While not required, they help the programmer structure the program. The general syntax for a data directive section is

```
[<label>]  begin_data      [<procedure_name>]  [<comment>]
           <directive_1>
               . . .
           <directive_n>
[<label>]  end_data        [<procedure_name>]  [<comment>]
```

▷ *What is the relationship between the need to separate data from code and the concept of stored-program computer?*

THE ARITHMETIC LOGIC UNIT AND ASSEMBLY LANGUAGE COMMANDS

The *central processing unit* (CPU) performs or *executes* the statements of a program, using the data stored in memory. Figure 2-1*b*, shows schematically that the CPU is logically composed of two principal subsystems:

the *arithmetic logic unit* (*ALU*) performs simple operations, such as the addition of two numbers, movement of a value from one storage location to another, or the comparison of two characters; and

the *control unit* determines which instruction is to be executed next.

In practice, the functions of these two units can be quite intertwined. Arithmetic will be needed in order to control, and control information will be used during complicated arithmetic operations. The distinction is related to the hll distinctions between control statements, such as conditionals, and operations, such as assignments. For the moment, we will refer to both subsystems by the collective name central processing unit.

The ALU is only capable of simple operations compared to those specifiable in hlls. Each assembly language instruction corresponds to one ALU operation. Assembly language commands, like those of hlls, can be broken into three principal categories:

data movement instructions,
data manipulation instructions, and
control operations.

Assembly language commands are much like simplified versions of hll commands: Each operates on data items declared in the declaration section; each performs one step of an algorithm or procedure; and each can be grouped with others to form a procedure.

DATA MOVEMENT

Data movement instructions in assembly language are classified into the same categories of data movement as were discussed in Chapter 1: internal-internal, internal-external, external-internal, and external-external (the last being irrelevant). Internal-internal is by far the simplest.

Internal Data Transfer

Think of a data movement command as an instruction to *copy* data from one location (called the *source*) to a second location (called the *destination*). The programmer must specify the item to be copied and the location to which it is being copied. The `copy` command has the format:

```
    copy    <source_item>⇛<destination_item>
```

which is interpreted as "copy the data stored at the location specified by `<source_item>` into that specified by `<destination_item>`." For example, given the `variable` directive

```
item2    variable:integer
```

and then the statement

```
    copy    reg0⇛item2
```

is roughly equivalent to the Hill statement

```
    assign  item2⇚<some value>
```

If `reg0` has (somehow, previously) received the value 5, the statement will result in `item2` also having the value 5. As was the case with the hll assignment statements, the `copy` command does not destroy the contents of the source location. Like Hill, GAL uses arrows to indicate the direction of data movement, but the syntactic direction is the opposite. That is, the first item specified (the source) is copied into the second (destination). This would actually seem more natural to a programmer who was not already used to higher-level languages in which assignment is performed "right to left." Figure 2-2 schematically illustrates the various forms of `copy`.

The `copy` statement can also move literal values into a storage location

```
    copy    #5⇛item3
```

is equivalent to the Hill

```
    assign  item3⇚5          ;
```

Even if the literal value is not numeric, the immediate sign is still used

```
    copy    #'A'⇛item3
```

places the character "A" into `item3`. Literals used in commands are also called

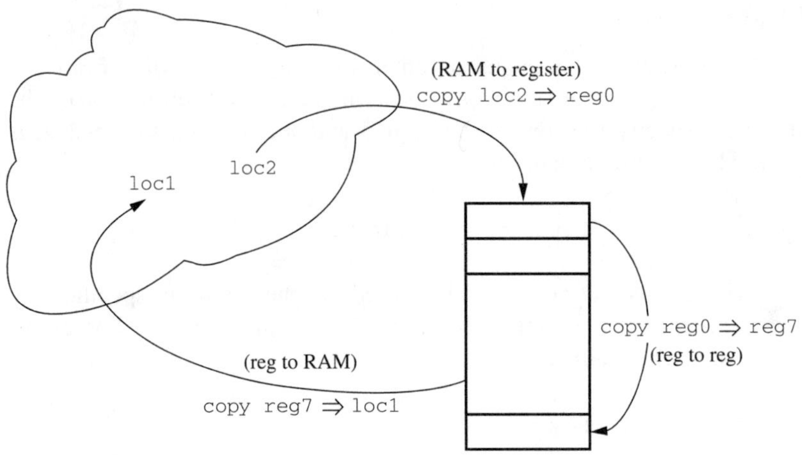

FIGURE 2-2
Forms of `copy`.

immediate values. The value itself immediately follows the command verb. There is no need to access a separate source location to obtain the value.

In general, literal values can be used wherever a reasonable interpretation of their use may be made. In the case of the `copy` command, it generally makes sense to copy a literal value into some other location. But since literals cannot change, you cannot copy a value into a literal. Thus, the destination operand must be either a register or a RAM location declared as a variable. Given the declarations

```
var1        variable:integer
var2        variable:integer
const3      constant:integer      5
```

the following are all legal `copy` statements:

```
    copy    reg0⇒var2         ;register to RAM
    copy    var1⇒reg2         ;RAM variable to register
    copy    const3⇒reg2       ;RAM const to register
    copy    reg2⇒reg1         ;register to register
    copy    #1⇒reg3           ;literal to register
```

But this one would be *illegal*:

```
                           ;↓ILLEGAL↓ because
    copy    reg0⇒#3        ;destination is literal
```

GAL makes one further restriction on the operands. In general, both source and destination may specify either main memory locations or register locations.

But in GAL, no more than one of those operands may specify a RAM location.[4] This apparently arbitrary rule reflects the mechanism for identifying operands. Because there are few registers, they are easy to specify. The number of distinct RAM locations, on the other hand, makes them more difficult to specify. For an English analogy, consider the difference between specifying a specific state within the United States (each has a unique name) and specifying a particular seagull on a beach. By restricting the number of RAM operands, the internal structure of the GAM machine can be similarly simplified.

> ▷ *Why is it also difficult to represent one item out of many in a computer?*

Thus, given the same declarations as above, the following would also be illegal:

```
                                 ;ILLEGAL because
copy            var1⇒var2        ;two RAM operands
copy            const3⇒var2      ;     ''
```

Although this restriction may seem problematic, it is easily circumvented by using a register as an intermediate storage location:

```
copy            var1⇒reg2
copy            reg2⇒var2
```

Finally, recall that instructions are stored in RAM memory. Therefore, since a literal value is actually a part of an instruction, it too is ultimately stored in RAM memory. Thus, a literal is a RAM operand in GAL. Therefore, the GAL statement

```
copy            #2⇒item2       ;ILLEGAL:literal to RAM
```

is also illegal.

As noted, few assemblers check for the úse of correct types. A program may not work correctly if data is moved without regard to its type. The `copy` statement allows the programmer to indicate explicitly the intended type of the data transfer. For example,

```
copy:integer      reg0⇒item2
copy:character    reg2⇒reg1
copy:integer      #1⇒reg3
```

[4]The reader is reminded that GAL is a generic language. Every specific assembly language will have its own (seemingly arbitrary) exceptions to these rules. In later chapters we will learn to explore the specific exceptions of a given language. In general, GAL is probably at least as restrictive as most languages; therefore, you will seldom get into trouble following the GAL rules.

This is a fundamental distinction between AL and hlls. While neither language will provide correct results if the programmer uses types incorrectly, hlls protect the programmer by providing an appropriate error message. In contrast, ALs attempt to follow the programmer's request without checking the type. The programmer should develop the habit of always explicitly indicating the type of the data.

GENERALIZING THE GAL SYNTAX. The `copy` can optionally have an identifier in the first column. Thus, its full syntax is essentially the same as for the data storage directives:

```
[<label>]     copy [:<type>]     <source>⇒<destination>
                                                  [<comments>]
```

In general, all GAL statements have essentially the same syntax:

```
[<label>]    <operation> [:<type>]    <operands>
                                                  [<comments>]
```

Each of the given fields can be generalized from the form seen thus far:

Any statement may have a label. The rules for labeling statements are the same as for labeling data items: an alphanumeric string, beginning with a letter.

Every statement must have an operation (called an *opcode*).

Most operations specify the type (integer, character, etc.).

Most require one or more operands (usually, two).

Any statement can be followed by a comment.

▷ *But, why would one want to label an executable statement?*

This consistency makes it easier to understand new statements as they are encountered. The syntactic structure provides a clear distinction between the operation and the operands. On the other hand, the simplicity implies that the content or meaning of a statement must be derived almost entirely from the meaning of the individual components. The structure of the statement provides little help. In Hill each command had a unique structure with named subfields filling unique roles. There is no unique structure for the individual GAL commands.

External Data Transfer

Movement of data between the computer and the outside world is one of the more complicated basic activities of a computer. In Hill the complications were hidden within the `read` procedure, which is capable of reading any basic data type or any number or combinations of data items, detecting errors, and skipping blank space. Assembly language provides only the most rudimentary of such capabilities. Therefore, handling the tasks equivalent to those provided by `read` and write statements is often one of the more complicated tasks of the assembly language programmer.

In the GAM machine, all transfers of data between the internal and external world are funneled through a register. That is, all data entering the GAM machine will enter at reg0, from where the program can copy it to any other internal location. For output, the program will place the data in reg0 before it can be output. Two built-in GAL procedures accomplish the I/O tasks.

> ▷ *The convention of channeling input through register 0 is not as arbitrary as it appears. What might its significance be?*

INPUT. Input is accomplished by the GAL procedure

```
input
```

which transfers a single *byte* (or character) of data from the keyboard to reg0. It is roughly equivalent to the Hill

```
read (<item_name>);
```

in which <item_name> fills the same role as reg0 and is assumed here to be of type char. Input is even closer to the Pascal statements:

```
<item_name>:= input↑;
get;
```

which also transfer a single byte or character of data from the keyboard to <item_name>. Alternatively, one may think of input as similar to the pseudo-GAL statement:

```
copy                keyboard⇒reg0     ;not valid
```

The exact syntax for GAL procedure calls has not yet been introduced, but input of one character from the outside generally requires two steps:

```
input
copy:character      reg0⇒<item_name>
```

That is, a character is moved from the keyboard into reg0 and from there into <item_name>. After executing an input, the newly read value may then be accessed by any further commands, just as if it had been placed into reg0 with a copy statement. It must be re-emphasized that input reads a character data item, not a numeric value. It assumes that the type of the input is equivalent to the Hill type char.

When most hlls read a character from the keyboard, the character appears on the screen. We say it is *echoed* to the screen. The keyboard is not directly connected to the screen. Rather, the screen reflects—or echoes—what was read by the program. One of the first distinctions that the GAL programmer will notice is that the input command does not echo the input character. Thus, when an input character is typed, it will not automatically appear on the screen.

OUTPUT. The GAL output procedure is similar to the input command in that it transfers a single character between internal and external locations. The program must first place data into reg0 and then call the output procedure

```
copy:character    item_name⇒reg0
output
```

which will result in a value previously placed in item_name being output to the next available position on the screen. It was necessary to copy the character into reg0, because output insists on the value being in that register, not in main memory (as item_name apparently is according to the syntax).

Output is roughly equivalent to the Hill command

```
write (item_name)
```

assuming that item_name was declared to be of type character. It is even closer to the Pascal sequence

```
output↑:= item_name;
put;
```

(where output here is not the GAL procedure but the Pascal file pointer of the same name). Two successive characters could be written "back-to-back" by

```
copy:character    one_thing⇒reg0
output
copy:character    another⇒reg0
output
```

(assuming the appropriate declarations).

Since input does not echo the characters to the screen, one could use output to duplicate the echo effect:

```
input
output
copy:character    reg0⇒where_you_want
```

or

```
input
copy:character    reg0⇒where_you_want
output
```

which are both roughly equivalent to the Hill statement

```
read (where_you_want);
```

which automatically includes the echo.

▷ *What might be an advantage the second GAL sequence has over the first?*

A Longer Example

The following code segment, `reverse`, reads in three characters and prints them out in reverse order. Remember that input is not automatically echoed.

```
    begin_data    for reverse
temp0   variable:character          ;two temporary
temp1   variable:character          ;storage locations
    end_data
reverse
    input                           ;read a character
    copy:char    reg0⇒temp0         ;save it
    input                           ;get the second
    copy:char    reg0⇒temp1         ;save it
    input                           ;and a third
                                    ;write the last item
    output                          ;immediately
    copy:char    temp1⇒reg0
    output                          ;now the middle one
    copy:char    temp0⇒reg0
    output                          ;finally the first char
```

Note several details about this segment:

- All of the data directives were grouped together at the front.
- Comments may be placed on any line.
- Blank lines can be used to separate lines that are not related to each other. This greatly increases the readability of assembly language programs.

DATA MANIPULATION

Arithmetic Operations

Data manipulation commands in assembly language are limited to single-step well-defined operations, such as the addition of exactly two numbers. They include simple arithmetic operations such as addition, subtraction, multiplication and division. All arithmetic operations are primitive; for example, addition or subtraction of exactly two numbers. There are no compound commands such as "add three numbers," which must instead be thought of as "add two numbers, then add a third one to their sum."

ADDITION. The addition operation produces the sum of two numbers. It requires two operands, which are added together yielding the sum as a result. Unlike `copy`, which has two basic operands, the source and the destination, specification of addition logically requires three objects

two numbers to be added (the *addends*), and
a result (the *sum*).

One might, therefore, expect AL instructions to have three operands, specified in a syntax, something like

```
        add   addend1 + addend2⇒sum   ;NOT quite correct
```

In fact, some older machines actually worked in this manner. However most assembly languages today, including GAL, use a *two-operand notation,* in which all operations require two or fewer operands. Since there are logically three operands, but only two are specified in the syntax, some operand must serve double duty. In GAL, the second input operand also serves as the destination for the result. The syntax of `add` is similar to `copy`:

```
[<label>]  add  <addend_1>⇒<addend_2>   [<comment>]
```

for example

```
        add   item1⇒reg0
```

The interpretation of the above command is "add the contents of `item1` to the contents of `reg0` and store the result in `reg0`." `Add` is the operation, and as with `copy`, the first operand is the source, and the second is the destination since the result always ends up there (even though both may logically be thought of as sources). The "⇒" emphasizes that, as with `copy`, the result ends up in the destination. Figure 2-3 shows the logical relationships.

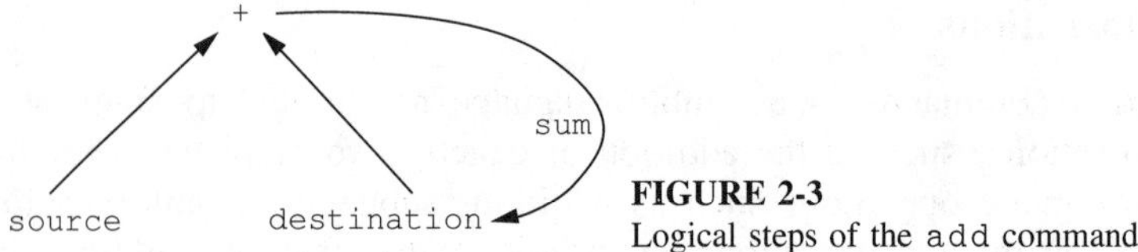

FIGURE 2-3
Logical steps of the `add` command.

As a result of the duplicate use of destination as a source `add` always destroys the result previously held in `item2`. This contrasts with addition in Hill, in which

```
assign          a⇐(b + c);
```

does not destroy either `b` or `c`. Thus, it is important to ensure that the operation will not destroy any contents of the destination operand that might be needed at some future point. Probably the most common way to accomplish this is to copy the contents of one addend into a register, and then perform the addition. Thus, the Hill statement

```
assign          sum⇐item1 + item2;
```

has the GAL equivalent

```
copy:integer    item1⇒reg4         ;preserve item1
add             item2⇒reg4
copy:integer    reg4⇒sum
```

The operands of the GAL `add` can be either main memory or registers. However, as with `copy`, no more than one operand may designate a RAM location. This restriction, like the corresponding problem with `copy`, can be solved by copying one operand into a register. Thus, the above code satisfies the restriction, as do

```
add            my_loc⇒reg1
add            reg2⇒your_loc
```

and

```
add            reg3⇒reg4
```

but

```
add            my_loc⇒your_loc     ;ILLEGAL
```

is not a legal GAL command.

As with the `copy` command, the GAL `add` can also take literal and constant operands. The same rules apply: since literals cannot change, the destination cannot be a literal, and since literals are stored in RAM, they cannot be added to RAM locations. Thus, if `const1` and `var1` are declared as an integer constant and integer variable respectively,

```
add             #5⇒reg1
```

and

```
add             const1⇒reg1
```

are legal, but

```
add            reg1⇒#5    ;ILLEGAL:changes literal
```

and

```
add            #5⇒var1    ;ILLEGAL:two ram operands
```

are not.

Finally, note that GAL does allow some seemingly bizarre uses of addition, such as the addition of two characters. This capability suggests that like `copy` the `add` operation may need a type specification. In fact, it is allowed:

```
add:<type>     <source>⇒<dest>
```

Although the operands of `add` are assumed to be integers by default, the programmer will find it useful to develop a habit of always specifying the type for every command.

> ▷ *Eventually we will discover some useful purposes for addition of items other than numbers. What possible use could there be?*

OTHER OPERATIONS. GAL also has operations for performing subtraction, multiplication and division. Like addition, each arithmetic operation logically has three operands:

Subtraction has

- two inputs: the *minuend* and the *subtrahend*
- a result: the *difference*

Multiplication has

- two inputs: the *multiplicands*
- a result: the *product*

Division has

- two inputs: the *dividend* and the *divisor*,
- a result: the *quotient*

> ▷ *Why do multiplication and addition each have two input operands with the same name, while division and subtraction each provide distinguishing names for their two input operands?*

The GAL commands for all four have structurally identical syntax:

```
<operation>:<type> <source>⇒<destination>
```

or more completely

```
[<ident>] <operation>:<type> <source>⇒<dest> [<comment>]
```

(Note: since any statement may optionally be preceded by an identifying label and/or followed by a comment, those two fields will be omitted from future generic examples. Similarly the type will be omitted when the intent is clear.) The GAL arithmetic operations have the obvious names

```
multiply         my_loc⇒regl
subtract         reg2⇒your_loc
```

and

```
divide           reg3⇒reg4
```

The syntactic rules of each are identical to those of addition. Each operation specifies two source operands and stores the result in the destination, which is the same as the second source operand. Any previous content of the destination is destroyed. The second source, which serves as a destination, will usually be called simply "destination" in spite of its dual role. For example the first of these may be read as "multiply the contents of `my_loc` by the contents of `regl`, leaving the result in `regl`." Like `add`, all GAL arithmetic operations assume the operands are integers unless otherwise specified.

ORDER OF OPERANDS. A simple question that may have occurred to the reader is "What is the GAL equivalent to the following Hill statement?"

```
assign           a⇐(b - c);
```

Is it

```
copy:int         c⇒reg3
subtract:int     b⇒reg3      ;lst operand is minuend?
copy:int         reg3⇒a
```

which would imply that the destination is subtracted from the source? Or, is it

```
copy:int         b⇒reg3
subtract:int     c⇒reg3      ;lst operand is subtrahend?
copy:int         reg3⇒a
```

which would imply that the source is subtracted from the destination?

This question has no simple absolute answer generalizable across all assembly languages. In fact, assemblers for different machines will have exactly opposite interpretations. There are at least two methods for answering this question:

1. Try it. Write a short program and check its results.
2. Look in the assembly language manual for a description of the operation.
3. (Best of all) do both!

A similar problem exists with division: Does

```
divide          reg3⇒reg4
```

mean "reg3 divided by reg4" or "reg4 divided by reg3"? In GAL, the operands are ordered so that an attempt to read the statement with an English interpretation will result in the correct description:

```
subtract     b⇒c
```

becomes "subtract b from c" (when you take something away, it is the original total that is changed). The destination is the minuend; the source will serve as the subtrahend. Similarly

```
divide          b⇒c
```

is read "divide b into c" (when you divide something up, the pieces are smaller than the whole). The destination will be the dividend; the source will serve as divisor. The general solution for any actual assembly language is left as a lab exercise. However, you should start right now to develop a habit of figuring out how things work in assembly language. There will be many aspects of assembly language that require such experimentation. Often the text (any text) will seem either vague or ambiguous. Often you simply will not be able to find the answer. Fortunately, assembly language provides several excellent tools for writing quick little test programs for the sole purpose of figuring out how the machine works.

▷ *A similar question: what is the quotient of 7/2. Is it 3 or 3.5?*

MORE COMPLICATED ARITHMETIC. In hlls, the user can express arbitrarily complicated arithmetic expressions by use of parenthesis and default precedence rules. In assembly language however, each statement corresponds to a single arithmetic operation between two operands. To represent a more complicated arithmetic expression, the programmer must specify each step of the operation as a separate statement—in the precise order in which they are to be executed. Thus the Hill statement

```
assign          a⇐b * ( c + d);
```

can be expanded into two Hill statements

```
assign          temp⇐(c + d) {for some variable TEMP}
assign          a⇐(b * temp)
```

which in turn is equivalent to the GAL statements

```
copy:integer    d⇒reg2
add:integer     c⇒reg2      ;reg2 is now serving as temp
multiply:int    b⇒reg2      ;now reg2 = b*(c+d)
copy:integer    reg2⇒a      ;final result goes into a.
```

Similarly, the Hill statement

```
assign          a⇐(b * c)/(e * f)
```

should be thought of as the three Hill statements

```
assign          num⇐(b * c):
assign          den⇐(e * f);
assign          a⇐num/den;
```

which in turn, might be accomplished in GAL as

```
copy:integer    c⇒regl
multiply:int    b⇒regl         ;leave num value in regl
copy:integer    f⇒reg2         ;and continue with calcs
multiply:int    e⇒reg2         ;reg2 is equivalent to den
divide:int      reg2⇒regl
```

Even though arithmetic operations default to type integer and all of the surrounding operations in the example were arithmetic, ALs do not recognize this fact when performing the `copy`. It is up to the programmer. Manipulation on other data types is also possible in GAL, but discussion of such manipulation will be postponed until a later section.

▷ *Is it odd that all input and output procedures are character-oriented, but all of the operations discussed thus far are arithmetic? Is that observation related to the postponement of other forms of data manipulation?*

THE CONTROL UNIT AND CONTROL OPERATIONS

As was the case with higher-level languages, the default order of execution of statements in assembly language is sequential: each statement is executed after the syntactically preceding statement (usually the statement positioned above the current statement in a listing of the code). The control unit manages the execution of commands. Normally the control unit fetches a command, executes it, fetches the next, and so on. Control can be altered by *control operations* that alter the *flow of control:* the selection of the statement to be executed next. Control statements do not alter data in the usual sense. They instruct the machine not to execute the syntactically next statement but to "jump" to some other statement instead. In Hill, the control statements included

conditionals	`(if-then-(else), case)`
iteration	`(while, repeat... until, for)`
subprogram calls	(procedures, functions)

The set of assembly language control statements is much smaller.

Jumps

In GAL, there is only one basic control operation, the `jump`:

```
jump:          →<newloc>
```

or

```
jump:always    →top_of_loop
```

where `<newloc>` is a label specifying some statement or location within the program. The destination of a `jump` statement must have a label, created in exactly the same manner as variable labels. For example,

```
top_of_loop    copy          temp ⇒ reg2
```

is a statement called `top_of_loop` (probably indicating that it is the first statement in a loop structure). In Figure 2-4, the statement executed after the `jump` would be the statement with the label: `newloc:`

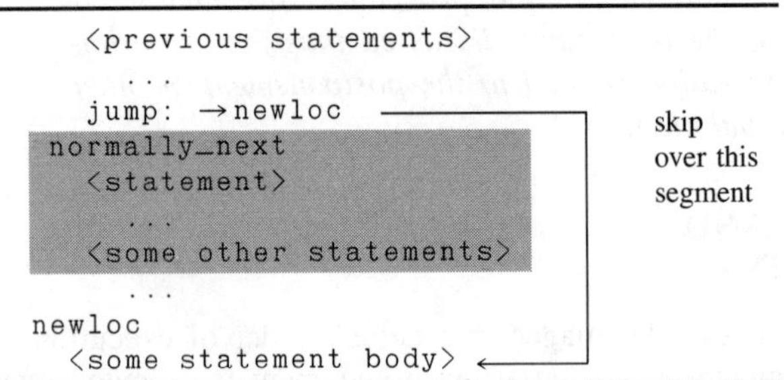

FIGURE 2-4
The `jump` control statement.

Or more concretely, the code

```
          copy:int       item1⇒reg0
          jump:always    →newloc
          copy:int       item2⇒reg0
newloc    add            reg0⇒reg0
```

copies `item1` into register 0, but the second `copy` is skipped, resulting in register 0 ending with twice `item1`, not twice `item2`. The added syntax, `always`, specifies that the `jump` will always be performed and never skipped. Also note in passing that since the `jump` is always taken and there is no label on the following statement, it is apparently impossible to ever get to the second `copy` statement; it is useless.

▷ *Is the "always" qualifier of the* `jump` *instruction a hint of things to come?*

Conditional Jumps

The vigilant reader will note that the `jump` as described thus far is a relatively useless operation if used alone. All control structures in Hill entailed a decision process: perform this block of code or do not perform this block; repeat this block or don't. To create useful control structures in GAL, the `always` may be replaced with restricted conditions for jumping. That is, a `jump` may or may not be performed, depending on some logical condition. `Jump` instructions that always jump are called *absolute* or *unconditional jumps;* `jumps` that may or may not jump depending on some condition are called *conditional jumps*. GAL contains conditions for `jump` statements equivalent to any of the legal test conditions in Hill control structures:

	Condition
`jump:equal`	jump if equal
`jump:less`	jump if less than
`jump:greater`	jump if greater than
`jump:less_eq`	jump if less than or equal
`jump:greater_eq`	jump if greater than or equal
`jump:not_equal`	jump if not equal

For example,

```
jump:equal    →over_the_rainbow
```

is read "jump to `over_the_raninbow` if equal." Note that although the syntax says "jump if two things are equal," it does not specify which two things. Nothing in the above syntax indicates which two entities are being compared. In some very real sense, that would require a four-field instruction, something like:

```
jump:equal    = first→second→to_location
                                        ;NOT CORRECT
```

which might be interpreted as jump to `location` if the two values `first_item` and `second_item` are equal. This is *not the case*. Instead GAL provides the `compare` statement

```
    compare              first⇒second
```

which compares `first` to `second` and determines if `first` is equal, greater than, or less than `second`. `Compare` does not change either the destination or the source operand; it only compares them. A conditional jump can then be used, to jump (or not jump) based on the value of the comparison. In the early examination of GAL, the two statements are always used in tandem:

```
    compare              first⇒second
    jump:equal           →newloc
another_statement
```

This example compares the contents of `first` and `second` and jumps to `newloc` if the two values are the same but falls through to the syntactically next statement, `another_statement`, if the values are not the same. Think of `compare` and `jump` as a single statement, requiring two lines. This two-line pair can be used to create GAL structures equivalent to any of the Hill control structures.

> ▷ *Is there a question of order in a* `compare` *analogous to the one involving the operands of a subtraction operation?*

The general syntax of `compare` is

```
    compare:<type>       <source>⇒<destination>
```

The semantic rules are exactly the same as for the previous statements: operands may be variables, constants, or literals; operands can be in RAM or register; one operand must be in a register; and the type should be explicitly indicated.

Emulation of Hill Control Structures

As primitive as these simple control structure tools seem, they are sufficient to produce every structure found in any higher-level language. In fact, a good approach to learning to program in assembly language is to build those equivalent structures. The structures can be used as building blocks for all programs.

CONDITIONALS. The general form of the simple Hill conditional statement is

```
    if <test>
      then <action>;
```

The `<test>` is usually a comparison between two values such as `(a = b)` or `(c < 2)`. The `<action>` is a block of code that is executed only if the test yields a `true` result. The conditional can thus be thought of as shown in the following:

```
if <test> is true
  then perform <actions>
  otherwise proceed immediately to the next statement.
```

The GAL `compare` corresponds roughly to the <test> and a conditional `jump` enables the program to bypass the <actions> when the test is false. Thus,

```
if (first = second)
  then <actions>
<following statement>;
```

can be represented in GAL as shown in Figure 2-5.

An important observation: the condition attached to the `jump (not_equal)` is the *logically opposite* of that specified in the Hill pseudocode `(=)`. The `jump` skips the <actions> and therefore is executed when the <actions> are *not wanted*. The `jump` transfers control to the statement immediately beyond the <actions>. Roughly, the `jump` acts as an `else`: it is taken if the condition is not true. When the pseudocode specifies an asymmetric comparison (e.g., "<" or ">"), this can be more confusing. The Hill structure

```
if (first>second)
  then assign first⇐second;
write  (first);                         {writes the lesser }
```

becomes

```
    copy             first⇒reg0
    compare          reg0⇒second     ;which was greater?
    jump:less_eq     →jump_it
                                     ;first was greater:
      copy           second⇒reg1     ;these two copy
      copy           reg1⇒first      ;from 2nd to 1st
jump_it
    output
```

The `jump` is taken when `first` is less than or equal to `second` which is to say, when `first` is *not greater than* `second`.

```
   compare      first⇒second
   jump:not_equal  →  <following statement>──┐
                                             │
      <actions>                              │
                                             │
<following statement> ←──────────────────────┘
```

FIGURE 2-5
The conditional if/then.

In general, simple conditionals are translated into assembly as

```
    compare          <test items>
    jump:<not true>  →<following code>
        <actions>
<following code>
```

For another concrete example, consider the Hill code (assume that all necessary declarations have been made)

```
    if (initial = 'A')                    {may write an "A"}
      then write (initial):
    write ('B');                          {always writes a "B"}
```

which is equivalent to the GAL sequence

```
    copy:char       initial⇒reg0
    compare:char    reg0⇒char_A        ;was it an "A"
    jump:not_equal  →skip_out          ;if it wasn't
                                       ;recall: output expects
          output                       ;character in reg0
skip_out                               ;gets here,
    copy:char       char_B⇒reg0        ;no matter what
    output
```

Conditionals with an `else` clause require two paths through the code, one that includes the `<then action>` and one that executes the `<else action>`. The general form in Hill is

```
    if <test>
      then <then action>
      otherwise <else action>;
```

The corresponding GAL code is shown in Figure 2-6. Note that there are two `jump` instructions:

- a conditional `jump`, which selects the `<then action>` or the `<else action>` by either skipping over the former, or simply "falling through"; and
- an absolute `jump` after the `<then action>`, which skips the `<else action>` and rejoins the two segments at the statement following the `<else action>`.

As with the simple conditional, the condition specified in the conditional `jump` was the logical inverse of that indicated in the pseudocode. The three segments `<test>`, `<then_part>`, and `<else part>` appear in the same order

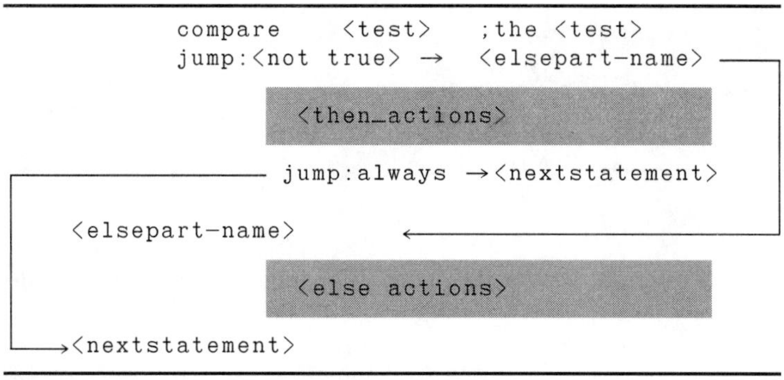

```
          compare     <test>     ;the <test>
          jump:<not true> →     <elsepart-name> ──┐
                  <then_actions>                  │
┌──────────── jump:always →<nextstatement>        │
│  <elsepart-name>          <─────────────────────┘
│                 <else actions>
└──→<nextstatement>
```

FIGURE 2-6
The conditional structure if/then/else.

in which they would appear in a Hill and are separated by blank lines for clarity. A more concrete example:

```
    if (my_initial <your_initial)
      then write (my_initial)
      else write (your_initial)
      . . .
```

becomes

```
    copy:char               my_initial⇒reg0
    compare:char            reg0⇒your_initial
    jump:greater_eq         →second_part
        output
        jump:always         →after_all
second_part
        copy:char           your_initial⇒reg0
        output
after_all
```

Iteration

Iteration structures or loops are blocks of code that are executed repeatedly. Therefore, a loop requires a jump backwards to a statement that has already been executed. Up to this point, all examples of `jump` instructions have jumped forward to code further down the listing, skipping over an unwanted segment. There is no reason that this must be the case. In AL, loops are constructed by jumping backwards (or upwards) into the section of code that has already been executed.[5]

[5]Note that when using an arrow to explicitly indicate the destination of a jump instruction, the derivation of the colloquial name for iteration, "loop," is much more obvious than when using hll constructs, which shield the user from the lower-level details.

```
→ top <first statement>
      <body>
      jump: →top

  next_statement
```

FIGURE 2-7
A general loop.

The generic loop structure shown in Figure 2-7 seems to create an infinite loop, analogous to

```
while (true) do
  <body>;
```

In practice, every loop must have an exit mechanism. Again, the GAL `compare` and `jump` pair is sufficient to create the exit mechanism for iteration structures corresponding to those of Hill.

PRETEST LOOPS. The defining characteristic of a pretest (or while) loop is that the test for continuation is made at the top of the loop body, before the body is executed. The Hill form of a while loop was

```
while <test is true> do
  <loop body>
<next statement>
```

The GAL equivalent is shown in Figure 2-8. The test is performed first, comparing the two values referenced in the test. When the condition is false, the conditional `jump` exits the loop to the statement immediately following the loop structure. The absolute `jump` at the end closes the loop by returning control back to the top of the structure.

```
→ <loop_top>
        compare <values in test>
        jump:<if test is false> → <next_statement>

                <loopbody>

        jump: always →<loop_top>
  <next_statement> ←
```

FIGURE 2-8
Pre-test loop.

As an example, consider a loop to find the sum of the even integers less than 15, which could be written in Hill as

```
assign  total⇐0;               {running total}
assign  counter⇐0;             {current value to be added}
while   (counter<15) do
    assign  total⇐total + counter;
    assign  counter⇐counter + 2;
```

The GAL equivalent is

```
    copy:int        #0⇒reg0       ;reg0 serves as total
    copy:int        #0⇒reg1       ;reg1 serves as counter
add_sum_loop
    compare:int     #15⇒reg1      ;while (count <15) do
    jump:less_eq    →out_of_it
        add         reg1⇒reg0     ;total⇐total+count;
        add         #2⇒reg1       ;count⇐count + 2;
    jump:always     →add_sum_loop
out_of_it           . . .
```

Things to notice: as was the case with conditionals, the test condition is reversed. Indentation is used to distinguish control from action. Registers make excellent counters.

POST-TEST LOOPS. The primary characteristic of the post-test (or until) loop is that the test is made at the end of the loop, thus ensuring that the body will be executed at least once. The general form of the post-test loop in Hill was

```
repeat
  <loop body>
until <test is true>
```

The GAL equivalent is given in Figure 2-9.

```
→ loop_top

     <loop body>

     compare <values in test>
     jump:<test is not true> → loop_top
  <nextstatement>
```

FIGURE 2-9
Post-test loop.

For a more specific example, consider a loop that reads and echoes input characters, stopping *after* printing the first blank to be found. In Hill this could be represented as

```
repeat
  read  (new_char);
  write (new_char);
until (newchar = ' ');
```

The GAL equivalent is

```
read_more
        input
        copy           reg0⇒new_char
        output
    compare:char       # ' '⇒new_char
    jump:not_equal     →read_more
```

COUNTER-CONTROLLED LOOPS. The counter-controlled (or `For`) loop executes a given number of times, rather than until some arbitrary test becomes true. It is characterized by an incremented counter. The general form in Hill was

```
for <counter>⇐<start> to <stop> do
  <loop body>
<nextstatement>
```

Recall that a counter-controlled loop is equivalent to a pretest loop in which the test involves a counter that is incremented once per pass through the loop. The above loop structure could then be rewritten in Hill as

```
initialize counter⇐start
while (counter ≤ stop) do
  <loop body>
  increment (counter)
<nextstatement>
```

One way to accomplish this in GAL is shown in Figure 2-10. For a more specific example, consider a segment designed to add the numbers from 1 to 10. In Hill, this could be accomplished with

```
assign  total⇐0;        {assumes proper declarations}
for count⇐1 to 10 do
  assign  total⇐total + count;
```

```
        ;assume start & stop have values

        copy:int  start⇒counter_reg
┌→ top_of_loop
│       compare:int counter_reg⇒stop
│       jump:greater →out_of_loop ──┐
│          <loop body>              │
│       add   #1⇒counter_reg         │
└────── jump:always →top_of_loop    │
                                    │
   out_of_loop  ←───────────────────┘
```

FIGURE 2-10
Counter-controlled loop.

In GAL, this becomes

```
    copy:int       #0⇒reg1           ;reg1 serves as total
    copy:int       #1⇒reg2           ;reg2 serves as count
sum_top
    compare:int    #10⇒reg2          ;test the loop
    jump:less      →not_in_loop      ;get out if
                                     ;done 10 times
         add       reg2⇒reg1         ;the real body
    add            #1⇒reg2           ;increment the loop index
    jump:always    →sum_top          ;the looping statement
not_in_loop
```

Subprograms

Imitation of hll subprogram structures requires two additional variations of the `jump` command. Consider the simplest case: a procedure with no parameters and no local variables. In Hill, there are two segments of code to consider, the procedure definition

```
    procedure <name>
    begin
      <body>
    end
```

and a calling sequence

```
    <previous statement>
    {call the procedure:}
      <name>
    <following statement>
```

Creation of an AL procedure definition is reasonably straightforward. Only one new tool is needed: a mechanism to return to the calling procedure at the spot from which the subprocedure was called. The general form of the procedure body is

```
<name>        ;recall that any statement can have a label
    <body>
    return
```

The `return` can either be written

```
    return              →caller
```

or more commonly, simply

```
    return
```

`Return` may be thought of roughly as replacing the final `end` statement in a Hill procedure. More precisely, `return` is like a `jump` that causes control to be returned to the statement following the statement that originally called the subroutine. Many hlls have exactly such a statement. Thus, as an example, a subprogram that prints three stars or asterisks might look like

```
star3
    copy         aster⇒reg0     ;assume aster holds "*"
    output
    output                      ;reg0 still holds the "*"
    output
    return
```

The calling statement, or jump to a subroutine, is also straightforward:

```
    jump:subroutine     →<name>
```

or

```
    jump:sub            →<name>
```

"Jump-to-subroutine" is a special form of the absolute `jump` command that records its own location. A subsequent `return` statement within the subroutine body can use that address to jump back (return) to that same spot.

▷ *Return addresses are stored in a stack, discussed later. Why use a stack?*

A segment of code including a call to the `star3` routine above might look like:

```
    copy         a_char⇒reg0    ;defined with constant "A"
    output
    jump:sub     →star3
```

```
copy        a_char⇒reg0
output
```

Its execution would print

```
A*** A
```

The full sequence of actions is

- prints a_char
- transfer control to the subroutine star3 (and save the return address)
- prints "*"
- prints "*"
- prints "*"
- return control to the main program (at the saved address)
- prints a_char again

Figure 2-11 schematically illustrates the flow of control.

PROCEDURES WITH PARAMETERS AND LOCAL VARIABLES. We actually saw two GAL subroutines earlier but did not acknowledge them as such: input and output. These two operations are very complex. GAL therefore provides the prewritten routines to deal with the low-level details. Therefore the correct syntax for call to these routines is

```
jump:subroutine     →input
```

and

```
jump:subroutine     →output
```

▷ *The observant programmer will recall that the Hill syntax for* read *and* write *is also that of a procedure call. What is the significance of that?*

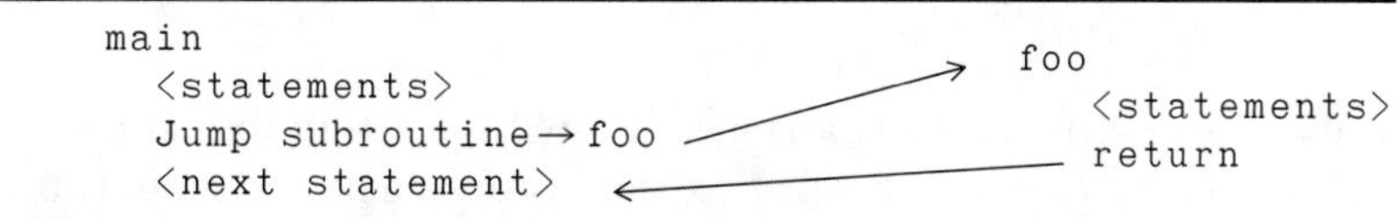

FIGURE 2-11
Control flow for jumping to a subroutine.

Apparently reg0 was used to pass the input or output parameter from or to the procedure. Thus the body of the procedure star3 above would actually look like:

```
star3
    copy:char   aster⇒reg0    ;aster passed to output
    jump:sub    →output       ;reg0 still holds
    jump:sub    →output       ;the "*"
    jump:sub    →output
    return
```

The addition of parameters adds only slightly to the complexity. The first mechanism for passing parameters that occurs to many programmers is the use of global parameters: let the calling program place a value in a specified global storage location. The procedure will then access the same location. In Hill, most programmers learned to avoid global variables. There is a very simple convention for continuing this practice, which corresponds closely to the rules of parameter passing of Hill, and which is also suggested by the input and output procedures. Parameters are passed through the registers. Some additional structure is still needed. Recall that in Hill, the actual parameters passed to a procedure must correspond in number and in position to the formal parameters used to define the procedure. For example, a procedure defined with three formal parameters must be called using exactly three actual parameters. The first actual parameter corresponds to the first formal parameter, the second actual to the second formal, and so on. In GAL, the first convention we will use is to

place the first (better to say zeroth) actual parameter in reg0
the next in reg1
and so on

Thus, the Hill procedure call

```
my_sub (arg0, arg1);
```

has an equivalent GAL procedure call, which looks like

```
copy        arg0⇒reg0
copy        arg1⇒reg1
jump:sub    →my_sub
```

Within the body of my_sub, reg0 is assumed to hold the zeroth formal parameter and reg1 the next. A procedure that expects two parameters should look for them in reg0 and reg1. The calling routine must place exactly the correct number of values in registers in exactly the correct order. The values placed there must also be of the type or representation expected by the subroutine. Note that the actual parameter is usually placed in the register by means of a `copy` statement. The value passed is thus a *copy* of the actual parameter. That is, it is a value (or `val`) parameter. Mechanisms for call by name (`var`) parameters will be discussed later. For example, consider the procedure `Line`, which prints out one line (80) of the character passed to it:

```
   begin_data                                  ;data for line
print_char                                     ;note location of
   variable:character                          ;local variables
   end_data
line
   copy:char        reg0⇒print_char            ;retrieve argument
   copy:int         #0⇒reg2                    ;reg2 holds count
print_loop
   compare:int      #80⇒reg2
   jump             less_eq→end_of_subroutine
      copy:char     print_char⇒reg0
      jump:sub      →output
      add:int       #1⇒reg2
   jump:always      →print_loop
end_of_subroutine
   return
```

The calling sequence might be

```
      copy:char         #'* '⇒reg0
      jump:sub          →line
      . . .
```

Note that the call to the procedure `output` from within the procedure `line` implies that procedures may be embedded, just as in a hll.

FUNCTION CALLS. Functions in Hill are very similar to procedures but differ in that (a) they are used in situations that call for a typed expression, and (b) they always return a single value. In AL, the first distinction is obscured, because each hll statement corresponds to several assembly language statements. In addition, there is no special command for function calls. Every reference to a subroutine—either procedure or function—must be contained in a single `jump-subroutine` statement, plus any statements to place required actual parameters into registers.

The single value returned by a function implies that the function must have a mechanism for delivering or returning values to the calling program. The simplest method is the mirror image of that used for passing arguments to the subroutine: the value is passed back in a register, normally `reg0`. The last action the function performs prior to returning is to place its value in reg0. The calling program must retrieve the value from the register. `Input` can therefore be viewed as a function. Consider the following Hill function, `larger`, which returns the larger of two values passed to it:

```
    function larger (first, second:integer):integer;
    begin
      if (first  >second)
          then assign larger⇐first
          else assign larger⇐second
    end;
```

which can be accomplished in GAL by

```
larger
    compare:int     reg0⇒regl       ;if (first  >2nd)
    jump:greater    →near_end       ; then reg0 is larger
                                    ;so keep it
        copy:int    regl⇒reg0       ;else return regl
near_end
    return
```

To call `larger`, the values must first be placed in the registers.

```
    copy:int     val0⇒reg0    ;assume all declarations
    copy:int     vall⇒regl
    jump:sub     →larger
    copy:int     reg0⇒outval
```

Notice that all statements involved in the parameter passing and function return were grouped together. As another example, consider the body of a function called `double` that doubles its input:

```
double                             ; the single result is left
    add        reg0 ⇒ reg0         ; in the same register
                                   ; in which the single input
                                   ; argument was received
    return
```

CALL-BY-ADDRESS PARAMETERS. The superficial effect of call-by-address (`var`) parameters—that the actual parameters are changed when the formal parameter values are changed—can be accomplished in an analogous manner:

- pass the values back in registers, and
- allow the calling program to save the results.

The first value returned should be passed back in `reg0`, the next, in `reg1`, and so on. Thus the Hill routine

```
procedure switch (var item1, item2:character)
variable
    temp:character;
begin
    assign    temp⇐item1;
    assign    item1⇐item2;
    assign    item2⇐temp;
end;
```

could be approximated by the GAL procedure

```
    begin_data
temp    variable : character
    end_data
switch
    copy      reg0⇒temp
    copy      reg1⇒reg0
    copy      temp⇒reg1
    return
```

The calling sequence is a bit more complicated since it must explicitly save the parameter values at the end of the procedure:

```
    copy        one_val⇒reg0
    copy        another⇒reg1
    jump:sub    →switch
    copy        reg0⇒one_val
    copy        reg1⇒another
```

At best, this is only superficially correct. It resembles the `input/output` parameters of Ada more closely than it does the `var` parameters of Hill or Pascal. There exist techniques that are both cleaner and more accurate for emulating `var` parameters, but these will be discussed later.

▷ *Can you think of an example in which this code would not generate the same results as would a Pascal procedure with* `var` *parameters?*

Local Variables, Modularity Constructs, and Good Programming

As with higher-level languages, local variables in assembly language programs should be grouped with the procedures that use them. In GAL, the statements of a procedure, function, or program can be grouped together by the following directives:

```
begin_code
```

and

```
end_code,
```

which are like the Hill statement pair `begin–end`, and not unlike the data directives `begin_data` and `end_data`. Thus, the structure of a typical program segment with data would appear as

```
          begin_data     for <procedure_name>
          . . .
          <all data directives>
          . . .
          end_data

<procedure_name>
          begin_code
          . . .
          <all executable statements>
          . . .
          end_code
```

However, these constructs only serve the programmer by making the intent clear. They do not guarantee proper structure. It remains up to the programmer to correctly construct programs.

Built-in Subprograms

In addition to `input` and `output`, GAL contains several other built-in procedures and functions that enable the programmer to build simple programs. The attentive reader may have wondered about the paradox: GAL seems to have operations for manipulating integers, but input and output operations seem to be restricted to characters. Four built-in functions help alleviate this problem.

CHARACTER-MANIPULATION FUNCTIONS. GAL includes built-in character-manipulation functions equivalent to the Pascal functions `succ` and `pred`. Given a character input, `succ` returns the character following the argument in alphabetic order; `pred` returns the character before it. The declarations can be thought of as

```
function succ (item:character):character
```

and

```
function pred (item:character):character
```

A Hill function call might look like:

```
assign  item⇐succ (item);
```

The calling sequence for succ is identical to that of any function created by the programmer:

```
copy:char    item⇒reg0
jump:sub     →succ
copy:char    reg0⇒item
```

TYPE-TRANSFER FUNCTIONS. GAL also contains the two built-in type-transfer instructions equivalent to the Hill:

```
function Ord (in_character:character):integer;
```

which returns the position of in_character in the collating sequence, and

```
function Char (in_value:integer):character;
```

which returns the in_valueth character. These two functions provide an excellent example of the need for care in specifying the type of arguments for many commands:

```
copy:char    #'A'⇒reg0        ;"A" is a
jump:sub     →ord             ;character but the
copy:int     reg0⇒some_int    ;result is an
                              ;integer
```

"REAL" ASSEMBLY LANGUAGES

Generalizations

The GAL language is exactly what its name implies: a generic assembly language. Likewise, there is no real GAM machine, nor any existing machine that uses a language exactly like GAL. Yet, these facts in no way suggest that one cannot or should not use GAL as a primary tool in the creation of assembly language programs for real machines. GAL's syntax is similar to the assembly language used in most machines. Paul Stookey once described the song *It's Raining* as "the only children's song which embodies every one of the essential ingredients of every single children's song." Similarly the concepts embodied in GAL are present in essentially every assembly language that might be available to the reader. The languages will vary in

- the details of syntax
- the specific restrictions upon operands
- number and size of registers and RAM locations, and so on.

The programmer must learn the specific restrictions imposed by the language and the machine being used. Often these will be idiosyncratic "quirks" that have no obvious reason for existence. Sometimes the study of local peculiarities will tell much about the given machine. However, every assembly language will be very close to GAL with respect to most of its features. Stated another way, GAL is to the assembly languages for the M68000, the i80386, or the Vax as Hill is to Pascal, Modula, C, or Ada. Both the language and the techniques developed in this chapter may be translated directly into any available machine language. Attention to the general rules of GAL will reveal much about any other assembly language you may use. First, consider the structural aspects, which can be generalized fairly easily.

COMMAND STRUCTURE. A simplifying feature of GAL, and most assembly languages, is that all statements have essentially the same syntax:

```
[<identifier>]  <operation>   <operands>   [<comments>].
```

Unlike the syntax of Hill, spacing is important in GAL. Any item in the first column is assumed to be an identifier; each field—identifier, operation, and operands—is separated by white space (blanks or tabs); and the entire statement must fit on one line. Every real machine will have its own syntactic peculiarities. Usually they will be quite close to GAL, but not quite an exact match. The following list provides some general guidelines. For each of these rules, GAL and most real languages will have very similar, if not identical, properties.

FIELDS. There are generally four fields to each assembly language statement. The fields are separated by white space: either blanks or tabs. Tabs are recommended because they create visually neater code, with corresponding fields lined up.

Statement label [optional]: an identifier that names the statement for reference by other statements such as `jumps` and subroutine jumps. The label must follow the general rules for identifiers (e.g., any string of alphanumeric characters, with the first alphabetic). Generally a statement may have one or more labels. Even the null statement (blank line) may usually have a label.

Operation or "opcode": a mnemonic name that indicates the particular operation. Generally the opcode provides a mnemonic aid in remembering the instruction. However it is frequently more terse than the opcodes of GAL (e.g., `mul` rather than `multiply`).

Operands. Generally all operands are lumped into a single field. No white space is usually allowed within the operand fields. The individual operand names should obey the conventions for identifiers. However, few—if any—languages include features such as the directional arrow distinguishing source and destination operands. The individual operands are separated by a simple separator, such as a comma.

Comments. Generally comments are allowed only to the right of all other operands. Often any text following the last operand is automatically treated as comment. A semi-colon or an asterisk often indicates that the remainder of a line should be treated as comment. A line containing only a comment is usually allowed, in which case it is usually preceded by a marker, (such as "*" or ";") so that the assembler will not confuse it with an operation name or statement identifier.

Memory and Data References

STORAGE DECLARATIONS. Most assembly languages do not allow the programmer to declare the type of a storage location (e.g., character or integer) for the simple reason that the language will provide no further type-checking. It will be up to the programmer to use the variable consistently. Generally, the programmer declares only the *size*—measured in bytes—of the variable, not the type. Generally one byte is needed for a character, two (sometimes four) bytes are needed for an integer, and four for a real value. Thus, declarations for an integer and two characters might appear as

```
an_integer      variable    2
one_char        variable    1
another_char    variable    1
```

a syntax that can easily be confused with constant declarations.

Identifier Names

Identifiers usually follow the same rules as for higher-level languages: they may contain any alphanumeric characters. Often the length of an identifier is limited to eight, or even fewer, characters. Generally identifiers may not be identical to any operation names or other "reserved words." The rules are generally the same as for GAL, except that the lengths may be restricted. The alphabet may sometimes vary slightly from the purely alphanumeric identifiers allowed by GAL: characters that are sometimes considered alphabetic include

`@, $, %, &, -, _,` and `/`

sometimes with special interpretation for some of the characters.

REGISTERS. Every language provides a naming convention for its registers. Generally these names must be distinct from any other identifiers or operation names. Register names are also usually much more terse, often: `R0 ... R7` or `D0 ... D7` ("D" for data).

LITERAL VALUES. Most assembly languages require that the use of any literal or immediate must be explicitly indicated. The typical mechanism is a special indicator character, such as # placed before the literal value. Thus,

```
Copy            #2⇒reg0
```

When a character is intended as a literal, it must also be enclosed in quotes:

```
Copy            #'2'⇒reg0
```

Warning: many assemblers will appear to allow the programmer to use a literal value without the indicator character, but they will seldom interpret the command as the programmer intended.

▷ *An interesting question: if the assembler does not interpret*

```
Copy            'A'⇒reg0
```

as meaning that the character "A" should be copied into register 0, what else might it mean?

OPERATION NAMES. Most assembly languages have very short operation names. Few if any languages use full English language names such as `jump` or `compare` for operations. Generally the actual names are considerably contracted from the full mnemonic, frequently to about three characters. Thus, `subtract` is more likely to be `sub` or `subt`; `multiply` is more likely to be `mult` or even `mul`. Table 2-1 contains equivalent commands for two common assembly languages. Generally, you will find that the GAL command is very close to the conceptual name of the operation; command names in other languages are usually abbreviations of that concept.

Jump Mnemonics

Most assembly languages include the conditional operand for `jump` statements within the operation code itself, rather than as a separate field. Thus

```
jeq             Loc
```

is used rather than

```
jump:equal      →loc
```

Usually the names of the testable conditions will be identical to those used in many hlls such as Fortran: `eq`, `ne`, `gt`, `ge`, `lt`, `le`. The `jump` mnemonic may be reduced to as little as the single letter "j" preceding the condition code. The absolute `jump`, "jump always," is often a distinct name such as `jmpa` (which may also be thought of as "jump absolute" or "jump always"). Also, the jump-to-subroutine command frequently has its own syntax, typically `CALL` or `srj`.

TABLE 2.1
GAL Operations and their equivalents on M680x0 and 180x86 machines

GAL		M68000		I80x86	
		Data transfer commands			
copy	<source> ⇒ <dest>	move	<source>, <dest>	mov	<dest>, <source>
load_address	<source> ⇒ <dest>	lea	<source>, <dest>	lea	<dest>, <source>
jump : subroutine	→ input	(no explicit command)		in	<reg>, <port>
jump : subroutine	→ output	(no explicit command)		out	<reg>, <port>
		Control commands			
compare	<source> ⇒ <dest>	cmp	<source>, <dest>	cmp	<dest>, <source>
jump : <condition>	→ <loc>	b<cc>	<loc>	jcc	<loc>
jump : always	→ <loc>	bra	<loc>	jmp	<loc>
jump : equal	→ <loc>	beq	<loc>	jeq	<loc>
jump : greater	→ <loc>	bgt	<loc>	jg	<loc>
jump : less	→ <loc>	blt	<loc>	jl	<loc>
jump : not_eq	→ <loc>	bne	<loc>	jne	<loc>
jump : greater_eq	→ <loc>	bge	<loc>	jge	<loc>
jump : less_eq	→ <loc>	ble	<loc>	jle	<loc>
jump : subroutine	→ <loc>	bsr	<loc>	call	<loc>
		jsr	<loc>		
return		rts		ret	
halt		stop		hlt	
		Arithmetic operations			
add	<source> ⇒ <dest>	add	<source>, <dest>	add	<dest>, <source>
subtract	<source> ⇒ <dest>	sub	<source>, <dest>	sub	<dest>, <source>
multiply	<source> ⇒ <dest>	mulu (unsigned)	<source>, <dest>	mul	<source> (accumulator assumed)
		muls (signed)	<source>, <dest>	imul	<source>
divide	<source> ⇒ <dest>	divu	<source>, <dest>	div	<source>
		divs	<source>, <dest>	idiv	<source>
		Logical operations			
and	<source> ⇒ <dest>	and	<source>, <dest>	and	<source>, <dest>
or	<source> ⇒ <dest>	or	<source>, <dest>	or	<source>, <dest>
not	<dest>	not	<dest>	not	<dest>
rotate	<source> ⇒ <dest>	rol	<disp>, <dest>	rol	<disp>, <count>
		ror	<disp>, <dest>	ror	<disp>, <count>

The tables compares GAL to subsets of the commands of two popular series of micro processors, showing the correspondence of commands. The two physical machines each have much broader instruction sets. For a full description of the languages, see the appropriate reference manual. While reading this comparison, pay close attention to the variations in semantics (such as order of operations) as well as to the surface syntax.

Common Variations on Legal Semantics

OPERANDS. Operands may generally be RAM memory locations (specified by an identifier), registers, or literal values. Many machines place restrictions on the operands for specific instructions. Frequent restrictions include

- at least one operand must be a register.
- the destination operand must be a register.
- both operands must be registers.
- no literals are allowed.
- only certain data types (or sizes) should be used.

On a given machine, restrictions may vary from one operation to the next. The only way to know for sure for any specific operation on any specific machine is to look it up in a reference manual for that machine. No two assembly languages have exactly the same syntax or semantics. However, the variations are relatively small and can be characterized fairly easily. You will need to use a reference manual to determine the specific rules for your machine. Although there are a number of possible differences, most can be categorized easily.

ORDER OF OPERANDS. Recall the discussion of the interpretation of the operands of the `subtract` command: the question was which operand was the subtrahend and which was the minuend. Unfortunately, there is no absolute standard order for operands of subtraction or any other operation. Thus,

```
subtract            first⇒second
```

may subtract the first from the second, or the second from the first. Similarly,

```
divide              first⇒second
```

may divide the first by the second or the second by the first. A particularly problematic operation is `compare`. In GAL, the comparison operator compares the source to the destination. It is not unusual for an assembly language to compare the destination to the source. The distinction is unimportant when comparing for equality, but when testing for inequalities, it is problematic. In such a language,

```
copy:int            #2⇒reg1
compare             #1⇒reg1
jump:greater        →school
```

would result in the jump to `school` being taken. That is, the statements test for (and jump if) the *second operand is less than the first*—which may seem exactly backwards. The programmer must look up the exact details from the appropriate assembly language reference manual.

SYNTACTIC GUIDES. Syntactic aids and guides, such as GAL's arrows, served as heuristics to help the programmer understand the operations to be performed. They contribute little or nothing to the semantics. Most assembly languages contain no such aids. Generally, all operands are separated only by commas, independent of the meaning of the command. No arrows, plus signs, spaces, etc. may occur in the operand field of any command.

BUILT-IN PROCEDURES. Generally, built-in procedures are not provided directly as part of assembly languages. Some development systems may include a library of useful routines, but there seem to be no standards.

POINTS TO PONDER

1. In your studies of higher-level languages, you no doubt were introduced to the concept of the *compiler.* However, for many students it is a very mysterious object. It somehow changes a hll program into another form called *internal representation, machine language,* or *object code*. In the process, it somehow informed you if there were syntax errors in your *source code*. After a successful compilation, you could run your compiled program or *object code*. One very rough description of a compiler might be that it is a program that transforms a hll program into an assembly language program. After compilation, the assembly language program is executed. This image is not exactly correct, but it is a major step in the right direction. You may be more familiar with an *interpreter.* It can similarly be described as an assembly language program that reads your hll statements and performs the required actions. That is, it interprets the statements and acts on them without translating them into another form. Again this description has the correct feel, even if it is not precisely correct.
2. If a compiler translates a hll into something like assembly language, what does an assembler do?
3. If `compare` does not alter either the source or destination, where does it store the results of the comparison?
4. Why do you suppose many GAL operations demand that at least one of the operands be a register?

SUMMARY

The assembly language model is much lower-level than the higher-level language model, meaning that the level of abstraction is lower and that individual commands are less powerful. The central processing unit of such a machine has a very limited set of actions that it can perform. Its two logical sub-units, the ALU and the control unit, perform actions and control the flow of actions respectively. Memory is composed of two primary forms: random access memory and registers. In spite of the restrictions, it is possible to duplicate in assembly language almost any structure—either data and control—familiar to the hll programmer. The "trick" to making successful control structures in assembly language is mimicry of Hill. Design an assembly language program exactly as you would a hll program: top-down, specifying first the general outline, advancing to pseudocode and finally to the specific language. The only aspect that has changed is that assembly languages require a finer level of specification. A well-written pseudocode should reflect the control structures available in the hll, which can be translated into assembly language. Brief summaries of the statements and commands of GAL follow.

Data Directives

general

```
<identifier>    directive:<type>
```

for variables

```
<identifier>    variable:<type>
```

for constants

```
<identifier>    constant:<type>    <value>
```

data delimiters

```
        begin_data
        end_data
```

Commands and Procedures

internal data movement

```
copy:<type>            <source>⇒<destination>
```

data manipulation

```
add:<type>             <source>⇒<dest>
subtract:<type>        <source>⇒<dest>
multiply:<type>        <source>⇒<dest>
divide:<type>          <source>⇒<dest>
```

control statements or jumps

unconditional:

```
jump:always            →<newloc>
or
jump                   →<newloc>
```

conditional

`jump:<condition>`	→ <newloc>
`jump:equal`	jump if equal
`jump:less`	jump if less than
`jump:greater`	jump if greater than
`jump:less_equal`	jump if less than or equal
`jump:greater_equal`	jump if greater than or equal
`jump:not_equal`	jump if not equal.

comparisons

```
compare <source>⇒<dest>
```

subroutines

```
jump:subroutine→<newloc>
return
```

procedure delimiters

```
begin_code
end_code
```

built-in functions and procedures

```
input
output
succ
pred
ord
char
```

EXERCISES

2.1. Determine for your assembly language the specification order for the operands of the `copy`, subtraction, and division operations. To do this, write a short program that inputs two characters, copies one to the other, and prints one out.

2.2. After completing Exercise 2.1, use the "look-it-up" approach to solve the same problem. If this is your first attempt at looking up a command in an assembly language manual, knowing the results from 2.1 will help you find and interpret the answer.

2.3. Armed with the results of Exercises 2.1 and 2.2, figure out the direction of operands for the other arithmetic operations.

2.4. Figure out the order of operands for the `compare` instruction.

2.5. Write a series of GAL statements expressing the positive root to a quadratic equation. Assume that the function SQRT is defined in the obvious manner.

2.6. Write GAL code to find the largest of three numbers. Try four numbers.

2.7. Using the built-in procedures input and output, create and use a GAL procedure `echo_input`, which inputs a character and echoes it to the screen leaving the result available to your program.

2.8. Write and use a GAL function to find the average of two integers.

2.9. GAL contains both absolute and conditional jumps for use within a program module. But for subprocedures, there is only an unconditional jump to subroutine. It seems that this could cause a problem for any attempt to create well-structured GAL code. For example, consider the Hill code segment

```
if (a < b)
        then switch (a, b)
```

in which `switch` is the name of a procedure. Logically, this is a conditional call to `switch`, which would be prohibited by the rule given. How can you get around this problem? Demonstrate an appropriate GAL sequence of code.

2.10. Write a pre-test loop in GAL that prints out the letters of the alphabet.

2.11. Write a GAL post-test loop that writes the letters up through "m".

2.12. Write a GAL counter-controlled loop that writes the first 15 letters of the alphabet.

2.13. Write GAL code that accepts a character and writes "D" if the character is a digit and "A" if it is alphabetic.

2.14. Write a GAL procedure that accepts two characters and writes out all of the characters between them.

2.15. Some machines have a command, `swap` or `exchange`, which is a variant of `copy`. It allows the contents of two locations (usually both must be registers) to be swapped in one operation. Describe the impact that such an operation might have on a higher-level language.

2.16. Exercises 2.5 through 2.14 asked you to write GAL code. Write the corresponding instructions in your own assembly language.

2.17. Exercises 1.13 and 1.14 asked you to write Hill code. Write the equivalent programs in GAL or your own assembly language.

2.18. Representations of the letters of the alphabet are sequential, that is,

```
char(ord('a')+1)='b'.
```

Figure out if the upper- or lowercase letters come first.

2.19. Since the characters are sequential (see Exercise 2.18) the upper- and lowercase versions of any letter must be the same distance apart. That is, `ord(uppercase) – ord(lowercase)=constant` for any letter. Write code to convert uppercase input into lowercase.

2.20. Find all of the jump instruction variations for your machine.

2.21. Write a paragraph about the `compare` command: Is it a control unit or arithmetic unit function?

CHAPTER 3

A SHORT GUIDE TO PROGRAMMING IN ASSEMBLY LANGUAGE

Chapter 2 described assembly language, using GAL as an example, and provided a number of program segments to demonstrate that most of the higher-level language building blocks—both data and procedural—have equivalents in assembly language. The chapter did not address the question of how to program in assembly language; that is, how to create programs that actually accomplish a specific task—and what to do if the program does not work. This chapter suggests a few general techniques for writing assembly language programs. It should be no surprise that the general concepts needed for creating working programs in an assembly language are almost identical to those employed in writing higher-level language programs. The major distinctions are that

- a lower level of detail must be specified, and
- more care must be taken to prevent errors.

WHY PROGRAM IN ASSEMBLY LANGUAGE?

Before we embark on major investigations of the methodology of assembly language programming, let's consider the question, "Why program in assembly language anyway?" There are three principal reasons for programming in assembly language; two have to do with what can be done and one is concerned with human understanding:

- *Efficiency considerations*. Because assembly language gives ultimate control over storage allocation, register utilization, and so on, the assembly language programmer can fine-tune a program to take advantage of special circumstances to create a program that is particularly efficient with respect to time or storage conditions. For example, the procedure `star3` in Chapter 2 could take advantage of the fact that it printed three identical characters to save two (redundant) `copy` commands.
- *Flexibility*. One price of higher-level languages is flexibility. Chapter 1 indicated that Hill had at least one construct that is not present in most familiar hlls: the `read` loop. What can a hll programmer who needs such a construct do? Assembly language offers few such restrictions. In assembly language, constructs are limited only by the programmer's imagination. The flipside, of course, is that the language offers little protection.
- *Understanding*. The use of assembly language can be compared to the use of a microscope: its finer level of detail exposes more of the machine to the programmer. The protection provided by a hll hides a great many aspects of the machine from the programmer, which can be good because it saves much anguish, but it limits the programmer's understanding of the underlying processes. For the purposes of a computer organization course, such understanding is the most important reason for studying assembly language. The rules and concepts of assembly language programming are presented with this goal of understanding in mind. There may come a time when the efficiency aspects of assembly language programming are the important reasons for selecting it, but those times are not now.

NAKED PROGRAMMING

Assembly language provides all the same capabilities as higher-level languages and at the same time provides the programmer with better insight. Unfortunately, that insight comes at a price: the lack of support services. One service that no assembly language provides very well is protection. The feeling is that of being tossed out into the world with no protection—of being naked. The novice assembly language programmer will experience many (often frustrating) new forms of error, and when such errors occur the feedback will seem less than informative. The following guides may help the novice respond to these new-found types of errors.

GENERAL PROGRAMMING GUIDELINES

An assembly language program is essentially the same sort of entity as a hll program: an *algorithm,* or an ordered sequence of instructions to a computer that, when executed, will accomplish a specific task. Therefore, the novice assembly language programmer should not be surprised that the process of creating an AL program is essentially the same as that of creating a hll program. The process contains exactly the same logical components:

- problem definition
- algorithm development
- coding
- documentation
- testing
- debugging
- verification

Many of these individual aspects are identical in hlls and ALs. For example, problem definition has nothing to do with the ultimate language in which the program will be written: The task must be understood in terms of restrictions, available input, desired output, special situations, and so on. If there is one essential piece of advice that every assembly language programmer should receive, it is

> *Don't forget what you already know about programming (from your studies of higher-level languages).*

When writing an assembly language program, the basic rules for attacking the problem are identical to those used by higher-level language programmers. Some good practices are reviewed here. (If they are unfamiliar, the reader is urged to consult one of the references cited at the end of Chapter 1.) Algorithm development is best conducted top-down. That is, an algorithm should first be specified in terms of very broad general steps. Then, these general steps should be successively refined until a level of detail appropriate for coding is reached. In AL, that level is finer-grained than it is in hlls, but that has absolutely no impact on the first few levels of refinement. In fact, an excellent approach to writing AL programs is to proceed exactly as if you were writing a hll program, until you have fully specified a hll or pseudocode program. That hll program may then be further refined into an AL program using the equivalences described in Chapter 2. Because every hll construct has an AL equivalent, this last step is very straightforward. An excellent form of documentation is to include the Hill or Pascal code equivalent to a given segment of code. For example,

```
;     Assign        rad⇐(b^2 - 4* a* c)
;
      copy          b⇒reg1
      multiply      reg1⇒reg1      ;b^2
      copy          a⇒reg2
      multiply      #4⇒reg2
      multiply      c⇒reg2         ;4* a* c
      subtract      reg2⇒reg1
      copy          reg1⇒rad
```

Much of what follows may seem to be belaboring the obvious. However, one of the most significant errors that assembly language programmers make is forgetting what they already know about programming. When the task seems to get complicated many new assembly language programmers forget about top-down design, well-structured code, good variable names, and so on. For example, the hll programmer who would avoid writing code with poor variable names

```
assign  p⇐q *  r + s    {poor names}
```

might be tempted to use those same names in an assembly program. These are dangerous mistakes to make in the naked and unprotected world of assembly language.

Problem Definition

Problem definition is perhaps the most overlooked step in the program development process. The right solution to the wrong problem is seldom satisfactory. Make sure that you understand the problem fully. In colloquial terms, this means "Ask a lot of questions!" Generally the user and the programmer are not the same person. It is the programmer's job to ask questions of the user. In the classroom situation, it becomes the student's job to ask questions of the instructor. You should describe the problem in terms of the input and output requirements. Is the input information realistic? Will it be available when needed? (A tax computation program should not ask the user: "How much do you owe in taxes?") Does the output satisfy the needs of the user? What are the logical relationships between the input and output?

In assembly language programming, extra care should be paid to the details of input and output in the problem definition. Since assembly language input routines are very limited, the programmer must determine the exact requirements of the input format. For example, Pascal will ignore leading blanks before an integer input. If these blanks are to be ignored, the AL programmer must provide the code to do so.

Because the assembler provides no type-checking, no error messages will be generated when the programmer makes an incorrect assumption about the type of a variable. Correcting the error when found may require rewriting sections of code. The programmer will need to document the types of all variables very carefully; such identification of types should pervade the entire programming process. The specification begins during problem definition, which is also the best time to create documentation.

Algorithm Development

Always write a pseudocode algorithm to solve the problem, just as you would for a hll program. The final pseudocode may need to be a little more detailed than you are used to because vagueness can get you into trouble even more quickly in assembly language than it can in a hll. Control structure and data definitions should be as well-specified as the algorithm itself. Assembly language procedures should be developed top-down, starting with the general outline and working toward a detailed description. The process of programming in AL contains nothing new to this point. In fact, this pseudocode algorithm can serve as the basis of much of your documentation.

Coding

The coding process is essentially identical to the hll equivalent for individual structures, but with smaller granularity. The general conversion process was covered in the last chapter. Some additional comments are included in the following sections, particularly about the roles of data abstraction, procedural abstraction and documentation. It is at this step that many new programmers first become aware of the lack of protection provided by the assembler. Programmers who are used to the modern protections provided by current higher-level language compilers (e.g., many programmers depend on compilers to find the "silly little errors and typos") may be rather annoyed by the seeming "lack of intelligence" on the part of most assemblers.

The result of the coding process will, of course, look very different, but the process is essentially identical: translate each step of a refined algorithm into a single step of the programming language. The basic distinction is that each of these steps is more finely specified, which means that there will be more steps and the listing of a code segment will be longer. The programmer should pay special attention to variable names and documentation of those names (a register name will provide no clue as to its function, so document its use). Maintain a clear list of all variables and constants showing the assumed type and the role in the program. Pick names that not only help the programmer remember the role but that also provide a clue as to the type. Use only standard control structures and document them carefully. Always keep the programmer's reference manual close at hand to look up the details of a given command.

STYLE. When coding assembly language programs, follow the general style rules you learned from your study of higher-level languages. (You may want to refer to the style guide provided as Appendix I, which is largely composed of rules found in hll style guides but reinterpreted for assembly language.) Do not succumb to the temptation to violate the rules simply because AL does not prevent you from violating them. Because assembly language does not provide built-in types or type-checking, control structures, sophisticated error checking, and so on, it is especially important to follow the points of style you have learned previously. The rules will help make the structure of your program clear. Although the rules are stated in terms of assembly programs, you will recognize most of them as direct paraphrases of rules that you learned in the study of higher-level languages.

Documentation

Document as you code—never wait until the program is complete to begin documentation. Concurrent documentation provides an essential tool for the other aspects of the programming process. Particular attention should be paid to variable and storage names, register usage, and control structures. A later section in this chapter will provides concrete suggestions for the form of this documentation.

Testing and Debugging

The major problem you will encounter in the early stages of learning to use assembly language is the lack of useful error messages. But eventually the few distinct run-time error messages provided to the assembly language programmer—when combined with the available debugging tools and the programmer's own intimate knowledge of the details of a program—will be more useful than those provided by most hlls.

ANTI-BUGGING. The best way to fix errors is to avoid them altogether. If that is not possible (and it seldom is), you should write code that anticipates possible sources of error. Some general guidelines follow.

CHECK POINTS. An *invariant* is a relationship that holds throughout your program (or segment). For example, a variable, `processed`, may contain the number of customers processed thus far. Determine points in your program at which the results should be predictable. These results may be as simple as the value of an index after leaving a loop. Use these points as a first line of defense against errors. You should identify these points before attempting to run your program. Provide output statements so that you can follow these values as the program executes. For example,

```
assign processed⇐0
<loop control>
  <increment processed>
  <do processing for customer number processed>
write (processed)
```

At each important point—the loop control, during the actual processing, or after completion of the processing—`processed` contains the number of transactions (complete or partial). The only instant at which the value is inaccurate is between the increment and process steps.

ASSUME THAT YOUR PROGRAM IS IN ERROR. You will usually be right. (And when you are wrong—you are right?[1]) This is not a criticism of you, the programmer. It is simply a fact of life about programs: they are almost always

[1]This quandary is a play on a famous logical conundrum called Russell's Paradox, after the British logician/philosopher Bertrand Russell (1872–1970). The paradox postulates the existence of the set that contains exactly those elements that belong to no set: an element is in the set if and only if it is not in a set.

wrong. If you assume that there will be errors, you can build-in the tools for detecting and identifying errors. These tools include both value checks and trace information. For example, in the above example, the program outputs the final value of `processed`, which should be the same as the total number of customers.

PLANS. Have a *testing* plan. You must be able to test every program. That means that you must be able to select input data that tests all possible cases. The best time to think about a testing plan is when you write the program—not when you realize that it does not work. Thinking about testing in advance will also help you to see flaws in your basic logic and specifications that you have overlooked. For example, in writing a program that calculates a square root, many programmers forget to deal with negative input. A test is likely to include large and small numbers, positive and negative numbers, and so on. In creating the plan, the programmer should ask "What do I want the program to do in each of these cases?" Conversely, make sure that all cases are covered.

A plan helps the programmer anticipate errors and spend less time attempting to figure out what is wrong. In the early stages of debugging, it is especially important to have simple test data for which you know the expected result. If you are emulating a hand calculator, do not simply test with the input 743*491 and check to see if the answer seems reasonable. Give it problems for which you know the expected result and compare. Use simple values and work up to more complex cases, so you can create a model or image of the circumstances under which you get the error. Be sure to remember (i.e., write down) the test data you use. After you attempt to fix an error, you will want to replicate the situation with the same test data. Otherwise you will not know whether the change actually fixed the error or if the second test data simply did not generate an error.

Select your test values carefully. They should not only verify correct results but should also bring incorrect results to your attention. For example, because

$$2 + 2 = 2 * 2 = 2^2 = \text{square}(2)$$

using 2 and 2 as test values may not indicate potential errors.

DATA ABSTRACTION

An area in which there are significant differences between assembly language and higher-level languages is abstraction. It is always possible to create a data structure or procedure to implement any abstraction. However, in AL that implementation usually requires a much lower level of abstraction. The differences manifest themselves in both data and procedural aspects of programming, as well as the documentation to support the abstractions. Although the general process is the same, the structure of assembly language does suggest a number of different programming rules. Assembly languages provide few, if any, tools designed to aid the programmer in abstraction of either data or procedures. The programmer must establish self-discipline rules to maintain appropriate levels of abstraction.

Type-Checking

Few ALs provide any type-checking of any form. Hill insisted that two addends in an arithmetic expression be appropriate types for addition (i.e., integers or reals). GAL does not check for such compatibility. If a storage location that is declared as sufficient for a character is used as the operand for an arithmetic operation, assembly language allows the operand, performs as meaningful an operation as it can, and returns the result—whatever it is. For example, given the following code fragments,

```
my_num          constant            'A'
another_num     constant            'B'
                 . . .
                copy:char           my_num⇒reg0
                add                 another_num⇒rego0
```

GAL would obediently add the characters "A" and "B" together, leaving the "sum" in register 0. No error message would be produced; no warning provided. Thus, an incorrect specification of the character "2" rather than the numeric value 2 will not be detected. An `add` command given the specification `'2'` as an operand will not add the number 2 but will actually behave as if it were adding 50.

> ▷ *Why might this particular number occur?*

Similarly, parameters of incorrect type, incorrect subscripts, or even "meaningless" declarations will not be detected. For example, the following declaration and statement are both legal:

```
my_num          constant:integer    'A'
                 . . .
                add     #'C'⇒reg0
```

but of very questionable meaning at this point.

> ▷ *Eventually we will be able to predict the meaning for such statements. Can you invent some meanings for this declaration?*

It is up to the programmer to declare constants and variables in a manner that will help ensure their correct use and to pay attention to the declarations when writing the program body. Here are three useful guidelines:

- Use naming conventions that make the type clear. For example,

```
char_A          constant:char       'A'
```

- Group declarations logically. Use care in the physical layout of the declaration section, using the `begin` and `end_data` directives or comments to mark off the declaration section.
- Avoid defaults. Always specify the type, in commands as well as in declarations.

- When you deliberately take advantage of assembly language's tolerance for mismatched types, always comment to show your intent.

Global Variables

Most hlls place some form of restrictions upon the use of global variables. The primary reason for such restrictions is the prevention of undesirable side effects. AL provides little prohibition or protection with respect to global variables. Once again, it is up to the programmer to establish a policy of self-protection.

REGISTERS. The most likely place for an assembly language programmer to get into trouble with global variable problems is in the use of registers. Consider this simple observation: There is only one set of registers, but a program may have several procedures. Each of those procedures uses the same set of registers. Some mechanism will be needed to guard against unexpected changes in memory values caused by multiple use. Clearly, the registers used to pass data to and from the subroutine may not be used concurrently for any other purpose. For example, if `reg0` contains a running total,

```
add          #1⇒reg0
```

that total will be lost when a parameter is passed to a subroutine in the same register,

```
copy         param⇒reg0
```

To avoid losing data, be sure to save the contents of the register first. But the problem is even worse than this suggests. Because the subprogram may also use any register, it has the potential to destroy any value left in any register by the calling program. For example, in the following sequence,

```
copy         param⇒reg5
jump:sub     →some_routine
copy         reg5⇒new_loc
```

`new_loc` will not have the same value as `param` if the routine, `some_routine`, alters register 5. The programmer must establish a convention regarding saving register values. One alternative is for the calling program to save any values that are held in a register and will be needed later to a RAM memory location prior to calling a subroutine:

save any important register values
pass arguments in registers
call subroutine
retrieve function values and var parameters
restore other registers

A reasonable alternative would be to establish the guideline that all subprocedures should ensure that all registers (other than those holding the arguments to the procedure) will be restored to their original content before returning to the calling program. The structure of each subroutine might look like this:

```
<start_of_procedure>
    save all registers
    main body of procedure
    restore registers
    return
```

Note, however, that this is only possible if the writer of the subprocedure agrees to the convention. When using a procedure written by another person, prudence is the watchword: Unless you have been assured otherwise (and have complete trust in those assurances), assume that the procedure might change the value. Either the calling program or the subroutine must save and restore the values. The latter will involve fewer lines of code (only one per procedure definition, not one per call) and some improved efficiency (only the registers actually changed need be saved). However, the writer of the calling program may not be sure that a subroutine written by another person will save the registers.

▷ *Compare these observations to the old adage "If you want it done right, do it yourself!"*

RAM VARIABLES. The use of global RAM variables can produce similar—though less severe—problem situations. Fortunately, in assembly language no two variables in a program may have the same name (contrast this with higher-level languages), so there is little chance of confusion from that cause. However, note that any change of the contents of a RAM variable in one procedure is likely to cause problems in any other procedure that uses that variable. In addition, because assembly language programs have a tendency to be quite long (in terms of the printed listing), it will be difficult to check the use of a variable to ensure that its type is defined correctly relative to its use if that variable is declared in any procedure other than the current one. Use RAM variables only in the procedure in which they are declared:

```
<declarations for main program>
begin_code
<main body>
end_code

<declarations of local variables for procedure 1>
<procedure 1>
return

<declarations for procedure 2>
<procedure 2>
return
```

DECISIONS ABOUT MEMORY USE. Several factors will influence the choice of main memory versus registers. In many cases, the assembly language itself will require that certain operands be kept in registers. But often the programmer will have a choice. The choice may be made on grounds of efficiency or on pragmatic grounds, such as reducing the likelihood of error. The following guidelines, based primarily on the latter considerations, will help the beginning assembly language programmer:[2]

- There are relatively few registers, so use them sparingly. There is much RAM memory: Use it generally.
- Registers are working locations, intended to help perform computations quickly. Avoid using them for long-term storage with little intervening use.
- Use registers for values requiring frequent modification, such as loop counters.
- RAM storage cells can have mnemonic names. Take advantage of this capability.
- Pass parameters in registers, never as global RAM variables.
- Some commands insist on register operands. Use registers for data that you know will be used by such operations.
- Some subroutines may modify registers, and data left in those registers by the calling program will be destroyed. Beware: some system routines may also modify registers. Even if you did not create subroutines that modify registers, a call to a systems routine might have the same impact.
- Registers are faster. If the situation truly calls for speed, use a register. However, for the beginning programmer, optimization of code should be clearly subordinate to the creation of clear, modifiable, correct programs.

Data Errors

DECLARATION ERRORS. A programmer may inadvertently specify a constant value that is inappropriate for the type. Hll compilers usually warn the programmer that this situation has occurred. Assemblers provide no equivalent protection. It will be up to the programmer to check the validity of all results. Even declared data may not be checked. For example, a programmer might wish to declare a constant containing the value 1 million:

```
income    constant:integer    1000000
```

[2]Throughout the early chapters of the book, rather dogmatic stylistic rules are presented. The purpose of providing absolute rules is to simplify the learning process. Later, as you become more skilled, many situations will develop in which there are overriding reasons to violate the rules. An analogy can be made to learning to drive: in the beginning, you are told "*always* drive on the right-hand side of the road." In time you discover that there are occasionally situations in which it is necessary or desirable to drive on the left: to pass, to go around an obstacle, and so on—but always with a cautious realization.

This number may be too large to fit in a single-integer storage location. In Pascal, the built-in constant, `maxint`, can be used to compare a value to the maximum permitted size, but an assembler might simply truncate the number, placing only the last several digits into the location `income` (a most distressing situation in this particular example).

PROCEDURAL ABSTRACTION

Few assemblers will check to see that standard conventions of program structure are followed. Among digressions that *will not be detected:*

- failure to provide a `return` (or `end`) statement from a subroutine
- failure to properly bracket a loop with `jump` statements
- inadvertent alteration of a loop-control variable
- `jumps` into or out of the middle of a procedure
- failure of a function to return a value
- incorrect number of parameters passed to a subroutine
- incorrect operand type

For example, the error in the following code will *not* be detected:

```
        copy        val1⇒reg0      ;pass a single parameter
        jump:sub    →dummy
        . . .
dummy
        copy        reg0⇒temp0      ;copy the first and
        copy        reg1⇒temp1      ;second parameters
```

`Dummy` apparently assumes that the calling program placed two values into the registers. It will then use the register contents accordingly, even though there is nothing meaningful there.

The best programming practice that the beginning programmer can develop to minimize these errors is to keep track of the program in terms of its hll equivalent: use hll statements as documentation and follow one simple guideline:

If you can't (wouldn't) do it in Hill, don't do it in assembly language.

For example, the control structures described in Chapter 2 were designed to help minimize control errors. The new programmer is advised to use them carefully until fully knowledgeable of all consequences of an action.

Control Structures

JUMPS. At first glance, the GAL `jump` instruction seems strangely like the "forbidden" `goto` statement of yesteryear. This is not really so strange as it may seem. Early higher-level languages reflected the constructs available in existing assembly languages; they simply inherited the available constructs. More modern hlls were written with program structure in mind, rather than the underlying machine. These languages downplayed or removed altogether the `goto` statement. On the other hand, one can learn to live with `jumps` quite well by following the earlier "if you can't do it in a hll, don't do it in AL" adage. That is, restrict all `jumps` to those that create structures directly corresponding to those of Hill. You have already seen that you could do so. If you restrict yourself to these forms for now, you should have relatively few control problems. When efficiency and flexibility issues start to become important, you may want to revise this rule, but the beginning assembly language programmer is urged to follow it very closely.

ITERATION. Chapter 2 indicated three basic iteration constructs: pretest, post-test, and counter-controlled. Avoid other structures. In general, exits from a loop should always come either at the end of the loop (post-test) or at the front (pretest). The only statements that should precede the `compare/jump` pair in a pretest loop are statements intimately involved in the comparison process. More complicated situations will sometimes involve more than simply the `compare` and `jump` pair for the test. For example, the Hill pretest loop:

```
while(a<(b+c)) do
  <body>
```

can be written in GAL as

```
start_compare_loop
    copy:integer        b⇒reg3
    add                 c⇒reg3         ;(b+c)
    compare:integer     a⇒reg3         ;while a <(b+c)
    jump:greater_eq     →out_of_loop

    <loop body>

    jump:always         →start_compare_loop
out_of_loop
```

Unless there is a very compelling reason, no loop should ever be partially executed. No loop should ever terminate by jumping to a location distant from its own body. This is exactly the set of constraints created by the loop constructs of higher-level languages. The destination of the exit `jump` from a loop should always be the statement that immediately follows the loop structure. Avoid "short-circuiting" the process until you are very comfortable with assembly language programming.

One final rule of thumb for creating control structures using `jumps`: for conditional statements, `jumps` are always forward (downward). Iterations always require at least one backwards (upwards) `jump`. If you draw the arrows corresponding to the `jumps`, they should reflect the nature of the construct (e.g., in a loop you should be able to see the loop).

NESTED STRUCTURES. Always nest structures; never let them overlap. In most most hlls, this issue does not come up because the language does not allow improper nesting. The rule of thumb is that the beginnings and ends of structures must act like a stack. The structure that starts first in the listing must end last. This rule applies to iterations, conditionals, or combinations of the two. Figure 3-1 illustrates incorrect and correct nesting. A general rule of thumb: if you can't draw in the flow-of-control arrows without crossing the lines, your structure is poor.

PROCEDURES. The calling sequence should form a structure. All the statements comprising the call sequence—the parameter copy commands, the actual call, and the retrieval of function value, if any—should be grouped together syntactically to indicate the structure. In writing the subroutine, place any local variables within a declaration block dedicated to that procedure. Thus located, they are clearly associated with the subroutine but are not located where they can be confused with the code (steps) of the procedure. The `return` from the subroutine should also be a structure. Group the statements that place results in registers with the actual `return` statement.

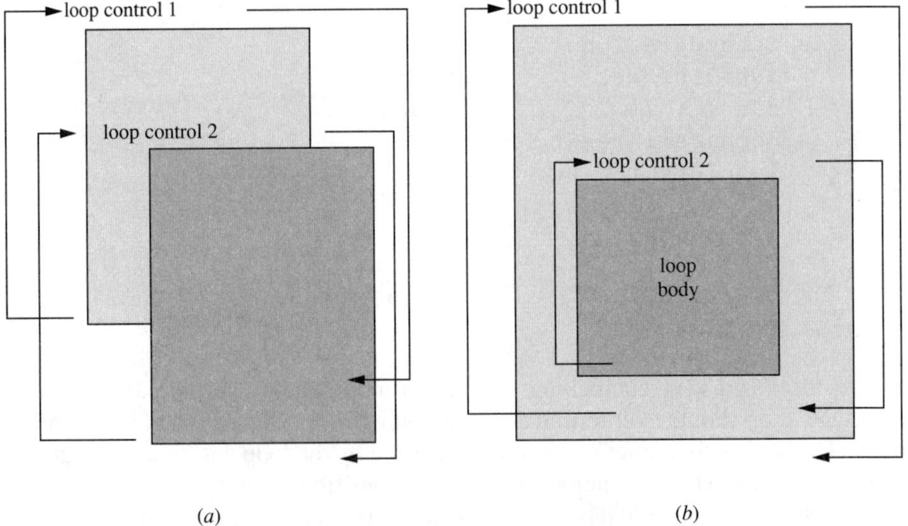

FIGURE 3-1
Program structure nesting. (*a*) Incorrect. (*b*) Correct.

Global Program Structure

Most hlls distinguish between program statements and data. Even though the program itself is stored in memory, there is no way that data can be confused with commands and vice versa. In assembly language, there is little equivalent protection. For example,

```
        copy            loc2⇒reg0
loc2    constant:int    17
        copy            loc1⇒reg1
```

is a syntactically legal—though probably useless—segment. However, when the program is executed, the machine will execute the first `copy` successfully and then die when it attempts to interpret the number `17` as if a command were stored next. This lack of protection may manifest itself in either of two errors, neither of which will be detected by the assembler:

- an unrecognized instruction error
- execution of an unexpected instruction

Which case occurs depends on whether or not the data can somehow be interpreted as an instruction.

DOCUMENTATION

One of the primary tools for maintaining abstractions available to the assembly language programmer is documentation. It is hard to over-document an assembly language program. When in doubt, document! Documentation just may be the assembly language programmer's single best defense. Be sure to document heavily. Several suggestions follow.

WHITE SPACE. Note the blanks included to separate the parts of the examples in the previous chapter. For example, in the conditional structures blank lines were used to separate the `<test>` from the `<action>`, and the `<action>` from the `<following code>`. Such spacing helps emphasize the structure of the program by indicating that some blocks of statements are more closely associated than are others. Additionally, indentation of the `<actions>` statements provides exactly the same information that indentation provides in hlls: that the `<actions>` form a logical block which is subordinate to the control statement.

Similarly, in the iteration example above, the code representing the body of a loop was indented and separated from that of its control mechanism by blank lines. The loop body and the counting mechanism should always be kept distinct; the first block for the body, the second block for the counting/control mechanism. It is best to separate the blocks with a blank line in addition to indenting the loop body. This is true for all three forms of loop, even though the control structure appears at different places relative to the loop body. For example, notice how the whitespace helps with one of the trickier structures—a "for loop":

```
        copy:int          start⇒regl

    top_of_loop
        compare:int       regl⇒stop
        jump:greater      →out_of_loop

            <loop body>       ;note:separated and indented

        add               #1⇒regl
        jump:always       →top_of_loop

    out_of_loop
```

ABSTRACTION. The abstraction capabilities of hlls reflect the tools necessary for good programming. Because assembly language does not provide these tools, the programmer should include them artificially by means of documentation. Include descriptions of the data structures and procedural abstractions that you use. Remember that the granularity of assembly language does not support these concepts. A `jump` statement by itself does not indicate clearly if it is a conditional structure or an iteration structure—you must make it clear. A very useful technique is to include Pascal or pseudocode as a documenting tool.

INTENT. Specify the *purpose* of each statement or block of statements. What was the goal in terms of higher-level intent? Compare the following attempts at commenting:

```
poor:  add #1⇒reg2     ;add 1 to reg2
```

and

```
better: add #1⇒reg2     ;reg2 holds the number
        add #1⇒reg2     ;of chars processed
```

The former adds nothing that any knowledgeable programmer cannot see directly from the statement. The latter both indicates why the statement is included and reminds the reader of the use of `reg2`.

Appendix 1 includes several specific suggestions for documentation techniques.

EXTENDING LANGUAGE CAPABILITIES

As stated previously, it is not the goal of this text to present assembly language as an efficiency tool. However the concept of efficiency cannot be completely ignored. Assembly language does provide an important window on efficiency issues not available to the hll programmer. Because AL offers few restrictions, it also allows more choices. Since many hlls do not include a `read` loop construct, we will consider that as an example.

The lack of a powerful `read` procedure in GAL such as that found in Hill makes the `read` loop even more important. The `input` procedure reads only single characters. Therefore, `read` loops will be needed not only for reading multiple lines and multiple items from a line but also for reading data types other than characters. The general form of the `read` loop in GAL is very similar to that of the while loop:

```
<read_loop_name>
    jump:sub         →input                ;read and
    copy             reg0⇒<item>           ;test control
    compare:char     <item>⇒<target>       ;structure
    jump:not_equal   →<end_of_read_loop>

        <body of loop>

    jump:always      →<read_loop_name>
<end_of_read_loop>
```

For a more specific example consider the following procedure that echoes all input characters up to but not including the first blank.

```
readmore
    jump:sub        →input
    copy            reg0⇒new_char
    compare:char    #' '⇒reg0
    jump:equal      →after_loop
        jump:sub    →output        ;new_char still in reg0
    jump:always     →readmore
after_loop
```

Consider two important observations about this example. First, it represents a new construct not available in many hlls. But the `compare/jump` statements are no longer the first two statements of the loop, as would be the case for the escape from a simple while loop. However, the only statement to precede them is the `input` statement—an integral part of the control mechanism of the `read` loop.

The read loop also provides an opportunity to consider the notion of efficiency. *Efficiency* is actually a technical term in computer science. Its most common measures are the quantity of memory used and the amount of time required to run a program (as a function of the quantity of input). One criterion that is *not* a measure of efficiency is the number of lines of code (although in assembly language, the correlation between the number of lines of code and the amount of memory used may be higher than in a hll). Another aspect that causes little concern is small changes in these measures. Suppose you have a machine that executes 1 million assembly language instructions per second and can store 1 million characters in RAM (both very modest assumptions today). A program that executed one fewer instruction than another would run 1 millionth of a second faster. A program that executed 10,000 fewer instructions would only run 1 hundredth of a second faster. In practice, code that is only executed once effectively adds nothing to the total computation time—put another way, no one could write so much code that the speed would matter if it were only executed once. In order to use significant amounts of time, code must be part of a loop. Suppose that you had a loop with the following structure:

```
loop_top                    ;termination example
      code
      point at which terminating condition is known
      more code
      loop bottom
```

Although it would be possible to exit the loop in the middle as soon as the terminating condition is reached, execution of only part of a single pass through the loop will be saved by doing so. That is, there is no gain in efficiency. It is possible that the logic will require that the lower portion of the loop not be executed, but that is not an efficiency issue.

On the other hand, in the above `read` loop the test could be shortened by comparing `reg0` without copying its contents to `new_char`. If the `copy` could be avoided, one step per pass through the loop would be saved, which might be significant.[3] Even more important would be variations that greatly reduced the number of passes taken through the loop. Similarly, the pretest loop needed two `jumps`, the post-test uses only one. Even though the extra jump is actually performed only once, the statement itself is executed on each iteration of the loop. The post-test loop is therefore more efficient, but the small savings should seldom dictate which structure to use. Always use the one that makes logical sense in the current situation, which is usually the form corresponding to your pseudocode.

ERRORS

Assembly language does not support abstraction issues very directly. One result of this is that additional errors are likely to be introduced that would not have occurred in a hll. Fortunately, the simplicity of the structure of the language and the precise control provided by assembly both help in the task of detecting and fixing errors.

---

[3]Although it turns out that the savings would be insignificant compared to the total cost of the input—a topic covered in Chapter 12.

Classes of Error

In Hill, the vast majority of errors can be classified as falling into three groups:

Syntax or compilation errors. These errors are detected by the compiler as it attempts to understand the code written by the programmer. Invariably, compilation error messages mean that some aspect of your code was not a legal construct in the hll you were using. Most frequently they result from incorrectly specified syntax or from incorrectly typed variables.

Run-time errors. These are errors that are not detected until the program is actually running. To create a run-time error, the program must be syntactically correct but have a significant logical problem. Typical run-time errors include illegal array subscripts and invalid input. A run-time error necessarily involves a detectable condition, such as division by zero or subscript out-of-bounds.

Logic errors. These errors produce no error message. They can only be detected by comparison of the actual and expected output. They therefore tend to be the ones that give programmers the most difficulty. For example, a statement intended to calculate the total pay for several hours of work might inadvertently be written as

```
assign    pay⇐hours + rate    {error in operation}
```

There is no detectable error, but the answer would be very disappointing to the employee.

It often seems to the new programmer that almost anything can cause an error in assembly language programming. In reality, a small number of mistakes account for a very large percentage of student errors. Thinking about the sources of error can lead, hopefully, to their prevention and certainly to their detection. Many of the distinctions are analogous to the above distinctions for hlls, between the types of error: assembler, linker, machine, and logical. Simply knowing which subsystem detected the error provides much information about the nature of that error. Assembler errors are analogous to compiler errors. They are detected by the assembler when it attempts to read your program. Linker errors can occur only for programs involving separately assembled modules. Machine errors or run-time errors occur when an attempt to perform a requested command results in an illegal condition. Finally, logic errors are manifested simply by incorrect results. Error messages will always provide some indication of their source. Learn to recognize the distinctions; it will save much grief. We take each of these classes in order and discuss the most common examples of each. Figure 3-2 illustrates the relationships.

Errors are to be expected in every programmer's life. Many of the techniques require information that will be covered in Chapter 4. What follows is a "quick-and-dirty" set of rules for dealing with error messages now.

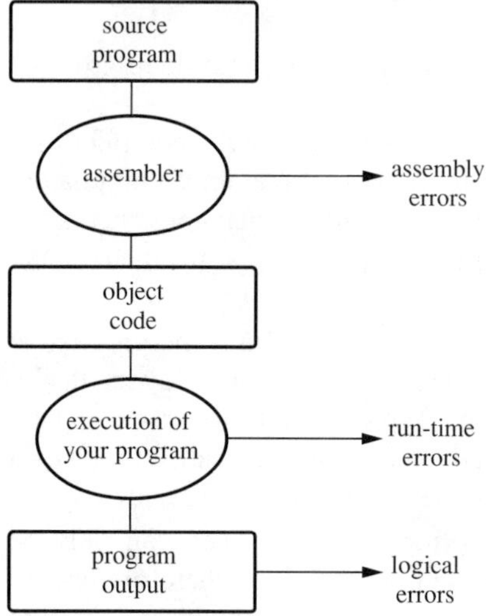

FIGURE 3-2
Relationship of errors to assembly and execution.

ASSEMBLY ERRORS. The assembler is to AL as the compiler is to a hll. Assembly errors correspond roughly to compile errors. The assembler will only generate an error message when it cannot determine any valid command that might be intended. Because AL commands are syntactically very structured, the most common root cause of such errors is a careless or misunderstood use of a command, such as

a misspelled identifier
a wrong number of operands
an illegal form of operand specification
a misplaced label

Many of the most common hll compiler error messages dealt with incorrect expressions, program structure, and type mismatches—none of which have analogies in AL. Assembler error messages are generated as the assembler attempts to read a user program. Therefore, assembly errors invariably imply that the code violates the rules of the assembly language itself. In all cases, the most important tool you will need for correcting the error is the formal specification from the assembly language reference manual.

The assembler must process all of the code in your entire program before any of it can be executed. Errors detected by the assembler almost always have a single interpretation: a statement did not correspond to the syntax of the language. You should look up the description of the syntax in the manual. Remember that most commands have few syntax rules; therefore a small set of precautions will go a long way toward preventing errors.

- Count the number of operands. It should agree with the number specified by the manual.

```
        add    first,second⇒sum    ;incorrect:3 operands
```

- Check the type of each operand. An incorrect type will seldom cause an assembly error, but it is convenient to check types when you check the number or operands.
- Make sure each operand is declared; also check the spelling.

```
my_var  variable:integer
        . . .
        add    myvar⇒reg0          ;error, misspelled
                                   ;identifier
```

- Make sure there is whitespace at precisely the required locations. Common errors are incorrectly placed labels and comments.

```
        section_name               ;error statement label
                                   ;indented
        add    reg0⇒regl
```

or

```
        add    reg0⇒  regl         ;error whitespace
                                   ;between operands
```

- Be wary of special syntax for literals, etc.

```
        add    l⇒regl              ;error no immediate sign
```

The description of an error detected by the assembler may also differ from the error that the programmer made. That is, the error message describes a problem with the assembler's attempt to interpret the instruction—not with the actual error that the programmer made. Some of the more common assembly errors follow.

Missing operand. The assembler believes that more operands are required for the indicated command than you provided. Several possible causes exist for this error:

1. An incorrect number of operands were specified for the command.
2. A blank space was inserted between the operands (and the assembler interpreted the blank as the end of the command).
3. You confused the command with one having a similar name (but a different syntax or number of operands).

Suggested action: compare the list of operands you used with that specified in the reference manual. Check the punctuation.

Illegal operand. Although the number of operands may be okay, one (or more) of them is not permissible for the operand specified. Recall that the error must be detectable from the syntax. Errors in data type will seldom be detected at this point.

1. An operand for the command must be a register, but a main memory operand was specified.
2. An operand for the command must be in main memory, but was specified as a register. For example, the GAL statement

```
add     item1⇒item2     ;error too many RAM operands
```

   would be illegal because GAL allows only one RAM operand.
3. An address that should not be modified was specified as the destination operand.
4. Some other mismatch occurred. For example, an immediate operand was intended, but the syntax did not indicate that it was an immediate.

Suggested action: check all storage declarations. Check order of operands. Check restrictions on the operands, such as register/RAM restrictions, or immediate restrictions.

Label not found. This means that an identifier was specified as an operand, but no statement or `variable` declaration with that identifier as a label could be found anywhere in your code. Possible causes, other than the obvious:

1. The label exists, but its first character was in a column other than the first. Most assemblers require labels to start in column 1; some allow markers for labels, in which case you should make sure that the label follows all rules for label identifiers and syntax.
2. Misspelled labels (watch for such small differences as `item_1` versus `item1`). Either the definition or the reference may be the one in error. Some assemblers may distinguish between upper- and lowercase characters.
3. There is another error in the labeled statement, causing that statement to be ignored.
4. The final `end_code` construct occurs syntactically prior to the label, causing assembly to stop assembling at that point, missing the needed label.
5. The labeled statement is in a separate module, but no indication was provided to the assembler (see also linker errors).

Suggested action: compare the label definition with the label reference. Note that a label may refer to any location: a statement (reference is probably a `jump`) or a storage declaration (reference can be any data movement or manipulation operation).

Duplicate label. A label was used twice. Typical causes include

1. Exactly what it says, you used a label twice.
2. You may have inadvertently used the same label in two different routines.
3. A command starting in column 1 may incorrectly be interpreted as an identifier.

Unable to open file. Typically this means that the desired sourcecode (program) file was incorrectly specified: it was not on the default disk or in the default directory.

1. The name of the file containing your program was misspelled.
2. The location (disk, directory, or folder) containing the file was incorrectly specified.
3. A secondary file reference violated one of the above.
4. On very rare occasions, there may actually be an error on the disk. Try duplicating the file.

Suggested actions. Compare the referenced filename with the actual filename. If you did not provide a full path-name, check the system's default path-name. Check syntax for specification of path-names.

Perhaps some of the most useful information to use for interpreting assembler errors is the recognition of what *cannot* cause an error at assembly time. Your program does not start to execute until the assembler has completely processed the code (see Chapter 7). Therefore no assembly error is due to errors in the execution of your code. Do not look where the answer cannot be. For example, assembly errors will not be caused by bad input to the program, infinite loops, improper comparisons, type incompatibility, and so on. Concentrate on the specification of the program on a command by command basis.

Linker errors. Hopefully, the beginning programmer will not encounter this class of errors. Linker errors are a result of incorrectly specified relationships between program segments contained in multiple files. Like the assembly errors, linker errors occur before the program begins to execute. (Linker errors are covered more thoroughly in Chapter 7.)

Machine or Run-Time Errors

If your program gets through assembly before encountering an error, congratulations—but you have now entered the difficult part. Errors may take three forms:

- the machine may die;
- you may discover a set of incomprehensible error messages; or
- you may get the wrong answer.

Machine errors are *not* errors caused by the machine, as the name seems to suggest. They correspond most closely to run-time errors in Hill. These errors occur only when code generated by the assembler (which is almost certainly correct legal machine code) results in an operation that cannot be performed. Because the operation cannot be performed, the machine stops. In AL—unlike many hlls—the detection of dangerous conditions does not cause a run-time error message. The programmer is completely on his or her own with respect to dangerous but legal conditions. The narrowness of the set of situations that can cause run-time errors—the instruction was syntactically valid but cannot be executed—can be used to help interpret the causes of those errors. In particular, the situation invariably involves some aspect that could not be known until run time. For example, it cannot be known that the divisor of a particular division operation will be zero until that statement is executed. What errors can be detected? Actually there are relatively few distinct situations and even fewer that the novice programmer is likely to encounter.

For the moment, you should debug in roughly the same way you did for hlls: provide test data, compare the actual and expected results, and try to figure out why the code did not do what you expected it to. Some additional pointers:

- Watch for any output that will indicate that your program worked partially. You can always add extra output to provide feedback as the program progresses.
- Do not forget that the machine may not echo the input (if you see no input echoed on the screen, it does not necessarily mean your answer is wrong).
- Keep everything as simple as possible.
- Check the following:

  the types of all operands
  for "double use" of registers (one register; two roles)
  look for missing control structure such as `returns`

Run-time errors are extremely machine-dependent. Although the following descriptions are intended to be very general, they may not apply exactly to any specific machine. There may be other error messages on a given machine, or different causes for the same errors.

Illegal address. It is possible to make a reference to a storage address that does not exist. Additionally, some existing locations are not appropriate for some operands. When an instruction attempts to access such an operand, but that operand is not correctly located, an address error is signaled. This situation can be caused in three ways:

1. A command, specifying a multibyte operand (e.g., an integer), references an operand that is declared as a single byte (e.g., a character). For example,

```
strange  variable:character
         . . .
         copy:int  strange⇒reg0  ;error mismatched type
```

Solution: make sure that all operands of all commands are declared using the same size as is expected by its use in the command. Beware of default lengths. Specify the length or type for all operands.

2. Data and statements are intermixed. A data directive before an instruction (without an intervening `begin` or `end` construct) can cause statements to be stored at illegal addresses. Most assemblers will attempt to prevent this from happening. However, if the program contains `constant` directives prior to instructions and these constants happen to declare an odd number of bytes, subsequent code may be incorrectly located. The error will occur when control transfers to statements following the constants (usually through a subroutine `jump`). For example.

```
item     constant     5
block    copy:int     strange⇒reg0
```

Solution: place data after code, or use `begin` and `end`, or other directives to make the boundaries of code and data blocks explicit.

3. Failure to specify the immediate sign ("#") can cause an immediate operand to be treated as an address or location. (The exact nature of this error will become clear in Chapter 7).

4. In Chapter 5, you will see one more possibility: An address register has been incorrectly incremented, causing it to point to an illegal address or even to a nonexistent address. It is usually up to the programmer to increment the address register correctly: by 1 to reach the next byte, 2 for the next word, and 4 for the next long. Note that the system may maintain a register for its own addressing purposes. If that register is inadvertently modified, address errors are likely.

Solution: the automatic increment and decrement modes can take care of some of this, and the built-in stack operations will alleviate some more of this problem.

Divide by zero. This error is exactly what it sounds like: a division was specified in which the divisor was zero. Since the machine cannot perform such an operation, it quits. Most frequently, this situation is caused by a logic error (the programmer did not check the divisor first). It can also be caused by an incorrect size of operand. For example,

```
long  variable    long_word
      . . .
      divide:int  long⇒reg0  ;possible divide by zero
```

Solution: make sure that the divisor is correctly specified. Make sure that it has been initialized.

Illegal instruction. This error also means exactly what it sounds like: the machine attempted to execute an instruction but found that the instruction it wished to execute looked like no valid instruction. How can this be? Every instruction that the machine attempts to execute is created by the assembler, isn't it? It seems that this could only happen if the assembler is in error. Nice thought, but not quite true. Recall that the assembler does no type-checking. If a jump statement has a variable or constant storage as its address, the assembler will often allow the jump even though it seems to be an obvious error. If a procedure does not have a `return` as its last statement, the assembler will generate code that is immediately followed by data. The computer attempts to execute successively each statement in the procedure. After the last statement, it will attempt to execute the data as if it were part of the procedure.

Solution: the error can usually be fixed by placing the `end_data` and `end_code` directives between the data and code segments. Also, check for a wayward `jump` instruction, one that specifies a jump to data:

```
        . . .
        jump:always     →item
        . . .
        end_code
item    constant . . .
```

This is perfectly legal from the assembler's point of view but almost certain to generate an error. Analogously, a data item placed between two instructions will cause an error as illustrated earlier.

Solution: use labels and markers that help distinguish between data and instruction.

Logical Errors

Logical errors can be the most difficult to deal with. No error message (nor any other explicit indicator) is generated, and the program continues to run as if it were correct. The most common symptom is simply an incorrect answer. A few other common symptoms and suggested solutions:

1. The machine "hangs" and does nothing. This is probably an infinite loop. Check the comparison for the loop-exit condition. Programmers frequently get it backwards. For example,

```
copy           initial⇒reg0    ;want to loop 10 times
compare:int    limit⇒reg0      ;while initial<limit do
jump:equal     →out of loop
               . . .
add            #1⇒reg0
jump:always    →top_of_loop
```

In GAL, this is an infinite loop if `initial > limit`. In a machine that compares `<destination>` to `<source>` , there is no problem.

2. Program ends early. Check for a simple jump being used rather than a jump-to-subroutine.
3. A procedure that you did not call is executed "accidentally." Check to see if all the procedures that you did call have `return` statements. For example, in

```
<procedure 1>
    <body>
    ;missing return statement
<procedure 2>
    <body>
```

control will fall through to `procedure 2`.

4. Simply incorrect results. Check all operand types or sizes. Check registers used by multiple procedures.

DEBUGGERS. The most valuable tool for assembly language debugging is called a *debugger.* This program can be used to investigate the current status of programs including the contents of registers and RAM storage locations, the current instruction, and the results of comparisons. Debuggers can be used to trace through the execution of a program or to find the status when an error occurs. For example when a program has an error, the debugger reports the general nature of the error, the location in the code of the error, and the content of memory and registers. Most debuggers display the memory and register content information in base-2 or base-16 representations, which are discussed in Chapter 4. Chapter 13 contains general rules for the use of debuggers.

> ▷ *Actually the debugger will usually point to the instruction after the error. Why would it point to the next, rather than the one that caused the error?*

PROGRAMMING IN "REAL" ASSEMBLY LANGUAGES

Variations on Commands

Although most languages have similar command sets, they vary in details, including the mnemonics, allowable operands, etc. For example, the `copy` command may be called `move`. Other machines use the names `load` and `store` to distinguish between `copys` to or from registers. Table 2-1 shows commands equivalent to GAL commands for two popular machines. Often a language has two commands that are very similar, with minor distinctions in meaning. Important or common examples include the following.

IMMEDIATE OPERANDS. Most languages require that instructions explicitly indicate literal or immediate operands. In addition to the immediate symbol, a language may have two distinct commands `add` and `add_immediate` that are both identical to the GAL `add` command except that `add_immediate` will only accept immediate operands. The programmer is expected to use the immediate version of the command, `addi`, whenever one operand is an immediate. Usually, the immediate sign (or other syntactic indication of immediate data) is required prior to the immediate data, even though the command's syntax indicates that the data is immediate. Commands that frequently have such immediate forms include the arithmetic operations, `copy`, and `compare`.

REGISTER/RAM DISTINCTIONS. On some machines, the operation name varies slightly for operations that allow register operands from those that allow RAM operands. Thus, one might find CMPM and CMPR for "compare memory" and "compare register".

STORAGE DECLARATIONS. In addition to variations in name, directives for reserving storage may differ in form. Some may make no distinction between `constant` and `variable` directives. Some may have an `initial_value` directive rather than the constant, which is also probably a more accurate description. Some may allow the declaration of large blocks of storage with a single directive, for creating arrays, and so on.

JUMP COMMANDS. Many machines have several variations on the `jump` command. A frequent variation is the `branch` command, which you may consider for the moment as being functionally equivalent to a `jump`. It sometimes confuses the novice assembly language programmer because on the one hand the `jump` seems very similar to the `branch` command, but on the other hand not all variations exist. For example, the M68000 machines have both `branch` and `jump` to subroutines, but only conditional `branchs`. The distinction between such variations will be discussed in Chapters 6 and 7.

REGISTER SAVING. Many assembly languages provide a command (probably called something like `store-multiple-registers`) precisely tailored for the problem of saving registers before entering a subroutine. Usually a single command can be used to save all registers needing protection.

OPERAND SIZE. Many assembly languages allow or require the programmer to specify the size rather than the type of the operands. The usual measure is the *byte*—just enough storage to hold one character. Typical operand sizes are one, two, or four bytes. These sizes may be specified as numbers. More often, there are machine-specific names for these sizes such as *byte, word,* and *long*; or *byte, half-word,* and *word.* Typically, the size option is specified as an extension to the operation name. Thus,

```
copy:byte    loc1⇒loc2
```

might specify that the copy operand should copy a single byte—one character—from `loc1` to `loc2`. As with the operation codes, most assembly languages have very terse extensions, such as

`b`	for	`byte`
`w`	for	`word` (2 bytes)
`l`	for	`longword` (4 bytes)

Note that the naming is not standard. For example, some machines have four-byte words with two-byte half-words. Usually, the programmer must determine exactly how much storage is needed for the particular operands that are being used. GAL's default assumptions are typical:

Type	**Required storage**
character	1 byte
integer	2 bytes
reals	4 bytes
string	varying size
array	varying size

Most languages have default lengths that are used if the programmer does not provide a length in the command. But the programmer should *never assume* that the default length is correct. Make it a practice to include the type or size specification on every command. For example, it would make sense for the add command to use word as the default length, but the default might be byte.

PROGRAM STRUCTURE. Few real languages provide `begin` or `end` directives for structuring the program. The programmer should take care to separate program and data and to separate the procedures from each other. In particular, data declarations and program statements should never be intermixed. The first line of every block of code should have a label, and the last line should be some form of exit or `return`.

READING A REFERENCE MANUAL

Programming necessarily requires a real language. To program effectively in any given assembly language, you will need a reference manual describing that language and an understanding of the previous chapter. The bible of every assembly language programmer is the programmer's reference manual. Every machine has a manual that explains each instruction: its syntax, its semantics, how it is coded, the restrictions on its operands, the size of operations, and so on. Learning to read the programmer's reference manual is an essential skill. Often a quick look into the manual creates the sensation that reading the contents must be a very formidable task, but it really is not difficult if you approach it properly. It is not necessary to read the entire description. You do not yet have all the background needed to read the typical assembly manual, but you have enough to get started.

Remember that a reference manual is just that—a reference manual. It is not a textbook. There is very little, if any, "how to" information in the manual. The manual simply provides answers to questions that the programmer needs to ask. The key is that the programmer must have a well-formed question to ask. "I don't know where to start" is not a well-formed question. You should use a reference manual to answer specific questions about the exact syntax, the specific results, the legal operands, and so on, of a specific instruction. That is, you should first develop a general generic algorithm, perhaps in pseudocode or even in Hill, then convert the algorithm into a generic assembly language such as GAL. Then and only then, you should look up and fill in the details of specific commands.

Most programmer's reference manuals have a section (usually the largest) devoted to the specifics of each assembly language instruction. It is to this section that the programmer must turn at this point. The first unfortunate aspect that the programmer will discover is that the section is typically organized alphabetically by command name, which is great if you know the command name but terrible if you do not. For example, if the `jump` command is called `branch` on some machine, the programmer will never find it by looking under "J".

Finding Command Descriptions

There are several approaches to finding the command you want.

1. First, attempt to find a command with the same name as the corresponding GAL command. More likely, the command will be an abbreviation of that name. The commands may be listed alphabetically by the abbreviation or by the full mnemonic for which the abbreviation stands.
2. Use Table 2.1 to find synonyms for the command you seek. If your machine is listed in the table you can simply look for the synonym. If not, look for synonyms used on other machines.
3. It is probably well worth your time to peruse the entire manual frequently, simply looking at the command names and any other details that attract your attention. Eventually you will develop a general sense of the names of available commands.
4. Be sure to watch out for variants of commands such as CMP (compare) and CMPI (compare immediate). Often both commands correspond to the same GAL instruction but differ in "little" details, such as the legal operands they may take.

Reading the Command Description

The entire description for a given command is probably a page or two long. Most of the description will seem Greek to you at first. But you should be able to find the following items, which are all useful.

INSTRUCTION NAME. There should be both a short form and a long form. The short form is the command or operation name that forms part of the language. The long form is a more readable English-like form for humans. For example, you might find `cmp` and `compare` or `add` and `add-binary`.

> ▷ *Computer arithmetic is really binary as we shall see in the next chapter. Why isn't it decimal?*

OPERATION DESCRIPTION. Again, there may be both a short form and a long form of the operation description. The former is designed to be a precise, unambiguous formal or mathematical description of the command. The latter will be in English prose. The beginning programmer will probably prefer the English description. With experience you will start to prefer the formal description for many purposes. The full description may include unfamiliar words and references. Start by paying attention to the ones that you do know and to ones that clearly refer to actions performed on the operands.

SYNTAX. The exact syntax of the command will be specified. The syntax will show the number of operands, the legal forms (RAM, register, etc.) of the operands and the relative position of the operands (e.g., does the dividend or divisor come first?).

SIZE. It will also show the legal sizes for the operands. Note that it is almost certainly the size and not the type of the item. If there is more than one size, you should always specify the size of the operands that you wish to use.

ADDITIONAL INFORMATION. The preceding items will usually be near the front of the entry. Much additional information will follow. However, most of it goes beyond the understanding of the beginning programmer. Do not worry about items you do not understand. Concentrate instead on finding the preceding items.

SUMMARY

Assembly language provides few of the protections that most programmers have grown to expect in higher-level languages. But programming naked—without such protection—may be useful both for reasons of efficiency and as a tool for understanding the inner working of computers. In general, the programming process is conceptually identical to programming in hlls, but there is less protection and are more details to deal with. The programmer should learn to structure programs to reflect the protections offered by higher-level languages. Pay close attention to the abstraction process, for both data and procedures. Use very careful documentation to make up for what the language does not enforce. Errors may be detected by the assembler, or when the program is running. The timing of an error may be as important for figuring out the problem as what the message said. In either case, there are relatively few possible errors from the machine's point of view. The programmer's reference manual for your machine is your most important tool.

EXERCISES

3.1. Translate any hll language program that you have into assembly language.

3.2. What is wrong with the following GAL instructions?

```
add      ⇒17
add      a⇒b⇒c
add      a⇒b
```

In the assembly language for your machine, attempt to duplicate the above incorrect statements.

3.3. Using your assembly language, attempt to create the assembler errors discussed in this chapter:

missing operand
illegal operand
missing label
duplicate label

What did the message say? Where did the message appear relative to the statement that caused it? What additional information was provided?

3.4. Using your assembly language, attempt to create the run-time errors discussed in this chapter:

divide by zero
illegal instruction
illegal address

Note how your machine responds to each type of error. What did the message say? When was it generated? What additional information did it provide?

3.5. In your reference manual, find the closest equivalent for each GAL instruction used so far. Find as many points of difference as you can.

3.6. Write subroutines to expand the basic power of assembly language:

```
power(base, exponent)
average(first, second, third)
```

Assume integer arithmetic.

3.7. The Hill post-test iteration construct `repeat-until` states its continuation criterion in the negative: "stop looping when the condition is *no longer* true." There is no necessary reason why this must be the case. It could have been stated as "loop as long as condition holds." Create such a positively stated post-test loop in assembly language. Similarly, create a negatively stated pretest loop: *iterate if condition does not hold.* Why did Hill and Pascal select the semantics they did?

3.8. Write a function terminator, that determines if a character is one that would normally end an input string, such as carriage return.

3.9. Write a routine that inputs a series of characters and writes as output the series of characters `succ(first)`, `succ(succ(second))`, `succ(succ(succ(third)))`, ... For example, given the input `abcd`, it writes `bdfh`.

3.10. Write a procedure that accepts an integer parameter and counts the number of times it can divide the result by two before getting a zero result. If it passes the number 500, it should return.

3.11. Recall that `char(ord('0') + small_number)` will produce the character corresponding to `small_number` if `small_number` < 10. Use this relationship to output the values in the previous problems.

3.12. Write a program that inputs two small numbers such that their sum is less than 10 and outputs the results.

3.13. Most humans feel that multiplication is more complex than addition. Is the same true for computers? Write a short program that performs 10,000 additions and one that performs 10,000 multiplications. Time them with a stop watch.

3.14. Read Appendix I: Style guide. Compare each rule to rules you learned for dealing with higher-level languages.

CHAPTER

4

NUMERIC REPRESENTATION AND COMPUTER ARITHMETIC

INTERNAL REPRESENTATION

Digital computers represent all data in binary; or, perhaps more accurately, all data is built up from just two basic values. (If you have attempted to use the debugger, you have already witnessed this.) Every number is represented using a binary representation and every character is represented as a sequence of binary values. Assembly languages provide mnemonic representations for the names of variables, procedures, and locations in code. Internally, computers keep track of such items by means of numeric addresses, which are also represented as binary numbers. So not only the content of memory locations, but the addresses of those locations are represented as binary numbers. It is relatively simple to create a storage mechanism that can hold exactly two values: one or zero (on or off, yes or no, true or false, in or out, etc.). In fact, essentially all internal arithmetic in modern computers is binary. This means that if we are able to look at the contents of variables or registers, we will find binary numbers. Further investigation of the internal workings of the machine requires an understanding of the representations used.

Review of Decimal Notation

Most of us are so familiar with the decimal number system that we normally do not think about the meanings of the conventions inherent in the representations. Recall that the decimal representation is a positional number system; that is, the decimal representation of any number specifies the value as a sum of the individual digits times powers of ten. The number 4321 is really

$$\begin{aligned} 4 \times 10^3 &= 4000 \text{ plus} \\ 3 \times 10^2 &= 300 \text{ plus} \\ 2 \times 10^1 &= 20 \text{ plus} \\ 1 \times 10^0 &= 1 \end{aligned}$$

In general, a number

$$d_n d_{n-1} d_{n-2} \ldots d_1 d_0$$

represents the value

$$\sum_{i=0}^{n} d_i * 10^i = \begin{cases} d_n & * & 10^n & + \\ d_{n-1} & * & 10^{n-1} & + \\ d_{n-2} & * & 10^{n-2} & + \\ & \cdots & & + \\ d_1 & * & 10^1 & + \\ d_0 & * & 10^0 & \end{cases}$$

Informally, the positions are named according to the numbers that they represent: thousands, hundreds, tens, and ones (or units). Alternatively, we could name them after the corresponding power of ten each represents: 3 (thousands), 2 (hundreds), 1 (tens), and 0 (units). Note that ten to the 0 is, in fact, 1 (more generally, by definition anything to the 0 is 1). The four positions in this example are numbered from 3 down to 0, rather than from 4 to 1. Mathematicians and computer scientists have a tendency to count from zero rather than one. (As this chapter continues, some of the reasons for this will become apparent to you.) Computer scientists also count positions from right to left, because the right-most digits represent the smallest numbers or, more specifically, the lowest powers of ten. By numbering the digits from right to left and beginning at 0, the number of each position is the same as the power of ten that it represents. The positions at the left represent the largest powers of ten and are therefore called *high-order* or *most significant* digits. The positions at the right represent the smallest (lowest) powers of ten and are therefore called the *low-order* or *least significant* digits.

The Arabic number system (the one commonly used today) also incorporates the important concept of *zero*. To represent a number as the sum of digits times powers of ten, you need to account for the case in which some specific power of ten is not involved. For example, the number 102 represents the value

$$1 * 10^2 + \underline{0 *} 10^1 + 2 * 10^0$$

This *place-holding* feature of the zero is a cornerstone of the power of the Arabic number system. It enables us to multiply by 10 by simply adding a zero as a new last digit.

$$12340 = 10 * 1234$$

Adding the zero moves each digit one position to the left, so that it now occupies the position representing the next higher power of 10. Similarly, we can divide by 10 by simply lopping off the last zero:

$$43210/10 = 4321$$

If the last digit is not a zero, its removal has exactly the same result as does integer division in Hill or Pascal. Thus,

$$1234 \texttt{ div } 10 = 123$$

Other Radices

The Arabic system is not wedded to base ten. In fact, the above discussion can be generalized to any base. In such discussions, the base is more frequently referred to as the *radix*. A value represented in a given radix R is represented by a series of digits between 0 and $(R - 1)$, inclusive. The number $d_n d_{n-1} d_{n-2} \ldots d_1 d_0$ represents the value

$$\sum_{i=0}^{n} d_i * R^i = \begin{cases} d_n & * & R^n & + \\ d_{n-1} & * & R^{n-1} & + \\ d_{n-2} & * & R^{n-2} & + \\ & \cdots & & + \\ d_1 & * & R^1 & + \\ d_0 & * & R^0 & \end{cases}$$

Shifting a number to the left (i.e., adding a zero at the right) has the effect of multiplying by R; shifting to the right (removing a digit at the right) of dividing by R.

Arithmetic calculations are performed in all radices in exactly the same manner as in base ten. For example, the following algorithm adds two numbers, A and B:

Addition

```
(starting at the right)
while there remain digits to be added
   add the current digit of A to the current digit of B.
   if the sum is less than the radix,
      then record that sum
   otherwise
      subtract the radix from the sum
      record the difference
      add 1 to the next digit of the first addend (A).
```

Or more formally

```
set num_of_cols ⇐ size of storage location
set column ⇐ 0
set temp ⇐ a[column] + b[column]
for column = 0 to num_of_cols − 1
   if temp < radix
      then
         sum[column] ⇐ temp
      otherwise
         sum[column] ⇐ temp − radix
         a[column + 1] ⇐ a[column + 1] + 1
```

▷ *When written formally, a small problem occurs: it seems that* `a[num_of_cols]` *might not exist, yet the last line could attempt to place a value there. What could be done to solve this problem?*

Experiment with this algorithm until you convince yourself that when using a radix of ten, this is exactly the same algorithm you have always used for adding two decimal numbers. Performing the algorithm on two base 7 numbers yields

$$\begin{array}{r} 432_7 \\ \underline{543_7} \\ 1305_7 \end{array}$$

Note the subscript 7, indicating that the numbers represent base 7 values. Similarly, subtraction, multiplication, and division are algorithmically the same for all bases. Subtraction uses a similar algorithm:

```
(starting at the right)
while digits remain to be subtracted
   if (current digit of subtrahend) > (current digit of minuend)
      add radix to current digit of minuend
      subtract 1 from next digit of minuend
   subtract current digit of subtrahend from current digit of minuend
```

Formal specification of the algorithm is left for an exercise, as are algorithms for multiplication and division.

BINARY REPRESENTATION

All representation within a computer ultimately requires bits of data. *Bit* is actually a technical term meaning *BInary digiT.* A bit is a quantity of storage just sufficient to hold one of two values. You can think of this pair of values in many manners: yes and no, on and off, zero and one, true and false, or even red-light and green-light. What is important is not the naming, but that there are exactly two values that can be represented—exactly the the number of distinct digits in a radix two (or binary) representation, hence the name *binary digit*.

Binary representations and arithmetic can be derived as special cases of the general radix representations and algorithms. Thus, a binary number can be represented as

$$d_n d_{n-1} d_{n-2} \ldots d_1 d_0$$

where each d_i is either 1 or 0. The interpretation of the number is

$$\sum_{i=0}^{n} d_i * 2^i = \begin{cases} d_n & * & 2^n & + \\ d_{n-1} & * & 2^{n-1} & + \\ d_{n-2} & * & 2^{n-2} & + \\ & \ldots & & + \\ d_1 & * & 2^1 & + \\ d_0 & * & 2^0 & \end{cases}$$

Adding a 0 at the right multiplies by 2. Dropping the right-most digit divides by 2 (div 2). There are some additional interesting properties of binary arithmetic. The first is that because the only two possible digits are 1 and 0, multiplication by a binary digit becomes a very simple task: multiplication of any number by 1 yields that number as a result; multiplication of anything by 0 is 0 (students of modern algebra will immediately recognize these as the *identity* and the *null* operands). The number 10101_2 is actually

$$\begin{array}{ccccc} 1 & * & 2^4 & + \\ 0 & * & 2^3 & + \\ 1 & * & 2^2 & + \\ 0 & * & 2^1 & + \\ 1 & * & 2^0 & \end{array}$$

but this is just

$$\begin{array}{ccccc} 1 & * & 2^4 & + & \\ 1 & * & 2^2 & + & \\ 1 & * & 2^0 & = & 16 + 4 + 1 = 21_{10} \end{array}$$

The price paid for this simplicity is that more digits are required to represent any given value in binary than in decimal. Arithmetic in a binary representation inherits the "simple representation but many digits" dichotomy. The sum of two binary digits can yield only three distinct results:

$$\begin{array}{r} 0 \\ +0 \\ \hline 0 \end{array} \qquad \begin{array}{r} 0 \\ +1 \\ \hline 1 \end{array} \qquad \begin{array}{r} 1 \\ +0 \\ \hline 1 \end{array} \qquad \begin{array}{r} 1 \\ +1 \\ \hline 10 \end{array} \quad \text{(0 and carry 1)}$$

The algorithm for addition of binary numbers is identical to that for decimal addition:

```
(starting at the right)
while there remain bits to be added
   add the current bit of A to the current bit of B.
   if the sum is less than two,
      then record that sum
   otherwise
      record (sum - 2)
      add 1 to the next digit of the first addend (A).
```

For a simple example,

$$\begin{array}{rcl} 1010_2 & = & 10_{10} \\ \underline{1100_2} & = & 12_{10} \\ 1\ 0110 & & \end{array}$$

Note that the extra 1 carries out of bit 3 when 1 + 1 are added. For a slightly larger example,

```
 1    111  1    {carries}
  101 0101 0101
  110 0011 0100
 --------------
 1011 1000 1001
```

Binary digits are often grouped into blocks of four bits for legibility. Note that assemblers will not allow you to place blanks with numbers.

▷ *Why groups of four bits rather than the three that are common with decimal numbers?*

Similarly, binary multiplication reflects the algorithm used for decimal multiplication:

```
 9              1001
*5   becomes    *101
--              ----
45              1001
               0000
              1001
              ------
              101101 = 45₁₀
```

Likewise, integer division of 42/6 becomes

```
          111     = 7₁₀
     ________
110 ) 101010
      110
      ---
      1001
       110
      ----
        110
        110
        ---
          0
```

Follow these examples and create others of the same level of complexity until you feel comfortable with binary arithmetic. Several exercises at the end of this chapter will provide such practice.

CONVERSION BETWEEN BASES

While computer arithmetic may always be performed using binary numbers, humans will continue to prefer decimal arithmetic. Although a programmer may feel completely comfortable with binary, most users of computer systems will not. Imagine the shock of parents receiving $10000000000 tuition bills for their 10100-year-old sons and daughters—the college tuition at an "inexpensive" public school and the age of the typical college student written in binary. It is therefore frequently necessary to convert from one base to another. There are several techniques for performing these conversions. The best method to use will depend on both the circumstances and individual preference, so it is useful to learn all methods. Before you investigate any of the methods, consider the following observation: whichever method you are using, you will be converting a number represented in one radix (called the source representation) into a second (called the destination representation). During the conversion process, you will perform calculations using some specific radix. This representation may be either the source or the destination representation, but most people prefer that it be base ten. The best method to use will depend on whether the working representation is the same as the source (e.g., you are converting from base ten to base 2 and working in base 10) or the destination representation (e.g., you are converting from base 2 to base ten and working in base ten). It may also depend on additional information that you have available.

▷ *How much is that typical tuition and how old is that typical student?*

Multiplicative Method

The multiplicative method relies on the positional properties of the Arabic representation common to all numbers in all radices. Consider the number

$$d_n d_{n-1} d_{n-2} d_{n-3} \cdots d_1 d_0$$

which has the value

$$R^n * d_n + R^{n-1} * d_{n-1} + R^{n-2} * d_{n-2} + R^{n-3} * d_{n-3} + \cdots + R^1 * d_1 + R^0 * d_0$$

Since R^0 is 1, this can be rewritten as

$$R^n * d_n + R^{(n-1)} * d_{n-1} + R^{(n-2)} * d_{n-2} + R^{(n-3)} * d_{n-3} + \cdots + R * d_1 + d_0$$

Factoring out an R, this can be rewritten again:

$$R * [R^{(n-1)} d_n + R^{(n-2)} d_{n-1} + R^{(n-3)} d_{n-2} + \cdots + 1 * d_1] + d_0$$

which, factoring another R, can be written

$$R * [R * (R^{(n-2)} d_n + R^{(n-3)} d_{n-1} + R^{(n-4)} d_{n-2} + \cdots + 1 * d_2) + d_1] + d_0$$

and so on, until we get

$$R * [\ldots R * (R * [R * (R * (d_n) + d_{n-1}) + d_{n-2}] + d_{n-3}) + \cdots + d_1] + d_0$$

This rewriting suggests an algorithm for converting between bases. Each digit d_i must be multiplied times R, i times. Thus, each digit must be multiplied by R one more time than the digit to its right. The general approach is to take the digits one at a time, starting at the left, multiplying by the radix, and adding the next digit. The algorithm itself is

```
total⇐0
while more digits exist
   total⇐total * source-radix
   total⇐total + next-digit
total is the converted number.
```

To perform the conversion, work in the *destination* radix. First, determine the representation in the destination radix for

- the source radix, and
- each legal digit of the source radix.

For example, to perform the conversion

111111_2 to base 10

first determine the representation of the source radix (2) and of each of the legal digits in the destination radix (10):

$$\begin{aligned} \text{base 2:} &= 2_{10} \\ \text{digits:} &= \\ 1_2 &= 1_{10} \\ 0_2 &= 0_{10} \end{aligned}$$

It is always trivial to represent a smaller radix in a larger one: the representation for each digit is identical in each base. Thus, when working in the destination radix, the next digit can always be used "exactly as it is found." Employing the algorithm on the example:

$$\text{total} \Leftarrow 0$$

digit_5 :

$$\text{total} \Leftarrow 0 * 2 = 0$$
$$\text{total} \Leftarrow 0 + 1 = 1$$

d_4 :

$$\text{total} \Leftarrow 1 * 2 = 2$$
$$\text{total} \Leftarrow 2 + 1 = 3$$

d_3 :

$$\text{total} \Leftarrow 3 * 2 = 6$$
$$\text{total} \Leftarrow 6 + 1 = 7$$

d_2 :

$$\text{total} \Leftarrow 7 * 2 = 14$$
$$\text{total} \Leftarrow 14 + 1 = 15$$

d_1 :

$$\text{total} \Leftarrow 15 * 2 = 30$$
$$\text{total} \Leftarrow 30 + 1 = 31$$

d_0 :

$$\text{total} \Leftarrow 31 * 2 = 62$$
$$\text{total} \Leftarrow 62 + 1 = 63_{10}$$

Since there are no more digits, the algorithm halts. Consider a second example: converting 101010_2 to base 10:

$$\text{total} \Leftarrow 0$$

digit_5 :

$$\text{total} \Leftarrow 0 * 2 = 0$$
$$\text{total} \Leftarrow 0 + 1 = 1$$

d_4 :

$$\text{total} \Leftarrow 1 * 2 = 2$$
$$\text{total} \Leftarrow 2 + 0 = 2$$

d_3 :

$$\text{total} \Leftarrow 2 * 2 = 4$$
$$\text{total} \Leftarrow 4 + 1 = 5$$

d_2 :

$$\text{total} \Leftarrow 5 * 2 = 10$$
$$\text{total} \Leftarrow 10 + 0 = 10$$

d_1 :

$$\text{total} \Leftarrow 10 * 2 = 20$$
$$\text{total} \Leftarrow 20 + 1 = 21$$

d_0 :

$$\text{total} \Leftarrow 21 * 2 = 42$$
$$\text{total} \Leftarrow 42 + 0 = 42_{10}$$

For a slightly trickier (for humans) example, consider the conversion of 16_{10} to binary, working in binary. First, the radix of the source can be represented in binary:

10_{10} is 1010_2

and there are only two decimal digits of interest in this case:

6_{10} is 0110_2 and

1_{10} is 1_2

Performing the computation in binary yields

	total $\Leftarrow 0$		
digit 1	total $\Leftarrow 0 * 1010_2$	=	0
	total $\Leftarrow 0 + 1$	=	1
digit 0	total $\Leftarrow 1 * 1010_2$	=	1010_2
	total $\Leftarrow 1010_2 + 0110_2$	=	10000_2

Because humans generally prefer to perform their arithmetic in base 10, the multiplicative method is useful for humans converting from base 2 to base 10. For computers, it is exactly the opposite. Computers generally perform arithmetic in base 2, so the multiplicative method is useful for converting from base 10 to base 2.

Additive Method

An even simpler technique for converting between bases is the *additive method*. Although it requires some extra knowledge—the representations in the destination radix of all the needed powers of the source base—this method can be a very useful and effective shortcut. The algorithm follows directly from the definition of radix arithmetic or from the multiplicative method. The general idea is that because a number is the sum of values, each represented as a digit, the number can be calculated by summing those values. Specifically, the algorithm is

```
total = 0
while there exist more digits in the source representation
   D⇐value represented by the next digit
   total⇐total + D
```

For example, Table 4-1 provides the equivalences needed to repeat the first example. Adding up the first six powers gives

$$111111_2 = 1 + 2 + 4 + 8 + 16 + 32 = 63_{10}$$

TABLE 4.1
Conversion tables

For binary to decimal conversion

n	binary = 2 to the *n*	hex	decimal
	0	0	0
0	1	1	1
1	10	2	2
2	100	4	4
3	1000	8	8
4	1 0000	10	16
5	10 0000	20	32
6	100 0000	40	64
7	1000 0000	80	128
8	1 0000 0000	100	256
9	10 0000 0000	200	512
10	100 0000 0000	400	1,204
11	1000 0000 0000	800	2,048
12	1 0000 0000 0000	1 000	4,096
13	10 0000 0000 0000	2 000	8,192
14	100 0000 0000 0000	4 000	16,384
15	1000 0000 0000 0000	8 000	32,768
16	1 0000 0000 0000 0000	10 000	65,536

For decimal to binary

binary	hex	decimal = 10 to the *n*	*n*
0	0	0	
1	1	1	0
1010	10	10	1
110 0100	64	100	2
0011 1110 1000	3E8	1,000	3
0010 0111 0001 0000	2 710	10,000	4
0001 1000 0110 1010 0000	18 6A0	100,000	5
1111 0100 0010 0100 0000	F4 240	1,000,000	6

as above. The number 101010_2 can be converted similarly:

$$\begin{aligned} 0 * 2^0 &= 0 + \\ 1 * 2^1 &= 2 + \\ 0 * 2^2 &= 0 + \\ 1 * 2^3 &= 8 + \\ 0 * 2^4 &= 0 + \\ 1 * 2^5 &= 32 \\ &= 2 + 8 + 32 = 42_{10} \end{aligned}$$

Notice that the zero digits simply do not enter into the calculation.

Obviously this method is only of use when the values of the individual digits are easily obtained (Table 4-1 also includes values for conversion up to 2^{16} and 10^6). When the source representation is binary, these values are often readily available, either from a chart showing the powers of two, or from the programmer's own memory (most assembly language programmers become familiar with the powers of two up to at least 10). Converting from decimal to binary does not work out so conveniently.

> ▷ *Why doesn't this algorithm work well for decimal to binary conversion? What can be done about that problem?*

Division Method

The division method is roughly the inverse of the multiplicative method. Therefore, it is not surprising that it works best for performing calculations using the source radix. For humans, this typically occurs for conversion of numbers from base 10 to base 2. The division algorithm is based on modular arithmetic and is especially easy to visualize when converting to base 2. Consider the meaning of the right-most digit of a binary number: it is the only digit that may represent an odd value; all other digits represent values that can be expressed as 2^n for some positive n. A 1 in the right-most position implies that the number is odd (it is the sum of$\ldots + 1$); a 0 means that the number is even (there are no odd numbers in the sum). Therefore, a binary number is odd if and only if its last digit is a 1. We can tell if a number N in base 10 (or any other radix for that matter) is odd or even by dividing by 2 and checking the remainder: a 1 indicates odd and a 0 even. Alternatively stated, the last digit is `N mod 2`. The problem is then reduced to finding the remaining digits.

Let's consider the quotient of that division. Recall that division by 2 in binary is equivalent to dropping off the right-most digit. If we can determine the representation of that quotient, we can represent the entire number. The quotient, `N div 2`, is itself a number, and like any number it must be odd or even and can be converted to binary by the same process. This yields a recursive definition for the binary equivalent of N_{10}:

$$N_2 = \begin{cases} N_{10} & \text{for } N < 2 \\ (N\text{div } 2)_2 \text{ followed by } (N \text{ mod } 2) & \text{for } N \geq 2 \end{cases}$$

Thus, the definition yields the general algorithm for converting a number into radix R:

```
let n be the number (represented in source radix)
while n > 0 do
   divide n by R
   output the remainder: (n mod R)
   n⇐the quotient: (n div R)
```

The algorithm yields the digits of the answer from right to left. For example, converting 100_{10} to binary yields

Calculation	**Output**
$n \Leftarrow 100$	
	$(100 \text{ mod } 2) \Rightarrow 0$
$n \Leftarrow (100 \text{ div } 2) = 50$	
	$(50 \text{ mod } 2) \Rightarrow 0$
$n \Leftarrow (50 \text{ div } 2) = 25$	
	$(25 \text{ mod } 2) \Rightarrow 1$
$n \Leftarrow (25 \text{ div } 2) = 12$	
	$(12 \text{ mod } 2) \Rightarrow 0$
$n \Leftarrow (12 \text{ div } 2) = 6$	
	$(6 \text{ mod } 2) \Rightarrow 0$
$n \Leftarrow (6 \text{ div } 2) = 3$	
	$(3 \text{ mod } 2) \Rightarrow 1$
$n \Leftarrow (3 \text{ div } 2) = 1$	
	$(1 \text{ mod } 2) \Rightarrow 1$
$n \Leftarrow (1 \text{ div } 2) = 0$	

Since the algorithm generates the numbers in reverse order (right-to-left), the result is

$$1100100_2$$

▷ *Since this algorithm generates the numbers in reverse order, will it be useful at all?*

Because the division method is especially useful when performing the conversions using the source radix, you will not be surprised to discover that humans find the division method to be most useful for converting from decimal to binary. It is also useful when we wish the computer (which you recall works using binary arithmetic) to convert base 2 numbers to decimal. To convert 1100100 to decimal, a computer could employ the same algorithm:

Calculation	**Output**
$n \Leftarrow 1100100$	
	$(1100100 \text{ mod } 1010) \Rightarrow 0$ $\{100_{10} \text{ mod } 10_{10}\}$
$n \Leftarrow (1100100 \text{ div } 1010) = 1010$	
	$(1010 \text{ mod } 1010) \Rightarrow 0$
$n \Leftarrow (1010 \text{ div } 1010) = 1$	
	$(1 \text{ mod } 1010) \Rightarrow 1$
$n \Leftarrow (1 \text{ div } 1010) = 0$	

$n = 0$, so the algorithm halts, and the answer is 100_{10}.

Subtraction Method

Like the additive method, the subtraction method is very simple but relies on pre-existing knowledge of the corresponding representations of selected values in the destination radix. It is essentially an abbreviation of the division method and as such is particularly useful for humans when converting from base ten to base 2. Assume that you have a table of the powers of the destination representation, as represented in the source. The subtraction method simply checks for the largest number in that table that can be subtracted from the total. That number must be part of the answer. The algorithm is

```
let current⇐largest number in table ≤ number to be converted
while current > 0 do
   if number > current
      then
         record 1 as next digit
         number⇐(number − current)
      else
         record 0 as next digit
   current⇐next value down in table.
```

Note that the subtraction method finds the digits from highest to lowest order; therefore works left to right. For example, Table 4-1 can be used to convert 100_{10} to *base* 2:

Current	**Compare**	**Subtract giving new number**	**Record**
64	$100 > 64$	$100-64 = 36$	1
32	$36 > 32$	$36-32 = 4$	1
16	$4 < 16$		0
8	$4 < 8$		0
4	$4 \geq 4$	$4-4 = 0$	1
2	$0 < 2$		0
1	$0 < 1$		0

The result is 1100100_2. As with the additive method, the subtractive method is practical because most assembly language programmers have learned many of the powers of 2 through experience.

Hexadecimal Representations

Consider a 12-digit binary number:

$$d_{11}d_{10}d_9d_8d_7\ldots d_3d_2d_1d_0$$

which is actually

$$\sum_{i=0}^{11} d_i * 2^i = \begin{cases} 2^{11} * d_{11} + \\ 2^{10} * d_{10} + \\ 2^9 * d_9 + \\ 2^8 * d_8 + \\ 2^7 * d_7 + \\ \cdots \\ 2^3 * d_3 + \\ 2^2 * d_2 + \\ 2^1 * d_1 + \\ 2^0 * d_0 + \end{cases}$$

Factoring out powers of 16: 16^0, 16^1, 16^2, $16^3, \ldots$, which are also 2^0, 2^4, 2^8, $2^{12}, \ldots$, gives

$$\begin{aligned} & 2^8 * 2^3 * d_{11} + \\ & 2^8 * 2^2 * d_{10} + \\ & 2^8 * 2^1 * d_9 + \\ & 2^8 * 2^0 * d_8 + \\ & 2^4 * 2^3 * d_7 + \\ & \cdots \\ & 2^0 * 2^3 * d_3 + \\ & 2^0 * 2^2 * d_2 + \\ & 2^0 * 2^1 * d_1 + \\ & 2^0 * 2^0 * d_0 \end{aligned}$$

$$\begin{aligned} = \; & 2^8 * (2^3 * d_{11} + 2^2 * d_{10} + 2^1 * d_9 + 2^0 * d_8) + \\ & 2^4 * (2^3 * d_7 + 2^2 * d_6 + 2^1 * d_5 + 2^0 * d_4) + \\ & 2^0 * (2^3 * d_3 + 2^2 * d_2 + 2^1 * d_1 + 2^0 * d_0) \end{aligned}$$

That is, the number is a sum of expressions of the form:

$$2^{4n} * D_i = 16^n * D_i$$

where D_i is a number between 0 and 15. But, that is just the definition of a base 16 number. So every binary number can be converted to a hex number by regrouping the digits. In general 2^n can be written as

$$2^n = 2^{4^{(n/4)}} = 16^{(n \text{ div } 4)} \times 2^{(n \text{ mod } 4)}$$

dividing a number into groups of four binary digits. Each base 16 digit corresponds to four binary digits. *Hexadecimal* (as base 16 is usually called) will thus provide an excellent abbreviation for base 2 numbers.

The number 12_{16} is $1 * 16^1 + 2 * 16^0 = 1 * 2^4 + 2 * 2^0 = 1 * 2^4 + 1 * 2^1 = 10010_2$

Prior to this analysis, we have only considered radices of ten or less. In those cases we simply used the decimal digits 0 to (R-1) for the possible digits of radix R. For base 16, we need 16 distinct digits. The normal convention is to use 0 through 9 in their obvious interpretation and to use the letters A through F to represent the values 10 through 15. The following table summarizes the values and representations.

Decimal	Hex	Binary	Decimal	Hex	Binary
0	0	0000	8	8	1000
1	1	0001	9	9	1001
2	2	0010	10	A	1010
3	3	0011	11	B	1011
4	4	0100	12	C	1100
5	5	0101	13	D	1101
6	6	0110	14	E	1110
7	7	0111	15	F	1111

The algorithm for conversion from base 2 to 16 is direct:

starting from the right,
  group the binary digits in groups of 4
  if necessary, pad with zeros on the left
for each group of four binary/digits
  convert the group into the corresponding hexadecimal digit.

Thus

$1100\ 0011_2$ is $C3_{16}$
$1010\ 1010_2$ is AA_{16}
$1000\ 1111\ 0111_2$ is $8F7_{16}$

and so on. The reverse conversion works in exactly the analogous manner:

For each hex digit
  Convert it into the corresponding 4 bit binary number
  {be sure to use all four bits, even for small numbers}
Concatenate the strings of digits into a single binary number

$17B_{16}$ becomes

$$1_{16} = 0001$$
$$7_{16} = 0111$$
$$B_{16} = 1011$$

The base 2 equivalent is $0001\ 0111\ 1011_2$.

STORAGE AND THE SIZE OF NUMBERS

For storage purposes, bits are grouped together into *bytes*—almost universally eight bits.

▷ *Why this particular number?*

Since each hexadecimal digit represents four binary digits, a byte can conveniently contain two hex digits. A group of four bits or half a byte—just enough to hold one hex digit—is sometimes called a *nibble*. Historically, when some machines had six-bit bytes, *octal* (base 8) arithmetic held a similar role: two octal digits would just fit in a six-bit byte. Today the use of octal arithmetic is of historical importance only.

A *logarithm* is a measure of the magnitude of a number. Most people are familiar with either base ten or base e (natural) logarithms. Computer scientists are more interested in base 2 logarithms. Roughly stated, a logarithm is the measure of the number of digits needed to represent a value in a given radix. The following table shows the largest number that can be represented with a given number of binary digits:

digits	binary			decimal equivalent
1	1	=	$2^1 - 1$	1
2	11	=	$2^2 - 1$	3
3	111	=	$2^3 - 1$	7
4	1111	=	$2^4 - 1$	15
5	11111	=	$2^5 - 1$	31
6	111111	=	$2^6 - 1$	63

In general, the largest number that can be written in n bits is the strings of n 1's, and it has the value

$$\sum_{i=0}^{n-1} 2_i = 2^n - 1$$

Thus, the log tells us how many digits are needed to represent a number. Log_{10} indicates the number of decimal digits, and $\log_2$ indicates the number of binary digits required. Note also that since the number zero can be represented using any number of digits, we can represent 2^n distinct values: 0 through $2^n - 1$, in n digits. This is another way of saying that

$$\log_2 \text{ of } 2^n = n$$

(Note that this definition of logarithm is not quite precise: 2^n actually requires $n + 1$ digits. N digits are sufficient to represent 2^n values, but one of those is zero.)

By investigating the size of the storage locations in a machine, we can determine much about allowable values. A byte—eight bits—is the standard storage location. Thus, a single storage location can hold $2^8 = 256$ distinct values: 0–255 if we assume they are integers. Clearly, this is not sufficient for most arithmetic. A GAM integer storage location contains a word—two bytes—16 bits; therefore a GAM integer can contain 2^{16} or 65,536 possible values. If we assume that the values are natural numbers, they would be 0 to 65,535. Again, the log of 65,536 is 16—the number of bits needed to represent the number. A four-byte (32-bit) storage location could hold $2^{32} = 4{,}294{,}967{,}296$ possible values. The log of that number is, of course, 32. (Do not memorize these numbers but do recall the earlier claim that assembly language programmers seem to learn the powers of two automatically!)

A particularly interesting number is $2^{10} = 1024$. Since this number is so close to 1000, computer scientists usually behave as if the two values were equal. While most people use the abbreviation K for 1000 (e.g., kg for kilogram), computer scientists use it to mean 1024. This provides an excellent means for specifying large numbers. A large number such as the quantity of RAM in a computer can be specified easily:

$$65{,}536 = 2^{16} = (2^6) + (2^{10}) = 64\text{K}$$

Because

$$\log x * y = \log x + \log y$$

large numbers can easily be specified or manipulated using logs. For example, a million is one thousand thousand. Thus,

$$\log (1{,}000{,}000) = \log (1{,}000) + \log (1{,}000) \approx 10 + 10 = 20$$

So representing that number must require 20 bits.

NEGATIVE NUMBERS

The discussion thus far assumes that all numbers are nonnegative integers. We will certainly need to represent negative binary numbers. Actually, the previous representation did not allow for *any* signed numbers, positive or negative. There are several possible choices for the representation of negative numbers.

First Attempt: Sign and Number

As a first attempt, consider what might be called the *obvious* representation: let the set of negative numbers be exactly the same as the set of positive numbers, with the single distinction that they have a negative sign. There are only two possible signs for a number: positive and negative. So use a single bit, say the left-most, as a sign bit: 1 for negative and 0 for positive. This choice preserves the expectation that the sign may be omitted for positive numbers. Thus the (eight-bit) positive integers are

$$
\begin{aligned}
0000\ 0000 &= 0 \\
0000\ 0001 &= 1 \\
0000\ 0010 &= 2 \\
0000\ 0011 &= 3 \\
&\cdots \\
0111\ 1111 &= 127
\end{aligned}
$$

and the negative integers

$$
\begin{aligned}
1000\ 0001 &= -1 \\
1000\ 0010 &= -2 \\
&\cdots \\
1111\ 1110 &= -126 \\
1111\ 1111 &= -127
\end{aligned}
$$

The attentive reader will notice that this leaves 1000 0000 $= -0$. Does that make any sense? There are two problems with this representation. The first—which is relatively minor, but more obvious—is that there are two values for zero: $+0$ and -0. This not only wastes a value but causes problems for arithmetic comparisons: should $-0 = +0$? The second, more troublesome result is that simple addition and subtraction must be performed using different algorithms for positive and negative numbers. Consider the problem created by the addition of two numbers of opposite sign:

$$
\begin{array}{rcr}
1010 & = & -2_{10} \\
\underline{+1001} & = & +\underline{-1}_{10} \\
(1)0011 & = & +3_{10} \neq -3_{10}
\end{array}
$$

Recall from algebra the rule for subtracting numbers of opposite signs: "change the sign and add." Computer addition, using a representation system such as the one above, requires two steps for addition: first compare the signs and then either simply add the numbers or perform a subtraction (with choice of subtrahend and minuend dependent on which number had a negative sign). Although this may seem normal (e.g., just like what a human must do), the two-step process can be avoided.

A Second Attempt: Ones' Complement

A partial solution to this problem uses a representation called *ones' complement*. In ones' complement notation, the representation for the negation of a binary number N is obtained by subtracting each *digit* of N from 1. That is, to find the ones' complement representation of the negation of

$$5_{10} = 0101_2$$

subtract each digit from 1

$$\begin{array}{l} 1111 \\ \underline{0101} \\ 1010_2 = -5_{10} \end{array}$$

Because the only values representable in a single binary digit are 0 and 1, the subtraction never needs to borrow. Note that the term *complement* means "the other part." Any digit and its complement add up to 1. The observant reader will note that subtraction from 1 always yields the opposite value: the complement of 1 is 0; the complement of 0 is 1. The representation of the positive numbers is identical to the unsigned number representation above, but the negative numbers are

$$\begin{array}{lcl} 1000 & = & -7 \\ 1001 & = & -6 \\ 1010 & = & -5 \\ 1011 & = & -4 \\ \ldots & & \\ 1110 & = & -1 \\ 1111 & = & -0 \end{array}$$

▷ *The notion of complement will reappear in Chapter 6. Why is it especially important in binary computers?*

This did not remove the negative zero problem, but it does simplify the computation of simple arithmetic operations with fewer complicated sign checks. Addition of numbers of opposite sign is performed in exactly the same manner. For example,

$$\begin{array}{rr} -4 & 1011 \\ +\underline{\;\;1} & \underline{0001} \\ -3 & 1100 \end{array}$$

is both simple and correct. However, if the addends are both negative, the sum will carry out of the sign bit, requiring an extra addition: 1 must be added to the result (as if it "wrapped around").

$$\begin{array}{rlrll} -2 & & & & \\ +\underline{-4} & \text{becomes} & 1101 & & \\ -6 & & + \;\; \underline{1011} & & \\ & & (1)1000 & = -0, & \text{so add 1:} \\ & & \underline{0001} & & \text{giving} \\ & & 1001 & & -6 \end{array}$$

To see why this works, note that the number 111 . . . 1 for n 1s is actually $2^n - 1$. Thus, the 1s' complement representation of $-N$ is

$$(2^n - 1) - N$$

But adding two negative numbers, $-N_1$ and $-N_2$, gives

$$\begin{aligned} & -N_1 + -N_2 \\ &= (2^n - 1) - N_1 + (2^n - 1) - N_2 \\ &= 2 * (2^n - 1) - (N_1 + N_2) \\ &= (2^{n+1} - 1) - (N_1 + N_2) - 1 \end{aligned}$$

Thus, the simple addition produced an answer that was 1 too low. In general, you can perform a complement representation in any radix representation. For example, by taking the complement of each decimal digit, we can obtain the 9s' complement. Such complements are also called *diminished radix complements*.

The major advantage of ones' complement representation is that addition is performed in essentially the same manner with positive and negative operands. Another way to view the same process is the traditional *number line* view, in which numbers get larger in absolute value as you get further from the origin, either positively or negatively. Thus, the effect of adding positive and negative numbers is not the same. Adding 1 to a positive number increases its magnitude, but adding 1 to a negative number decreases its magnitude. With ones' complement representation, the addition operation is independent of the sign.

The Final Solution: Two's Complement

The solution for removing the double representation for zero will also simplify the problem of addition even further. Define the *two's complement*[1] representation of a negative number to be one more than its ones' complement. Thus, to determine the two's complement of a number,

> complement each bit, and
> add one.

Thus, considering a four-bit example, we get

$$\begin{aligned} -7 &= -0111 = 1000 + 1 = 1001 \\ -6 &= -0110 = 1001 + 1 = 1010 \\ -5 &= -0101 = 1010 + 1 = 1011 \\ -4 &= -0100 = 1011 + 1 = 1100 \\ \ldots \\ -1 &= -0001 = 1110 + 1 = 1111 \\ -0 &= -0000 = 1111 + 1 = (1)0000 = 0 \end{aligned}$$

---

[1]Note the difference in punctuation between *ones' complement* and *two's complement*. The distinction is that the ones' complement (recall that *complement* meant "the other part") is obtained by subtracting the value from 2^{n-1}, which is a series of n ones (plural). The two's complement is calculated by subtracting from 2^n—a single power of two.

This last value suggests some important characteristics of computer arithmetic. Each data item is stored in a fixed-size location. If the result of an operation requires more digits than the storage location can hold, the extra digits overflow from the location and are lost. This is exactly what happens on an automobile odometer when 99,999 miles becomes 0 miles: There is no place for the extra digit, so it is lost. Therefore 0000 is the two's complement representation for minus zero—exactly the same as the positive zero. In two's complement there is only one zero.

Note that this example appears to leave 1000 unused. But if the conversion algorithm is applied to 8 (pretending for a moment that it is unsigned), it yields

$$-8 = -1000 = 0111 + 1 = 1000$$

There is no positive number, that gives 1000 when complemented. We can check this by adding 1 to 1000 giving

$$\begin{array}{r} 1000 \\ 1 \\ \hline 1001 \end{array} = -7$$

Thus in four bits, a negative sign-bit followed by all zero digits must be −8.

In general, n bits can represent 2^n distinct numbers. With unsigned arithmetic, this is usually

$$0 \text{ to } \sum_{i=0}^{n-1} d_i * 2^i = 2^n - 1$$

Using signed arithmetic, one fewer digit is available and the largest positive number is

$$\sum_{i=0}^{n-2} d_i * 2^i = 2^{n-1} - 1$$

The most negative number is, therefore, -2^{n-1}. Thus with eight bits, the range of possible signed numbers is

$$-2^7 = -128 \text{ to } (+2^7 - 1) = 127$$

With 16 bits, the limits are

$$-32{,}768 \text{ to } +32{,}767$$

Usually, we simply approximate this to ±32K. With 32 bits, the limits are

$$-2{,}147{,}483{,}648 \text{ to } +2{,}147{,}483{,}647$$

or roughly minus and plus 2 billion.

The operations for performing an addition are identical for both positive and negative numbers. Furthermore, the operations are identical for both signed and unsigned representations. This means that a computer need not even know if the number was intended to represent a signed or unsigned number.

SIGN EXTENSION. Note that in two's complement notation, any negative number starts with a 1, no matter how many digits are required. If you need to represent a four-bit number as an eight-bit number, simply add 1s to the left. In conventional arithmetic, you have always done the equivalent with positive numbers: adding zeros to the left. It is simply the reverse for negative numbers. Leading 1's are not significant. Carries of 1 off the left-hand end are also insignificant. Consider a few examples:

$$\begin{array}{rrl} & -4 = -0100 = & 1100 \\ + & -2 = \qquad\quad = & \underline{1110} \\ & & (1)1010 = -6 \end{array}$$

Note the bit that was carried off the left-hand end. If the space available to store the result is limited, the bit is simply thrown away. Addition of opposite signs causes no problem:

$$\begin{array}{rrl} & -4 = & 1100 \\ + & +2 = & \underline{0010} \\ & & 1110 = -2 \end{array}$$

and

$$\begin{array}{rrl} & -2 = & 1110 \\ + & +4 = & \underline{0100} \\ & & (1)0010 = +2 \end{array}$$

The bit carried off the left-hand end is lost, without interfering with the sum.

COEXISTENCE OF REPRESENTATIONS

As noted earlier, Pascal requires that every storage location has a type, and the user may only place values of the proper type into any location. Assembly language makes no such distinctions: Any storage location can hold any type of data. We have just seen that we can think of a series of bits as designating a binary number, or we can abbreviate the number by writing its hexadecimal equivalent. In addition, any storage location may be thought of as an n-bit unsigned number or as a sign plus an $(n - 1)$-bit number. It is up to the programmer to keep track of the form of the stored value. The problem becomes even more complicated when we introduce character data.

Characters are represented in computers using an arbitrary assignment of bit pattern to characters. Today, the most common representation is the *ASCII* (*American Standard Code for Information Interchange*) representation scheme. In this representation, each printable character (and some that are not printable) is assigned a bit pattern that corresponds to that character. For example,

A is 0100 0001
B is 0100 0010
C is 0100 0011

These values could just as easily represent binary numbers (65, 66, and 67_{10} in this case). The user must know what the bits in a storage location represent, so that the data can be interpreted as an integer, character, or some other form.

To a large extent the selection of this particular representation is arbitrary. In fact, there are other commonly used representations such as *EBCDIC (Extended Binary Coded Decimal Interchange Code)*. It is necessary to represent each letter by some combination of bits, but it could have been any combination. There is, however, some rationale to the choices. First, the size of the code is eight bits. Eight is the log of 256, so eight bits provides 256 possible configurations. Note that the number of combinations is independent of the specific interpretation that we place upon the bit pattern. On the other hand, consider the printable characters: 26 lowercase letters, 26 uppercase letters, 10 digits, many (about 32 on a typical keyboard) punctuation marks, and such things as the blank character and the return character—at least 96 distinct characters. That requires at least seven binary digits, since

$$2^6 = 64 < 96 < 2^7 = 128$$

Even seven bits does not allow for much expansion for special nonprinting (control) characters. So ASCII uses eight bits. Technically, ASCII uses only seven bits, and all possible seven-bit combinations have been assigned. Many implementations now use eight bits, both to gain the extra representations and because eight bits turns out to be easier to work with.

▷ *As usual, when given a choice, computer scientists always pick an exact power of two. Why?*

Given an ASCII alphabetic character, the representation of the alphabetically next character in ASCII can be calculated if we choose to represent the bits using hexadecimal—that is, we write down the hex equivalents of the binary representations. The letters become

$$A = 0100\ 0011 = 41_{16}$$

$$B = 0100\ 0010 = 42$$

$$C = 0100\ 0011 = 43$$

and so on. By interpreting the bit configurations as binary numbers rather than ASCII characters, the uppercase letters turn out to be in numeric as well as alphabetic order, with the hex equivalents ranging from 41_{16} to $5A_{16}$. Note that this does not say that the character "A" is equal to 41_{16}, only that the representations are the same. The lowercase letters "a" to "z" form a similar series corresponding to the hex numbers 61_{16} to $7A_{16}$. This is especially interesting because it implies that every lowercase letter—when viewed as a number—is $20_{16} = 32_{10}$ more than the corresponding uppercase letter. The digits also form a series ranging from 30 to 39_{16}. Note that this provides some insight into the distinction between the binary number 1 (which is stored as 0000 0001) and the character "1" (which is stored as 0011 0001).

Looking further, one can observe that blank (20_{16}) is less than any alphabetic character, as is the carriage return (0D). Other interesting characters include the bell (07), horizontal tab (09), and delete (7F). Table 4-2 shows the full set of ASCII representations.

▷ *Study Table 4-2 carefully. What patterns and interesting relationships can you find?*

Because the letters and digits all form sequences, it is possible to perform addition on characters. Thus, we can see above that "A" + 1 = "B"; "B" + 1 = "C";

TABLE 4.2a
Table of ASCII characters

		First (left) digit							
		Binary :000	:001	:010	:011	:100	:101	:110	:111
Second digit		**Hex** 0	1	2	3	4	5	6	7
Binary	**Hex**	**Control codes**		**Printable characters**					
0000	0	null	dle	space	0	@	P		p
0001	1	soh	dc1	!	1	A	Q	a	q
0010	2	stx	cd2	"	2	B	R	b	r
0011	3	etx	dc3	#	3	C	S	c	s
0100	4	eot	dc4	$	4	D	T	d	t
0101	5	enq	nak	%	5	E	U	e	u
0110	6	ack	syn	&	6	F	V	f	v
0111	7	bell	etb	'	7	G	W	g	w
1000	8	bs	can	(	8	H	X	h	x
1001	9	ht	em	)	9	I	Y	i	y
1010	A	lf	sub	*	:	J	Z	j	z
1011	B	vt	esc	+	;	K	[	k	{
1100	C	ff	fs	,	<	L	\	l	|
1101	D	cr	gs	-	=	M	]	m	}
1110	E	so	rs	.	>	N	^	n	~
1111	F	si	us	/	?	O	_	o	del

Notes: *ASCII codes are only seven bits (bit 7 = 0)

*Some machines use an extended ASCII in which case, a 1 in bit 7 indicates a special character

TABLE 4.2b
Meanings of control characters

Control code definitions			
Value	**Mnemonic**		
00	null	:	empty string
01	soh	:	start of header
02	stx	:	start of text (msg)
03	etx	:	end of text (msg)
04	eot	:	end of transmission
05	enq	:	enquire
06	ack	:	acknowledge
07	bell	:	(ring the) bell
08	bs	:	backspace
09	ht	:	(horizontal) tab
0A	lf	:	line feed (down only)
0B	vt	:	vertical tab
0C	ff	:	form feed
0D	cr	:	carriage return (back to the left)
0E	so	:	shift out
0F	si	:	shift in
10	dle	:	data link escape
11	dc	:	device control
15	nak	:	negative acknowledge
16	syn	:	synchronize
17	etb	:	end of transmission block
18	can	:	cancel
19	em	:	end of medium
1A	sub	:	substitute
1B	esc	:	escape
1C	fs	:	file separator
1D	gs	:	group separator
1E	rs	:	record separator
1F	us	:	unit separator
7F	del	:	delete character

"a" = "A" + 32_{10}; and so on. ALs place no restriction on such mixing of types. On the one hand, it enables many shortcuts—on the other, it opens up whole new worlds of mistakes. We must understand that the internal representation is a series of bits. The "value" of that series of bits depends on the way in which we interpret the bits: as a binary number or as a character. The programmer must remember what interpretation is used in each circumstance. Assembly language provides no checking. Consider the following error:

```
zero   constant:char '0'
       . . .
       add              zero⇒reg0
```

Although most hll compilers would generate a type-mismatch error, most assemblers will obediently generate code that adds the character '0' (or 32_{10}) to the register. (Obviously, naming conventions and documentation are very helpful in such situations.) Any arbitrary interpretation could be placed on strings of bits. Thus 0100 0001 represents the character "A" and the number 65. It could also represent the color "blue", the country "Spain", or the student "Kilroy". In most hlls the compiler ensures that once a variable is declared to be an integer, character, or enumerated type, it is always interpreted consistently. In AL, that consistency is up to the programmer. Similarly, when the programmer creates an enumerated type, the hll compiler takes responsibility for creating an assignment of mnemonic values to internal representations. Again, in AL this is up to the programmer.

Of particular interest will be the representations of the *Boolean values* `true` and `false`. By tradition, a 1 bit is interpreted as `true` and a 0 as `false`.

IMPLICATIONS FOR "REAL" LANGUAGES

Although some numbers require more storage space than others, assemblers do not perform any automatic storage sizing. The programmer must determine the size of all stored data as well as the representation. While a default size will certainly exist, it may not be appropriate for the current purposes of the programmer.

Because the size is often more important for understanding an operand than is the declared type, future examples will often incorporate the size rather than the data type:

`byte` for one-byte operands such as `char`
`word` for two-byte operands such as `integer`
`long` for four-byte operands such as `real`

for example,

```
copy:word     Reg0⇒reg2
```

Most real languages use a similar convention.

Humans generally prefer to use decimal numbers. Therefore, most real languages allow humans to use decimal as the default representation for constants, immediates, and so on. However, we will soon find occasions in which we wish to code a binary or hexadecimal number explicitly. You may enter a number in base 2 or 16 in any place where it is legal to enter a decimal number simply by writing the number followed by B for Binary or H for Hex. Thus

```
test_item     constant:int   1010B
```

and

```
add     #0A2H⇒reg2
```

are legal GAL commands. Notice that the latter example started with a zero to avoid confusion with a possible variable named `a2h`, although the immediate symbol serves the same purpose. The hex representation equivalent to the decimal value 11 must be coded `#BH`, B for 11 and H to indicate that it is a hex value. Most assembly languages include similar conventions. (Some variations: `x` or $ for hex and % for binary. Some languages prefer the radix indication to precede rather than follow the value: `x12ab`.)

SUMMARY

Although we humans tend to prefer to think in terms of decimal arithmetic, computers generally use binary. But that presents few problems. The algorithms for manipulating numbers are the same no matter what base is used to represent them. Conversion between any two bases is straightforward using one of the standard conversion algorithms.

Hexadecimal representation is convenient for representing the contents of computer memory cells because they form an excellent middle-of-the-road compromise. Hex is far more concise than binary, but the conversion is straightforward: four binary characters are one hex character. On the other hand, two hex characters can represent a single ASCII character. An n-bit number can represent 2^n different values; the log of 2^n is n.

Any given string of binary digits can be interpreted in several ways: as a positive integer, as a signed integer, as a character, and as a logical value or a real number (as will be seen later).

EXERCISES

In addition to the following exercises, mini-project II-1 in Appendix II is particularly relevant to the material in this chapter.

4.1. Write algorithms for general radix multiplication and division.

4.2. Use the algorithms from Exercise 4.1 to perform additions in base 5, 7, 2, and 16.

4.3. A string of characters could contain just digits. Write a program to add two strings of digits using the multiplicative algorithm from the chapter. Note that the program must convert each digit to a binary value before adding it into its total.

4.4. Convert each of the following numbers from base 10 to base 2 using the division method:

123, 255, 1024, 100, 16000

Convert them again using the subtraction method.

4.5. Convert each of the numbers in Exercise 4.4 from base 10 to base 16 using the multiplicative method. Convert them again by converting them first to base 2 and then to base 16.

4.6. Convert each of the following numbers from base 2 to base 10 using the multiplicative method:

10 1010, 11 100 0111, 1000 0000, 1111 1111

Convert them again using the additive method.

4.7. Convert each of the following numbers from base 10 to base 2 using the multiplicative method:

127, 99, 85, 111

4.8. Convert the following from base 16 to base 2:

ABCDEF, 98765, 1F2E3D

4.9. Taking advantage of equivalent representations, write a function equivalent to the Pascal SUCC, which returns the alphabetically next character.

4.10. Write functions equivalent to the Pascal functions ORD and CHR. Comment on any interesting implications of the code that you wrote.

4.11. Write a program that converts a series of decimal digits into the binary equivalent.

4.12. Write an output routine that can output a value (larger than 10) as a decimal number.

4.13. Write a subroutine that can output the contents of one byte as a two-digit hexadecimal number.

4.14. Write a function that converts alphabetic characters from upper- to lowercase. Write one that performs the opposite operation.

4.15. Write a function that creates the two's complement of a number.

4.16. Specify the subtraction algorithm formally in manner similar to that provided for the addition algorithm.

4.17. The chapter cited $\$10000000000_2$ as a typical tuition at a public university. How much is this in more familiar terms? It cited 10100_2 as the typical age of a college student. What is this number?

4.18. Prove by induction that the largest unsigned integer that you can represent in n bits is $2^n - 1$. Prove that the largest base k number that you can represent in n digits is $k^n - 1$.

4.19. How many bits are needed to represent a billion? A trillion? How many if the numbers must be signed?

4.20. Derive the ten's complement representation for signed decimal numbers. Also derive the nines' complement.

4.21. Consider the binary numbers

01010101 and 11100011

What values do they represent as signed numbers? As unsigned numbers? Show that the addition algorithm works for either interpretation. Show that the subtraction algorithm also works.

4.22. Define an algorithm for multiplying by 2^n. Use that algorithm and the definition of binary representation to define a general algorithm for multiplication by a binary number [e.g., $17 * 12 = 17 * (8 + 4) = 17 * (2^3 + 2^2)$].

4.23. Show that two's complement arithmetic works for subtraction as well as addition.

4.24. What is this?

(A: A computer scientist ordering three beers.)

CHAPTER 5

STRUCTURES: DATA AND CONTROL

Chapter 2 described assembly language equivalents for most of the basic structures provided by most higher-level languages. Chapter 3 provided basic guidelines for the programming process in ALs. This chapter investigates the construction of more complicated structures: control structures such as case statements, and data structures such as arrays, records, and pointers. Two additional organizational aspects—*condition codes* and storage of *addresses*—support the implementation of these structures.

DATA STRUCTURES

All hlls provide a mechanism for building aggregate types—arrays, records, and lists—from the basic data types—integers, characters, and so on. Assembly languages also provide a method for building aggregate data structures—all using pointers. One ironic aspect of higher-level languages will suggest itself immediately: the support tools needed for implementing arrays and pointers are identical in AL, but some hlls provide only arrays but not pointers.

▷ *Why would that be?*

Details of Implementation: Addresses

Every storage location has a unique address—an integer between 0 and some upper bound, say $2^{16} - 1$ ($\sim$ 64K). Since this address is a number, it can be held in a storage location, either RAM or a register.

> ▷ *Is there a convenient relationship between the size of a register and the magnitude of the upper bound of legal memory?*

An address can be manipulated in any way that other numbers are manipulated: a value can be added to or subtracted from an address; an address can be replaced by another address. The address of a storage location serves as a unique identifier for that location, that is, it is a pointer to that location in much the same way as a Hill pointer variable points to a Hill storage location. Such manipulation of addresses provides access to arrays and records, and facilitates linked lists and the passing of `var` parameters.

The command

```
load_address     <location>⇒<regn>
```

places the address of a named RAM storage location into a register. For example,

```
load_address     block⇒reg3
```

will load the address of `block` into register 3. A note on nomenclature: recall that `load` is often used for `copy into` a register.

> ▷ *"Copy address" would not be quite correct since the address is more calculated than copied. How can it be calculated?*

Pointers

Although the `load_address` command makes it possible, the human user does not need to know the actual location of `block`. The knowledge that the program can determine the location is sufficient. `Reg3` has become a *pointer* to the array `block`: it contains the address of the array, and therefore it also holds the key to finding it. The human need not know where `block` is, just that `reg3` points to it. This is exactly analogous to pointer variables in Hill. One can use a hll pointer without knowing its exact contents, just the interpretation of that content as a pointer to some data structure. Pointers allow the programmer to refer to a location *indirectly,* using the address that has been loaded into a register. Reference to items pointed to by a register is called *indirect addressing* because the manipulated object is only referenced indirectly: the command names a register, which in turn holds the address. Such an indirect address is indicated syntactically by the same notation as was used by Hill: an up-arrow: `↑`. For example,

```
copy          reg3↑⇒loc1
```

can be read as "copy the contents of the location pointed to by register 3 into `locl`." Thus the pair of statements

```
load_address      block⇒reg3
copy:char     reg3↑⇒locl.
```

has the same logical result as does

```
copy:char     block⇒locl
```

Figure 5-1 illustrates the relationship. (Of course, the former has the side-effect of altering the register). The pointer can be changed to point to the next cell by incrementing it by the size of the cell. Thus,

```
add           #1⇒reg3
copy:char     reg3↑⇒loc2.
```

would cause the next character of `block` to be moved into `loc2`.

As with the pointers of Hill, the semantics of GAL pointers produce subtle syntactic variations. It is necessary to have a means of reference both for the

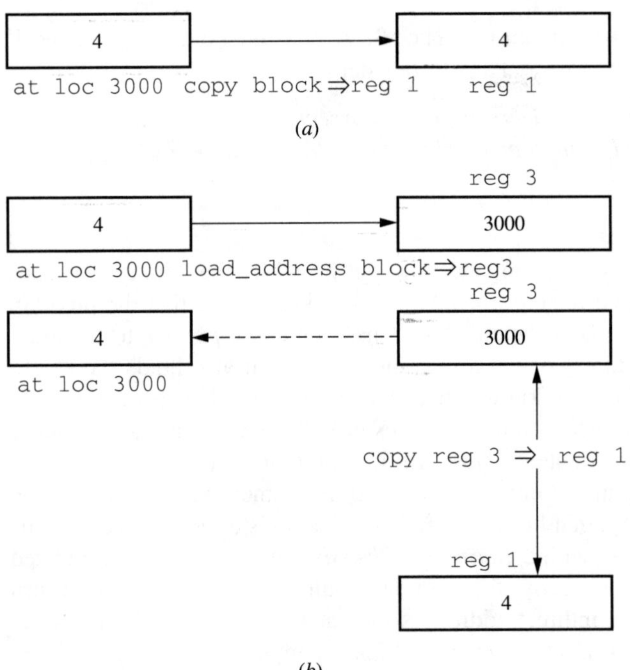

FIGURE 5-1
Indirect addressing compared to direct addressing. *(a)* Direct. *(b)* Indirect.

pointers themselves and the things to which they point. Thus GAL, like Hill, uses its normal—or simple—notation when manipulating the actual pointer itself:

```
Hill                     GAL
```

for referencing a pointer, to set it:

```
ptr⇐. . .                load_address   item⇒reg3
```

or increment it:

```
ptr⇐ptr↑.next            add            #1⇒reg3
```

but uses a distinct notation to refer to the item pointed at:

```
item⇐ptr↑                copy           reg3↑⇒item
```

Figure 5-2 illustrates the differences. Note that when using pointers, the size of the operation refers to the the size of the actual operand—the item pointed at, the item being manipulated—in this case `block`. It does *not* refer to the size of the address held in the register. When the operation manipulates the pointer itself, the size of the operation refers to the size of the address (the pointer). The similarity of the phrase "pointed to by . . ." to the Hill or Pascal term "pointer" is no accident. The hll pointer is exactly the same thing: a representation of the address in which an item is stored.

Arrays

An array is an ordered collection of data. Since it is ordered, the elements of the array can be numbered : 0, 1, 2, 3,. . . . If an array `block` of bytes is stored in memory at location `loc`, then

the first item of the array is at location (`loc` + 0) = `loc`
the second is at location (`loc` + 1)
the next at location (`loc` + 2)
then (`loc` + 3), (`loc` + 4), . . .

STRINGS. Because every memory location is numbered, the position of any item in an array can be calculated from the location of the beginning of the array, and the relative position of the item within the array. In the current example, if `block` is stored beginning at location 1234 (i.e., `loc` = 1234), then

`block[0]` is at 1234
`block[1]` is at 1235
`block[2]` is at 1236
`block[3]` is at 1237 . . .

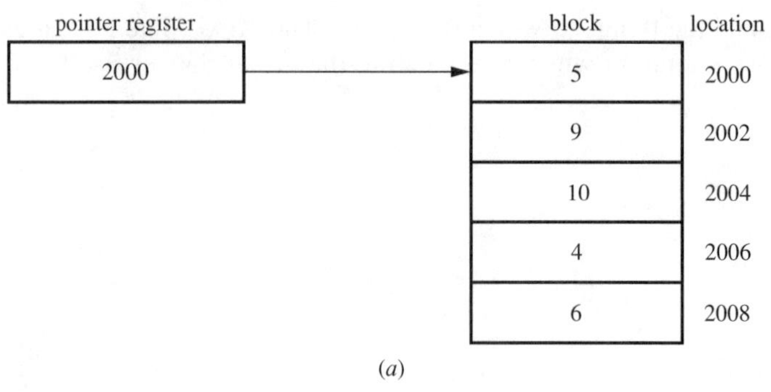

(*a*)

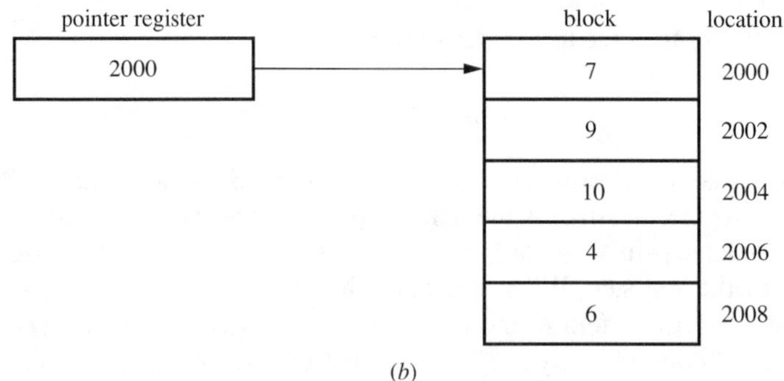

(*b*)

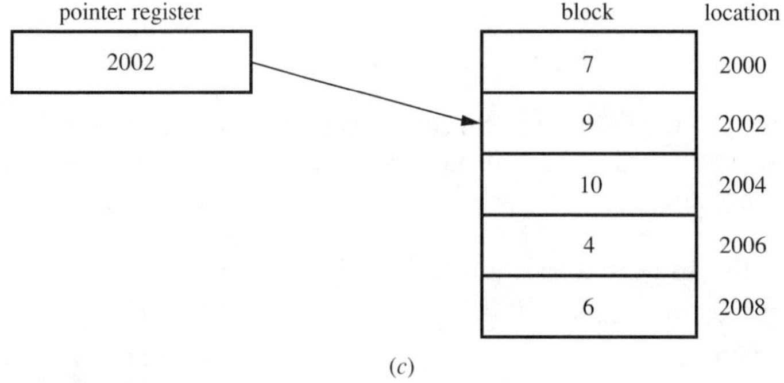

(*c*)

FIGURE 5-2
Pointer manipulation *(a)* after `load_address block`. *(b)* after `add #2⇒pointer_reg↑`. *(c)* after `add #2⇒pointer_reg`.

To refer to a specific cell of an array, two factors are needed:

- location of the array
- position within the array (also called *displacement*)

The address of a given cell is the address of `block` plus the displacement. Note that this view of arrays provides insight into computer scientists' preference for starting counting at zero: the zeroth item in an array is one with a displacement of zero from the beginning. If the first position in the array were numbered as position one, this calculation would be slightly more complex.

> ▷ *What would the needed calculation be for arrays starting at cell number 1?*

Once the program knows the location of the array, it can determine the location of all other locations in that array: they sequentially follow the first. For example, consider an array of characters (i.e., a *string*) called `message`. The following code will print out all characters of a 10-character message by sequentially accessing each element and outputting the one character:

```
    begin_data
message
    constant:char       'hello msg.'
    end_data

    load_address  message⇒reg3   ;register 3 now points
                                 ;to the message
    copy:int      #0⇒reg4        ;reg4 counts the
                                 ;characters printed

string_top
    copy:char     reg3↑⇒reg0     ;get one character
    jump:sub      →output        ;and print it
    add           #1⇒reg3        ;point to next character
    add           #1⇒reg4        ;count # of chars printed
    compare:int   #10⇒reg4       ;if not all 10 chars yet
    jump:greater  →string_top    ;then loop for rest
```

The relationships between the pointers and the array are illustrated in Figure 5-3. In this code segment

```
    copy          reg3↑⇒reg0
```

has a meaning equivalent to the pseudo-Hill statement

```
    assign        reg0⇐reg3↑;
```

(i.e., `reg0` gets the value that `reg3` points to) and

```
    add           #1⇒reg3
```

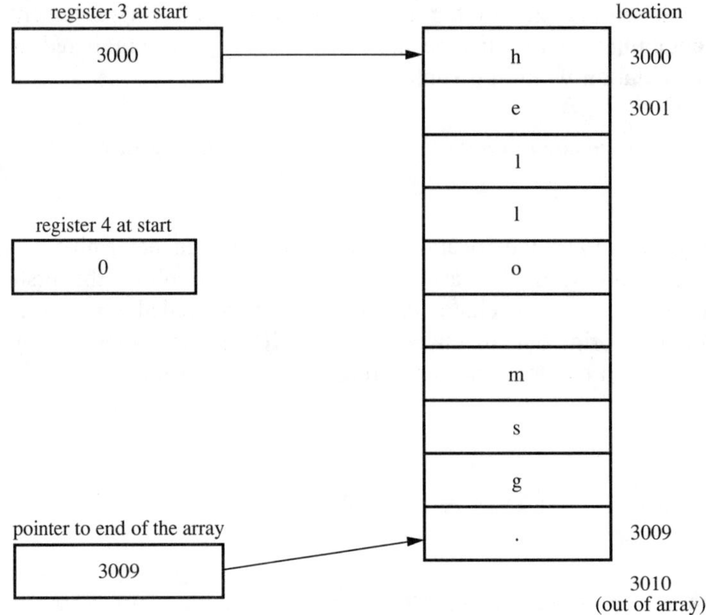

FIGURE 5-3
Pointers to an array.

changes the value of the pointer so that it points at the next item, much like a cross between

```
    assign    reg3⇐reg3↑.next
```

and

```
    assign    counter⇐counter + 1;
```

Arrays of characters are commonly called *strings*. Each cell of a string requires exactly one byte. Arrays of integers would be handled in analogous manners, but using a word (two or four bytes) of storage for each cell. Thus if the zeroth location of an array of (two-byte) integers is at `loc` then the first will be at (`loc` + 2), the second at (`loc` + 4), and so on. Stepping through an array can be accomplished by adding 2 to the address at each step. AL will not keep track of the size of the operands. It is up to the programmer to increment the pointer register by the correct amount at each step. One could also work backwards through an array by subtracting 2 rather than adding as each cell was fetched, but the details are left as an exercise. Many common array problems require setting all cells of the array to the same value, typically zero or blank. This can be done with a loop, very similar to the one above, with the pointer incremented by 2 at each pass through the loop.

▷ *Some hlls refer to strings as packed arrays. Why? Can you picture a way to keep track of the size of cells in arrays automatically?*

```
    begin_data
block
    variable:integer20                ;twenty integer locations
    end_data
    load_address     block⇒reg3      ;register 3 now
                                      ;points to the array
    copy:int         #0⇒reg4         ;reg4 shows how many
                                      ;have been initialized
fill_top
    copy:int         #0⇒reg3↑        ;put zero in one cell
    add              #2⇒reg3         ;increment the pointer
    add              #1⇒reg4         ;and the counter
    compare:int      #10⇒reg4        ;if not all 10 characters
    jump:greater     →fill_top       ;yet, then loop for rest
```

One variation on this technique is interesting as an illustration of the pointer process. A single value placed into the array prior to the loop can be propagated all the way through the array, copying the new value in each cell into the next. The following block of code fills a character array with blanks. (The syntactically odd line

```
    copy              reg3↑⇒(1+reg3)↑
```

should be read as "copy the item pointed to by `reg3` into the location one byte beyond the item pointed to by `reg3`," or "copy each byte into the next position.")

> ▷ *The algorithm in this paragraph turns out to be not particularly efficient—why not?*

```
;assume all declarations have been made
    load_address     string⇒reg3      ;register 3 now points
                                       ;to message
    copy        blank⇒reg3↑           ;put a blank in
                                       ;1st location
    copy        #0⇒reg4               ;reg4 keeps track of
                                       ;progress so far
string_top
    copy        reg3↑⇒(1+reg3)↑       ;copy location pointed
                                       ;to by reg 3 into
                                       ;next location
    add         #1⇒reg3               ;increment the pointer
    add         #1⇒reg4               ;and the position counter
    compare     #10⇒reg4              ;if not all 10
                                       ;positions yet then
    jump:greater     →string_top      ;loop to get the rest
    end_code
```

PRE- AND POST-TEST LOOPS FOR ARRAY PROCESSING. Counter-controlled loops are not always practical for tasks such as printing a string of characters. The programmer would need to count the characters in the string at the time the code was written—an error-prone process at best. Long messages would be especially difficult. If the message were modified, the counting process would have to be repeated. Fortunately there are other ways to process an array, for example, a post-test loop could output the characters until the next character is a ".":

```
    ;post test array process example
        begin_data
message constant:char 'hello msg.'
period  constant:char '.'

    begin_code
    load_address   message⇒reg3 ;reg3 pts to the message
  string_top
    copy:char      reg3↑⇒reg0   ;copy and print
    jump:sub       →output      ;print it
                                ;current character
    add            #1⇒reg3      ;increment the pointer
    compare:char   reg3↑⇒period ;if not all characters yet
    jump:not_eq    →string_top  ;loop for the rest
```

Alternatively, a pre-test loop could print while the current character is a letter and quit as soon as the next character comes alphabetically before "A". That is, it prints "Hello". A blank would stop the printing, as would any of the alphabetically early punctuation marks such as "!" or "?". There are some punctuation marks that come after the uppercase letters, such as "[" and "{", which would not cause termination of printing.

```
;pre-test array processing
        begin_data
message constant:char 'hello msg.'
letterA constant:char 'A'

    begin_code                             ;reg 3 pts
    load_address     message⇒reg3     ;to message
 string_top
    compare:char     letterA⇒reg3↑    ;blank comes
                                       ;before 'A'
    jump:greater_eq →out_of_loop
    copy:char        reg3↑⇒reg0       ;print a character
    jump:sub         →output          ;print it
    add              #1⇒reg3          ;increment the pointer
    jump:always      →string_top      ;then loop to get the
                                       ;rest
  out_of_loop
```

INDEXED ADDRESSING FOR ARRAYS. Arrays are not always accessed in sequential order. It is frequently necessary to access an arbitrary position within the array. The position can always be found by adding together the position index and a pointer to the front of the array. However, this could require three steps, including the repeated reloading and destroying of the pointer:

Load the address of the beginning of the array
Add the displacement corresponding to the desired position
Use the new pointer value to access the array cell

Either the beginning address will need to be recalculated each time an array element is used or two registers will be needed: one to save the beginning address and one for the current reference. If two array items are needed by one command, such as

```
    assign        block[x]⇐block[y]
```

then three registers are needed. Many languages allow an additional addressing mode, called *indexed addressing*. In this mode, two address registers are used together to form a single pointer, one register called the *base* is set to the beginning of the array. A second register acts as an index to the array. It contains the displacement from the beginning of the array to the currently referenced cell. Thus, block[10] of a character array might be accessed by

```
    load_address    block⇒reg4
    copy            #10⇒reg5
    copy            (reg4+reg5)↑⇒. . .
```

meaning that the two registers should be treated as a single-address pointer. There is no need to destroy the base pointer. The technique is especially useful for accessing corresponding positions of two arrays. For example, to copy one 10-cell integer array to another:

```
    load_address    block1⇒reg1    ;ptrs
    load_address    block2⇒reg2    ;to the two arrays
    copy            #18⇒reg3       ;10th cell is 18 bytes
                                   ;(9*2) after first
loop_top
    copy            (reg1+reg3)↑⇒(reg2+reg3)↑
    subtract        #2⇒reg3
    compare         #0⇒reg3        ;current cell number 0?
    jump:less_eq    →loop_top
```

Stacks and Queues

Address pointers can also be used to implement *stacks* and *queues*. Recall that a stack is an abstract data structure in which data is stored and retrieved on a first-in last-out basis. New data is said to be placed on top and only the top item can be retrieved. Suppose a block of 1000 memory locations is reserved for a stack:

```
stack        variable:byte     1000
```

A pointer to the bottom of the stack could be established by using a register to hold the address of the beginning of the reserved storage:

```
             load_address      stack⇒reg0
```

An item can be pushed onto the stack by placing the value into the location where the pointer points, and then incrementing the pointer:

```
push         copy              item⇒reg0↑
             add               #1⇒reg0
```

Figure 5-4 shows the results of these steps.

Pushing values onto the stack in this manner leaves the top-of-stack pointer pointing to the empty position on top of the stack, which is consistent with the initial state in which the pointer points at the (top of) the empty stack. Values may be popped off the stack by reversing steps. However, since the pointer points to the empty position above the stack, it must be decremented before, rather than after, removing the data from the stack.

```
pop          subtract          #1⇒reg0
             copy              reg0↑⇒item
```

The stack is empty whenever the pointer points to the original top-of-stack location. Thus the Boolean function `empty` could begin

```
empty        load_address      stack⇒reg4
             compare           reg0⇒reg4
             jump:equal        →. . .
```

The two items being compared in this case are the pointer addresses themselves—not the items to which the pointers point. The comparison asks, "Does the pointer point at the bottom of the stack?" The following code incorporates all of these steps in a single, more complete example. The procedure reads several letters of input, stores them in a stack, and prints them out in reverse order, stopping when it finds a blank character.

> ▷ *The latter case would certainly yield true results whenever the former does. Would the inverse also be true?*

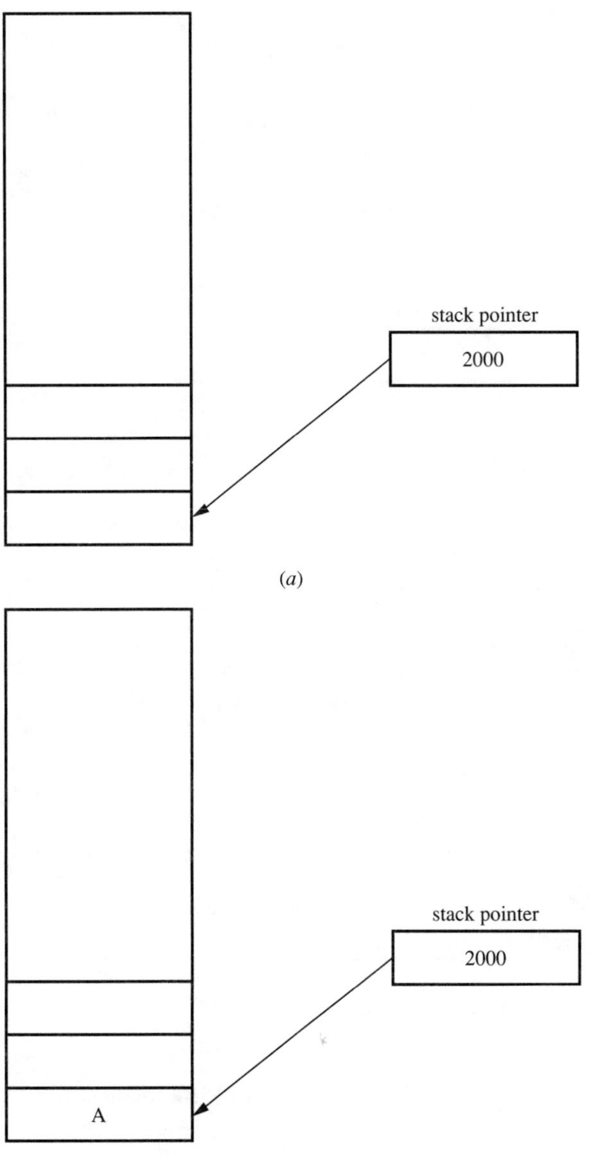

FIGURE 5-4
Use of a stack *(a)* after initialization. *(b)* after `copy item⇒SP↑`.

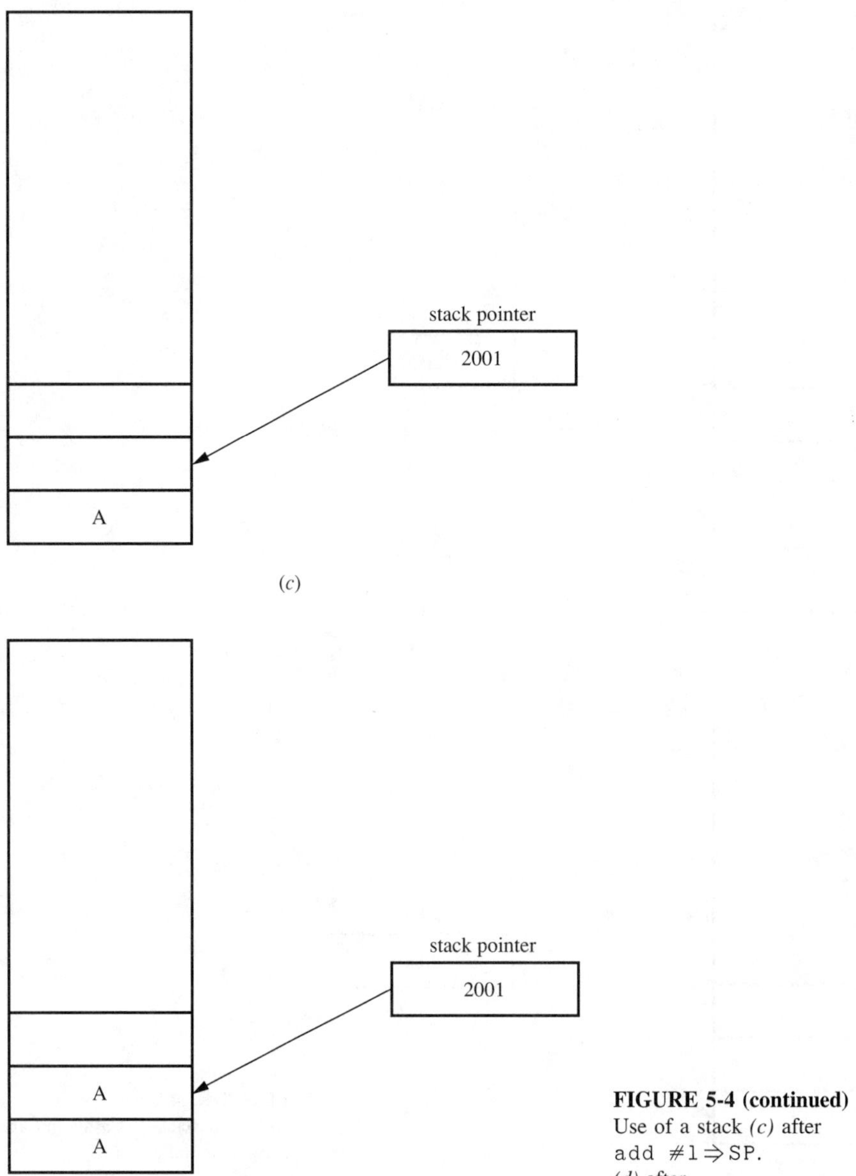

FIGURE 5-4 (continued)
Use of a stack *(c)* after `add #1⇒SP`.
(d) after `copy item⇒SP↑`.

```
;assume stack declared with sufficient storage
    begin_code
reverse
    load_address     stack⇒reg7
inloop
        jump:sub     →input
        copy:char    reg0⇒reg7↑      ;push the character
        add          #1⇒reg7         ;increment the tos ptr
    compare:char     #' '⇒reg0       ;was it a blank?
    jump:not_eq      →inloop
outloop
        subtract     #1⇒reg7         ;decrement the tos ptr
        copy:char    reg7↑⇒reg0      ;get the character
        jump:sub     →output         ;and print it
    load_address     stack⇒reg3
    compare          reg7⇒reg3       ;any left?
    jump:greater     →outloop
```

QUEUES. Queues can be implemented in AL in a manner directly analogous to the implementation of stacks. One pointer is required to point to the front of the queue and another to point to the back. Both pointers initially point to the same location. When new values are added to the queue, the back pointer is incremented. When new values are removed from the queue, the front pointer is incremented. The stack is empty when both pointers point to the same address.

One problem with the basic implementation of a queue is that it will eventually run out of space. Since both pointers are incremented—and never decremented—the storage and retrieval activity must continually move in one direction. An alternative is the *circle queue*. In a circle queue, items are pushed on the back and pulled from the front as usual. However, a fixed number of locations are reserved for the queue. When pushing one additional item onto the queue would exceed the upper bound of the reserved area, it "wraps around": the new item is placed at location zero of the queue. This does assume that items will be pulled off fast enough so that the queue never overflows, or contains too many items. The check could be accomplished by comparing the position with the known end of the allocated area:

```
;CIRCLE Q: FIRST ATTEMPT
;assume:front_ptr, and end_ptr are
;legal pointer operands;
;begin_queue & end_of_queue are
;the two end_points of the queue:
    load_address     end_of_queue⇒end_ptr   ;
    add              #1⇒front_ptr
    compare          front_ptr⇒end_ptr      ;at the end?
    jump:less_eq     →process_normally
    load_address     begin_queue⇒front_ptr ;set to front
process_normally
```

The programmer can improve time efficiency (possibly at the expense of space efficiency) by taking advantage of the internal representation of numeric values, as described in the Chapter 4. Suppose an unsigned integer is held in a single byte. It can take on the values 0 to $2^8 - 1 = 255$. If 1 is added to 255, an overflow occurs, leaving the result as zero:

$$\begin{array}{r} 1111\ 1111 \\ +\ \underline{0000\ 0001} \\ [1]\,0000\ 0000 \end{array}$$

This observation can be used to create an automatic wraparound, with no need to check to see if the upper bound has been reached. The programmer first places the beginning of the queue at an address divisible by 256 (address mod 256 $=0$). The last eight bits of the address will be zero. When the initial pointer to the queue is loaded, it will also end with eight zero bits. Items can be pushed onto the back of the queue by

```
;CIRCLE Q:SECOND ATTEMPT
    add:byte          #1⇒back_ptr
    copy:byte         item⇒back_ptr↑
```

`Back_ptr` will always point between the front of the queue and the end of the storage area, 256 bytes later.

▷ *How can a programmer specify an internal address?*

Record Structures

Records are blocks of logically related data. A single record can be easily simulated in assembly language by declaring its parts to be syntactically contiguous:

```
name                string           10
age                 variable:integer
phone               string           7
```

Each field can be referenced by the distance from that field to the start of the record. Thus, if `reg2` points to the front of the record:

```
load_address        name⇒reg2
```

then age is located 10 bytes later. Thus, a person can be made 5 years older by

```
add                 10⇒reg2              ;now points to age
add                 #5⇒reg2↑
```

Many assembly languages allow this to be accomplished with a single statement

```
add                 #5⇒(10+reg2)↑
```

which has the additional advantage that it leaves `reg2` pointing to the front of the record, not to `age`. Similarly, `phone` can be referenced as

```
        . . .           (2+10+reg2)↑
```

This is essentially the same as the indexed addressing mode used with arrays, except the compound address is composed of a base register and a fixed *displacement*. By use of the base-displacement addressing mode, the essence of structured types can be captured. A base pointer can point to any instance of a structure, and the displacement pointer can be used to specify a given field. Since all instances of a given type will be identical, one displacement pointer can be used to designate corresponding fields of identical structures. Using pointers, it is also easy to pass structured variables as parameters. (Many languages also allow a similar addressing mode called *based* for such situations. Based addressing is discussed in Chapter 7.)

Linked Lists

The typical hll technique for creating a linked list uses records with two fields: data and pointer. The pointer field always points to the next item in the list. A special pointer `null`, indicates that the pointer does not point at anything. The same technique can be used in assembly language. Suppose that `list` is to be a linked list of integers. Each node in the list needs two fields: an integer value and a pointer.

```
node   variable:integer
       variable:address
```

Assume for discussion that integers and addresses are all four-byte storage locations, as illustrated in Figure 5-5. A procedure to add all of the nodes in a list would need to access each node in succession, add the value of the node to a running total and, if there is another node, access that node and repeat:

```
;assume all data declarations are complete
      copy          #0⇒reg4      ;reg4 will hold
                                 ;running total
      copy          start⇒reg3   ;assume start pts to
                                 ;first node
loop_top
      compare:int   #0⇒reg3      ;is it the null ptr?
      jump:equal    →all_done    ;if so, quit
        add         reg3↑⇒reg4   ;add current node to total
        add         #4⇒reg3      ;access the pointer
        copy:int    reg3↑⇒reg3   ;point to next node
      jump:always   →loop_top
all_done
   . . .
```

This example assumed that the list had already been created. In some hlls, a function such as `new` is provided to "find space" for a new pointer-controlled variable and return a pointer to that space. One way to achieve a similar effect might be to create a list of all of the available free space. Suppose `pool` is a reservoir of nodes, that is, it is a storage area declared large enough to contain the number of nodes that are needed (1000 nodes would require 8000 bytes). And assume that zero is used as the null pointer value. In this case, the initial list of free space could be created by making each free location point to the next:

```
   load_address  pool⇒reg0   ;pts to front of 1st
                             ;data field
   copy       reg0⇒reg1      ;also points there
   add        #4⇒reg0        ;reg0 now pts to 1st
                             ;ptr field
loop_section
   add        #8⇒reg1        ;reg1 pts at next free record
   copy       reg1⇒reg0↑     ;the ptr field pts to
                             ;next record
   add        #8⇒reg0        ;reg0 points to next
                             ;ptr field
   jump:   . . .             ;back to loop_section
```

The `new` and `dispose` functions could use this list to maintain the list of free locations.

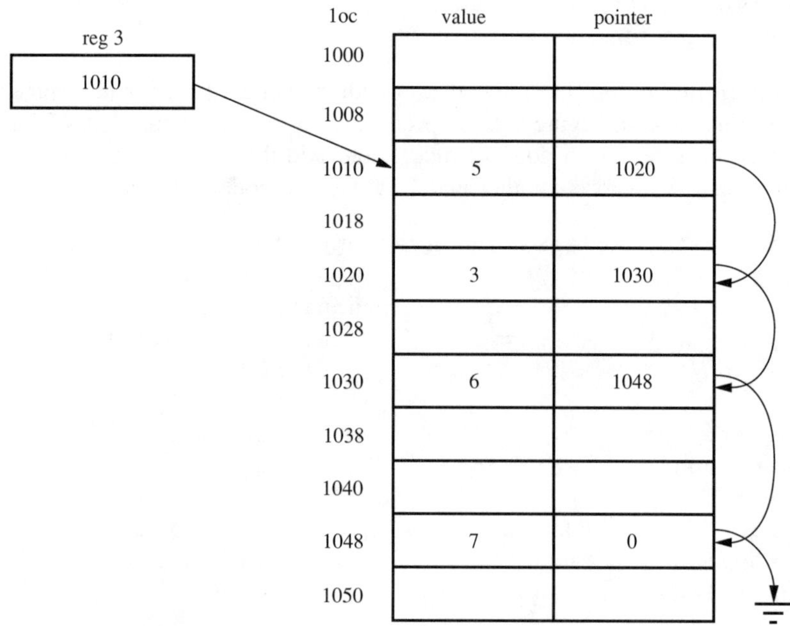

FIGURE 5-5
Pointers to a linked list.

Parameter Passing

STACK-BASED PARAMETERS. An important use of stacks is as a data structure for passing parameters to subroutines. The parameter passing method introduced in Chapter 2 had one very significant drawback: registers are a scarce commodity, and any procedure requiring several parameters could easily use up a significant percentage of the available resource. By using a stack for that purpose, the registers can be saved for other purposes.

Assume that a stack has been declared and that `reg0` has been set to point to it as above. Suppose a procedure `A` wishes to call a procedure `B` that requires two parameters. The calling procedure `A` can pass the two parameters by pushing them onto the stack, one at a time, before it calls `B`:

```
A     copy          val_1⇒reg0↑
      add           #2⇒reg0            ;assuming 2 byte parameter
      copy          val_2⇒reg0↑
      add           #2⇒reg0
      jump:sub      →B
```

When the called procedure `B` begins, it simply copies the parameters from the stack:

```
B     subtract      #2⇒reg0            ;assuming 2 byte parameter
      copy          reg0↑⇒local_2      ;note reverse order
      subtract      #2⇒reg0            ;
      copy          reg0↑⇒local_1
      <body of B>
```

In addition to the savings of registers, there are a number of additional advantages to this form of parameter passing. With register parameter passing, each routine passed parameters in the same registers. Therefore, before calling a second subprocedure, a procedure must protect all of its parameters. With stack-based parameter passing, the parameters are safely stored on the stack until they are needed. Recursive procedures are very awkward (indeed impossible in any direct manner) with register-based parameter passing because some mechanism must exist for saving the intermediate state descriptions.

> ▷ *What are the basic requirements needed for implementing recursive procedure definitions?*

CALL-BY-ADDRESS PARAMETERS. Pointers may be used to pass call-by-address `var` parameters to routines. Chapter 2 claimed that the superficial effect of `var` parameters could be accomplished by passing the value back at the end of the subroutine. We are now in a position to see (1) why the method of Chapter 2 was not quite correct, (2) why `var` parameters are often called *call-by-address* parameters, and (3) how to accomplish the task correctly.

The correct interpretation of a var or call-by-address parameter requires that the procedure should manipulate the original data item itself, not just a copy of it. The procedure expects the address of the item, not the value of the item. When a parameter is passed by copying the parameter into a register (or onto the stack), only a copy of the "value" of the actual parameter—not the parameter itself—is placed on the stack. But if the calling program passes the address of the actual parameter, the called routine has access to the original parameter itself. Any changes to the parameter made by the subroutine will affect the original parameter directly, and immediately—not at the return from the procedure. Thus, if the calling sequence is

```
load_address     item⇒reg0      ;VAR parameter
jump:sub         →dummy
```

and dummy includes the code

```
add              #10⇒reg0↑
```

the add statement in dummy will add 10 to the location pointed to by register 0, that is, item. Contrast this with the traditional call-by-value parameter passing, in which a copy of the value of the actual parameter is passed to the subroutine

```
copy             item⇒reg0      ;VAL parameter
jump:sub         →dummy
```

and dummy includes the code

```
add              #10⇒reg0
```

In this case, item is not changed.

Another situation in which var parameters are used is for passing large quantities of data, such as arrays. The Chapter 2 approximation of var parameter passing would not work for that case. Passing an entire array in registers would be impossible for any but the smallest arrays, but the address of any array can clearly be passed as a single item. In fact a pointer to an array is the method already used for accessing the cells of the array. Any changes made to any part of the array would be reflected in the original array. Note that use of an address parameter for an array is a double winner: not only did it save the many registers that would be needed to pass all of the values, but it saved the time needed to copy the parameters. The changes would also take effect immediately since the original is the item actually being manipulated. Address parameters are doubly convenient for arrays since pointers are needed to manipulate any array.

With this corrected implementation of address parameters, there is no need for values to be passed back at the end, which is also more practical for the calling program. The implementation of Chapter 2 required that the calling routine explicitly access any `var` parameters after completion of the subroutine. Although the extra step may provide a reminder to the programmer that the parameter was referenced by its address, it certainly increased the logical complexity, as well as the total time for the calling sequence.

PROGRAMMERS' NOTE. AL provides no checking for either method of parameter passing. It does not check for the var-value distinction nor the method of passing: register or stack. It is up to the programmer to assure consistency.

CONTROL STRUCTURES

Condition Codes and the Condition Code Register

As introduced in Chapter 2, conditional jumps used for loop control and conditional statements required a `compare–jump` pair of assembly language statements. The first compared two values and, depending upon the results of the comparison, the `jump` statement could jump (or not jump) to the destination. The curious reader may have wondered at that time, "But how does the `jump` statement find the result of that comparison?" After all, the `jump` and the `compare` are two separate statements. The very curious reader may even have attempted to write code that contained a conditional `jump` with no preceding comparison. That reader found out that while no error message occurred, no predictable results were encountered either. The explanation of this quandary is that most machines contain another register: the *condition code register* (*CCR*). The condition code register is similar to the previously discussed registers, except that it is not normally accessed directly by the programmer. Values are placed into the register by the `compare` operation and examined by the conditional `jump`. Thus, the logical description of the `compare` operation itself has two parts:

compare two values
place the result into the condition code register

Or more formally, in a Hill-like notation:[1]

```
*assign    condition_code_reg⇐test
```

For example, the GAL

```
*compare   regl⇒reg2
```

[1]The * notation used here indicates that the statement does not really correspond to Hill. In general, starred statements do not have higher-level language equivalents but merely represent a concept using a Hill-like notation.

might be thought of as

```
*assign    condition_code_reg⇐(regl > reg2)?
```

Note that comparisons in GAL differ from the logical comparisons of hll in that any of three (rather than two) possible values—greater-than, equal, or less-than—may be returned as the condition code.

▷ *The exact internal representation for conditionals is covered in Chapter 6. Based on the representations of the previous chapter, what would you expect the CCR to look like?*

The conditional `jump` statement simply checks the condition code register and jumps if the value found there corresponds to the test condition specified in the `jump`. Thus, if the condition code register contains `equal`, then any `jump` specifying an `equal` comparison (`equal`, `greater-than-or-equal`, or `less-than-or-equal`) would jump. If the CCR specifies `less than`, commands to jump on `less`, `less-than-or-equal`, or `not-equal` would all result in a jump being taken. The conditional `jump` could, therefore, be described as

```
if (CCR contains <condition> )
   then perform jump
   otherwise do nothing
```

Note that the `compare` statement modifies the contents of the condition code register but does not change the value of its operands. The `jump` statement looks at the CCR but does not modify its content.

While it would have been possible to create case and other control structures without the CCR, its addition provides much clearer and more understandable structures.

Simplified Test and Jump Situations

The `compare` statement is not the only statement that sets the condition code register. All operations that produce a result value (e.g., `add`, `subtract`, but not `jump`) reflect that value in the CCR. The values are set exactly as if the comparison

```
compare    <result>⇒#0
```

were executed immediately after the arithmetic command. Thus, if an `add` or `subtract` produces a zero sum or difference, the condition code register is set as if an equal comparison had been made.

A counter-controlled loop can count the number of cycles through the loop that remain. Control exits from the loop when the number reaches zero:

```
loop_top
    subtract        #1⇒reg2          ;reg 2 is loop counter
    jump : equal    →out_of_loop     ;no compare!
                    <body>
out_of_loop
```

Case

The `case` statement in Hill takes the general form

```
    {test is an expression to be evaluated}
    do case <test> of
      <val_1>:<action_1>
      <val_2>:<action_2>
      . . .
      <val_n>:<action_n>
      otherwise:<escape action>
    end case
```

and is equivalent to the series of “if-then-elseif”s:

```
    if (<test> = <val_1>)
      then <action_1>
    else if (<test> = <val_2>)
      then <action_2>
      . . .
    else if (<test> = <val_n>)
      then <action_n> . . .
      else <escape action>
```

From this equivalence it is a straightforward task to build an assembly language structure that corresponds to the series of `ifs`. (See Figure 5-6.)

It was easy to perform the straightforward and naive conversion from Hill to GAL using the equivalent `if-then-else` structure. However, this approach did introduce an added problem of clarity: the *snake*. Notice how the control structure for the case statement was spread over a large block of code, with actions and control statements intermixed. About three control statements were needed for each possible case value—before and after the code representing the actions for that case. A complicated case structure could force a reader of the program to look through several pages of code to follow the path through the structure. This reading takes the form of following a long series of jumps around each of the nonapplicable cases. If all of these jumps were indicated with arrows from `jump`

```
;case - first attempt
 copy     test⇒reg3          ;save in convenient loc
 compare  val_1⇒reg3         ;check first value
 jump:not_eq →try_val_2      ;skip if not the case
     <statements for case: test = val_1>
 jump:always  →end_of_case   ;avoid remaining cases
try_val_2
 compare  val_2⇒reg3         ;check second value
 jump:not_eq →try_val_3      ;skip this one
     <statements for case: test = val_2>
 jump:always  ⇒end_of_case   ;avoid remaining cases
try_val_3
 ...
try_val_n
 compare  val_n⇒reg3         ;check last value
 jump:not_eq →otherwise_section
     <statements for case: test = val_3>
 jump:always  →end_of_case   ;avoid remaining cases
otherwise_section
 <statements>
end_of_case
```

FIGURE 5-6
Snake.

statement to target, the result would be a snake-like path through and around the individual cases. The clear meaning of the hll `case` statement (do one and only one of the following possibilities) is totally obscured from the AL reader. There is no indication that the code forms any recognizable structure.

To avoid this problem, follow the same guiding principles applied to the simpler control structures: *separate control from action*. Place the majority of the control statements at the front of the block, followed by each of the possible cases shown in Figure 5-7. With this change, all of the comparisons are now grouped together into a single block representing the control structure for the `case` statement. The reader of the program can easily recognize the block of comparisons and branches as a multi-valued decision (i.e., it is a `case` statement). There is no need to follow the snake through all of its twists around the various possible cases.

The new representation also provides a safety feature. In both representations, `reg3` held the value being compared. The first representation presents a potential error-producing situation. The control statements along the snake's body all assume that `reg3` contains the case index. If the body of any one of the `case` actions used `reg3` for any reason, that register would be altered for all future comparisons. That situation should not actually occur, since only a single segment should be executed, with no further comparisons being made. However, that may be nontrivial for the programmer to verify. Such improved structure clarity is often accompanied by reduction in the likelihood of errors.

```
;case second attempt
 copy    test⇒reg3    ;access index. compare  val_1□reg3
 check first value
 jump:equal  →case_1  ;it is val_1...go to case_1
 compare  val_2⇒reg3 ;check second value              case
 jump:equal   →case_2 ;it is val_2                    select
 ...
 compare  val_n⇒reg3  ;check nth value
 jump:equal   →case_n
 jump:always   →otherwise_section
case_1
 <statements for case: test = 1>
 jump:always   →end_of_case   ;avoid remaining cases
case_2
 <statements for case: test = 1>
 jump:always   →end_of_case   ; avoid remaining cases
case_3
 ...
case_n
 <statements for case: test = val_n>
 jump:always   →end_of_case   ;avoid remaining cases
otherwise_section
  <statements>
end_of_case
```

FIGURE 5-7
Case.

The `otherwise` clause is a very valuable part of the structure, even if it simply prints out an error message. It will aid in avoiding or fixing errors. Note that the `otherwise` command is represented here in a very natural way: when all of the conditional jumps have failed, control falls through (via the absolute `jump`) to the `otherwise` section.

CASES WITH RANGES. Grouping all of the `compare/jump` pairs together may occasionally provide one further benefit. Recall that a `compare` statement leaves its results in the CCR, and the `jump` statement does not modify that register. It is therefore possible to perform one comparison followed by two conditional jumps, each based on the same comparison. For example, consider a `case` statement in which each value was not a single value but a range of values:

```
case test of
    (test < 0):<action_1>;
    (test = 0):<action_2>;
    (test > 0):<action_3>;
end_of_case
```

In GAL, this could be implemented as:

```
              compare:int    #0⇒ test
              jump:greater   →action_1
              jump:equal     →action_2
                                          ;not greater
              jump:always    →action_3 ;or eq = less
    action_1  . . .
              jump:always    →out_of_case
    action_2  . . .
              jump:always    →out_of_case
    action_3  . . .
              jump:always    →out_of_case
    out_of_case     . . .
```

The single comparison placed a result into the CCR. Each of the subsequent jumps then examined the CCR, using the same condition code value to determine if a jump should be taken. This saved two of the three comparisons. Note that the third `jump` statement

```
jump:always   →  action_3
```

could have been eliminated by placing `action_3` prior to the other actions. However, good programming style dictates that the order of statements in a program should closely resemble the order exhibited in the pseudocode.

Historical note. The observant programmer may recognize the above construct as the `arithmetic if`, an archaic construct found in Fortran and other early higher-level languages. The construct has fallen out of favor because it is not only a "forbidden `goto`" but a "double `goto`" at that. It is used here precisely because it illustrates the way in which many constructs found their way into higher-level languages. Assembly languages made the above comparisons very simple to construct. Early higher-level programmers were used to such constructs from their assembly language experience. They expected the savings in time obtained by avoiding the repeated comparisons and wanted analogous constructs in higher-level languages. Since they were also easy to construct, they were incorporated into early higher-level languages. In reality, the minor time savings was not worth the potential for convoluted code.

Conditionals Involving Compound Tests

Not all tests used in `if-then-else` statements or in `while` or `until` loop control are simple tests like the ones used earlier. Sometimes, the test is compound:

```
if (<test1> or <test2>)
   then <actions>
```

for example,

```
if(3 < x < 4)
  then<actions>
```

which must normally be written

```
if (x > 3) and (x < 4)
  then <actions>
```

The `<action>` is performed only if both of the two tests are `true`. The same logical structure can be built in AL by performing each of the tests separately but providing the same destination for each attempted jump:

```
    copy                x⇒reg3
    compare             #3⇒reg3       ;is 3 ≥ x?
    jump:greater_eq     →out_of_if
    compare             #4⇒reg4       ;is 4 ≤ x?
    jump:less_eq        →out_of_if
         <then_actions>
out_of_if
```

The failure of either test causes control to jump around the `then-clause`. If the compound test is a disjunction:

```
if (x > y) or (x < z)
  then <actions>
```

the `then-clause` should be executed if either (or both) of the tests are true:

```
     copy               x⇒reg3
     compare            y⇒reg3        ;is y ≥ x?
     jump:less          →then_clause  ;yes - do it
     compare            z⇒reg3        ;is z ≤ x?
     jump:less_eq       →out_of_if    ;yes - skip it!
then_clause
          <then actions>
out_of_if
```

The two tests were treated in opposite manners: the first jumped to the `then-clause`; the second around the `then-clause`.

▷ *Why are these two cases treated in different manners?*

Suppose a language had only simple conditional jumps (e.g., jump-on-less-than, but not jump-on-less-than-or-equal). The more complicated conditional jumps could be imitated using structures such as these combined with the fact that values stay in the condition code register (left as an exercise).

NOTES ON "REAL MACHINES"

Operand Mismatch

An understanding of the use of addresses internally (rather than mnemonic labels) helps clarify a frequent paradox experienced by beginning assembly language programmers. An address refers to an internal location with RAM—usually a byte. But many data items—and the operations that manipulate them—require more than a single byte of storage. For example, integers usually require two bytes. Obviously, both bytes cannot be located at the same address. One is at the given address and the second at the byte next to it, usually in the higher-numbered position.[2]

It is the programmer's responsibility to match the size for operations with the size of its intended operands. Consider an error generated when accessing a two-byte integer contained in RAM as if it were a single-byte operand. Suppose location 2000 contained the value generated by the GAL directive:

```
item            constant:integer  85  ;(note: 85₁₀ = 55₁₆ ).
```

Then, memory contains

location	contents
2000	0055

which might be more clearly indicated as

2000	00
2001	55

The integer requires two bytes, starting at location 2000. Thus, it is actually located in both bytes 2000 and 2001. The "most interesting" part of this value is the 55; the leading zeros are not very interesting. Suppose this value is accessed as a one-byte operand:

```
copy:integer     #0⇒reg2
compare:byte     item⇒reg2
```

---

[2]When the higher-order byte is stored at the lower address, it is sometimes referred to as *big endien* (the big end is stored first). Some machines do store the lower-order byte first, thus 123_{16} stored at `loc` would be stored `23` in `loc` and `01` in `loc+1`. This representation, known as *little endien* (the little end is stored first) is useful because the first-encountered byte in an operand field (address or immediate) following the instruction is always the low-order byte—independent of the size of the operand. (The terms *big endien* and *little endien* are a play on words first used in *Gulliver's Travels* by Jonathan Swift to refer to those who argued that eggs should be broken at the big or little ends. Does this suggest that some think the argument is silly?)

The second operation expects a single-byte operand. Therefore, the byte at location 2000 is fetched as `item`. The resulting comparison yields an unexpected true value, because only the single byte at the RAM address is compared to the single byte in the register. It may seem that no one would be so careless. But consider this question: What are the default sizes for the operations? What would the result be of

```
copy              #0⇒reg2
compare           item⇒reg2     ;?
```

It is very easy to make such mistake if you rely on default sizes.

Consider an even more surprising comparison:

```
copy:integer      #256⇒reg2
compare:byte      item⇒reg2
```

In this case `reg2` contains $256_{10} = 100_{16}$:

```
0000 0100
```

The last eight bits are all zero. Thus the comparison again acts as if the operands were equal, because all the bits that were actually compared were identical. Consider an operation which accesses two bytes, but the operands are declared as single-byte operands

```
item     constant:character     'A'
next     constant:character     'B'
         . . .
         copy:character         item⇒reg2
         compare:word           item⇒reg2
```

This seems as if it should certainly produce an equal comparison. After all, it compares an item with itself. However, after the `copy`, `reg2` will contain

```
0000 0041
```

the representation of `A`. The `compare` attempts to compare two bytes of `reg2` with two bytes of RAM, starting at the location of item:

```
reg2     item
0041     4142
```

which clearly are not the same. Figure 5-8 summarizes the type-mismatch problem.

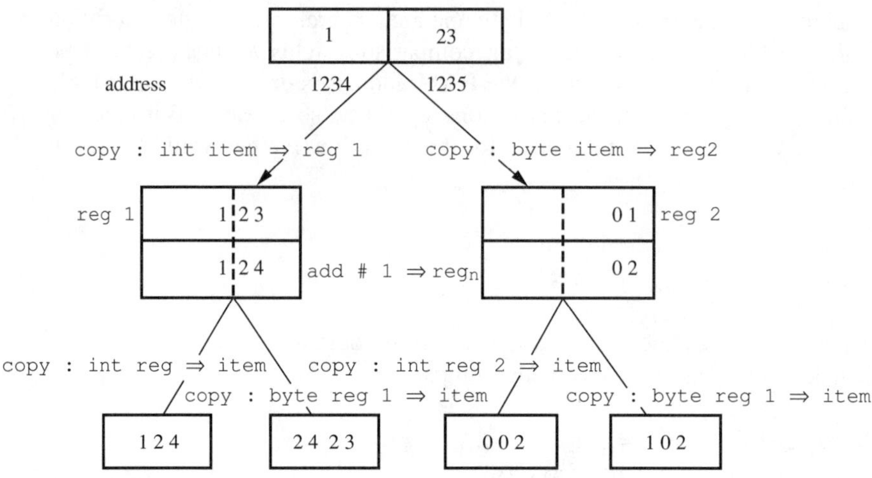

FIGURE 5-8
Errors caused by improper type specification

Machine Architectures

ADDRESS REGISTERS AND COMMANDS. Many machines have a distinct set of registers, called *address registers,* for holding address pointers; the general purpose registers may then be called *data registers*. Often special or at least distinct commands exist for manipulating the address registers and the general purpose registers. For example, the destination of the `load_Address` command may be restricted to address registers. Similarly, there may be two distinct sets of commands:

```
add        add_address
copy       copy_address
compare    compare_address
```

and so on, in which, each operation can take only the appropriate registers as operands. The careful programmer will check to see if such a special naming system exists.

SYSTEM STACKS. Many machines have a special stack "built-in." That is, there may be a designated register that is used as a "system stack pointer." Often space is prereserved by the system for this stack. Use of such a stack has some obvious advantages and disadvantages. It is very useful because it has been predefined. Routines written by multiple programmers can use the stack consistently. Standard parameter passing conventions are established, and so on. However, if a program inadvertently pushes more (or less) data onto the stack than it takes off, the results can be catastrophic: usually resulting in a dead system that must be completely rebooted. Any routine that has placed values on the stack can no longer access its information. Variables may be passed to subroutines using the system stack. However, care should be exercised.

▷ *In Chapter 7, we will see that the system stack is likely to be used as part of the procedure-calling mechanism, in which case the return address will end up on top of the stack—not the parameter placed there by the programmer. How might that be a problem?*

AUTO INCREMENT. The most common data structures—arrays, stacks, and queues—are all processed sequentially (arrays frequently; the others, always). Any such access requires two statements,

one for the access
one to increment the pointer

This combination is so common that many machines provide an addressing mode called *auto-increment,* which accomplishes both steps in a single statement. The statement

```
copy      item⇒reg2&inc
```

can be read as "copy the source to the destination (as usual), but then increment the address in register 2 so that it points at the next item in the array or stack." In a loop that processes an array, this would save one step in every iteration of the loop.

Popping items from a stack requires that the relative positions of the two steps (decrement pointer and get value) be reversed. Therefore, the analogous addressing mode, *auto-decrement* will normally perform its two suboperations in the reverse order:

```
copy      reg2&dec⇒item
```

should be read "decrement the pointer register and then fetch the item pointed to."

DECREMENT AND JUMP. Many machines provide a command that reduces even further the complexity of comparisons for loop control. The decrement and jump command actually performs three steps in one: it decrements a counter, compares the result to zero, and jumps if the result is not zero. (Some machines allow even further variations.) The command is especially useful for building counter-controlled loops.

Language Specifications

INDIRECT ADDRESSING NOTATION. The "↑" does not exist on most keyboards. Usually the related symbol "^" does exist, but few languages incorporate that specific notation. Two alternative notations for `reg2↑` are

```
(reg2)
```

and

```
@reg2
```

ADDRESS SPECIFICATION. Some assembly languages have an explicit notation for "the address of x" for use when it is important to emphasize that it is the address and not the contents of that address that is intended. For example, the `load_address` command may require a syntax such as

```
load_address    address (item)⇒reg2
```

STRINGS. Some languages represent strings as a length and array record.

length
array of length characters

Others store them as a string with a terminating character at the end. Some allow the programmer to specify which of the two should be used.

SUMMARY

Complexities in both data structures and procedural structures can be handled with a small number of additions to the generic model. The condition code register enables better manipulation for the comparisons needed for building more complicated control structures such as case and compound conditionals. Understanding its use can reduce the number of comparisons needed both by jump on the basis of the results of operations and by using one test to control multiple jump options. The use of addresses as pointers enables the construction of arrays, records, stacks, queues, and lists. It also provides an improved parameter-passing mechanism and enables call-by-address parameter passing. The additional command, `load_address`, and the additional addressing mode, indirect, provide support for these abstract structures. In each case, a register is used to hold the address of the data structure, and references are made to the location indirectly.

EXERCISES

Mini project II-4 in Appendix 2 is applicable at this point.

5.1. Write a program that reads a series of input characters and for each determines if it is an uppercase character ("A"–"Z"), a lowercase character ("a"–"z"), a digit ("0"–"9"), or something else.

5.2. Write a program to convert uppercase letters to lowercase—making sure that it is a letter that is being converted.

5.3. Assume there were no "jump on greater than or equal" command. Write a series of GAL statements equivalent to it. Use only one `compare` command.

5.4. Declare a string in your assembly language. Use a debugger to find out how the length of the string is represented.

5.5. Write a procedure to print out an entire string.

5.6. Write a program to convert from a large binary number to a series of decimal values using the division algorithm. Recall that that algorithm generates the digits in reverse order, so if you want to print them out, you will need an array to hold them in order to print them out.

5.7. Write a program to find the smallest value in a 100-cell array.

5.8. The disjunctive conditional statement

```
if (x > y) OR (x < z)
  then <actions>
```

was emulated by using two tests, one of which jumped around the then-clause and one of which jumped to the then-clause. Reconstruct the code segment with two tests jumping to the then-clause (and one skipping it).

5.9. Define and use procedures `push` and `pop`.

5.10. Define a stack `stack` and use it in a recursive procedure `fac` that calculates the factorial of its parameter n:

$$fac = \begin{cases} 1 \text{ if } N \leq 1 \\ N * fac(N-1) \text{ if } N > 1 \end{cases}$$

5.11. Define a hll data structure for storing data about a student, say name, class, phone number, and GPA. Define three students Tom, Dick, and Harry. Specify based address references for each field for each student.

5.12. Suppose the legal indices for an integer array are 1 to 100. Give a formula for the actual position of the ith cell of the array, based on the stating address of the entire array (note that there is no cell number 0).

5.13. Build two versions of the routine `swap`, which accepts two parameters and switches their values. The first version should use value parameters and the second should use address parameters. Comment on the success or failure of each.

5.14. Write expressions for calculating the address of cell `i,j` of an `NxM` matrix.

5.15. Use the result of 5.11 to calculate a matrix product. The product C of two $n \times n$ matrices A and B is defined by

$$c_{ij} = \sum_{k=1}^{n} a_{ik} * b_{kj},$$

Write a program to calculate the product. Note that it will need three nested loops.

5.16. If arrays were to be numbered starting at 1, the code to reference cell i of an array would be slightly trickier. Provide code to reference the ith character of a string, assuming the position of the first character is called `string[1]`. Extend the code to word and long cell sizes.

5.17. Write code that verifies that the sum of `n` values is the same if added forward or backward. The code should add `n` items of an integer array, first adding the cells in increasing position number, and then by decreasing position number.

PART III

THE MACHINE LANGUAGE MODEL

Structurally, machine language is very closely linked to assembly language. In fact, there is an almost one-to-one correspondence between the statements of assembly language and those of machine language. But, there are also clear differences. While the assembly language model was indeed closer to the machine than was the higher-level language model, it still is a model constructed with an eye toward the human user. Both the syntactic structure and use of mnemonic names in assembly language aid the human user. Machine language maintains the same logical structure as assembly language, but the representation is oriented toward the machine, not toward the human. It is even less ambiguous than assembly language—if that is possible. The individual fields of machine language instructions are compactly constructed according to very precise rules. It is possible to provide a rigorous description of the steps by which a computer interprets and executes machine language instructions. By studying the machine language model, we will gain our first insight into how a computer actually performs the operations as instructed by the human. Additionally, we will gain a better understanding of the assembler, compiler, and other software that processes the human-oriented source program, creating an object program that can be understood by the computer.

Chapter 6 investigates the relationship between machine language and the machine, illustrating concepts with examples from a generic language, GEML, and its equally generic machine, GEM. Like GAM and GAL of earlier chapters, GEM and GEML possess all of the properties of every machine and machine language but look like no specific existing machine. Once we see the internal representation of the commands we can finally ask what may be the central question of this text: "How does a computer process instructions?" Chapter 7 then investigates the software used to map the assembly language model onto the machine language model. This examination will reveal characteristics of assembly language that we have ignored to this point.

CHAPTER 6

THE MACHINE LANGUAGE MODEL

ARCHITECTURAL OVERVIEW

The machine language model resembles the assembly language model in both power and functionality. Similarly the GEneric Machine (GEM) used in the examples corresponds closely to the GAM machine used to explicate the assembly language model. Its hardware has the same logical substructures: CPU: ALU and control unit; memory: registers and RAM; and so on. It has the same capabilities: it can move, manipulate, and compare data items, and can control which instructions will be performed. The example machine language, GEML (GEneric Machine Language), contains instructions corresponding almost exactly to the legal instruction set of the GAL language: `add`, `compare`, `jump`, and so on. But it has two significant and immediately obvious differences:

- Its instruction set is machine, not human, oriented.
- It contains three additional registers:

  the *program counter*

  the *instruction register*

  the *systems stack pointer*

The most important (but not the most obvious) distinction between the models is that the internal workings of a machine can be inspected at the machine language model, both literally—by observation—and intellectually—by reasoning about how it must work. Because this structure is defined much more rigorously, or in more detail, than earlier abstractions, it enables the investigation of the details necessary to process a machine language (ml) instruction. This investigation provides an understanding not only of ml but also of ALs, and indeed of higher-level languages. When reading about ml constructs the reader should always consider the question, "What does this tell me about the AL model?" As the representation becomes more precise, it necessarily becomes more detailed. The detail provided in the text is designed to provide a uniform illustration of the concepts; to make them more concrete in a simple form.

The Fetch/Execute Cycle

As with the more abstract models, instructions are held in main memory. A program is a collection of such instructions, executed by the machine sequentially from first instruction to last. Although this process can be viewed in exactly the manner that we viewed execution of hll or AL code—each statement is executed sequentially, and so on—at the ml level, instructions can be examined more closely. For example, execution of each command actually requires several substeps. An endless loop of these substeps is known as the *fetch/execute cycle* (also called the machine cycle, execute cycle, instruction cycle, or instruction fetch cycle). Previous abstractions assumed that execution of an instruction was an atomic or primitive action—one that did not subdivide any further. The concept of the fetch/execute cycle distinguishes the ml model from the earlier abstractions, because it allows for dissection of single instructions. The general cycle is

```
while (forever) do
   1. fetch the instruction
   2. increment the program counter
   3. decode the instruction
   4. fetch the operands
   5. perform the operation
   6. store the results
```

This step-by-step breakdown seems to create more questions than answers, such as

1. Fetch the instruction.
   Where is the instruction?
   Why does it need to be fetched? Isn't it okay where it is?

How does the machine keep track of the location?
Where does it put the instruction it has just fetched?

2. Increment the program counter.
   What is the program counter?
   What does the program counter count?
   Increment by how much?
   Where does the program counter point now?
3. Decode the instruction.
   Why does the instruction need to be decoded?
   How does it get decoded?
4. Fetch the operands.
   What does it mean to fetch?
   Is this fetching distinct from the fetch in step 1?
   Where are the operands?
   How many are there?
   Where do we put them when we fetch them?
5. Perform the operation.
   Is this the central step?
   Couldn't the machine simply have done this part?
   What part of the machine performs the operation?
6. Store the results.
   Where from?
   Where to?

While (forever)
   Repeat from where?
   Is it really an infinite loop?
   Why or why not?
   How do these steps accomplish any instructions at all?

MACHINE LANGUAGE

The first source of answers to the above questions is in the machine language itself. Every machine language instruction contains all the information needed to perform a command: the operation specified, all the operands, the size of the operands, and additional information about the representation of the operand, such as the use of registers or RAM. AL commands contained the identical information. However, the syntax of AL commands is designed to be very readable by humans. The fields are explicit and easy for the human to view: operation and operands are separated. The syntax allows mnemonic names, comments, and so on, all of which helps create a relatively human oriented language. Comments and labels are distinctly human oriented. Ml commands, on the other hand, are represented in the form most readily accessible to the machine itself: a string of bits. The string is composed of several fields, of various sizes, each containing specific information about the command. For example, the GEML fields are from left (high-order) to right (low-order) bits:

field	bits	size
operation	31–28	4 bits
(unused)	27–26	2
size	25–24	2
mode	23–20	4
(unused)	19	1
register operand	18–16	3
RAM operand	15–0	16

for a total of 32 bits (4 bytes or one long word). The first observation to be made is that this representation is apparently very compact. In contrast, if the GAL instruction

```
add      loc⇒reg3
```

is thought of as a string of characters, it would require 12 (or more depending on the interpretation of white space, etc.) bytes. Any single field of a GAL instruction may have required four or more bytes. Chapter 4 explained that a given pattern of bits could be interpreted in many ways: signed or unsigned numbers, characters, etc. Ml simply adds one more interpretation: each field is interpreted as a partial description of the instruction. The general definitions of the fields follow.

Operation (Opcode)

The *operation code* or *opcode* identifies the particular operation—`copy`, `add`, `jump`, `return`, and so on—that is to be performed. Every AL operation has a unique opcode in ml. When the machine executes ml code, it determines the instruction by examining this field. In GEML, the field is four bits long and is therefore sufficient to represent $2^4 = 16$ distinct values, in this case, 16 possible instructions. Figure 6-1*a* contains the full list of GEML commands. From the figure, we see that the GAL command

```
add      loc⇒reg3
```

has the partial GEM equivalent

```
1000 ---- ---- ---- ---- ---- ---- ----
```

That is, the `add` command starts with 1000 and is followed by an additional 28 bits.

▷ *What are the differences between the GEML commands and the commands of GAL? How do the opcodes for the assembly language that you use contrast with the GEML instructions? What do these differences imply about your language?*

FIGURE 6-1*a-b*
GEML machine language instructions

(a) Nibble 7

GEML command		Mnemonic
Hex	**Binary**	
0	0000	`Halt`
1	0001	`Copy`
2	0010	`Load_address`
3	0011	`Trap`
4	0100	`Jump`
5	0101	`Compare`
6	0110	`Jump to Subroutine`
7	0111	`Return`
8	1000	`Add`
9	1001	`Subtract`
A	1010	`Multiply`
B	1011	`Divide`
C	1100	`And`
D	1101	`Or`
E	1110	`Not`
F	1111	`Rotate`

(b) Nibble: 6
Contents: size

Hex value	Binary	Interpretation
0	0000	`byte`
1	0001	`word [2 bytes]`
2	0010	`long word [4 bytes]`

Operands

REGISTER OPERAND. Each AL operation has associated with it, a specific number of explicit operands: two for an `add`, one for a `jump`, and none for a `return` from subroutine. GEML shares GAL's restriction that no more than one of the operands could be located in main memory. The machine takes advantage of this restriction by representing the two operands in different manners. The register operand field specifies the operand, if any, that is stored in a register. Since GEM has only eight registers, GEML can specify a register using only three (log (8)) bits (Figure 6-1*d*). Thus, three bits are reserved for this field. Filling in the register field for the above example gives:

```
1000 ---- ---- -011 ---- ---- ---- ----
```

FIGURE 6-1*c-e*
GEML Machine Language Instructions

(c) Nibble 5
Contents: operand mode

Mode mnemonic	Bit position	0 means
indirect	23	not indirect
immediate	22	not immediate
direction	21	register is destination
RAM	20	no RAM operands

		Interpretation			
Hex value	**Binary**	**Indirect?**	**Immediate?**	**Register operand is**	**# Ram operands**
0	0000	no	no	destination	0
1	0001	no	no	destination	1
2	0010	no	no	source	0
3	0011	no	no	source	1
4	0100	no	yes*	destination	0*
5	0101	no	yes	destination	1
6	0110	no	yes*	source*	0
7	0111	no	yes*	source*	1
8	1000	yes	no	destination	0
9	1001	yes	no	destination	1
A	1010	yes	no	source	0
B	1011	yes	no	source	1
C	1100	yes	yes*	destination	0*
D	1101	yes	yes	destination	1
E	1110	yes	yes*	source*	0
F	1111	yes	yes*	source*	1

* = incompatible/impossible combinations

(d) Nibble: 4
Contents: register operand

Hex value	Binary	Interpretation
0	000	reg0
1	001	reg1
2	010	reg2
3	011	reg3
4	100	reg4
5	101	reg5
6	110	reg6
7	111	reg7

(e) Nibbles 3–0
Register operand address

(16 bit absolute address)

RAM. There are many more RAM locations than register locations. GEM's operand field is 16 bits long, which is sufficient to identify $2^{16} = 65,536 = 64K$ possible storage locations (numbered 0 to 65,535). Apparently that is the number of possible RAM storage locations in GEM. The description of the GAL assembly language suggested that it is more difficult to identify one object out of many than it is to identify one out of a few. This distinction has a direct impact on GEML: over five times as many bits are required to represent a RAM operand address than a register address. This explains one important reason why GAL and GEM allow only a single RAM operand: 32 bits would be needed just to represent the operands if two RAM operands were allowed. Continuing the example, suppose that `loc` was assigned the address 123_{16}. The RAM address field can now be completed:

```
1000 ---- ---- -011 0000 0001 0010 0011
```

▷ *Convince yourself that the representation of the address is correct. How might the address be selected?*

In some cases, an instruction may not have any operand located in RAM: both operands are in registers or the operation has only a single operand. In such cases the RAM operand field may be used in other ways, as described later in this section.

Size

The size field indicates the size of the operands for the instruction: byte, word, or long word. In GAL, some instructions such as `add`, had a default type. Others such as `copy` and `compare` required an explicit indication of the type of the operands (character or integer), which in turn dictated the size as byte or word. Every ml instruction must explicitly specify the length—not the type—of its operands. The two operands of an operation will generally be the same size. It is not clear what it would mean to compare an eight-bit number to a 16-bit number. In GEML, the size field indicates the number of bytes in each operand (expressed as a power of 2):

Value		Length						
00	⇒	2^0	=	1 byte				
01	⇒	2^1	=	2 bytes	=	1 word		
10	⇒	2^2	=	4 bytes	=	2 word	=	1 long word.

The default type of the GAL `add` instruction was integer, which requires two bytes. Thus, two more bit of the example can be completed:

```
1000 --01 ---- -011 0000 0001 0010 0011
```

▷ *Of the four possible bit combinations, size uses only three. What interpretations are possible for the missing combination?*

The size field of GEML instructions provides some insight into the nature of GAL instructions. First, GAL included the implicit assumption that each type had an inherent length: one byte for characters and two for integers. GEM, like other machine languages, does not concern itself with the type, only the size required for the type. The size must be explicitly encoded in every GEM instruction; there are no defaults (any bit necessarily holds some value). This in turn dictates that each GAL instruction actually requires a type—perhaps by default. At first it may seem odd to specify the length of the `add` instruction in ml. After all, `add` must add two integers, which each require one word of storage. However, we are not restricted to that narrow definition of addition. Addition of bytes or long words is also possible. Although seemingly odd, this is actually a useful concept. A byte can hold 256 distinct values. Therefore, if it was known that only small numbers were to be added (for example, a counter used as an index for 20 iterations of a loop), single-byte additions could be used, with a resulting saving in storage (and perhaps time). At the other extreme, two-byte integers can only represent numbers up to 64K. This would clearly be unsatisfactory for the census bureau, charged with keeping track of the population of the United States. Four-byte integers could hold numbers up to 2^{32} or about 4 billion, which would be much more practical.

Mode

Mode is the most complex and interesting of the fields. It is actually a collection of details describing the interpretation of the operation and its operands. For each operation, the mode field specifies characteristics of the operands such as type of memory (RAM or register), use of indirect references, or presence of immediate values. This field will vary from machine to machine more than any other. The conceptual details represented in the mode field are present in any given AL instruction but may not be explicitly stated as were the name of the operand and the operands. Each of the bits in the mode field of a GEML instruction specifies a given characteristic of the instruction.

OPERAND MEMORY TYPE. Like GAM, GEM requires that no more than one operand be located in RAM. For two-operand instructions, this leaves two possible combinations:

- one operand is in RAM and one is in a register, or
- both operands are in registers.

The GEML memory type bit indicates the number of operands located in RAM, either 0 or 1. The remaining operands must be in registers. Thus,

RAM (bit 20): number of the operands stored in main memory
0: if both source and destination are in registers
1: if one operand is in memory

Since the example,

```
add     loc⇒reg3
```

involved a RAM operand, the bit must be a one, giving

```
1000 --01 ---1 -011 0000 0001 0010 0011
```

A command to add two registers would have a zero in that bit, generating an interesting question: how are the operands of an instruction with two register operands specified? The answer is that one register is represented in the RAM address field. The RAM operand field contains more than enough bits to represent any register, but not vice versa.

DIRECTION. The direction bit distinguishes the source and destination operands. The distinction between

```
add     reg2⇒somewhere
```

and

```
add     somewhere⇒reg2
```

is that the first adds a register source to a RAM destination (changes RAM), and the second adds a RAM source to a register destination (changes the register). Since each GEML instruction has distinct register and RAM fields, the direction bit can uniquely specify the interpretation of each as source or destination:

Direction (bit 21): direction of operation relative to the memory types
0: register operand represents the destination.
1: register operand represents the source.

In the example, the destination, `reg3`, is a register. Thus, the direction bit contains a 0

```
1000 --01 --01 -011 0000 0001 0010 0011
```

If the command had been

```
add     reg3⇒loc,
```

bit 21 would be a 1. The direction bit is meaningful even if both operands are registers. In that case, it specifies which of the two registers is the destination. For purposes of the direction bit, the operand encoded within the RAM field is treated as if it were a RAM operand, even if it is a register.

IMMEDIATE. The next bit indicates the presence of immediate data. Recall that in GAL, literal data is indicated by the symbol # preceding the operand. In GEML the immediate data itself is physically stored within the RAM operand field.

Immediate (bit 22): form of a RAM operand
0: if the RAM operand specifies a memory address
1: if the operand represents immediate data.

Since the example

```
add    loc⇒reg3,
```

does not have an immediate operand, the immediate field is a 0, yielding

```
1000 --01 -001 -011 0000 0001 0010 0011
```

An immediate operand follows the body of the instruction *immediately,* hence its name. For example,

```
add    #h123⇒reg3
```

is only slightly different from the above example:

```
1000 --01 -101 -011 0000 0001 0010 0011
```

INDIRECT ADDRESSING. The last mode bit is used to specify that a register operand contains not the data but a pointer to the actual operand. Chapter 5 described such indirect address pointers and their use, indicated in GAL by an up-arrow: ↑ .

Indirect (bit 23): register addressing mode
0: the register operand contains an actual value
1: the register operand is an address (indirect) pointer to the actual data.

Since there is only one such bit in GEML, it apparently applies only to the register operand. If there are two register operands, the indirect bit refers to the operand stored in the register field (the one not stored in the RAM field). GEM does not allow two indirect operands. The example,

```
add    loc⇒reg3,
```

does not use indirect addressing. Therefore the bit is zero:

```
1000 --01 0001 -011 0000 0001 0010 0011
```

If the instruction had been

```
add     loc⇒reg3↑
```

meaning add the contents of `loc` to the location to which `reg3` points, the representation would be

```
1000 --01 1001 -011 0000 0001 0010 0011.
```

Notice that such an instruction specifies the addition of two RAM operands: one specified by an address contained in the instruction itself, and one pointed to by a register. But the GAL language did not allow two RAM operands. Apparently, the restriction on the number of RAM operands is really a restriction on the number of RAM addresses that can be *specified* within an instruction, not on the number of RAM operands that can be *accessed*.

The remaining three bits are not used (perhaps they are reserved for future use) and are normally set to zero. The full representation of the `add` example is

```
1000 0001 0001 0011 0000 0001 0010 0011
```

which can be abbreviated using hexadecimal as

```
81 13 01 23.
```

For purposes of describing machine language instructions, the more compact hex notation is generally used, rather than the longer binary representation. Programmers soon become comfortable making the translations as needed. (The mode is summarized in Figure 6-1*c*.)

Some Examples

Examination of a few variations on the previous example will help convince the reader that any AL command has a ml equivalent. Each of the following examples differs from the original example in exactly one field:

```
    add          #H123⇒reg3     ;immediate operands
is  1000 0001 0101 0011 0000 0001 0010 0011 = 81 53 01 23

    add          reg3⇒loc       ;RAM destination
is  1000 0001 0011 0011 0000 0001 0010 0011 = 81 33 01 23

    add:byte     loc⇒reg3       ;short operands
is  1000 0000 0001 0011 0000 0001 0010 0011 = 80 13 01 23

    add          reg1⇒reg3      ;two register operands
is  1000 0001 0000 0011 0000 0000 0000 0001 = 81 03 00 01.
```

and

```
    subtract    loc⇒reg3   ;different opcode:subtract
is  10010001 0001 0011 0000 0001 0010 0011 = 91 13 01 23.
```

In GEM and most mls, the meaning of each field is almost identical to that of the corresponding field of the AL. For most commands, the operation and operand fields correspond exactly. The size field appeared explicitly in some GAL instructions, such as `copy`, but was implicit in others, such as `add`, which assumed by default that the operands would be integers (and therefore two bytes). Information equivalent to the mode is also present in GAL but is indicated by the syntax, rather than contained in its own field: the operand identifier implicitly indicated whether it was a register (`regn`) or was located in RAM. A # sign indicated an immediate value. Direction is determined by the order in which the operands are specified, and so on. In fact, machine language commands actually correspond very closely to assembly language commands: every machine language command corresponds to a unique assembly language command and (almost) vice versa. Each syntactic subpart of an assembly language command is represented by some portion of the machine language command. The order may differ and certainly the appearance will differ. But the correspondence is always present. Further reflection suggests that there may be more possibilities in ml than there are in AL. Some of these new possibilities represent true extensions, such as addition with single-byte operands. Others are excluded as meaningless. For example, the GEML instruction

```
0001 0001 0111 0011 0000 0000 0000 0101
```

would correspond to the meaningless GAL instruction

```
copy         reg3⇒#5
```

In general, the exact behavior of meaningless instructions is unpredictable. There are two possible behaviors. Most machines will not process instructions that are meaningless, even if the syntax appears to allow it. When such instructions are detected, they will generate an "illegal instruction" message and halt. Others may not even check a bit that could lead to meaningless results. In the previous example, once GEM has determined that the destination specifies a RAM operand, it may not check the immediate bit since an immediate value would be meaningless. While the assembler (Chapter 7) can perform such checking when it converts a AL program to ml, there is little reason for the machine to check such details every time it executes an instruction.

Some meaningful instructions do not seem to fit the general format specified above. Generally, this means that some of the fields are left empty (zero). For example, an operation involving two register operands, uses the RAM address to specify the second register. Thus, the first 13 bits of the address field will be unused. For example,

```
add          reg1⇒reg2
```

is represented as

```
1000 0001 0000 0001 0000 0000 0000 0010 = 81 01 00 02.
```

In other assembly languages the format of instructions may vary with the amount of space required for the operand. We will ignore that complication for the moment. In general, GAL and other languages may use the available space in different manners for different operations.

The GAL `jump` instruction does not specify a register operand, but it does require a test, or value, resulting from a comparison. Note that there are actually three logically possible results of a comparison:

`<operand 1>`	is equal to	`<operand 2>`
`<operand 1>`	is greater than	`<operand 2>`
`<operand 1>`	is less than	`<operand 2>`.

The three bits normally used to specify a register can be used to specify the conditions under which a jump will be made. GEML uses the three register bits to specify the above three conditions: a one in a given position means a jump should be made if that condition holds. Thus:

bit pattern	**jump on condition**
001	less than
010	greater than
011	not equal (less than or greater than)
100	equal
101	less than or equal
110	greater than or equal
111	always (equal or greater than or less than)

The last pattern above deserves some special attention. The pattern 111 means

```
jump if ((less than) or (greater than) or equal)
```

A little reflection shows that those are the only possible conditions. Thus, the jump always is accomplished by specifying all possible conditions. Some machines have distinct instructions for `jump` always and `jump` conditionally. The perceptive reader may have noticed that there is yet one more possible bit pattern: "000". But that pattern must mean to jump if the comparison yielded a value that was

```
(not equal) and (not greater than) and (not less than)
```

That is, the pattern specifies that the instruction should "never jump," or more explicitly, it should "do nothing." Such an operation is called a *no-op* (no operation). Many languages have an explicit `no-op` instruction. GEM programmers may simply use this "never jump" instruction to accomplish the same purpose.

> ▷ *What possible need would a programmer have for a "do-nothing" instruction?*

The reader should attempt to write GEML commands equivalent to many of the GAL commands until convinced that the conversion is always possible. For example, try all the possible `subtract` commands or the variations on `jump`. It should be equally possible to perform most of the same conversions in a "real" assembly language (but beware, the correspondence is not always as obvious).

Implications for Real Machine Languages

Compared to "real machines," GEML is actually relatively easy to read. There are five fields: operation, size, mode, and two operands. The first four of these are each contained in single nibbles. In a hexadecimal representation this means that each of the first four hex digits represents a single field and the last four digits indicate the RAM operand. Other languages may not be so easy to read. The fields may overlap nibble—and therefore hex digit—boundaries. Different instructions may even have different field definitions: they may vary in number of fields, size of fields, and interpretation of fields. Any given machine language will have its own specific syntax. Every instruction will always contain enough information to be unambiguous, even out of context. Variations are possible in attributes such as the manner in which immediate or indirect operands are represented, the size and direction are specified, and so on. A given machine may have capabilities that vary slightly from those of GEM, but GEM's syntax includes most of the kinds of information available on most machines. For example, small machines may only allow operands of one or two bytes. Some larger machines allow eight-byte operations. Some machines allow multiple RAM operands for some instructions, some do not have immediate values, and so on.

While GEM's instruction set is representative of many (or most) real machines, and many of its restrictions are characteristic of real machines, some of the restrictions are artifacts of GEM itself. For example, GEM allows no more than one indirect operand. Many real machines do allow two such operands. The structure of GEML simply did not provide a mechanism for representing that situation.

> ▷ *What basic definitional characteristic of GEML must be changed to allow two RAM operands? Which other restrictions could just as easily have been removed?*

In some real languages, not all instructions have the same length. The order of the fields differs from GEML—and may even differ within the specific language. Specific restrictions on the fields may differ; there may be more operations, more registers, more modes, etc. The mode fields may even combine in different ways. For example, the direction bit is often implicit in other fields of the command: explicit source and destination fields may be used rather than register and RAM operands with direction.

> ▷ *How can a field be located in different positions for different commands?*

ARCHITECTURE: STORAGE AND COMMUNICATION

Registers

As we have seen, GEM uses a six-step fetch/execute cycle to interpret and process each instruction. To accomplish the above steps, it incorporates three additional special-purpose registers:

- the *program counter* (PC)
- the *instruction register* (IR)
- the system *stack pointer* register (SP)

as well as the previously mentioned

- *condition code* register (CCR)

and three "hidden" operand registers, which are not accessed explicitly by GEML commands but are necessary to describe the fetch/execute cycle:

> `source_1`
> `source_2`
> the `result` register

These registers are instrumental in answering the questions asked at the beginning of the chapter. Although all of these special purpose registers are in fact registers, they are not normally accessed in the same way as the general purpose registers we have previously encountered. Generally, the programmer will never explicitly use any of these registers as an operand in any instruction. But they will be used implicitly by every instruction that is executed. The first two of these special-purpose registers—the program counter and the instruction register—are particularly important for understanding the fetch/execute process by which the processor executes the ml instructions. Their use is fundamental in every cycle. You have seen the next two registers—the condition code and stack-pointer registers—briefly in Chapter 5. They are essential for controlling the execution of the program and will be examined here in more detail. While the first four registers are almost universal, the last three hidden registers, which provide temporary storage during execution of a single fetch/execute cycle, are idiosyncratic of GEM.

PROGRAM COUNTER. The *program counter* (*PC*)[1] serves as a pointer to the current instruction. It contains the address of the first byte of that instruction. If there are 64K bytes in memory, the `PC` must be 16 bits long. At the beginning of execution of a program, the `PC` is set to the address of the first instruction in that program. As each instruction is executed, the `PC` is incremented to point to the following instruction. Since GEML instructions are 32 bits long, the `PC` will normally be incremented by four after each instruction.

> ▷ *How might the PC receive its initial value? What other restrictions and interactions exist between the size of the machine and the size of operand fields? Why increment the PC by four rather than 32?*

INSTRUCTION REGISTER. The *instruction register* contains a copy of the current instruction, copied from main memory. Recall that each instruction is a series of bits containing the coded information: opcode, operands, size, and mode. As such, it can be copied from memory to a register. Since GEM instructions are 32 bits long, its instruction register must also be 32 bits long.

OTHER REGISTERS. The `source` registers hold the operands after they have been fetched, and the `result` register holds the result until it can be stored in its ultimate destination. Each of these registers must be large enough to hold the operand, which can be 8, 16, or 32 bits. Since any of the three operand sizes could be stored in a 32-bit register, these registers each have 32 bits in GEM.

---

[1]Note that the term *PC,* meaning *program counter,* is much older than any personal computer.

The Bus

All the registers are connected through an internal communication channel called the *bus* (or internal bus),[2] which serves as a conduit for passing information from one register to another. The bus greatly simplifies the total construction of the CPU. Without such a central information conduit, a very large number of register-to-register connections would be required. Suppose some machine has a total of eight registers, and that at some point the content of any single register may need to be copied to any other register. The first register would need seven lines to connect it to each of the other seven registers. The second would need an additional six lines (it is already connected to the first, so that line need not be reconnected), and so on (see Figure 6-2*a*). In general an n-register machine requires

$$(n - 1) + (n - 2) + \cdots + 1 = \frac{(n - 1) * n}{2}$$

separate lines: 28 in the case of the eight-register example. If instead there is a common path to which all registers are connected, only n distinct connections are needed. A telephone system provides a simple analogy. If every phone needed to be connected to every other phone, many more distinct lines would be needed (1000 phones would require some 500,000 lines). With a central telephone office, each phone need only be connected to that central office (1000 lines). Of course, some additional means will be needed to connect an incoming call to the right outgoing line (see Chapter 9). Figure 6-2*b* illustrates the improvement.

An Expanded Fetch/Execute Cycle

Many of the original questions about the fetch/execute cycle can now be answered, and the cycle can be described in more detail.

1. *Fetch the instruction.* All the instructions making up any program have been stored in RAM memory. The current instruction is fetched from its RAM location and copied into the instruction register, where it can be examined (recall that registers are much faster than main memory). The program counter contains the address of the instruction and thus serves as a pointer (a in Figure 6-3) to that instruction. The processor looks first at the `PC` to obtain the address of the next instruction. It then looks in RAM—using the `PC` as a pointer to find the appropriate address—and copies the content to the instruction register (b in the figure). The process by which the data is copied from RAM to a register will be expanded in Chapter 10.

   ▷ *Compare the concept of copying the instruction into the* `IR` *with that of executing a* `copy` *instruction. What is the relationship between the use of the* `PC` *as a pointer to an instruction and the use of a register as a pointer to an array location?*

---

[2]The internal bus is distinct from external system or memory buses, which you may be familiar with. The former is for communication only between the internal subparts of the CPU. The latter is used for communication with memory or with external devices such as disk drives.

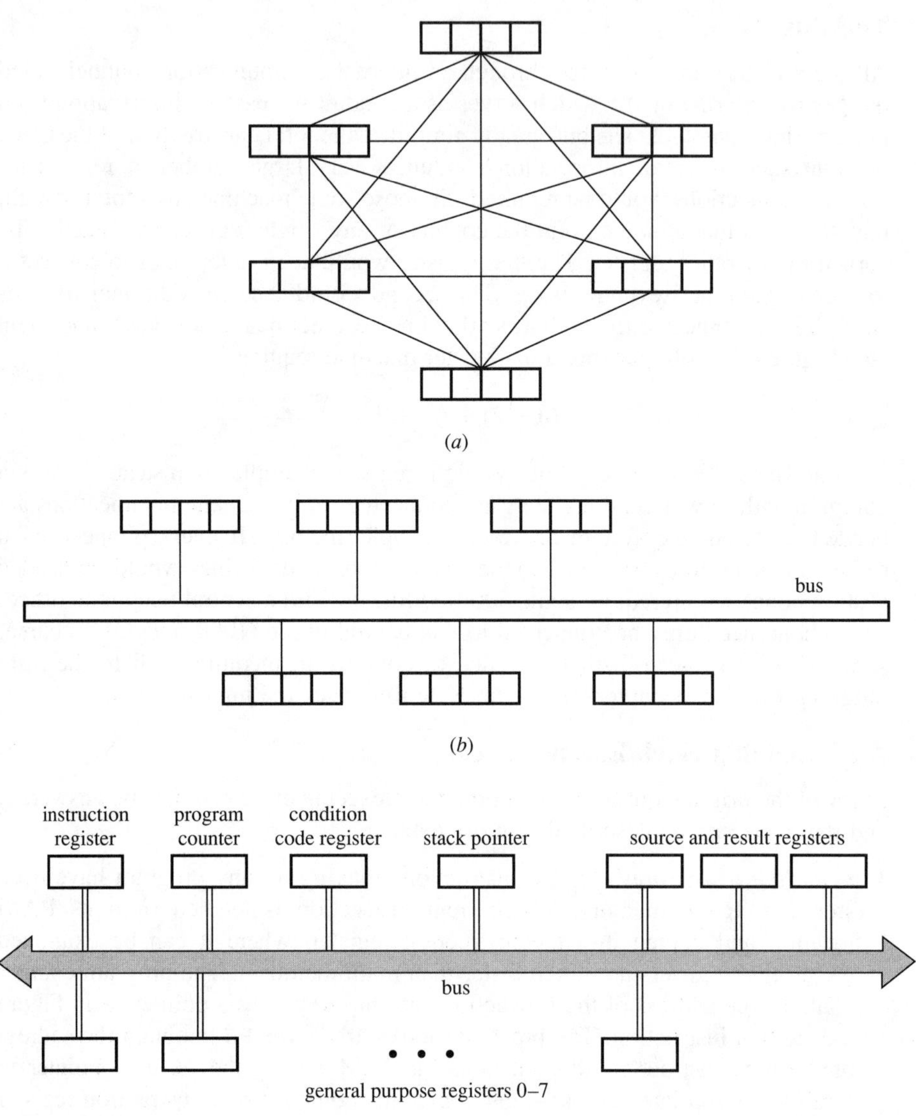

FIGURE 6-2
Connecting registers. (a) first step without a bus (b) first step with an internal bus (c) GEM's registers and bus

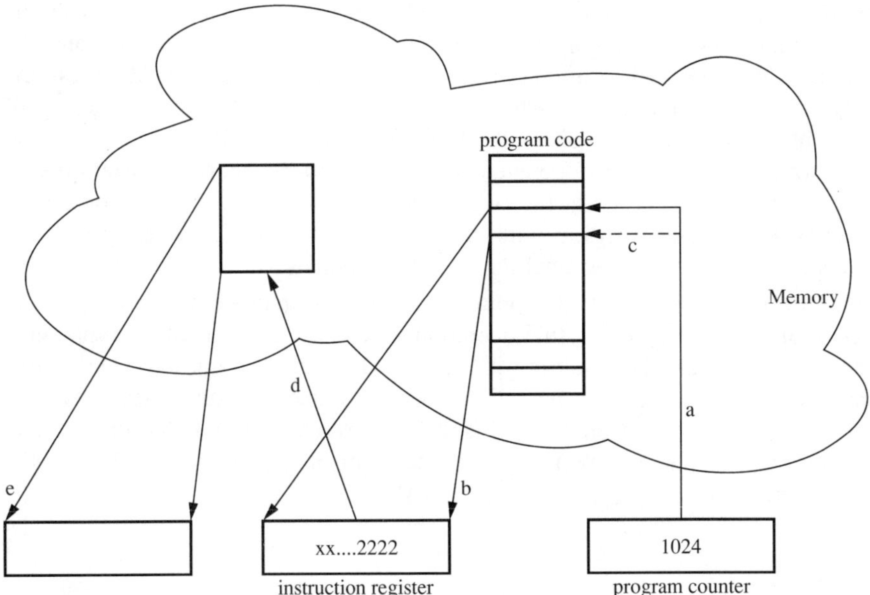

FIGURE 6-3
Program counter as pointer to memory

2. *Increment the PC*. The `PC` always acts as a pointer to the instruction. After each instruction has been fetched, the `PC` must be made to point to the *next* instruction. Fortunately, the instructions are usually stored in the order of execution, so the address of the next instruction may be calculated easily. The `PC` is incremented by the size of a single instruction—in the case of GEM, the length of each instruction is four. The updated `PC` will then point at the next instruction (`c`).

3. *Decode the instruction*. The operation or opcode field of each instruction uniquely identifies that instruction. The mode field also provides specifics of the particular instruction. By looking at these fields for the instruction now held in the instruction register, the machine determines what specific actions need to be performed in the remaining steps. In GEM, this means the leftmost four bits of the GEML instruction are examined to determine the operation and the mode bits are examined to determine the nature of the operands.

4. *Fetch the operands*. To perform an operation, the operands must be readily available. The body of the instruction specifies where these operands are presently stored: the mode indicates if the operands are stored in a register, a RAM location, or as immediate data within the instruction; the RAM or register operand field specifies which register or RAM location. At this step, GEM copies each operand from its present location into the two `source` registers. If the operands are in registers, the fetch is very simple: the operands are copied through the bus from the specified general purpose register to the appropriate source register. In the case of RAM operands, the data must be copied from

RAM to a source register (e in Figure 6-3) in much the same manner as the instruction was copied from memory: the address is sent to memory and the value in the specified location is returned. The address for a RAM operand is part of the instruction and is therefore held in the IR (d). In the majority of commands, there are two operands. In GEM, one is copied to source_1 and one to source_2. Both operands are copied into the source registers one at a time via the bus. Clearly the two values must be sent separately otherwise their values would interfere with each other. Thus, step four really has two substeps corresponding to fetching the two operands.

5. *Perform the operation*. At this point, all needed operands have been copied to the source registers. The actual operation specified by the instruction may now be performed, and the result left in the result register. Figure 6-4 shows this step schematically. It may be a little surprising that this step represents such a small portion of the total workload. The perform step is determined solely by the opcode and is independent of the form of the operands. That is, the "perform" steps of

```
        add     #5⇒reg2
        add     loc⇒reg1
        add     reg2⇒reg1
and     add     reg3⇒loc
```

are all identical. The fact that operands were originally stored in different forms of memory, and accessed through various modes is irrelevant. In fact, this is the only step of the cycle that is unique to a particular operation.

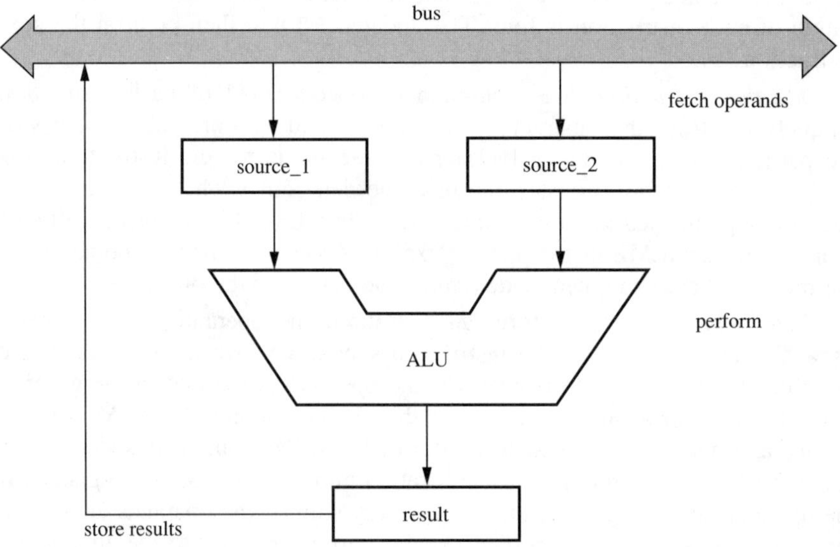

FIGURE 6-4
Path through ALU

6. *Store the results.* The operation result is now in the `result` register, but it must be copied to the location specified by the destination operand of the instruction. Fortunately, that address is still identified by the `IR` and is therefore readily available (normally it is the same as one of the operands). The result is copied through the bus either to the appropriate register or into RAM — whichever is specified by the mode.
7. *Loop.* The body really does proceed essentially forever. If the loop stops, execution of all code stops. Thus, the loop is an endless loop as long as the computer is executing.

A DETAILED EXAMPLE. Suppose at some point, the registers and RAM have the contents shown in Figure 6-5 (initial state). RAM locations starting at 1000_{16} contain instructions, the first of which adds the contents of loc 3210 to register 2. Location 3210 contains an integer 1, register 2 contains a 3, and the `PC` presently points to the instruction at location 1000_{16}. (Only relevant RAM and register content is shown.)

FIGURE 6-5
Add.

Initial state

			CPU registers		
PC	=	1000	Reg0	=	
IR	=		Reg1	=	
source_1	=		Reg2	=	0000 0003
source_2	=		Reg3	=	
Result	=				

RAM contents

address	contents	note
...		
1000	8211 3210	;add:integer loc⇒Reg2
1004	5152 0000	;compare:int #0⇒reg2
...		
3210	0001	
3212		

Step 1: fetch the instruction

			CPU registers		
PC	=	0000 1000	Reg0	=	
IR	=	**8211 3210**	Reg1	=	
source_1	=		Reg2	=	0000 0003
source_2	=		Reg3	=	
Result	=				

Step 2: increment the PC

			CPU registers		
PC	=	**0000 1004**	Reg0	=	
IR	=	8211 3210	Reg1	=	
source_1	=		Reg2	=	0000 0003
source_2	=		Reg3	=	
Result	=				

(continued)

FIGURE 6-5
(continued)

Step 3: decode the instruction (no changes)

Step 4: fetch the operands

			CPU registers		
PC	=	0000 1004	Reg0	=	
IR	=	8211 3210	Reg1	=	
source_1	=	**0000 0001**	Reg2	=	0000 0003
source_2	=	**0000 0003**	Reg3	=	
Result	=				

Step 5: perform the operation

			CPU registers		
PC	=	1004	Reg0	=	
IR	=	8211 3210	Reg1	=	
source_1	=	0000 0001	Reg2	=	0000 0003
source_2	=	0000 0003	Reg3	=	
Result	=	**0000 0004**			

Step 6: store the results

			CPU registers		
PC	=	0000 1004	Reg0	=	
IR	=	8211 3210	Reg1	=	
source_1	=	0000 0001	Reg2	=	**0000 0004**
source_2	=	0000 0003	Reg3	=	
Result	=	0000 0004			

RAM contents (unchanged)

address	contents	note
...		
1000	8112 3210	;add:integer loc⇒Reg2
1004	5152 0000	;compare:int #0⇒reg2
...		
3210	0001	
3212		

1. *Fetch the instruction*. All the instructions are stored in RAM memory, but only one can fit in the instruction register at a time. The program counter contains the address of the needed instruction: `1000`. At step 1, the instruction `8112 3210`, located at location 1000, is copied into the `IR`. Note that nothing else is changed; neither the contents of location 1000 nor the `PC` is altered. The instruction is *copied,* not removed from the location. The process can be described formally in a sort of pseudo GAL[3]:

```
*copy     pc↑⇒IR
```

[3]Pseudo-GAL is used only to make the process more explicit. It is not intended to imply that each command is made up of a series of assembly language commands. The "*" in front of each command serves as a reminder that it is not actually GAL code. Chapter 15 provides an interesting alternative interpretation of the substeps

GEML instructions are four bytes long. Therefore, four bytes—locations 1000 to 1003—are copied into the instruction register.

> ▷ *Why is it essential that the instruction be copied and not moved in this step?*

2. *Increment the program counter.* The next instruction must start at the next possible location 1004. Thus, the program counter is incremented by 4 to 1004. The `PC` no longer points to the current instruction, but to the next instruction (`compare` in this case). This does not cause a problem since the `PC` has already served its purpose for the current instruction: the contents have been copied into the instruction register.

> ▷ *Debuggers normally indicate the next, rather than the current, instruction. What is the relationship between that and the timing of the increment step? Are there situations in which it may be undesirable to increment the* `PC` *before executing the instruction?*

To increment the `PC`, it is necessary to perform an addition. The same adder ALU that is used for `add` instructions could be used for this purpose. The `PC` must be sent to one source register, and the integer 4 to the other. The adder then generates the sum and leaves it in the result register. Finally the value is copied back to the `PC`. The entire process could be described in a pseudo-GAL:

```
*copy     pc⇒source_1
*copy     #4⇒source_2
*add      ;source_1 & 2 are the implicit operands
*copy     result⇒pc
```

3. *Decode the instruction.* Since the `IR` contains the entire instruction, it contains the opcode: $8_{16} = 1000_2 =$ `add` in the leftmost (7th) nibble (4 bits). The processor examines that nibble to determine that the instruction is an `add`. The 1 in the next (6th) nibble indicates that the operands are of length two bytes. GEM knows the number of operands from the definition of addition. The 5th nibble contains the mode, indicating that one operand is in RAM and one in a register.
4. *Fetch the operands.* There are two operands to fetch. The first, or source, is located in RAM at address 3210. The address is contained in the instruction, but the operand itself is in RAM. At this point GEM fetches the first operand, 0001, from location 3210 and places it in the `source_1` register. Fetching the operand from RAM is essentially the same as fetching the instruction in step 1, except that (1) the result is placed in a source register rather than the instruction register, and (2) the address from which the fetch is to be made is held in the low-order 16 bits of the `IR` rather than the `PC`. The instruction also specifies that the destination operand is

located in register 2. The contents of the register 2 are then copied to the source_2 register. The length of the operands was two bytes so the source registers are padded with zeros on the left. The pseudo-GAL might look like this:

```
*copy   3210⇒source_1    ;3210 is address, not a value
*copy   reg2⇒source_2
```

5. *Perform*. The current instruction is an add. Its operands have already been placed in the two source registers. The adder ALU can now perform its task: adding the contents of its two source registers and leaving the sum in the result register.

```
*add    ;source_1 and source_2, the implicit operands
```

6. *Store the results*. The contents of the result register, 4, are then copied into the destination. In the add command, the destination is also one of the input operands, reg2. The contents of the destination will be irrevocably altered.

```
*copy   result⇒reg2
```

7. *Loop*. The above steps repeat endlessly, with one small—but all-important—difference: the PC now contains 1004. Thus, when step 1 is executed again, the compare instruction stored at location 1004 will be loaded into the IR rather than the add. The PC will be incremented to 1008. The compare will be decoded, and so on.

IMPLICATIONS FOR OTHER INSTRUCTIONS

Data Manipulation Instructions

VARIATIONS ON ADD. Virtually every ml instruction is executed in exactly the same manner. It is relatively easy to imagine most distinctions. For example, the add instruction may involve operands of different sizes:

```
add:long      loc⇒reg2
```

which would be stored internally as

```
8212 3210
```

This instruction differs from the previous example only in the size bit. The only difference in the fetch//execute cycle is in the fetch-operand and store-result steps, which move four bytes rather than two. In pseudo-GAL,

```
*copy:long   result⇒reg2
```

Similarly, if the operand size had been one, only one byte would be moved. All other steps are identical to the above example. If the operands are of other forms, they are fetched and stored from alternative locations. For example, to process

```
add:int        reg2⇒loc
```

the operands would be fetched in the reverse order, placing the contents of register 2 in the `source_1` register and ultimately storing the result in `loc`.

If the source operand is immediate:

```
add            #1⇒reg2
```

the operand is loaded directly from the operand field of the IR. In pseudo-GAL,

```
*copy:word     ir⇒source_1
```

There is no need for a second fetch from memory, since the operand has already been copied into the `IR`.

▷ *Does this have further implications on the name of the mode "immediate"?*

OTHER DATA MANIPULATION COMMANDS. All data manipulation instructions, such as `add`, `subtract`, `and`, `or`, behave in exactly the same manner. The only step that distinguishes a `subtract` from an `add` is the perform step. The command

```
subtract       loc⇒reg2
```

differs from the original example only in the opcode:

```
9211 3210
```

The machine decodes the opcode as `subtract`, but the fetch/execute loop will differ only in the perform step; the incrementing of the `PC`, fetching of operands, and storing of results are all identical.

▷ *Are there instructions for which the process does not seem to work?*

Data Movement

COPY. Although the processing of every instruction uses exactly the same fetch/execute cycle, some instructions, such as `copy`, apparently involve one or more degenerate steps. In the case of `copy` all steps proceed in an analogous manner through the fetching of operands. Notice that although there are two operands, only one—the source—has a significant value at this point. By definition, there is some value in the destination, but it is not used. In fact, whatever that value is, it is about to be destroyed. The contents of the destination need not be fetched. Additionally, there will be very little to "perform": the source is simply copied to the result register. The fetch/execute cycle for `copy` can be thought of as follows:

1. Fetch the instruction: copy it into the `IR`.
2. Increment the `PC`, by adding 4 to its current value.
3. Decode the instruction (determine it is a `COPY`).
4. Fetch the source operand into the `source_1` register (note that the destination operand is not fetched).
5. Perform: copy the `source_1` register (which now contains a copy of the source operand) into the `result` register.
6. Store the result register into the destination location, specified by the destination field of the current instruction in the `IR`.

It is logically possible to shortcut this step by copying directly from the source register to the destination. The description above maintains a consistency of description across all operations.

> ▷ *In a later chapter we will see that such a shortcut probably will not result in any actual savings or speed up. Can you figure out why?*

Some machines have distinct operations, `load` and `store`, for copying from RAM to register and vice versa. In GEML, the instructions differ only in the direction bit of the mode field. The other forms of data movement, input, and output, are accomplished by means of subroutine calls and therefore will be covered after the discussion of control operations.

LOAD_ADDRESS. `Load_address` is unusually interesting. Like all commands, `load_address` must explicitly contain the address of the source operand. But that address is exactly the value that is to be loaded into the register. Thus, the execution of `load_address` starts out exactly like `copy`. When the operand is to be fetched, the address itself is simply loaded into the source register:

Step 4. Fetch the operands: copy address from `IR` to `source_1`.
Step 5. Perform: copy from `source_1` to `result`.
Step 6. Store: copy from `result` to the specified register.

> ▷ *At first glance, it may appear that this command could be accomplished as if it were a copy-immediate instruction. But ponder this question: how was the address determined?*

Control Operations

JUMP. The `jump` instruction is a control instruction and therefore seems to be quite different from data manipulation instructions such as `add`. However, jumps are accomplished using exactly the same fetch/execute cycle. The `jump` instruction alters the `PC` to achieve the jump action. Consider, first, the absolute or unconditional `jump`:

```
jump:always     →somewhere.
```

Suppose the `jump` instruction is contained at location 2000_{16}, and that `somewhere` is located at 3456_{16}. Assuming that the `PC` started out at 2000, the actions taken at each step of the cycle (shown in Figure 6-6) are

1. Fetch instruction. The `jump` instruction is copied from location 2000 to the `IR`.
2. Increment the `PC`. As with any other instruction, the `PC` now points at the next instruction, at 2004: exactly the instruction that would be executed if there were no `jump`; the instruction that *should not* be executed next.

FIGURE 6-6
Jump

Initial state

			CPU registers	
PC	=	0000 2000	Reg0	=
IR	=		Reg1	=
source_1	=		Reg2	=
source_2	=		Reg3	=
Result	=			

RAM contents

address	contents	note
...		
2000	4017 3456	;jump:always→somewhere
2004	5241 0000	;some next instruction
...		
3456	...	;somewhere

Step 1: fetch instruction

			CPU registers	
PC	=	0000 2000	Reg0	=
IR	=	**4017 3456**	Reg1	=
source_1	=		Reg2	=
source_2	=		Reg3	=
Result	=			

Step 2: increment PC

			CPU registers	
PC	=	**0000 2004**	Reg0	=
IR	=	4017 3456	Reg1	=
source_1	=		Reg2	=
source_2	=		Reg3	=
Result	=			

(continued)

FIGURE 6-6
(continued)

Step 4: fetch operands

			CPU registers	
`PC`	=	0000 2004	`Reg0`	=
`IR`	=	4017 3456	`Reg1`	=
`source_1`	=		`Reg2`	=
`source_2`	=	**0000 3456**	`Reg3`	=
`Result`	=			

Step 5: perform operation

			CPU registers	
`PC`	=	0000 2004	`Reg0`	=
`IR`	=	4017 3456	`Reg1`	=
`source_1`	=		`Reg2`	=
`source_2`	=	0000 3456	`Reg3`	=
`Result`	=	**0000 3456**		

Step 6: store results

			CPU registers	
`PC`	=	**0000 3456**	`Reg0`	=
`IR`	=	4017 3456	`Reg1`	=
`source_1`	=		`Reg2`	=
`source_2`	=	0000 3456	`Reg3`	=
`Result`	=	0000 3456		

RAM contents (unchanged)

address	contents	note
...		
2000	4017 3456	`;jump:always→somewhere`
2004	5241 0000	`;`
...		
3456	...	

3. Decode. The instruction is recognized as an absolute `jump`.
4. Fetch operand. The operand is simply the address to which control should be transferred—the address of the next instruction to be executed. This address is contained in the last 16 bits of the `jump` instruction—which is already in the `IR`. The address 3456 is copied to the `source_2` register (source_2 because it is like a destination).
5. Perform the operation. The address is simply copied from `source_2` to the `result` register. So the perform step simply copies the jump address from the instruction register to the result register, via the destination register. The result register now points to the desired next instruction.
6. Store the result. The purpose of the `jump` instruction is to alter the flow of control from the syntactically next statement to some other statement. The next instruction performed will be whatever is fetched in step 1 during the *next* fetch/execute cycle, which in turn will be whatever the `PC` points to at that time. To achieve this, the `result` is stored in the `PC`: the `PC` gets the value 3456. Although, the programmer normally cannot access the `PC` directly,

there is no logical distinction between storing a result in the `PC` and storing it in some other register:

```
*copy        result⇒PC
```

Thus the `PC` now contains the destination specified in the `jump`. When the loop reaches step 1 again, the instruction at the destination of the `jump` will be fetched.

LOOP. Since the `PC` now contains the destination of the `jump`, 3456, the instruction at that location will be executed next. The fact that the `PC` temporarily contained an erroneous address does not matter. On the other hand, suppose we attempted to avoid that temporary erroneous content by postponing the increment `PC` step until after the operation had been performed (step 5). The perform step would cause the `PC` point to the desired location, but the delayed increment would then change the `PC` incorrectly to be the desired value plus 4. This is one reason the `PC` is incremented so early in the cycle.

▷ *Are there other reasons for performing the increment at that point?*

The Condition Code Register and Conditional Jumps

Conditional `jumps` are usually paired with a `compare` operation. The conditional jump must react on the basis of that comparison. Every ml operation is a self-contained entity, interpreted individually by the above six-step fetch/execute cycle. In GAL, the `compare` instruction places its result in the condition code register (CCR), for use by the following conditional `jump` instruction. The `compare` operation leaves a result in specific bits of that register, and the conditional `jump` examines those bits. For the moment only two of those bits are relevant:

- the *Equal* (or *Zero*) bit, and
- the *Less_Than* (or *Negative*) bit.

The full conditional `jump` operation requires two full fetch/execute cycles. In the first cycle, `compare` sets the `equal` bit to 1 if the two operands compared are equal and clears the bit to 0 if the operands are not equal. If the source is less than the destination, the `less_than` bit is set to 1, otherwise it is cleared to 0. The two bits taken together can indicate all three possible results of a comparison:

10 = `equal`
01 = `less than`
00 = `greater than`

▷ *Two bits are capable of representing four distinct combinations, so why are there only three possible results here? What is the missing combination?*

The conditional `jump` instruction describes the conditions under which the jump should be executed: `equal`, `not equal`, and so on. In the next fetch/execute cycle, the conditional jump will compare its target conditions with those held in the CCR and will jump or not jump accordingly. Consider the process of executing a `compare` and `jump` pair of instructions (Figure 6-7).

CYCLE 1 The first four steps of the fetch/execute cycle proceed as normal for the `compare` instruction, after which the instruction register contains the `compare`; the `PC` points to the next instruction (the `jump`), and source registers contain the two items to be compared.

1. The `compare` instruction is fetched.

2. The `PC` is incremented to point at the conditional `jump` instruction.

3. The instruction register is decoded to determine that it is a `compare` instruction.

FIGURE 6-7
Conditional Jump

Initial state

			CPU registers		
PC	=	0000 2000	Reg0	=	
IR	=		Reg1	=	
source_1	=		Reg2	=	0000 0000
source_2	=		Reg3	=	
Result	=				
CCR	=				

RAM contents

address	contents	note
...		
2000	5162 0000	;compare:integer #0⇒reg2
2004	4011 3456	;jump:equal→somewhere
...		
3456	...	

Step 1: fetch instruction

			CPU registers		
PC	=	0000 2000	Reg0	=	
IR	=	**5261 0000**	Reg1	=	
source_1	=		Reg2	=	0000 0000
source_2	=		Reg3	=	
Result	=				
CCR	=				

Step 2: increment the PC

			CPU registers		
PC	=	**0000 2004**	Reg0	=	
IR	=	5261 0000	Reg1	=	
source_1	=		Reg2	=	0000 0000
source_2	=		Reg3	=	
Result	=				
CCR	=				

(continued)

FIGURE 6-7
(continued)

Step 4: fetch operands

			CPU registers		
PC	=	0000 2004	Reg0	=	
IR	=	5261 0000	Reg1	=	
source_1	=	**0000 0000**	Reg2	=	
source_2	=	**0000 0000**	Reg3	=	
Result	=				
CCR	=				

Step 5: perform operation

			CPU registers		
PC	=	0000 2004	Reg0	=	
IR	=	5261 0000	Reg1	=	
source_1	=	0000 0000	Reg2	=	0000 0000
source_2	=	0000 0000	Reg3	=	
Result	=	0000 0000			
CCR	=	**0001**	[equal bit is set]		

Step 6: store results[nothing happens here]

			CPU registers		
PC	=	0000 2004	Reg0	=	
IR	=	5261 0000	Reg1	=	
source_1	=	0000 0000	Reg2	=	0000 0000
source_2	=	0000 0000	Reg3	=	
Result	=	0000 0000			
CCR	=	0001	[equal bit is set]		

Cycle 2
Step 1: fetch instruction

			CPU registers		
PC	=	0000 2004	Reg0	=	
IR	=	**4100 3456**	Reg1	=	
source_1	=		Reg2	=	
source_2	=	0000 0000	Reg3	=	
Result	=	0000 0000			
CCR	=	0001	[equal bit is set]		

RAM contents

address	contents	note
...		
2000	5162 0000	;compare:integer #0⇒reg2
2004	4011 3456	;jump:equal→somewhere
...		
3456	...	;somewhere

Step 2: increment PC

			CPU registers		
PC	=	**0000 2008**	Reg0	=	
IR	=	4100 3456	Reg1	=	
source_1	=		Reg2	=	
source_2	=	0000 0000	Reg3	=	
Result	=	0000 0000			
CCR	=	0001	[equal bit is set]		

(*continued*)

FIGURE 6-7
(continued)

Step 4: fetch operands

			CPU registers	
PC	=	0000 2008	Reg0	=
IR	=	4100 3456	Reg1	=
source_1	=	**0000 0001**	Reg2	=
source_2	=	**0000 3456**	Reg3	=
Result	=	0000 0000		
CCR	=	0001	[equal bit is set]	

Step 5: perform

			CPU registers	
PC	=	0000 2008	Reg0	=
IR	=	4100 3456	Reg1	=
source_1	=	0000 0001	Reg2	=
source_2	=	0000 3456	Reg3	=
Result	=	0000 3456		
CCR	=	0001	[equal bit is set]	

Step 6: store results

			CPU registers	
PC	=	**0000 3456**	Reg0	=
IR	=	4100 3456	Reg1	=
source_1	=	0000 0001	Reg2	=
source_2	=	0000 3456	Reg3	=
Result	=	0000 3456		
CCR	=	0001	[equal bit is set]	

RAM contents

address	contents	note
...		
2000	5162 0000	;compare:integer #0⇒reg2
2004	4011 3456	;jump:equal→somewhere
...		
3456	...	

4. The two operands to be compared are fetched into the source registers.
5. At this step, the comparison itself is performed by subtracting the destination from the source, leaving the difference in the `result` register. This step is performed in exactly the same manner as if the command had been a `subtract` instruction. The conditional branch can determine the results of the comparison by inspecting the `result` register. Subtraction of equal quantities will result in a difference of zero; subtraction of a smaller number from a larger number results in a positive difference; and subtracting a larger number from a smaller number yields a negative result.

Rather than store the results in the usual manner (and destroy the destination operand), a "summary" of the results is placed into the condition code register, as follows:

- The `equal` or `zero` bit is set if the result is zero. If the two compared values are equal, the result of the subtraction would be zero. If the answer is zero (all bits are zero), 1 is stored in the zero bit. If the answer was not zero, the zero bit is set to 0.

> ▷ *This may seem like a tricky operation, but it is logically very simple. Can you imagine the technique?*

- The `less_than` or `negative` bit is set if the result was negative. If the source was smaller, the subtraction yields a negative number. The negative (or less than) bit is then set to 1. If the destination is smaller than the source, the subtraction yields a zero (positive) result in the sign bit and the negative bit will likewise be cleared to zero. Since all negative numbers will have a "1" in the sign bit, the sign bit of the result can simply be copied into the `negative` bit.

6. No further action is taken, as the results have already been placed in the condition code register.

CYCLE 2 The conditional `jump` simply unwinds the preceding logic. Jump-on-equal asks "Did the previous comparison yield equal results?" by checking to see if the zero bit was set. Jump-on-less checks to see if the negative bit was set, and so on. With respect to the fetch/execute cycle, the conditional `jump` is accomplished in exactly the same manner as an absolute jump.

1. Fetch the instruction. The `PC` now points to the conditional `jump` instruction. Note that the instruction itself contains the address that might be jumped to.
2. Increment the `PC`. The `PC` now points at the instruction that will be executed next if the condition proves *false:* the one at 2008.
3. Decode instruction (as conditional `jump`).
4. Fetch operands. The conditions for jumping are specified in the register operand field of the instruction (bits 18–16). These conditions are copied to the source register as an operand.
5. Perform. The jump conditions are compared to the zero and negative bits in the condition code register. Recall that the instruction had three bits of condition but the register contains only two.

The equal bit in the `jump` instruction asks "Is the zero bit of the CCR set?"
The less-than bit asks "Is the negative bit set?"
The greater-than bit asks "Are both the negative bit and the equal bit clear?"

Thus, if the `jump` specifies equality as a jump condition (`equal`, `greater_eq`, or `less_eq`) and the CCR indicates an equal or zero result, the jump will be made. In that case, the destination address is copied from (the low-order bits of) the `IR` to the `result` register. In the example, the `jump` specifies equal and the equal bit is set. The destination address is then copied to the result register.

6. At the final step, if the appropriate bits were set in the condition code register, the destination address is copied from the `result` to the `PC`. That is, if the CCR matches the test specified in the conditional `jump` instruction, it behaves exactly as does the unconditional `jump`. If the CCR bits did not match, no action would be taken. This implies that the `PC` would not change at this step. Fortunately, the `PC` has already been incremented (at step 2) to point to the instruction following the conditional `jump`. Thus "no action" yields the desired result: no jump is made and the syntactically next instruction will be executed next. (repeat). The instruction executed next will depend on the content of the `PC`, which will be either the instruction (positionally) following the `jump` instruction or the instruction specified as the destination of the `jump`.

JUMP REVISITED. When you step through a program using a debugger, the instruction displayed is always the next instruction to be executed—not the one just executed. This is because the `PC` always points at the next instruction (except for a very brief interval between steps 1 and 2 of the cycle). If an error occurred during the processing of a `jump` instruction, the debugger might seem to imply that the next instruction to be executed is the one after the `jump`—which in fact would never be executed at all, even if there had been no error.

OTHER COMMANDS AND THE CCR. There is no mechanism to enforce the requirement that the conditional `jump` always follows a `compare` command. One might ask "What would be in the CCR if there has been no `compare` instruction?" The `compare` command sets its value as a result of a subtraction operation, the exact result of which is actually thrown away. One might also ask "What happens with a full subtraction?" It turns out that storing the results in the CCR is actually a side-effect, and can be performed independently of other storage results.

▷ *Does this mean that it is possible to do two things in parallel?*

The subtraction operation also sets the condition code bits according to the results of the subtraction: zero, negative, or positive. That is, subtraction has exactly the same effect on the condition code register as does the `compare` command. In fact, they are the same operation through the perform step. Only in the store-results step do they differ. The results of almost any arithmetic operation will set the bits in the condition code register, depending on the result of the operation: zero, positive, or negative. This has two important implications. First, it explains why we insisted in GAL that the conditional `jump` always follow the compare *immediately.* Otherwise, some intervening operation might alter the condition code register. Second, the `compare` may be omitted if a conditional `jump` is to be made based on a result of an arithmetic operation. Thus,

```
label   . . .
        . . .
        subtract          #1⇒reg3
        compare           #0⇒reg3
        jump:greater      →label
```

can be rewritten

```
label   . . .
        . . .
        subtract          #1⇒reg3
        jump:less         →label
```

which will loop until the result of the subtraction is less than zero (the test was reversed because the original `compare`, in effect, subtracted the result from zero). Many programmers will nonetheless conclude that there is less chance of a misunderstanding if the `compare` is always explicitly included.

The Stack Pointer and Procedure Calls

Up to a point, the jump-to-subroutine instruction works exactly like the absolute `jump`. But implicit in the concept of a subroutine jump is the return of control to the calling program at the completion of the subroutine. Specifically, control should be returned to precisely the point at which it left the calling routine or, even more precisely, to the statement immediately following the jump-to-subroutine. The jump-to-subroutine instruction must provide a mechanism for returning control to the location from which the `jump` was executed. To accomplish this task, execution of a jump-to-subroutine contains an additional suboperation: save the address to which control should return after completion of the subroutine.

For a subroutine jump, the first three steps of the fetch/execute cycle are identical to those for the regular `jump` instruction (Figure 6-8 provides an example).

1. Load the jump-to-subroutine instruction into the `IR` (Figure 6-8*a*).
2. Increment the `PC` to point at the instruction syntactically following the `jump`. Note that this happens to be precisely the instruction to which control must be returned after completion of the subroutine (Figure 6-8*b*).
3. Decode the instruction, recognizing it as a jump-to-subroutine.

At this point, the first distinction can be found: there are two operands.

- The subroutine address is explicitly encoded in the statement (and is, therefore, in the `IR`, and
- The return address is presently held in the `PC`.

Thus the cycle may proceed.

4. Fetch the operands. Copy the return address from the `PC` and the subroutine address from the `IR` into the source registers.
5. There is really no perform step, other than to pass the values through. This instruction seems to have two "results": the subroutine address and the return address, but there is only one result register. It can be viewed as if one of the results is stored in this step. To avoid losing the return address, the old `PC`

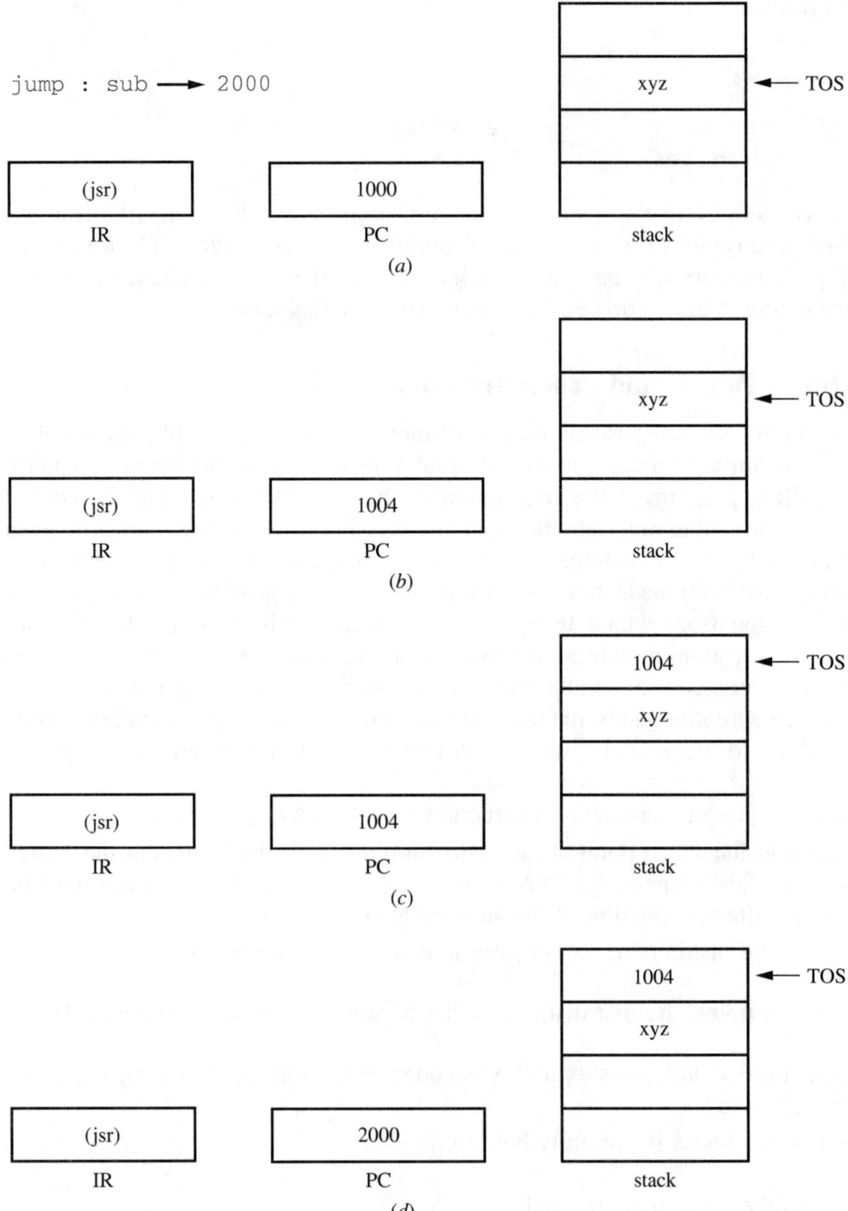

FIGURE 6-8
The jump to subroutine command.

contents must be saved before the subroutine address can be placed into the PC. So at this step, the contents of the PC are saved into a designated location, called (for the moment) return_address. For now you can think of this location as a register, or RAM, or whatever: we will consider exactly how this location is specified in the following section.

```
*copy     PC⇒return_address     ;(Figure 6–8c.)
```

So, the address of the return location will be available when it is needed.

6. Save the result register (same as low-order bits of the IR) into the PC:

```
*copy     source_1⇒PC           ;(Figure 6–8d).
```

The PC now points to the subroutine.

On the next fetch/execute cycle control will have transferred to the subroutine as desired, exactly as with any other jump, and the return_address is available for use by the return instruction. After the subroutine is executed, the return instruction is eventually encountered. Its execution proceeds much like a jump. However, its destination is not contained in the command but is the return_address saved earlier by the jump-to-subroutine instruction.

1. The return instruction is fetched into the IR.
2. The PC is incremented. Note that it now points past the end of the subroutine (either at code that is part of another routine or to a storage location that contains data, not code).
3. The IR is decoded, revealing the instruction as a return.
4. The only operand is the return address, saved by the earlier jump-to-subroutine. It is copied from return_address to the source register.
5. The return address is copied from source register to result register.
6. The result is saved in the PC. On the next cycle, the instruction fetched will be the address originally saved by the jump-to-subroutine: the address following that jump.

THE RETURN ADDRESS. Thus far, the exact nature of the storage location return_address is not very clear. There are a number of possible mechanisms that could be employed. Let's examine and reject several of these mechanisms, starting with the simplest assumption: return_address is simply a memory (either register or RAM) location, similar to any other. This works fine as long as the program never nests its subroutine calls more than one deep. But suppose the main program called subroutine SubA, and SubA called SubB. The first jump to SubA would place an address in return_address. The subsequent jump to SubB would also store its return address in return_address, destroying the address stored by the first subroutine call. It is therefore necessary that there be more than one location for return_address. Now suppose that every

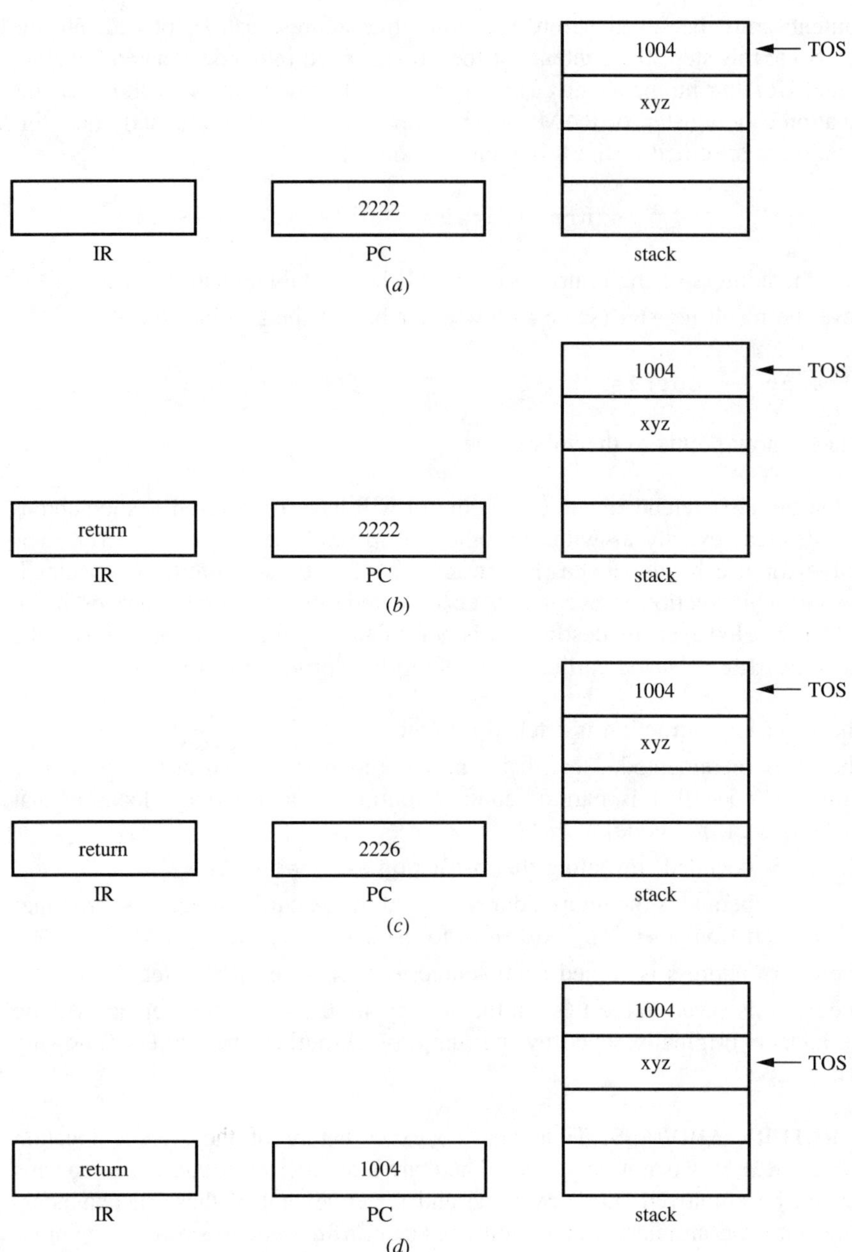

FIGURE 6-9
Return.

subroutine had its own `return_address`. Perhaps this could be accomplished by placing `return_address` in a register. The first action of every subroutine would then be to save the address in a local variable. However, this solution cannot account for recursion. Every time a program attempted to recurse, it would destroy its previously stored `return_address`.

▷ *What is the great problem with not supporting recursion? Early higher-level languages did not permit recursion. What can we conclude about the mechanisms these languages used for recording the return address of subroutines?*

The solution can be seen in the structure of nested program calls. The most recently called subroutine must be the first one to end. That is, subroutine calls have a LIFO nature and are suitable for a stack; GEM maintains a built-in system stack for that purpose. The system stack is implemented as a region of RAM memory, capable of holding many such return addresses. A special register, the *system stack pointer* (`SSP` or simply `SP`) is essentially a special address register that always points to the top of the stack (i.e., the `SP` contains the address of the top of the stack). Thus, the subroutine-jump instruction simply *pushes* the return address onto the stack, and the `return` instruction simply *pops* the needed return address off the stack. The two instructions can now be briefly resummarized.

Jump-to-subroutine

Steps 1–4: As previously defined
Step 5: Copy new address from `PC` to result
Push return address on stack
incremented stack pointer
copy address operand onto stack
Step 6: As before: copy subroutine address from source register to `PC`

Return

Steps 1–3: As for all instructions
Step 4: Pop operand from stack to destination register
copy address from stack to source register
decrement stack pointer
Steps 5–6: As previously defined: copy return address from source register to `PC`

IMPLICATIONS FOR THE ASSEMBLY LANGUAGE MODEL

Types of Operands

We have seen that operands may be specified by any of several addressing modes: register, memory, immediate, indirect, and so on. At this point we can begin to understand some of the implications of using the various forms by considering each of these addressing modes in turn. We will concentrate on step 4 of the fetch/execute cycle: "fetch the operands."

Register and RAM operands. Register operands are easier to access than RAM operands. So far, we have seen at least three reasons for this.

- First, since there are more RAM locations the address is necessarily larger. Therefore, specifying a specific address in RAM requires more storage.
- More importantly, while RAM is external to the CPU, registers are contained within it; therefore distances are shorter, signals smaller, and coordination easier.
- Finally—and most importantly—since there are very few registers, it is more economically feasible to build speed into them than to speed up the large quantities of RAM. The relatively fast CPU must request the value from the relatively slow memory portion of the GEM machine. While every instruction must be fetched from memory, only some operands must be fetched. In general instructions with register operands will require less time to complete an entire fetch/execute cycle, even though the time required for the actual performance of the specified operation is identical. If the destination is in RAM, the time will be even slower since the operand not only needs to be fetched but also needs to be stored in RAM when the operation is complete.

An early section of the chapter suggested that the restriction on the number of RAM operands (to one in GAL) was because the specification required more bits in the instruction. The current observation reveals a second reason: it would be slower. A data manipulation instruction with two RAM operands would require four memory accesses:

1. fetch the instruction
2. fetch the first operand
3. fetch the second operand
4. store the result

Immediate operands. Since an immediate operand is coded directly as part of the instruction, by the time it is needed, it must already be in the instruction register (in step 1). The fetching of such an operand is actually a register fetch and should therefore be as fast as a register operation and faster than if the operand were in main memory. The GEML restriction on the use of immediate data as if it were a memory operand is therefore due to the representation in that machine rather than with the fact that memory is slower. Other languages may allow immediate and RAM data in a single instruction.

Indirect addresses. On the other hand, indirect addresses look like register addresses in the instruction. The instruction specifies a register, containing only the address of the operand. To fetch an indirectly specified operand, the correct register is selected; the contents of that register become the address, and then a memory access is made to that address. Thus, indirect address operands must be *at least as slow* as directly addressed operands. The GAL restriction was not necessary; it only provided consistency.

THE VON NEUMANN BOTTLENECK. The observations about the number of fetches required and relative speeds are not mere chit-chat or random observations about the various instructions. The total number of memory fetches required can be the dominant factor in determining the speed of a program. Since memory fetches are the slowest part of the operation, they can become the bottleneck of the entire cycle. In fact, this critical point is called the *von Neumann bottleneck*. Some have observed that this problem is the Achilles heel of modern computers.

WASTED MOVEMENT? Many GEM instructions may seem to waste much data movement. For example, the `copy` operation seems to copy data from the source operand to the source register to the `result` register to the destination address. Is this not inefficient? Couldn't the operand have been copied directly from source to destination? Actually, the internal movements are very fast. What little cost is incurred by these extra movements is regained from the efficiency provided by the uniform handling of all instructions. Without this uniformity, a special operation would be required to copy the data directly from address to address. No such special action is required in an architecture such as GEM's. Chapters 11 and 14 will investigate alternative approaches to this problem.

Understanding Errors

We can now better understand the nature of run-time errors and why so very few distinct error messages are generated during execution. Error messages only result when the machine is unable to perform one of the steps of the cycle.

ADDRESSING ERROR. For some reason, one of the fetch steps (1 or 4) was unable to access the address. Perhaps the address specified a location beyond the highest existing memory location; perhaps there is something wrong with the memory at that address. Perhaps incrementing the PC caused it to overflow. In our examples, the size of the PC was—conveniently—defined to be just sufficient to address all of memory. In larger machines this might not be feasible (a 32-bit PC could legally address four gigabytes of memory). If the PC pointed beyond the highest existing memory location, the first step of the cycle would fail since no instruction could be fetched. Similarly, an address field could indicate an address that does not exist. In that case, the fetch-operand step of the instruction would fail.

ILLEGAL INSTRUCTION. Even if an instruction is fetched, it may not be successfully decoded (step 3). In such a case, an illegal instruction message is generated. This error might also be generated if the modes are not legal or meaningless for the operation (needed for step 4). This message is often perplexing to the programmer. How can an illegal instruction be generated by the assembler? Shouldn't the assembler recognize bad syntax in the GAL instruction and not generate bad GEML code corresponding to bad GAL code? Actually, the error is more likely to be generated by code that isn't really code at all. For example, data in the middle of a poorly structured program might inadvertently be fetched as code. If the PC points at data, that data—whatever it is—will be loaded by the next instruction fetch. If the value in the opcode field of a fetched instruction does not represent any legal instruction for the machine, the f/e cycle cannot decode the instruction. The GEM machine adroitly avoids this problem. Since it has exactly as many instructions as there are distinct values possible in the opcode field, no error is possible. It is easy to imagine that more complicated machines may have instruction sets that do not cover the full set of possible values—not every instruction set can have exactly 2^n instructions.

PERFORMANCE ERRORS. Sometimes, even though a legal instruction is found and decoded, the operation itself cannot be performed (step 5). For example, division by zero is not defined. Therefore an error should be generated if the denominator for a division operation is zero. It is possible that addition could generate an error if the result were too large to represent in the allotted space (although 128 can be represented in one byte, the sum of 128+128 cannot). Most machines do not generate an error message for that situation, leaving it for the programmer to detect the anomaly. This has both positive and negative results. It does allow the programmer to take advantage of modular arithmetic (recall the circular queue example from Chapter 5), as well as avoiding the question of signed or unsigned arithmetic operations. On the other hand, the constant need for vigilance toward such errors can complicate the programmer's task.

> ▷ *What is the relationship between modular arithmetic and overflow problems?*

IMPLICATIONS FOR "REAL" LANGUAGES

Not every machine uses fixed-size fields. This seems impossible. How could the machine know how much of the instruction to fetch? How would it know if some particular bits were operands for the current instruction or the opcode for the next instruction? David Huffman showed that if two representations are relatively unique at any point, they can be distinguished (Huffman codes are also important in the theory of computation and complexity of information). Suppose that a machine had instructions of two distinct sizes, say four bytes and six bytes. The first bit could indicate if it was a long or a short instruction (recall that GEML has an unused bit next to the opcode). With such a representation, commonly used instructions could have shorter representations and less commonly used instructions could have longer representations. If the short instructions are used more commonly than long instructions, the total length will be shorter. If the total quantity of instructions that must be fetched is smaller, the run-time will also be faster. This seems to violate the time-space tradeoff. A very simple representation might include something like

```
0000    ;copy:         the first of eight common
                       instructions
0001    ;add:          all with four-bit opcode
...     ;              all starting with a 0 bit
0111    ;branch
1000 00 ;load_address:the first of 32 longer
        ;              instructions
1000 01 ;              all starting with a 1 bit
...     ;              and having a six bit opcode
1111 11
```

The allowable addressing modes may vary from instruction to instruction. In that case, each instruction can be constructed with its own unique representation of addressing modes, thus avoiding the space that GEM needed for nonexistent addressing modes. An operand with only two addressing modes need only devote two bits to that representation. An operand with four possible modes will need a two-bit representation; three bits if there are eight legal modes, and so on.

INCREASING THE ADDRESS SPACE. All GEM instructions are four bytes long. If the first instruction is located at an address divisible by four, all instructions will be at addresses divisible by four. In binary every instruction address would end with 00. Since all instructions end with the identical two bits, these bits are actually redundant or unnecessary; the address could be determined without the two low-order bits. This is equivalent to adding two bits to the possible addresses for each instruction, which in turn is equivalent to multiplying the size of the address space by 4. A machine that accessed its instructions in that manner could access 64K*4 = 256K bytes of RAM. Unfortunately, this technique does not increase the address space for GEM operands, since they are not necessarily located at multiples of 4. Also it introduces another potential run-time error: illegal address. Any attempt to reference a location that is not divisible by 4 will result in an address error.

▷ *Does this suggest that instructions and operands should be stored separately?*

READING COMMANDS AS HEX CODE. If GEML instructions are viewed as hexadecimal numbers, every field fits into a single nibble. Moreover, no nibble refers to more than one field. Thus, any GEML instruction can be read easily by looking at its hex representation. Figure 6-1 (a–e) includes the nibble-by-nibble interpretation of GEML instructions. Other languages are not so neatly structured. The internal representation may pack multiple fields into a nibble or allow fields to cross nibble boundaries. Debuggers often provide a disassemble command, enabling the programmer to interpret an instruction more easily. Even with a debugger that does disassemble, there will be times when the programmer must be able to disassemble some instructions. For example, you may be in the debugger, with your program about to execute a `jump` instruction. Although the `jump` instruction may be disassembled for you, the statement to which it jumps may be a mystery.

SUMMARY

The machine language model may be viewed as a direct image of the assembly language model. Since the machine language is the internal or machine-readable form, it would be more accurate to say that assembly language is an image of machine language. The latter has fields corresponding to each item of information in AL. Ml includes more architectural constituents—most notably the instruction register, program counter, condition code register, and stack pointer. The basic unit of time in the assembly language model was, roughly, the instruction. In the machine language model, each instruction is divided into several steps, collectively called the fetch/execute cycle. Instructions are thought of as strings of binary digits, not as mnemonic commands. During the fetch/execute cycle, a single instruction is fetched from memory, the PC is incremented, the instruction decoded, the operands fetched, the operation performed, and the the result stored. The process then repeats. All of the instructions, including the control instructions, can be explained using this cycle.

EXERCISES

6.1. GEM has 16 instructions (opcodes). If mode is considered to be part of the instruction, how many total instructions are possible?

6.2. Give the GEML machine language equivalents for the following GAL instructions:

```
subtract:integer  reg2⇒reg3
return
load_address      item        ;assume item is located
                              ;at loc 3000.
rotate            #5⇒reg2     ;no you do not need to
                              ;understand the command
                              ;to translate it!
```

6.3. Repeat Exercise 6.2 for your real machine.

6.4. Are there items in addition to the return address that might be usefully stored on the system stack?

6.5. Consider the representation of immediate data in GEML instructions. Consider in particular the field used to represent the immediate data itself. Careful examination of this representation will reveal a previously unmentioned restriction on GEML and, therefore, on GAL operands. What is the restriction?

6.6. There are two distinct GEML instructions that are both equivalent to the GAL instruction

```
add          reg2⇒reg3.
```

Create both and describe their differences.

6.7. The `jump never` is a form of `no-op`. Create at least three others.

6.8. For each of the examples of GAL-to-GEML conversion presented in this chapter, perform the same conversion on the "real" assembly and machine language of your machine. Use the assembly language reference manual as your guide.

6.9. Build a table like the one in Figure 6-5 for three instructions in your assembly language.

6.10. The requirement of some systems that instructions and some forms of data be located at even addresses often seems very odd to the novice programmer. One possible explanation could be that by using only even address, the effective size of the address space has been doubled. How could that be? (Also note that additional reasons will appear later.)

6.11. Discuss the `halt` instruction in terms of the fetch/execute cycle.

6.12. Study the GEM instructions in Figure 6-1, looking for patterns in the opcodes.

6.13. Perhaps the unused bits (e.g., 28) of the GEML language were intended to be available for expanding the language. Given its position between the opcode and the register operand, give two possible uses for the bit. Describe numerically the expansions that would be made possible by use of the bit.

6.14. GEML allowed only one indirect address per instruction. Some real languages allow two. Modify GEML to allow two indirect addresses.

6.15. Write a short code segment to determine if your machine uses big-endien or little endien representation.

6.16. Step through an instruction containing subroutine calls. Find the stack pointer and check its contents. When an address gets placed on the stack by a jump-to-subroutine, find the contents of the return address and disassemble it.

6.17. GEML is a primitive language with only 16 instructions. Make a list of instructions that you have used in your language that have no GEML equivalent. For each, find a way to accomplish the same instruction with GEML.

6.18. If you are using a microprocessor, there are very likely some instructions or operand types that seem to be missing. List two instructions that you think your machine should have but which it apparently does not.

6.19. Determine for your machine language whether or not the instruction length is constant. If not, make a list of the aspects that impact the length.

6.20. This chapter suggested that the fixed-length GEM instructions had the advantage of creating an easy way to expand the address space. Give a disadvantage.

6.21. GEML has several instances of wasted fields. Make a list of unused fields in GEML. Attempt to design a language that does not waste these fields. What are the issues that you must deal with? Does your real assembly language have wasted fields?

6.22. For the commands in your own assembly language closest to the GAL commands

```
add            reg2⇒reg3
subtract       item⇒reg3
copy:int       loc⇒reg3
copy:byte      reg3⇒loc
```

create the equivalent ml commands. Check your result either from the assembler listing or using a debugger.

6.24. How many bits would be needed for ml instructions in a machine that allowed two RAM operands and had a 16-Mb address space?

6.25. If it is true that memory operands are slower, it should be possible to detect the difference. Perform 50,000 additions in which the operands are both in registers. Do the same for one operand in memory. Was there a difference? Does it matter which operand was in RAM?

6.26. Similarly, multiplication should be slower than addition. Compare 50,000 additions to the same number of multiplications.

6.27. Does an operation such as addition or multiplication require more time if the numbers are large? Demonstrate your answer.

CHAPTER
7

THE ASSEMBLER AND RELATED SOFTWARE

OVERVIEW

Previous chapters have contained periodic references to the *assembler*— but without explanation. Apparently, the assembler somehow processes an assembly language program. It provides the link between the assembly language and machine language models of computation. In this chapter, we first investigate the role of the assembler and then other related software. From the study of this software we can gain a further understanding of both assembly and machine languages.

Humans generally prefer to write in a higher-level language or, at least, in assembly rather than machine language, while computers require that programs be represented in machine language. The process of translating code from AL, which is relatively human-oriented, into the more machine-readable machine language is called *assembly,* and the program that accomplishes it is the *assembler.* Assembly is one step in the chain of producing a working program. The programmer writes the *source* or assembly code, using an editor. The source code is fed as input to the assembler, which creates *object* or machine language code. Often the two versions of the program are called the *source module* and the *object module,* respectively. With very few exceptions, each assembly language instruction is converted into a machine language instruction on a one-for-one basis. This translation can be carried out by the assembler in a straightforward manner. Each assembly language statement contains all of the information needed to create the corresponding machine language instruction:

- The operation *mnemonic* specifies the op-code.
- The operand *type* indicates the size of the operand.

• The operand *syntax* shows the addressing mode:

the order of operands distinguishes source and destination operands,
operand names indicate register or RAM addressing, and
special symbols indicate indirect or immediate addressing modes.

The assembler provides the important "missing link" between the machine language and assembly language models of computation. Understanding the tasks of the assembler provides understanding of the relationships between these two models and essential insight into the relationships between the assembly and higher-level language models.

THE ASSEMBLER

The assembler is actually a program that reads the source file, which contains the original assembly language program. Remember that this file is a stream of ASCII characters. As the assembler reads each statement, it generates machine code corresponding to the source statement, one field at a time. It can determine the op-code from the mnemonic instruction name, the addressing mode from the syntax, the operands from the operand field, and the size from the size field. Each field is represented in a few bits of the total machine language instruction. Assembly of a single instruction can be compared to the inverse of the decode step of the fetch/execute cycle. However, the assembler must translate all instructions of an entire program before any of them are executed. Consider the following example.

Given the GAL code

```
subtract            reg2⇒reg2
compare:integer     #5⇒reg2
```

a GAL assembler would build the corresponding GEML code by translating the GAL code one field at a time, as shown in Figure 7-1*a*. The assembler stores this as the first instruction and proceeds to process the second instruction, shown in Figure 7-1*b*. Since a GEML instruction requires four bytes, the assembler places each instruction four bytes after the location of the previous instruction. Thus, if the first instruction were placed at location 1000_{16}, the results to this point would be stored in RAM as

location	**contents**
1000	9102 0002
1004	5152 0005

Generally, the assembler not only translates the assembly language source code into machine language object code, but it also produces a listing of the

```
operation name: subtract
                1001 ---- ---- ---- ---- ---- ---- ----
register operand: reg2
                1001 ---- ---- -010 ---- ---- ---- ----
mode: not immediate, no indirect address, direction, no RAM operands
                1001 ---- 0000 -010 ---- ---- ---- ----
size: default size for subtraction is integer
                1001 --01 0000 -010 ---- ---- ---- ----
RAM operand field (actually a register in this case)
                1001 --01 0000 -010 0000 0000 0000 0010
  padding: 3 unused bits (zeros)
                1001 0001 0000 0010 0000 0000 0000 0010
                  = 9102 0002₁₆
```

(a)

```
operation name: compare
                0101 ---- ---- ---- ---- ---- ---- ----
register operand: reg2
                0101 ---- ---- -010 ---- ---- ---- ----
mode: not indirect, immediate, direction: toward register, one RAM operand,
                0101 ---- 0101 -010 ---- ---- ---- ----
size: specified by integer
                0101 --01 0101 -010 ---- ---- ---- ----
second operand: the immediate 5
                0101 --01 0101 -010 0000 0000 0000 0101
  padding: 3 unused bits (zeros)
                0101 0001 0101 0010 0000 0000 0000 0101
                    = 5152 0005₁₆
```

(b)

FIGURE 7-1

machine language code it generated. A programmer who is very familiar with the machine language can actually use this listing to recognize errors. More useful, however, are the error messages generated by the assembler. When the assembler cannot translate an assembly instruction into machine language, it generates an error message informing the human of the problem. It does so only for those assembly commands for which it is not possible to generate any machine language instruction. For instructions that seem odd or dangerous or otherwise improper, the assembler will generate no message; it will simply generate the "odd" machine language. For example, error messages are generated when

- An identifier is used as an operand, but no definition may be found for the identifier.
- An illegal form is specified (e.g., an immediate value as a destination).
- Operands are missing (e.g., `add reg2⇒`).

- Too many operands are provided (e.g., `add reg2⇒reg1⇒reg3`).
- The operation is not defined (e.g., `foo reg2⇒reg3`).

No message is generated for situations such as improperly sized fields

```
copy:character     #'AB'⇒reg2
copy:character     #1000⇒reg2
```

In the first case, the operand seems to be two characters long, but the size specification calls for one byte to be copied. The assembler will assume that the programmer had a good reason for requesting the partial transfer (perhaps as a reminder that the operand to be copied was the first character of "AB," and the second character was to come later). In the second case, the number 1000 will not fit into a character location. The assembler simply uses the last eight bits of the immediate value as the operand. Similarly, in Figure 7-1 the assembler must assume that the programmer really did intend to subtract `reg2` from itself.

The reason for this seemingly bizarre refusal to help is that the assembler assumes that programmers know what they are doing (a rather bold assumption!). In fact, we will see examples in which the programmer will actually want to perform an instruction that on the surface seems improper. Such conflicts should be reserved for situations in which the programmer is confident of the results. One reason for programming in assembly language is precisely to take advantage of this ability to maintain multiple views of operands. For example, `succ` and `pred` can be handled very rapidly if the character is treated as a number. The successor can always be obtained by adding 1, with no jump-to-subroutine and no `return`. `Pred` can be calculated by subtracting 1.

▷ *The assembler is probably written in assembly language. How can that be?*

THE TWO-PASS ASSEMBLER

Address Identifiers

The two preceding examples could be assembled in isolation. The assembler could assemble each of those statements using no knowledge of any other statement in the program. Neither instruction had a variable or constant as an operand. However, any instruction that refers to a mnemonically-specified main memory address (e.g., a `jump` or any operation with a RAM operand) cannot be assembled in isolation. The machine language code must contain the address of the memory location where that operand is stored. Assuming that the assembler works through the AL code from top to bottom, it may or may not have determined the machine address of an identifier by the time a reference is encountered. In particular, such an assembler will know all of the addresses it has encountered prior to (above) the current statement, but none that it will not encounter until later (below the current line). Consider the following code segment:

```
loc_1    <statement_1>
         <statement_2>
         jump:always     →loc_1
         <statement_4>
         jump:always     →loc_2
         <statement_6>
loc_2
```

By the time the assembler reaches the first `jump` statement, it will have translated the top two instructions, generating a total of eight bytes of code. If those bytes are stored beginning at location 1000_{16}, the code generated thus far will be

location	**value**	**translation of**	
1000	xxxx xxxx	loc_1	<statement_1>
1004	xxxx xxxx		<statement_2>

where each x indicates one nibble of completed machine code. The assembler has already seen `loc__1`, the target of the `jump`. Therefore, it knows where `loc__1` has been stored, and it can determine the exact machine address needed for the jump:

```
1008    4007 1000                ;(assuming GEM syntax)
```

Symbol Tables

To keep track of the identifiers it has seen, the assembler maintains a list called a *symbol table* containing symbols (identifiers) encountered, together with the corresponding addresses. When the assembler encounters a labeled statement such as `loc_1`, it adds the label and the address where it is stored to the symbol table. After `<statement_1>` has been assembled, the symbol table contains

symbol	**address**
loc_1	1000

When the assembler later finds a reference to a label, such as the destination of the first `jump` statement, it can find the address in the table and insert it into the instruction currently being generated. However, when the second `jump` is encountered, the situation is different. The total code generated at that point will be

location	**value**	**translation of**		
1000	xxxx xxxx	loc_1	<statement_1>	
1004	xxxx xxxx		<statement_2>	
1008	4700 1000		jump:always	→loc_1
100C	xxxx xxxx		<statement_4>	

and the symbol table is the same as before. The assembler has not yet seen `loc_2`. It cannot know the address needed for the operand and therefore cannot completely translate the instruction.

Consider, as a more concrete example, an extension of the code already translated:

```
top_of_loop
    Subtract             reg2⇒reg2
    compare:integer      #5⇒reg2
    jump:always          →top_of_loop
another_statement
```

The code and symbol table corresponding to this code would be generated in the following order:

	code		**symbol table**	
1	**addr**	**content**	**symbol**	**addr**
	1000	9102 0002	top_of_loop	1000
2	**addr**	**content**	**symbol**	**addr**
	1000	9102 0002	top_of_loop	1000
	1004	5512 0005		
3	**addr**	**content**	**symbol**	**addr**
	1000	9102 0002	top_of_loop	1000
	1004	5512 0005		
	1008	4007 1000		
4	**addr**	**content**	**symbol**	**addr**
	1000	9102 0002	top_of_loop	1000
	1004	5512 0005	another_sta	100C
	1008	4007 1000		
	100C			

Each time the assembler encounters an identifier while processing the code, it looks up the identifier in the table and inserts the corresponding address into the current ml instruction. However, this simple procedure assumes that the identifier definition is encountered prior to its use as the operand of a statement. Forward jumps (used in conditional structures and loop exits), subroutine jumps, and references to data items all create situations in which the target has not been encountered—and hence is not in the symbol table—at the time it is referenced. At first glance, it might seem that such problems could be avoided if the code were assembled in the opposite direction: from back to front. Unfortunately, the symmetrical problem still exists. To see that, consider the case in which the entire program is one large loop. The last statement in the program must reference the first statement.

The Two-Pass Solution

The usual solution for this dilemma is the *two-pass assembler.* The first pass builds the symbol table; the second pass uses the symbol table to create the final code. During the first pass, the assembler does not convert each instruction into machine language but only builds the symbol table. To do this, it must maintain a running total of the quantity of storage required by all of the code up to the current instruction. This total is kept in a *location counter* (LC). As each new AL instruction is encountered, the LC is incremented by the length of the corresponding machine language instruction, which, for GEML, is always four (other machine languages in which the length of instructions is not uniform are only slightly more complicated: each assembly language statement always contains all of the information needed to determine the length of the corresponding machine language instruction). As the defining statement for each new identifier is encountered, the assembler makes an entry in the symbol table containing the identifier and the current value of the LC. When it encounters `constant` and `variable` declarations, it increments the LC by the size of the declared data items. The instructions do not need to be translated at this point. After the first pass in the preceding example, the symbol table will be complete, but no code will have been generated:

symbol	**address**
top_of_loop	1000
another_sta	100C

▷ *What is the relationship between the use and function of the LC and that of the PC?*

On the second pass, translation proceeds sequentially through the assembly language instructions as before. When the assembler encounters any instruction containing a RAM reference in an operand field, it looks up the appropriate address in the symbol table and fills in the field. Since the table is completed before any code is translated, the symbol should always be present. Failure to find the symbol indicates that there is no such symbol defined anywhere in the program, so the assembler can generate an error message to that effect. In the example, the assembler processes the first two statements, which do not involve any identifiers, exactly as before. It fills the last two bytes of the `jump` statement by looking the symbol up in the table and inserting the corresponding values into the RAM operand field of the instruction. Returning to the first example, when the second `jump` statement is reached, the total code generated is

location	value	translation of		
1000	xxxx xxxx	loc_1	<statement_1>	
1004	xxxx xxxx		<statement_2>	
1008	4007 1000		jump:always	→loc_1
100C	xxxx xxxx		<statement_4>	
1010				

and the symbol table contains

symbol	address
loc_1	1000
loc_2	1018

so the remaining code can be filled in.

location	value	translation of		
1000	xxxx xxxx	loc_1	<statement_1>	
1004	xxxx xxxx		<statement_2>	
1008	4007 1000		jump:always	→loc_1
100C	xxxx xxxx		<statement_4>	
1010	4007 1018		jump:always	→loc_2
1014	xxxx xxxx		<statement_6>	
1018		loc_2		

▷ *Some may feel that the frequent table look-ups may be expensive in terms of time during assembly. What relevant techniques do you recall from your previous studies for reducing this overhead?*

The symbol table is the last remaining link between the mnemonic names used in an assembly language program and the actual addresses at which the items are stored in the machine memory. When the program is complete, the symbol table can be thrown away. Unfortunately, this means those mnemonic names are unavailable during execution. It is also instructive to notice what is *not* in the symbol table. Most important, it does not include the type or size of each operand. Without the declared size of an operand, it is impossible for the assembler to check for the correct operand size as it translates the operations. It would of course be possible to add a third column to the symbol table, but historically this has not been done, in part because AL programmers are sometimes avoiding the constraints imposed by the protection rules of higher-level languages.

> ▷ *What does the use of a symbol table suggest with respect to the maximum length of identifier names? What inferences can be drawn from the use of the symbol table about the requirements that Pascal places upon declarations?*

EXECUTING THE ASSEMBLED PROGRAM

In principle, after the assembler converts a program to machine language, the program can run immediately. During assembly, the program being executed is the assembler. The program to be run next is the object program that the assembler has just created. What needs to be done to accomplish this? There are numerous techniques, but the essential steps remaining are

a. store the object program in main memory—at the appropriate address
b. initialize the PC to point to the first instruction of the program
c. start the execution process
d. ensure that the machine will behave properly when the program terminates

Assemblers seldom (on modern machines, perhaps never) work in exactly this way. Nonetheless, it is instructive to start by imagining a machine that works in this manner.

First attempt. In the simplest model, the assembler takes care of step (a) by storing the object program into memory as it is generated. Presumably, it places each instruction at the appropriate location. The simplest way to accomplish (b) is to place the newly generated code at the location that immediately followed the last instruction of the assembler:

> first location of the assembler code
> ...
> last instruction of the assembler
> first location of the new object program

Then, as soon as the assembler finished executing, control would "fall through" to the just-created object program, which would start to execute automatically. At the end of the assembly process, the PC points to the new object program. Thus, step (*c*) is taken care of automatically: the fetch/execute cycle is already running. Figure 7-2 illustrates a more general approach.

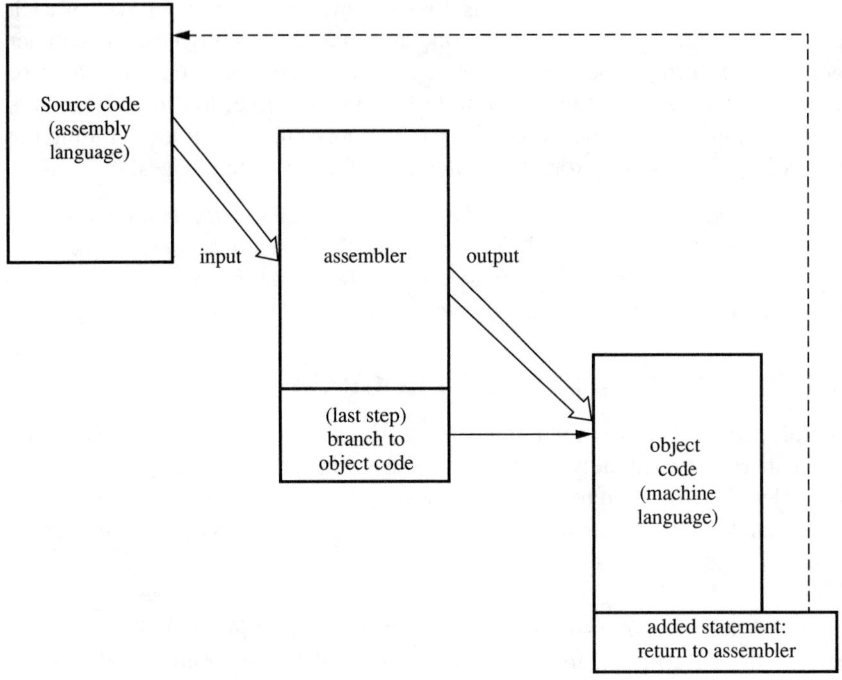

FIGURE 7-2
Transfer control to object program (first attempt).

One way to accomplish step (d) is to add one additional instruction at the end of the object code:

```
jump:always    →somewhere–in–the–assembler
```

which would return control to the assembler when the program was complete. Alternatively, control could be returned to the system by the same method.

However, this approach has at least two problems. First, it requires that there must be sufficient memory to hold both the entire assembler and the entire object program, which is quite wasteful of memory. It requires that both programs be resident at the same time, when by definition only one will be needed at a time. The assembler is finished when the object program begins, so why should it be kept around? Second, there is no guarantee that the object program will complete its execution gracefully. The assembler could not tell which instruction in the source code was intended to be executed last—*or* if the intended last instruction will in fact be last. Some mechanism should be provided to return to the system gracefully. What should happen when the program ends? (Although, GAL does in fact contain a `halt` instruction, `halt` is not a satisfactory ending, for it requires human intervention before the fetch/execute cycle may start again.)

Second attempt. For a marginally better solution, note that the program was assembled using addresses based on the assumption that the program would be started at the given address. Now that the program is assembled and stored at the address, the assembler can cause the object program to run simply by jumping to the first statement in its code. In the last example this could be accomplished with the instruction equivalent to

```
jump:always     →top_of_loop
```

or more accurately

```
4007 1000
```

since there is no reason for the assembler to produce assembly rather than machine code. There is no reason why this location could not occupy the same main memory segment that the assembler occupied. As long as the portion of the assembly code that was overlaid had completed before the object code was stored on top of it, there would be no problem. Perhaps the assembler generates all of the code and copies it to a disk. It then copies the code from the disk to the desired location, overwriting the translation portion of the assembler in the process.

When the program completes execution, it should return control to the system. This can be ensured if the assembler treats the object program as a subroutine, using a

```
jump:subroutine     →top_of_loop
```

rather than a simple jump. That is, the assembler performs a jump-to-subroutine to start execution of the object code. If the assembler also inserts a return at the end of the program, control will return to the assembler after execution of the object program. Only a very small part of the assembler would need to be resident for that final step. The assembler then regains control and can return control to the system in a more graceful manner.

There are still problems with this scenario. One is that the programmer may not have created a well-structured source program. It is not always possible to determine which statement of a program will be executed last. The next section will explore some partial solutions.

▷ *This fact can be proven mathematically and is equivalent to the halting problem.*[1] *Can you think of other significant ramifications of this problem?*

---

[1]The *halting problem* is one of the most famous conundrums of computer science. In its simplest form it states that in general it is not possible to determine in advance whether a given program with given input will always terminate (halt) or will run forever.

Compilers and assemblers are actually very similar entities. Chapter 2 suggested that a compiler might accomplish its goal by translating a higher-level language into assembly language. At this point it should be clear that, although that would theoretically be possible, the assembly language code so produced would then need to be translated into machine language. The normal output of a compiler is machine language code, as is the output from an assembler.

LINKERS AND LOADERS

Although it is always possible for the assembler to insert a `return` at the physical end of the object code, it is not possible to guarantee that that statement will ever be executed. In most systems, two additional pieces of software—the *linker* and the *loader*—address such problems by further processing the object program after assembly, but before it is executed.

Loaders

The addressing problem is even trickier than it first appears. First, it would not be desirable to assemble the code every time you wished to run it.

> ▷ *Can you imagine the problem if you had to assemble the editor or the assembler each time you wish to run those programs? Why is the latter an especially interesting problem?*

Once assembled, it would be desirable to keep a copy of the object code and simply load it whenever you needed it. That would require a different technique from the assemble-and-jump technique described in the previous section. Or suppose you are creating software for use by other users and you expect a large number of copies to be created for use on several computers. These computers, although essentially identical, may have small variations in the hardware or resident systems software. For example, one might have more RAM memory; one might have a disk driver for a hard disk and one for a floppy disk; or one might have more resident fonts; or one has a startup routine that runs first whenever the machine is turned on. Whatever the variations, one potential side effect is that the systems software on the machine will require more of memory on some machines than on others. If one machine has more memory than another, the legal address space for the program will reflect that difference. A *loader* or *linking loader* can help solve these problems.

The basic concept of a loader is simple. The assembler saves the object code on a disk rather than in memory. It then terminates without completing the full task of starting the program. When the loader is executed, it copies the object code from the disk into memory. At this point the situation becomes identical to the earlier situation involving an object module that was loaded by the assembler. The loader can simply finish the task in the same manner as the original assembler: place a return at the end of the object program and jump to the object program

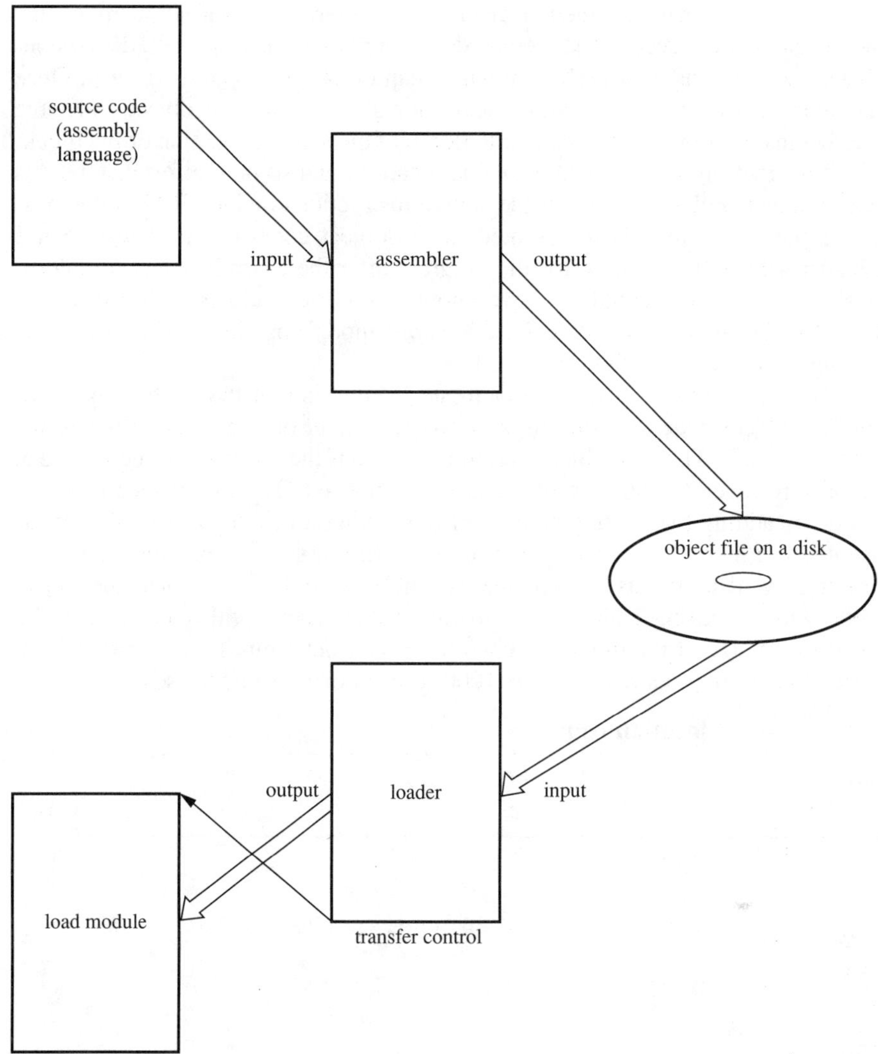

FIGURE 7-3
Loader first attempt.

as a subroutine, as illustrated in Figure 7-3. This would apparently still require that the loader remain resident while the object program ran, but that would not be so great a problem as with the assembler since the loader must be a much smaller program.

RELOCATABLE ADDRESSES. Unfortunately there is a much bigger problem. Although a loader, as its name implies, does load the code into memory at the appropriate location, it has a much more important function. Before a program can be loaded into memory, the loader must first determine where in memory that program should be placed. (The method does not matter for the current discussion. Perhaps it asks the user, or perhaps it has a map of all the system software). Once it has identified a block of memory with enough room for the object code, the loader begins by copying the first instruction into the starting location of the block, the next instruction into the next available location, and so on. Unfortunately, this creates a major problem: many of the source instructions include RAM operands. Each of those operands is represented in the object code as an address. Since the loader selects the location for the program after the assembler has completed its task, the assembler could not have known the correct addresses for all of the labels. The loader must create a *load module*, modifying the object module by changing every address within the module.

The important observation to facilitate loading is that the relative locations within the object code are constant and not dependent on the location where the module is loaded. The assembler, therefore, acts as if the module will be loaded at location zero (even though it knows that it will not be). The loader then modifies the code by adding the starting address of the module to each internal address, as illustrated in Figure 7-4. If the system in the earlier assembly example employed a loader as well as the assembler, the assembler would have created the object module with a starting address of zero rather than 1000, with addresses in the range 0 to the size of the module. When the loader determines that location 1000 is a suitable starting address, it adds 1000 to each of those addresses:

	location	**code**
input to loader		
`code`	`0000`	`<code>`
	`...`	
	`0080`	`----0120 (reference to location foo)`
	`...`	
`[foo]`	`0120...`	
output from loader		
`code`	`1000`	`<code>`
	`...`	
	`1080`	`----1120 (reference to location foo)`
	`...`	
`[foo]`	`1120...`	

In addition to addresses of instructions, the loader must also alter any references to those addresses contained in any instruction. This includes the addresses of RAM operands, destinations of jumps, and the address operand of a `load_address` instruction. To do that, the assembler must inform the loader

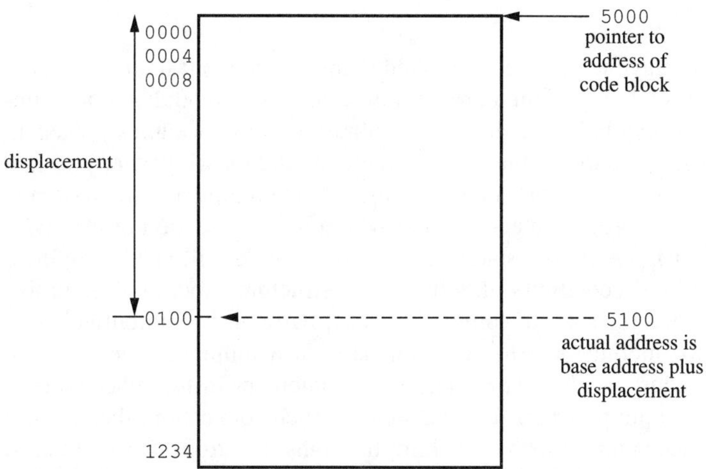

FIGURE 7-4
Base and displacement addressing.

which items must be modified. Addresses that can be modified by the loader are sometimes referred to as *relocatable* (this term should not be confused with the related concept *relocatable code* described in the following section). Addresses that indicate the actual address explicitly are called *absolute addresses*. Conceptually, the determination of which addresses need to be changed could be made in any of several ways. Presumably, the loader could, in effect, reassemble the code to determine which bits represent relocatable addresses. One way to accomplish the conversion would be for the assembler to produce a reference table listing the relative locations of each of the commands that had modifiable addresses. The table consists simply of a list of addresses. The loader adds a displacement to each location indicated by the table. For the preceding example, the table would consist of the single entry:

```
relative references
0082
```

where 0082 specifies the operand field of the command that referred to `foo`. The loader places all code in memory, adds the starting address to the value at 0082, and jumps to the beginning of the first module, in the same manner as did the first version of the assembler.

Although loading in this manner is not a conceptually complicated task, it could be relatively expensive. Once a program is working correctly, the assembler need never be executed again, but such a loader must be executed every time the machine language program is to be executed. Since the majority of instructions contain a RAM operand address, this could necessitate a significant quantity of work every time the program runs.

Linkers

The assembler itself may face a problem related to the relocation task of the loader. On occasion, it is desirable to build a program in segments or modules. For example, the programmer may build a collection or library of subprocedures for use in many programs. It seems undesirable to reassemble the library with every program that uses it. To make the situation worse, the task of developing a large system is often split among many programmers, each of whom writes a section of the code. In such situations, it is likely that statements in one module will need to refer to identifiers declared in a second module. True, well-structured code will minimize the number of such references, but some references, particularly subroutine calls, are necessary if two modules are to communicate. At a minimum, one module will contain a procedure—call it `foo`—and some statement in the other module will need to perform a jump to `foo`. If there were no such connection, there would be no reasonable mechanism for ever making the transition from one module to the other. If a library contains the bodies of several functions and procedures, the main program needs the names (or addresses) in order to call those subprograms. Finally, when building a large program, the programmer will probably build it in segments. Once a given segment is complete and working, future assemblies should not need to reassemble the working segment.

EXTERNAL ADDRESSES. Labels used in one module but defined in another are said to be *external references*. A simple two-pass assembler for the assembly of a main procedure that calls subroutines from an externally defined library would generate error messages if it found external references, because the externally defined symbols will not be found in the symbol table for the main program. On the other hand, the procedure identifiers presumably do appear in the symbol table generated during assembly of the library. In effect, it is necessary to link the symbol table of the library with that of the main procedure. This task is accomplished by means of a *linker*. Essentially, the linker behaves as an extended version of the second pass of the assembler. The linker uses the symbol table from each module to fill in the references found in the other. If a library contained procedures `log`, `exponent`, and `root`, the linker must fill the addresses of these routines into each statement of the main program that references them.

In the simplistic approach, the assembler saves the identifiers that will be needed even after the second pass is complete. If the only external references were identifiers defined in the first module and used in the second (and never the other way around), the task could be handled in a relatively straightforward manner. In theory, the assembler could accept, as input, the symbol table for the previously assembled module and incorporate it into its own symbol table. However, such an approach would require that the modules be completed in a specified order: the target of every external reference must be defined and assembled prior to the referencing statement. But, just as individual instructions could refer to locations above or below the location counter, it is possible that each module will contain references to identifiers defined in the other, making any ordering impossible.

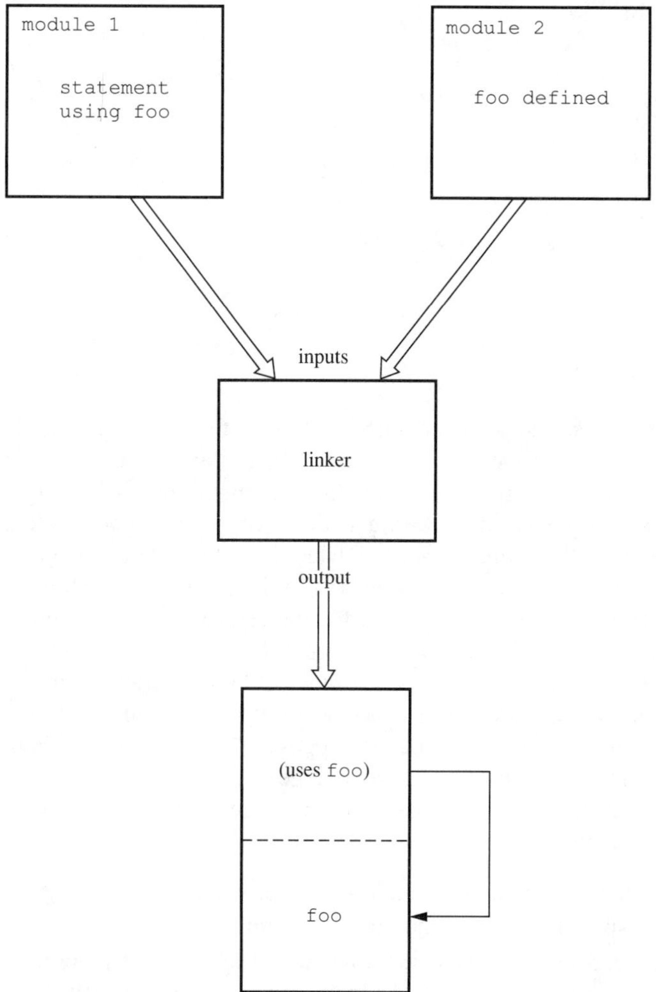

FIGURE 7-5
Logical structure of a linker.

The task is both easier and more complicated than this first description implies. Generally, a linker will match only identifiers that are explicitly marked as intermodule references. Each module may contain directives indicating which references are for external use. The library module containing the definitions of subroutines or other identifiers will contain an *externally referenced* directive. This directive indicates which identifiers defined within the module will be needed (referenced) by some other module. A module that uses those definitions should contain a corresponding *externally defined* directive. The externally defined directive informs the assembler that although a label is used within the code of the current module, it is not defined within that module. The general form is illustrated in Figure 7-5. In more detail:

```
    A       ;module A
            externally defined:       foo
            ...
            copy    foo⇒reg3
            ...
            end_code

    B       ;module B
            externally referenced:    foo
            ...
foo
          constant:word 17
            ...
            end_code
```

Each module must be stored in a separate location. Otherwise the module loaded second would wipe out the first one. To avoid that situation, the module assembled second must have information about the length of the first. If two modules are to be linked together, the starting address of at least one module is usually unknown at assembly time. Prior knowledge of the starting address would require either that the length of the first be known at the time the second is assembled or that an arbitrary address be picked for the second. The first option would not be practical if the modules were assembled by separate individuals. The second option, use of an arbitrary address, would not be a desirable solution if there were more than two modules or if space were at a premium. Selection of an arbitrary starting address for a module presupposes that there is sufficient room for previous modules—even if they are very large.

The object module generated by the assembler is more complex than originally indicated. It has four logical components:

- assembled code: the almost complete machine language code
- a value indicating the size or length of the code segment
- an unresolved references table: for each identifier noted as externally defined, this list contains the relative addresses of statements that use that identifier.
- externally available labels: including all symbols defined within the module but marked as externally referenced, together with the address within the module corresponding to that symbol.

The object modules corresponding to the source modules A and B might appear

module A

```
code         0000   <code>
                      ...
             0080   <incomplete statement involving foo>
             ...

unresolved (externally defined) references
foo          0082

length:      100
```

and

module B

```
code          0000    <code>
              ...
              0020    xxxx (foo)
              ...

externally referenced indentifiers
foo           0020
length:       80
```

The linker has two jobs:

- establish the relative positions of the two modules, recalculating all addresses, and
- match the externally referenced identifiers of one module with the externally defined identifiers of the other module.

The linker accepts as input each object module generated by the assembler. It builds a single load module by combining the object modules sequentially. For each module, it calculates a starting address. For the first module, it is zero; for the second, it is the length of the first; for the third, the combined lengths of the first and second; and so on. Address references are updated in the same way the loader recalculated addresses—by adding a displacement to each address. Note that each externally referenced location has been relocated. Therefore, the externally referenced identifier table is incremented by exactly the same amount. Generally, the starting address of at least one module is not known until they are linked together.

In the example, module `A` is 100_{16} bytes long and module `B` is 80 bytes long. The assembler has no way of knowing the length of module `B` when it is assembling module `A`, and vice versa. The first task of the linker is to adjust the addresses in the individual modules to reflect their relative location when incorporated into a single working module. Assume that in the example, the addresses in module `A` are initially between 0000 and 00FF, and that the original addresses in the library module `B` also started at zero: 0000 to 0080 (as with a loader, when a linker is to be used, most assemblers build the code as if the object module were to start at location zero). The linker adds the length of module `A` = 00FF+1 = 0100 to each address reference in module `B`, including each address defined in module `B` but referenced in module `A`. That is, the linker must create a single block of unambiguous addresses:

Module A & B combined

```
code        0000   <code>
            ...
            0082   0000 (reference to foo)
            ...
            0100   <code>:start of module B
            ...
foo         0120   ...

unresolved (externally defined) references
foo         0082

externally referenced identifiers
foo         0120

length:     180
```

The linker then replaces each unresolved external reference with addresses found in the externally referenced table for the other module. It simply fills in the correct address for each external reference. In the example,

Module A & B combined and resolved

```
code        0000   <code>
            ...
            0082   0120 (reference to foo)
            ...
            0100   <code>:start of module B
            ...
foo         0120   ...

length:     180
```

the linker fills in the value 120, the updated address of `foo`, into the statement that began at location 0080 (with RAM operand field beginning at 0082). If there are several modules, the task is only slightly more complicated. An unresolved identifier might be found in any of several modules. However, since all of the external reference tables are combined into one, multiple modules can be linked sequentially. It seems that conflicts could possibly arise if identical identifiers are used in multiple modules. This would defeat some of the benefits of modular construction. Fortunately no problem occurs unless the identifier is listed as externally addressable in multiple modules.

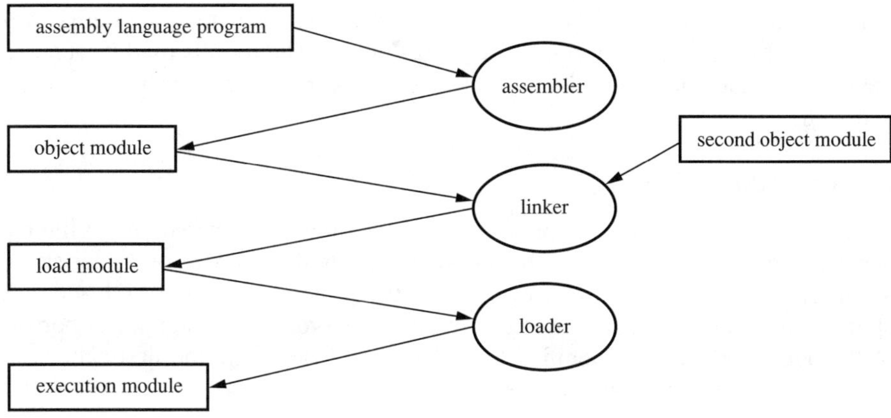

FIGURE 7-6
Relationship between software tools and program modules.

After linking, a loader may load the entire linked module just as it loaded a single assembled object module. The final loaded module is called the *execution module*. The loader is to the linked load module as the linker was to the assembled object module. The sequence of steps therefore can be summarized as in Figure 7-6. In some systems, a single program called a *linking loader* can perform the task of both the linker and the loader.

ASSEMBLY, ADDRESSING, AND MACHINE ARCHITECTURE

The entire assemble-link-load sequence suggests some variations on the internal structure of the basic machine. A few minor changes in the internal representation of addresses and the use of pointers will greatly improve the assembly process.

Binding

An identifier may be associated with its ultimate machine address at several points in the assembly-through-loading process:

- The assembler may specify an absolute address.
- The linker may modify the address to reflect relative position of modules.
- The loader may modify the address to reflect the location of the execution module.

The actual association of a machine address with an identifier is called *binding*, and the chronological point at which binding occurs is called the *binding time*. This is the same term *binding* used in the context of higher-level language to refer to the point at which the value of an actual parameter to a subroutine was bound to an identifier specifying a formal parameter. The term is used throughout mathematics and computer science to refer to such connections between identifiers and values.

Relative Addressing

There is a second partial solution to some of the problems inherent in the linking and loading process. When binding is postponed until the linker or loader steps, all addresses must be modified every time the program is linked or loaded. A slight modification of the hardware can reduce this problem. A significant portion of the addresses that are modified by linkers and loaders are the destinations of `jump` statements. For example, the loop

```
2000    loop_top
2004        compare             . . .
2008        jump:greater        →out_of_loop
200C        . . .
2010
2014
2018
201C
2020        jump:always         →loop_top
2024    out_of_loop             . . .
```

contains two `jumps`. The exact destination address of each `jump` is not known at assembly time since all addresses may be altered by the linker or the loader. However, the position of each statement is known *relative* to the rest of the object module. In particular, the *relative distance* from each `jump` statement to its destination can easily be calculated at assembly time by counting the number of instructions between the `jump` and its destination address. Although the absolute address will change, this relative distance will remain constant when the module is linked and loaded, because the entire module is moved as a block. Two statements that are 20 bytes apart in the object module will be 20 bytes apart in the final execution module. A small change in the `jump` instruction—both its representation and execution—can take advantage of this consistency. This variant of `jump` accomplishes a transfer of control by *adding* a relative distance to the PC rather than completely replacing its contents with a new absolute address. The original `jump` instruction could be described in pseudo-GAL, as:

```
*copy      operand⇒PC
```

while the new variant can be described as

```
*add       operand⇒PC
```

The original GEM architecture accomplishes the first (conditional) `jump` in the example by replacing the contents of the PC (which was 200C at the time) with the new destination address, 2024, causing `out_of_loop` to be the next statement executed. The example loop contains six instructions between the first `jump` and its destination. The six instructions require $6 * 4 = 24_{10} = 18_{16}$ bytes of storage. The modified version of `jump` simply adds 18 to the PC:

```
200C + 18 = 2024.
```

During the fetch/execute cycle, the processor fetched the conditional `jump` when the PC held 2008, but the PC is incremented to 200C before the instruction is actually executed. In terms of the fetch/execute cycle, the relative `jump` becomes

1. fetch `jump` instruction at 2008
2. increment PC to 200C
3. decode instruction
4. fetch operands: PC = 200C and displacement = 18
5. add 200C and 18
6. store sum = 2024 in PC

`Out_of_loop` is at location 2024, 18 more than the contents of the PC at the time of execution. Similarly the absolute `jump` at the end must subtract $9 * 4_{10} = 24_{16}$ from the PC. The `jump` statement is located at 2020, but the PC is incremented to 2024 before the `jump` is executed. `Top_of_loop` is at 2000, 24 less than the current content of the PC. The PC becomes

```
PC = 2024 - 24 = 2000 = address of top_of_loop
```

To enable the processor to use the relative `jumps`, the assembler calculates the relative distance of each jump and places that value into the instruction rather than the absolute destination. Then, if the program is loaded at location 3000 instead of 2000, the relative distance of the `jumps` would still be +18 and −24, even though the absolute addresses are different. With such an addressing mechanism, the loader need only determine the program location, copy the code into that location, and set the PC to point to the first instruction. There is no need to alter every relocatable address, because the relative distances did not change. Such addressing is called *PC-relative addressing* because the address is specified relative to the current address held in the PC. Programs that use such relative addressing are said to be *relocatable* because they can be located anywhere in memory and still work.

An interesting—but confusing for the new programmer—aspect of relative `jumps` is that the machine language representation for two instances of a `jump` will vary, even though the source code for each was identical. Given the code

```
        jump:always      →middle
        ...
middle
        ...
        jump:always      →middle
```

the first machine language instruction will have a positive displacement operand, and the second will have a negative.

Relative addressing offers additional potential fringe benefits. The first is a potential savings in storage. In a well-structured program, the majority of jumps (other than subroutine jumps) should be to locations that are relatively near the current location. Most control structures, such as loops and conditionals, are small, with relatively few intervening instructions. A relative `jump` can usually be accomplished by adding a *small* number (positive or negative) to the PC. In one byte, signed numbers from -128 to +127 can be stored. Thus a single-byte operand can specify a jump forward or backwards of approximately 128 bytes (32 instructions in GEM). A one-byte absolute address, on the other hand, would dictate that the entire program—not just the current control structure—fit within 256 bytes. The GEM model specified a fixed-size for all operands and therefore cannot take advantage of that savings. A machine instruction with a four-bit opcode, and four bits for the mode, and four bits for the relative address would fit in two bytes. Similarly a jump incorporating a two-byte relative address could jump to any location within 32K bytes of the current address (forward or backward). Chapter 6 indicated that the fetch/execute cycle was one of the few places where savings of space and of time could often occur simultaneously. Space savings results in a faster program since fewer instruction bytes would need to be fetched.

A second advantage of relocatable code is in multi-tasking or multi-user machines. In any machine that runs multiple programs at a time (see Chapter 11), whether it allows one or more users, the programs all have to be loaded together. It is impossible to know in advance exactly what other programs will also be loaded. Relocatable code removes the difficulty for these systems, just as it did for the single-program system.

Based Addressing

Although PC-relative addressing reduces the address problem for linkers and loaders with respect to `jump` commands, many of the addresses specified in a program are not `jump` destinations but operands to be added, copied, or otherwise manipulated. Essentially, the same modification can be used for operand addresses. There are two related methods used to accomplish this. First, suppose all of the data storage locations for a program were placed as a block at the front of the program. Further suppose that a register were made to point to that block by initializing it with the address of the first of those storage locations. Each of the storage addresses could be described by its position relative to the first data item and, therefore, relative to the pointer register. For example, suppose data items are stored as follows:

```
2000  my_int           constant:integer
2002  another          constant:integer
2004  and_one_more     constant:integer
2006  a_char           constant:character
2007  two_char         constant:character
```

If `reg3` is set to the value 2000, it becomes a pointer to the first of the data storage locations, `my_int`. Any instruction can then access `my_int` by using the register as an indirect address.

```
copy:int    my_int⇒regl
```

has the identical result as

```
copy:int    reg3↑⇒regl
```

The register is said to be a *base register* since it points to the base of the data section. The remaining identifiers in this case are stored two, four, six, and seven bytes after the first. `Another` is located at the location that is two more than the location pointed to by `reg3`. It could be copied to `regl` by

```
copy:int    reg3⇒reg2
add         #2⇒reg2
copy:int    reg2↑⇒regl
```

Of course, a step could have been saved by adding 2 directly to `reg3`, but that would have destroyed `reg3`'s value as a pointer to the entire data section. The distance from a storage location to the base address is its *displacement*.

```
copy:int    2+reg3↑⇒regl
```

yields an equivalent result to the above and is interpreted as "copy the contents of the location two bytes after the location pointed to by register 3 into register 1." If the representation is standard throughout the program, an assembler can translate each storage reference into a "base plus displacement" representation. For every identifier, the symbol table includes its relative address; the displacement is identical to that relative address. The address field therefore specifies the relative address or displacement from the beginning of the data section rather than the absolute address. In format, this is essentially identical to the indexed addressing mechanism, described in Chapter 5. In the indexed addressing mode, the base register points to a structure and the index (usually a register) is used to access the individual elements of the structure. In the based mode, the base register points to the beginning of the data block. The displacement (usually an immediate or constant) distinguishes between the data items.

The final technique for relative addressing is very similar, combining PC-relative addressing with base register addressing. In this method, the PC is used as a base address for all data references—not just the jumps. This is possible in spite of the fact that the PC is continually changing. Consider the following example:

```
2010          copy     temp⇒reg2
2014          add      temp⇒reg2
...
2040 temp     constant:integer     5
```

From any given statement, each variable and constant is a fixed distance—like the other commands. The assembler can calculate this distance just as it can for jump destinations. As with jumps, multiple assembly language statements that refer to a single data item will have different displacements in their machine language translation. In the example, the distance from the `copy` to `temp` is

```
2040 - 2010 = 30.
```

When the `copy` command is finally executed, however, the PC will point to location 2014, so the relative displacement from the PC to `temp` is actually

```
2040 - 2014 = 2C
```

at the perform step for the `copy` command. When the `add` is executed, the displacement is only 28. Since the relative displacement will be the same no matter where the code is placed by the linker or loader, it can be determined at assembly time: the symbol table contains the address of all symbols, the location counter contains the current address as the code is generated; the displacement is the difference. The assembler, linker, and loader do not need to know where the `add` command will be placed. All that is needed is a guarantee that the relative positions of the commands and the operands are fixed. References to identifiers defined in other modules are a bit more complicated. The relative address will depend on the work of the linker and cannot be determined until the relative locations of all of the modules are determined. The final relative address can then be calculated.

Whichever method is used to implement relative addresses, one instruction in particular develops a new significance: the `load_address` instruction. It is apparent that the `load_address` is one mechanism by which a relative address can be converted into an absolute address. The address is computed as the sum of the base register and the displacement, and it is this sum that is loaded into a register.

LINKING HIGHER-LEVEL LANGUAGE PROGRAMS TO ASSEMBLY LANGUAGE PROCEDURES

Sometimes, a programmer writes a program in assembly language for efficiency reasons. Fortunately, optimization of a single segment of code will result in almost all of the efficiency that is to be gained. Put another way, most compilers generate very efficient code. The human programmer is not likely to do much better. Even if the human can do better, there is little point in doing so unless the code will be executed often enough to result in substantial savings. There are two general classes of circumstance in which such efficiency is likely:

- The higher-level language may prohibit the user from performing some important step.
- The code contains a very tight loop, executed many times. Improvements in the segment will be magnified manyfold by the loop.

Most parts of most programs could be written in a higher-level language with no significant loss of efficiency. Very small portions of a program account for most of the execution time. The commonly used rule of thumb is that 10 percent of the source code is responsible for 90 percent of the execution time. If the programmer could simply optimize that 10 percent of the code, almost all of the possible improvements would be achieved. The immediate question arises: can a higher-level language call an assembly language procedure (or vice versa)? The answer is a distinct and emphatic Yes. The task can easily be accomplished by the linker with very few additional restrictions. The first restriction is that the language development software—assembler and compiler—must share a format for their object code. If both generate an object module of the same format (including the external reference tables, etc., as well as the object code itself), the linker will not care which software generated the module. It can link modules from two source languages just as easily as two modules from the same language. In fact, in any given system, such a convention normally exists.

> ▷ *The above observation is related to the principle of locality, described in Chapter 10. What observations could help the programmer recognize the sections of code that could be optimized?*

The second requirement is trickier, placing the responsibility on the individual programmer. Every hll has established standards: size and representation for variables, strings, arrays, and so on, and established conventions for interprocedure communication, such as the order of arguments to a procedure, the use of register or stack-passing conventions for arguments, or the situations when pointers are used rather than actual values. Fortunately, the programmer's reference manual for any given hll will normally contain a statement of these conventions. The programmer need only obtain the conventions and follow them precisely. For example, the hll reference manual might include the following summary:

- Passing conventions

  all parameters passed on a stack,
  pushed in order of definition

- Sizes

  character: 1 byte
  Boolean: 1 byte
  integer: 2 bytes
  real: 2 bytes
  long_integer: 2 bytes
  structures: sum of their parts

- Value or pointer

  value parameters: copy of the value is passed
  address parameters and structures: pointer is passed

- Functions: result returned on the stack

DIRECTIVES TO THE ASSEMBLER

Assembly language corresponds to machine language on an almost—but not exactly—one-to-one basis. The assembler translates assembly language *commands* directly into the corresponding machine language instructions. The largest class of assembly statements that cannot be translated directly is called *directives*. Prior to this point both terms, *command* and *directive,* have been used, but no formal distinction has been drawn between them. Directives are assembly language statements that do not have machine language equivalents but simply provide directions to the assembler specifying how it should perform its task. Directives look much like assembly commands, but no machine code is generated by a directive. For example, an assembly language program might include the directive

```
addressing = pc_relative
```

which indicates that the assembler should generate PC-relative code rather than absolute addresses. You are already familiar with some directives, for example, the `variable` and `constant` statements. Perhaps the two most important directives are

- macro definitions, which are interpreted as abbreviations for use in future commands, and
- conditional assembly statements, which restrict assembly of the following segment.
- Other directives include string format directives, which tell the assembler how it should represent strings;
- alignment directives, which tell the assembler to place next item on a word boundary; and
- include directives, which tell the assembler to assemble an additional file as if it were inserted at the current point.

Variable and Constant Directives

The `variable` and `constant` statements are actually directives. They do not correspond to any executable machine language statements; no machine instruction has the interpretation "create a variable." The `variable` directive simply reserves space. The presence of a variable declaration tells the assembler to add a symbol to the symbol table and increment the location counter during the first pass. Constants are also directives: no op-code is generated. In addition to the actions suggested by a variable statement, the given value is simply inserted in the program. After the first pass of the assembler, the following code

```
            jump:always     →past_them
conl        constant:word   37
varl        variable:word
past_them
```

will have generated

program		**symbol table**	
loc	code	identifier	loc
1000	xxxx	conl	1004
1004	0025 (hex)	varl	1006
1006	0000	past_them	1008
1008			

Macros

The programmer can create a sort of shorthand representation, called a *macro,* for frequently used assembly language constructs. A macro serves as an abbreviation, perhaps with arguments, for a block of assembly code. Once a macro has been defined, using a *macro definition* statement, it may be used any number of times within the assembly language program. For example, to clear (set to 0) the low-numbered registers, a programmer might use the macro

```
clear_um     macro       =
             subtract    reg0⇒reg0       ;anything minus
                                         ;itself is 0
             subtract    reg1⇒reg1
             subtract    reg2⇒reg2
             end_macro
```

The macro can then be used anywhere in a program by referring to it by name

```
             <previous_statement>
             clear_um
             <next_statement>
```

The macro definition should be interpreted as an instruction to the assembler telling it to replace each occurance of macro, `clear_um`, with the body of the macro (the three `subtracts`) before assembling the line. Macros can have parameters. For example, it is frequently necessary to switch the contents of two storage locations, using a temporary storage location. A macro, `switch`, used for this purpose could be defined as

```
switch     macro       first,second,temp   =
           copy        first⇒temp
           copy        second⇒first
           copy        temp⇒second
           end_macro
```

The formal parameters for the macro are replaced by the actual parameters when it is expanded. The macro expansion is really a three-step process:

- replace the name of the macro with the body of the macro;
- replace each formal parameter with the actual parameter; and
- assemble the resulting text.

The replacements are purely syntactic string substitutions. The macro definition itself is really just a template for use by the assembler. No machine code is generated by the macro definition. However, at any later point in the program, wherever it is necessary to switch two values, the *macro call* can be used as if it were an assembly language instruction. The assembler *expands* the macro into AL code by substituting the body of the definition for the call. The code

```
        copy            #5⇒item1
        switch          item1,item2,save_place
        jump:always     →somewhere
```

is expanded to

```
        copy            #5⇒item1
        copy            item1⇒save_place      ;expansion
        copy            item2⇒item1           ;expansion
        copy            save_place⇒item2      ;expansion
        jump:always     →somewhere
```

before it is assembled into machine code. Notice that each formal argument of the macro is replaced by the corresponding actual argument. The expanded code is then assembled as if it were the original code delivered to the assembler.

Macros have two very important uses. Obviously, a macro can shorten the assembly language program as it appears in a listing. More importantly, it can create code that is easier to understand by grouping assembly language statements into logical units. For example, consider the macro

```
call    macro           routine,param   =
        copy            param⇒reg0
        jump:sub        →routine
        end_macro
```

which could be used to call the subroutine `foo`, passing it the single parameter, bar, with the statement

```
        call            foo,bar
```

which would be expanded to

```
        copy            bar⇒reg0
        jump:sub        →foo
```

before assembly.

These advantages are very similar to the modularity provided by procedures and functions, but there are important differences between macros and procedures. A subroutine is only coded once, but every macro call is fully expanded into the entire macro body. As an example of the difference, consider a code segment `eight_times`, which multiplies a number by 8 by doubling itself 3 times. As a procedure, `eight_times` looks like this:

```
eight_times                          ;assume argument in reg0
    add            reg0⇒reg0
    add            reg0⇒reg0
    add            reg0⇒reg0
    return
```

The subroutine `eight_times` could be used to multiply a value by 512 (= 8^3) by calling it three times:

```
    copy           #5⇒reg0
    jump:sub       →eight_times
    jump:sub       →eight_times
    jump:sub       →eight_times
```

The definition and three calls required a total of eight lines of assembly code. On the other hand, a macro definition of `eight_times` looks like

```
eight_times
    macro          loc  =
    add            loc⇒loc
    add            loc⇒loc
    add            loc⇒loc
    end_macro
```

To use the macro to multiply by 512 one would write

```
    copy           #5⇒reg0
    eight_times    reg0
    eight_times    reg0
    eight_times    reg0
```

which requires nine lines of assembly source code. So far the two approaches look approximately the same. However, the macros are expanded to

```
    copy           #5⇒reg0
    add            reg0⇒reg0      ;first reference
    add            reg0⇒reg0
    add            reg0⇒reg0
    add            reg0⇒reg0      ;second reference
    add            reg0⇒reg0
    add            reg0⇒reg0
    add            reg0⇒reg0      ;third reference
    add            reg0⇒reg0
    add            reg0⇒reg0
```

which bring the total to 10 assembled object statements; multiplying by 2^{12} would generate 13 lines. Unlike a subroutine, each use of a macro expands all of the statements within the macro definition. Only the source code is actually shorter. Since the macro is expanded before assembly, the full object code contains the full body of the expanded macro for each instance of its use. The expanded body is said to be inserted *in line*. In general, macro expansions will require much more machine code than will subroutines. On the other hand, there is no `jump` needed to reach the body of the macro, nor any `return` needed to get back to the main procedure. The macro will therefore run a (very) little faster.

Some additional distinctions: a macro is more flexible than a subroutine. When a subroutine is written, the specific parameter-passing technique (passing in `reg0` in the example) is firmly established. The macro could just as easily have had its argument in `reg2` or `reg7`. The expansion would have generated the correct code. On the other hand, this flexibility can lead to errors. Once a subroutine is debugged, the programmer can ignore the internal details. Since every instance of a macro is expanded, use of a macro can generate an error if the internal details are ignored. In GAL, the macro call

```
        eight_times   my_item
```

would generate an error because the first line would would be expanded to:

```
        add           my_item⇒my_item
```

which would not be a legal GAL instruction (two RAM operands).

Macros can be used to define other macros. For example, the macro

```
push    macro         value =
        copy          value⇒(reg0)     ;assume reg0 is stack
                                       ;register
        add           2⇒reg0           ;assumes word length
                                       ;operands
        end_macro
```

could be used in a new definition of the `call` macro, which uses stack-based parameters

```
call    macro         routine,param    =
        push          param
        jump:sub      →routine
        end_macro.
```

Parameters other than "operands" can be passed to a macro. For example, the macro

```
copy_type
        macro         type,from,to     =
        copy:type     from⇒to
        end_macro
```

could be used by the programmer to ensure that all copy commands included a `type`. A "missing argument" error message will be generated if it is omitted, which is much better than an incorrect value with no message!

A subroutine is necessarily composed of an integral number of lines, and the arguments to a subroutine are necessarily items to be manipulated by the subroutine. Macros have no such boundaries. For example, a macro could be a single word. Suppose the programmer wanted to make it clear that arguments were passed using `reg0`. The macro `param_reg` would allow that name to be used in place of `reg0`:

```
param_reg     macro              =
              reg0
              end_macro
```

The original program could then contain the line

```
              copy    item⇒param_reg
```

which would be "expanded" to

```
              copy    item⇒reg0
```

In fact, this use of macros is so common that many machines have a second macro structure (typically called `equate`) for the specific use of equating a user-defined symbol to some previously existing symbol. This form is slightly simpler because the translation is a one-step, rather than two-step, process. An `equate`-type macro is especially useful for representing constant values that appear repeated in a program. For example, the bounds of a 10×10 matrix—and all of the appropriate indices to the matrix within the program—can be specified with the statement

```
size     equals   10
```

If a new size is needed, `size` can be redefined to the new size. All statements using `size` are automatically adjusted when the program is reassembled.

Conditional Assembly

On occasion, the programmer knows there will be distinct situations that may arise in the future that differ from the present. For example, a program may need to run on two machines, one of which has considerably more memory than the other. It may be desirable in such a situation to reserve a block of storage, the size of which reflects the quantity of memory available. One way to do this would be to provide two complete versions of the program. A more elegant method is to provide two versions for just those parts that differ and to assemble only one—whichever block was appropriate to the situation. *Conditional assembly* provides exactly such a capability. For example, two storage declarations might be provided together with a test:

```
          IF (size >1000) then assemble:
item      variable:integer    100
          ELSE assemble:
item      variable:integer    10
          END_CONDITIONAL
```

Although it appears that the name `item` was defined twice, only one of the lines will be assembled depending upon the conditions in the test. The `if`, `else`, and `end_conditional` statements are not lines to be assembled but directives specifying which other lines are to be assembled. The assembler first evaluates the test. If the result is true, it assembles the first (then) item. If the test is false, it assembles the second (else) item. The test `(size >1000)` may involve any information available to the assembler. Since the entire assembly process is completed prior to execution of the program, the test cannot contain any information that will not be available until execution time. Frequently, the assembler itself is allowed to have assembly variables that can be tested. In the example, `size` is apparently such a variable. Assemblers may provide two methods for assigning values to assembly variables. First, the `equate` (or related directive) may be used to set the value explicitly:

```
size      equals  100
```

If `size` is then used in an assembly statement, `100` is substituted for `size` before the statement is assembled. If this `equate` is inserted prior to the conditional assembly, the second option is taken. On some machines, values can be passed to the assembler at the time the assembler is called:

```
assemble    mycode,size=100
```

which is useful because there is no need to edit the source code itself to set the value. Of course a single test value may be used multiple times within an assembly.

Conditional assembly may be combined with macros, to enable variations in the code to be used throughout the program. One particularly useful combination allows macros with a varying number of parameters. For example, consider the following version of `add`, which allows the programmer to establish the byte as the default size:

```
new_add     macro     item1,item2,size    =
            if (size = null) then assemble
                add:byte    item1⇒item2
            else assemble
                add:size    item1⇒item2
            end_conditional
            end_macro
```

If the third argument is not passed, it becomes `null`, causing the assembler to make the first interpretation.

Miscellaneous Directives

Most assembly languages provide a number of options for programmer control. Some common directives include the following.

INCLUDED CODE. Another common assembly directive, `include`, allows code from a second source file to be inserted into the primary source file for assembly purposes. If source file `B` had the lines

```
<statement_b_1>
<statement_b_2>
. . .
<statement_b_n>
```

and the primary file contained the statements

```
<statement_a_1>
include B
<statement_a_2>
```

the result would be exactly the same as if the line `include B` was replaced by the statements in the file B.

```
<statement_a_1>
<statement_b_1>
<statement_b_2>
. . .
<statement_b_n>
<statement_a_2>
```

Such a directive would be useful if all of the code in segment `B` were fully debugged and the programmer wanted to keep it "out of sight and out of mind." Unlike linked modules, the entire segment `A` and `B` will be assembled. In that sense, it is closer to a macro. The code is first expanded to include the extra file and then assembled. It is also common to place all of the macros into an *include* file.

FORKS. Normally, data is stored at the location corresponding to the position of its directive in the assembly code. If one item is declared prior to another, it will be physically located in front of the other. This positioning rule applies to commands, data, and combinations of the two. However, some machines insist that all code be broken into two segments called *forks:* a data fork and a program fork. The former holds all variables; the latter holds all code and constants. As a program is assembled, all statements and constant directives are assembled and placed in order as expected. However, all variables are grouped together in a second module: the data fork. The items in the variable fork can change. The task of separating variables from code may be accomplished by the assembler or left to the programmer. The important reasons for this separation are discussed in Chapter 11. For the moment, simply observe that the items in the program fork (commands and constants) cannot (or more precisely, should not) change their content. In terms of the addressing modes, it is typical for the program fork (including the constants) to use PC-based addressing, since all are stored near to where the PC points. The data fork will typically use a register- (not the PC-) based addressing mode. Typically, a single register will point to a block containing all variables. Figure 7-7 illustrates the concept.

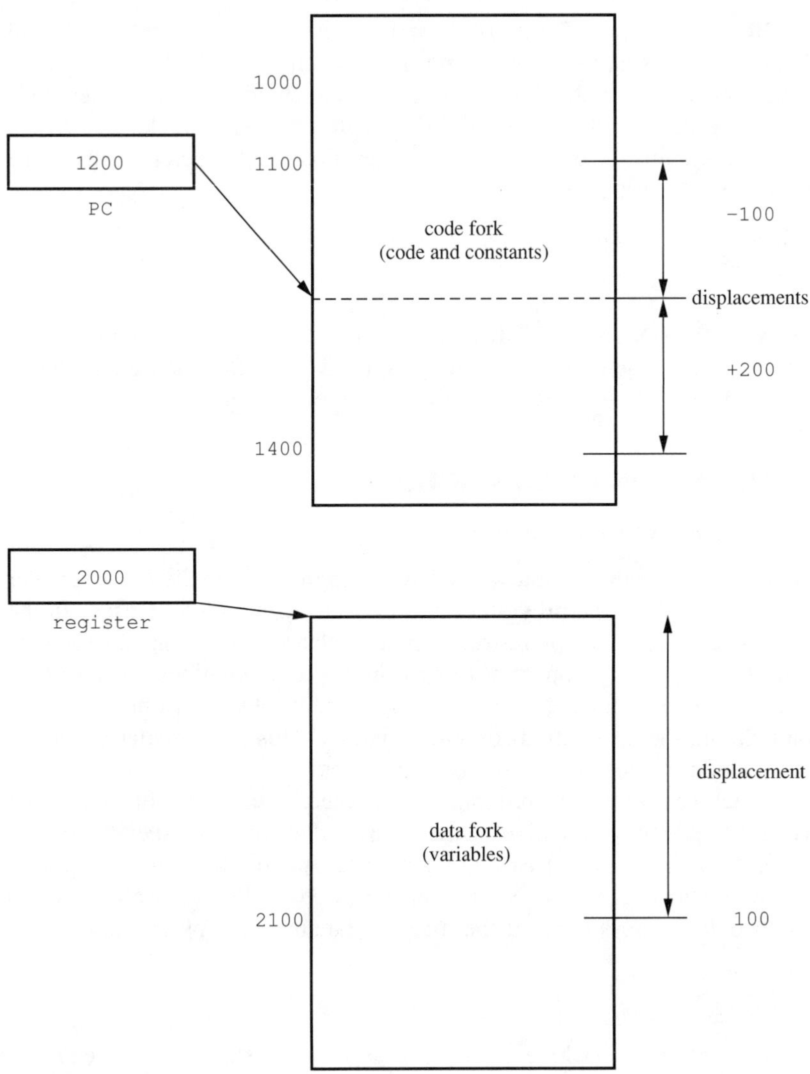

FIGURE 7-7
Forks.

EXTERNAL DEFINITIONS. Usually any symbol that is externally defined must be explicitly indicated. Similarly any identifier to be referenced from another module must also be indicated. The directives *external definition* and *externally referenced* are used for this purpose.

ALIGNMENT. Machines that require that all instructions start on even boundaries normally have a directive to specify that the next command should be an even boundary.

> ▷ *How could it be otherwise?*

STRING FORMAT. Chapter 5 discussed techniques for processing arrays and strings. Many machines allow the programmer to specify how the lengths or end-points of strings will be stored. The two most common choices are (1) the length is explicitly stored as the zeroth byte of the string, with the first character in the next location, and (2) the final character is a special termination character—usually the null character (`null` = 00_{16}).

> ▷ *What does method (1) suggest about the maximum length of a string?*

MODE OR ADDRESSING DEFAULTS. Many machines allow the programmer to specify aspects of the assembly process ranging from the default addressing mode (absolute, based, PC-relative, etc.) to default storage addresses.

PROGRAMMING ON REAL MACHINES

Relative versus Absolute Addresses

Many machines allow both absolute and relative jumping. Normally the assembler provides a mechanism for the programmer to indicate which is to be used. In the M68000, for example, `branch` instructions are relative and `jump` instructions are absolute. It is especially important to have jumps-to-subroutines, because in a well-structured program they are far more likely to be located far from the current instruction than are the destinations of simple jumps. This is particularly true for subroutines located in separately assembled modules.

Some machines allow the programmer to specify the form of addressing by means of an assembly directive. Others insist that you use specific forms. For example, some machines insist that code be relocatable (therefore, requiring relative `jumps`). The assemblers for such machines probably do not allow you to specify an absolute address (even if the machine language seems to allow it).

Understanding Errors

It may seem strange that machine errors such as illegal instruction or illegal address can occur in an object program derived from an assembly language program. At first, such a break-down may seem almost inconceivable in the modern computational process (despite ample evidence to the contrary in the form of error messages). After all, machine code represents the output of an assembler, and presumably the assembler has been thoroughly debugged. It seems hard to believe that the assembler might make an error in the code that it generates. It is possible—although not likely—that an error could arise from poor assembly. A far more likely source of problems are coding errors on the part of the programmer—errors that the assembler could not reasonably be expected to detect. Some simple examples:

- Data is inserted between statements of the program:

```
      jump:equal     →next
      constant        5
next ...
```

  The user may have used the `constant` as a mechanism for generating some special instruction. Further, the assembler has no way of determining whether or not the `jump` will always be taken. If the `jump` is always taken, there is no problem. If a conditional jump is not taken, the constant value 5 will be fetched in the following cycle, most likely producing an "illegal instruction" error.
- The jump to absolute address,

```
      jump:always    →12345
```

  could cause attempted execution of a nonexistent address. The assembler may have no knowledge of the quantity of memory available (particularly in the case in which the code is assembled on one machine for use on another).
- Assuming that `loc` specifies a valid instruction address, the `jump`

```
      jump:always    →loc + 1
      ...
loc   ...
```

  would likely result in a misaligned instruction being fetched. If instructions each have four bytes and an instruction starts at `loc`, no instruction can possibly start at `loc + 1`. The assembler cannot detect such invalid uses, since the code will be relocated during linkage and assembly. Successful assembly implies that the code is valid assembly language, but not necessarily a valid machine language program.

Most assembly errors involve the translation from assembly language into machine language and were discussed in a previous chapter. The use of some directives opens up new error possibilities. The macro can produce "hidden errors" requiring that the programmer expand the macro by hand to see what incorrect code would be generated.

LINKING ERRORS. An understanding of the overall assembly process also helps to clarify some of the nonassembly errors. Normally it is impossible to link unless the assembly step was successful. The "good news" delivered by linker errors is that assembly was successful: the individual modules must be syntactically correct. The most common linker error is an "unresolved external reference" error. Simply stated, this error indicates that one module expected to find the definition of some symbol in another module, but no identifier was found. The most common sources of the error are (1) a misspelled identifier in one module or the other, and (2) an omitted "externally referenced" directive in the defining module. A second potential linker error may occur if the linker fails to find a file containing one module. Typically, the file was incorrectly specified.

LOADER ERRORS. Loader errors should be quite rare. Assuming that the link step was successful, few errors can occur when loading. Two possibilities are that not enough memory is available for the program, and that files were incorrectly specified.

RUN-TIME ERRORS. Improperly included or linked segments can introduce new forms of error. Incorrect assumptions about default addressing modes can cause unpredictable results. For example, an ill-formed jump to an address in another module cannot be detected by the assembler. Macro expansions can often create code that is not what the user intended.

SUMMARY

The assembler is a program that translates an assembly language source program into a machine language object program. Most assemblers require two passes in order to resolve forward identifier references using a symbol table. A linker can be used to link multiple object modules together into a single-load module, which can be loaded into the machine as an execution module by the loader (or the two processes can be combined in a linking loader). In order to facilitate the work of the linker and loader, PC-relative and based-addressing modes are often used.

Directives can be given to the assembler to control various aspects of the assembly process. Macros can be defined and later expanded into actual code segments, producing easier-to-read source code. Conditional assembly allows a program to be assembled in different ways in varying situations. Other directives can specify addressing modes, data formats, and so on.

EXERCISES

(Appendix 2 includes a project very relevant to this chapter: build a GAL assembler. However, that project is best postponed until after Chapter 9.)

7.1. Take any segment of code you have written and play the role of assembler for several lines of code. Compare your results with the output of a real assembler.

7.2. Assemble two small blocks of code separately. Play the role of linker by changing the addresses in one to create a single larger block.

7.3. Compilers for higher-level languages also use symbol tables to keep track of identifiers. Some languages, such as Pascal, require that all identifiers be defined at the beginning of the procedure in which they are used. What impact does such a requirement have on the symbol table and its use?

7.4. Take any program that you have written and create two files. Separate the subroutines from the main program, placing them into the two separate files. Add the appropriate external reference and definition directives. Assemble the two programs and link them together.

7.5. Write the following macros:

(a) `write`, which outputs its single argument
(b) `call2`, which calls any subroutine requiring two arguments
(c) `pop`, which removes the top item from the stack
(d) `push`, which places a value on the stack

7.6. For any convenient higher-level language, look up the argument passing conventions in the reference manual. Write a bubble sort in that language that uses a procedure `switch`. Define `switch` in your assembly language, link the two together, and run them.

7.7. Some assemblers attempt to "optimize" the code they generate by making minor changes. For example, an `add` instruction may be changed to an `add`-immediate instruction. Look at the machine language output from your assembler and see if you can find any such changes.

7.8. What does the concept of the two-pass assembler suggest about languages such as Pascal and Modula?

7.9. Many higher-level languages insist that reserved words such as command names not be used as identifiers for variables or constants. Are the same restrictions necessary in assembly language?

7.10. The GEM machine has fixed-length instructions. If it had relative addressing, how far from the current instruction could a jump transfer? If the relative address specified instructions, how distant a jump would then be possible? How could the jump be accomplished since addresses must really be in terms of bytes?

7.11. For each GAL instruction that is not identical to the nearest corresponding assembly language on the machine you use, write a macro that adds the GAL instruction to your assembly language. For example `subtract` can be defined something like

```
subtract     macro         source,dest =
             sub.w         source,dest
             end_macro
```

7.12. What is wrong with the following macro definition? Can it be fixed?

```
test         macro         value =
             subtract      #1⇒value
             test          value
             end_macro
```

7.13. If a program has 1000 defined symbols, how long will a naive search of its symbol table take? Can it be optimized? How?

7.14. Write a very simple assembler for a subset of GAL, containing only the arithmetic operations, integer sizes, and register operands. (Note: with no RAM operands, it need not be two-pass.)

7.15. Suppose three modules, A, B, and C, of length 300, 1000, and 100, respectively, are fed to a linker. For each module, how much must be added to all internal values? If they are then loaded at location 2000 with a non-relocating loader, what are the final displacements?

7.16. Consider a simple example of relocating code:

```
beginning
    set pointer to beginning
    copy from pointer↑ to pointer plus 1000↑
    increment pointer
    branch to beginning if not all copied
    branch to beginning plus 1000.
```

Write a code segment, move it with a mover like the above, and branch to it.

PART IV

THE DIGITAL LOGIC MODEL

All models to this point—the higher-level language, the assembly language, and the machine language models—have been essentially similar with respect to both procedural and data abstractions. The primitive actions at each model corresponded to user instructions. The primitive objects reflected the data types commonly associated with higher-level languages. Some of the primitive actions are actually fairly complex: arithmetic operations, decoding, copying data from one location to another, and holding a value in a register. Section IV marks a distinct departure from those models. To understand why a new descriptive method is necessary, the reader should reflect on questions such as: "I know how to add numbers in a given base, but how can a computer accomplish this task?" "I know that when a value is placed in memory, it stays there until it is replaced with a new value, but how is memory constructed to guarantee that result?" "The fetch/execute cycle is a series of steps, but how are the steps coordinated?" "The opcode is contained in only a portion of a byte, but the operands of machine instructions are all at least a full byte, so how can the opcode be accessed?" "I know that computers are *binary,* but why are they binary? And what does that have to do with programming?"

In this section, we will see that all computer operations, such as the steps of the fetch/execute cycle, can themselves be broken down into a series of suboperations, all of which can be described using a very small number of basic logical tools. Boolean algebra is a mathematical system of two values: `true` and `false`. Since computers are also based on a system of two values, Boolean algebras form an ideal mechanism for describing the behavior of digital computers. Chapter 8 investigates the basic abstract properties of Boolean algebras. For many readers, it will serve as a review. For others, it will serve as a very brief introduction. Chapters 9 and 10 then investigate how those basic principles can be used to construct or describe the individual logical components of a computer.

CHAPTER 8

LOGICAL OPERATIONS

Metamathematics is the study of the foundations of mathematics: an attempt by a discipline to establish its ultimate roots. The foundations of computer science can be found in the study of discrete math. It seems that ultimately most (or at least, a great many) issues of computer science can be described in terms of discrete mathematics. Computer organization is no exception. All the aspects covered this far—registers, memory fetches, addition, conditional jumps, etc.—can be described in terms of a small set of logical operations. Therefore, we now take a short detour from the study of computer organization to review (or for some, to see for the first time) some of the logical foundations of computer science that we will need in the following chapter.

BOOLEAN ALGEBRA

Boolean Constructs in Higher-Level Languages

Most higher-level languages include a representation of the logical or Boolean data type: a type whose values are either `true` or `false`. At a minimum, hlls include Boolean values as part of the control mechanism for program execution. Conditional and iteration statements involve a Boolean test such as

```
if <test>
    then <action>
```

in which the `<action>` is performed if (and only if) the `<test>` has the value `true`. This is summarized:

conditional value	result
`true`	`<action>` taken
`false`	`<action>` not taken

An if−then−else statement could be represented by a similar diagram, with the last line replaced by

```
false        <else-action> taken
```

Hlls also allow compound tests:

```
If (<test_1> and <test_2>)
  then <action>
```

in which case the <action> is not performed unless both <test_1> and <test_2> are true. A two-test conditional can be diagrammed as

conditional values		**result**
test_1	test_2	
true	true	<action> taken
false	true	<action> not taken
true	false	<action> not taken
false	false	<action> not taken

Although some programmers may not be quite so familiar with further uses of the Boolean type, most hlls provide a full range of Boolean capabilities, including storage declarations (both variables and constants), assignment capabilities, functions for combining logical data, and relations for computing logical values based on data of other types (e.g., the relation less applied to two numeric operands yields a Boolean value: (3 < 4) is true). Thus, the statement

```
assign   test⇐(3<4)
```

would place the value true into the variable test. The function

```
function test_it (a, b:real):Boolean;
```

will return a value of true or false depending upon some tests performed within its body. Chapter 5 showed that all of the common Boolean control operations of hlls can be simulated by careful use of compare/jump combinations. This chapter investigates the logical data type, its mathematical interpretation, as well as its representation and use within a digital computer.

Basic Operations

An *algebra* is a system consisting of *objects,* which have values, and *functions,* or *mappings,* from the set of possible values onto the set of values. In the algebra that you all know (and love) from high school, the objects are the numbers and the functions are the arithmetic operations such as addition and multiplication. A *Boolean algebra* (named for the British mathematician, George Boole (1815–1864), who first formally described such systems) is an algebra, or formal system, for the manipulation of objects that can take on only two distinct values. Typically, the two values are called `true` and `false`, but they could also be any other pair of values. As will soon become obvious, the definitions of the common Boolean functions assume that the values are interpreted as `true` and `false`. Variables or constants can have Boolean values.

In addition to the objects, an algebra has a system of operators or functions for manipulating the objects within its universe. Recall that, mathematically, a function is a mapping from one set to another. Thus, a typical Boolean function, `b`, is a mapping:

$$\texttt{b}:\{\texttt{False, True}\} \times \{\texttt{False, True}\} \rightarrow \{\texttt{False, True}\}$$

That is, a binary Boolean function maps two Boolean values onto a single Boolean value. The basic Boolean functions or *operators* are *conjunction* (`and`), *disjunction* (`or`) and *negation* (`not`).

A *proposition* or *formula* is an expression composed of

- a Boolean literal, constant or variable (simple expression);
- two Boolean expressions connected by Boolean operators `and` or `or`; or
- a Boolean expression preceded by `not`.

An expression

<bool_val> <operator> <bool_val>

is true if `<operator>` applied to `<bool_val>` and `<bool_val>` is `true`. The behavior of the Boolean functions is described by the following table:

operands		**result**		
a	b	a AND b	a OR b	NOT a[1]
false	false	false	false	true
false	true	false	true	true
true	false	false	true	false
true	true	true	true	false

[1]The wide variety of symbols used for these operations can be confusing. For example,

(a or b) is represented as ($a \vee b$) or as ($a + b$);
(a and b) by ($a \wedge b$) or ($a \cdot b$); and
(not a) can be any of -a, ~a, ¬a, a', or $\bar{a}$ (pronounced "a bar")

To avoid confusion, I attempt to use the English language names for the operations wherever possible.

Such tables are called *truth tables,* because they indicate the conditions under which an expression yields a `true` result. Notice that this table is essentially the same as the tables used earlier to describe the behavior of conditional statements. The above table can be summarized as

`a and b`	is true if and only if both `a` and `b` are true.
`a or b`	is true if either `a` is true, or `b` is true.
`not a`	is true exactly when `a` is not true.

Continuing the analogy with numeric algebras, disjunction and conjunction are apparently *binary* operations (like addition and multiplication) and negation is a *unary* operation (like a unary minus). Unlike the common numeric algebra, both the domain and the range of functions are finite. Thus, a complete enumeration of a Boolean function requires a very few lines. On the other hand, the arithmetic function, addition, is infinite. There is an infinite number of possible inputs and an infinite number of possible outputs. No purely tabular or descriptive definition is possible. Procedural definitions are necessary to describe the behavior of arithmetic functions. Truth table descriptions are useful partly because they allow us to categorize formulae.

A formula is said to be a *tautology* if it is always true—that is, if all the entries in its truth table are true. For example, the formula (`a or (not a)`) is a tautology:

`a`	`not a`	`a or (not a)`
F	T	T
T	F	T

Therefore either `a` or its negation must be true. A formula with all false values in its truth table is called a *contradiction.* It can never be true. For example, `a` and `not a` cannot both be true:

`a`	`not a`	`a and (not a)`
F	T	F
T	F	F

Two formulae are said to be *equivalent* if they have the same truth table. Since (`a and b`) and (`b and a`) have the same truth tables:

`a`	`b`	`a and b`	`b and a`
F	F	F	F
F	T	F	F
T	F	F	F
T	T	T	T

they must be equivalent, which implies that conjunction is commutative.

The Boolean operations within an algebra all behave exactly as their counterparts do in hll conditional statements. With the possible exception of disjunction, they also reflect the common sense definitions of the terms. Conjunction requires both values to be `true`; negation yields the opposite value of its argument. Disjunction yields a true result if either of the operands is `true`, including the situation in which both operands are true. That is, although the English word "or" might be used to imply that only one of two possibilities is true, the logical `or` does not have that distinction. The English sentence, "Either I am going to study or I am going to the party" might be interpreted as implying that I will do one or the other, *but not both*. As can be seen from the truth table, the logical conjunction allows for the possibility that I will both study and go to the party. Because disjunction includes the conjunctive situation, it is sometimes referred to as *inclusive disjunction* or an *inclusive or*. Computer scientists and mathematicians also use a variation called *exclusive or,* which corresponds more closely to the English "or" and is described by the truth table:

a	b	a exclusive-or b
F	F	F
F	T	T
T	F	T
T	T	F

The inclusive interpretation for `or` provides a more consistent interpretation. For example, consider the Boolean expression `(a or a)`. Intuitively, this expression should be `true` in exactly those situations for which `a` is `true`, but the exclusive interpretation would require that that expression be always false.

Propositional Calculus

The *propositional calculus* is a set of operational rules, by which a formula can be proved to be a theorem, that is, a tautology. Most of the rules take the form:

if `<exp1>` is a theorem
then `<exp2>` is also a theorem.

For example the rule of *simplification* states that

if `(a and b)` is a theorem
then `a` is a theorem.

The rule of *adjunction* states that

if `a` and `b` are both theorems
then `(a and b)` is a theorem.

The propositional calculus is very closely related to Boolean algebra. In this simple form a calculus rule is roughly equivalent to the statement that, in a truth table, the consequent will be true wherever the antecedent is true. The propositional calculus also allows for conditional proof techniques such as proof by contradiction, in which one assumes that a proposed theorem is false and generates a contradiction.

Constructed Operations

Because Boolean operands have only two possible values (`true` and `false`), binary Boolean operations have only four (2^2) possible input combinations. Thus, it is always a simple task to describe a Boolean operation completely with a truth table such as the above. One might wonder what other logical operations exist and how many of them have recognizable names. Since there are four possible combinations of Boolean operands (FF, FT, TF, TT), and each combination could map to one of two distinct values (T or F), there must be $2^4 = 16$ possible binary functions. Table 8-1 shows the full set.

> ▷ *Suppose we interpret F as zero and T as one. What will that tell us about the correctness of the number of possible functional results? What similarities exist between Table 8-1 and the definitions for* `and` *and* `or` *given earlier?*

Half of the functions have simple and obvious names:

F_1 is conjunction
F_7 is disjunction
F_{10} and F_{12} both represent negation (`¬b`, and `¬a`, respectively)
F_3 is identically `a`
F_5 is identically `b`
F_{15} is the tautology (universally `true`)
F_0 is the contradiction (universally `false`)

IMPLICATION. A particularly important function is called *implication* and denoted: `A → B`. Function F_{13} is read as "A implies B," or "if A then B." The definition of implication can be confusing at first: implication is `true` unless it is demonstrably `false`. The only case in which implication is false is that in which the first argument or *antecedent* is true but the second argument or *consequent* is false. Implication is summarized in the following truth table.

operands		**result**		
`a`	`b`	`a implies b`	`not a`	`(not a) or b`
false	false	**true**	true	**true**
false	true	**true**	true	**true**
true	false	**false**	false	**false**
true	true	**true**	false	**true**

TABLE 8-1
Logical functions

Operands		All possible functions			
first a	second b	#0	#1	#2	#3
F	F	F	F	F	F
F	T	F	F	F	F
T	F	F	F	T	T
T	T	F	T	F	T
names		universally FALSE	conjunction		identity
construction		a and (not a)	a and b	a and (not b)	a

first a	second b	#4	#5	#6	#7
F	F	F	F	F	F
F	T	T	T	T	T
T	F	F	F	T	T
T	T	F	T	F	T
names			identity	a xor b	disjunction a or b
construction		(not a) and b	b	(a or b) and not (a and b)	

first a	second b	#8	#9	#10	#11
F	F	T	T	T	T
F	T	F	F	F	F
T	F	F	F	T	T
T	T	F	T	F	T
names		nor*	bi-implication a iff b	negation	implication b →a
construction		not (a or b)	(a and b) or ((not a) and (not b))	not b	(not b) or a

first a	second b	#12	#13	#14	#15
F	F	T	T	T	T
F	T	T	T	T	T
T	F	F	F	T	T
T	T	F	T	F	T
names		negation	implication a →b	nand*	TRUE
construction		not a	(not a) or b	not (a and b)	a or (not a)

* The functions *nor* and *nand* have special significance that will be seen in Chapter 9.

This table also shows that the implication

`(a implies b)` (also written `(a→b)`)

is equivalent to the disjunction

`((not a) or b).`

▷ *Can you convince your self that* F_{11} *is the companion function:* "`b implies a`"?

The interpretation of logical implication is that if the antecedent is true, the consequent also must be true. Note that the preceding statement does not say anything about the situation in which the antecedent is not true. The implication itself is said to be true if the antecedent is not true; the implication is true if the antecedent is true and the consequent is true, but it is also true if the antecedent is false. The implication is only false in the situation in which the antecedent is true but the consequent is false. This definition permits some seemingly outrageous statements to qualify as true. For example: "If Millie is really the president, then I'm 150 years old" or "If wishes were horses, then beggars would ride." In both cases the antecedent is false, so the implication is true. These statements are said to *vacuously satisfy* the implication. Conversely, true antecedents can provide some seemingly contradictory combinations. "If Carl is my brother, then my name is Greg" and "If Carl is not my brother, then my name is Greg" are both true statements because the consequent of each is true.

Logical implication can also be understood as the support mechanism for one of the most famous forms of logical argument, the *syllogism*. A syllogism is a logical argument of the form:

if x is `true`
    then y is `true`
and it is `true` that x,

therefore

y is true

For example, "a square is a rectangle and has equal sides" could be written as

if (shape is a square)
  then (shape is a rectangle)

and

if (shape is a square)
  then (shape has equal sides).

Therefore, if it is also true that

(shape is a square),

we can conclude that

(shape has equal sides).

Formally, the above is described by the propositional calculus rule *modus ponens,* which states that if an implication is true and its antecedent is true, then we can conclude that the consequent is true. Schematically,

$$\frac{\begin{array}{l} a \rightarrow b \\ a \end{array}}{b}$$

If `a` is not true, the rule cannot be invoked. Therefore interpreting `a → b` as true is completely consistent. The inverse rule does not say that if `a` is false we can conclude `b` is false. Rather the rule *modus tollens* states that if `b` is false, we can conclude that `a` is false:

$$\frac{\begin{array}{l} a \rightarrow b \\ \neg b \end{array}}{\neg a}$$

Logical implication contrasts with the similar appearing `if-then` construct in most programming languages. In a conditional statement, the `<action>` clause is executed if *and only if* the `<test>` is true. A false `<test>` causes the `<action>` to be skipped. The logical `if`, on the other hand, says nothing about the case in which the antecedent is false.

CONSTRUCTION OF FUNCTIONS. All Boolean functions can be constructed easily from the basic set: conjunction, disjunction, and negation. (We will see later that you could survive with only two of the three. More important, we will eventually see that another alternative set of operations is not only equivalent, but more useful for the practical construction of computer systems.) For example, F_4 can be written as `(not a) and b`. Many of the functions can be created by combining the basic function in more than one way. For example, consider F_6, which can either be

`(a or b)`

or

```
(b or a)
```

as can be seen from their truth tables:

a	b	(a or b)	(b or a)
false	false	**false**	**false**
false	true	**true**	**true**
true	false	**true**	**true**
true	true	**true**	**true**

That is, they are equivalent.

▷ *We have now accounted for 9 of the 16 functions. Can you create the remaining 7?*

The fact that the above two expressions yield the same function demonstrates that logical disjunction is *commutative*. Logical commutativity is exactly the same concept as algebraic commutativity of addition or multiplication. In a similar way we could demonstrate that conjunction is commutative:

`(a and b)⇔(b and a);` (read "⇔" as "is equivalent to ")

Both conjunction and disjunction are associative:

```
(a or (b or c))⇔((a or b) or c)⇔(a or b or c)
(a and (b and c))⇔((a and b) and c)⇔(a and b and c);
```

Conjunction *distributes* across disjunction

```
(a and (b or c))⇔((a and b) or (a and c))
```

and vice versa:

```
(a or (b and c))⇔((a or b) and (a or c))
```

Many such combinations are, in fact, famous as logical theorems. For example, the equivalence of

```
not (a or b)
```

and

```
(not a) and (not b)
```

is known as De Morgan's Law (after the nineteenth century logician Augustus De Morgan). The law can be demonstrated or proved by writing the truth tables for the two expressions:

operands			**result**			
a	b	a or b	not (A or B)	not A	not B	(not A) and (not B)
false	false	false	**true**	true	true	**true**
false	true	true	**false**	true	false	**false**
true	false	true	**false**	false	true	**false**
true	true	true	**false**	false	false	**false**

Since the truth tables for the two expressions are identical, the functions must in fact be the same functions. There is a second version of De Morgan's Law:

```
not(A and B)
```

is equivalent to

```
(not A) or (not B).
```

In fact, it turns out that truth table equivalence can be represented as bi-directional implication or *bi-implication*. That is,

```
(a ⇔ b)
```

is the same as

```
(a⇒b) and (a⇐b)
```

The proof is included in the Exercises.

All possible functions—no matter how complex—can be represented as simple combinations of the basic named functions—usually in several ways. The most important lesson to be drawn from this discussion is that any Boolean function can be built up from the set previously discussed. It will turn out that virtually any computer operation can be described in terms of a series of Boolean operations.

Arbitrarily complex Boolean expressions can be built up to represent almost any condition that a mathematician might desire. For example, suppose a researcher was conducting three tests—`test1`, `test2`, and `test3`—and desired to know if exactly two of the three tests were true (but did not care which two). One could solve the problem with a program that performed each test, counted the number of true tests, and compared the sum to 2. Alternatively, one could ask the question by describing all possible situations in which exactly two tests were true. The query can be built up from simpler queries.

1. Are `test1` and `test2` both true? `(test1 and test2)`
2. Is `test3` false? `(not test3)`

Thus,

```
(test1 and test2) and (not test3)
```

asks if the first two tests are true and the third is false. There are two other possible situations: only the second test is false and only the first test is false. The Boolean expression corresponding to these conditions is analogous to the above. The full expression can be constructed as the disjunction of the three conditions since only one of the three need be true:

```
[(test1 and test2) and (not test3)] or
[(test1 and test3) and (not test2)] or
[(test3 and test2) and (not test1)]
```

The above logical expression describes a single (although complicated) test that answers the question, "Are exactly two of the three tests true?" Many persons find such declarative problem statements easier to use than the algorithmic or imperative description given earlier. Some programming languages are based on such representations. More importantly for the present context, such declarative descriptions turn out to be much more useful for describing the low level internal operations of a digital computer.

▷ *Note that there are three arguments in the above query. Therefore the table will have more rows. How many?*

LOGIC OPERATIONS IN ASSEMBLY LANGUAGE

Assembly and machine languages include representations for the Boolean values:

`1 for true`
and `0 for false`

and for commands analogous to each of the basic logical operations

`and`, `or` and `not`.

As in the Boolean algebra underlying these operations, the first two operations are binary and the third is unary. Like other assembly language commands with which you are already familiar, the GAL logical commands have the form:

```
<operation>    <source>⇒<destination>
```

As before, the operation is performed using `<source>` and `<destination>`, leaving the result in the `<destination>`. In the case of negation, there is only one operand, so the result replaces that operand.

Boolean Logic and Control Concepts

Boolean commands can be used to create complex logical tests. For example, if one wished to construct the AL equivalent of

```
if (test_1 or test_2)
    then...
```

the code could be created as in Chapter 5:

```
    compare             test_1⇒true
    jump:equal          →then-clause         ;true, so do it
    compare             test _2⇒true
    jump:not_equal      →past-then-clause    ;don't do it
then-clause ...
    ...
past-then-clause
```

An alternative, suggested by Boolean algebra, takes the form:

```
    copy                test_1⇒temp
    or                  test_2⇒temp
    compare             temp⇒true             ;true if either
                                              ;is true
    jump:not equal      →past-then-clause
```

As indicated in Chapter 6, operations other than `compare` alter the condition codes. In particular, most logical operations do so. In particular, the zero bit is set as it is for arithmetic operations—set when the answer is zero and cleared when the answer is not all zero. When a logical operation produces a `true` (or 1) result, the zero bit is cleared. The preceding code could be abbreviated:

```
    copy                test_1⇒temp
    or                  test_2⇒temp
    jump:not_equal      →past-then-clause
```

To understand this conditional jump, consider the usual interpretation of `true` as a single 1 or "on" bit. `False` is a 0 or "off" bit. Recall that the `compare` command works by subtracting one operand from the other, yielding zero if they are identical. It sets the zero bit when the result is zero. The jump-on-equal tests for the zero bit and jumps if it is 1. Analogously, the `or` command sets the zero bit if the result is false (zero). Thus a jump-on-equal will also jump if the zero bit was set due to a `false` result from an `or` command. It will skip the jump if the bit was cleared due to a `true` result. Jump-on-equal can thus be thought of as jump-on-false, and jump-on-not-equal as jump-on-true. The actions can be summarized as

result of `or`	zero bit is	jump-on-equal will
true	clear (0)	not jump
false	set (true)	jump

All the more complicated logical expressions discussed previously have analogs that can be expressed in assembly language.

```
((not a) or b)
```

can be calculated as:

```
copy    a⇒temp
not     temp
or      b⇒temp
```

(This may appear to be `(b or (not a))`, but the commutative law says the two expressions are equivalent.) For a more complicated example, consider the following demonstration of De Morgan's law (first form):

```
;       not (a or b)⇔(not a) and (not b)
copy    a⇒temp              ;a
or      b⇒temp              ;a or b
not     temp                ;(not (a or b))

copy    a⇒temp2             ;a
not     temp2               ;(not a)
copy    b⇒temp3             ;b
not     temp3               ;(not b)
and     temp2⇒temp3         ;((not a) and (not b))
```

`Temp` and `temp3` should have the same value at the end of this sequence, no matter what combination of values are in `a` and `b`.

▷ *Can you write assembly language equivalents to all of the above logical functions and rules?*

Multiple-Bit Logical Operations

As with all previous assembly commands, the smallest operand for a logical operation is one byte—eight bits, which seems odd since a logical value requires only one bit. Actually, this anomaly is exploited to advantage by most machines. Each operation manipulates the entire content of the operands bitwise in parallel. Bit 0 of the first operand and bit 0 of the second operand are manipulated to yield bit 0 of the result: bit 1 with bit 1, and so on. Thus, for a one-byte operand, eight logical operations are performed in *parallel* (that is, at the same time). For example, in conjunction each bit of the result byte is obtained by `and`ing the corresponding individual bits of the two operands.

	FFFF TTTT
`and`	FFTT FFTT
yields	FFFF FFTT

or more traditionally

	0000 1111
`and`	0011 0011
yields	0000 0011

At first glance, this appears incredibly wasteful. Why manipulate eight bits when only one manipulation is needed? Since the operations can be performed in parallel, no time is lost, and since the smallest operand that can generally be addressed is a byte, no real space is lost. It is possible to pack several logical values into a byte, but for the moment assume that a single logical value is stored in the low-order (right-most) bit of each operand. By selecting a consistent position, the "interesting" bit of each operand is always in the same location. Further assume that the rest of the bits are all initialized to false (or zero). Then, the possible operands for an `and` operation are

	(both false)	(one false)	(other false)	(both true)
`a`	0000 0000	0000 0000	0000 0001	0000 0001
`b`	0000 0000	0000 0001	0000 0000	0000 0001
`(a and b)`	0000 0000	0000 0000	0000 0000	0000 0001

Since all seven lead bits are always zero, the conjunction of those bits is always zero. Therefore, the lead bits have no effect on the result. Alternatively stated, the `and` operation has no effect on the leading zeros. In this case, the conjunction of two full bytes is nonzero in exactly those cases in which neither operand is zero, that is, the case in which both operands had 1's in bit 0.

> ▷ *Suppose that a machine could address any bit individually. What effect would such an assumption have on the addresses for the machine?*

Disjunction behaves similarly:

`a`	0000 0000	0000 0000	0000 0001	0000 0001
`b`	0000 0000	0000 0001	0000 0000	0000 0001
`(a or b)`	0000 0000	0000 0001	0000 0001	0000 0001

Unfortunately, negation will not behave so nicely, since it will convert all leading zeros to ones:

`a`	0000 0001	0000 0000
`(not a)`	1111 1110	1111 1111

which is not zero in either case. A condition code will not distinguish between the two values (both presumably are negative if treated as numeric values).

An Additional Logical Operation: xor

Recall that when computer scientists use the term `or`, they normally mean an *inclusive-or.* The "or" that most people use is the exclusive-or "one or the other, but not both" (as in "either I'm going to do my homework or I'm going to fail"). Another way to describe exclusive-or is that an exclusive-or is true if exactly one of the operands is true. The exclusive-or, usually denoted `xor` (or ⊕), is easily constructed from the other logical operations as shown by the table:

a	b	a XOR b	a or b	a and b	not (a and b)	(a or b) and (not (a and b))
F	F	**F**	F	F	T	**F**
F	T	**T**	T	F	T	**T**
T	F	**T**	T	F	T	**T**
T	T	**F**	T	T	F	**F**

Therefore, exclusive-or is indeed "one or the other, but not both," that is,

```
(a or b) and (not (a and b))
```

Similarly, the equivalence could also be demonstrated by writing the code:

```
copy    a⇒temp          ;a
xor     b⇒temp          ;(a xor b)

copy    a⇒temp2         ;a
or      b⇒temp2         ;(a or b)
copy    a⇒temp3         ;a
and     b⇒temp3         ;(a and b)
not     temp3           ;(not (a and b))
and     temp2⇒temp3     ;(a or b) and
                        ;(not (a and b))
```

`Temp` and `temp3` should have the same values.

Uses of Logical Commands

Sometimes new assembly language programmers find it difficult to envision uses for logical operations. Most of them are not likely to spend much time proving the equivalence of logical expressions. In general, logical operations can be used in the same manner as Boolean variables and expressions are used in hlls. The most common such use is in complicated control tests for conditional and iterative structures. In the example given at the beginning of the chapter, the question

```
if (test1 or test2)
   then . . .
```

could be replicated in assembly language with equal ease using either Boolean operations or multiple `compares`. However, with more complicated test questions (for example, the earlier question about exactly two of three tests being true), constructing control structures that handle the conditional directly can be exceedingly complicated. Boolean operations reduce the problem to the calculation of a single Boolean value and a single `compare` statement. In addition, most hlls restrict the exit points from loop constructs. On occasion, a condition for exit is detected in the middle of a loop. By storing the condition in a Boolean variable, the test can be made at a later (legal exit) point in the loop body. The following section introduces some new uses for logical operations.

LOGIC AND MASKS

Logical operations apply to all bits of the operands, but sometimes we wish to apply the operation to only selected bits. A mechanism is needed to select the single bit of interest. For example, after a negation operation, a compare statement apparently does not give the appropriate result. When more than one bit within a byte contains logical data, the extraneous bits must be hidden. Interestingly, the logical operations themselves provide a mechanism for selecting individual bits. A *mask* created from an `and` or an `or` can hide the undesired bits. Consider the mask:

FFFF FFFT

Used as one operand of a conjunction, this mask will "hide" all bits other than the first (right-most) of the second operand. Since the left seven bits of the mask operand are all false, any value `and`ed with those bits must necessarily yield a `false` result. Thus, the only bit that can possibly have a `true` result is the rightmost bit:

operand	FTFT FTFT
mask	FFFF FFF**T**
yields	FFFF FFF**T**

and

operand	TFTF TFTF
mask	FFFF FFF**T**
yields	FFFF FFF**F**

The bit result will be true if both operands are true for that bit. Since the fixed operand has a true in the last bit, the result will be true in exactly those cases for which the remaining operand also has a true in that bit.

And-Masks

Masks used with `and` operations are called *and-masks*. The use of the mask created a result for which all the bits were false or "masked out," and only one bit yielded an interesting result. The mask can be viewed metaphorically as a wall with windows only in selected positions. False bits correspond to the wall—they block the contents of the operand (forcing the result to be zero or false). True bits are like the window—they allow the value of the operand to pass through. After performing a mask operation, only the bits in the windows can be seen; all others are false. Figure 8-1 illustrates the concept schematically.

Traditionally, masks are denoted using 1s and 0s rather than `T`s and `F`s. This allows the programmer to specify a mask as a binary or hex number. The preceding examples could have been written as

mask	0000 0001	=	01_{16}
operand	0101 0101	=	55_{16}
yields	0000 0001	=	01_{16}

and

mask	0000 0001	=	01_{16}
operand	1010 1010	=	AA_{16}
yields	0000 0000	=	00_{16}

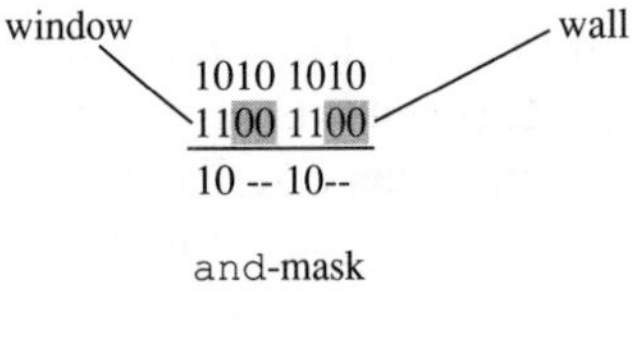

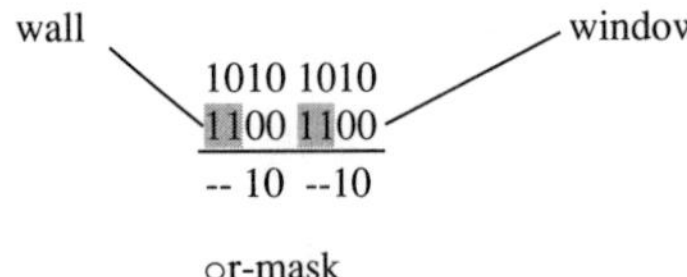

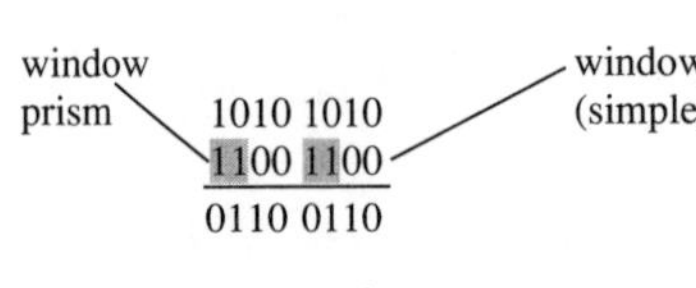

FIGURE 8-1
Masks as walls and mirrors. (*a*) `and` mask (*b*) `or` mask (*c*) `Xor` mask

One obvious use of such a mask is the removal of all bits in the operand except for a single logical value. Such removal eliminates the problem with negation noted earlier:

`a`	0000 0001
`(not a)`	1111 1110
mask	0000 0001
yields	0000 0000

Thus, even though negation changes all the bits, a mask can be used to hide those not involved in the current operation. Masks can also remove the restriction that logical values be stored in only the last bit and that all others be zero (false). An appropriate mask makes it possible to look at any single bit:

FFFF FFTF hides all but bit 1
TFFF FFFF hides all but bit 7.

If all eight bits of a byte contained logical values, eight different masks could be used to access the eight distinct values.

▷ *The reader should verify that this is true. Suppose that two variables* `a` *and* `b` *each contained several logical values. Is it possible to perform a series of logical operations, such as the earlier examples, on one position, without altering any other bits?*

A third use of masks is for transforming data from one form to another. If an operation should affect only a portion of a byte, masks can be used to alter that portion—even though the operation may not seem to be Boolean in nature. Recall that the character digits are represented in ASCII as the hex numbers 30 to 39. That is, the second hex digit corresponding to each character is precisely the numeric value of the character. In binary, the range is

0011 0000 = 30_{16} to
0011 1001 = 39_{16}

If the first digit could be removed, the remaining value would be the binary representation of the original digit. The `and`-mask

FFFF TTTT or 0000 1111

can be used to remove the first hex digit, because those bits are always `and`ed with false. The second (interesting) hex digit is always passed through the mask because its bits are `and`ed with true values. Thus,

	0011 0101	= 35_{16} = 5_{ASCII}
`and`ed with	0000 1111	= $0F_{16}$
yields	0000 0101	= 05_{10}

The same result could have been obtained by subtracting 30_{16} from the ASCII character. The mask operation is more transparent. Clearly, the operation manipulates *portions* of the byte. Additionally, in the event of an input error, this method will usually generate a reasonable numeric value. For example, "A" masked as above will yield a 01_{16}.

> ▷ *Of course there are also disadvantages to converting by masking. Can you name one?*

Finally, consider the following familiar problem. The upper- and lowercase ASCII characters are distinct characters, which can be inconvenient for situations such as the following. A program asks the user whether or not to continue. The user may type "Y" or "y". The distinction between upper- and lowercase requires the program to check for both possibilities: "Y" and "y". Notice that the uppercase "Y" is

$$59_{16} = 01\underline{0}1\ 1001_2$$

and the lowercase "y" is

$$79_{16} = 01\underline{1}1\ 1001_2$$

The only difference is in bit 5. If all other bits match, either value—a one or a zero—in bit 5 will yield some form of "y". Thus, the bit can be ignored and only the remaining bits compared. A mask of

$$1101\ 1111 = DF_{16}$$

allows all values to be passed through—except for bit 5 (which becomes 0). If the initial value was a uppercase "Y", the mask operation produces

$$\begin{array}{lll} \text{“Y”} = & 01\underline{0}1\ 1001 & = 59_{16} \\ \text{mask} & \underline{1101\ 1111} & = DF_{16} \\ & 0101\ 1001 & = 59_{16} \quad = \text{“Y”} \end{array}$$

The result is unchanged. On the other hand, if the initial value was a lowercase "y", the operation is

$$\begin{array}{lll} \text{“y”} = & 01\underline{1}1\ 1001 & = 79_{16} \\ \text{mask} & \underline{1101\ 1111} & = DF_{16} \\ & 0101\ 1001 & = 59_{16} \quad = \text{“Y”} \end{array}$$

Again, the result is an uppercase "Y". The value resulting from the mask need only be compared with the uppercase "Y".

This technique works for converting any lowercase letter to any uppercase letter. The uppercase ASCII letters all have either a 4 or a 5 as their first hex digit. Every lowercase letter has exactly the same second digit as its uppercase counterpart, but its leading hex digit is always 2 greater than the corresponding digit of the uppercase letter—either a 6 or a 7. Notice that

4 is $01\underline{0}0_2$ and 5 is $01\underline{0}1_2$
while 6 is $01\underline{1}0_2$ and 7 is $01\underline{1}1_2$

In each case, the only difference is in bit 1 of the nibble—bit 5 of the byte. Thus, this masking technique can always be used for converting lowercase letters to uppercase letters.

Finally, `and`-masks provide a method for accessing portions of a byte. One important use for such an access is for breaking a machine language instruction down into its constituent fields. The assembler must construct machine language instructions one field at a time, and the fetch/execute cycle must decode the instructions one field at a time. Although `and`-masks are not actually the mechanism employed during the instruction fetch cycle, they are related to the actual method used. Or-masks (described in the following section) could be used during assembly to construct (assemble) the machine language instructions. For example, consider the GAL and GEML assembly and machine representations of an `add` instruction:

```
add:byte     loc⇒reg3
```

is

1000 0000 0001 0011 0000 0001 0010 0011 = $80\ 13\ 01\ 23_{16}$

Masking with

$\underline{1111\ 0000\ 0000\ 0000\ 0000\ 0000\ 0000\ 0000}$ = F0 00 00 00

yields

1000 0000 0000 0000 0000 0000 0000 0000 = 80 00 00 00

effectively isolating the opcode.

Or-Masks

The logical `or` operation can also be used to construct a mask. Recall that if either operand is true, `or` produces a true result. So for any bit in the mask (fixed operand) that is true, the result must also be true. For any bit that has a false in the mask, the operation will yield a true result if and only if the second operand has a true in the corresponding bit. Thus, an `or`-*mask* will also behave like walls and windows, but in the opposite manner: true (or 1) values in the mask act as walls, forcing true results. False (or 0) values in the mask act as the window allowing the value in the other operand to pass through. The mask:

mask	FFFF TTTT	or	0000 1111	= $0F_{16}$
applied to	TFTF TFTF		1010 1010	= AA_{16}
yields	TFTF TTTT		1010 1111	= AF_{16}

An `or`-mask has applications roughly inversely related to the uses of the `and`-mask. A binary number less than 10 always fits in four bits and can be converted to the corresponding ASCII decimal digit by inserting 0011 in front of it. The `or`-mask is ideally suited to insert these two bits:

$$\begin{array}{lll} & 0000\ 0110_2 & = 6_{16} = 6_{10} \\ \texttt{or}\text{-masked with} & \underline{0011\ 0000} & = 30_{16} \\ \text{yields} & 0011\ 0110_2 & = 36_{16} = 6_{\text{ASCII}} \end{array}$$

Similarly, uppercase letters can be converted to lowercase letters by forcing bit 5 to be a 1. Thus,

$$\begin{array}{lll} & 0100\ 1110_2 & = 4E_{16} = \text{“N”} \\ \texttt{or}\text{-masked with} & \underline{0010\ 0000} & = 20_{16} \\ \text{yields} & 0110\ 1110_2 & = 6E_{16} = \text{“n”} \end{array}$$

Finally, an `or`-mask can be used to insert a single Boolean value into a storage location without impacting the remaining values. For example, the mask

0000 0100

when `or`ed with a second operand, will force bit 2 of the result to be a 1. The mask contains a 1 in that position, and only a single `true` is needed for the result of an `or` to be `true`. All other bits pass their own values through the mask, since zero or “something” is always that “something.” Thus, the `or`-mask can be used to set a Boolean value in a single bit within a location without disturbing any other bit in the location:

    or–mask
`or` original content of location

yields

original content with 1 at position designated by mask

The assembler can use such a technique to build the machine language instructions. As each portion of the assembly language instruction is interpreted, the corresponding field in the machine language instruction can be set by `or`ing the entire machine language instruction with the mask corresponding to the appropriate machine language field. For example, if the GAL instruction is

```
copy    reg2⇒reg3
```

several fields can be filled in with the commands

```
copy    #0⇒command                ;clear all fields
or      #H1000 0000⇒command       ;set the op code
                                  ;to "copy"
or      #H0002 0000⇒command       ;set the register
                                  ;field to 2
or      #H0000 0003⇒command       ;set 2nd opnd
                                  ;field to 3...
```

Xor-mask

There is one more commonly used mask based on the basic logical operators. Instinctively, one might expect it to be a `not`-mask. However, that cannot be the case since the masking operations are created from a binary logical operation by holding one of the operands fixed. The `not`, however, is already a unary operation. Thus, if one operand is held fixed, there is no other operand left to mask out. Fortunately, the results that might be expected from a `not`-mask—inverting selected bits—can be obtained using the exclusive-or. Recall that exclusive-or yields a true result if and only if exactly one of the operands is true:

value	0011
`xor`	0101
yields	0110

If a mask contains a 0 in a given position, at most one operand (the other) can contain a 1 in that position. So the operand will be "passed through": 1 if the operand has a one, and 0 otherwise. Now suppose the mask contains a 1 in a given position. If the remaining operand also contains a 1, both operands are 1 and the exclusive-or yields 0 or `false`. If the second operand is a 0, only one operand is `true`, so the exclusive-or yields a `true` result. Thus, an exclusive-`or`-mask allows some values to pass through unchanged and others to be inverted. Maintaining the window analogy from above, an exclusive-or-mask with a 0 bit acts like a window, allowing values to pass through unchanged. In contrast, a 1 bit in the mask acts like a prism, inverting any bit that passes through.

For example, an exclusive-or-mask could be used to change the case of any letter. The mask

0010 0000

would allow every bit except bit 5 to pass through untouched. Whatever is in bit 5 will be inverted. Thus

	0100 0100	=	$44_{16} = D_{\text{ASCII}}$
masked against	0010 0000	=	20_{16}
`yields`	0110 0100	=	$64_{16} = d_{\text{ASCII}}$

and

	0110 0110	=	$64_{16} = d_{\text{ASCII}}$
masked against	<u>0010 0000</u>	=	20_{16}
yields	0100 0100	=	$44_{16} = D_{\text{ASCII}}$

Similarly, an exclusive-or-mask can be used to *toggle,* or flip, a single logical value. The mask

0000 0001

will flip the value in bit 0, leaving all other values untouched. Thus,

a value	1111 0000
masked with	<u>0000 0001</u>
yields	1111 0001
masked again	<u>0000 0001</u>
yields	1111 0000

which was the original value. Finally, an exclusive-or-mask composed of all 1s behaves exactly like `not`:

a value	1010 1010
masked with	<u>1111 1111</u>
yields	0101 0101

SHIFT OPERATIONS

Manipulations at the bit level are seldom supported in higher-level languages. True, Boolean operations are supported, but the programmer generally has no control over the internal representation. One cannot access multiple Boolean values as a unit, compressing related variables into a single byte. All the assembly operations explored thus far have an analog in higher-level languages. A family of operations that have no analog in hlls is the shifting operations. Although there are several varieties of shifting operations, they all share the common result: all bits of the operand are shifted one or more positions to the side.

The simplest shift operation moves each bit one position to the left. Thus

0001 0001

becomes

0010 0010

Shifting again would yield

0100 0100

In the simple form of shift, zero-bits are always added at the right-hand end of the operand. Bits at the left-hand end are shifted out and are lost forever. If the above value was shifted two more times, the successive results would be

1000 1000

and

0001 0000

The left-most 1 is lost when it shifts out of the operand. Any byte shifted eight or more times will necessarily contain all 0s.

Shifting can be used with a mask to examine each bit of some byte, one at a time. Using an `and` mask of 0000 0001 produces a one in bit 0 if and only if the operand has a one in that position. The mask can then be shifted, yielding 0000 0010 as the new mask. When this new mask is `anded` against the same operand, the result contains a one if the operand has a one in bit 1. Note that the storage location must be copied to prevent destruction of the remaining bits:

```
copy   #00000001⇒mask    ;mask apparently is a register
copy   a⇒temp            ;suppose A =  1010 1010
and    mask⇒temp         ;yields       0000 0000

shift  mask              ;mask is now  0000 0010
copy   a⇒temp
and    mask⇒temp         ;yields       0000 0010
```

A similar result could be obtained by shifting the operand under the mask, rather than shifting the mask.

An interesting feature of shifting such masks is that they generate their own mechanism for loop control: after (no more than) eight shifts, the mask will contain all 0s. Therefore, a loop can be controlled as follows:

```
while (mask <> 0) do
    perform masking operation
    use result
    shift mask left.
```

Variations

Two variations on simple shifts include the following.

SHIFTS OF MULTIPLE BITS. Shifts of multiple bits require a second operand indicating the number of bits to be shifted. They save the programmer the trouble of specifying repeated shift operations and certainly execute faster than a loop of single shifts, but they do not add any fundamentally new capabilities. The programmer can always accomplish a shift across multiple bits with a loop, shifting one position each pass. In GAL and GEML, operands can be shifted up to eight bits. The register field (which is unused, since shift has only one true operand) is used to specify the number of bits to be shifted.

SHIFTS TO THE RIGHT. There is no simple way to use left-shifts to shift an operand to the right. Therefore assembly languages also allow an explicit right-shift, which adds this new capability. The value

0100 1101

shifted right one bit is

0010 0110

In GEM, the direction bit is used to distinguish between left and right shifts.

Shifts and Arithmetic

In decimal arithmetic, placing a zero after a number results in a number 10 times larger than the original. Similarly, in binary placing a zero after a number doubles the magnitude of that number. Thus a "quick-and-dirty" method for doubling a number is

```
shift it one place to the left.
```

Shifting it two places multiplies by 4; shifting by three, 8; and so on.

	0000 0011	=	3		
shifted once	0000 0110	=	6	=	3*2
twice	0000 1100	=	12	=	3*4
and three times	0001 1000	=	24	=	3*8

This does assume that the resulting number fits within the allowed storage location. Similarly, numbers can be divided by 2 simply by shifting to the right one position. It is interesting that this is exactly "integer division" as defined in higher-level languages. That is, shifting

	0000 0101	=	5
one place yields	0000 0010	=	2

The fractional part is lost. If you look up the execution time for multiplication or division on a real machine, you will note that they are among the slowest operations for execution. If multiplication by a power of 2 is needed frequently, shifting can save some time.

▷ *Why might shifting be faster than multiplying?*

Rotate

A *rotate* is exactly the same as a simple shift, except that bits shifted out the left end are not lost. They rotate back in at the right end, as shown in Figure 8-2. At each step, the value placed in bit 0 is the value just rotated out at the left end,

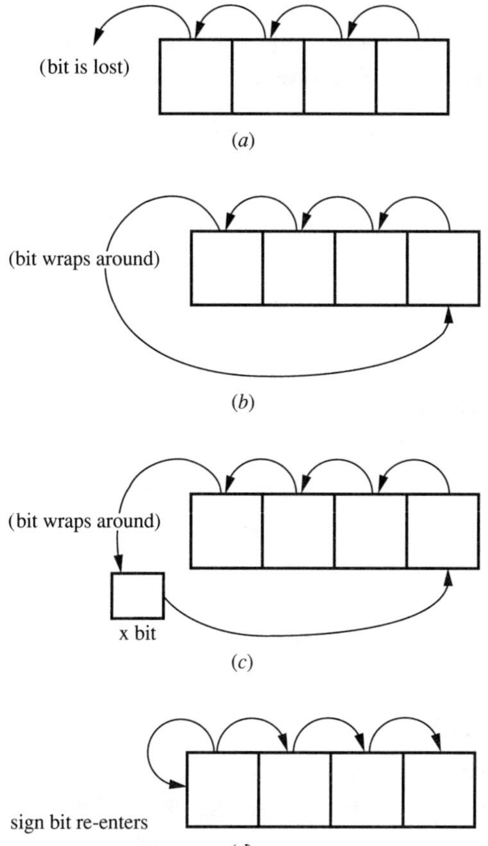

FIGURE 8-2
Shifting operations in a four-bit register. (*a*) shift left 1 bit (*b*) rotate left 1 bit (*c*) rotate left 1 bit with extend (*d*) arithmetic shift right 1 bit

rather than always being zero. The difference can easily be seen by contrasting the earlier example of shift with rotate.

	in a rotate	**in a shift**	
	0001 0001	0001 0001	
becomes	0010 0010	0010 0010	
	0100 0100	0100 0100	
	1000 1000	1000 1000	(no difference, yet)
and finally	0001 000$\underline{1}$	0001 000$\underline{0}$	

Figure 8-2 shows the relative effect of shift and rotate. Rotate commands "salvage" the left-most bit, creating many simplifications. In particular, operands themselves can be rotated (rather than the mask or a copy) without loss of the multiple Boolean data items contained therein. After rotating a mask all the way around (i.e., as many bits as the size of the operand), the original mask will have been restored. It will not need to be re-initialized should the program need to examine the location again.

A rotate operation in a single direction can be use to accomplish the results of either shifts or rotates, either to the right or the left. For example, shifting left three positions is similar to rotating left three positions and masking out the right-most bits:

```
shift    3⇒reg0
```

is equivalent to

```
rotate    3⇒reg0
and       #1111 1000⇒reg0
```

▷ *How can you verify this claim?*

Shifts to the right can also be accomplished with rotates to the left, and masks:

```
shift_right    3⇒reg0     ;assumes 1 byte operands
```

is equivalent to

```
rotate_left    5⇒reg0
and            #0001 1111⇒reg0
```

IMPLICATIONS FOR "REAL" ASSEMBLY LANGUAGES

The Generic Assembly Language contains only the single form: `rotate`. `Shift` must be accomplished through careful use of `rotates`. A summary of the GAL `rotate` command:

opcode	F_{16}	=	rotate
register field	n	=	number of positions to shift

RAM operand: always contains the operand, even if it is a register.

mode

direction	0 = left; 1 = right
RAM	0 = operand specifies a register; 1 a RAM operand

GAL provides only `and`, `or`, and `not`. There is no exclusive-`or`. All three commands obey the general format, with no special fields required:

op code	**mnemonic**
C_{16}	`and`
D_{16}	`or`
E_{16}	`not`

Most real languages provide a richer set of basic instructions. The redundancy emphasizes the importance of logical operations.

Condition Codes

Every logical instruction on GEM—and most real machines—(including `or`, `and`, `not`, `rotate`, and `copy`) sets the condition codes to reflect the value stored in the destination. The zero bit is set if the entire operand is zero and the negative bit if the high-order bit is 1. These values reflect exactly the same conditions for which the values would be set in the case of arithmetic operations. On other machines some instructions, such as `copy`, may not set the condition codes. The best way to check on any individual machine is to look up the command in the programmer's reference manual.

Further Variations

Two additional variations that may be found on some real machines include the *arithmetic shift* and the *shift with extension.*

THE ARITHMETIC SHIFT. This command is used for performing arithmetic manipulation and is identical to the logical shift described earlier, except that it preserves the sign bit. Recall that negative numbers always have a 1 in the left-most bit. Two's complement numbers have leading 1s just as positive numbers may have leading 0s. Although, we observed earlier that shifting to the right was equivalent to dividing by 2, this would not hold for negative numbers. Shifting a negative number to the right and setting the left-most bit to zero would produce a positive number:

$$1111\ 1111 = -1$$

shifted right one position is

$$0111\ 1111 = 127$$

The arithmetic shift to the right solves this problem by propagating the sign bit into the left. If the sign is zero, 0s are added at the left, if it is one, 1s are added. Thus

$$1111\ 0000 = -16$$

arithmetic shifted one is

$$1111\ 1000 = -8$$

Thus, the arithmetic shift right is identical to the logical shift to the right unless the left-most bit is a 1. An arithmetic shift to the left would be identical to a logical shift left.

SHIFT WITH EXTENSIONS. Most machines provide operand sizes of one, two, or four bytes. What if one wants to shift really large operands, for example eight bytes? Some machines provide sign-extended operations for this purpose. Think of a sign-extended `shift` or `rotate` as an operation whose operand is extended to include one extra bit: 9 instead of 8, 33 instead of 32. Consider an extended-left-shift. The operation proceeds exactly like a regular left-shift, except that the left-most bit is not lost but is shifted into the extra bit (however the

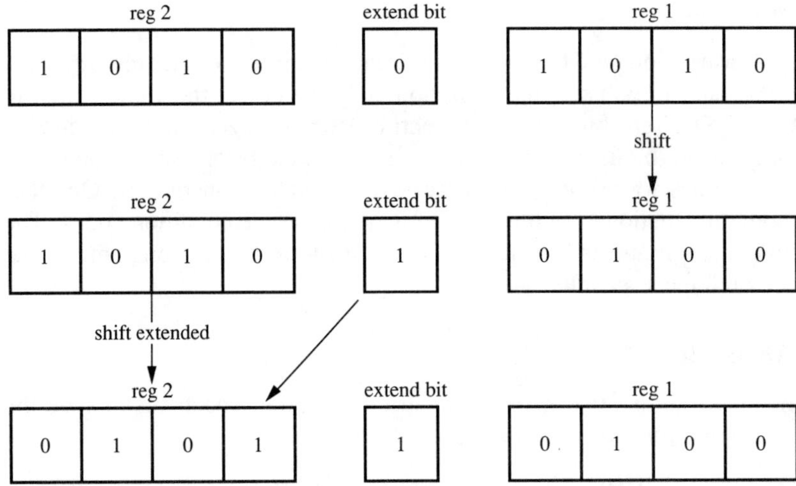

FIGURE 8-3
Double register shift using extend.

previous content of the extra bit is lost). Although there is no obvious distinction between the two on the surface, the extra bit is accessible by a later command. For example, if the next command was a rotate left, the left-most bit would rotate into the extra bit but the current extra bit would rotate into the right-most bit, thus achieving a double-length rotate. Figure 8-3 shows the process. The extra bit is usually held in the status register, so that it can also be examined by other commands.

SUMMARY

Boolean algebras are logical systems of two values, usually denoted `true` and `false`. From a small set of logical functions—`and`, `or`, and `not`—it is possible to build up any logical function. Truth tables and the rules of propositional calculus can both be used to prove the equivalence of logical expressions. Computers support logical operations to enable control statements to have some flexibility. In addition to the three basic operations, most machines support exclusive-or. Like their arithmetic counterparts, logical operations set bits in the condition code register. Since most computer operations have operand sizes of at least one byte, they work on a "bit-by-bit" basis; therefore, they can be used as masks. `And`-masks can be used to force certain bits to 0; `or`-masks to force bits to 1; and `xor`-masks to invert selected bits. The shift and rotate commands add flexibility to the logical operations by moving values between bit locations.

EXERCISES

8.1. The two forms of the distributive law of Boolean algebra are stated as:

$$(A \ and \ (B \ or \ C)) \Leftrightarrow (A \ and \ B) \ or \ (A \ and \ C)$$

and

$(A\ or\ (B\ and\ C)) \Leftrightarrow (A\ or\ B)\ and\ (A\ or\ C)$

Use a truth table to prove the distributive law.

8.2. The two forms of the associative law of Boolean algebra are stated as:

$(A\ and\ (B\ and\ C)) \Leftrightarrow ((A\ and\ B)\ and\ C)$

and

$(A\ or\ (B\ or\ C)) \Leftrightarrow ((A\ or\ B)\ or\ C)$

Use a truth table to prove the associative law.

8.3. The two forms of the commutative law of Boolean algebra are stated as:

$(A\ and\ B) \Leftrightarrow (B\ and\ A)$

and

$(A\ or\ B) \Leftrightarrow (B\ or\ A)$

Use a truth table to prove the commutative law.

8.4. An important rule of logical proof is called *modus ponens*. Essentially, it states that given an implication A implies B, and given the antecedent A, then B must necessarily be true. Build a truth table for the conjunction of the two conditions A and (A implies B). In effect, *modus ponens* states that we cannot have any row in which the A is true, but the conjunction of A with the implication is false. What does this tell us about B?

8.5. Build all functions from Table 8-1 using only the logical operations `and`, `or`, and `not`.

8.6. Suppose there were no shift (or rotate) right. Write generic assembly language statements that could accomplish a shift of one position to the right.

8.7. Compare the methods for converting between upper- and lowercase outlined in this chapter with the method often used in higher-level languages. Compare them in terms of the number of steps required. What does this say about higher-level languages and assembly language?

8.8. Build a truth table demonstrating that function F_{11} in Table 8-1 is B → A.

8.9. Recall the division algorithm for converting between bases. If the target radix is 2, the mod test is equivalent to asking if the low-order bit is 1 (or alternatively if the number was odd). The division is equivalent to shifting right one bit. Write a program to print out the binary contents of a storage location. Use only logical operations: `shifts` and `ands` rather than `divides` and `mods`, masks to select a bit and convert it to ASCII, and `shifts` to examine different bits.

8.10. Demonstrate the second form of De Morgan's law: (*a*) using a truth table, and (*b*) as a short program.

8.11. Repeat 8.10(*b*), but place all three values `a`, `b`, and `c` in a single byte. Use masks as needed to keep them separate.

8.12. Write explicit GAL code (which only has the rotate command) equivalent to commands that shift data. Further restrict the GAL command to left shifts. Attempt to create code equivalent to an arithmetic right shift.

8.13. In the next chapter, you will see that most computers are built using the logical operations `nand` and `nor` rather than `and` and `or`. `Nand` means "not and" and is defined by

```
a nand b ⇔ not (a and b)
```

By De Morgan's law, it could also be defined as

```
a nand b ⇔ (not a) or (not b)
```

`Nor` is defined analogously. Show that each of the functions in Table 8-1 could be constructed using only `nand`, `nor` and `not`.

8.14. Show by means of a truth table that *modus tollens* is a reasonable rule.

8.15. Show by means of a truth table that truth table equivalence

```
(a ⇔ b)
```

is the same as

```
(a⇒b) and (a⇐b)
```

8.16. Several examples in the chapter (definition of `xor`, De Morgan's law) showed that two expressions were equivalent by writing the code that would calculate each of the two values. In order to test the result one would have to write a generator that sent all possible combinations of values to the two expressions. Build such a generator for the `xor` and De Morgan's law examples.

8.17. Play assembler: write code using logical operations to build `add` and `copy` instructions within a single long-word storage location.

8.18. Use shift operations to create a multiplication subroutine.

CHAPTER 9

DIGITAL CIRCUITS

Chapter 8 discussed the relationship between Boolean operators and assembly or machine language instructions. We saw that it is possible to build up complex logical operations from a minimal set of logical primitives. Boolean logic can also be used to describe the internal operation of a digital computer. It is probably not immediately clear to most readers how the Boolean operators can be used to answer questions about the fetch/execute cycle. Indeed, one additional concept is needed: a representation of time.

Instruction processing cannot be explained by introducing new instructions—each of those instructions must also be subject to the same cycle with all of the same substeps. To describe these steps, another representation is needed. Each of the Boolean operations described in Chapter 8 has a direct analog as a component of an electronic circuit. Throughout computer science, one builds complicated programs from a minimal set of basic operations of a programming language. Similarly, complicated digital electronic machinery can be built from a very primitive collection of basic components. To investigate the details of a computer any further, one must consider the underlying constructs from which the overall machine is constructed. We will investigate these operations only as far as the logical description of the primitive parts, generally leaving the electronics and physics for another course.

INTRODUCTION TO DIGITAL CIRCUITS

Just as we think of a bit as containing one of two values, we can think of a signal as being either present or not present at any point in a circuit. The signal could be represented by the presence of a current or a voltage, as on or off, as a high voltage or a low voltage (although "high" is certainly a misleading terminology, since a "high" voltage is a small fraction of a volt). For simplicity, we will usually say the signal is present or not present, that it is on or off. An "on" signal will be treated as true or one, and an "off" signal as false or zero.

For the moment, we will ignore many physical or electronic details involved in the construction of digital electronic devices and concentrate on the logical principles embodied in that construction. For example, we will ignore real-world limitations caused by the speed of light, resistance in a wire, attenuation of a signal, or noise. While the laws of physics cannot be ignored in the actual construction of a machine, construction of a logically correct model of computation does not require an extensive knowledge of physics. Just as the Newtonian model of mechanics and the higher-level language model of computation provide very good approximations for their purposes, the digital-circuit model will provide an excellent model for our purposes here. For example, the model helps us understand why computers are binary rather than decimal. Binary representations only require a machine that can distinguish between the presence or absence of a signal. If we assume that "present" means above the threshold of the measuring device, "presence" then means "detectable." Decimal values, on the other hand, would require that the device be able to measure multiple signal levels, one corresponding to each decimal value.

Basic Constructions

Like a simple program involving only assignment, input, and output statements, a very small portion of the necessary logic can be visualized just on the basis of simple "light switch" circuitry. For example, a circuit to copy a value from one storage location to another, shifting it by a single bit-position, might be constructed in Figure 9-1. The shift could take place during the perform step of the fetch/execute cycle, transferring the bits from a source register to the result register. It should be clear that several aspects of more complicated circuits have not yet been accounted for: how does the CPU signal that it is time to perform the step? What happens after the signal is shifted? How does the register maintain the values after executing the step? How are more complicated operations constructed?

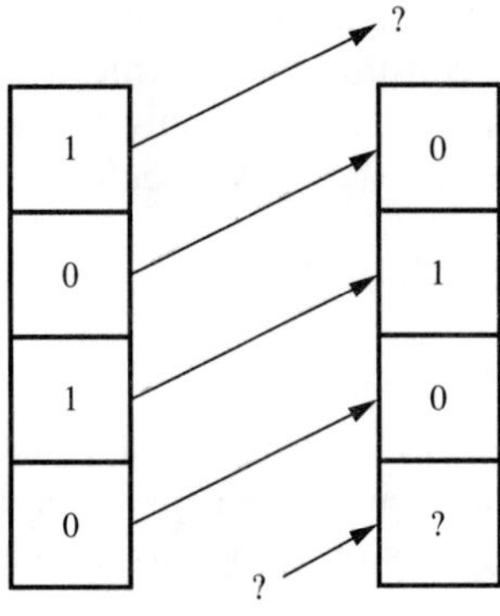

FIGURE 9-1
A very simplistic shifter.

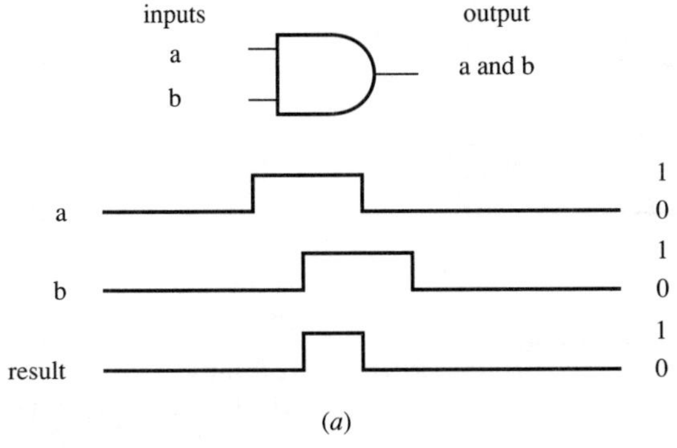

FIGURE 9-2
Basic gate constructs. (*a*) an AND-gate.

The primitive digital-circuit operations are exactly equivalent to the logical functions discussed in Chapter 8. As with the logical representation, a small set of primitive circuit constructs, called *gates,* provides a set of building blocks sufficient for all needed structures. Figure 9-2a represents an `and`-gate. `A` and `b`, at the left, represent two Boolean input signals, usually represented as 1 and 0. The result at the right represents the conjunction of the two values (1 iff both `a` and `b` are 1). The three lines at the bottom provide a schematic representation of the behavior of the gate as a function of time. Each of the three lines—`a`, `b`, and `result`—represent the value of the signal at corresponding time intervals. The normal state for each input is zero. When either `a` or `b` becomes 1 individually, no change is observed in the result. But when both are 1 at the same time, the result `(a and b)` also becomes 1.

An `or`-*gate,* drawn as in Figure 9-2b, yields a true (or 1) result if either of the inputs is true (or 1). It is directly analogous to the logical function `or`. This figure also indicates both the schematic notation and the relationship of input and output signals. The output of the `or`-gate is high if either one (or both) of the input signals is high. A `not`-*gate,* shown in Figure 9-2c, inverts its signal: if the input is on (or 1), the output will be off (or 0); and if the input is off the output will be on. In the electronics literature, you will sometimes also see a very

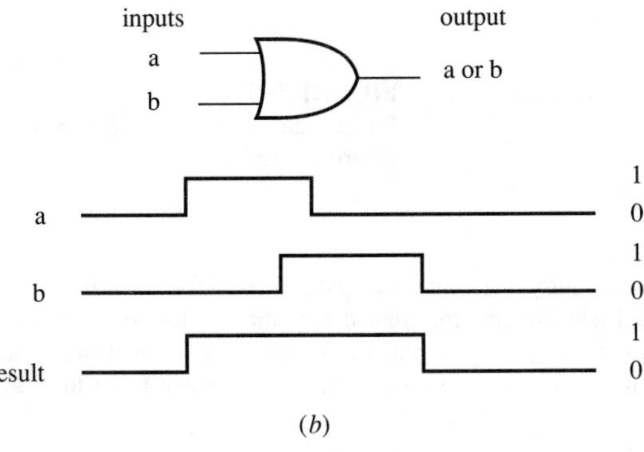

FIGURE 9-2 (cont.)
Basic gate constructs. (*b*) an OR-gate.

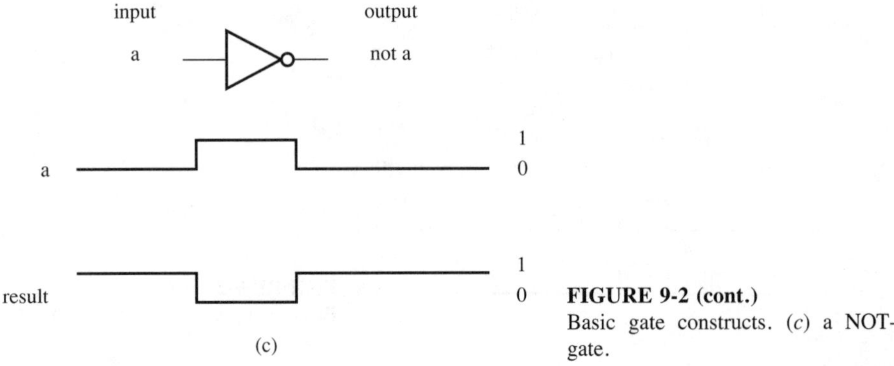

FIGURE 9-2 (cont.)
Basic gate constructs. (*c*) a NOT-gate.

similar-looking construct: the *noninverting buffer,* or simply, *buffer* (Figure 9-2d) included in schematic diagrams. It is used as an amplifier (a variation is used as a mask). Do not let the similar appearance confuse you. Without the negating circle, no inversion is implied. Since this symbol adds no further logical capabilities, we will not discuss it further here.

▷ *How could a device with no power from its input produce a positive signal as its output?*

Equivalence to Boolean Algebra

With just these simple gates, circuit diagrams can be constructed that are equivalent to any of the expressions or truth tables illustrated in Chapter 8.[1] For example,

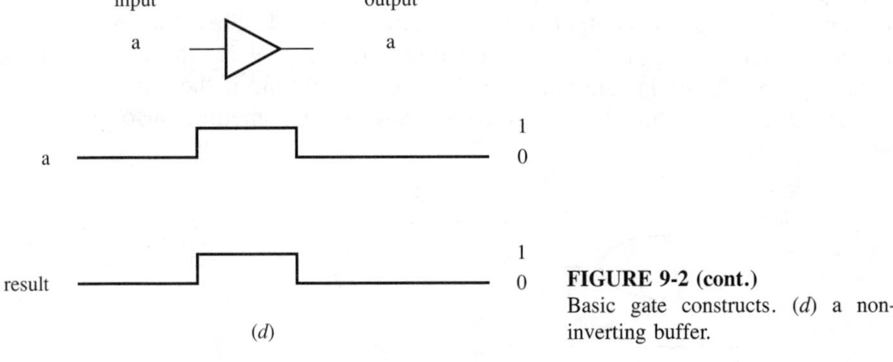

FIGURE 9-2 (cont.)
Basic gate constructs. (*d*) a non-inverting buffer.

---

[1]Although this statement is true, in reality a slightly different set of gates is used for constructing the circuits in a digital computer. The set used here reflects the logical operations with which humans are more comfortable. The set actually used in creating digital machines—and the reason for the distinction—is described in the appendix to this chapter. The two sets can be shown to be logically equivalent.

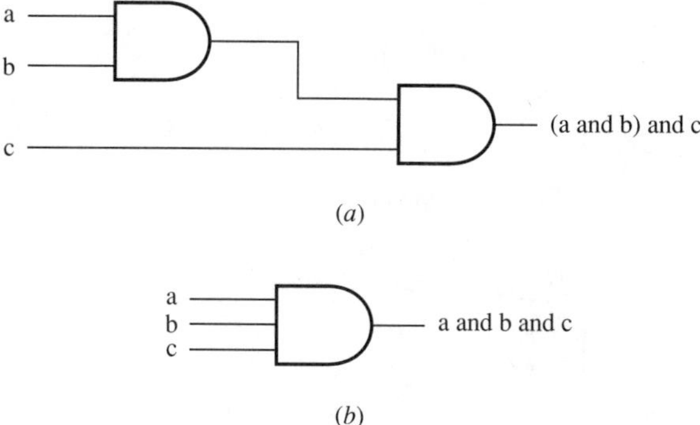

FIGURE 9-3
Conjunction of three values. (*a*) Construction from two and-gates. (*b*) as an atomic symbol.

the associative property of conjunction implies that the conjunction of three items can be constructed by `and`ing two of the three and then `and`ing that result with the third value, as in Figure 9-3a. The schematic representation for the conjunction of three items is often abbreviated as in Figure 9-3b.

Similarly, we can create an exclusive-or by building it from its definition:

```
(a xor b) ⇔ (a or b) and (not (a and b))
```

Figure 9-4 shows a construction for an exclusive-or. Note that a connection between two lines is denoted with a heavy dot. Lines that simply cross do not

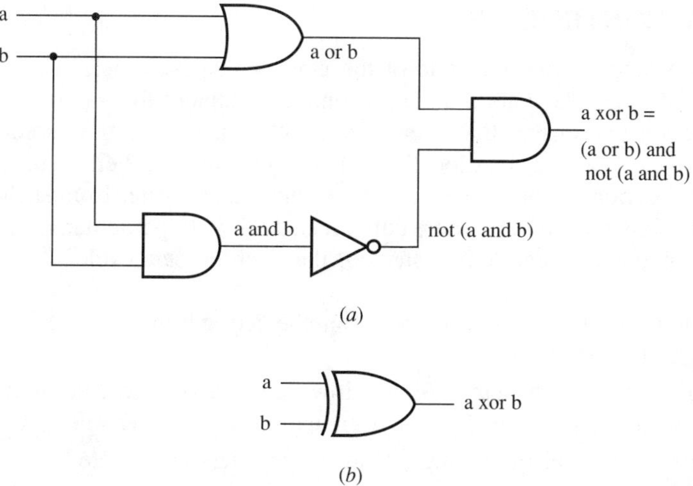

FIGURE 9-4
The exclusive or. (*a*) Constructed from primitive components. (*b*) as an atomic unit.

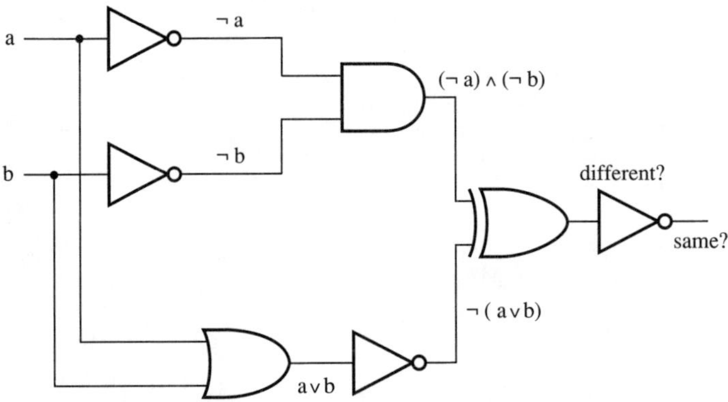

FIGURE 9-5
Circuit demonstration of De Morgan's law.

represent connections. The exclusive-or is often denoted as in Figure 9-4b, which we treat simply as a black box, and is assumed to contain circuitry equivalent to that of Figure 9-4a. As a final, more complicated example, Figure 9-5 shows circuitry that could demonstrate De Morgan's law. The overall circuit is equivalent to either the truth-table or program representations of the same law in Chapter 8. The two subportions of the circuit will always produce the same result; the exclusive-or of the two parts must always be false and its negation must always be true.

> ▷ *Is there an analogy between the use of a single symbol to represent a more complicated circuit and the use of a single procedure name to represent a complicated process or function?*

BUILDING THE CONTROL UNIT

The notion of control implies that the state of the world changes, which in turn implies the concept of time. The control unit of a computer includes those portions of the central processor that ensure that events are synchronized, that the appropriate next instruction is selected, that locations change or maintain their values, that the appropriate location is found, etc. In order to build a computer from such simple devices, it is necessary to build more complicated tools. In particular, each of the following problems is suggested by steps of the fetch/execute cycle:

- How is information copied from one place to another? (e.g., in the fetch instruction and fetch operand steps)
- How is one item selected from many? (e.g., How does the opcode determine which operation should be performed? How is an appropriate register selected?)
- How can a value be held over time? (e.g., How are registers constructed?)
- How can a circuit detect that it is time to perform its task? (e.g., What controls the order of steps in the fetch/execute cycle?)

- How are circuits built that do not seem to be logical in nature? (e.g., Can addition be performed using only logic?)

We will now build circuits capable of performing each of the basic tasks: we will then use them to build a larger circuit corresponding to the entire fetch/execute cycle.

The Bus

Chapter 6 introduced the internal bus, a common path that connects all registers. It would theoretically be possible to connect registers with a bus composed of a single line. However, a register contains multiple bits (e.g., 16 or 32) of information. Generally the entire contents of a register are moved together. A single-line connection would require that the bits be transmitted sequentially, one after the other. Since all (or at least many) of the bits are transmitted together, parallel lines would improve the efficiency. Think of the bus as a bundle of parallel wires, one corresponding to each bit in a storage location. Generally the bus has as many lines as there are bits in the standard registers or storage locations in the machine. Each of the system registers is logically connected to the bus, as shown in Figure 9-6a. Bit 0 of each register is connected to bit 0 of the bus; bit 1 to bit 1; bit 7 to bit 7. The concept of bus will occur in other contexts. In fact, there are several busses in a typical computing system. When there is any chance of confusion, the bus described here will be called the *internal* or *common bus*. The term *bus* may encompass more than just the data lines connecting the registers. In some cases, the term is used broadly to include additional lines, such as the control lines, indicating which register is to send and which is to receive the bus data. In other uses, the term will refer not only to the physical lines and connections, but also to the full protocol used to communicate over the bus. For simplicity, we use the term here to refer only to the data lines. When the contents of any register are sent onto the bus, they are, in effect, broadcast throughout the bus. Without some form of coordination, there could clearly be chaos. Multiple registers might

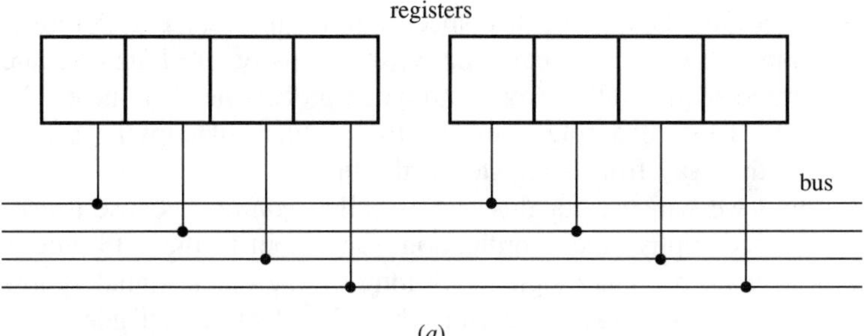

FIGURE 9-6
Connecting registers. (*a*) Bit by bit.

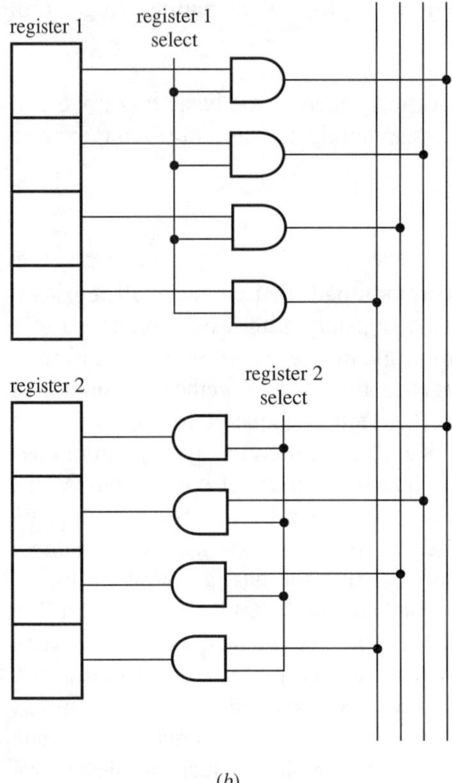

FIGURE 9-6 (cont.)
Connecting registers. (*b*) Gated registers.

simultaneously place their signals on the bus (presumably resulting in some value that resembled the disjunction of the values in the registers). All registers would receive the signal and therefore be set to the same value.

Signaling an Event in Time

Each step of a process must take place at a specific point in time. For example, the steps of a program are executed sequentially; the steps of the fetch/execute cycle are also performed sequentially. Any coordinated process needs a means for sequencing events. As a first example, consider the problem of copying a byte from one point to another, say from a register to the bus.

The primary tool we will use for this task is called *gating,* because it uses parallel `and`-gates to accomplish the coordination. One input to the `and`-gate is data. The other is a *clock* or *select* signal. As long as the clock signal is low (0), the output of the gate is always low. But when the clock signal goes high (1), the output becomes "true and something", and "true and something" is just that "something." That is, the select signal, like a true in an `and`-mask, allows

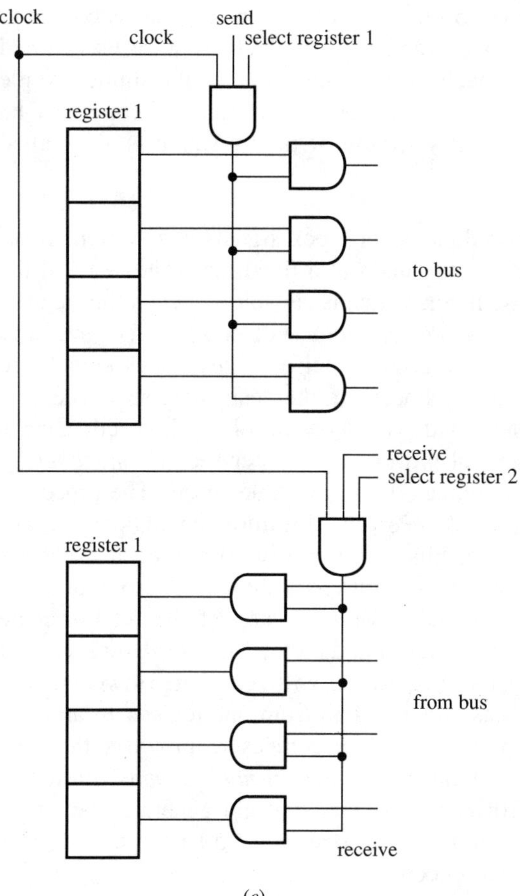

FIGURE 9-6 (cont.)
Connecting registers. (*c*) Simultaneously gated registers.

the data signal to pass through.[2] And-gates used for passing data can be *ganged* or grouped together to pass data between two multi-bit locations such as registers. Figure 9-6b shows two registers connected to the bus using ganged and-gates. The registers are no longer directly connected. There are and-gates on each connecting line. As long as the clock/select signal is 0, the output of each of the gates is always zero. No signal flows from the register to the bus. When the select signal

[2]In practice, a clocked noninverting buffer is used for this purpose. In the underlying electronics, there is an important difference between a selected and-gate and a buffer. The latter is actually constructed from a *tri-state device* capable of representing the states: high, low, and "disconnected." There are practical engineering reasons for the difference (like simplicity and speed), but the logical result is the same: a data value is allowed to pass through only when a control signal is present. We will continue to use the and-gate to emphasize the similarity to an and-mask. (Exercise 9.12 illustrates the difference).

goes high, each gate allows its signal to flow. Each bit of the register is copied to the corresponding bit of the bus. Since exactly the same clock pulse was `and`ed with each bit of the source register, each bit is simultaneously transmitted to the bus, and then to the second (destination) register. The process of copying data into a location by gating it with a short selection or timing signal is also called *strobing*.

THE CLOCK. The source of all coordination or clock signals is a system *clock,* whose sole function is to generate timing pulses at a fixed rate. The heart of the clock circuit is typically a crystal oscillator, which is capable of generating regular signals with great accuracy. The line from the clock will normally be low. At a regular interval, the clock will generate a brief 1 "pulse." These clock signals are used to ensure that the appropriate actions occur in the designated sequence.

The unit *hertz,* or cycles per second, is a measure of clock speed. Clocks on most systems today generate several million signals per second (*megahertz*). It is this rate that is often quoted to indicate basic machine speed. The processor of a machine with a 20 megahertz clock receives 20 million signals per second. This does not necessarily mean the machine can perform 20 million instructions per second. Each instruction may require several clock pulses. One obvious first approximation of timing is one clock pulse for each step of the fetch/execute cycle: one pulse to fetch an instruction, one to update the PC, etc. However, that is not precisely correct for several reasons, as we will see later. However, it is true that a single CPU action, such as copying data from one register to another, will generally require one clock pulse. An inverse measure provides the time interval between pulses, which is generally measured in *nanoseconds* (billionths of a second). A machine with a 10 megahertz clock would generate one signal every 100 nanoseconds; a 20 megahertz clock, one every 50 nanoseconds (the signal itself would last just a few nanoseconds).

Maintaining Values over Time

The discussion thus far does not explain how data values can be maintained over time, how data is accessed from memory, or the distinction between sending and receiving. The importance of the first of these questions can be seen from Figure 9-2, which implies that signals are transient in nature. In fact, it would clearly be impossible to establish a permanent connection between any two locations, because the two locations would always have the same value. Therefore, when a transient signal arrives at a register, it must somehow be trapped or held. The value received must survive after the connection is broken.

FLIP-FLOPS. The mechanism for holding onto a signal goes by the unglamorous name of *flip-flop*. A flip-flop is a bi-stable circuit, meaning that it can maintain either of two stable conditions. The simplest form of bi-stable circuit is a simple ring composed of two inverters or `not`-gates, as shown in Figure 9-7. Whatever value exists at point `a` in the circuit will be inverted twice, resulting in the original

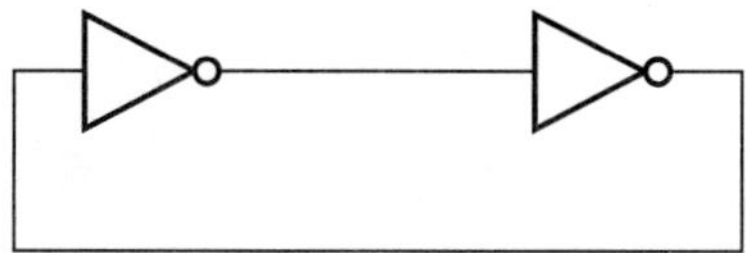

FIGURE 9-7
A simple bi-stable circuit.

value being fed back into the device. Unfortunately, there is no way to control which value this circuit holds.

A flip-flop provides exactly the desired additional capability: when a signal arrives, the flip-flop enters a state known as `set`. It stays in the `set` state until it is *reset* by a second (distinct) signal. Figure 9-8a shows a basic flip-flop, called an *S-R latch* after the two input signals, `set` and `reset`. As long as these signals are both zero, the basic flip-flop behaves exactly as the double inverter circuit. When and only when a signal arrives, the circuit behaves differently. To understand the transition, trace a signal through the circuit:

0. At the start, time = t_0, the flip-flop is in some state (that is, each labeled point in the flip-flop is either 0 or 1). The initial state does not matter, but note that every signal must be either high or low and be consistent with its neighbors.
1. Assume that at time t_1 a `set` signal (1) arrives at S.
2. The disjunction therefore becomes true (at intermediate point `a`). The other input to the `or`-gate does not matter—the result of the disjunction will be true.
3. The signal from `a` is negated, giving false at `b`.
4. By assumption, no signal is entering at the `reset` line `R`. Thus, both `R` and `b` are false, and the lower disjunction yields false at `c`.
5. That signal is negated giving true at `Q`, which is fed back into the upper `or`-gate. For the moment, it is irrelevant that this second true signal has arrived.
6. Eventually the transient signal `S` will cease. This will have no impact on the flip-flop, since `Q` is true. The disjunction of `S` and true is true. `S` has actually become irrelevant. The signal `Q` has taken over `S`'s task.
7. With `Q` true, `a` is still true; `b` false, etc.
8. The output of the flip-flop is available at `Q` with no impact on the flip-flop.

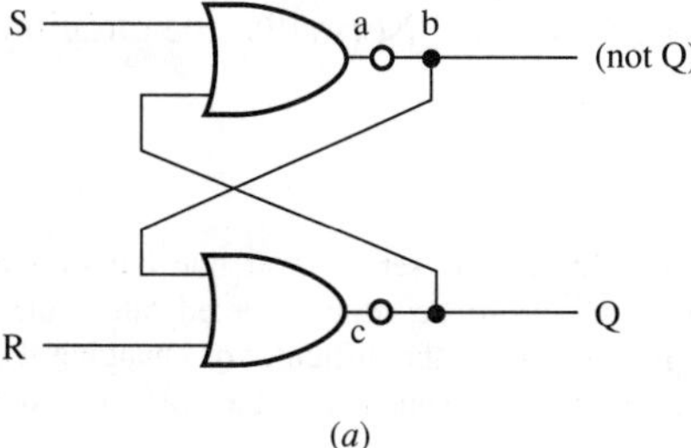

FIGURE 9-8
Flip-flops. (*a*) Basic SR latch.

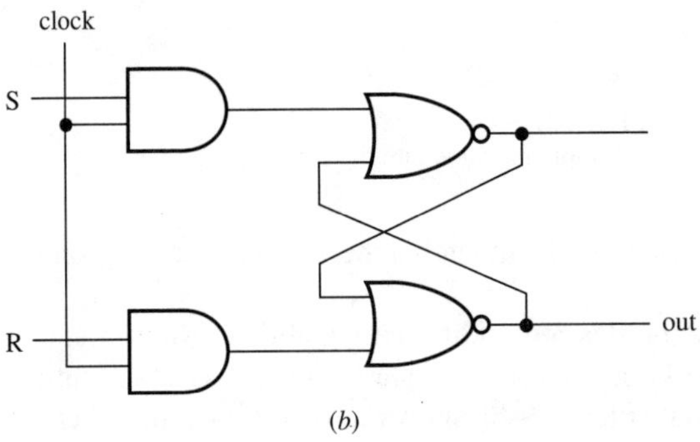

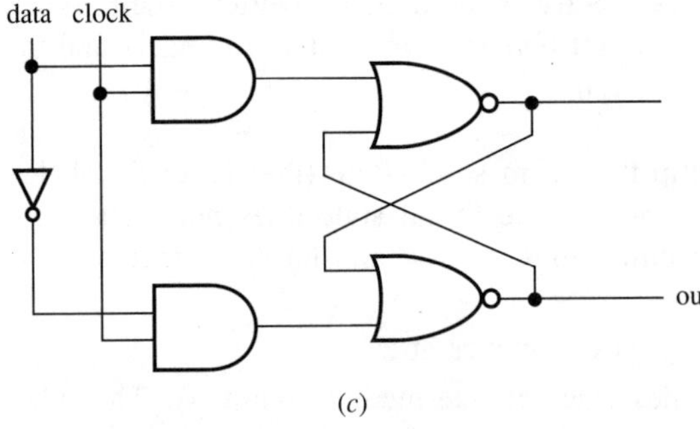

FIGURE 9-8 (cont.)
Flip-flops: (*b*) Clocked SR flip-flops; (*c*) D flip-flop.

No matter what the initial state of a flip-flop is, a `set` signal will cause the flip-flop to enter the `set` or 1 state, and to stay in that state even after the `set` signal has ceased.

The observant reader will already have noticed that the flip-flop is completely symmetrical. This symmetry provides the mechanism for terminating the `set` state. A signal at the `reset` line `R` will cause `c` to become true and `Q` to become false, thereby cutting off the support to the upper or-gate. The signal will become high at `¬Q` and low at `Q`. On the other hand, if a second `set` signal is received before a `reset`, no change will take place in the system. That is, placing a 1 where there is already a 1 causes no apparent change. It is unclear what would happen if `set` and `reset` signals were somehow simultaneously sent to the flip-flop. The final state would depend on which signal terminated later. Hopefully, such a condition, called a *race condition,* will never occur.[3] Normally, the circuitry

[3]In practice, state changes are not signaled by the high value on the set or reset line but by the change from low to high or vice versa. Such flip-flops are said to be edge-triggered rather than level-triggered. The advantage of edge-triggered flip-flops stems from the difficulty of changing the state at a precise instant in time. There is no logical or conceptual distinction in the current model between edge-triggered or level-triggered flip-flops.

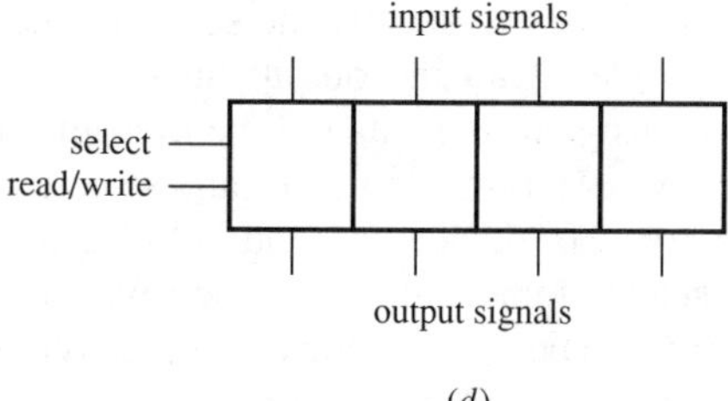

FIGURE 9-8 (cont.)
Flip-flops. (*d*) A complete four-bit register.

is designed to ensure that it won't, since the obvious use for a flip-flop is as a bit in a register. Whenever a signal is sent to a register, only one signal should be sent to each bit, which implies that only one signal should enter the flip-flop.

Unfortunately, the above configuration does not seem to be quite correct for use as a storage location. A signal arriving at a register (e.g., as in Figure 9-6) is either a 1, or a 0. That value, whichever it was, should be maintained by the register. But setting or resetting a flip-flop requires a 1 signal on exactly one of two lines. The incoming signal cannot simply be inverted, since inverting a null signal would send a reset signal rather than the needed "no change." The solution to this problem requires two steps. A clock pulse can restrict incoming signals to the appropriate times (Figure 9-8b) when `and`ed as in the previous section. Additionally, a single input value of 0 or 1 can be converted to the appropriate `set` or `reset` by splitting the signal and inverting one of the two resulting signals. There will always be one true and one false signal. Normally, the clock will be false and therefore both inputs will be 0 (Figure 9-8c). But when the clock signal is high, one of the two lines delivers a 1 to the flip-flop. Such a flip-flop is called a *D-flip-flop,* since it takes a single data input.[4] A register can thus be built using a ganged set of D-flip-flops. Sending the signal to a flip-flop register is essentially the same as shown in Figure 9-6c, but each bit is constructed internally as in Figure 9-8c. Since the same clock or select signal is sent to each bit, a register may be represented as in Figure 9-8d. Thus, a D-flip-flop is exactly what is needed: a device to hold on to a signal after it has been received.

Signaling One Event of Many

Sometimes it is necessary to indicate that one particular event should occur. For example, the processor must indicate that data should be copied from register A (rather than register B), or that an addition should be performed (rather than a subtraction).

[4]Note that some authors use the term *latch* to refer to flip-flops of the sorts discussed here. They reserve the term flip-flop for edge-triggered latches. Others use latch to refer only to the S-R latch, and flip-flop to refer to the D-flip-flop.

SELECTING A PATH. Path selection is accomplished in exactly the same manner as time-selection: with an and-gate. For example, if all the output lines from a specific register are anded with a *register select* signal, the data will be transferred if and only if the select signal is high. Generally, selection of a device and selection of time occur in tandem: "it is now *time* for *this* device to send." In such a case, both the clock signal and the device select signal must be anded with the appropriate data line, as shown in Figure 9-6c. The single clock pulse arriving at the source and the destination ensures that the send and receive signals are simultaneous.

The control must also indicate which register should send and which register should receive. For example, if it is desired to send a signal from the result register to general register 1, three simultaneous signals need to be sent to each of the registers involved:

- a clock signal indicating the time (to both registers)
- a register selection signal
- a send or receive signal

These signals are anded together indicating that one specific register should send (or receive) at a specific time.

Decoding Signals

It is often necessary to interpret a group of bits as a single signal. For example, every instruction in the generic machine contains a three-bit field indicating the register operand of the command. However, that register has a single select line on which it expects a signal telling it to send (or receive) data. This multi-bit number must be decoded or translated into a single instruction select signal. The tool needed to accomplish this task is a *decoder*—a device for accepting a multi-bit signal and producing a single signal to send to the destination. In this case, there are three bits, which can represent $2^3 = 8$ different registers. Each of the eight registers needs its own select line. The decoder must, in effect, accept a three-bit input signal and produce eight separate single-bit outputs, seven of which are false and exactly one of which is true (one will always be true—there is no such thing as "none of the above"). The trick is to treat the incoming lines as a single binary number and each outgoing line as if it were individually numbered. The output line corresponding to the number in the input bits is set high. Figure 9-9 shows such a decoder. The input lines are treated as if they were a miniature bus. The output lines are connected to and-gates, each of which is connected to each input bit. For each gate, a unique combination of the input signals are negated. If all three input lines are 0, the uppermost output gate inverts each 0, and the conjunction is of three 1's and is therefore true. Every other output gate has at least one false conjunct and therefore produces a zero. Similarly, an input of 001 produces a true signal on output line 1, and an input of 111 produces a true signal on output line 7. Every

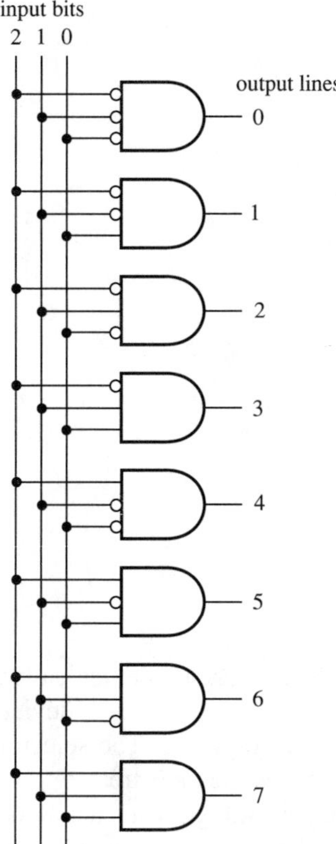

FIGURE 9-9
A three-bit decoder.

possible combination of input bits is accounted for. So one output line will always have a true signal. Decoders can be made in any size n, with n input lines and 2^n output lines. The current example illustrated a three-bit decoder for selecting a register. As a second example, note that each machine language instruction has an opcode field containing the opcode of the operation to be performed. In the generic example, the opcode has four bits; therefore, the decoder will have four input and $2^4 = 16$ output lines.

▷ *How can one distinguish between the much larger number of RAM locations?*

Merging Signals

On occasion it is necessary to merge many signals into one. In fact, this is essentially the process of placing the values from individual registers onto the bus: one specific register is selected and its value is copied to the bus. At some other instant, a different register could be copied onto the same bus. Although the combination of register select and clock signals does accomplish this logically,

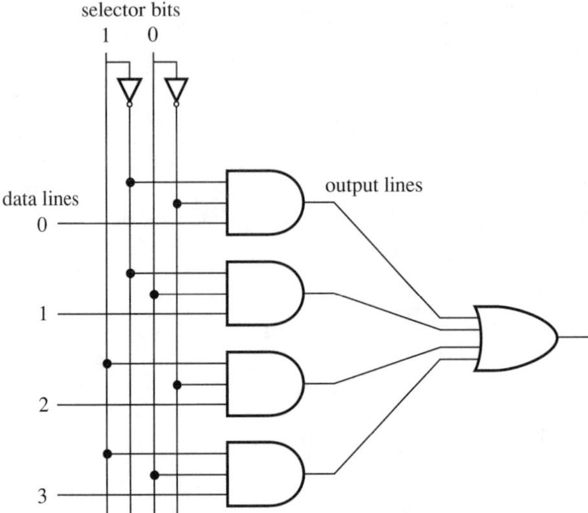

FIGURE 9-10
A four-channel multiplexer.

many such merging operations are performed by a general merging device called a *multiplexer* (sometimes *mux* for short). Generally, a multiplexer is a device that receives 2^n single-bit data signals, plus an n-bit selector value. The selector value uniquely specifies a single data line. The selector values are treated very much like a decoder's input. However, each data line is `and`ed with a unique combination of selector bits. Only one input line will be selected by combining with a true selection signal, so all result lines can be `or`ed together to produce the combined output. Figure 9-10 shows a typical four-bit to one-bit multiplexer. The register-to-bus connections can be thought of as a ganged set of multiplexers, each multiplexer merging the outputs of a single bit position from each register.

Multiplexers have another interesting use: converting parallel signals into serial signals. This may be necessary if, for some reason, there is a need to transmit the contents of a register to a location not served by a full bus, but through a single line. The multiplexer can be used to send all eight bits of a register by cycling the selector bits through all the legal values 0 through 7. Thus bit 0, 1, . . ., 7 would be sent in sequence. Chapter 12 illustrates additional uses for parallel-to-sequential conversion.

CONSTRUCTING AN ALU

The digital circuits named and described in the previous section form the building blocks for the control unit. The control structure must also have some operations that it can invoke. The *arithmetic logic unit* (*ALU*) of a computer is the part that performs the essential arithmetic and logical operations. Every such operation can also be created using combinations of digital logic operations—even those that seem to be purely arithmetic and unrelated to digital logic. The term ALU is used both to refer to the circuit that performs one specific arithmetic or logical operation and to refer to the collection of all the individual ALUs.

Logical ALUs

It is easy to imagine an ALU for performing any of the logical operations. The two operands are connected bit-wise with ganged gates of the appropriate type. Figure 9-11 shows an `and` ALU. But most machine instructions do not specify logic operations. How can those operations be constructed from logic gates?

The Adder ALU

As an example of an ALU, consider the hardware needed to perform an addition operation. Of course, addition is an arithmetic, not a logical, operation. It is, however, performed in binary, bit by bit. For each binary digit, the results can be described as:

a	b	carry	sum
0	0	0	0
0	1	0	1
1	0	0	1
1	1	1	0

For each pair of bits, there is a one-bit sum and a one-bit *carry.* The carry is only generated when the sum of the two bits cannot fit into a single bit, i.e.,

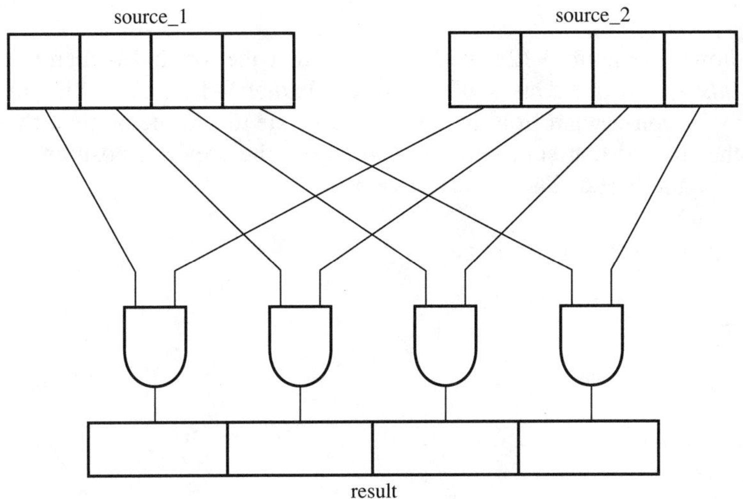

FIGURE 9-11
An AND ALU.

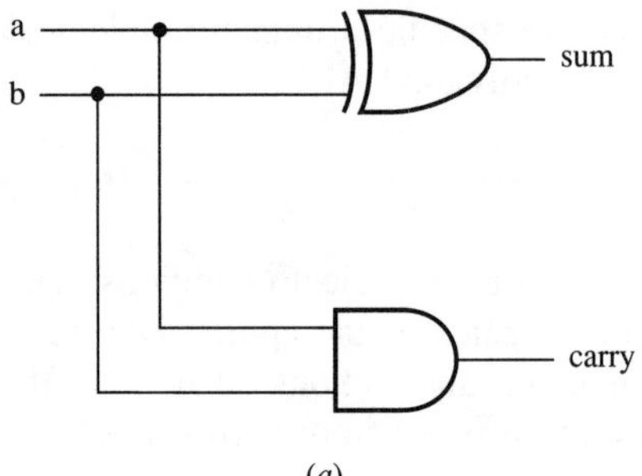

FIGURE 9-12
The adder. (*a*) construction of a half adder.

when it is 2. Alternatively, the two output bits can be viewed as a two-bit binary number representing the sum. Both of these functions are easily created from logical operations. The sum is just the exclusive-`or` of `A` and `B`. That is, `A+B` is a 1 iff exactly one input is a 1 (both 0 clearly yields 0, and both 1 yields $2_{10} = 10_2$, which is 0, and carry 1). The carry is the conjunction of the two inputs (unless both inputs are one, there is no way the sum of two one-bit numbers can be greater than one). Digital circuitry that accomplishes both results for single-bit inputs is shown in Figure 9-12a. For a full addition, the carry bit from each position must be added to the next bit. That is, after adding the two bits together, it is necessary to perform a second addition to add in the carry bit (from the previous addition). For example,

```
    0 1 0 1
    1 1 1 0
    -------
    1 0 1 1   (sum)
    1 0 0     (carry from previous column)
    -------
(1) 0 0 0 1
```

The `add`, as shown in Figure 9-12a, performs only half the job and is therefore called a *half adder,* illustrated as a black box in Figure 9-12b. A (1-bit) *full adder* can easily be constructed from two half adders: one to add the original two bits and the other to add that sum with the carry from the previous position, as diagrammed in Figure 9-12c. The sum is obvious:

$$\texttt{sum}_i = (\texttt{a}_i + \texttt{b}_i) + \texttt{carry}_{i-1}.$$

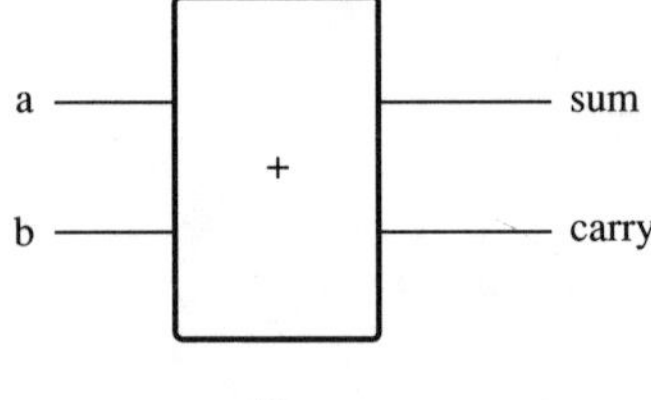

FIGURE 9-12 (cont.)
The adder. (*b*) black box representation.

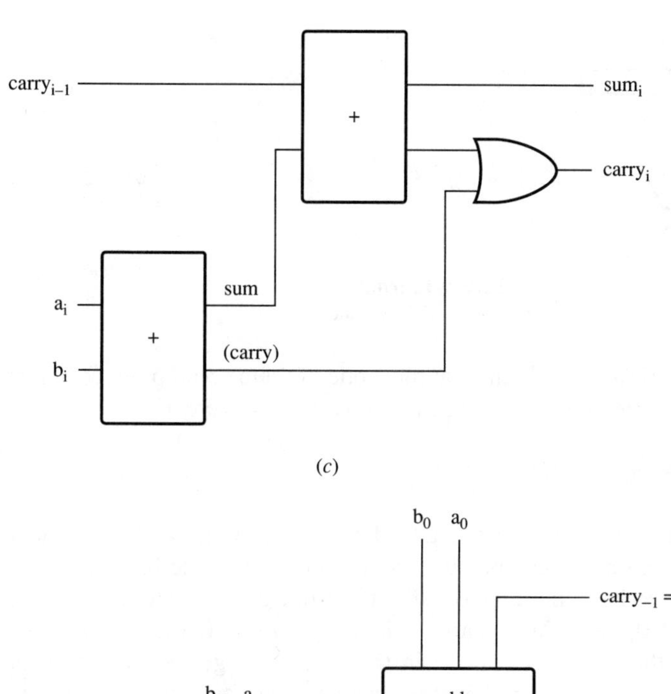

(*c*)

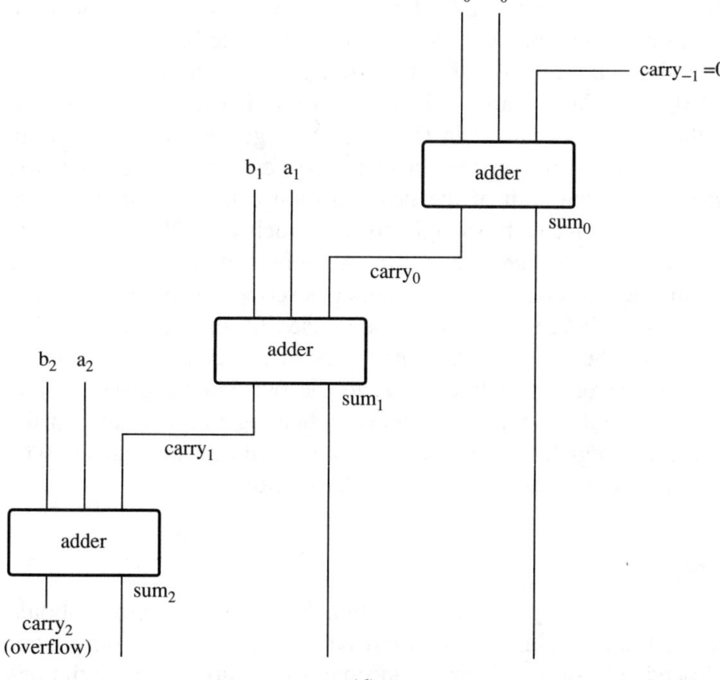

(*d*)

FIGURE 9-12 (cont.)
The adder: (*c*) A full one-bit adder constructed from two-half adders; (*d*) A three-bit full adder.

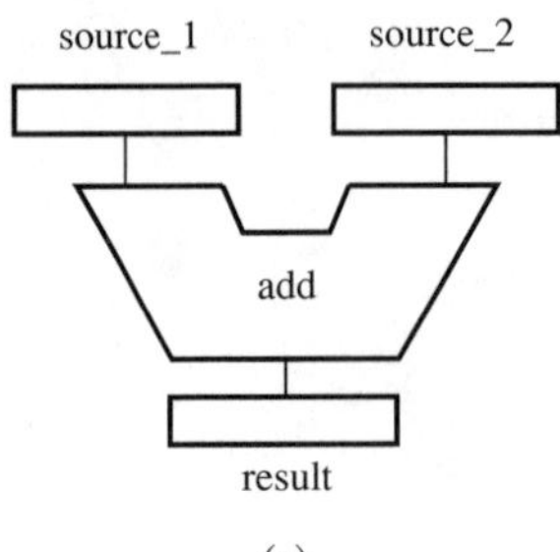

FIGURE 9-12 (cont.)
The adder. (*e*) The adder ALU.

The two carry signals are `or`ed, since at most one of them could produce a nonzero carry. Even if all three signals a_i, b_i, and $carry_{i-1}$ were 1's,

$$(a_i + b_i) = 10_2$$

yields a half-sum of 0, which when added to the carry-in, will not produce a carry-out. A multi-bit adder can be built from a series of single-bit adders. Figure 9-12d shows a three-bit full adder constructed from three single-bit full adders. Notice that for bit 0, carry-in = carry_{-1} is simply zero. If the last bit contains a non-zero carry, the result will not fit in the given storage location, causing an overflow. In an adder constructed in this manner, the carry from each position must be determined before the sum of the next position can be calculated. The results therefore ripple or cascade from right to left. Such an adder is therefore sometimes called a ripple or *cascading adder.* A more complicated but faster adder is described in the Exercises. The full adder described in Figure 9-12d is usually drawn as in Figure 9-12e (the odd shape is used to represent any ALU). The general operation of the adder ALU, when viewed as such a black box, is incredibly simple: the control unit delivers data to the two input registers of the ALU. A device select signal is sent to the adder indicating that it is to add the contents of the two input registers, and leave the sum in the result register. The control unit causes the result to be copied to the destination.

A Logical Shifter

This chapter opened with a very simplistic shifter. Subsequent sections should have made it clear that such a shifter would not be very useful. At a minimum, it certainly would need selection and timing mechanisms. Further, the variations on shift commands described in Chapter 8 also accept directional and magnitude arguments. Figure 9-13 shows a shifter that allows shifts to either the right or the left. The lines D_0 through D_3 contain the input data. The Left/Right line controls which direction the data is to be shifted, 0 for right and 1 for left. Each of the data inputs is `and`ed with both the Left/Right control line and its inverse (separately). For each data bit only one of the directions will pass through the `and`-gate. Thus, each of the `or`-gates receives exactly one signal (even at the ends). Note that the

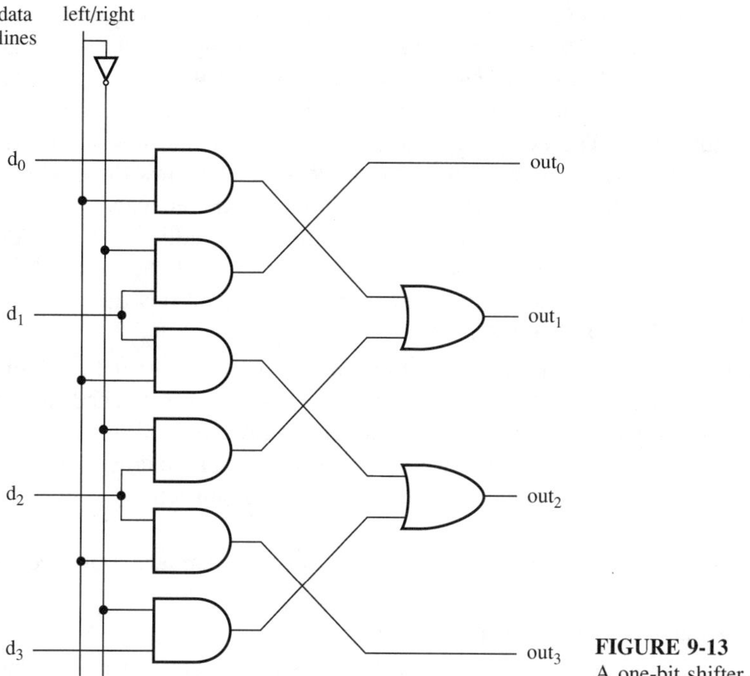

FIGURE 9-13
A one-bit shifter.

result of shifting bits off the end of the register is exactly the same as specified for the assembly command `shift`. To shift multiple positions, more complexity is needed. Schematic drawings for more complicated shifts are left as exercises. In analogous manners, circuits for each of the ALUs corresponding to machine language instructions can be built from simple gate structures. Additional ALUs are included in the Exercises.

THE FETCH/EXECUTE CYCLE REVISITED

We now have most of the tools needed to perform a typical pass through a fetch/execute cycle. The major exception is the specific mechanism needed for memory access, which is not covered until the next chapter. For the moment, assume that the address of the data needed from memory must be placed in an intermediate location called the *memory address register* (*MAR*) and that data fetched from memory is copied to an intermediate location called the *memory buffer register* (*MBR*). The mechanisms for fetching data from memory will affect the details of the cycle, but now we can certainly paint a clearer picture than was obtained in Chapter 6. Each step of the process can be investigated in more detail than before:

1. *Fetch the instruction.* The instruction must be fetched from memory (as described in Chapter 10). To accomplish this, the address of the instruction must

first be copied from the PC to the MAR. The controller then requests that the contents of that location be fetched. The memory fetch operation leaves the instruction in the MBR, from where it is copied into the instruction register. Each of these two data transfers is accomplished by a mechanism like the one shown in Figure 9-6c. The PC receives a register select signal, a send signal, and a timing pulse. The conjunction of the three signals allows the contents of the PC to be sent to the bus. Simultaneously the MAR receives a register select signal, a receive signal, and the same timing pulse, allowing the MAR to load the signal from the bus. Since each register receives the same clock signal, the transfer takes place in one clock cycle. (Total: 2 bus transfers for the step—PC to MAR, and MBR to IR.)

2. *Increment the PC*. The PC must be made to point to the next instruction. This can be accomplished by adding the length of the instruction (just fetched) to the current contents of the PC. Fortunately, in the generic machine all instructions are the same length, four bytes, and we have already constructed an adder. So the PC could be incremented by the following series of substeps:

   - Copy the PC to source_1 of the adder ALU (all copies are accomplished as above).
   - Copy the value 4 to source_2 of the adder.
   - Allow the adder to form the sum. This requires an adder such as the one shown in Figure 9-12 (can probably be completed between clock pulses, and is therefore effectively free).
   - Copy the result back to the PC (can take place at the next clock pulse). (Three bus transfers.)

3. *Decode the instruction*. A four-bit decoder is used to determine the instruction. The decoder values can be copied directly from the four high-order bits of the IR (instructions never come from any other location). One of 16 select lines is activated and will remain so for the duration of the cycle (no flip-flop is needed since the value will be output from the decoder as long as the appropriate bits of the IR contain the opcode). Additionally, a three-bit decoder will determine the register operand, and the mode bits will be analyzed individually. It is these decoded values that act as "select" signals (see step 5 below). This step is effectively instant (no bus transfers).
4. *Fetch the operands*. Assume for the moment that both operands are contained in registers. One at a time, they will be copied into usable locations:

   - The source operand. This requires a decoder to decode the three bits of the instruction that specify the source operand. The result is used to select the appropriate register for sending the source operand, which is copied into the `source_1` register.
   - The destination operand. A similar decode selects the destination register that is to be copied to the `source_2` register. Note that since both operands are

copied through the bus, they must occur sequentially not simultaneously. (2 bus transfers.)

If one operand is located in RAM memory, a memory fetch will be required as described in the next chapter. The fetch would leave the result in the MBR, from which the copy would have been made, requiring at least one extra bus transfer: address field of IR to MAR, then MBR to source.

5. *Perform the operation.* Each ALU now has direct access to the operands in `source_1` and `source_2`. Every single command can be built up from logical primitives just as the add command was. Many operations can be completed in less than the time between clock pulses. In such cases, apparently no time is needed for the instruction. That is, no clock pulse is needed for step 5. Each of the ALUs can perform its operation in parallel—as long as only one actually attempts to store the result onto the `result` register. The decode operation in step 3 singled out one ALU to do so. A multiplexer circuit—using the results from the ALUs as data and the opcode from the IR as a selector signal—may be used to transfer the result. There is, therefore, no conflict. (Effectively instant.)
6. *Store the results.* This process is identical to each of the previous register-to-register movements: the value is copied from the result register onto the bus and from there into the appropriate destination. If the perform step requires less than one clock pulse, this step can take place at the pulse after step 4. (Usually, one bus transfer.)

(Loop will be ready to repeat at next clock pulse.)
Figure 9-14 illustrates portions of the step by step flow of data and control.

Time Requirements

Each of the preceding steps includes an indication of how many bus transfers were needed. Since each bus transfer must take place individually, each such transfer requires at least one clock pulse. Thus the bus transfers provide some measure of the time required for the step, measured in clock pulses. Several of the events indicate that the event should be "effectively instant." This does not mean that the process requires no time—just that the amount of time is less than one clock pulse. In such a case, the data is ready to be accessed at the next clock pulse. Therefore, the step can be treated as "free." Total times required for the example were

step	pulses	
1.	2	`PC⇒MAR; MBR⇒ir (+ memory fetch time)`
2.	3	`PC⇒source_1; #4⇒source_2; result⇒PC`
3.	0	`(but decoded IR⇒ALU select lines)`
4.	2	`reg0⇒source_1; regl⇒source_2`
5.	0	`(add is fast)`
6.	1	`result⇒regl`

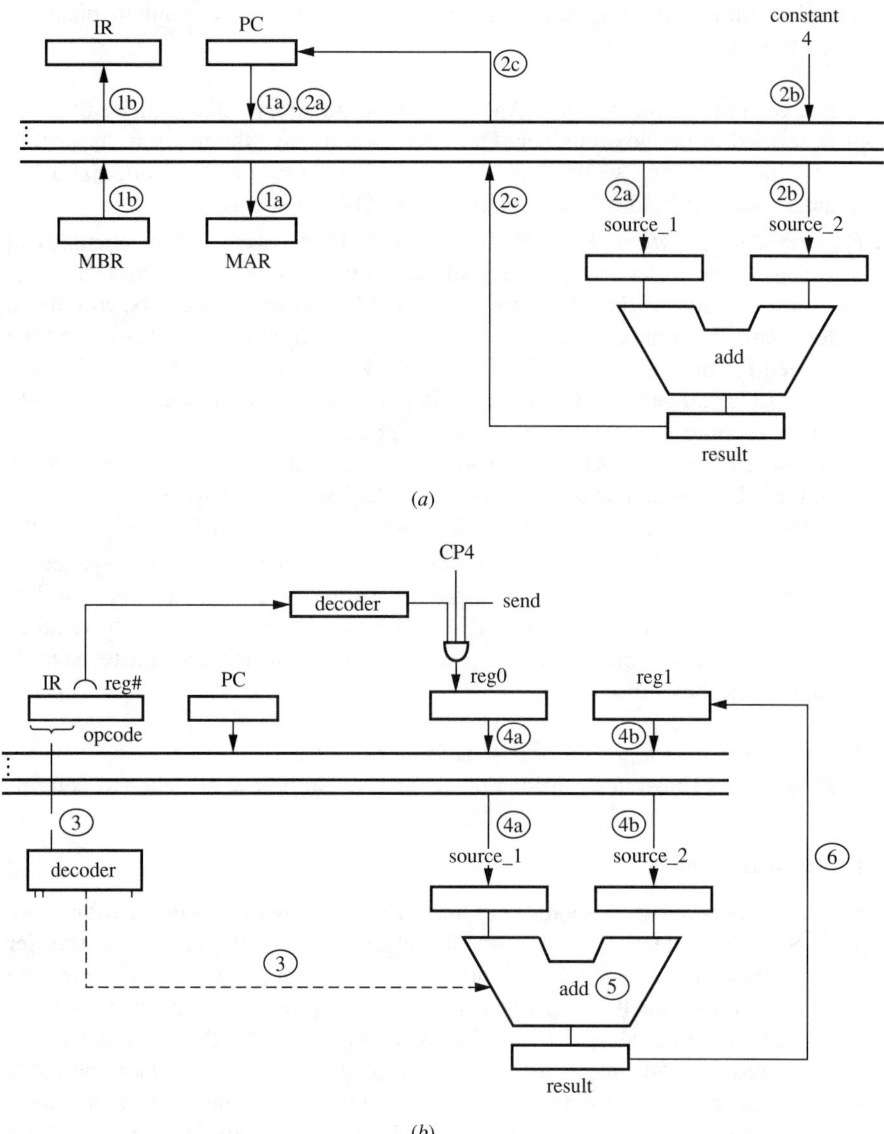

FIGURE 9-14
Construction of the controller: (*a*) Fetch portion of cycle; (*b*) Execute portion of cycle.

It would seem that something like eight clock pulses are needed for such an instruction. A 16 megahertz clock would generate 16 million pulses per second and therefore 2,000,000 such operations could be performed each second. That would mean that each instruction required

$$\frac{8}{16 * 10^6} = \frac{0.5}{10^6} \text{ seconds or 0.5 microseconds}$$

Alas, life is not so simple. Most noticeable will be the cost of memory access, which (as we shall see in the next chapter) is expensive relative to the steps described above. Therefore, the instruction fetch step and any operand fetch involving memory will require extra time. Cost variations will also be found in the "perform" steps of instructions such as multiplication, which are relatively expensive in terms of time, and in instructions with memory-based operands. On the positive side, we will discover some design improvements that will speed up the process slightly. The driving force, however, will be memory fetches.

▷ *What would the impact on the number of clock pulses be if an operand was referenced indirectly?*

This completes the digital-logic picture of the fetch/execute cycle, excluding memory references. For the first time, we have a model that can provide us with some measure of the *cost* of running a program. In terms of time, a program that requires more clock pulses is more expensive. Previous measures that students may have thought useful, such as the number of lines of code or the use of particular system features, are all clearly misleading. Clock pulse is as close to an absolute measure as we have seen. Most reference manuals provide a summation of the number of clock pulses required for each instruction. (Because the various addressing modes require different lengths of time to fetch the operand, some manuals provide separate instruction and memory fetch times, leaving the user to calculate the total time required.) The number of clock pulses, together with the clock rate, can be used to calculate how long a section of code should run. Similarly, given the machine language representation of instructions, the size of a program can be determined from the number of actual instructions. In a course on "analysis of algorithms" you will learn (or will have learned) alternative formal methods of mathematical analysis for estimating the order of magnitude of the running time for a program without actually writing the code.

APPENDIX: WHY NANDS AND NORS RATHER THAN ANDS AND ORS

As noted earlier, all needed logical structures can be built up from the three operations: `and`, `or` and `not`. It was also indicated that the same results could be accomplished using a related but distinct set of operations. These operations are `nand`, `nor`, and `not`. In fact, these operations more accurately reflect the logical structure of electronic computers. While electronic circuit theory is beyond the scope of this text, it is interesting to see why `nand`s and `nor`s are used in preference to their more understandable counterparts. In the following pages, we explore this alternative representation to see why it is actually the representation of choice.

`Nand` means "`not and`" and can be described by the truth table:

a	b	a and b	not (a and b)
0	0	0	1
0	1	0	1
1	0	0	1
1	1	1	0

Similarly, `nor` is "`not or`":

a	b	a or b	not (a or b)
0	0	0	1
0	1	1	0
1	0	1	0
1	1	1	0

Figure 9-15a shows the common schematic representation for both operators.

De Morgan's laws can be used to show that `and`s and `or`s can always be built from `nor`s and `nand`s and vice versa:

Constructing an `and` from a `nor`:

```
(a and b)⇔¬¬(a and b)           ;double negation

         ⇔¬((¬ a) or (¬ b)) ;De Morgan's Law

         ⇔(¬ a) nor (¬ b)     ;definition of nor
```

Constructing an `or` from a `nand`:

```
(a or b)⇔¬¬(a or b)

        ⇔¬ ((¬ a) and (¬ b))

        ⇔(¬ a) nand (¬ b)
```

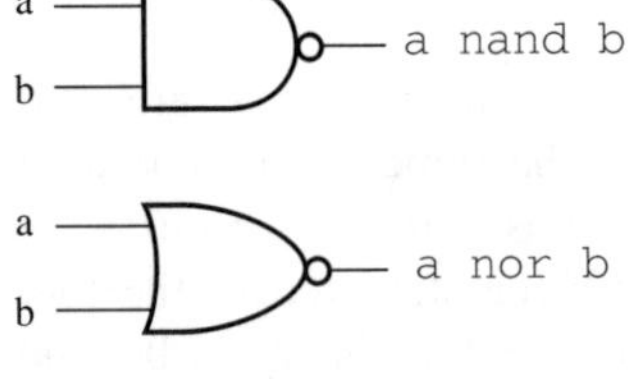

FIGURE 9-15
NAND and NOR. (*a*) Basic NAND and NOR-gates.

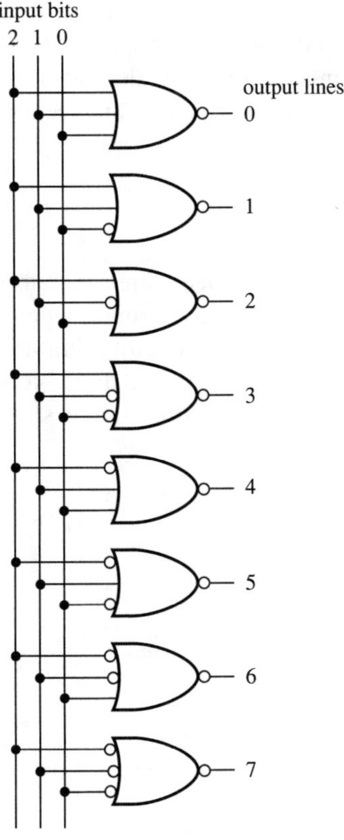

(*b*)

FIGURE 9-15 (cont.)
NAND and NOR. (*b*) Three bit decoder constructed from NOR-gates.

Constructing a `nor` from an `and`:

```
(a nor b)⇔(¬¬ a) nor (¬¬ b)
         ⇔not ((¬¬ a) or (¬¬ b))
         ⇔(¬ a) and (¬ b)
```

Constructing a `nand` from an `or`:

```
(a nand b)⇔(¬¬ a) nand (¬¬ b)
          ⇔not ((¬¬ a) and (¬¬ b))
          ⇔(¬ a) or (¬ b)
```

Thus, either form is equally powerful. With a little work, one could rewrite all the examples from the past two chapters—-code, truth tables, and circuitry—to create components based on nands and nors that are exactly equivalent to those based on ands and ors. For example, Figure 9-15b shows a three-bit decoder built with nots and nors.

Universal Operators

Both nands and nors have a surprising property: one does not need three operators at all. In fact, all digital circuitry could be constructed using only a single type of gate. The single operator nand is sufficient for describing any circuit; similarly for nor. To see this, all we need demonstrate is that any one of our three basic operations can be constructed from nand-gates. The following truth tables show the needed results:

`not a ⇔ a nand a:`

a	not a	a and a	a nand a
0	0	0	1
1	1	1	0

`a and b ⇔ (a nand b) nand (a nand b):`

a	b	a and b	a nand b	(a nand b) nand (a nand b) (from above)
0	0	0	1	0
0	1	0	1	0
1	0	0	1	0
1	1	1	0	1

`a or b ⇔ (not a) nand (not b):`

a	b	a or b	not a	not b	(not a) nand (not b) (from De Morgan's law and the definition of not above)
0	0	0	1	1	0
0	1	1	1	0	1
1	0	1	0	1	1
1	1	1	0	0	1

A similar result can be obtained for nors. Thus, an elegant simplicity can be gained by restricting the circuitry either to nands or to nors. Figure 9-16 shows nand-gates used to construct each of the basic operations.

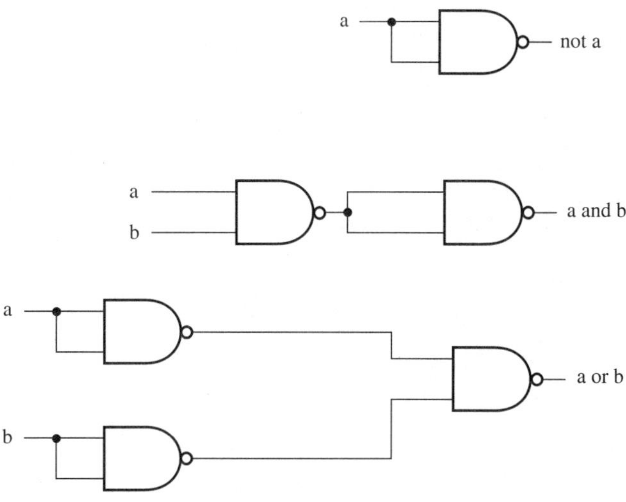

FIGURE 9-16
Construction of the traditional functions from NANDs.

Transistors

There is also a pragmatic reason for building computers from the negated forms: it is easy to construct `nand`s and `nor`s from transistors (or, historically, from their predecessor, the vacuum tube). A transistor is a semi-conductor, which means that it conducts current—but only under a specific condition: that it receives a signal from a second source. Figure 9-17a represents a basic transistor. A simple transistor has three connections to the outside world: a collector, with value V_c, which can be thought of as input at the collector; the emitter, with value V_e, which might be thought of as output; and a base, with input V_b. It is this last input that is responsible for the name *semi-conductor.* When V_b is high, the transistor behaves as a conductor, effectively creating a closed circuit between collector and emitter. Thus, if V_b is high, V_e will equal V_c. If V_b is low, the transistor turns off and acts like an open circuit or an infinite resistance. As drawn, the transistor behaves as an `and`-mask: if the base signal is high, the signal at the collector can be passed through to the emitter; but if the base is low, no signal is passed through at all.[5] Actually, it is the relative value of the base and emitter that determines whether a signal can or cannot pass through the transistor. Because of problems with extraneous signals in the close environment of a computer chip, the transistors are generally configured in a slightly more complicated manner, which provides greater electronic efficiency. In particular, the collector and emitter do not hold their obvious roles.

[5]Compare this to the earlier discussion of the use of `and`-gates versus buffers for gating information onto a bus.

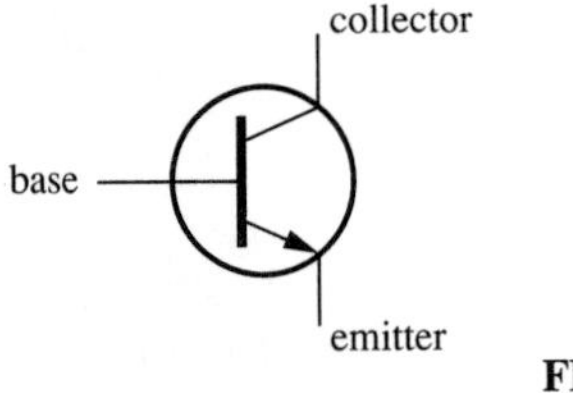

FIGURE 9-17
Transistors. (*a*) Basic transistor.

transistor signals

V_c	V_{in}	V_{out}
0	0	0
0	1	0
1	0	0
1	1	1

NOT. Figure 9-17b shows a transistor embedded in a very simple circuit. The jagged line represents a resistor, R. The resistance of R is selected such that it is greater than that of the transistor when the transistor is in its open state (V_b high) but less than the transistor in its closed state (V_b low). Thus, when V_b is low, V_c is disconnected from ground and is essentially connected only to the $+1$ source. It is therefore high. But when V_b is high, output $= V_c$ is effectively connected to ground and is therefore low. This configuration thus behaves as a `not`-gate, with V_b as input and V_c as output.

NAND. Figure 9-17c shows two transistors connected in series. If V_1 and V_2 are both high, both transistors become conductors. V_{out} is effectively connected to ground through the two transistors and is therefore low. But if either V_1 or V_2 is low, the corresponding transistor becomes a nonconductor, the connection to ground is broken, and V_{out} becomes equal to V_{hi} or true. Thus, V_{out} is high unless both V_1 and V_2 are low. That is precisely the definition of `nand`:

```
a nand b⇔ not (a and b)⇔(not a) or (not b)
```

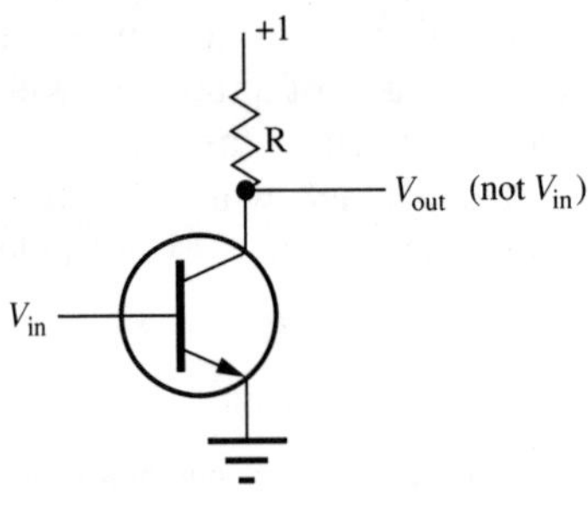

FIGURE 9-17 (cont.)
Transistors. (*b*) Used to create a NOT-gate.

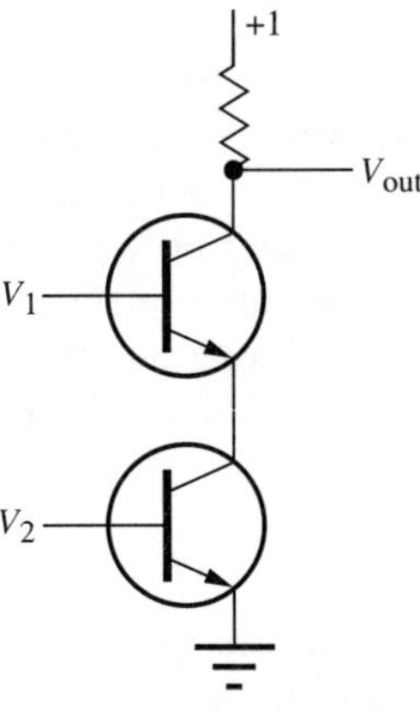

FIGURE 9-17 (cont.)
Transistors. (*c*) Used to create a NAND-gate.

The circuit in Figure 9-17c must therefore be a `nand`-gate.

NOR. Figure 9-17d shows two transistors connected in parallel. If either V_1 or V_2 is high, V_{out} is connected to ground through the corresponding transistor and is therefore low. V_{out} can only be high if both inputs are low. This is precisely the definition of `nor`:

```
a nor b⇔not (a or b)⇔(not a) and (not b)
```

The circuit must therefore be a `nor`-gate.

Thus, the three forms of gate—`not`, `nand`, and `nor`—are all easily and efficiently constructed from simple transistors. These forms are therefore used in preference to the equivalent, but more human-oriented, `not`, `and`, and `or` combination.

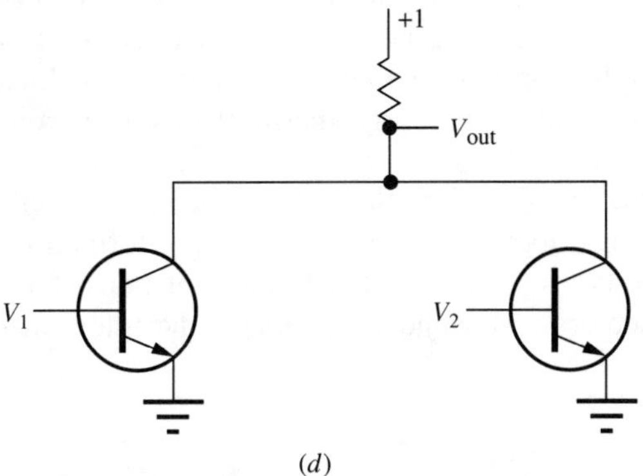

FIGURE 9-17 (cont.)
Transistors. (*d*) Used to create a NOR-gate.

INTEGRATED CIRCUITS. Individual transistors (as separate devices) are no longer used for construction of digital computers. Since the middle 1960s, when IBM introduced its System 360 series of computers, *integrated circuits* containing multiple transistors on a single chip have been used for computer construction. In less than 25 years, the number of transistors that can be placed on a single chip has grown to hundreds of thousands, even millions. The name integrated circuit evolved into *very large scale integrated* circuit or *VLSI*. During that time, the size of computers has changed, but the logical foundation by which they are constructed has not.

Speed Factors

In addition to the `nand` and `nor` constructs, several other factors impact the construction of real machines. One of the most important is speed. Clearly, speed is essential for any modern machine. One problem with the logic as described is the length of clock pulse required. Faster speed requires both shorter intervals and shorter clock pulses. On the other hand, the clock pulse must last long enough for an action to be completed. For example, when copying data from one register to another, a clock pulse must remain high long enough that a full transfer of data is assured. This means that the source register must be selected when the signal to the destination register ceases. Otherwise, the destination will receive all zeros. To make the process more efficient, many devices such as latches are "edge-triggered," meaning that the device changes state whenever input changes, rather than as a result of the absolute level of the input. Because the device is sensitive to the change in value rather than the actual value, the precision of the clock signal is not so important. A signal need not arrive at exactly a precise time. Any student seriously considering the study of computer engineering should investigate these differences.

SUMMARY

All basic Boolean functions have equivalent circuits. The circuits equivalent to the primitive logic operators `and`, `or`, and `not` are called gates. Any of the basic logical structures can be built using the corresponding digital circuits. The constructs—called ALUs—necessary for the basic computer operations, such as `copy` and `add`, can be built from logic gates. Similarly, the mechanism for controlling events in time, such as the sequence of steps in the f/e cycle (the control unit) and flip-flops for holding values, decoders for selecting one of many, multiplexers for merging several signals, and clocks for providing timing information, can be built from a small set of gate types. Because of the nature of transistors, in actual machines the logical connectors `nand` and `nor` replace the traditional `and` and `or`.

EXERCISES

9.1. In Exercise 8.1, you proved the distributive law of Boolean algebra. Create a circuit diagram equivalent to that proof.

9.2. In Exercise 8.2, you proved the associative law of Boolean algebra. Create a circuit diagram equivalent to that proof.

9.3. In Exercise 8.3, you proved the commutative law of Boolean algebra. Create a circuit diagram equivalent to that proof.

9.4. Build circuits equivalent to each of the remaining functions in Table 8-1 using only the logical connections `and`, `or` and `not`.

9.5. Repeat Exercises 9.1 through 9.4 using the operations `nand` and `nor`, rather than `and` and `or`. Repeat the process once again, using only `nands`.

9.6. Build circuit diagrams similar to the `add` ALU created in this chapter for performing other operations:

- subtract
- and
- or
- not

9.7. An encoder is the opposite of a decoder: it accepts a signal on the mth of 2^n input lines and generates the binary number m on n output lines. Draw a diagram for an eight to three-bit encoder.

9.8. Show that `nor`-gates are universal.

9.9. Diagram a half adder, using only `nand`-gates.

9.10. Recall that negative numbers are normally represented in two's complement form. Show that the adder as described in this chapter will work equally well for negative numbers.

9.11. Expand the shifter in Figure 9-13 so that it can shift multiple bits.

9.12. Draw two transistor diagrams: one representing an `and`-gated data line and the other simply as a tri-state buffer. Compare the logical and practical differences.

9.13. Figure 9-16 shows the construction of the traditional Boolean operations using `nand`-gates. Do the same using `nor`-gates.

9.14. A basic clock generates signals at a fixed rate on a single output line. Sometimes it is desirable to have separate signals on each of n lines: a signal on line n represents clock pulse n. Build such a clock from the basic clock and using other tools of this chapter.

9.15. For large numbers (e.g., 32 bits), the delay for a cascading adder can be significant. While it is generally beyond the scope of this text to investigate architectural nuances that can result in local speed-up, it is worth investigating a faster method here as an illustration of the interrelations between Boolean logic, digital electronics, and logical operations. The problem with the cascading adder is that the full sum for each position is dependent upon the carry from the next lower-order position. If the dependence upon carries can be removed, the cascade problem could likewise be removed. Therefore, we could attempt to represent each arithmetic (1-bit) sum as a logical expression free of references to carries. Fortunately, there is a base point from which to start:

$$S_0 = A_0 \oplus B_0$$

since there is no carry into bit 0. Likewise

$$C_0 = A_0 \wedge B_0$$

But

$$S_1 = (A_1 \oplus B_1) + C_0$$

so, substituting for C_0

$$S_1 = (A_1 \oplus B_1) + (A_0 \wedge B_0)$$

and, likewise the definition of

$$C_1 = (A_1 \wedge B_1) \text{ or } ((A_1 \oplus B_1) \wedge C_0)$$

can be expanded. Complete the representation for C_1 free of references to carries. Build similar representations for S_2 and C_2.

9.16. Draw a circuit diagram for a multi-byte shifter. It should have two control lines indicating a shift displacement of from one to four bits.

9.17. Suppose that you have a processor with a 2 megahertz clock. How many nanoseconds between clock pulses? A 5 megahertz clock? 40 megahertz?

9.18. Draw a circuit diagram for a one-bit full adder without using the atomic representation for the half adder.

9.19. Draw a timing diagram for the adder that you constructed in Exercise 9.18.

9.20. Draw a timing diagram for a flip-flop.

9.21. Draw a transistor diagram for an `and`-gate. For an `or`-gate.

9.22. Figure 9-14 does not indicate all of the needed connections (e.g., the logical connection from IR to second operand register), nor all of the clock pulse and select signals. Complete the figure.

CHAPTER 10

MEMORY

Previous chapters described two principal divisions of memory: registers and main memory or RAM. Most recently, Chapter 9 investigated the construction of registers as part of the central processing unit. This chapter first investigates the larger RAM memory at a similar level of detail. Most programmers are familiar with RAM memory as "main memory" or "the memory," which suggests that memory is a single amorphous entity. However, main memory, like other entities discussed previously—registers, the control unit, and the arithmetic unit—can be described in more detail using digital logic. The chapter then discusses additional forms of memory and investigates the various levels that make up the *memory hierarchy.* All forms of memory share certain common characteristics. They form a repository for data. They are organized as addressable bytes and words. The CPU can send data to individual words or bytes and can request the current contents of any word or byte. Individual locations are distinguishable: by their addresses in the case of RAM, and by name in the case of the registers. Each of the additional memory levels has analogous characteristics, but each also has advantages and disadvantages.

The final sections of the chapter discuss practical issues of memory construction, such as the detection and correction of errors, as well as some historical observations that help explain some of the common terminology.

PRIMARY MEMORY

Technologies used for manufacturing RAM have evolved over the years, but the general relationships between RAM and registers have remained essentially constant. In particular,

- RAM access is slower than register access.

- There are more RAM cells than register cells.
- Restrictions usually apply to allowable RAM access at the ml level.

This relationship, of course, has a direct impact on both the possible and preferable programming techniques. In GAL, for example, register-based operands result in faster execution, and therefore most instructions require that at least one operand be in a register. Although there are several factors dictating memory speed, one simple fact of life accounts for much of the distinction: cost. Faster components are more expensive than slower components—if only due to supply and demand, since every rational consumer prefers the better (faster) product. This universal truth can help us understand the nature of memory. What is economically feasible for two or eight registers is not practical for a million bytes of main memory. A designer of a microcomputer may not hesitate to include eight items if they cost $1 each, but a million such items would be out of the question. Many other factors, ranging from the larger address required for RAM memory access to the relative distance the signal must travel (at one time memory was housed in a separate cabinet from the CPU), are also involved; we will see some of them later.

A Quick Review of Register Memory Construction

Recall that each bit of a register is constructed using a flip-flop. The flip-flop can hold the value as long as it is needed (unless power is cut off, or other data is inadvertently placed in the register). Data can be loaded into all of the bits of a register in parallel by strobing it in from a source (typically, through the internal bus). The contents of a register can similarly be read by sampling the output lines of each bit. Data can be transferred from one register to another by simultaneously directing one register to send its value to the bus and a second to receive a value. Note that this requires a set of `send` lines, one per register, to signal a register to send its contents, and a second set of `receive` lines to instruct a register to load values from the bus. Registers are not connected directly to each other but must share a common communication pathway (bus).

RAM Memory

In theory, RAM memory could be constructed and addressed in exactly the same manner as register memory: each cell could be constructed as a single register, with individual register-select signals and read/write signals to select the operation for the selected "register." Several problems (in addition to the obvious cost) exist with this model.

FLEXIBILITY. Would single-byte operations necessarily be restricted to the low-order byte of the "RAM-register"? If so, it seems that only half or a quarter of the memory cells could be accessed directly for byte-size data. If not, some additional indicator would be needed to specify high- or low-order bytes within the RAM-register. Conversely, it is not clear that records or other larger entities could be accessed conveniently in fixed-sized locations.

ACCESS. A second—and ultimately more important—distinction is the access techniques required for the two methods. The number of bits required to identify a RAM location is significantly larger than for a register. With only eight general purpose registers, the generic machine can specify a register using a total of eight distinct register select lines and, more importantly, three bits of an instruction fed to a decoder. Clearly 64K distinct select lines for 64K storage locations is prohibitive. Sixteen bits of an instruction are needed to specify that many locations. That implies that the size of the address required to identify a specific memory location has approximately the same order of magnitude as the information to be stored in the location. Alternatively stated, the CPU will need to transmit as many bits to specify the address as it sends to store in that address. Some form of bus structure will be needed for the address as well as the data. To write to RAM, the CPU must transmit two values (the address and the data) from CPU registers (e.g., the PC or the IR) to memory simultaneously. Surprisingly, this simple observation of the difficulties caused by address size provides part of the solution to the problem.

COORDINATION. Finally, memory is not part of the CPU. It is a separate entity (observation: on most machines, you can easily add more memory but not new instructions). All of the structures supporting the fetch/execute cycle—registers, internal bus, control unit, and ALUs—were part of a single entity, the CPU. They are logically and physically contained in the same unit. Memory is a separate entity and cannot be controlled directly by the CPU in the same manner as the subparts of the CPU itself. While the CPU may request data from memory, it is up to memory to ensure delivery. Typically, memory will not return a result to the CPU within a single clock pulse. The addressing techniques used for registers would require the CPU to maintain the address signals for the entire memory fetch period, which in turn would prohibit any further activity until the value was returned. When the content finally is returned, the address signal must immediately be discontinued, to avoid bus interference with the returned value. Access to RAM memory will clearly require some additional and more specialized or complicated logic than was needed for registers.

Reading from RAM Memory

In essence, the process of reading data from memory has two basic steps. A memory-read command, specifying an address, is broadcast to all memory locations by the CPU. The appropriate memory location—and only that location—responds by sending its contents to the CPU, which can then load the value into the desired destination. A more efficient overall operation is possible with the addition of two intermediate steps. The problems of address specification and multi-clock pulse fetch time can be minimized by the introduction of two special registers that act as buffers: the *Memory Address Register* (*MAR*) and the *Memory Buffer Register* (*MBR*). (For purposes of this discussion, assume that each of these registers and each cell of RAM is eight bits long.) From the perspective of the CPU, a memory fetch can logically be regarded as a function

```
fetch(MAR:integer):bitstring
```

which, when passed an address, returns a bitstring equal to the contents of that address.

There are two buses for communication between the CPU and memory: the *address bus* and the *data bus*. These two buses are sometimes collectively referred to as the *memory bus* (indeed some systems have only one bus serving both purposes) or the *system bus* (often this term refers to a more general bus that can communicate with other entities in addition to memory). Figure 10-1 shows the logical relationships between the registers, buses, and main memory. Note that the memory registers are connected to both the internal bus and to the memory bus.

The address contained in the MAR is broadcast through the address bus to memory. Effectively, the connections between the address bus and memory function as a single large decoder, providing the *memory select* signal to a single memory cell. That cell then transmits its contents back to the MBR via the data bus. Since only one cell attempts to return a value, the connections to the data

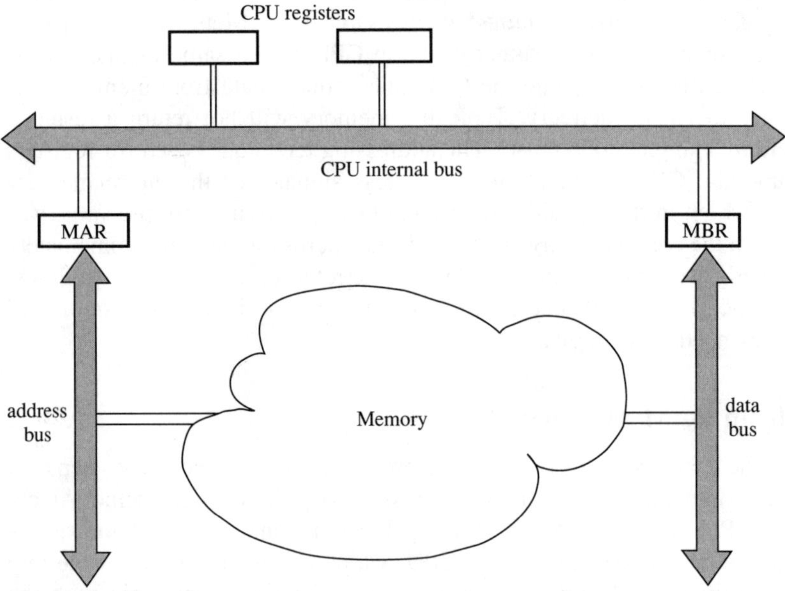

FIGURE 10-1
The memory bus and memory registers.

bus effectively function as a large multiplexor, returning only the signal from the selected cell. The substeps of a memory fetch operation can be summarized:

1. The CPU copies the desired address into the MAR. Typically, the address is copied from the PC (for instruction fetches) or the IR (for operand fetches). This process is identical to a copy between any other pair of registers.
2. The address is then sent from the MAR onto the memory bus. In effect, the address is broadcast to all memory locations. Two additional signals are sent simultaneously: A *memory-read* signal (usually designated RD[1]) indicates that the requested operation is a read, and a *select* or timing signal synchronizes the fetch. At this point the CPU relinquishes control of the fetch operation. The memory locations are connected to the bus as if it were an eight-bit decoder. That is, only one location will actually receive a signal indicating that its content is desired for a read. The single location receiving the appropriate address signal, the select signal, and the memory-read signal will return its contents. Figure 10-2 shows details of the logical connections for a small memory of four-bit cells.
3. The designated memory cell copies its contents onto the data bus. The combined RD and select signals serve the same role as the register-select signals do for register transfers. From there, the value is copied into the MBR. This process is analogous to the transfer of data from one internal register to another. Note that all other cells are effectively blocked from placing their data on the data bus by the lack of a memory-select signal.
4. Finally, the CPU copies the MBR register into the desired destination register (IR in the case of an instruction fetch, a source register for a data fetch).

Figure 10-3 expands the description of the memory steps 2 and 3. Each bit of the selected memory cell receives the strobed signal RD and the memory select. The select and RD signals are `anded`[2] with each of the parallel output lines from the flip-flops and delivered to the data bus. The combined select lines restrict the output to that from a single data cell. In theory, it might be possible to perform a memory fetch operation without the MAR and MBR. That would

---

[1]Sending the signal to a destination outside of the CPU presents a practical problem: the CPU and the memory may be created by different manufacturers. While the details of the internal logical construction of the CPU are immaterial to the system external to the CPU, memory requests are external and therefore a standard protocol will be needed. The signals RD and select are such standard signals. RD distinguishes read requests from write requests. The distinction between internal and external signals is analogous to that between variables internal to a procedure and the parameters to that procedure.

[2]In practice, the connecting gate is not an `and` (which allows two possible output values), but a tri-state device, which outputs 0 or 1 corresponding to values in the flip-flop or an open circuit value for unselected cells. Logically, the results are equivalent.

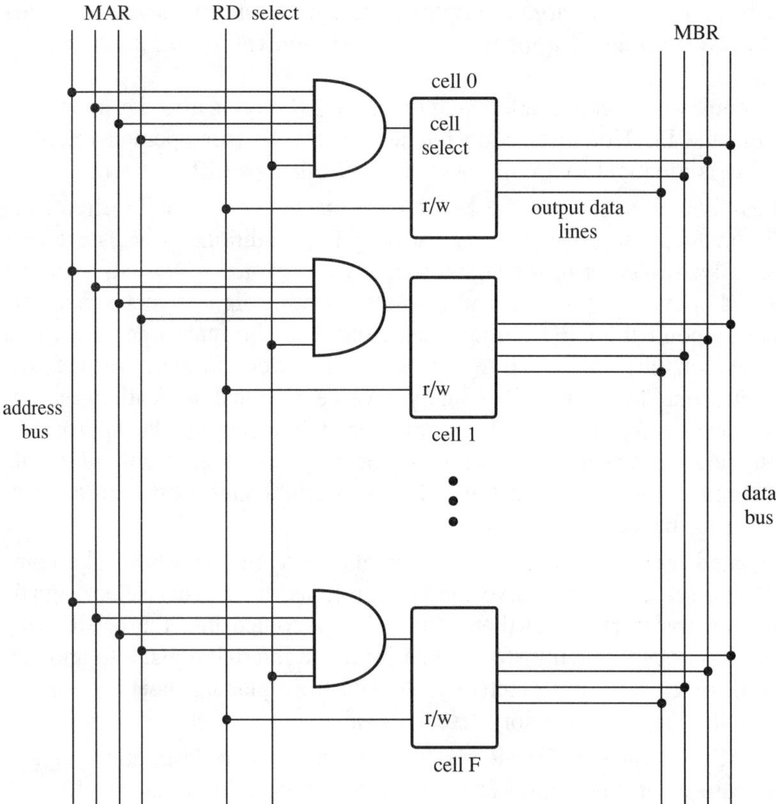

FIGURE 10-2
A 16-cell four-bit cell memory.

require very precise timing and would prohibit further CPU activity until the result was returned. Not all memories are created equal; in particular, some are faster than others. Building such timing information into the CPU timing might also prohibit incorporation of faster memory as it became available in the future.

If a single bus were used for broadcasting the desired address and for returning the contents (occasionally, but not usually, the case today), two distinct timing events would be required: one for sending the address and one for returning the content. Otherwise, the two values would interfere. Use of the same bus would also dictate that the quantity of available memory be intimately related to the size of the memory locations. If each memory cell is eight bits, an eight-bit bus is needed. Therefore, $2^8 = 256$ memory locations can be addressed. Sixteen-bit buses would allow 64K 16-bit cells to be accessed.

▷ *An address space restricted by bus size sounds problematic given the size of today's machines. What are some possible solutions?*

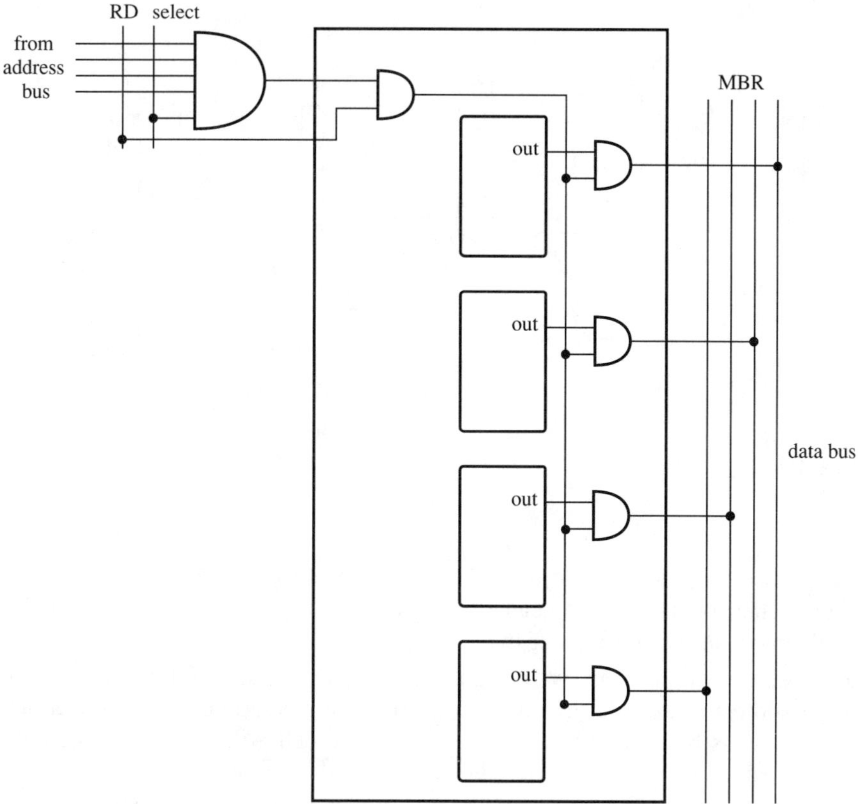

FIGURE 10-3
Read signals for a single cell.

Memory Write Operations

For storing data into a memory location, a memory-write event is needed, requiring a similar—but slightly more complicated—series of steps. The data to be stored and the address at which to store it must be sent to memory in parallel. This operation would be considerably more complex without the existence of the two memory registers. The essential steps are

1. The CPU copies the address of the desired memory cell to the MAR.
2. The CPU copies the value that is to be placed in that location to the MBR.
3. Three simultaneous events occur next. The address is transmitted from the MAR through the address bus, the contents of an entire data byte are sent from the MBR through the data bus, and a *memory-write* signal is broadcast on a separate line. In practice, the write signal is the negation of the `RD` signal. A simultaneous memory-select signal and `(not RD)` is interpreted as write.

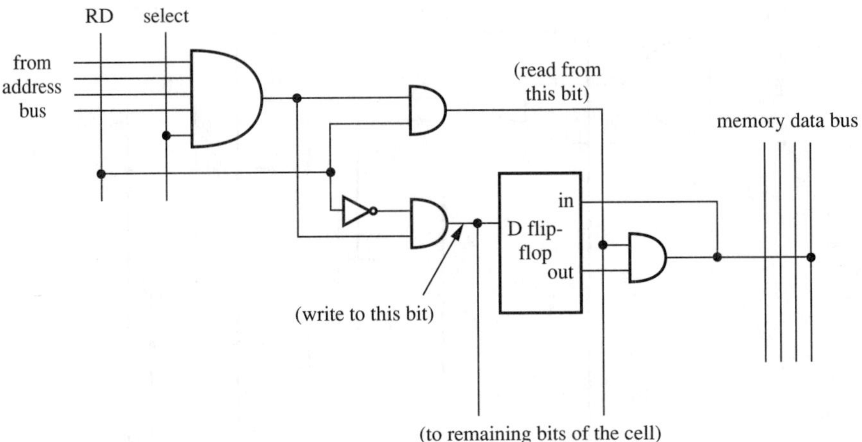

FIGURE 10-4
Logic for a single bit.

Select is set high to indicate that a memory operation is needed. RD indicates whether that operation is a read (high) or a write (low). This ends all CPU involvement in the write process.

4. On receipt of the memory write signal, the single cell selected by the address in the address bus loads the value from the data bus. Again, the connections to the address bus act as a decoder, so only one cell will respond to the data transmitted. Each line of the data bus corresponds to a unique bit position, so the contents of each line of the data bus are loaded into the corresponding bit in the memory cell. Figure 10-4 shows the added complexity for a single bit.

Logical simplification was achieved at a cost of slower access. The data cannot all be accessed simultaneously by the CPU, but the MAR and MBR serve to hold the data until both address and data are ready to be transmitted. This extra step makes the operation practical. In addition, the intermediate step frees the CPU to perform additional tasks while the memory fetch operation is in progress.

Interaction of Primary Memory and the Fetch/Execute Cycle

OVERLAP OF FETCH AND INCREMENT STEPS. The four distinct substeps of a memory fetch provide an additional explanation for the slower access speed of RAM operands relative to other steps of the fetch/execute cycle. On the other hand, the requirement of the four steps does not imply that the CPU must be idle during all of the steps of a memory fetch. Once the CPU has requested a value from memory, it can continue processing other information in parallel with the memory fetch—if it is clear that no conflict could occur. In fact, this is always the case during an instruction fetch. Consider the first two steps of the fetch/execute cycle:

1. Fetch the instruction.

2. Increment the PC.

Once the address of the desired instruction has been copied to the MAR, the current address in the PC is no longer needed by the CPU. Thus, the "increment the PC" step can logically begin at any time after the MAR has been loaded. In fact, the entire PC update can be accomplished before the memory fetch is complete. Typically the logical substeps are as shown in Figure 10-5.

Using a bus, it is possible to copy a register to two distinct destinations simultaneously. Thus, the first two logical steps of the cycle begin simultaneously. In fact, the entire second logical step of the fetch/execute cycle can normally be completed before the first logical step. Unfortunately, the third step of the cycle, decode, cannot begin until completion of the first step because the result of the memory fetch is needed before any decoding can begin. Taking advantage of the potential parallelism between fetch/execute steps provides significant time savings, but there is a limit to such savings. Since every instruction must be fetched from memory, the total fetch/execute time must be larger than the memory fetch time. We saw this restriction earlier as the von Neumann bottleneck.

No similar savings is possible during the fetch-operand or store-results steps. In theory, since no result is returned to the CPU after a memory write, the CPU could continue processing immediately after sending a write signal in the store result step. This would create an overlap between the actual performance of a memory write operation and the next fetch/execute cycle. Unfortunately, the next cycle begins with the fetch instruction step, which first copies the PC to the MAR. It is imperative that the MAR does not change until the memory write operation is complete. Therefore, the CPU and memory actions cannot be overlapped here.

RELATIONSHIP OF CLOCK SPEED AND MEMORY ACCESS TIME. The timing in Figure 10-5 assumes that the addition operation requires less than one clock pulse interval. More significantly, it assumes that the memory reacts to a

CP	f/e step 1	f/e step 2
1	copy PC to MAR	and to ALU-source register
2	send memory read signals	
		send increments to second source register
		perform an addition
3		copy new value to PC
	MBR receives instruction	
4	copy instruction from MBR to IR	
5	start decode process.	

FIGURE 10-5
Relationship of PC-increment and instruction-fetch steps.

read request and returns a value within two clock pulses: the address is placed in the MAR at clock pulse 1, and the fetch request sent at CP2. The value was available in the MBR by CP4. This may not be a very realistic assumption. Suppose a machine has a 20 megahertz clock. The interval between clock pulses would then be $0.5*10^{-7}$ seconds or 50 nanoseconds. If the access time for memory is 120 nanoseconds, three clock pulses must elapse before the data can be retrieved. In such a case, the CPU is said to be *memory waiting*. Since steps of the f/e cycle require an integral number of clock pulses, a speed-up requires that the access be reduced to 50 nanoseconds. RAM access will be somewhat of a bottleneck, even if the RAM itself is extremely fast. In the limit, two clock pulses are required: one to copy the address to the MAR and one to retrieve the value from the MBR. (Exercise 10.11 explores this limit further.)

EFFECT OF BUS SIZE. Analysis of the fetch/execute cycle with various bus sizes provides an important indication of the speed of the machine. Suppose a machine has 32-bit instructions. If the data bus also has 32 bits, an instruction fetch is straightforward. However, if the bus has only 16 bits, two full memory fetches are required to fetch one instruction. The fetch and increment steps then might look like:

step	action
1a.	fetch first 16 bits of instruction
2a.	increment PC by 2
1b.	fetch last 16 bits of instruction
2b	increment PC by 2

Since a memory fetch is the most expensive part of the cycle and since an instruction must be fetched every time it is executed, a reduction in the bus size by half will approximately double the overall execution time. The net logical result is the same, but it requires twice as much time to achieve. Processing data items of a size larger than the bus (e.g., 32-bit words with a 16-bit bus) will slow down the processing in a similar manner, but the impact will not be so great since not every instruction fetches a data item. Similarly, RAM destination operands are also costly since they require two RAM accesses: one to fetch the operand and one to store the results.

> ▷ *This is a good point at which to think about the legal modes on your machine. Does it allow two RAM operands? Can the destination of arithmetic operations be a RAM location?*

Not all seemingly obvious extensions of the preceding observations yield similar results. Processing data items smaller than the data bus does not speed the process up at all, since all bits of the item are fetched or written in parallel. Eight bits and 16 bits each require one fetch on a 16-bit bus. Larger address buses do provide a similar—but much smaller—speed-up since the entire address can be transmitted in one step. Any reduction in the size of the address bus slows the machine down by complicating the fetch process (see the following section). If instructions are smaller than the data bus, some speed-up is possible by fetching more than one instruction at a time. Similar concepts (called *pipelining*) are explored briefly in Chapters 15 and 16.

Bus Size and Memory Size as Conventional Machine Descriptions

The size of the address bus dictates the size of the memory that can be addressed. With a four-bit bus, 16 bytes can be addressed; an eight-bit bus allows access to any of $2^8 = 256$ bytes. This is clearly insufficient for any real computer. A 16-bit bus can specify $2^{16} = 64K$ locations, which is still not sufficient for any modern computer, and a 32-bit bus would enable filling $2^{32} = 4$ billion locations, which should do for the near future (although there do exist machines with larger address spaces). Similarly, the size of the data bus dictates the amount of data that can be processed at one time. The four-bit data bus used in earlier examples allowed four-bit data cells; an eight-bit bus, eight-bit cells; a 16-bit bus, 16-bit cells and a 32-bit bus, 32-bit cells. While it is clear that more than 16 bits are needed to process most interesting problems, it is also expensive to create large buses. For example, among Macintosh computers, only the Mac II line has full 32-bit memory buses; among IBM-compatible machines, only those with an 80386 or later CPU have full 32-bit memory buses.

This bus limitation helps define one popular classification for microcomputers. Eight-bit machines have eight-bit buses, 16-bit machines have 16-bit buses, and so on. On the other hand, the size of the general purpose registers is also used to classify machines as eight-bit, 16-bit, etc. Thus, some machines with larger internal buses than memory buses have been referred to by a bus-size/register-size pair, such as 8/16 or 16/32-bit processors. Machines are also classified according to the amount of memory that they can address (usually measured in bytes). A 64K machine has 64K addresible memory locations. If those locations are bytes, the machine can have 64K bytes of memory. If the locations are 16-bit (two-byte), presumably the machine could have 128K bytes of memory.

There seems to be an apparent contradiction in the preceding discussion. In the early days of microcomputers, there were many machines described as 64K / 8-bit microcomputers. But more than eight bits are required to address 64K of memory. Similarly, one can now find 16-bit machines with several megabytes of memory. For example, the Mac Classic has 2 Mb of RAM and a 16-bit bus. How can this be? A 16-bit bus can address only 64K unique memory locations.

One possible explanation is that the address and data buses have different sizes. It would seem that a 64K machine needs a full 16-bit bus for the address but may use only an eight-bit bus to store the data. A better answer to this paradox is that a smaller bus is actually used than seems necessary at first. Consider the four-bit memory from Figure 10-2. This time, connect 16 rows of 16 bytes each for a total of 256 (2^8) bytes of memory to the bus. Figure 10-6 shows this configuration. Note that the configuration is now effectively three dimensional: two dimensions for the cell location and one for the bits within a cell. Each cell is connected to the address bus twice: once corresponding to the high-order bits of its address and once corresponding to the low-order bits. Selection of a cell will require two sets of address signals on the bus. First, the high-order bits are broadcast, selecting a block (row) of cells. Second, the low-order bits are broadcast, selecting a single cell within each block. The signals are anded together, so that only the byte that

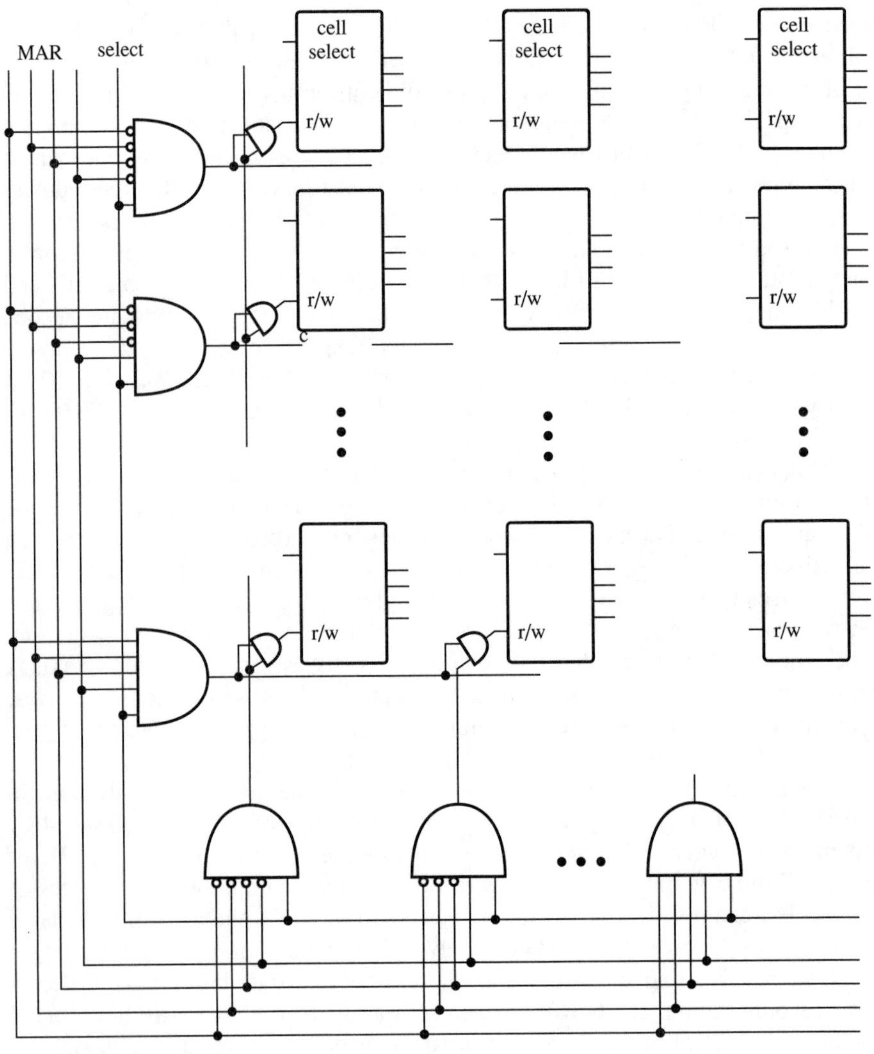

FIGURE 10-6
Coincident decoding.

receives both signals is selected. The contents for that byte are sent on the data bus as before. This process using split addresses, called *coincident decoding,* requires an extra step but dramatically increases the address space (effectively squaring it). Four bits could be used to address $256 (= (2^4)^2)$ bytes; eight bits could address $64K (= (2^8)^2)$ bytes; and 16 bits could address $4Gb (= 2^{16})^2$ bytes. Theoretically, a 32-bit machine could address $(2^{32})^2 = 16$ quadrillion bytes.

▷ *The first or high-order signal must be held until the second or low-order signal arrives. This requires a latch. In an earlier section, we rejected such a latch in favor of the MAR/MBR concept because of the cost or complexity of including so many extra latches. Why is that not a problem in this situation?*

MEMORY AND REGISTER ALLOCATION. The experienced assembly language programmer can take advantage of the relative qualities of RAM and register memory. A data item that will be accessed repeatedly in a short time frame is best placed in a register. The register accesses will be faster, but a data item that is only accessed occasionally should be placed in main memory to preserve the relatively scarce register resource. Occasionally, items can be made to migrate. For example, suppose several consecutive operations manipulate a running total, which then is not accessed for an extended period of time. The total can be copied from main memory to a register, used in several calculations, and then copied back to main memory (if it has changed value).

Modern Variations on Primary Memory

All common memory variations correspond logically to the model described above. However, there exist many variations in physical implementation. For example, *magnetic cores,* the original form of RAM (see "Historical notes" at the end of this chapter), became obsolete in the 1970s, replaced by electronically maintained solid-state or semiconductor memory. Such memory comes in various forms, including variations in technology used to create the digital logic, physical size of the circuitry, and even logical construction of a single bit. But the general logic principles have not changed.

One immediate distinction between modern semiconductor memory and magnetic core is that magnets do not require any electrical power to maintain their contents (only to change the content). A flip-flop requires power to maintain its content. Any interruption in power will cause a loss of memory content. All modern memory, register or RAM, is *volatile* in that an interruption in power (intentional or otherwise) will destroy the contents of memory. Memory composed of flip-flops is called *static RAM* because once a value is placed in memory, the logic (flip-flop) maintains that value until either a new value is placed there or the power is interrupted. It is not so static that it will survive power interruptions.

DRAM. A popular variation on static RAM is *dynamic RAM* memory (DRAM or D-RAM). Dynamic RAM is not more capable of being changed than is static RAM. The two are logically equivalent: addressing, storage, and retrieval are accomplished in essentially the same manner, and each bit is represented by a simple logical circuit. DRAM, however, holds its value in a small capacitor (a capacitor is an electrical device capable of storing energy, in the form of an electrical charge, for a period of time), rather than in a flip-flop. If the capacitor holds a charge, a 1 value is present; no charge indicates a 0. However, capacitors cannot hold their charge (and hence the value) without loss indefinitely. Therefore, DRAM memory contains additional circuitry to refresh the charge (value) periodically. Although there is a cost for this additional refresh capability, the total circuitry for a single bit is much simpler than a flip-flop, hence the cost per bit is much lower for DRAM. The cost of the additional refresh circuitry is essentially the same no matter how much memory is refreshed. Therefore, DRAM is particularly economical in machines with large memory capacities. Finally, since speed costs money, it should be no surprise that DRAM is slower than static RAM.

SEMICONDUCTOR TERMS. Most memory is constructed of semiconductors. The number of buzzwords describing specific semiconductor technologies has exploded in recent years. Although the terms apply to semiconductor technology in general, the computer user probably encounters them most in discussions of memory. Each technology has its own advantages and disadvantages. *Transistor-transistor logic* (*TTL*) is the oldest and most standard of the semiconductor technologies. *Emitter-coupled logic* (*ECL*) provides very high speed. *Metal-oxide semiconductors* (*MOS*) can be very compact, and *complementary metal-oxide semiconductors* (*CMOS*) have lower power requirements. The density of logic components has steadily increased over the years. Each significant improvement seems to bring a new acronym. Today, *LSI* (large scale integration) has largely given way to *VLSI* (very large scale integration).

READ-ONLY MEMORY. A minor variation on memory is *read-only memory* (or *ROM*). Read-only memory is logically identical to regular RAM memory with two exceptions:

- data in ROM cannot be changed, and
- data is not lost when power is interrupted.

Such memory is useful for code that will be needed every time a machine is used. To picture the logic of such memory, it is helpful to envision one of the earliest versions of this form of memory. Read-only memory was originally created as a coordinate grid on a plastic (non-conducting) card. Data was encoded as patches of metallic (conducting) surface on the non-conducting grid. Conducting locations represented 1s and nonconducting, 0s. The most primitive construction method started with a grid containing all 1s. The "programmer" scraped the undesired bits (conducting patches) off of a card using a knife, leaving patches only where 1-bits were desired. The read-only memory could then be read by checking to see if a given bit location would conduct a signal. Clearly, no instruction from the CPU could change the configuration of conducting and nonconducting patches. Today, ROM, like RAM, is created using semiconductor technology. The full circuitry for the read-only memory is permanently encoded on a chip during manufacture.

Many CPUs do not necessarily detect the difference between ROM and conventional RAM. This means that an attempt to write into a ROM location would not generate an error condition: nothing would happen. Recall that no signal is returned to the CPU from memory during a memory write operation. A subsequent attempt to read the same location will result in the original data being read. This situation can be very confusing to the programmer and suggests that absolute addressing may be a dangerous technique.

Instructions contained in read-only memory are sometimes referred to as *firmware*—neither hardware nor software. (But beware of an alternate—and more fundamental—definition of the term firmware described in Chapter 15.) Such memory usually contains essential information, such as start-up data (see bootstrapping in Chapter 11), or built-in functions for use by all applications. Such read-only code provides both advantages and disadvantages. Large segments of code can be permanently embedded in the machine. This saves considerable time at start-up, as well as reducing the size of the externally stored start-up program. Additionally, on some machines, reads from read-only memory may be slightly faster than from conventional memory. On the other hand, bugs in such code are considerably harder to fix since the entire chip containing the code must be replaced and a new version manufactured. ROM updates require an actual physical modification to the machine. Contrast this with the simple delivery of a new disk required for a software update. Thus, code in read-only memory can be thought of as cast in stone—or at least in silicon. Manufacturers do not normally place code into read-only memory until they are very confident that no bugs remain.

Several further variations on read-only memory exist—many of them with rather paradoxical names. All of these variations share the basic ROM properties: the programmer cannot normally alter the content and data is not lost when power is removed.

Programmable read-only memory (PROM). Perhaps a better way to think of PROM is "write once" memory. Data, once stored in PROM, behaves as ROM-based data. Normally, the programming of PROM requires special hardware. The data in the PROM is said to be *burned* into the chip. Using standard mass-produced PROMs, a system manufacturer may build the necessary firmware to control a system. If an error is later discovered, the code can be rewritten and burned into new PROM chips, which can then replace the original. This is clearly less expensive than designing an entire new ROM chip.

Erasable programmable read-only memory (EPROM). Generally EPROM is erasable through noncomputational techniques such as irradiating it with infrared light. EPROM can be used for special-purpose hardware. The machine can be configured and will maintain that configuration until reprogrammed. It is read-only in the sense that the data is not lost when power is removed and that it requires special operations to perform a write. EPROMs have occasionally been referred to as "write-seldom" memory.

▷ *Are there uses for EPROM other than video games?*

Electrically erasable programmable read-only memory (EEPROM). EEPROM can can be erased by sending a signal to the ROM, rather than using ultraviolet light. It sounds like regular RAM memory, but the write speed is much slower. A synonym is *EAROM* (*electrically alterable read-only memory*).

THE MEMORY HIERARCHY

Throughout this book, registers and main memory have been treated as two distinct entities. In reality, they can be thought of as variations of a single concept. One is larger; the other is faster and more tightly integrated into the processing of the CPU. A better model of the relationships between registers and RAM can be obtained by placing them in a larger hierarchy consisting of at least four possible levels and five dimensions.

Figure 10-7 summarizes speed, flexibility, size, volatility, and cost relationships between RAM, registers, and other forms of memory. For example, registers

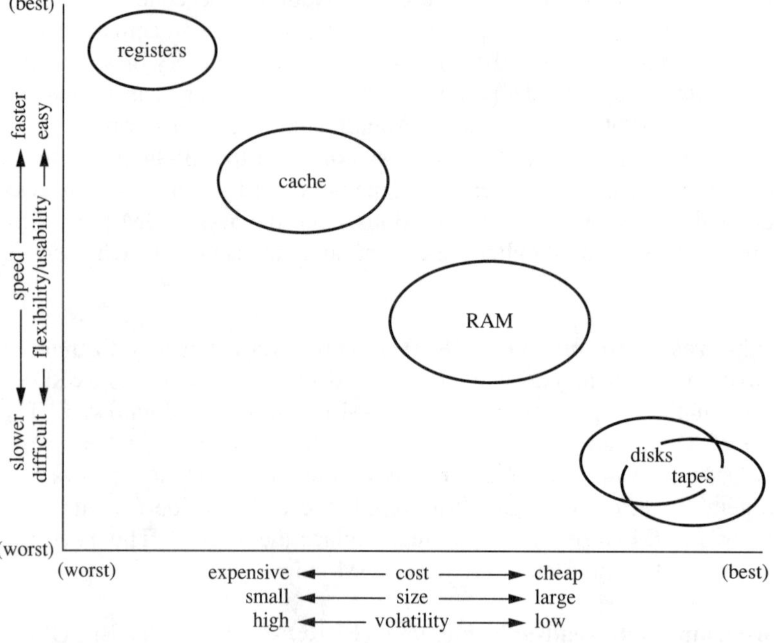

FIGURE 10-7
The memory hierarchy.

are faster than RAM and more directly usable by the CPU, as reflected in GAL by the fact that an instruction can have two register operands but no more than one RAM operand. In addition, access of RAM operands requires the intermediate registers MAR and MBR. However, there is literally a price to pay for those advantages: registers are more expensive to manufacture. In addition, the limited number of registers makes it more difficult to leave values in registers for extended periods of time without saving the values in main memory. The same relationships extend to less familiar forms such as secondary memory and cache memory. The characteristics of the additional forms of the hierarchy provide a continuum along each of the dimensions. In general, the faster the form of memory, the more it costs per storage location. Economics dictates that fewer cells of the more expensive forms can be provided. Neither register nor RAM storage can maintain values after the power is cut off. Secondary or external memory, while much slower than either register or RAM memory, has the added advantage of being nonvolatile. Values can be left in secondary storage devices for indefinite periods of time. An integrated system must take advantage of the tradeoffs offered by this continuum.

In terms of time, memory reads and writes are among the most expensive operations for any computer. The sheer volume of memory locations dictates that economical (and therefore slower) technologies are used. On the other hand, memory reads are probably the most common internal operation in any computer. Every instruction to be performed must be read from memory. Additionally, many instructions—perhaps the majority—require that at least one operand be read from, and/or written to, memory. This requires a careful balance between the dollar cost of memory and the time cost of accessing that memory. One result of these tradeoffs is the existence of additional levels in the memory hierarchy. One is already familiar to you: external, or *secondary memory,* such as a disk or a tape. Figure 10-7 shows that external memory is larger and slower than main memory (but fortunately much cheaper). Secondary storage is useful therefore in situations requiring very large quantities of memory. It is also nonvolatile. A fourth level of memory, called a *cache* (pronounced "cash"), fits between registers and RAM memory in the hierarchy. Cache memories are usually transparent to the user, even in assembly or machine language. (In fact the name cache comes from the French *cacher,* "to hide.") They are useful for speeding up processes that require frequent access to a relatively fixed subset of memory.

The memory hierarchy has implications for both the design of computers and the design of programs. Memory dollar cost is a limiting factor in the design of a machine, but access time is a limiting factor in making efficient use of a machine. Figure 10-8 illustrates the hierarchy more concretely. For each of levels of the hierarchy, the chart shows the speed or access time measured in seconds; the quantity or size of the total memory measured in bytes; and the cost per byte of storage. Cost and access speed are very clearly related. Cost and size of memory are inversely related. The cheaper a mechanism is, the larger the unit that can be incorporated. The price, speed, and volume characteristics of the hierarchy are defined by the technology. The final characteristic must be up to the programmer of the system. The fastest (but most expensive) memory should

memory type	speed (secs)	quantity (bytes)	cost $/byte
registers	10^{-8}	10^{1}	
cache	$2 * 10^{-8}$	10^{3}–10^{5}	10^{-3}
primary	10^{-7}	10^{6}–10^{7}	10^{-4}
secondary		10^{7}–10^{9}	10^{-5}
seek	10^{-1}–10^{-2}		
transfer	10^{-4}–10^{-5}		

FIGURE 10-8

be used most frequently. Seldom-used data should be placed on the slower, but cheaper, devices.

CACHE MEMORY

Machines have substantial amounts of relatively slow RAM memory and very little relatively fast register memory. Any interesting program is certain to be too large to fit entirely in registers and must reside in the slower RAM memory. This is an unfortunate restriction since every instruction requires at least one fetch from RAM. If the program could somehow be stored in registers, a very significant speed-up would result. While that is clearly impossible, there is a compromise solution. *Cache memory* is an intermediate form, faster and more expensive than RAM, but slower and less expensive than registers.

The general principle is that frequently accessed memory items should be kept in the faster cache. Less-frequently used items should be kept in main memory. Cache memory is significantly smaller than main memory, so selection of what data should be stored in cache is a nontrivial problem. In general, instructions are probably the most frequently accessed items, so they are prime candidates for cache. In fact, some caches are explicitly called *instruction caches*. Unfortunately, the instructions by themselves are too large to fit in cache. The primary tool for addressing the problem is known as the *principle of locality.* Simply stated, this principle says that memory accesses will tend to cluster together, or that once a given location has been accessed, future accesses to nearby locations (or the same location) are very likely. To see why the principle works, observe that the most frequently accessed memory items are the instructions. Instructions tend to be executed in syntactically sequential order. When execution is not in syntactic order, the jump is most often to a relatively nearby location (conditionals and loops). Loops can be defined as repetition of the same code. A subroutine call may jump to a very distant instruction, but once in the subroutine the principle applies to the statements of that subroutine. Even operand references tend to obey this principle. When one cell of an array is accessed, very often many of them will be accessed. All the local variables of a single procedure are probably stored as a group.

In theory, the programmer could ensure that the faster memory contained the more frequently accessed data items. In practice, it is far better to allow the machine to take care of the allocation. When an instruction is fetched in a cache machine, it is not loaded directly into the instruction register but is copied into the cache, and from there to the instruction register. More importantly, the entire block of code containing the instruction is loaded into cache—not just the one instruction. When the next instruction is needed, it is already in the cache and can therefore be accessed very quickly. Assuming that several instructions are executed from the same block, the savings on each instruction will more than offset the time required to load the additional locations into cache. In the case of a tight loop, for example, very substantial quantities of time can be saved, because every instruction is executed many times with no additional cache loads.

Cache memory does increase the complexity of a memory access, but not as much as one might expect. The simplest form of cache memory requires that cache contain blocks of storage. Suppose, for example, that a machine has a single 1K block of cache and 64K of main memory. A 16-bit address can be broken into two fields:

tag or block number (high-order six bits)
byte position within the block (low-order 10 bits)

The cache has associated with it the tag for the block that it represents, as shown in Figure 10-9a. When any memory access is requested, the high-order bits are compared against the tag. The 10 low-order bits of the address specify a single byte position within cache. If the tag for the block is the same as the six high-order bits of the address, the cell is the correct one and the value at the displacement address is retrieved. If the tag does not match, a new block corresponding to the tag is copied from main memory to cache. The desired cell is then fetched. In cases where the tags do not match, access will be considerably slower than simple memory access. But the principle of locality implies that these cases will be the exception. The increased speed of the majority of accesses more than offsets the overhead.

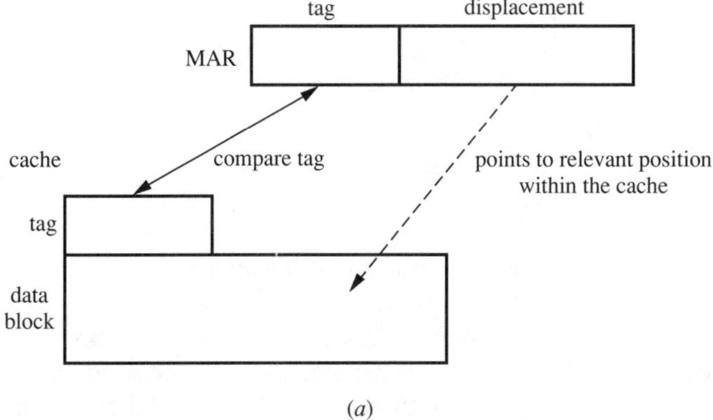

FIGURE 10-9
Cache memory access. (*a*) single cache.

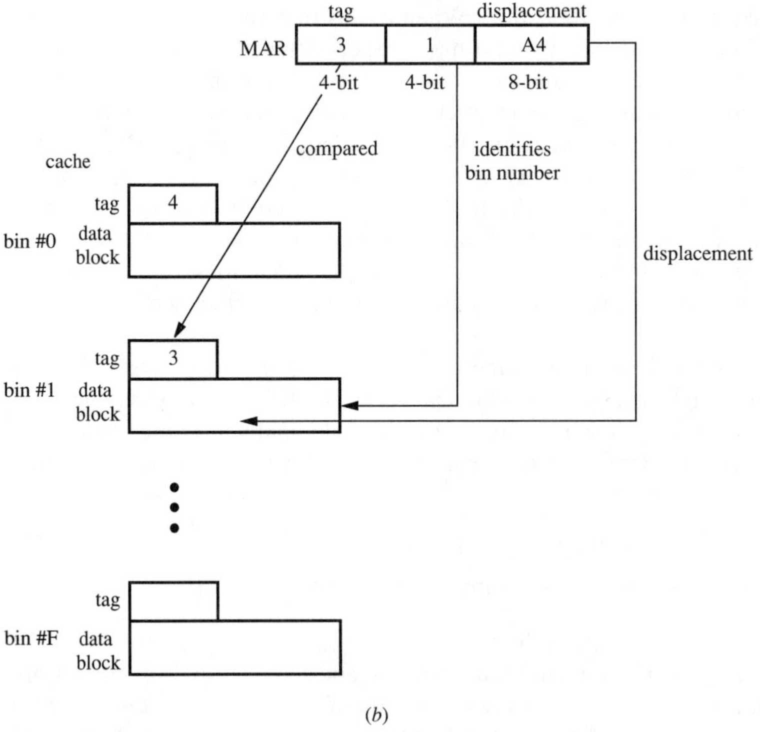

FIGURE 10-9 (cont.)
Cache memory accesss. (*b*) multiple segment cache.

If there are multiple blocks of cache, the algorithm can be improved by assuming that each block of cache can match only certain blocks of RAM. Consider a 64K machine with 16 blocks of cache, each 256 bytes long. Again, a full address is 16 bits long. Assume the 256 possible blocks of RAM are numbered according to their high-order bits:

block	**addresses**
00:	0000–00FF
01:	0100–01FF
. . .	
FF:	FF00–FFFF

Addresses will have an eight-bit tag and an eight-bit displacement, as shown in Figure 10-9b. Restrict each block of cache, N, so that it can hold only those blocks of RAM with the value N in bits 11–8 of their address, that is, those blocks with N as the second digit of the block identifier. When memory is accessed, only the leading four bits need to be compared with the tag. The second four bits are necessarily identical. Notice that by restricting the second four bits rather than the first, adjacent logical blocks can be in cache at the same time—a reasonable goal, given the principle of locality. A second approach to cache access, called *associative mapping,* searches cache for a tag corresponding to the address.

SECONDARY STORAGE

Secondary storage or external memory may sound at first like a misnomer, since there are at least two or three faster forms of memory in every machine. Secondary memory is clearly slower than either registers or main memory, so why not tertiary memory—or even n-ary memory for some larger n? In practice, registers are not generally thought of as storage devices—more like working locations. Main memory is the primary storage location of data during execution of a program. Cache memory is a relatively recent invention (also one that is frequently invisible to the programmer in most models of computation). External memory is secondary to RAM as an important visible depository of data. It sits at one end of the memory hierarchy: usually at least a few orders of magnitude larger than main memory, several orders of magnitude slower, and an order or two less expensive. The first and last of these properties provide its principal advantage; the middle property, its principal disadvantage.

Properties and Uses of Secondary Storage

Secondary memory has two features that cannot be provided by RAM memory as discussed up to this point. First, while RAM memory may not be large enough to hold all of the data that a program needs, secondary storage can be arbitrarily large. One million bytes of RAM sounds like a considerable quantity. But consider a matrix designed to hold relationships between any two of 500 data items. A 500 by 500 matrix contains 250,000 cells. If each cell is a four-byte number, the matrix requires all million bytes of memory (without leaving any room for code). A program needing this data could keep all, or part of, the matrix in secondary memory. It will be slower, but at least the task can be accomplished. More programs today need secondary storage for this reason than most student programmers suspect. Programs with a million lines of code (and therefore several million bytes of memory) are not uncommon. Several large databases now have over 10^8 records.

The second major advantage of secondary storage is its nonvolatility. Data in secondary memory is not lost when power is interrupted. If data will be needed at a later time, it must be stored in secondary memory. For example, an instructor's grade sheet must be updated after every assignment. A program that does not save these grades from week to week is useless. Or consider the program development process as discussed in Chapter 7. A program must reside in main memory during execution. However, if the program is to be run again at a later time, it must be saved. A programmer writes a program using an editor or word processor. The editor is a program that considers the source program to be data, which should be saved—at least until it is compiled. Thus, an editor can create externally stored data. A compiler can read that data and create object code, which it, too, stores externally. A loader can read that object code and place it in main memory. In fact, the data need not even be kept on the same computer.

A program can be written on one machine and stored on an external disk, which can be removed, attached to another computer, and read. Thus, a companion of nonvolatility is transferability. Once the data is stored externally, it can be made accessible to other machines. Thus, secondary storage can be used to store data to be used later by the same or a different program; the same or a different machine. Without secondary storage, it would be impossible to distribute software, save data for extended periods of time, or make backup copies.

Logical Organization of Secondary Memory

Like RAM memory, secondary storage consists of a large number of addressable byte-sized locations. Under direction of the processor, data can be stored into, and read from, any location. As with RAM memory, data can be read from a device by providing the address of the needed information. Data can be written to a device by sending both the value and the location at which it should be stored. The syntax for access is different, and the "secondariness" of the media is apparent because assembly languages do not provide any mechanism for manipulating secondary memory directly.

Secondary storage is not logically necessary for execution of a computer program, but it is necessary as a practical consideration. The storage devices for secondary memory are external to the computer itself logically if not physically. Even on computers with so-called internal disks, the term "internal" simply means the two objects, computer and disk, were placed into one cabinet. Inside, the disk drive is in fact physically distinct from the computer itself.

External memory cannot be accessed with a single computer operation. It is, therefore, not only too slow for general memory use but is unacceptable for program storage during execution. Execution of every statement requires at least one, and sometimes more, memory access. Any form of memory that cannot be accessed within a single cycle is clearly useless for currently executing instructions. The current chapter, therefore, addresses the logical concepts needed to comprehend secondary media as memory. Chapter 12 discusses the external devices and their access mechanisms in more detail.

Data can be freely copied from primary to secondary memory and back, but only by explicit instruction. From the perspective of a program, the data on a secondary storage device can be copied to or from main memory where it can be manipulated. Every hll contains explicit commands for this purpose:

```
assign    external_location⇒internal_location
```

or

```
assign    internal_location⇒external_location
```

Generally the mechanisms for accessing secondary memory are considered to be input/output operations. Certainly, the usual syntax for requesting access more closely resembles an I/O command than it does an assignment command. In most higher-level languages, the access routines reflect that nature:

```
input(external_location⇒internal_location)
```

or

```
output(external_location⇐internal_location)
```

Some assembly languages, including GAL, provide analogous procedures. No other instruction in the language may have operands located in external memory. Generally, the internal location must be a RAM location, although some machines have special registers for this purpose. Since secondary memory can only be accessed via the `input` and `output` commands, any manipulation of externally stored data must involve extra steps. For example, consider the command

```
add     reg2⇒item
```

If `item` is externally stored, it must be copied into main memory, the addition performed, and finally copied back to secondary storage:

```
*copy    external_item⇒internal_temp    ;input
*add     reg2⇒internal_temp
*copy    internal_temp⇒external_item    ;output
```

Access Methods

The two general classes of secondary storage differ in their accessibility. One class, called *random access* storage (or random access devices), is logically equivalent to RAM memory. Any location can be accessed for either reading or writing at any time (although by only the designated forms of the `copy` command). As long as the program knows the relative location of a data item within a file, it can access the item as above. The most common form of random access device is called a disk. The second form of secondary memory is not random. With *sequential access* devices, only one data cell can be accessed at a given time: the one that sequentially follows the previous access. Often storage and retrieval cannot be intermixed.

The choice of access method will depend, in part, on the programmer's original need for secondary storage. If the data will be needed in an order other than sequential, random access is clearly needed. If a program needs more temporary storage than is available in RAM, or if frequent access to that data will be necessary, random access storage again will be most appropriate. If the purpose is to maintain a backup or to transport data between machines, sequential access is likely to be more appropriate.

Random Access Devices

Today, the most common form of secondary storage is the disk. Disk capacity for a single device may vary from about 100,000 bytes to over 1 billion bytes (one gigabyte). Access speed is in the range of 10^{-2} seconds for a "floppy disk" on a home computer and 10^{-3} seconds for a large diskpack on a mainframe computer. Independent of capacity, speed, or physical construction, all disks work in logically the same manner. A disk may be either removable or nonremovable. If it is removable, data may be physically transferred to another machine. Also, if the disk itself is removable, the total volume of data available is limited by the number of available disks, not by the number of devices for reading disks. On the other hand, removable disks may create an added delay if the disk must be *mounted* prior to access.

Physically, a disk can be visualized as a cross between a phonograph record and an audio tape. Like the record, a disk contains information on its entire surface—which is two-dimensional, enabling the random access. Data is arranged in concentric circles or *tracks*. A device for reading and writing, called a *read/write head* (or simply a *head*), can be positioned on any track. As the disk rotates, each position on the track, or *track address,* passes under the head. By the combination of the head moving and the disk rotating, every address on the disk can be accessed. When the head is at a given location, data can be written and later retrieved from the same location. Figure 10-10 shows the essential details. As with primary memory, the processor requests the contents of a cell by sending the needed address and a read request to the disk drive.

The external address will necessarily be more complex than a RAM address. The address of a storage location on a disk is measured in terms of its track position rather than a simple absolute address. For a specific file, the disk address is calculated when the file is *opened*. The disk-driver software makes all necessary translations using a *directory,* so the programmer generally does not need to worry about the translation. In addition, secondary memory is logically divided into *files*. (The term file is directly related to the same term as used in the language Pascal.) A file is a collection of data items of the same type (for now, assume the type is character). Each file contains a collection of data that is somehow related. When a program needs to access data on the disk, it must provide an address composed of two parts:

- the file identification
- the location within the file

The typical forms are

```
input(file_name & position⇒internal_location)
```

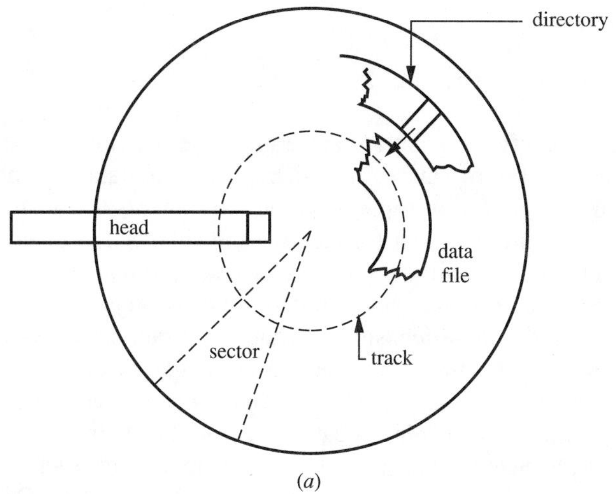

(*a*)

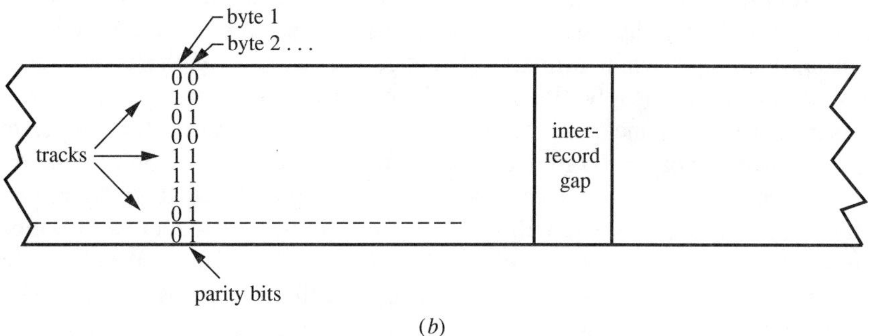

(*b*)

FIGURE 10-10
Secondary storage media: (*a*) disk; (*b*) tape.

and

```
output(file_name & position⇐internal_location)
```

With a file of characters, position is roughly the displacement equal to the number of bytes past the beginning of the file, very much like the displacements used to describe arrays in assembly language. External addressing is covered in more detail in the I/O chapter.

Sequential Address Devices

On a sequential access device only one data cell can be accessed at any time: the one sequentially following the most recent access. The data location is, therefore, implicit. The data access statements take the form:

```
copy    file_name⇒internal location
```

or

```
input(filename⇒internal location)
```

There is no need to specify the position, since only one position can be accessed. Sequential files are useful for tasks in which blocks of data are moved from external to internal storage, for example, printing the contents of a word-processed book chapter (although probably not for creating the chapter). A tape drive is the best-known sequential device, although others such as card readers have also been used. Random access devices may also contain logically sequential files.

A tape is essentially one-dimensional. That is, all data is stored as one long consecutive stream of bytes. In order to read a particular byte, the tape must be read from the beginning, passing all previous bytes under the read head. There is no nice way to jump to a specific location as you can with a disk. Unlike a disk, the tape must physically start and stop its movement with each access. This means that the time required to access a single location is high. On the other hand, it is simpler: there is no need for the processor to send an address since the address is always known by assumption. Like disks, tapes are much too slow for use as primary storage. Their primary advantage is that they can store very large volumes of data very cheaply. Tapes are always physically removable, and the media itself is relatively inexpensive. They are now used primarily for long-term backup and for transporting large quantities of data from one location to another.

If a file on a tape is `open`ed, the read head will be positioned at the beginning of the file. Each subsequent read will advance the head past the data read. (Notice that we say "advance the head" even though it is the tape, not the head, that moves). In addition, it may be necessary to request that the operator physically mount a tape on the drive. Although it is relatively simple to keep multiple files on a single disk drive open (accessing the second file requires only that the read head be moved), accessing two files on a single tape would be almost impossible, since the head can be at only one location.

Data Migration

The integration of secondary storage into the memory hierarchy is an important task needed for good performance. A user can use the disk as an extension of RAM. For example, if a program uses a very large array, it can keep the array on a disk. Then it can copy one row at a time into RAM memory, manipulate the data in the row, and write it back. Note that this does restrict the available program logic. All of the manipulations for one row should be made while that row is in RAM. Chapter 11 describes some methods for achieving automatic *migration* between primary and secondary memory.

Migration to secondary is part of a more general data migration between the levels of the memory hierarchy, as exemplified by RAM to cache migration. Most programmers discover a frequent need to exchange data between main memory and registers. There simply is not enough register memory to hold all of the data needed at a given time. The programmer must explicitly save the register into main memory and load other data from main memory to the registers. Cache memory depends on automatic migration. Similar operations and relations exists between the other levels. A programmer might read large segments of data from secondary storage, manipulate the data using primary memory, and finally store the results again into secondary storage so that new data can be manipulated. A computing system can also move data gracefully from one level of storage to another invisibly to the human user. For example, if data could be moved transparently from secondary to primary storage before it was needed, the apparent size of (fast) primary memory would be increased.

The seemingly oxymoronic term *disk-cache* refers to one form of data migration. This term attempts to capture some of the best properties of each form of the two forms of memory. A disk-cache is a RAM segment that holds frequently accessed items from secondary storage. When an item is read from secondary memory, an entire block is copied to the disk-cache. Future requests for data from the disk may be found in the cache, speeding up disk access in a manner analogous to the way that regular cache speeds up RAM access. A disk-cache is distinct from *RAM-disk,* in which a specific disk file (or files) is copied to RAM. The program then treats the RAM file as if it were a secondary storage. A RAM-disk speeds access to the particular file but does not automatically update the external copy. Thus, RAM-disks are often used for files that must be accessed frequently, but seldom changed.

ERROR CONDITIONS

Errors within a digital circuit are extremely rare and can for all practical purposes be treated as nonexistent. However, when data is stored for extended time or transmitted over relatively long distances, errors, while still the exception, do occur. Flaws in the magnetic surface of secondary memory—introduced in the manufacturing process or by damage due to mistreatment—can cause data to be lost. Exposure to a magnetic or electric field can alter data stored in either primary or secondary media. Transmission of data introduces the possibility of flawed communications media. Such problems include "noise" on a phone line, or loose connections to the wire between an external device and a computer. The number of bytes of memory implies that even a very low probability event will occur occasionally. The possibility of such errors dictates that—at the minimum—some mechanism exist for detecting the error. Better yet, there could be a method for not only detecting the problem but also correcting it.

Parity

Detection of small errors turns out to be relatively easy. The internal representation of every data item is composed of bits, and each bit can have only two distinct values. If a bit is corrupted, there is only one incorrect value that it can become: a 1 becomes a 0 and vice versa. All that is needed to detect an error is a count of the number of 1 bits. If there is an error, the number of 1-bits will change.

data bits	parity bit
0 0 0 0 0 0 0 0	0
0 0 0 0 0 0 0 1	1
1 1 1 1 1 1 1 1	0
1 1 1 1 0 0 0 1	1

FIGURE 10-11
Examples of even parity.

An extra bit, called a *parity* bit, is used to detect any such change. The parity bit is set so that the total number of 1 bits will be even (called *even parity;* an *odd parity* bit would force the number to be odd). Whenever data is stored in the cell, the number of 1's is counted. If the number is even, the parity bit is set to 0, maintaining the even number. If there is an odd number of 1 bits, the parity bit is set to 1, making the total number of 1's even.

When data is read from the cell, the parity can be checked. If a single bit had been corrupted, the number of 1's would have changed either up one (a 0 became a 1) or down one (a 1 became a 0). In either case, the parity would be incorrect and an error message could be generated. There are two small problems with parity. First, if two bits were corrupted, the parity would not be impacted: two additional or two fewer 1's would still result in an even number of 1's. Likewise, if a 1 became a 0 and a 0 became a 1, the parity would not change. The parity bit would still indicate that the value was correct. Second, although parity can detect an error, it tells the system or the user only that there was an error in a particular cell. It provides no information that would enable processing to continue. The system must interrupt execution with a data error.

Self-Correcting Codes

What is needed is a data representation that not only detects errors but provides sufficient information to correct the problem. The simplest way to create such self-correcting code is with a double parity construction. For example, suppose that in addition to the byte-oriented parity bit just described, there was also a bit-position parity bit, as illustrated in Figure 10-12. The bit-position parity bit functions in a manner exactly the same as the byte parity bit, but measures the parity of a given bit-position for each of several cells. In Figure 10-12, the bit measures the parity for eight cells. Thus, if there is an error in bit 3 of cell 4, two different parity bits will detect an error: one detects the cell, and the other, the bit position within the cell. Together, they uniquely identify the exact bit in error. Since there are only two possible values for any given bit, the correct value for the erroneous bit must be the opposite value from what it currently has. Therefore, the bit can simply be inverted. It is interesting to note that the double parity concept will work even if the error is in a parity bit.

The simple parity bit added one bit per cell. Assuming the usual cell size of one byte, simple parity bits add $n/8$ bits, or 12.5 percent, to n bytes of storage. A machine using exclusively ASCII characters could, presumably, use the eighth

data bits	byte-position parity check
0 1 0 1 0 1 0 1	0
1 0 1 0 1 0 1 0	0
1 1 1 1 1 1 1 1	0
0 0 0 0 0 0 0 0	0
1 1 1 1 0 0 0 0	0
0 0 0 0 1 1 1 1	0
1 1 1 1 1 1 1 0	1
0 0 0 0 0 0 1 0	1
bit-position parity checks	
0 0 0 0 0 0 1 1	0

FIGURE 10-12
A simple error-correcting code.

bit as a parity bit, but the normal practice is to add a ninth bit to every byte. With the self-correcting parity scheme, assuming the horizontal and vertical parity bits check the same number of data bits, $2N + 1$ parity bits are needed for an $N \times N$ cell. The number of bits needed increases as the square root of the cell size. For one-byte cells, 17 parity bits are needed for eight data bytes. An overhead of 25 percent is a small price to pay for error correction.

Hamming Codes

The double parity bit would work fine for, say, reading a sequential block of data from secondary storage. Unfortunately, it is not very well-suited for random access memory. Every read access of the memory would require that two data cells be examined: the target cell and the parity cell. In most cases, the two cells would not even be adjacent. Memory writes would be even worse, requiring that the parity cell be rewritten with every memory write. That would require that all of the cells in the parity group be read to calculate the new values.

A better, but slightly more sophisticated, error-detection code is a *Hamming code* (named for their inventor, Richard Hamming). The essential concept of a Hamming code is that sufficient control bits are stored with each cell to uniquely pinpoint any errors in the cell. This is accomplished by using several parity bits, each checking several of the bits. Each bit is checked by a unique combination of parity bits. To investigate how this might work, consider a simple cell with three parity bits corresponding to the data bits as follows:

parity bit	checks
p_0	checks bits $0,1,3,4,6,p_0$
p_1	checks bits $0,2,3,5,6,p_1$
p_2	checks bits $1,2,3,7,p_2$
p_3	checks bits $4,5,6,7,p_3$

An error in any given bit will generate parity conflicts as follows:

error in bit	generates conflicts in
0	p_0, p_1
1	p_0, p_2
2	p_1, p_2
3	p_0, p_1, p_2
4	p_0, p_3
5	p_1, p_3
6	p_0, p_1, p_3
7	p_2, p_3
p_i	p_i, for $i = 0 - 3$

Note that it is necessary to check the parity bits. An error in any data bit causes two errors. An error in a parity bit shows up uniquely in that bit. Since any valid combination of parity conflicts uniquely identifies the bit in error, that bit can be corrected by inverting it. Any other combination of parity-bit conflicts indicates that there was more than one error. Hamming showed that four parity bits is the minimum number that can detect and correct single errors in an eight-bit data code. In general, he showed that the number required is

```
parity bits = 1+ log(data bits)
```

Thus, the relative overhead for such self-correcting codes is reduced as the size of memory cells increases. A 32-bit cell would need $1 + \log(32) = 6$ parity bits. Of course the chance of an error in a 32-bit word is larger than in an eight-bit word.

Hamming codes of the type described work for single errors and are therefore called *single-error correcting* (SEC) code. Similar codes exist that can correct single errors but detect double errors (SEC-DED) or even detect and correct larger numbers of errors. These improvements require correspondingly more parity bits. The minimum number of single-bit corrections required to change one code into another, in particular to change an incorrect code into a correct code, is called the *Hamming distance* between the two codes.

CORE: AN HISTORICAL NOTE

Although magnetic *cores* became obsolete in the 1970s, the term *core* is still used occasionally to refer (incorrectly) to memory, sometimes to mean a single bit of memory but more often as a generic term referring to the entire main memory of a computer. To understand the term and its relation to modern forms of RAM memory, it is interesting to review the early technology of computer memory.

Classically, a magnet was used for each bit. Magnets can be polarized in either direction by exposing them to an electric field. Thus, one byte could be composed of a row of eight small magnets, each wrapped in a wire. Note that magnetization and polarization are "all-or-nothing" phenomena. If the current provided is less than some threshold, no polarization occurs. Similarly, providing extra current will not polarize the magnet further, nor will polarizing a magnet previously polarized in the same direction produce a change.

Even the (logically) small computers of the first generation had thousands of bytes of memory and tens of thousands of bits. Individually wrapping that many magnets would have been bulky, time-consuming, and expensive. Additionally, individual wires from the CPU (or even from a bus) to every bit would also be cumbersome. The solution was ring-shaped magnets called *cores,* illustrated in Figure 10-13a. Rather than wrapping each magnet with a wire, the wire was passed through the center of each magnet. Current in opposite directions generates electric fields in opposite directions. Thus, the magnet could still be polarized in either direction, but the wiring was reduced significantly.

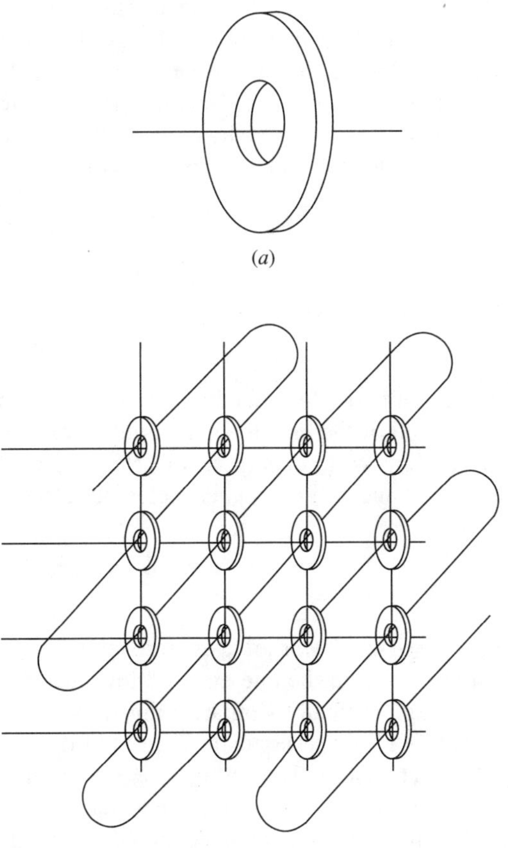

FIGURE 10-13
Core memory.

The advantage is obtained by arranging memory as a matrix. Two wires pass through each core—one vertically and one horizontally—as in Figure 10-13b. A unique pair of wires—one vertical and one horizontal—threads each core. If a small current (slightly less than the threshold) is run through one wire of each orientation, only a single unique core receives a field due to both wires. All other cores receive either no field or an insufficient field and are therefore unaffected. In the figure, a signal through the third vertical wire and second horizontal wire would result in the third bit of the second byte being set.

Reading the value in a bit was a "trick" operation. The inverse of polarizing a magnet by means of a current is creating a current by placing the magnet within a changing magnetic field. This works only if the field moves with respect to the wire. Physically moving either the magnets or wires was clearly an undesirable operation. "Moving" the field by changing the polarization of the core was a better solution—but it unfortunately would destroy the contents of the core. Fortunately, if the field changes, it does induce a current that can be detected. Furthermore, any binary value can only change to one other value. Thus, if there was a change in the magnetization of the core, it could be detected. To read a value from a core, the computer attempted to set that core to 1. If there was a change, the core must have contained a 0; if there was no change, it must have contained a 1. Unfortunately, the content of the locations was destroyed by reading it. The core then contained a 1, no matter what value was previously there. Fortunately, the former value had been read, so the core could be reset by replacing that value back into it. The algorithm is

```
For bits 0 to 7

        write 1 to bit of memory
        set value to not (signal on detection wire)
        write value to bit
```

Notice that the detection wire, shown in Figure 10-13b, runs through all bits. With a separate detection wire for each position, all of the bits of a cell could be read in parallel. Since every read required an implicit write operation, the classical read operation was especially slow. Occasionally, one still encounters references to the reset or restore portion of the read cycle.

SUMMARY

The registers and RAM memory form just two levels of a multilevel memory hierarchy. The levels are characterized by speed on the one end and low cost and low volume at the other end. RAM, although logically similar to registers, has a distinct construction. It is not part of the CPU but responds to requests from the CPU for memory reads and fetches. Data is transferred to and from RAM through the two parts of the memory bus, and the two special-purpose registers: MAR and MBR. Variations on the "standard" semiconductor memory include dynamic memory or DRAM, (which is actually even more common than static RAM) and read-only memory.

Two additional levels in the hierarchy are cache memory and secondary memory. Although it is usually invisible to the programmer, cache fits between registers and RAM in the hierarchy. Migration between RAM and cache is usually automatic. The principle of locality makes such automatic migration possible. Secondary memory is at the slow, but inexpensive, end of the hierarchy. The two principal forms of secondary memory are disks, which are random access, and tapes, which are sequential.

EXERCISES

10.1. Consider the process of creating memory with only one memory bus. What additional features would need to be included in each memory cell in order for it to function? Consider the process of writing one byte of data to a specific cell with an eight-bit address.

10.2. Compare the order in which the open, close, input, and output statements appear in two programs. The first program should update existing data in an external file. The second program should use an external file as temporary storage, saving data in the file until some later point in the program.

10.3. You cannot write to read-only memory. But what happens if a program inadvertently attempts to do so? Answer that question by describing, in detail, the steps of the memory write cycle.

10.4. Construct a simple parity-checker circuit using exclusive-ors.

10.5. Add even parity bits to the following cells:

10110010
11100011
10101010
11111111

10.6. Add self-correcting parity bits to the answers in Exercise 10.5.

10.7. Hamming's algorithm for selecting parity bits for an N-bit cell is:

Find the total bits required: $N + 1\log(N)$.
Number positions from the *left,* starting at 1
Bits with numbers $= 2^i$ for some i are parity bits.
For each data bit
  find the binary representation of the position of the bit
  for each 1 in that representation
    the corresponding parity bit should check this bit.

Use the algorithm to select parity bits for a 16-bit cell.

10.8. Suppose a machine had a clock rate of 16 megahertz and every instruction required eight clock pulses. Suppose memory access time was 100 nanoseconds. How many clock pulses would a machine have to wait when fetching an operand? What would it be for 150 nanosecond memory? Eighty nanosecond memory?

10.9. Suppose that the execution time required for an instruction is 200 nanoseconds plus the operand fetch times, and that memory access requires 100 nanoseconds. How long will each of the following commands require to execute?

```
add             reg2⇒reg3
add             mem_loc⇒reg3
add             reg2⇒mem_loc
copy            reg2⇒loc_1
copy            loc_1⇒reg2
copy            loc_1⇒loc_2
load_address    mem_loc⇒reg3
compare         mem_loc⇒reg3
```

10.10. Suppose the memory access time is 100 nanoseconds. How many cells could be fetched per second? Assuming that a `copy` command from memory to register is completely dominated by the time for fetches, how long would it take to copy one 10,000-word term paper from memory to registers, one byte at a time? (Do not forget the instruction fetch, but ignore any looping costs.) How long would it take from a floppy disk with 10^{-2} second access time?

10.11. Suppose there existed a special PC-increment adder. When passed the contents of the PC, the adder adds four and returns the result. Diagram the relationship between such an adder and the PC. Describe two ways in which this adder could be used to speed up the fetch/execute cycle. What is the limiting factor?

10.12. Discuss the impact of Big-Endien and Little-Endien representations on addressing. In particular, what is the advantage of the Little-Endien format in machines using coincident decoding?

10.13. Recall the rule: 90 percent of of execution time will involve 10 percent of the code. Assume that you have a cache capable of holding 50 percent of your code. If an instruction of a running program is selected at random from the listing, what is the probability that it will be in cache? If execution was stopped after a random number of steps, what would the probability be that the next instruction would be in cache? Repeat the questions assuming that only 5 percent of the program fits in cache.

10.14. Suppose a disk has 100 tracks, each with ten 512-byte sectors. Track 0, sector 0 contains a directory of files. All files are stored as contiguous blocks. Write an algorithm for calculating the disk address of a data item given a file name and offset within the file.

10.15. Describe and explain the apparent discrepancy between the number of of parity bits needed for cell-oriented self-correcting codes and Hamming's demonstration of the minimum number of bits needed for self-correcting codes.

10.16. Suppose a machine had instructions longer than the bus width. Describe the impact on the fetch time of instructions.

10.17. Write programs to compare the relative speeds of the register, RAM, and secondary memories. Copy a value 10,000 times into and out of each form of memory. Time the process for each.

10.18. Look up the bus size and register size for your machine. Predict the difference in time required to move 1-, 2-, and 4-byte chunks of data between RAM and register storage. Attempt to perform the moves 10,000 times. Compare the predicted times to those that you found empirically.

PART V

THE INTEGRATED SYSTEM MODEL

The previous four sections used language models to investigate the underlying hardware. They progressed through various models from the higher-level language model through assembly and machine language down to the digital logic model, providing successively finer levels of detail but always using abstractions of the classical von Neumann machine. Section I briefly considered a system model of computation in which a computer is interpreted as a black box that accepts high-level commands. No model has reexamined the system view since then. This section brings us full circle, reconsidering the global aspects of computing systems in an attempt to understand the integration of the other models. In particular, it examines the mechanisms that insulate the programmer from the lower-level abstractions of the machine, and the mechanisms necessary for effective communication between the computer and the outside world. It provides an overview of potential improvements that are possible through minor variations on the generic models.

All previous models have been processor-based, with an implicit or explicit assumption that all aspects of computation can be understood in terms of a von Neumann-style CPU. The system view includes those parts of a computer that are logically external to the von Neumann model. However, not all aspects of a working computer system can be well understood within this model. This final section attempts to provide an overview, placing the CPU in context: in the context of time, as a machine that begins and ends execution; in the context of users, as a machine that communicates; in the context of processes, as a machine that provides support services.

CHAPTER 11

THE COMPUTER AS A SYSTEM

The previous 10 chapters discussed the machine and its components at levels of abstraction ranging from the higher-level language model down to the digital logic model. Unfortunately, the reader very likely has a nagging feeling that something is still missing. Although each of the models of the hierarchy does describe a coherent entity, in each there seems to be less than meets the eye of the user. Remaining questions include

- How does the entire process begin? All discussion of the fetch/execute cycle, for example, has assumed that the process was already in progress. The instruction to be fetched was always the "next" instruction—never the first instruction. The PC somehow pointed to the first instruction, but no model explained how this was accomplished.
- Assemblers translate assembly language programs into machine language programs. Where did the first assembler come from? What language was it written in? If it was assembled, by what? Similarly, a loader loads the object program, but how was the first loader loaded?
- Each model has assumed the existence of prewritten routines for input and output. What is the nature of those routines? Why was I/O treated special?
- It has become clear (slowly) that the debugger is itself a process. Normally, the user's program does not call the debugger. How does the processor switch control from the user program to the debugger and back?

- Similarly, many machines provide auxiliary services, such as a clock, which is displayed on the screen. Is there a process that runs the clock? If so, how can the processor run two programs simultaneously?
- As described, a computer has only one processor and only one instruction register. But many microcomputers allow more than one task to run at a time, and larger systems allow multiple simultaneous users. How can multiple users share resources such as registers?
- The programmer issues a command to start an editor or an assembler. What object receives that command? Is it a program? If so, how exactly does it invoke the editor program?
- Some machines allow the user a choice of devices for entering commands (e.g., a mouse and a keyboard). Input commands in all previous models wait for input from a single device. How can any program read from either of two devices at a given point?

The answers to these quandaries can be found in the study of a broad spectrum of software, collectively known as the *operating system* or simply the *system*. The system model provides yet another abstraction of the machine. This model, however, is not so much a level of abstraction as a form of glue that holds the other models together. The first section of the book alluded to the system as a "black box model of computing," a level that is above the higher-level language model. But it is more than that. *System* is a generic term that refers to the software (and sometimes aspects of hardware) that enables the programmer to make transitions between levels. The methods of implementation and the collected subsystems that make up a system are as varied as the machines they serve, but every system provides specific tools or services, including:

- A high-level model of the machine, with consistent access to all applications. Modern system designers push this consistency further with uniform models to which each application package should adhere. The Unix system carries the concept further still, providing a single coherent model that is independent of the hardware on which it runs.
- Protection for the user from the low-level details of implementation.
- A mechanism enabling the machine to initialize itself.
- A built-in collection of prewritten tools for standard operations such as I/O.
- "Hooks" to allow the user to access needed programs and tools.

Most computer science curricula include an upper-division course on operating systems that explores the techniques for delivering the essential services. This chapter acts as a preview to advanced operating-systems courses, exploring those aspects of the system that provide insight into the abstract models of previous chapters. The discussion should provide a sense of the "glue" that holds the hardware abstractions together, and de-mystify most aspects of computation that previous models hand-waved away. The chapter does not categorize system responsibilities into the classical subsystem organization. Rather, it organizes system features into three groups, based on user perspective:

- interface and utility services—the visible routines that bridge the gap between models, particularly those that enable human-machine communication.
- process initialization and termination—the means by which an entire process or program begins and terminates.
- the invisible or virtual machine aspects that make a machine appear more powerful than the earlier views would predict.

THE VISIBLE OR INTERFACE SERVICES

At the highest—and most visible—level of abstraction, a computer is a black box. The user gives commands and the black box responds. This model is, in fact, entirely appropriate and sufficient for a wide class of users (e.g., the home computer user, who views the machine as a combination word processor, spreadsheet, and checking account recorder). The system software is the interface that makes such a view possible. It stands between the user and the machine, acting as a translator, mapping commands based on one abstraction into commands of a lower abstraction.

The system-level interface between user and machine is the *command language*. On the majority of machines, the command language appears to be a simple, straightforward language in which the user may request specific general actions of the machine. This top-level interface is simply a translation program that accepts user input in the form of "English-like" (or at least, derived from English) commands and calls the appropriate programs or routines to accomplish the task. If the user commands

```
edit    my_doc
```

the command language processor simply calls the program `edit` and informs that program that it is to work with a file called `my_doc`. On some newer microcomputers (e.g., Macintoshes and IBM PCs running Microsoft Windows), the command language takes the form of an iconic manipulation language in which objects are referenced by pointing at icons, and actions are requested by analogs to the corresponding real-world actions (e.g., moving an icon to the trash can to "throw it away" or delete it). In short, the system command language can be viewed as a function that maps the black box model into a machine language model. Essential visible actions that can be found in every command language interface include

- information routines
- file manipulation routines
- inter-user communication

- security and integrity tools
- general service utilities
- ability to access an arbitrary program

INFORMATION SERVICES. The user may inquire about the status of almost any aspect of the system. Typical systems can answer queries about the names or properties of the user's files, the availability of external devices, the time of day, other users on the system, and the status of programs. It can even provide information about the interface to other system services (e.g., `help`).

FILE SERVICES. The system helps the user maintain data files with tools for copying a file from one location to another or combining two files into a third. The user can rename a file, list a text file on a terminal or printer, append one file to the end of another, or delete a file. File services include commands for inquiring about available files (e.g., `directory`) and creating new files.

GENERAL SERVICE ROUTINES. Most systems provide some number of commonly used utilities—tools that a programmer might need as building blocks for larger programs. For example, `sort` routines are a typical utility for sorting the records in a file. Monitoring programs allow the programmer to check on the status of a specific job, or the relative capacity or saturation of an entire system. Even mundane tools, such as calculator or calendar programs, assist in the overall task of the programmer. Other commonly available routines include time measuring routines for either processor or "wall-clock" time, memory usage routines (e.g., how much memory does my program use?), accounting routines (for measuring costs on systems that recharge users for the computing services), device query routines (Is there a printer available?), etc.

▷ *Why are wall-clock and processor time different?*

INTER-USER AND INTER-MACHINE COMMUNICATION SERVICES. Users need to communicate with one another. The operator must warn users of impending shutdowns; two users working jointly on a single program need to communicate about the status of their individual modules. Students need to turn in homework to faculty in a machine-readable form. Similarly, users of distant machines need to communicate to share programs or data. The alternative requires the user to copy data onto a transportable media (e.g., tape or floppy disk) and physically transport it to the distant site. Inter-user communication includes mail service, which enables one user to send an entire message to a second user; phone service, which enables one user to "talk" to another, effectively locking two terminals together, so that whatever is typed at one also appears at the other; and shared-access facilities, in which one user can access a file owned by another user (with permission). Computers can be *networked* together, enabling communication between users of distant machines. On many systems the mechanism for communication appears identical for local users on the same machine or distant users across the country. Chapter 16 also briefly explores aspects of networks.

▷ *How can two computers be connected? What problems might exist in terms of memory access or processor synchronization?*

SECURITY AND INTEGRITY. *Security* is protection against unwanted access to privately held data or programs. Typically, users are not allowed to log onto a machine unless they identify themselves and prove their identity by means of a *password*. System security prevents unauthorized persons from accessing data for any reason, either malicious or benign. The system allows the user to end a secure session by logging off. The companion problem of security is *integrity:* protection against incorrect mutations of data. The best-known integrity service is *backup:* the creation of a second copy of files in case the original is accidentally lost. The user may explicitly request backup copies of important files. Multi-user machines normally provide automatic backup of all files on a regular basis. *Journalling* is the creation of a log of all steps in a user's work session. If the product of the session is somehow destroyed before completion, the journal file can be used to reconstruct an equivalent object.

INVOKING PROGRAMS. Through the command language, the user can request that a program be executed. Typical commands for starting programs are `run xyz` or `execute xyz`. The execute command is especially significant for two reasons. First, this command enables the user to move from one model of computation to another. When the user requests execution of a program, the user's view of the world changes from the system black box model to a view matching the requested program. The apparent capabilities of the machine change, as do the mechanisms for interacting with the machine. When the user requests a word processor, the expected machine capabilities become text-processing capabilities, such as text search, insertion, or deletion. When the user requests a compiler or an assembler, the view must include the rules of the hll or assembly language. Execute commands include within their domain programs written by the user. The specific program need not be known to the system designers. This means that the user can extend and redefine the capabilities of a computer—or more precisely, the current model of a computer. Any program, once created, is accessible by direct request to the operating system. Many systems allow the users to modify their own black box model further, by providing a mechanism for creating macro programs of command language statements. Command language macro programs are analogous to assembly language macros: collections of instructions invoked by a single identifier. With such macros, the user may build a higher-level interface tailored to individual needs.

PROGRAMMING LANGUAGE INTERFACES. System services also include prewritten procedures for performing standard tasks that are necessary for every program. For example, every program needs input and output routines. It makes little sense for programmers to re-invent the wheel continually. Therefore, most systems provide a package of routines with a standard (and documented) interface. Many of these routines are available to user-written programs at any language level. Such routines not only save the applications programmer work but permit the programmer to maintain a consistent machine model. The hll programmer need not know the internal details of an operation, simply the results. A jump to an input routine, called a system service request, can be thought of as a jump "into" the system—a call to a standard routine for performing I/O operations. Common callable system routines include character or record input and output routines; device status checks; and device control (screen, tapes, disks, modems, etc.). These may include graphical tools, mouse controls, memory control tools, etc. Generally, the system utilities available to users at the command level are also accessible through language interfaces (although usually with less convenience). The system taken as a whole, then, is both higher-level and lower-level than user-written programs. Figure 11-1 helps illustrate this relationship.

EXCEPTIONAL SERVICES. In addition to requested services, the system also provides exceptional services—services initiated by sources other than the user. The system intercedes to protect the user from undesirable conditions. Although each system routine may have built-in diagnostic routines, some errors cannot be anticipated. The system must also field these errors and produce usable messages for the user—even in a user-written routine. The mechanisms for this protection do not seem possible within any of the previous models. For example, an attempt to divide by zero will invariably produce an error message. Assuming the machine is equipped with hardware for division, it seems unlikely that every division operation should invoke a subroutine call. If there was no subroutine in which the error checking could be buried, and the user did not write explicit error-checking code, where did the message come from?

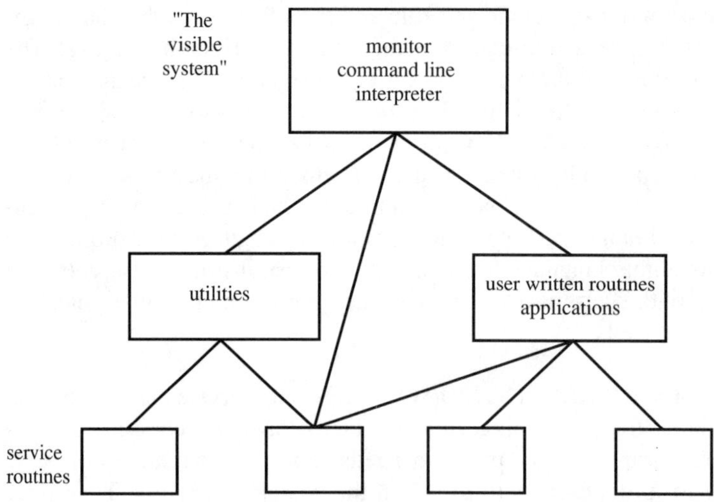

FIGURE 11-1
Relationship of the system to user programs.

BOOTSTRAPS

The first problem that system software must face is getting itself started when the user turns on the hardware. Each of the preceding models has conveniently ignored this problem. The machine language view simply assumed that the PC somehow pointed to the starting location. At the other end of the spectrum, assemblers and loaders started user programs by jumping to them—but nothing explained how the assembler started. Clearly, there must be a special mechanism to initialize a program. Indeed, there must be a special mechanism to start the system. The compiler, the editor, and even the system itself are all programs. How were those programs invoked for the first time? To load the first program, it seems necessary to have a "pre-first" program whose sole job is to load the first program. Since this program must virtually start itself from nothing, it is called a *bootstrap* program (from the expression "Pick yourself up by your bootstraps."[1] Try to imagine that act!).

The bootstrap program itself has two steps: copy the "first program" into memory and execute that program. Construction of a simple pseudocode bootstrap program (leaving the creation of an assembly language boot-program as an exercise) is possible given a few simple assumptions:

- The "first program" will be the system.
- A default external device contains the system program to be loaded. Assume the input device is character-oriented, logically equivalent to a simple keyboard. That is, it transmits single bytes as data. (Input has been treated as a subroutine in all previous discussions. The details of this subroutine are discussed in the next chapter. Assume for now that they are simple and straightforward.)
- Input from the device is not restricted to (7-bit) ASCII codes but can include any eight-bit value.
- There exists a bit-pattern, say FF_{16}, that does not occur within any instruction of the system program. This bit-pattern will serve as a termination signal.

The bootstrap algorithm might look like Figure 11-2.

---

[1]That expression was made famous by the nineteenth-century American novelist Horatio Alger, whose stories of the American Dream focused on rags-to-riches histories. The lead characters—with names suggestive of their own humble beginnings, such as Ragged Dick or Tattered Tom—"picked themselves up by their bootstraps" by raising themselves from virtually nothing or nowhere to positions of prominence. The many variations and contractions of the term *bootstrap* all derive from the same common origin. The verb form of bootstrap evolved as a reference to the actions needed to get the bootstrap loaded; the present shorter verb *to boot* is simply a contraction of bootstrap. *Boot disk, boot block,* and *boot program* are the disk, block, and program containing information needed for the boot process.

```
assign counter⇐100₁₆;              ;point to location
                                   ;where program will
                                   ;be stored
repeat                             ;fetch & store one
   input (RAM(counter)⇐device)     ;byte of program
   assign counter⇐counter +1       ;point to next location
until (next input = FF₁₆)          ;check for end marker
jump    →RAM(100₁₆)                ;to start of program
```

FIGURE 11-2
A simple bootstrap program.

The bootstrap program copies each byte of the system program from the input device to a pre-specified storage area (starting at address 100 in the example). When the bootstrap sees the termination mark, it jumps to location 100—the location where the first instruction of the program was just stored. The newly loaded system will thus start automatically at completion of the bootstrap program. Instead of loading the full system, some bootstraps merely load a more sophisticated boot program, which in turn will load the full system and set any necessary parameters. A more complex boot program may ask for time and date information or user identification. It may check to see what devices are connected to the computer, etc. On a typical microcomputer, the boot program causes the entire system program to be loaded from a disk. The boot program is usually sophisticated enough to find that program on an external disk; it may even be able to scan several disks in search of the system routines.

The bootstrap program itself must somehow be loaded into memory. In modern computers, the bootstrap program resides in read-only memory, placed there by the engineering team that designed the computer. Every machine has a low-level system initialization or power-up procedure—a hard-wired process—in which the various electronic components are initialized when power is first turned on. This circuitry takes care of the digital logic-level details such as initializing registers (recall that a flip-flop is bi-stable; consistency dictates that each bit be initialized one way or the other), including the PC. This is easiest to envision if one assumes that the first desired address will be location 0. That requires only that the PC be cleared at startup. Thus, when the fetch/execute cycle starts, the very first instruction fetched will be the first instruction of the bootstrap program.[2]

[2]An historical note: prior to the invention of ROM, it was necessary to enter the bootstrap program by hand—every time the machine was powered up. A common technique involved the use of an array of toggle switches—switches that had two possible positions, one interpreted as 1 and the other, 0—collectively called the *switch register.* The programmer could enter an address as a binary number into the switch register. By pressing a button, the address represented in the switches could be copied to the PC. The programmer could then enter another value into the switches—this time a binary representation of the first machine instruction of the boot routine. Pushing a deposit button

The essence of the bootstrap program involves one of the most fundamental and powerful ideas in computing: a program can be represented, stored, and manipulated as data. In this case, the bootstrap loads a system program as if it were data, copying it byte-by-byte from a disk. It then immediately jumps to the location at which it stored the program, assuming now that it is code.

PROCESS TERMINATION

Normal Termination

When a program is complete, it must somehow terminate or stop processing. The simplest—and least exciting—method for a program to terminate normally would be for the program to execute a "halt" or "power-off" instruction. The user could then restart or reboot the machine for another program. A slightly more satisfactory approach requires that the program end with a `jump` or `return` statement, abandoning control to the system (`return` would be preferable, since the destination address need not be known by the user-program). Chapter 7 suggested essentially the same approach for execution of a user-program by an assembler or loader but concluded that the approach had an inherent problem: the assembler or loader must remain resident while the user-program was executed, resulting in a significant waste of storage. In the present case, the operating system will presumably remain resident as a service provider. Therefore, no added overhead is incurred.

Abnormal Termination

The more interesting case is *abnormal termination*. Even though good programming practices dictate the use of consistency checks, no user can anticipate every possible error. Since errors can and do occur at execution time, the processor must provide some mechanism for dealing with them. When an error or other *exceptional condition* occurs, execution of the program should not continue. For example, if an instruction attempts to divide by zero, an instruction is fetched but it corresponds to no opcode, or an operand is located at an illegal address, continued execution of the program is pointless. No reasonable result can be expected. Nor could a program reliably return to the system, since the stack contents might not be meaningful (for example, the program may have called a subroutine prior to the error, leaving parameters and an extra return address on the stack). The

---

caused the new contents of the switch register to be copied into memory at the location to which the PC now pointed (i.e., the first location of the boot program). The entire boot program could be entered in this manner—one binary instruction at a time. After all of the instructions had been entered, the PC could be reset to the beginning of the boot program. Pushing a start button caused the fetch/execute cycle to begin. It was not a particularly pleasant task but was necessary to start the process—and certainly an improvement over entering a full program by hand.

simplest solution would be to modify the fetch/execute cycle slightly by adding an error flag:

```
while (no error) do            { was "while true do" }
   fetch instruction
   { body of f/e cycle }
   store results.
```

When an error occurred during execution of an instruction, the error flag would be automatically set and execution would halt before the next cycle. Unfortunately, this solution also seems unsatisfactory—although probably all too familiar. The user must then restart the machine. At least two alternatives seem more satisfactory—or at least more user-friendly:

- return to the system, perhaps with an error message, or
- enter a debugger.

Both of these options require that some mechanism exist to invoke a new procedure whenever an exceptional condition occurs.

Traps and Interrupts

Higher-level language programs do encounter errors, which may generate error messages of one form or another. Most programmers assume that higher-level language compilers provide explicit code for the detection of such problems. At the assembly or machine language level, however, errors generally invoke the debugger. Since the user usually did not write the code that checked for an error and called the debugger, something more complex must be involved. A hardware mechanism for automatically intercepting and handling errors is a *trap*. Traps are a subset of a more general form of break in the fetch/execute cycle called *interrupts*. A trap is an interrupt generated internally from within a program, usually—but not always—as a result of an error.

> ▷ *We will investigate the larger class of interrupts later. What circumstances, other than an error, might interrupt a program?*

If, at any point in the cycle, an error is detected, an interrupt or trap flag is set. The flag is simply a bit that is hard-wired to those units that can detect the error. For example, a divide instruction can include circuitry to check the denominator. If all bits are 0, it sets the trap bit. An `add` instruction can detect an overflow of unsigned numbers checking for a carry out of the highest-order bit. The current instruction is aborted, and the fetch/execute loop (as described to this point) terminates. With a modified version of the fetch/execute cycle, not all execution stops, only execution of the current program. In the case of assembly language programs, the debugger generally begins execution when an error is encountered. Although, it is possible to envision the debugger as an external big brother, most readers have probably figured out that it, too, is a program running on the same computer as the erroneous program. Therefore, control must be transferred from the user program to an error-handling routine such as a debugger. Since that also is a program, the fetch/execute cycle apparently continues—but executing a different program. Transfer to the error-handler is much like a subroutine jump:

- the current PC content is saved, and
- the PC is set to point to the interrupt handling routine.

The cycle then continues. Since the PC now points to the interrupt-handling routine, that routine will be executed. However, there are two important distinctions between a subroutine jump and a trap:

- The user explicitly asks for the former by including a machine instruction to do so, but the latter may occur at some unexpected or exceptional time, and
- The trap may never return to the program.

Since the transfer is accomplished without an explicit instruction from the user program, the mechanism to accomplish the transfer must be built into the fetch/execute cycle. A slightly better description of the cycle might be

```
while (true) do
   if (error_trap_flag is not set)
      then
         { original body of f/e cycle }
      else
         push PC onto stack        { the "return" address}
         (turn off error_trap_flag)
         load error-handler address into PC
```

Thus, the fetch/execute cycle is not absolute, as it was described previously. The machine language model of the cycle is accurate as long as there is no interrupt, but when there is an interrupt, the cycle behaves in a completely different manner. At that point, it takes the actions needed to jump to the interrupt service routine and to ensure that it can recover after it has processed the trap. The `error_trap_flag` is turned off so that a single error will not cause further interrupts. Finally, the current PC (which, of course, points to the next instruction that would have been executed had the interrupt not occurred) is saved in a temporary storage location. The address of the service routine is placed in the PC. The fetch/execute cycle may then continue as usual. However, the next instruction executed is the first instruction of the interrupt service routine (where the PC now points). Processing of the service routine continues until that process is complete.

▷ *Note that, if the* `then_clause` *did not turn off the* `error_trap_flag`*, this model would be functionally identical to the first version, discussed earlier. Would that version ever be preferable to this version?*

The interrupt service routine may either return to the top-level system or enter a debugger. In either case, it will normally display an error message. If control is to return to the top level of the system, the service routine should restore all registers to appropriate values. The values left in registers by the user-program cannot be relied upon. Copies of the important system values must have been stored before the user-program commenced. The restore operation is simple:

```
for all registers
   copy values from system-register-storage-area ⇒ registers
copy address of main system process ⇒ PC
```

The error-handler will generally save the user values from the registers including the status register:

```
for all registers
   copy values from registers ⇒ user-register-storage-area
      (including PC)
```

This step is so essential that it is often included as one of the hardware steps of invoking the trap:

```
while (true) do
   if (error_trap_flag is not set)
      then
         { original body of f/e cycle }
      else
         push PC onto stack        { the "return" address }
         (turn off error_trap_flag)
         copy registers ⇒ user-register-storage-area
         load error-handler address into PC
```

These values can be accessed by the error-handler. For example, they may be displayed for the programmer to see. The debugger provides some opportunity to fix errors, or at least discover the nature of the problem. Note that the register values displayed by a debugger are the values saved in the `user-register-storage-area`, not the actual registers, which are of course then being used by the debugger routine. Many debuggers allow the user to request that control return to the user program at the point following the interrupt. This is not always possible. For example, if the interrupt was caused by an erroneous jump instruction to an illegal address, there is no point in restarting the program.

In case recovery is possible, the environment should be re-created exactly as if control had never wavered. In that case, the last instructions of the debugger routine should restore the registers and jump to the saved PC address, returning control back to the user-program. The registers and stack are also restored to their pre-error values. The next instruction executed will be the instruction following the source of the interrupt. Most machines include a special machine language instruction, `return_from_interrupt`, designed specifically for this purpose. It is distinguished from a regular `return_from_subroutine` instruction in that it restores all registers—including the status register. Note that if the problem still exists (e.g., if an address error was generated by a PC that did not point at an instruction, it is unlikely to point at an instruction after being incremented), execution of the next instruction will result in immediate re-entry into the error-handling routine.

Some machines transfer control to a single debugger routine when any error is detected. Other machines distinguish between the various errors. In either case, debuggers normally provide the user with an error message. To inform the error-handler which error occurred, several interrupt bits are used rather than a simple flag. In its simplest form, the flag is replaced by a byte of storage (probably in a register, perhaps part of the same status register that contains the condition codes). Each bit represents a single possible error: a 1 in a given position indicating that a specific error has occurred, perhaps:

bit 0: address error (instruction fetch)
bit 1: address error (operand fetch)
bit 2: illegal instruction
bit 3: divide by zero

As long as this byte is all 0s, the cycle proceeds normally; when it is nonzero, the jump is taken to the interrupt handler. Thus, the loop control is

```
while (true) do
   if (interrupt byte = 0)
      then { regular f/e body }
      else { error interrupt }.
```

Note that the value of the interrupt value will continue to be available in the register so that the error-handler can use the value to provide a useful message. For example, suppose the user-program includes the following segment:

address	**instruction**	
2000	copy	#0⇒reg0
2004	copy	#0⇒reg1
2008	divide	reg0⇒reg1
200C	copy	reg1⇒reg2

The fetch/execute cycle would proceed normally through the first two `copy`s. During the `divide`, the error would be flagged. At the next cycle, the final `copy` would not be fetched. Instead, the contents of all registers, including `reg0`, `reg1`, the status register, and the PC, would be saved. Note that the PC now has the value 200C. The divide-by-zero bit of the status register would be cleared without changing any other status bits. If the error-handler needs to return control to the user program, it need only restore the registers. The PC will automatically point to the correct location.

Interrupt Vectors

In some cases, separate error-handlers are used for each type of message, in which case, the preceding technique seems inherently inefficient. First, the hardware explicitly set a separate and distinct error flag. The trap mechanism then grouped all of the flags together into a single byte to be passed to the error-handler. The handler then tested the byte to see which error occurred. The error-handler must determine which of the separate errors occurred. In theory, the fetch/execute cycle could include multiple tests and multiple jumps. Unfortunately, this approach focuses attention on another problem: each of the distinct error-processing routines must be stored at a unique address. If those addresses are "hard-coded" into the processor, any address changes would be catastrophic. If an error-handler needed to be rewritten (to fix a bug or for some other improvement), the starting address of that or another error-handler might change.

There is a way to avoid this problem: an *interrupt vector.* Although the details—including the length—of the interrupt-handling routines may change in a new release of system software, the specific list of errors is not likely to change. The system contains an array of addresses, one position for each interrupt-handler:

trap number	**displacement**	**error description**	**actual address of routine**
0	0	address error (instruction fetch)	1234
1	2	address error (operand fetch)	1800
2	4	illegal instruction	2222
3	6	divide by zero	2468

Although the address at which a routine is stored may change, the relative positions of the pointers in the vector need not change. If a routine does change, the addresses in the table can be changed without modifying the locations of the pointers themselves. To make the interrupt vector work effectively, the system designers guarantee that the address of the interrupt vector and the relative position within the vector for each routine will be maintained during future releases of the system. Thus, in the example, illegal instruction is always at displacement = 4. When a trap occurs, the processor does not jump directly to location 2222.

Instead, it finds the address in position 4 of the table and then jumps to that new address. In pseudo-GAL,

```
*load_address   table⇒reg0          ;address of table
*copy           trap-number⇒reg1    ;displacement for
                                    ;illegal-instr. routine
*shift-left     #1⇒reg1            ;multiply by two bytes
*add            reg1⇒reg0          ;now points to position
                                   ;in interrupt vector
*load           reg0↑⇒reg2         ;finally points to routine
*jump:always    →reg2↑             ;to illegal-instr routine
```

The destination of the `jump` instruction is specified as an indirect operand. Some machines contain an additional addressing mode called *double indirect* that allows vector addressing to be accomplished in a single step:

```
jump:always     →reg_n↑↑
```

In the case of the example interrupt vector, the needed statement might be

```
jump:always     →(displacement + reg0↑)↑
```

Other machines include a specific trap handling instruction which combines all of the steps.

Priorities

Multiple interrupts can occur simultaneously. Perhaps, an overflow occurs when adding, and an address error occurs when attempting to store the result. Perhaps an error occurs during execution of the error-handler. Clearly, only one interrupt may be processed at a time. In addition, one error could interrupt a user program and in turn be interrupted by a second error. To handle such situations, some systems include *priority* levels for each interrupt. That is, some interrupts are more important than others and are therefore processed first. When an interrupt occurs, the highest priority (most important) interrupt is used as an index into the interrupt vector. Only the single bit corresponding to the selected interrupt is turned off. Therefore, the lower priority interrupt flag remains set.

Normally no interrupt handler can itself be interrupted by a lower-priority interrupt. Otherwise, if there were two simultaneous interrupts, the higher-priority routine would be entered, but it would then be immediately interrupted by the lower-priority interrupt, which remained set. One simple solution is to prioritize the individual interrupt bits from high order to low order. Therefore, the fetch/execute control must look more like this:

```
while (true) do
   if (interrupt byte ≤ current_interrupt level)
      then { regular f/e body }
      else { interrupt }
```

Note that in the case where there are no active interrupt-handlers, the interrupt level is 0, and this loop structure becomes identical to the previous description.

INTERRUPT MASKS. A programmer may wish to ignore certain classes of interrupt. For example, a machine generates traps on overflow in addition. The programmer may wish to ignore the overflow as a means of achieving modular addition. A program or error-handler may mask out unwanted interrupts by use of an *interrupt mask*. The mask is structured exactly like the interrupt byte itself. A program can set and clear individual bits in the mask with `copy` or logical masking operations. Each position of the mask indicates whether or not the corresponding interrupt is currently allowed. If a 1 indicates that the interrupt is allowed, the fetch/execute control becomes:

```
while (true) do
  if ((interrupt byte AND mask) ≤ current_interrupt level)
    then { regular f/e body }
    else { interrupt }
```

Thus, if the above overflow interrupt is in bit 4, the interrupt byte is

0001 0000

and the mask is

0101 0100

and the conjunction yields

0001 0000

which implies that the interrupt-handler should be called unless it is already handling an interrupt of level 4 or higher. If the mask did not have a 1 in bit 4, the conjunction would be false and an interrupt routine called.

System Calls

If a programmer wishes to enter the debugger at a specific point in a program for debugging purposes, any illegal instruction form could be inserted into the code at this point. Many machine languages provide an explicit `trap` instruction that allows the programmer to interrupt the machine deliberately and call the debugger as if an error occurred. A deliberate trap is known as a *system call*. In GAL, the trap instruction has the form

```
trap <number>
```

where `<number>` specifies which routine is desired. In effect, the programmer is calling a system subroutine—in this case, one that is normally invoked by an error interrupt. Such a trap to the debugger is useful in any situation in which the programmer knows that the program is producing incorrect results but is not sure why or precisely where the error is. The programmer could also signal other errors. For example, suppose that the user had created a shortcut division routine that used shifts rather than divides. The routine could signal a divide-by-zero error if the shift displacement was zero. Since conditions such as overflow do not always represent disastrous errors, most machines do not automatically generate interrupts when they occur but simply set a bit in the status register. A user-program could test for overflow and generate its own trap or system call. The interrupt may duplicate an existing entry in the interrupt vector or represent a distinct entry.

System calls can also be used for non-error calls to system routines. For example, the system may make 100 special-purpose subroutines available to the user. These routines can also be invoked using a generalization of the interrupt vector, called a *jump table*. Each user `trap` instruction includes a trap number as an operand. The trap instruction uses that number as a displacement into a jump table for system service routines—in the same manner as the error traps used the interrupt vector—making an indirect jump to the desired system service routine.

VIRTUAL MACHINES: THE INVISIBLE SERVICES

Many of the most important services that the system provides are, by their nature, supposed to be invisible to the user at almost any level. A familiar example of an almost invisible service is "background printing," the printing of a document while the user continues to perform some other task. Background printing is not quite invisible because the user is usually aware that although the program in use acts as if the document has been printed, the printer—sitting right next to the programmer—is still busily printing the document.

The existence of invisible services suggests that one cannot categorize all of the tasks of an operating system in terms of the human interface. Nor are the hardware aspects, such as bootstrap routines and process termination, adequate for describing the software-dominated system. Independent of the perspective of the user, every operating system must provide several general categories of service, including

- process management
- memory management
- processor scheduling
- file management
- disk scheduling

A typical course in operating systems could be organized around this categorization. However, the focus of this text is not operating systems but computer organization. A more useful categorization for our purposes can be generated by the question:

> "How does system software transform the various models of computation?"

The remainder of the chapter illustrates the value of interrupts as a tool for transforming one model of computation into another. For the most part, the models discussed in the first 11 chapters can be thought of as a single model, viewed at varying levels of detail. A model in which the user sees a machine that is logically or quantitatively different from the hardware machine is called a *virtual machine*. Thus, a virtual machine is a machine that appears to be something other than it actually is. Like each of the earlier models, a virtual machine can provide a very reasonable conceptualization. The fact that the machine is not physically identical to a programmer's model is irrelevant to the immediate problem or solution—so long as the machine performs consistently with the logic of the model. Typically, a virtual machine appears to the user as a classic von Neumann machine—but one that differs in specific quantitative details, such as size of memory or number of CPUs, from the actual hardware machine available. An essential tool for all virtual machines is the interrupt, used previously for error processing.

Time Sharing: A Virtual Machine Possessing Multiple Processors

Time sharing is the creation of virtual CPUs by dividing the available time, providing small chunks to each virtual processor. Most users are at least vaguely aware that some sort of resource sharing must be possible on mainframe computers. Consider a room containing 20 users, each working at a terminal connected to the same mainframe computer. Each user is allowed to maintain the fiction that he or she is the only user of the entire machine. The user may be using an applications package, a higher-level language, or even an assembly language. In each case, the machine seems to behave as if it is the user's private tool. Even stepping through a machine language program will not reveal the truth that only a small fraction of the machine cycles belong to the individual programmer.

For a "quick-and-dirty" introduction to time sharing, imagine a machine with two users. Each has a program running on the machine. Each program uses a fraction of the machine's resources: memory, external devices, and processor cycles. Assume that program A is physically located in memory locations 1000–1FFF and that program B is in locations 3000–3FFF. Each has a distinct portion of memory, and each is unaware of the other's memory locations. To maintain the illusion of sole possession, each program must behave as if it has sole use of the registers and of the fetch/execute cycle. As the programs begin, this is true for one of the users, A, as illustrated in Figure 11-3*a*. At that point, the other user, B, is in a state called *ready* or *waiting* (the term "wait state" is often reserved for memory waiting situations). Eventually they will switch roles: B will run, while A is ready and waiting, as in Figure 11-3*b*. This *context switching* requires

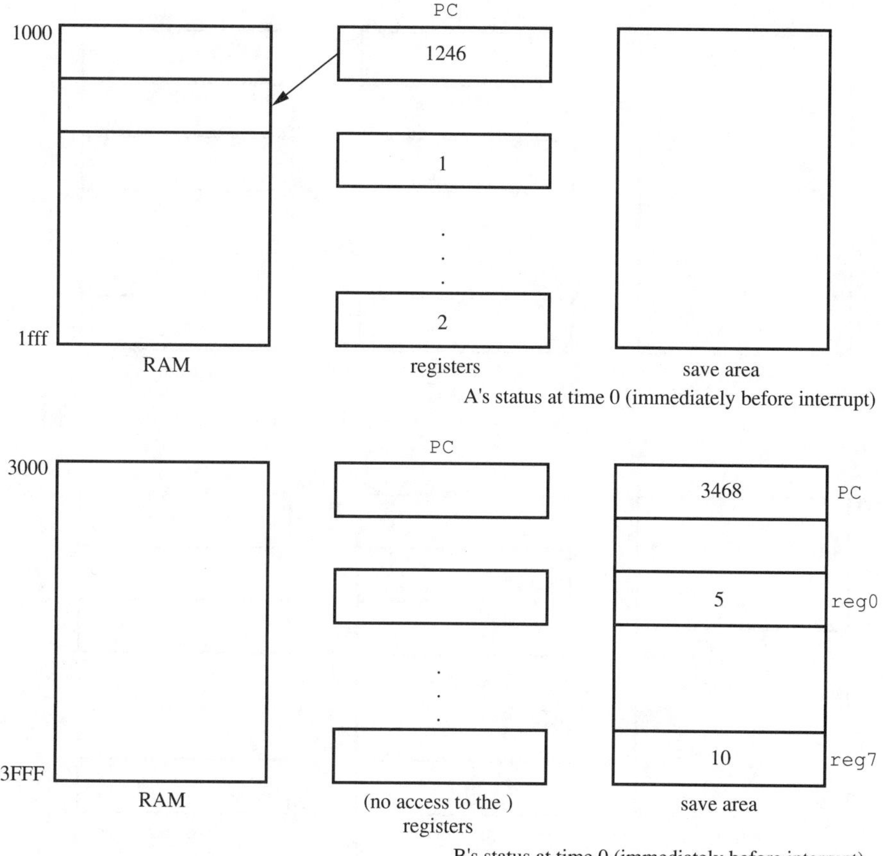

FIGURE 11-3
Time sharing (*a*) before A is interrupted.

(among other things) that the PC be changed to point to B's program. The process is invoked by the system clock, which generates an interrupt signal, conceptually identical to the trap discussed above except that it is generated by the clock, a source external to the program. The sequence of events is

- The clock sends an interrupt signal to the CPU.
- The interrupt-handler saves the status of the running job and starts the other job.

At each interrupt, the interrupt-handler switches the roles of the two users, placing B in the active role and A in the waiting role, etc. The interrupt-handler must ensure that the *state* of the program—all relevant and changeable aspects—

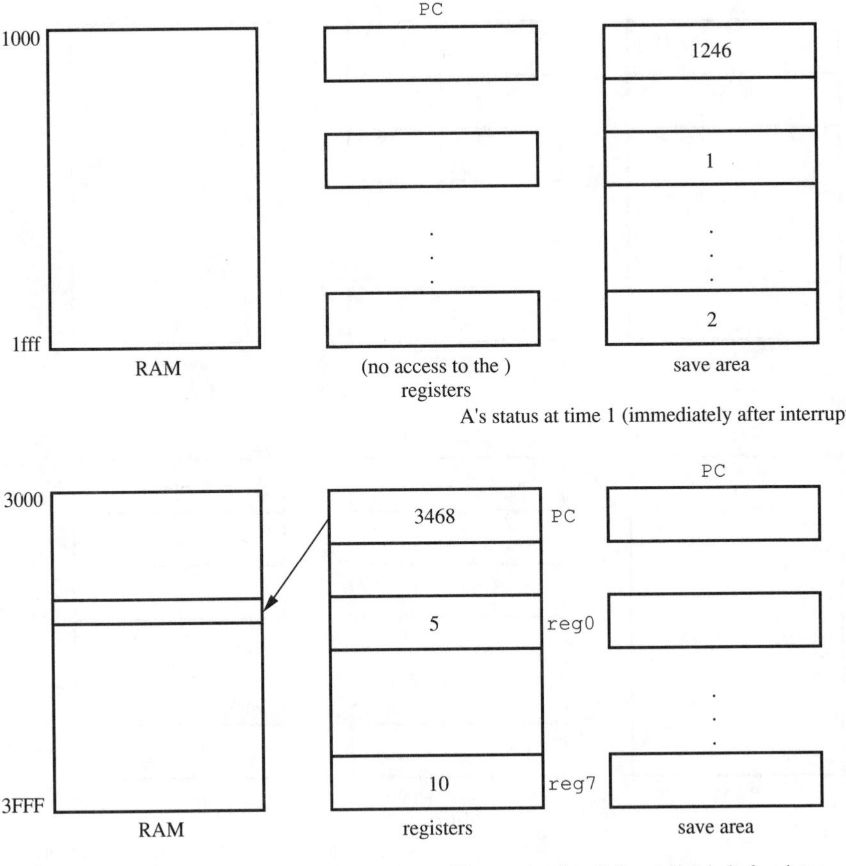

FIGURE 11-3
Time sharing (*b*) after A is interrupted.

is saved while the program waits. The state of a program includes the contents of all memory locations—both RAM and register—and a pointer to the next instruction to be executed. Since each program has its own distinct primary memory area, there is no need to save a program's RAM. But each one may use any of the registers—data registers, PC, IR, and status register. Only copies of the registers must be saved. The address of the next instruction is held in the PC and is therefore automatically saved when the registers are saved.

> ▷ *Why does time sharing provide an additional reason for preferring symbolic addresses over absolute addresses, even when programming in assembly language?*

The interrupt-handler maintains a save area for the register contents—they are not pushed onto the system stack. If they were, B's registers would be pushed on top of A's at the next interrupt. The significant steps of the interrupt-handler are

- Save the registers for the active (old) process.
- Load the previously saved register values for the new process.
- The PC is normally the last one loaded. Control will automatically transfer to the new process. At the next cycle, the next instruction for program B will be fetched since the PC now points to that instruction. Program B then runs as if the CPU is its own private machine until the next system clock interrupt, when the process is reversed.

The entire process sounds incredibly inefficient. In fact, there is a price to be paid, but it is much smaller than it may seem. If the machine can perform 10^6 instructions per second (a modest rate) and if interrupts are generated at one every 10^{-2} seconds, each user receives a 10,000 instruction *time slice,* minus the time required to process the interrupt. As described, the processing time is minimal—probably less than 100 instructions. Thus, the program is allocated 9900 instructions in one time slice. For short operations, the difference is imperceptible. The threshold of human perception enables a person to distinguish between 0.1 and 0.2 seconds. In that time, each of the two users receives 5 to 10 time slices, so a person would not notice any degradation in a process executing less than 50,000 instructions. In longer programs, of course, the process would run approximately half as fast as on a dedicated machine. Time sharing relies on the fact that most of the individual user commands involve very small requests.

Control can be switched between programs for other reasons. For example, after a program requests input, significant time may be wasted while waiting for the relatively slow input device. This observation is a prime motivator for time sharing machines. Many (perhaps most) programs spend more time waiting for input and output devices than they do in actual execution. Consider (as perhaps the worst example) input from the keyboard. A human will respond, at best, in a few tenths of a second, but it could take many minutes. Time-shared CPUs have their greatest advantage because most programs need to wait frequently for such I/O events. When a program requests an I/O event, it can be interrupted exactly as if it had timed out (see Chapter 12). The interrupt-handler can then give control to some other program. After all, the first program cannot use the CPU now anyway. The second program executes while the first waits for input. Control can be returned to the first process after its input has arrived, and either the second program has timed out or it has also requested input. This savings is truly free time—CPU time that would have been wasted while waiting for the I/O event had there been no time sharing.

In some systems, tens, or even hundreds, of users can time share and never be explicitly aware that they do not have complete control of the machine. When the number of users approaches some upper limit, or when many of the users have programs that are *execute* or *CPU bound* (i.e., that generate few I/O requests and therefore seldom give up the CPU voluntarily), the overall performance of the system will begin to degrade. In fact, it will simply seem to slow down—but the system never fully admits that multiple users are present. The general term for the task the system must perform in manipulating multiple processes in a time-sharing machine is called *process management*. Virtually all systems today—even single-user systems—provide at least some amount of time sharing. For example, a single-user, "single-process" system may have only one process available to the user. It may have an additional process, which maintains a wall clock, providing the current time to the user. Chapter 12 discusses important uses for time sharing in the input/output context.

Virtual Memory: Increasing the Apparent Size of RAM

The quantity of memory available to a given program on a given machine is clearly a fixed commodity. Every system has an upper bound on the quantity of memory that can be installed. Suppose that 98 percent of a user's work can be done in a given quantity of memory, say one megabyte, yet periodically that user must run a large program that requires two megabytes. One solution is to buy the extra megabyte of RAM. This is a rather wasteful solution: since the large program is only run occasionally, most of the time the extra memory will be unused. A *virtual memory* machine provides a compromise for precisely such situations. A virtual memory system is one that has a fixed quantity of memory but appears to the user (and the user's program) as if it had significantly more.

The key inspiration for virtual memory is that although a program must reside in RAM, only one statement can be executed at a time and only a small segment in any short period of time. Therefore, some fraction—perhaps most—of the code and data for a given program is actually kept in the larger secondary, rather than primary, storage. Unfortunately, secondary storage is not a useful place to keep a program or its data while a program is executing because external storage is extremely slow compared to RAM. The trick is to attempt to keep the code and data that is in current use in primary memory and to keep those parts that are not needed immediately in secondary storage. The process is logically very similar to data migration from RAM to cache. Suppose a two-megabyte program is divided into 100 segments, each 20,000 bytes long (1/100 of the entire program). A one-megabyte machine can hold 50 of the 100 segments, so 50 are placed in RAM and 50 are placed on a disk. As long as the current instruction (and any data it accesses) resides in memory, the program can proceed as in all previous examples. Eventually, the program will attempt to access a location that is actually on the disk and not in main memory (but, recall the principle of locality). The attempt to access data not in RAM generates an interrupt called a *page fault*. The interrupt-handling routine performs an exchange: the required segment[3] is read in

[3]Technically, a *page* is a fixed-size section of memory. A *segment* is variably sized (usually corresponding to program structure). The term *page fault* is used to indicate that the needed parcel is not currently available in RAM—independent of the logical organization of virtual memory as pages or segments.

from disk and stored in primary memory. Since all the memory is already in use, one segment of code or data must be removed from memory to make room for the new segment. It is saved on the disk, and the two segments are said to be *swapped*. Figure 11-4 illustrates the concept.

In the model as described, the available memory for each program is apparently filled to capacity when the program starts. That approach is a form of *anticipatory* paging: the system has anticipated that the segments would be needed. In practice, many segments will never—or seldom—be needed. It certainly is difficult to guess which new segments will be needed (the principle of locality is of limited help in anticipating previously unused segments). Therefore, segments are usually not even brought into memory until they are needed (or demanded, hence the method is called *demand paging*). Either way, virtual memory does require some additional hardware and a modification of the addressing mechanism, but in theory such modifications can be minimal. Recall that some computers distinguish between items that should not change, such as constants and code, and locations that might change, such as variables. If data and code are kept in separate segments, the task can be simplified. Suppose that the system requires that every data segment be held in memory (clearly this solution will not work if the

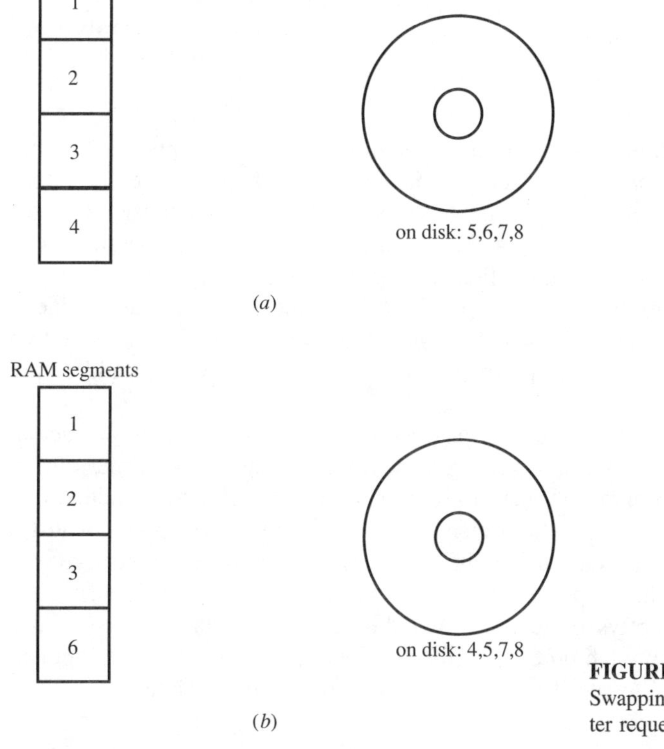

FIGURE 11-4
Swapping (*a*) at time t = 0. (*b*) after request for segment 6.

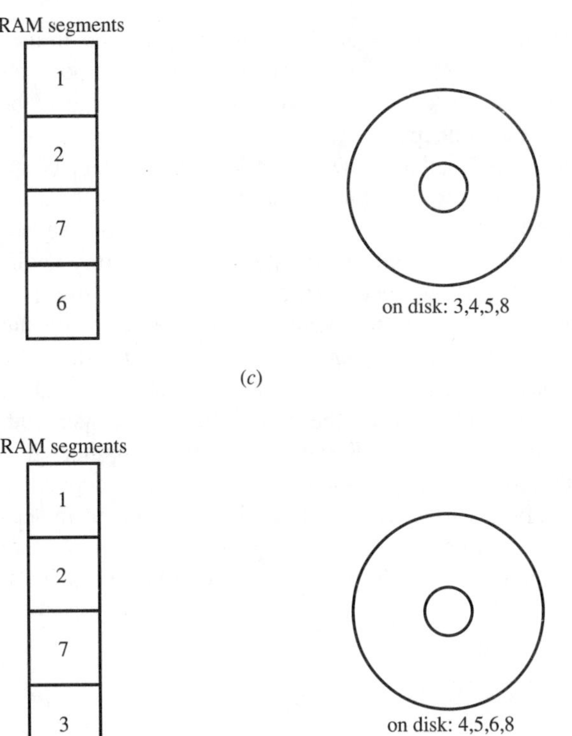

FIGURE 11-4 (cont.)
Swapping (*c*) after request for segment 7. (*d*) after new request for segment 3.

large size of the program is due to large quantities of data). Suppose also that the program requires that every code segment (e.g., each procedure) be either completely in main memory or completely swapped out to secondary storage. Once execution of a code segment has begun, the instruction fetch operations can be assured that the next instruction will always be in main memory. Only the jump-to-subroutines (and returns) may have problems. The machine must determine if the target address of a jump is actually contained in memory. Thus, these two forms of instruction will need to perform a more complicated form of addressing to check the residency of the code.

The nature of the virtual memory process suggests that more than one actual segment of code might reside in a given physical location at various times during the execution of the program. When a program wishes to refer to an address, it must be able to refer to a specific logical location within a program—not just a specific physical address. Virtual memory addresses therefore are typically composed of a segment and displacement pair (similar to a base and displacement used for referencing arrays or records, and the tag and displacement of cache memory). The memory fetch process performs an extra step in which the segment is looked up on a table to see if it is in memory or on the disk. Note that a given segment of code might be used multiple times during execution of an entire program. Each time it is needed it might be copied into distinct physical locations. If the program uses PC-based addressing, it does not matter if the segment is in the same physical location each time.

Virtual memory and time sharing often keep close company. If a machine has 32 megabytes of memory, it may also have 100 current users, all of whom not only believe they have sole use of the CPU but also believe they have two megabytes of their own memory. In reality, each may have only a quarter of a megabyte. From the collective view of all the users, the 32 Mb of memory would appear to be 200 Mb. The task of maintaining each user's virtual memory space is called *memory management*.

A variation on virtual memory is shareable code. On a multi-user system, it is common for more than one user to execute the same program at the same time. The system could react in several ways: it could refuse to load the program for the second requester, since someone else is already using it; or it could make a second copy for the second user. The first approach seems restrictive and not very user-friendly. The second approach would duplicate large quantities of code. A representation called *shareable code* enables a single copy of a program to be loaded and multiple versions of it to run. Such code must be stored using two forks: a code fork and a data fork (see Chapter 7). The code itself should not change as the program is run. Therefore, all users may share a single copy of the code fork. The data fork, however, contains data specific to an individual execution of the program. Each user has an individual data fork. The data fork is usually much smaller than the code fork. Therefore, the virtual machine may easily appear to the collective set of users to be several times its actual size. Segregation of changeable from nonchangeable code has one final advantage in a virtual memory machine. If a segment has not changed while it has been in RAM, there is no need to copy it to disk when the segment is swapped out. Thus, placing items together which will not change helps make virtual memory more efficient.

▷ *Next time you use a multi-user system, call the appropriate system information routine—probably called something like* `finger` *or* `show users`*—to see what programs most users are currently executing. There is a good chance that several (or most) will be using the mail facility or a text editor. What does this suggest about the need for shared code?*

Virtual Input and Output

Perhaps the most essential of the virtual services provided by operating systems is virtual input and output. The routines `input` and `output` are standardly provided by the system and act as hooks for a user-program. Both are also among the slowest actions on any system. The system provides an apparent reduction in this delay, thereby providing better throughput of programs. It takes care of all the details, enabling the programmer to think in terms of a higher-level model. In a hll, this higher-level model allows the programmer to think of an input object as an integer or a real number or a string; in assembly language, the programmer usually manipulated characters.

The system I/O routines provide even more useful services. The system fields all I/O requests—requests for input from users. At the same time, data arriving from a device generates interrupts, allowing other system routines to field all of the arriving data, even if several I/O events arrive with no intervening requests. The system simply places them in a buffer queue. When the user next requests an input, the system delivers the item at the front of the queue, rather than from the device directly. Thus, the system provides a form of virtual I/O, with events appearing to the program as if they occur on request. Chapter 12 examines the details of I/O devices which make this process possible.

Virtual I/O provides valuable support for time-sharing systems. When a process requests an I/O event (especially a very slow one, such as a keyboard input), the user surrenders control of the processor until after the input has actually arrived. The user is never aware that the program is not even running at the moment and therefore is not handling the I/O device directly. The system activities needed to provide a virtual I/O environment for the user are collectively called *I/O management,* or sometimes *event management*. Chapter 12 investigates some of the mechanisms for I/O management from the user-program's perspective.

Like the language-based models of earlier chapters, a virtual machine provides a very reasonable tool for conceptualization. The programmer need not understand the underlying details. As long as the actions of the virtual machine can be predicted based on the model, it provides a valuable service. An interesting aspect of most common virtual machines is that the virtual machine invariably appears to the user as the classic von Neumann machine, discussed throughout this text. Yet, the underlying machine represents variations on the original concept. One of the most surprising statements about virtual machines is that the underlying behavior is actually nondeterministic. The exact series of steps performed in the execution of multiple programs may not be repeatable because interrupts may occur at different points in the execution. Normally, this has no impact on the user, who sees a deterministic von Neumann machine.

Interrupt-Driven Programs

Viewed from the outside, the nature of the code in a system seems very unusual. The view of the system program is not one of a sequential or procedural program as those with which most students are most familiar. The system program does not seem to be directing a series of actions. Rather, it seems to be reactive. When an event occurs, the system reacts by providing some service and then steps back into the background. It is as if the system is controlled by the interrupts—and it is. If one attempts to describe the system routines using traditional pseudocode, the general logic of the system's service routines can be described roughly as

```
while (true) do
   while (no events occur) do;          { wait and do nothing }
   { if it gets here, an interrupt has occurred }
   do case (interrupt value) of
      interrupt handler #1
      . . .
      interrupt handler #n
```

Chapter 12 investigates applications of such code for user programs. Such virtual I/O models can also help explain how programs can receive input from any of several devices: the system fields all interrupts and handles each as a separate case.

POSTSCRIPT: GOOD PROGRAMMING PRACTICES REVISITED

A curious observation: most "good programming practices" are justified on the basis of the human problem-solving and programming processes. Yet, it seems that many may also improve overall system performance. For example, in all programming models, the user is admonished to avoid confusing or spaghetti code. The usual explanation is that it is extremely difficult for a human to understand such code for the purposes of debugging or modification, which is certainly true. Yet, there is actually a second set of reasons for many such rules. In a virtual-memory machine, excessive jumping to distant locations will result in frequent page faults and therefore slower execution. Similarly, the user is encouraged to use symbolic identification for addressable storage rather than absolute addresses. In a time-sharing machine, it is essential that the system be able to locate code according to its own—and not the programmer's—needs. Modular code not only allows the programmer to focus attention on the currently relevant details of a program, but it also enables the code to be assembled in modules, saving time. The final observation of the chapter is left as a question for the reader to ponder: Which came first, the chicken or the egg? Did system requirements drive the "good programming practice" concepts or vice versa? It is worth the effort to investigate other programming practices for such dual explanations?

SUMMARY

The name operating system applies to the collection of programs that insulate the user from the computer hardware. A bootstrap program is the first program to execute when a computer starts to run. It loads the system software and then starts the system running. The bootstrap normally resides in ROM, and the hardware initialization process sets the PC to point to the routine. An interrupt is a signal that causes temporary or permanent suspension of a process. Interrupts can be caused by errors, external requests for resources, or user request. Traps are interrupts generated from within a program, which can be used to detect and respond to errors. The interrupt mechanism is also useful in creating virtual machines such as virtual memory (memory appears larger than it really is) and time-sharing (appear to be more CPUs) systems. Such virtual machines improve the throughput and performance of the physical hardware.

SUGGESTED READING

Comer, D., and T. Fossum. *Operating system design*. Englewood Cliffs, N.J.: Prentice-Hall, 1988..
Deitel, H. *An introduction to operating systems*. Reading, Mass.: Addison-Wesley, 1984.
Peterson, J., and A. Silberschatz. *Operating systems concepts*. Reading, Mass.: Addison-Wesley, 1985.

EXERCISES

11.1. Among other things, the start-up electronics must initialize the PC and status registers. Draw a circuit that, when turned on, sets the contents of a four-bit register to all 0s. Most machines also have an "initialize" switch that causes the same action whenever the switch is pushed. Such a switch could simply send a signal indicating that it was pushed. Add a switch to your circuit.

11.2. Create a GAL program equivalent to the boot program described in Figure 11-2. Assume that `input` and `output` are the only prewritten I/O subroutines.

11.3. The discussion of the time-sharing virtual machine suggested that the cost of processing the clock interrupt was minimal. Given the pseudocode outline included in the discussion of time-out interrupts, outline GAL or GEM code to process the interrupt. Using the timing model in Chapter 10, estimate the amount of time required for the interrupt routine.

11.4. Suppose you are to implement a system-command interface language. The language specifications include the statement `Run xyz` that, when entered, should cause the program `xyz` to be executed—for an arbitrary program `xyz`. Assume that the program `xyz` is not known when you implement the language. Assume that `xyz` does exist at the time some future user attempts to execute it. Using tools that you have seen, such as loaders and jumps with register-based target addresses, outline a procedure to invoke the needed program.

11.5. Suppose a machine provided a double-indirect addressing mode: the actual operand is pointed to by the location pointed to by the apparent operand. Use such a command mode for building and referencing a jump table.

11.6. Does your machine support virtual memory? If you don't know, devise an experiment to figure out if it does. Does it time share between users? Between multiple processes for one user? If you don't know—find out.

11.7. What is the trap number for the debugger on your machine? What other important system calls are user-accessible?

11.8. GAL apparently did not specify indirect as a legal addressing mode for the `jump` instruction. But there is no reason why the mode should be illegal in GEML. Write a GEML instruction that specifies an indirect `jump`. Double indirect certainly was not included. Propose a syntax for double-indirect jumps in GEML.

11.9. Search your system manual for system service routines of each of the types: information, file manipulation, inter-user communication, security, and integrity. Use at least one of each.

11.10. Find the list of system traps that can be deliberately invoked from your program. The list may include I/O routines for nontraditional devices such as the mouse and graphics tools for drawing on the screen. If so, write a routine that draws a rectangle and then determines if future mouse clicks are in the rectangle. Do not use routines built into your assembly language—use the traps.

11.11. Find a list of distinct error types for your machine. Test what your system does in each case.

11.12. Find the interrupt vector for your machine. (The programmer's reference manual should tell you the address.) Write your own routine to respond to an interrupt. First, check to see if you can write an address into the interrupt vector. Then write your routine and place its address into the vector. Generate the interrupt and test your routine. The routine need not do anything fancy, perhaps load some values into registers and call the debugger. Be sure to select an interrupt that will not prevent your machine from running.

11.13. Write a routine that displays the time on the screen. It should be invoked by the clock interrupt. (Note that you will probably inhibit all other time-dependent actions of your machine.)

11.14. If your machine allows time sharing, test it. Write two (or more) compute-bound programs. The programs should perform many (enough to measure with a wall clock—even if you are the only user) computations and signal to you when they are done. Run several copies of the program simultaneously and measure the slowdown. (If using a multi-user system, it would be courteous to check with the system manager first.)

11.15. Measure the virtual I/O. Write a program that waits before it reads. Enter several characters before the program has a chance to read them. Did the system successfully handle the input?

11.16. Suppose a machine can execute 10^6 instructions per second. Suppose there are 100 users. Suppose context switching requires 1000 instructions. How many instructions per second does a single user see?

11.17. Write an interrupt-driven program. It should accept input from either the keyboard or a mouse. The program can be as simple as one that writes out a message stating either what key you pressed or where on the screen you clicked the mouse.

11.18. Suppose a virtual machine has 1 megabyte of actual RAM available to the user and that the user is running a 10-megabyte program. What are the odds that a random location is in RAM? If a program has been running for some time, how does the principle of locality change the relative odds that the next instruction to be executed is in RAM?

11.19. Most machines have a hardware interrupt button. How must that button be related to traps and software interrupts?

CHAPTER 12

INPUT AND OUTPUT

In Chapter 1 data transfer operations were classified into three meaningful groups based on the location of the source and destination of the data to be moved. The GAL instruction `copy` sufficed for all internal transfers—those in which both source and destination were either register or RAM locations. Intervening chapters examined the implementation of `copy` but largely ignored the subroutines `input` and `output`, which accomplish data transfers to or from the external world. The details of external I/O do not fit precisely into any of the abstract models. I/O cannot be described solely through the fetch/execute cycle because the CPU has no direct control over the external world. The operations of input and output were described as procedures at all language levels—allowing the details to be effectively swept under a rug. The concrete or physical appearance and structure of modern computers also blur the details of internal/external data transfers. Prior to the invention of microcomputers, the distinction was somewhat clearer: A terminal that is separated from the computer itself is clearly an external device as are keyboards and disk drives that reside in separate cabinets. Does a write to the screen in a single combined unit require an external output operation? Does a read from an internal disk require an external input operation? In terms of the models developed to this point, the answer in both cases is yes. The computer and its *peripheral devices* (for short, *peripherals*) are logically distinct entities, each with its own properties and characteristics.

Input and output are essential components of any computing system. Without input and output, all of the preceding chapters would be useless. I/O provides the only means by which computers and people can communicate. Every computer program processes data; every interesting program can process more than one set of data. Input is the only mechanism to get unique data to the program. Every program produces results, and without a mechanism for delivering those results to the external world, a computer would be like the cartoon philosopher who sits on the mountain top and thinks—providing no useful information to any other person. The mechanisms of I/O differ somewhat from the internal operations of a machine. This chapter provides an overview of both the similarities and the differences between the processor and the peripherals.

An *interface* is the point—logical or physical—at which the two devices, computer and peripheral, connect. Therefore, the interface must be consistent with each of two inconsistent entities. For example, external data transfers operate in a time frame so much slower than any internal operation that direct implementation of an I/O command as a machine instruction is impossible. Most of the examples thus far have assumed system clock rates measured in megahertz—or even tens of megahertz—and instruction rates on the order of a million or more per second. Chapter 10 showed that access to main memory required several clock pulses and that memory fetches are, therefore, a major bottleneck in machine speed. However, in contrast with external data transfers, internal memory fetches are lightning fast. A very fast typist may type 100 words per minute, which, assuming five characters per word and a space between each pair of words, translates to about 10 characters per second. A machine capable of 10^6 operations per second can perform 10^5 machine operations in the time required to input a single character from a keyboard. Even screen output, which is not limited directly by human capabilities, is excruciatingly slow from the CPU's perspective. A classic terminal screen can display 24 lines of 80 characters, or about 2000 characters. A fast model of such a terminal might fill its entire screen in a second. Since that is certainly much faster than any human could read the entire screen, there probably is not much point in filling it any faster. Even 2000 characters per second is 500 times slower than the 10^6 instructions per second found in a typical personal computer and as much as 10^5 times slower than a powerful workstation. The mechanisms for input and output will have a significant impact on the overall performance of the machine. Not only will the I/O slow the machine down, but apparently it will interfere with the continuous execution of the fetch/execute cycle.

THE LOGIC OF I/O: SIMPLE READ AND WRITE OPERATIONS

Suppose a program needs to write to the screen (or to any other external device: disk drive, magnetic tape, paper tape, punched card, knotted rope, etc.). The built-in procedures `input` and `output` have hidden many problems that must now be considered:

- The information must somehow be sent to—or at least placed where it is accessible to—the external device;

- A mechanism must exist to ensure that the external device actually receives the information; and
- A mechanism must exist to deal with the time disparity between internal and external data movement.

First Attempt: I/O Registers

The initial model will use an input device such as a keyboard, and an older style hard-copy terminal for output (for the younger reader who may never have seen one of these devices, imagine a typewriter that is driven not by a keyboard but by a computer, or a printer that prints each character as soon as the program outputs it). Such devices handle one character at a time. Each keystroke on a keyboard sends one character to the computer. The computer generates a separate signal for each character on the output terminal. The two built-in functions of GAL, `input` and `output`, provide exactly that capability. In the hll model, the `get` and `put` functions of Pascal accomplish this same task. The problems of I/O can be simply stated in terms of the AL model, "How do the procedures `input` and `output` actually work?"

Assume, as a first approximation, that there exist two additional special-purpose registers called the input and output registers, each accessible by the CPU. Further assume these registers are also accessible by an external device. Whenever a value is placed in the output register by the program, it is automatically sent to the output device. Whenever the input device sends a character to the processor, that character is automatically placed in the input register. These registers are directly analogous to the memory buffer register. All data moving between the CPU and main memory passes through the MBR; all data moving between the CPU and the external world passes through the I/O registers. The GAL language has built-in procedures for I/O, but the implementation of these procedures is obscured because no commands or syntax mentioned thus far can access these special registers. The body of the procedure `input` must be logically equivalent to

```
input;version I                          ;assumes register-based
    copy          Input_reg⇒reg0   ;parameter passing
    return
```

The external device transmits a character to the input register. The input procedure then moves that character to register 0 to be returned to the calling program. Similarly, the body of the procedure `output` must be logically equivalent to

```
output;version I
    copy          reg0⇒output_reg
    return
```

INPUT. This view does present some minor linguistic problems. For example, no GAL code has been specified for representing the new registers. Such problems are superficial and can be circumvented by use of an additional mode bit or by creation of new commands (alteration of the GAL and GEM languages is left as an exercise). The more significant problems created by this approach are problems of synchronization or coordination. Consider the `input` command in the context of a program that inputs one character. The `input` command normally appears syntactically after an output command requesting the input:

```
jump:sub    →writeline   ;"please enter a character."
jump:sub    →input
copy        reg0⇒...
```

The key of the input operation is the `copy` statement, which moves the input from the input register to a generally accessible location, such as `reg0`. Even assuming that several machine instructions actually intervene between the last `output` command and the `input` command (return from `output`, jump to `input`, etc.), the processor will reach the actual input statement long before the human has had a chance to touch a key (human reaction times are measured in tenths or hundredths of a second, not microseconds). If the `input` command is executed as soon as it is encountered, it will treat whatever value is currently held in the input register as the input. The program will proceed—even though no real input has yet been entered. Some mechanism must exist to enable the machine to wait for the human. At least two techniques are possible within the existing model. The first improvement employs an intervening loop to wait a specified quantity of time while the human enters the input.

```
input;version II
  copy               wait_time⇒counter[1]  ;an arbitrary
                                           ;number

wait_some_time                            ;loop to kill time,
  subtract           #1⇒counter           ;counting down from
  jump:greater_eq    →wait_some_time      ;wait_time before it
                                          ;performs

  copy               input_reg⇒reg0       ;the original body
  return
```

[1]Although the GAL language permits only one main memory operand, mnemonic names are used throughout this chapter for clarity. Consistency could be obtained by substituting a register name for the variable `counter` throughout.

Version II is also unsatisfactory. The program must necessarily assume the worst case, which might be quite long if the human had gone for a cup of coffee. Any lesser assumption will occasionally produce an error. One alternative is to wait for a change of value in the input register. The input procedure can compare the current to the original value in the input register to check if a new value has appeared

```
input;version III
    copy            input_reg⇒old        ;persumably this is
                                         ;an old value
wait_for_change
    copy            input_reg⇒reg0       ;loop while nothing
    compare         old⇒reg0             ;new arrives
    jump:equal      →wait_for_change
                                         ;reg0 now contains
    return                               ;the input value
```

One significant problem remains: version III cannot detect two successive identical input characters (a frequent occurrence in the case of such characters as 0, blank, return, etc.). This problem can be avoided by clearing the input register before testing for input. The ASCII *null* character, composed of all zero bits, is ideal for this purpose. It represents no printable character and requires no space if displayed.

```
input;version IV
    copy            null⇒input_reg       ;initialize register
wait_for_change
    copy            input_reg⇒reg0       ;loop while nothing
    compare         null⇒reg0            ;is new
    jump:equal      →wait_for_change
                                         ;reg0 now contains
    return                               ;the input value
```

For most situations, version IV is logically correct and will work with no other logical problems. A few further practical problems remain. First, if the human somehow managed to type an input character before execution of the `input` statement, that character would be lost because the first statement of the procedure clears the input register. This may not seem likely, but in many systems it is often possible to type input even before it has been requested. (The problems of interactive input is addressed further in a later section of the chapter.) A second practical problem is that of "wasted time" while looping and waiting for the human. The interface between the fast and slow components of the system was accomplished by slowing down the faster component. Although many early machines did exactly that, the observant programmer probably suspects that most machines today do not work in this manner. Finally, the approach seems to limit the number of I/O devices possible. Each device requires an additional register and a corresponding increase in selection logic.

▷ *If you have never noticed that input is often queued, you should attempt to create the situation. It can be done at almost any level. Enter a system or program with which you are familiar. Answer a question that you know is coming before the program prompts you for an answer. What happens?*

OUTPUT. Output requires similar coordination. Checking for a value change in the output register is not practical for output because the program, not the external device, changed the content. On the other hand, timing the rate of output can be useful. Each device has a maximum speed at which it can accept data (referred to as its *baud rate,* explained more fully later). For example, a hard-copy device can accept output only as fast as it can move the typing mechanism (print head, type ball, type keys, etc.). There is no advantage to outputting characters any faster than that rate. Indeed, data could be lost if the processor transmitted output faster than the device could accept it. If the CPU wrote several characters in rapid succession (i.e., faster than the output device can print), some of the characters would be lost. If a machine must output multiple characters to a device, it should wait long enough for the device to process each character fully:

```
output;version II
    copy                rate⇒counter
wait_some_time                               ;wait the
    subtract            #1 counter           ;appropriate
                                             ;amount of time
    jump:greater_eq     →wait_some_time

    copy                reg0⇒output_reg
    return
```

where `rate` depends on the baud rate of the device and the cycle time of the machine. The loop kills sufficient time so that the device may be assumed to be ready for the next character. For example, if the output device can accept 2000 characters per second and the machine executes one million operations per second, 500 machine operations should be used up by the loop. If the loop contained only the two instructions decrement and conditional jump, `rate` would apparently be 250.

DEVICE PERSPECTIVE. I/O is a two-way street. An output device must be able to recognize two consecutive instances of the same character. Duplicate characters cause the same problem for the output device as they did for the processor's input routine. Although the processor may place an identical value into its output register twice in succession, that does not change the output register at all. Conversely, on input to the processor, there is no assurance that the device will not generate a second character before the processor has processed the first one. Each communication requires a sender and a receiver. The output device receives the data output from the processor. From the perspective of the device, that data is input. An input device transmits data to the processor, and from the perspective of the input device, the data is output. Therefore, an output device can accept the data into its own input register and clear that register when the value has been displayed—the same procedure by which a host processor accepted its input. And an input device may need to delay before transmitting to the processor.

Additional problems remain. An output device may somehow get delayed. For example, hard-copy devices require more time to perform a carriage return than to print a character. Consecutive returns must certainly slow the device down. Presumably, the standard rate for the device is based on the normal situation rather than the worst-case situation. If so, the processor must determine that a device has fallen behind and delay output slightly. How can this be accomplished? Similarly, the absolute delay mechanism for output seems quite wasteful. Why should the output procedure always wait? If no character has been output recently, it should be able to output without a delay.

I/O Ports

Although the I/O register approach will work—indeed, has worked on many computers—it has a number of undesirable features. Total performance seems slow: one device is always waiting. Additionally, a separate register is needed for each I/O device. Although the total number of I/O devices is relatively small, the address specification for many additional registers could be problematic. More registers mean longer addresses. Since I/O devices are slow, it seems pointless to dedicate the fastest form of memory to their use. Finally, specific opcodes or modes must be reserved for the I/O commands. This makes the decoding step of the fetch/execute cycle more complex.

Memory-mapped I/O. A special form of memory location called an *input/output port* enables memory-mapped I/O. With respect to the actual data transfer, an I/O port behaves exactly like an I/O register: data received from an external source is placed into an I/O port, from which it can be copied to other internal locations. When the CPU places data into the port, the data is transmitted to an external device. I/O ports have an additional component: They actually consist of two bytes (typically, an even-odd memory pair):

- The *data byte* is logically identical to the register discussed above.
- The *status* or *control byte* reflects the status of the data byte.

A `true` in the status byte of an input port indicates the presence of new (unprocessed) data in the data byte. A `false` indicates that no new (unprocessed) data has been received in the data byte. For output, a `true` in the status byte means that the CPU has placed data in the data byte, but the device has not yet processed it. For input, `true` means that the device has placed data in the port, but the CPU has not yet accepted it. The two bytes of a port are physically connected

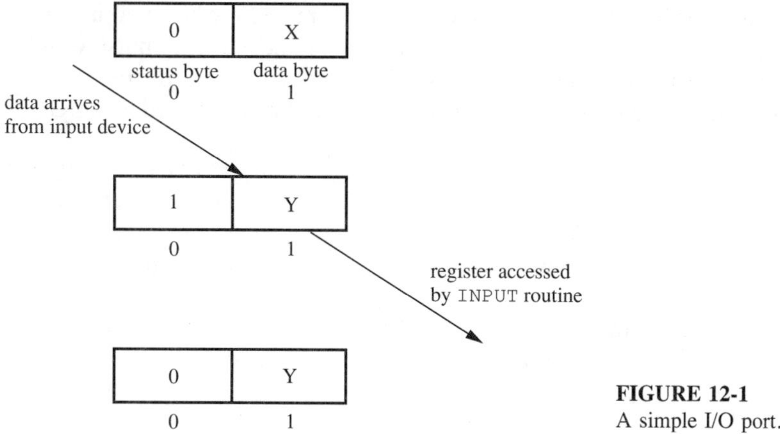

FIGURE 12-1
A simple I/O port.

so that the arrival of new data in the data byte automatically sets the status byte `true`. Whenever the data byte is read, the status byte is cleared to `false`. Figure 12-1 illustrates the input sequence. (Construction of the digital circuits for such a connection is left as an exercise.) The status byte of an input port can be set by action of the input device and cleared by action of the CPU. The status byte acts as a *semaphore*—a yes-no signal between the two devices. Output works in exactly the opposite manner: the status byte is set when the processor places data in the port and cleared when the output device accepts the data.

From the processor's perspective, input from the keyboard-like device can be handled through the logical steps:

```
while (status byte = false) do;      {wait for input}

copy data byte ⇒ destination         {the last two steps}
set status to false                  {are concurrent}
```

The CPU simply goes into a tight loop waiting for the status byte to become true. Once the value changes, control proceeds to the data transfer. If data is already present when the process starts, the test condition will be false, so the loop is not executed. As a GAL procedure, the process is

```
input;version V – I/O port
    compare       #false⇒status_byte     ;any input yet?
    jump:equal    →input                 ;no, so wait
                                         ;yes, so copy
    copy          data_byte⇒reg0         ;the data input
    copy          #false⇒status byte     ;concurrent with
    return                               ;clearing status
                                         ;byte
```

Presumably, the keyboard must execute a related process whenever a key is pressed. Logically, the keyboard also has access to the port. It must wait to transmit a character until the processor has acknowledged receipt of the previous character by clearing the status byte. This process could be described using GAL:

```
keyboard_send                                   ;describes behavior
                                                ;of device itself
    compare       true⇒status_byte              ;wait for port
    jump:equal    →keyboard_send                ;to become free

    copy          character⇒data_byte           ;
    copy          true⇒status byte              ;concurrent step
    return
```

Synchronous transmission. Notice that two entities must each monitor the status byte. The CPU must check to see if new data has arrived, and the device must check to see if the last data has been read. Either the device must be able to send queries to the port requesting the current content of the status byte or the processor must transmit the content of the status byte to the device without a request. Theoretically, an acknowledgement can be sent automatically from the processor when the status byte is reset (logically, the status byte is transmitted to the keyboard). One technique is called *data ready/data acknowledge*. Each device signals to the other any changes in its status byte. Thus, when the CPU reads an input character from a port, the change of the status byte is transmitted back to the input device as an acknowledgement that the character has been received. The device need not request the information. When the input device sends a character to the processor, it sets its own status byte and resets it when acknowledgement is received from the computer. Two small problems remain. This method seems to require twice as many signals as one would expect. In addition, if the human (who cannot be controlled by the processor or the device) enters several characters in rapid succession (perhaps by hitting multiple keys almost simultaneously), there must be a mechanism to save characters. The device cannot send the second character until the processor has accepted the first. What does it do with the second character while it waits?

BAUD RATE. The first problem is normally circumvented by establishing a mutually acceptable rate for transmitting data. The system designer guarantees that the processor can process characters if they arrive at a preset rate, called its *baud rate*. The input device delivers characters no faster than the baud rate. This convention removes the need for the data ready/data acknowledge protocol since the input device is assured that the processor will be ready when the data arrives. Baud rate, as used here, measures the bits per second that can be transmitted.[2]

---

[2]Technically, *baud rate* refers to the frequency of an analog signal in cycles or phase shifts per second. Generally a signal, originally digital but transmitted over an analog line, will be transmitted such

For output, the restrictions are reversed: the device speed is the limiting factor, and the processor must make sure that it does not deliver characters faster than the device can handle them.

OUTPUT. Output operations can be accomplished using exactly the reverse sequence of steps. The processor generates output, which is received as input by the external device. The status byte is automatically set to `true` by the `copy` command. This ensures that the processor never writes when the device has not yet received the previous character. In GAL, the above code for an `output` subroutine may look like:

```
output                                          ;i/o port version
wait_to_output
    compare        true⇒status_byte
    jump:equal     →wait_to_output

    copy           reg0⇒data_byte               ;these two steps
    copy           true⇒status_byte             ;are concurrent
    return
```

The status byte contains a true after the last step, ensuring that no further output operations can be made until the data has been received by a device.

From the perspective of the device, the same process looks much like the process for input to the processor:

```
output_device_receiver
    compare        false⇒status_byte            ;any data yet?
    jump:equal     →output_device_receiver

    copy           data_byte⇒reg0               ;accept the data
    copy           false⇒status_byte            ;concurrent step
    return
```

The status byte logic solves both of the earlier coordination problems. The CPU will never write characters too quickly for an output device to handle,

---

that each cycle of the analog signal has either a high or low amplitude representing a 1 or a 0 respectively. In that case, baud rate is synonymous with bits per second. It is possible to divide a cycle into more than two value ranges, thereby transmitting multiple values, and therefore, multiple bits per cycle. In this case, the bits per second will be a multiple of the baud rate. Although we probably drive the electrical engineers crazy, in practice computer scientists generally use the terms *bits per second* and *baud rate* interchangeable, since what we really care about is the performance of the data transfer, that is, bits per second. Another almost synonymous term is *bandwith,* a measure of information-carrying capacity of a path. Bandwidth is normally measured in bits per second, the same as baud rate.

because it must always wait until the device has indicated that it is ready to accept them by clearing the status byte. The device can always determine if there is an unprocessed character in the port by waiting until the status byte becomes true. Writing a large number of characters in succession still creates a minor problem: the processor must wait for the device to be ready before it outputs each character.

MULTIPLE DEVICES. I/O ports can be addressed as memory locations, increasing the number of input or output ports that are possible. In a machine with multiple I/O devices, the ports would typically be arranged as an array of even-odd pairs. For example, the screen might be at locations 0 and 1, the keyboard at locations 2 and 3, a disk drive at 4 and 5, and so on. The I/O procedures must have an extra parameter to specify the device. For example,

```
input(port_number,item)
```

The appropriate port could be accessed by translating the name into an offset address. In effect, the calling routine calculates the address of the port and passes the appropriate pointer to the input routine. The input routine uses the pointer to find the appropriate status and data bytes (a specific example is included as an exercise). Ports, therefore, also provide a solution to the problem of multiple devices. On some machines, I/O ports are treated as a separate memory address space.

Interrupt-Driven I/O

The port model is logically correct and works with no serious logical problems. The problems of waits for output and of "pre-inputted characters" are ones of efficiency, not correctness. However, this efficiency may be a practical problem. Both ends of the communication process must periodically wait. The CPU must wait to send output and the device must wait to display the output; the keyboard may need to wait before transmitting, and the CPU must wait for the input. Since there is normally a significant delay between an input request and the arrival of the data, programs could theoretically use some of that "wasted" time by computing during the interval:

- write request for input,
- perform some miscellaneous computations, and
- input answer to request,

thus taking advantage of otherwise "dead" time. The "miscellaneous computations" would replace the time-wasting loop of previous versions of `input`, enabling constructive work to proceed while waiting for input. Although many early programmers certainly wrote programs that worked in this manner, few systems today require the programmer to explicitly interleave the I/O and processing tasks. Such coding would certainly lead to incomprehensible code, with input commands widely separated syntactically from the messages requesting the input. Furthermore, the amount of time required for input is not very predictable. It is, therefore, difficult (or impossible) to estimate the quantity of work that can be performed between two I/O operations.

The "wasted" time is actually saved only if the processor can perform some other task while waiting. Although the modular logic recommended for modern programming often provides little opportunity for interleaving tasks, such situations do exist. Consider, for example, a problem involving a large table of numbers, each element of which requires a significant amount of computation. The program must compute the values, print out the table, and keep the table for some future computation:

```
compute table;
print table;
further_process_table;
```

The first segment performs no output and is executed at full processor speed. It is said to be *compute-bound*. The second segment, composed entirely of I/O operations, must run at a speed dictated by the output device. It is said to be *I/O-bound*. During the compute-bound phase, the I/O device is idle; during the I/O-bound phase, the CPU is largely idle. The programmer could rewrite the code, interleaving the two procedures and allowing both devices to work during their extended wait times:

```
for each element of the table
   compute element;
   print element;
further_process_table;
```

Unfortunately, such a rewrite requires that the programmer construct the program according to processor constraints rather than logical organization. Interrupts, similar to the ones discussed in Chapter 11, can be used to interleave the compute and I/O portions automatically. After requesting an I/O operation, the processor continues to perform additional operations. When the device is ready, it interrupts the processor. Suppose a program needs to read in a multiple-digit integer, simultaneously converting the series of ASCII characters into a binary number. Recall the algorithm for such conversions:

```
for each digit:
   obtain the next digit,
   double the previous total and
   add in the digit.
```

The new digit is not needed for the doubling step. It is logically possible to request the next digit, double the previous sum, and finally add in the next digit when it arrives. That is, the multiplication step is, in effect, overlapped with the data transfer. While it would, in principle, be possible for the programmer to identify all such situations and rearrange the algorithms, it clearly would make the coding much more complex. Interrupts are ideal for this task.

A QUICK REVIEW. An interrupt is a mechanism by which the fetch/execute cycle may be temporarily suspended and restarted using a new machine configuration (i.e., new register contents). For purposes of I/O, the external device must cause an interruption of the main procedure. The I/O event is then processed and control returned to the main procedure. In effect, the sequence of events surrounding an I/O request becomes

main process	**interrupt routine**
requests I/O event	
continues processing other data	
	interrupt main process
	process I/O event
	I/O interrupt ends
	control returns to main process
continues from where it was interrupted.	

When the CPU receives an interrupt, it saves all registers. The interrupt routine itself terminates with a `return_from_interrupt` instruction, which restores the registers, including the PC. In the I/O port model, the receipt of data automatically sets the status byte. In an interrupt model, that event also generates an interrupt—a signal that the device has delivered a character. The significant distinction between an interrupt signal and a simple status byte is that the interrupt signal is a message delivered to the CPU, not simply left in a memory location. A rough analogy can be made to the distinction between a telephone and a mailbox. You must check your mailbox periodically to see if you have received any mail, but the telephone rings when you have a call. On the one hand, you do not need to check the telephone periodically to see if anyone is calling you. On the other hand, a mailbox won't interrupt what you are doing: you can check it when you feel like it. In the simple I/O port model, it was up to the CPU to check the port to see if it was ready. Using an interrupt, the CPU is notified directly that the port is ready.

USING INTERRUPTS FOR INPUT. The problem with the I/O port version of input was that it did not work if data arrived before it was requested. The two-step interrupt-driven input procedure eliminates that problem. First, the interrupt service routine accepts the data from the port.

```
input_interrupt_service_routine
     copy     data_byte⇒buffer      ;no need to loop
     copy     false⇒status_byte     ;(concurrent)
     copy     true⇒data_ready       ;to be checked by input
     return_from_interrupt
```

The service routine is activated by an interrupt from the external device. When data arrives, the main program is interrupted and the service routine is executed. When the program asks for data by calling the input routine, the data may already be in the buffer. The actual `input` routine looks much like the port-driven input routine, except that it checks a `buffer` and `data_ready` flag rather than the actual I/O port.

```
input                                       ;first interrupt
                                            ;version
  compare         true⇒data_ready           ;wait for data
  jump:not_equal  →input
got_it
  copy            buffer⇒reg0               ;always have data
                                            ;by this point
  copy            false⇒data ready
  return
```

Although this mechanism works for the previously problematic situation in which data arrived early, it fails to help if the data request arrives first (unfortunately, the more likely situation). In that case, execution proceeds normally: the main program calls the input routine, which promptly enters a loop waiting for data. It works, but there is no saving. If the program could voluntarily give up control, some other task could execute while the first program waits for input. A special command, `trap`, enables the program to interrupt itself, indicating that it cannot presently proceed. Some other (presumably unrelated) task gets control. Eventually, a character is received, causing an I/O interrupt, which in turn starts the input-interrupt service routine. At that point, the main process need not wait since input has necessarily already arrived. The input-interrupt routine gets the character from the port, places it in the buffer, and signals that it has done so. The `return_from interrupt` command allows some other process to proceed. When the input routine restarts, there is necessarily data in the buffer and its next command takes it (turning off the flag, resetting it for the next input event). A typical sequence of events is shown at the top of the next page. The revised input routine looks like

```
input                                   ;improved interrupt
                                        ;version
  compare     #true⇒data_ready          ;has it arrived early?
  jump:equal  →got_it                   ;yet, go get it
  trap        self_interrupt_signal     ;no data yet, so wait
got_it
  copy        buffer⇒reg0               ;always have data by
                                        ;this point
  copy        #false⇒data ready
  return
```

process 1	process 2	interrupt handler
process normally		
request input		
(input routine generates an interrupt)		
		gives control to process 2
	take control	
	execute until . . .	
		input arrives
		interrupts process 2
		interrupt routine fetches value
		signals process 1 that data is ready
continues from the interrupt		

This improvement allows the system to use the waiting time productively, but it does not solve the problem of several characters transmitted in rapid succession. A second character might arrive before the interrupt routine has completed the first task.

OUTPUT. Interrupt-driven output also requires two procedures: an output request routine and an interrupt service routine. The former replaces the standard `output` routine. It leaves the data in a temporary buffer and signals that it has completed its task by setting a flag.

```
output                                          ;interrupt version
    compare        false⇒data_ready             ;can it just print
    jump:equal     →do_it_now                   ;yes, go do it
    trap           self_interrupt_signal        ;no, so wait
 do_it_now
    copy           Reg0⇒buffer
    copy           true⇒data_ready
    return
```

The interrupt service routine handles the interface with the external device and delivers the data to the port. The interrupt service routine is activated by the arrival of a device-ready signal at the port. Since the interrupt is only called when the device is ready to accept data, it does not need to check the status byte or to loop.

```
output_interrupt_service_routine
    compare        false⇒data_ready ;any data to be output?
    jump:equal     →output_interrupt_service_routine
    copy           buffer⇒data_byte
    copy           false⇒output_data_in_buffer
    copy           true⇒status_byte
    return
```

Output is a two-step process that is almost invisible to the user. The user simply places data into reg0 and performs a subroutine jump to the output routine as before. The output routine accepts the data but does not actually transmit it to the external device. Instead, it signals that data exists and should be output. If the device is ready, the service routine immediately interrupts the main procedure and transmits the data to the device. If, however, the device is not ready, nothing happens until the device_ready signal is received. At that point, the service routine interrupts the main process and outputs the data. If the device is not ready to accept the data, the program can continue processing without going into a wait-loop. Unfortunately, even this approach does not work if the program attempts to send several characters in rapid succession.

The call to the output routine is identical to that in a machine with no interrupts. In fact, the entire interrupt process is invisible to the user. While most machines incorporate interrupts for a number of purposes, they are not included in any of the models investigated in earlier chapters. The output-interrupt service routine that actually delivers the data to the port contains the instructions:

```
output interrupt_service
   copy        buffer⇒data_byte
   copy        true⇒status_byte          {automatic}
   copy        false⇒data_ready.
   return
```

After both processes have been executed, the desired goal has been attained: the data item has been copied (through the buffer) to the device, and the data_ready flag was set and then reset again.

Buffers

There remains one final problem. The interrupt-driven I/O method as described enables productive work to be accomplished between I/O events but does not solve the problem of multiple events of one type occurring in rapid succession. In the case of loops involving input or output, the savings created by using such interrupts is somewhat limited. The total elapsed time from first character transferred to last is still governed primarily by the quantity of time needed for the external device to process the entire set of characters. For example, while printing an 80-character line, a machine could do some extra processing between each pair of output characters. Unfortunately, as soon as the second output character is ready, the main procedure must stop and wait for the first character to be completely processed. Otherwise, writing the second output character into the buffer could result in the loss of the first output character.

One solution to the mismatch between processor speed and device speed is to create multi-character buffers—queues of characters waiting to be output to the device. Recall that a queue is a first-in-first-out data structure. In this case, it will hold data waiting to be processed in order of arrival. Rather than wait for the device, the output routine places the character at the back of the buffer—

and proceeds as if the character had actually been written to the device. The interrupt service routine removes and transmits characters from the front of the queue whenever the device is free. The two routines can be written

```
input                                          ;buffered
    compare        true⇒data_ready
    jump:equal     →get_it
    trap           self_interrupt
get_it
    copy           front↑⇒reg0
    add            #1⇒front
    copy           false⇒data_ready            ;no self_interrupt
    return
```

and the interrupt server as

```
input_interrupt_service
    copy           data_byte⇒back↑             ;get the data
    add            #1⇒back                      ;increment pointer
    copy           true⇒data_ready              ;something in queue
    return
```

The use of a queue increases the number of storage locations shared between the two processes. This introduces a new potential problem. If an interrupt occurs between the time the input routine removes a byte from the buffer and the point when it updates its pointer, the pointer will be off by one—meaning that data could be lost. It is essential that the interrupt not break the main program between detection and access of new data. Similarly, if an interrupt occurs during execution of the interrupt service routine, it cannot be expected to function properly. At best, two consecutive input characters are likely to be stored in the same location and then the pointer updated by 2. To prevent these situations an *interrupt enable* flag is turned off whenever the process should not be interrupted.

BUFFER OVERFLOW. As described, both pointers to a queue are nondecreasing functions; they are incremented but never decremented. It is not feasible to provide an arbitrarily large segment of RAM for the queue. One solution is to create a circular queue. In such a queue, modular arithmetic is used to create a queue that "wraps around." When a pointer reaches the end, it is automatically reset to the other end (implementation details are left as an exercise). Circular queues work very well, but the fixed bounds focus attention on another problem: buffer overflow. If a buffer holds 256 characters, the program must never fall more than 256 characters behind the actual arrival of data from the device. If it does, data is lost because the relative positions of the two pointers become inverted. Use of a buffer construct other than circular will not solve the problem as long as the maximum size is fixed.

Output is treated in an analogous manner. The only surprising aspect is that the interrupts are "device ready" interrupts—messages that the device can now accept data. (The details are left as an exercise.) For buffered output, the process is similar but incorporates a subprocedure `basic_output`, which can be used by the interrupts service routine or the output routine.

Finally, suppose that a large quantity of data arrives in a short time—not so fast that the interrupt service routine attempts to interrupt itself, but rapidly enough so that the main program cannot process it. Eventually the buffer will fill up and overflow. If no protective measure is taken, data will be lost when the buffer is overwritten. One technique for preventing this loss uses the *transmit on/off* (`XON/XOFF`) protocol. When an input buffer is nearly full, it transmits a XOFF signal to the device, effectively saying "Do not send any more data." The device must respond to the signal by halting transmission of data. When the host program has removed sufficient data from the buffer so that the danger of overflow is reduced, the processor sends a XON signal indicating that the device may again send data.

Direct Memory Access

For some situations, neither programmed I/O nor interrupt-driven I/O seems to be a very desirable method. For outputting a long string of characters, programmed I/O requires total suspension of all other processing while the entire string is printed. On the other hand, interrupt-driven I/O carries a very high overhead. Reading a 500-byte paragraph into 500 consecutive locations in main memory would require 500 such interrupt steps. An improvement is possible when the data to be transferred is stored in consecutive locations. In *direct memory access* (DMA), the driver for the external device actually has access to main memory through the memory bus. The CPU requests a transfer from a DMA driver by sending it a message containing

- the memory location where the block of data will reside (presently resides in the case of output) and
- the quantity of storage.

The driver maintains its own internal registers, which serve the same roles as the MAR and MBR. The driver places one byte of input data into its MAR and the address where it should be stored in its MBR. When it is ready to transfer a byte, it breaks the processor's fetch/execute cycle and steals a single cycle (yes, it is actually called *cycle stealing*) from the CPU to transfer the byte to or from the memory location. It then executes a memory store and updates its MAR. The time stolen is just sufficient to transfer one data item to or from memory—the same as the time required to fetch an instruction. That is no more than one full fetch/execute cycle and significantly less than the amount of time needed for either programmed or interrupt-driven I/O.

The simple I/O port described earlier is a single designated memory location. The external device does not actually need access to the memory bus to communicate with the port. In order for a DMA device to place data directly into arbitrary memory locations, the device must have access to all such locations—not just to the port. The device must access these locations in a manner identical to that used by the CPU. This requires use of the memory bus. This in turn creates a new problem if the CPU and the I/O device both attempt to use the bus at the same time. This undesirable situation is a simple form of *bus contention* and must be controlled via some form of *bus arbitration* procedure. Fortunately, DMA involves a very simple form of arbitration. Requests for bus access from the I/O device are actually infrequent. In the earlier example, the 500-byte record will generate a potential (potential because it is theoretically possible that the request will slip neatly between two CPU bus requests) 500 bus-contention situations. Each such request results in the current memory cycle being preempted by the I/O request rather than the CPU request. The time lost for each byte transferred is one fraction of an instruction cycle. No significant time is lost as would be for processing a full interrupt. The relatively infrequent I/O request gets priority, in part because if the I/O request is held up, the data will soon be replaced by the next data item, resulting in lost data.

DEVICES FOR HUMAN-MACHINE COMMUNICATION

I/O devices can be divided into three groups according to their typical use. The first half of the chapter assumed that the I/O devices communicated with humans. This most visible class of devices includes several other variations. Two other classes of I/O device are storage devices and devices for intermachine communication.

Keyboards

The input half of a terminal is the keyboard, with which you are quite familiar, and which has been the model for input thus far. Almost universally, the keyboard is composed of keys that are activated either electronically or magnetically when pressed. Modern keyboards have small imbedded processors that translate the combination keys and maintain their own small buffer queues. If the user types characters prior to the requests for data from the computer, some small number could be buffered in the keyboard. It is important to remember that the keyboard and the screen are logically distinct devices, even if contained in the same cabinet. The illusion that they are a single device is maintained by most application packages and higher level languages, which automatically *echo* input from the keyboard to the screen. At the assembly language level, it becomes apparent that input from the keyboard and output to the screen are two distinct actions. It is up to the program to echo the input if that is desired.

Screen Devices

Few terminals today are hard-copy devices. Modern *video display terminals* (*vdt*) are logically and electronically more complicated than printing terminals (although the latter were mechanically more complicated). The device displays output on a screen or *monitor* using a *cathode ray tube* or *CRT,* as shown in Figure 12-2. The image itself is created by means of an electron beam that sweeps horizontally across the screen, controlled by a varying-intensity electric field. The screen is coated with phosphors, which can be energized by the electron beam and appear to light up when sufficiently activated. When a phosphor is struck by a beam of high intensity, it lights up; when the intensity is low, it does not. The internal logic of the vdt coordinates the horizontal sweep, increasing and decreasing the intensity of the beam at the appropriate instants to create bright and dark points (*pixels*) on the screen. After sweeping across one entire horizontal row, the beam returns (*horizontal retrace*) to the left side. It repeats the sweep, one row lower. This scanning process is called a *raster scan.*

A phosphor stays lighted for only a moment, so it must be continuously refreshed. In a typical CRT, the entire screen is painted by the electron beam 30 to 60 times per second. When the entire screen has been scanned, it repeats from the beginning. In a terminal with, say, 300 rows of 500 pixels each, a total of 150,000 bits is needed to describe the screen. A total of 600,000 bytes per second must be processed to keep the screen fully refreshed. Any attempt to reduce this rate of pixel painting runs into problems. Reducing the number of pixels results in reduced screen resolution (the image looks less like characters and more like a collection of larger dots). Decreasing the decay rate of the phosphors (and therefore the required refresh rate) results in images that appear to linger (like a cartoon drawing of a speeding car) after the original has been removed. And if the refresh rate is dropped too far (much less than 60 refreshes per second), the image becomes jerky, like an old-fashioned motion picture. One partial solution is an *interlaced* raster scan. In effect, an interlaced raster paints every other scan line during one vertical scan. On the next vertical pass, it processes the remaining lines. Each individual pixel is scanned only half as often, but if its image starts to fade before it is refreshed, the human eye will not detect it because the adjacent pixels have been reactivated. Many modern workstation-style terminals have an even larger challenge: screens containing a million pixels (1024 by 1024) are not uncommon today.

The raster intensity can be controlled by either of two general methods. In a character-oriented terminal, the screen is logically divided into rows of characters (typically 25 rows of 80 characters). Each character position consists of a grid of pixels, perhaps 6 by 8. In this case, the entire screen would contain 400 rows of 480 pixels each. The terminal contains enough memory to represent each pixel

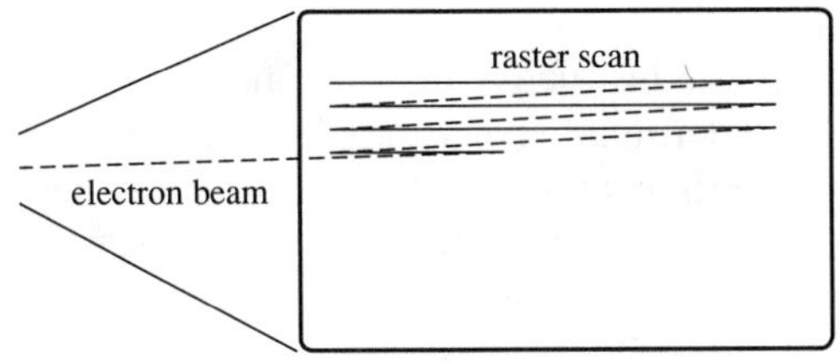

FIGURE 12-2
A raster scan device.

with a bit: 1 for on and 0 for off. The internal logic also contains templates for each printable character. For example the template for an "A" may be

```
00011000
00100100
00100100
01111110
01000010
10000001
```

An empty screen has a *bitmap* consisting of all zeros. In that case, the beam will uniformly have a low intensity. Printing an "A" requires some of the bits in the current location to be set to 1. When a terminal with an empty screen receives an 'A', it modifies the beginning of the bitmap by inserting the template for the "A." Typically, terminals have an internal processor that accepts the input as ASCII characters, generates the pattern corresponding to each arriving character, and copies the template into the bitmap. The memory for the entire screen is filled by adding new templates at the appropriate locations.

Color stations have three separate sets of phosphors and three electron beams, one each for red, green, and blue. Three phosphors are physically very near each other and appear to the human eye as a single pixel. More bits per pixel are required for color—typically typically 4 to 16. Using n bits per pixel, a screen can display 2^n distinct colors. Normally the colors can be selected from a much larger *pallet*.

On workstations or microcomputers with built-in screens, *bitmapping* can be used to maintain the screen content. Output commands to the screen actually generate a bitmap for the character directly in a section of RAM memory dedicated to the screen. There are no templates as with a character-oriented screen. The advantage is that the program can write characters in any font, size, or style that may be desired. The program is not constrained to use the fonts and styles for which the terminal has built-in templates. The output can appear exactly like a printed document and is, therefore, referred to as *what you see is what you get* (*wysiwyg*) output. The disadvantages are that significantly more bits must be generated by the processor for a given amount of display, and significantly more processing is needed to update the picture when new characters or images are added. The raster device memory is accessed directly by the CPU. Writes to the device are accomplished by writing into that memory. Delivery of data from the screen memory to the screen can be accomplished either by the CPU or by a special screen processor. The latter clearly improves the performance of the CPU, but at the cost of added hardware.

TERMINAL = SCREEN + KEYBOARD. It is instructive to think about the logic that must exist within a traditional ASCII terminal. For example, it must have a counter, which points to the current insertion point on the screen. Each new character must add 1 to the counter. The ASCII character set contains several characters that are not treated as simple printable characters. A backspace character must subtract one from the counter. A delete must subtract 1 and set all pixels corresponding to the current position to zeros. A line feed must add 80 to the pointer. A carriage return must perform the calculation: 80*(position `div` 80), etc. The ASCII chart includes many other special characters, including

hex	character	meaning
00	nul	no character
07	bel	ring the bell (buzzer) on the terminal
09	ht	horizontal tab
0C	ff	form feed
1B	esc	escape character

The terminal must process each of these individually. Since the screen is not directly connected to the keyboard, the program must echo the character to the screen. It is occasionally up to the assembly language programmer to intercept the control character and control the screen. Many terminals have the ability to display each character in a variety of ways: light on dark or dark on light, continuous or blinking, bold, italic, etc. For example, inverting a character can be accomplished by negating all of the relevant bits. The `esc` character is often used for this purpose.

HARD-COPY TERMINALS. Output to paper is another form of human-readable output. Each character is printed individually. Hard-copy terminals can be either single-character impact or dot matrix devices. In the former, a solid-character template is struck against an inked ribbon, copying its image onto the paper. Older hard-copy terminals are essentially typewriters driven by the computer. In newer versions of the impact-printing terminal, a single *hammer* is fixed and the character templates move under the hammer. *Daisy wheels* and *print chains* are of this sort. In dot-matrix printers, individual needles are struck against the paper to form the image from many dots, logically similar to the construction process of screen devices. The dot-matrix printers may either use an inked ribbon or electrostatic paper to form their images. Depending on the terminal, there may be anywhere from 7 to 24 needles vertically arranged.

PRINTERS. Hard-copy output devices that print entire lines or pages at one time are called printers. The more common (in the past, but probably not for much longer) forms of printers are impact printers, which operate on principles similar to impact and dot-matrix terminals. *Line printers* are so called because they print a full line at a time. Such printers have a separate hammer for each column. Large line printers, used with mainframe computers, can print 600 to 1000 or more lines per minute.

Increasingly popular today are *laser printers,* which use a technology almost exactly equivalent to xerography, except that the source is electronic rather than photographic. A high-voltage charge is placed on the surface of a rotating drum. A laser light beam is used to "draw" the image for the page on the surface of the drum, modifying the charge. The drum surface is bathed in toner, which is electrically attracted to the charged surface. Finally the image is transferred to a sheet of paper that is heated to bind the image permanently. A typical laser printer can print 4 to 16 high-quality pages per minute.

Many laser printers use scripting languages such as Postscript to describe the output image. From a computer organization point of view, perhaps the most significant difference between laser printers and other hard-copy devices is that output is transmitted not character by character, nor print line by print line, but as a complete image (bitmap) or as a linguistic description (e.g., Postscript) of the image.

Pointing Devices

Modern workstations and microcomputers have two primary user-input devices. In addition to the keyboard, a *deictic* device is used to communicate positional information to the computer. Deictic simply means pointing. By far the most common pointing device is the *mouse*. Internally, mice work by either of two general means: mechanical or optical. Logically, the mouse is a pointing device, rather than a character-input device like the keyboard. This means that when the button is pressed, the mouse delivers a logical record to the processor:

```
mouse_record
    x_coordinate
    y_coordinate
    button_press_info (which button, or how pressed)
```

Normally, this record is handled with an interrupt processor using a buffer just as the keyboard is handled. In practice, the mouse driver provides continuous feedback to the screen device. This feedback tells the user where the mouse is at any time. The physical mouse itself has two essential subparts: a tracking mechanism and one or more selector buttons. The tracking mechanism measures movement in the mouse position. The mechanism may be a physical ball, which rolls when the mouse is moved on a surface, or it may be a photo cell that measures movement on a grid-like surface. Either way, the mouse transmits information about its movement to the computer. The system routine that receives this input generates a cursor on the screen, which indicates the current logical location of the mouse. The selector button may be used to input the current location to a program. Just as with character input, interpretation of the data depends on the program being executed. It is generally interpreted as "at this location," which may mean simply to move the insertion point of a text editing program to that location, or to perform the command whose name (or icon) is displayed on the screen at the location where the mouse is currently located.

There are several other forms of pointing device. A *trackball* is logically identical to a mouse. The user rotates the ball directly rather than moving it across a surface. A *joystick* is similar, but usually movement of the joystick represents the rate of change of position of the cursor rather than just the change. Some terminals are equipped with a touch-sensitive screen. When the screen is touched, it delivers a record similar to that from the mouse, indicating the location at which the screen was touched. In all cases, it is up to the program to translate the deictic information into an action. This observation is also true of character input, a fact that is not always obvious to the beginning programmer.

DATA OR INTERRUPT-DRIVEN PROGRAMS. Many programs can accept either keyboard or mouse input at a given moment, either as synonyms (a mouse location might be equivalent to a succession of arrow keys; a menu item might be selectable by clicking the mouse on the location or by typing the name specified in the menu), or as alternate commands (some commands are typed; others are entered with a mouse). How can this be? How can a program be simultaneously waiting for input from two distinct sources? Once again, the system input interrupt routines intervene on behalf of the user. Many systems include system routines to check the status of an I/O device. A typical program segment that can accept input from either of two devices might look like

```
while true do
   if input exists on device 1
      then {respond to the input}
   if input exists on device 2
      then {respond to that input}
```

The loop will alternate between checking one device and then the other. Such a program is not so much a series of steps as it is a set of logical antecedents and consequents. This is clearly a user-level variation on the interrupt-driven aspect of the operating system and can also be viewed as a limited version of the message-passing facilities of object-oriented languages. Because it is becoming a more common form of programming, many newer languages include message-passing constructs explicitly tailored to this approach.

STORAGE DEVICES

Not all input and output is intended for direct communication with humans. In addition to human-computer communication devices, there exist two additional classes of input and output: data storage devices and data communication devices. The former refers to the physical realizations of secondary memory and the latter to communications between two computers or other electronic devices. Some of these other devices, such as a disk drive, are already familiar as secondary memory. On the one hand, storage devices are a form of memory, as described in Chapter

10. On the other, each device may interact with the processor logically, much like the terminal keyboard or screen. This section examines the common secondary storage devices from the perspective of the input and output operations that use them. From that perspective, the major distinction between storage devices and the human-oriented devices discussed above is that storage devices are intended to transmit large blocks or information as a package. The normal use of such a device involves a request for a large number of bytes of data to be transferred as a block from the device to the computer and vice versa.

Random Access Devices

A disk has a magnetic surface (like recording tape), which rotates on a center shaft at rates ranging from about 300 revolutions per minute for a floppy disk to over 3000 rpm for a large disk drive. The surface is logically divided into concentric circles, called *tracks* (40 to 80 for a floppy disk to a few hundred for a large hard disk). The disk drive has one or more read/write heads, which can be positioned over a given track. In a disk drive with one head, the head must be moved to the desired track. In others, one head is permanently located over each track. Each track is divided into sectors containing a fixed number of bytes, say 512. As the disk rotates, each sector of a track eventually comes under the head.

Disks are often called random-access devices because, like random-access memory, any location on the disk can be accessed at any time. They are also called direct-access devices because access does not require sequentially processing all elements of a file—it is direct. An important distinction between direct-access devices and human-interface devices is that the device must be explicitly asked for access to a specific location. In the case of a keyboard, the program waits for information to be received from the keyboard, but no explicit request needs to be sent to the keyboard. For disk access, the program must send a request to the *disk driver,* asking for data at a particular address. A full address for a piece of information on a disk is a triplet: *track, sector,* and *displacement* within the sector, illustrated in Figure 12-3. The driver retrieves the data and transmits it to the computer. The disk address—track, sector, and displacement—is not the same as a memory address. Fortunately, the system software performs most of the needed overhead to accomplish the needed translation. A hll `open` command finds the address of the beginning of a file. On each subsequent access to a direct-access file, the device driver calculates a displacement from the starting address. The driver keeps track of where on the disk a given piece of data is located relative to the read head. Figure 12-3 repeats the essential details from Figure 10-10.

To aid this process, each disk contains a *directory,* located in a standard location, perhaps track 0, sector 0. The directory indicates the starting location for all files on the disk. The `open` statement, must be executed prior to any attempt to access the file. It returns the disk address of the file, which is stored as a pointer accessible by the `input` and `output` routines. When the driver receives subsequent access commands, it calculates the physical location on the disk and

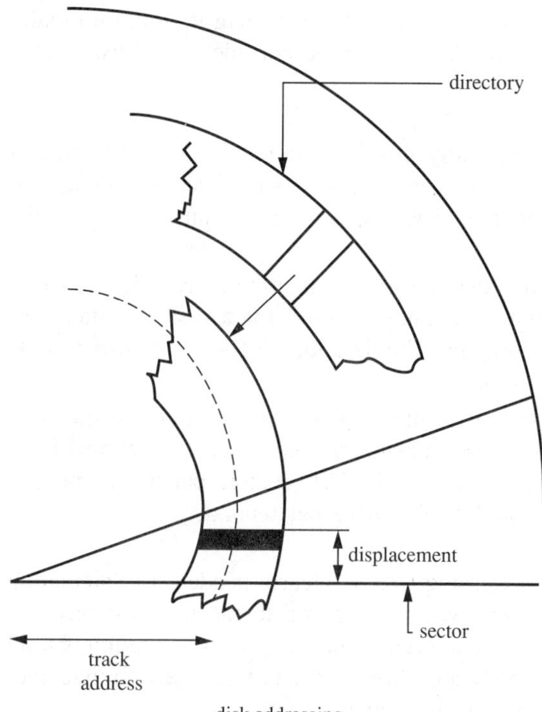

FIGURE 12-3
Disk format and addresses.

retrieves the data. Note that this process requires that a program must specify in advance which external files it will be using. Since each program uses different files and the actual physical location of any file may vary over time, there is usually no practical way in which the program can specify the exact location of an externally stored file. It is necessary to locate the logical file on the external media before the transfer. The locating process is relatively expensive (access to the directory takes as much time as any later request). It is more efficient to locate the file once and allow built-in routines to keep track of the external location. Similarly, a `close` statement

```
close(filename)
```

can be used to indicate that the program will not use the file again. In particular, it flushes all unread data from the buffer. Most higher-level languages will automatically invoke all needed close statements at the end of a program; assembly language programmers must normally close files explicitly. Generally it is a good idea to close a file when it is no longer needed. If a program ends abnormally, the automatic closing procedure may be skipped, leaving the file in an unusable state.

The time required to read a disk is considerably less than it would normally require a human to enter data. Nonetheless, it can be considerable. Disk delays are divided into three classes:

- *seek time:* the time needed to physically position the read head at the correct track. This is where multi-head disk drives have a significant advantage. A seek can take as much as 0.1 seconds (100 ms) if the head must be moved the maximum distance.
- *rotational latency:* the time for the disk to rotate so that the correct data position reaches the head—on the average, the time required for a disk to rotate 180 degrees. For a disk rotating at 300 rpm, this is about 0.1 seconds; for a 3000 rpm disk it is 0.01 seconds (10 ms).
- *transfer time:* the time for the data to actually be transferred through the head and transmitted to the computer. The transfer rate is a direct function of the rotation rate. For example, a disk with ten 500-byte sectors per track, rotating at 300 rpm, can read 5*10*500 = 250,000 bytes per second.

Additionally, some system processing time is clearly needed for calculating the correct addresses. This is minimal when compared to the time for physical movement. For example, a disk turning at 60 revolutions per second requires 8.33 msec for the rotational latency alone. In a million-instruction-per-second machine, that is time enough for 8333 machine instructions.

Disks can be made faster by reducing any of these three delays (note however that the last two are necessarily linked). The seek and latency time are independent of the amount of data transferred. For small data transfers, those two items account for essentially the entire read time. For this reason, entire sectors are often read into buffers. Individual items can then be "read" from the buffer with no further disk latency. Some disks have been made with multiple heads to reduce the seek time (or eliminate it altogether if there is a head for every track). Most have two sides, with a separate head for each surface. A disk drive can have several disks mounted on a single shaft. All surfaces rotate together, but there is a separate head for each surface. In such systems a *cylinder* is composed of the corresponding track from each surface. Since the heads typically all move in a synchronous manner, once a head has been placed on a given track, all data from the entire cylinder can be read without further head seeks. Many organizational schemes exist for the physical arrangement of data on the disk for reducing the total read time. For example, a *disk array* consists of a set of disks with logically consecutive data distributed across all of the disks. For example, the ith disk in an array of four disks might contain byte i of each word of the logical data set. When the driver receives a request for a word of data, it requests one byte from each drive. The four bytes are processed in parallel. Arrays of small but inexpensive disks have been built that outperform their larger and more expensive counterparts. Fortunately, such aspects are normally invisible to the programmer. They are usually discussed in courses on file structures or operating systems.

Disks may be classified as hard disks or floppy disks (or diskettes). The rigidity of the hard disk allows much higher rates of revolution—and, therefore, of data transfer. The distinction with respect to the nomenclature is that the former are generally made of rigid metal that enables them to rotate at a faster rate. The latter are more flexible (or floppy). Some floppy disks are not floppy at all because they are enclosed in a rigid plastic protective case. These are often called *microdiskettes*. In practice, the important distinction between hard and floppy disks are speed (hard disks are faster), capacity (hard hold more), price (hard cost more), and portability (floppies are usually easier to transport). A *Winchester disk* is a relatively small hard disk permanently sealed to keep out dust. By keeping out the dust, the disk head can be placed closed to the disk surface, enabling finer resolution of the bits on the disk and, therefore, greater capacity and greater speed.

OTHER RANDOM-ACCESS DEVICES. A *compact* or *optical disk* (or CD ROM) is logically and physically similar to a regular disk storage device. Like a regular magnetic disk, it is direct-access, revolves at a high speed, and has a head, which can be positioned at any track. There is at least one important physical distinction that does impact the logical structure. A compact disk is an optical device. Data is read from it by means of a laser beam reflected against its surface. The surface was permanently "pitted" by a high-power laser process during manufacture and cannot be written to by a user program. Such a device is useful for static information distributed from a central source, but not for variable information or user storage. On the other hand, the quantity of data that can be stored on a single disk is very large—half a gigabyte or more for CD ROMs designed to work with microcomputers. That is an order of magnitude larger than standard hard disks available for use with the same computers; enough to hold a complete encyclopedia, or the entire software library of most major software houses. But the price of this volume is speed: the CD ROM is an order of magnitude slower than most conventional disks.

One variation of the CD ROM is called a *WORM* (write once, read many). The user can write on a WORM a single time. The data is permanently etched on the surface. Such a disk is useful if the user generates large volumes of static data. The cost of such disks is falling rapidly, and they may eventually be cheap enough so that we might call them WORMTA (write once, read many, throw away) disks.

Sequential Access Devices

Some data does not demand random access. For example, data must be periodically backed up for safekeeping. In this case, a non-direct-access device can be used. The most common such device is a *tape drive*. A tape is essentially one-dimensional and therefore cannot reasonably be used if the data will be needed in an order other than sequential. Particular files on a disk can also be defined as sequential. As with a disk drive, the computer must explicitly request data from the tape drive; but unlike a disk drive, only the physically next data item can be read. When a sequential file is opened, the file pointer is set to the beginning of the file. Often such requests require human intervention to physically mount the tape. Subsequent reads simply increment the pointer. (See Figure 12-4.)

Tapes today are generally used for back-up or for physically shipping large quantities of data. Although tapes are generally regarded as somehow inferior to disks today, historically they have been around longer than disks and have contributed much to the vocabulary of I/O operations. Unlike a disk drive, a tape cannot turn continuously; it must start and stop with each request. Data cannot be reliably transmitted during the time the tape is accelerating or decelerating. There is a read delay while the tape accelerates (and a section of wasted tape called the *inter-record gap,* on which nothing can be written). To alleviate this problem, data from tapes is generally read an entire record at a time. A record is any group of bytes that can be read in this way. Thus, a single physical read operation is needed for moving an entire record. This concept is further expanded on by combining it with the concept of buffer discussed earlier. Each physical record—the data read in a single physical read operation—is composed of multiple logical records—the quantity the program thinks it is reading. At the first read request, the entire physical record is read into a buffer. Each subsequent read simply moves a logical record from the buffer and updates a pointer to the next logical record.

> ▷ *What is the relationship between this concept of "record" and the Pascal notion of record?*

OTHER SEQUENTIAL DEVICES. An *optical scanner* is a device that can read data optically or visually. Most people are familiar with the mark-sense forms used for standardized tests, etc. Newer devices can read printed characters. Such a device can save the user considerable time when the available data happens to be in human-readable form. One form of optical scanner has existed for years: the scanners used to read the IDs on checks. This type of optical scanner requires that the material be originally produced for machine use as well as human use.

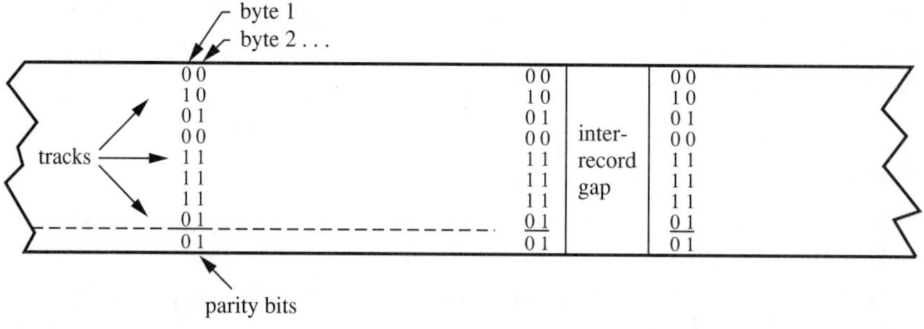

FIGURE 12-4
Tape addresses and format.

Bar code readers, such as those found in supermarket check-out counters, are also optical scanners designed to read optical material intended for machine use. Optical scanners that can read almost arbitrary text are now available. They are not perfect but can generate reasonably accurate data and are therefore useful in situations in which a human will eventually edit the material.

INTERMACHINE COMMUNICATION

Some devices for intermachine communication are probably familiar to most people—but not as I/O devices. They take the form of scientific instruments, control units in automobiles, etc. The external devices with which computers communicate may also be other computers. The most familiar situation for many programmers is that of one computer acting like a terminal to a second. Many software programs exist to enable a microcomputer to be set up to emulate a terminal. In this case, output from one computer is input to the other. Each machine views the other as a device. One aspect of such intermachine communication may seem surprising. Even though this communication requires no mechanical movement as is necessary with most devices discussed previously, this form of I/O is also slow relative to internal data movement. The reasons include data conversions from internal format to transmission format, the relative distance signals must travel, and noise on the channel that must be overcome. (Distance itself does not cause a major delay, but relays, error corrections, data conversions, signal amplification, etc., do.)

Modems

Occasionally the computer and the I/O device are separated by considerable distance. For example, a college mainframe computer may have terminals at remote campus locations, or one computer may communicate with another computer over the phone line (such as a microcomputer used as a terminal to talk to a mainframe or a bulletin board). When it is necessary to communicate over such distances it is often desirable to convert the digital computer signal into an *analog* signal—one in which a continuum of possible values can be transmitted. Phone lines, for example, are designed for carrying voices. Phone signals are manipulated in analog form. A *modem* (*mod*ulator/*dem*odulator) is a device for converting a signal from digital to analog or vice versa. Logically, a modem is invisible to the computer—it is simply part of the connection between the computer and its I/O device (which may be another computer). That is, the modem is not so much a logical device as a part of the communication path between two machines. It is important to realize that from the computer's perspective the modem does not exist. There is no logical distinction between two devices connected with or without a modem. The modem is simply the device that enables the signal to get from one location to another in a reliable manner. These observations are true whether the modem is integrated into a computer or added as a separate unit.

Intercomputer Communication

With or without modems there exist several levels of computer-to-computer communication. One important class of such communication is *computer networks*. In a computer network, two or more computers are connected so that they can pass messages back and forth and/or share external devices. For example, a user on one computer can send a message to other users of computers on the same network. A disk connected to a network may be accessed by multiple computers. This means that a program running on one computer can write data into a file. A second program, running on another computer, can read that data. Networks come in two generic forms: *local area networks* (*lan*) and *wide area networks*. The former usually links computers with an enterprise—within a classroom or a building. Wide area networks connect computers over larger geographical areas—across the country or around the world.

Of course, networking machines creates another set of communications problems. For example, how does one computer specify to the network which other computer it wishes to communicate with? A number of procedures or protocols, such as *Ethernet*, have been established to facilitate such communication. The study of networks and of distributed processing investigates these topics further.

A program can be established on one computer to run in a coordinated manner with other computers. The best known example of such coordination is automated bank-teller machines. Each machine is able to access a central computer to verify the user's bank balance and to communicate transactions. The machines belonging to various banks are connected, so that if a customer of bank A uses a machine from bank B, the latter bank's machine simply contacts the first bank's machine to verify and communicate all relevant information about the transaction. Such integrated networks of machines are said to engage in *distributed processing*. A second form of distributed processing that many students will be familiar with is automatic registration for classes. A local computer may act simply as a terminal to a mainframe, or it may act as an intermediate device, keeping track of a student's tentative requests, checking feasibility in terms of time overlap, etc., and finally transmitting the completed request to the host machine. In such a system, much of the low-level processing can be *downloaded* from the single central computer to the numerous peripheral machines.

If machines work together in an even more coordinated manner, it is called *parallel processing*—parallel because the programs running on two processors run at the same time or in parallel. The communication needed between parallel computers is often extensive and requires special new forms for processing and controlling the data flow. The topics of networking and parallel computation are addressed briefly in Chapter 16.

Instrumentation and Control

In addition to other computers, I/O is also necessary between a computer and specialized external devices. A scientific measuring device may produce thousands or even millions of measurements in a very short time period. It is clearly undesirable for a human to transcribe the output of such a device into a computer; therefore, the task is frequently automated. A little reflection should convince you that from the processor's point of view, there is no logical distinction between data arriving from an automated measuring device in a wind tunnel, or a picture from an interplanetary vehicle or from a keyboard. The former may arrive faster, and at more regular intervals, but there is no distinction of any importance to the logic of the program.

Similarly, output from a computer can be sent to an external device, such as a robot arm or an automated control valve in a factory. Or the output could be used for something as mundane as turning lights on and off. Again, the logic of a program is not impacted by the destination of the data. There may be distinctions in device speed or range of legal values, but no logical distinction.

COMMUNICATIONS LINKS BETWEEN DEVICES: A POTPOURRI OF COMMUNICATION TERMS

The computer user frequently feels bombarded with technical terms, which may appear in only limited contexts. The world of input and output seems especially prone to this phenomenon. What follows is a brief introduction to many of the terms that seem to come up in the context of I/O. The descriptions are intended to be glossary-like, designed not to provide full understanding but to provide a definition in case the reader comes across the terms in other reading.

DATA CHANNEL. A data channel is a specialized I/O processor. The CPU can be connected to a data channel and the data channel connected to one or more I/O devices. The channel can take care of much of the mundane work of I/O, freeing up the main processor for its "real" job: processing data. The complexity of the channel depends on how much of the I/O task is to be downloaded to the channel. For example, DMA drivers must perform extensive address calculation and bus interaction.

PARALLEL/SERIAL. Although internal movement of data within a computer is generally performed in parallel, it is not always feasible to do so between devices. Cables composed of 8 to 10 parallel wires (often called ribbon cables because of their physical appearance) are quite expensive. On the other hand, the external device itself may be so slow that there is nothing to be gained by sending a parallel signal. When data is to be transmitted in serial, a parallel-to-serial converter is needed. Chapter 9 describes one logical structure that could provide the service: a multiplexor with a clock signal that sequentially specifies each bit to be transmitted. An even simpler method uses a logical shifter, perhaps with an extend bit. After each shift, the bit that dropped off is transmitted. Special registers, called *shift-registers,* are designed for this purpose.

DUPLEX: FULL/HALF. Full duplex lines are capable of transmitting data in each direction simultaneously. They are far more common today than half duplex lines, which can only send signals in one direction at a time and they require a handshaking protocol to ensure that the devices at each end do not attempt to transmit data simultaneously.

SYNCHRONOUS/ASYNCHRONOUS. When a computer sends a message to its peripheral device, the device may not know that the message is coming. If the device needs a moment to recognize that a signal is coming in, some data may be lost. It is essential that the message be received in its entirety. Therefore, some mechanism is needed for coordinating the communication. One method requires that the sender notify the receiver that a character is coming via a special signal (say, an all-1 byte) and then transmit the character immediately thereafter. At any random point in time, there is no guaranteed synchronization between the two devices. Therefore, such communication is called *asynchronous*. If the two devices are synchronized by a mutual clock signal, they are said to be *synchronous*. In practice, synchronization can also be achieved either by continuous transmissions of empty characters or by block transmission. The signal is synchronized at the beginning of a block of data that is transmitted sequentially.

I/O TRANSMISSION DEVICES. Collectively, the register and port models as described thus far are sometimes called *programmed I/O,* because the I/O process is under CPU program control, directed by the input or output procedure (in contrast with the method described in the next section). A wide variety of hardware devices are manufactured to serve as I/O ports for programmed data transfer. The most common classes of such devices are *Parallel Input/Output* or PIO (transmits all bits of the data byte simultaneously over eight parallel lines), *Universal Asynchronous Receiver Transmitter* (*UART*), and *Universal Synchronous Asynchronous Receiver Transmitter* (*USART*) devices (which both transmit the data serially, one bit at a time, using a single data line). The latter two are universal in the sense that a single design will work for many types of peripheral or CPU. "Parallel" and "serial" indicate that the bits of the data byte are transmitted simultaneously or in sequence. "Synchronous" and "asynchronous" refer to the bit-level coordination method between sender and receiver. In addition to the functions previously discussed, these devices typically have the ability to detect errors and inform the CPU by setting the status byte to an error value distinct from true or false.

HISTORICAL NOTES

Punched Cards and Paper Tape

Chapter 11 described the bootstrap process, including one very early form of input device: the toggle switch. Programmers realized the problems of such input devices very early on. The two major drawbacks were speed and storability. Every time input was needed, the programmer had to input the data directly. What was needed was a machine-readable format that could be physically stored so that data (or commands or programs) could be entered with little or no human intervention. Two early physical forms were paper tape and punched cards. The punched card may be considered to be the grandparent of most future input mechanisms. In fact, the original punched card predates the computer itself by well over half a century. The concept was first employed for information processing by Herman Hollerith, founder of the Tabulating Machine Company, to help process the 1890 census data. The Tabulating Machine Company eventually became the International Business Machine Corporation and donated its name as the popular name for punched cards: the IBM card. Hollerith's own name appears in older versions of Fortran as a format specification for literals.

The format of the IBM card was 80 columns (a width that has persisted to this date in many terminal designs and versions of some programming languages), each with 12 fields, which could be punched or not punched. The early card readers read the cards by means of wire brushes. The card passed over the brushes, which would make contact with terminals wherever there were holes in the card. Later readers used photoelectric cells to detect the holes. The physical movement required for punched cards greatly limited the speed of card readers (10–20 cards a second was pretty good. In fact, the speed was normally stated in *cards per minute*). But the real limiting factor of the punched card was that it was not interactive; Using a keypunch the programmer typed all of the needed lines—including any needed data—*prior* to submitting a program. This meant that the programmer must anticipate the entire program run. Correction of an error required physically searching the *deck* of cards for the line, removing the card from the deck, completely retyping it (although keypunches did provide a mechanism for duplicating the correct columns), placing a new card in the deck, and finally submitting the job. Job submission was typically by means of handing it to an operator who loaded it into a card reader. This noninteractive mode is called *batch processing* and is still used today (although the data resides on a disk, not on cards) for special purpose tasks such as running a large, expensive program overnight. It was not unusual for such a task to have a *turnaround* time of many minutes or hours or—in extreme cases—days. The very long delays were due to total system load, but it is easy to see that the nature of the process itself would take minutes for the I/O operation in the typical situation. Many anachronisms still exist as holdovers from the days of punched cards: some persons use "CC" for (card) column. Cards were very column-dependent. The EBCDIC alternative to ASCII is closely correlated with the punched-card codes. Some people still refer to system control statements as "control cards". Fortunately, punched cards are fading from most of our memories—and with them the strange naming conventions.

Paper tape was a similar medium, with data encoded by means of holes punched in the paper. Since it was a tape, there was no built-in size limit of 80 columns. Paper tape was sometimes used for bootstrap programs. An interesting aspect of paper tape was that hard-copy terminals were sometimes equipped with tape punches that could punch on tape a copy of the data printed on the page. This tape could later be used to reenter data rather than retyping.

Pascal's Get and Put

The Pascal language contains two input primitives, `get` and `put`, designed in part to provide insight into the I/O process. Unfortunately, Pascal was designed prior to widespread acceptance of interactive I/O. The "insight" provided may have been helpful to punched-card users but now confuses as many of today's students as it helps. The actual model for `get` and `put` resembles punched cards, or perhaps disk I/O, more than it does a modern interactive terminal. With that it mind, it may be useful to review the mechanisms by which Pascal accomplishes its I/0 (See Figure 12-5).

The Pascal `read` operation for a single character is equivalent to the following two steps:

```
assign item⇐file_pointer↑;
get(file pointer);
```

In the first step, the value currently pointed to by the file pointer is moved into the input variable. Then the `get` procedure moves the file pointer to the next item in the file. This definition of read contains the implicit assumption that the file pointer somehow points to something prior to execution of the read statement. The definition of Pascal states that the `open` statement actually reads the first character into the computer and initializes the file pointer to point to that character. This clearly cannot be the case with interactive input. If it were, the program would stop at the `open` statement and wait for the user to type the first input character. However, if that input comes from cards, at the beginning of execution the system can easily copy the first card into a buffer and set the file pointer to the

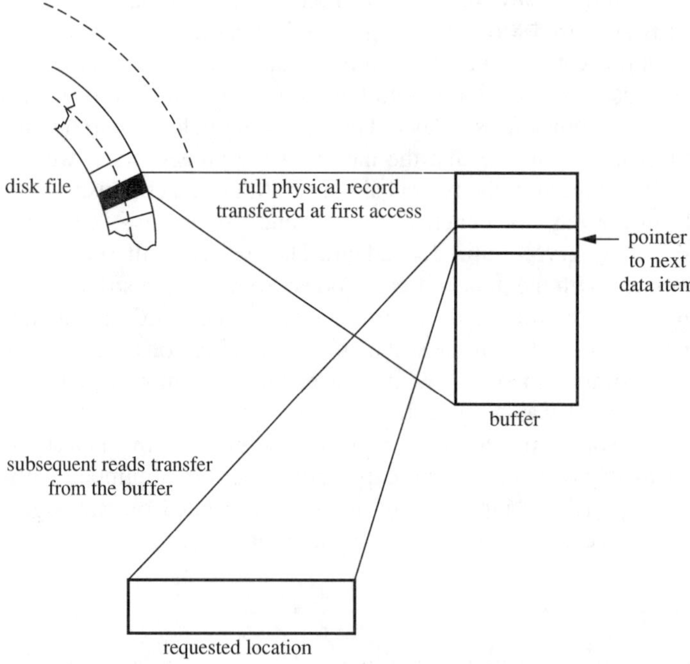

FIGURE 12-5
An I/O buffer.

first character in the buffer. Suddenly, the entire process make sense. The first read will move the value pointed to by the file pointer into `item`. `Get` will then move the pointer to the second character on the card.

A number of techniques have been developed for Pascal to circumvent the problems. A typical solution, called *lazy I/O,* delays setting the file pointer until it is absolutely necessary. In such a system, the `open` statement does not initialize the file pointer. In effect, the order of steps in the `read` procedure are simply reversed.

```
get(file pointer)
assign item⇐file_pointer↑;
```

SUMMARY

Input and output operations cannot be fully described in terms of the fetch/execute cycle. Some method is needed for coordinating the processor and the external device. Simple coordination can be achieved through I/O registers or I/O ports, but because of the speed differences any robust system must rely on interrupts. Interrupts have the advantage that the system can perform useful work while waiting for an I/O device to be ready. They also suggest a relatively new approach to programming: interrupt or data-driven programs. Buffers can be used to further improve the performance of I/O operations. Direct memory access allows an I/O device to place data directly into RAM.

Devices can be categorized according to the nature of the communication: human-machine interaction (keyboards, screens, mice), data storage (disks, tapes), and machine-to-machine communication (modems, networks). The general area of I/O devices provides many of the most visible examples of the changes that have occurred in computing over the past 25 years.

EXERCISES

12.1. Modify the GEM machine language so that the copy command can make reference to the I/O registers. What changes were necessary? Are safeguards needed to ensure that no other operation may access the register? What if other operations were allowed such access?

12.2. Modify the GAL language to create explicit register I/O commands. What additional modifications needed to be made to the language to accomplish this?

12.3. Provide two distinct criticisms of the following claim: One mechanism for a (I/O register-oriented) machine to detect an input character is to wait for a return to be typed, signaling that there must now be input in the input register.

12.4. Suppose a computer had multiple I/O devices numbered 0 through n, and that the port for the first device was at memory address M (and M+1). Give an equation that describes the locations of the status and data bytes for a given device. Modify the I/O port version of the assembly language input routine to accept a device number, calculate the port address, and retrieve the data from the port. Finally, set up a list of equate constants for a hypothetical list of devices and pass the device identification using these constants.

12.5. Suppose an interrupt vector starts at location `vector`, and contains 10 (four-byte) addresses for the various interrupt routines. Write code that will jump to routine number n, using only address modes that are legal in the GAL language. What additional addressing mode could be useful for this purpose?

12.6. Most vdt devices are capable of *scrolling* the output—as each new line is added, the existing lines of output are each moved up one row to make room for the new line. The topmost line scrolls off the top. The terminal must maintain an internal memory structure to represent the entire screen. If a terminal had 25 80-character rows and each character required eight rows of six pixels, a first approximation might be simply an 480 by 25 array of bytes (one byte representing each "vertical slice" through a character). The problem with this arrangement is that every time the screen scrolled one row, all 12,000 bytes would have to be moved. Even if the device is slow compared to memory, 12,000 data movements might be very expensive. Create an alternative data structure for the screen memory that would eliminate this problem.

12.7. For various experiments in psychology, reaction times are measured. For some experiments, an accuracy of .01 second is needed. Assuming 60 refreshes per second, what is the shortest time in which a new image can appear on the screen? What does this say about the use of CRTs for such experiments?

12.8. Construct, at the digital electronic level, an output port composed of a data byte and a control byte. The control byte should reflect current status of the port: true if there is data to be output and false if there is not. You may assume that only the CPU will place data into the port and that only the device will attempt to read the data byte. *Hint:* recall that reads and writes to memory locations generate memory select and read/write signals, both of which the location would receive.

12.9. Modify the `output` and `output-interrupt` routines to use a curcular queue. The straightforward method requires that the pointers front and back be compared against some maximum size each time they are incremented. If the pointers are each one byte in size and the queue has 256 locations, an automatic wraparound can be achieved. Try to create this form. What additional precautions are needed in the case of a circular buffer?

12.10. At the time when card readers were common input devices, computers frequently had six-bit bytes. With 12 fields per card-column,

(*a*) How many distinct values could be stored in a column?

(*b*) How many bytes could be stored on a card?

12.11. Write GAL routines for buffered output, both the output routine and the output interrupt service routine.

12.12. Suppose a keyboard has 64 keys plus a shift key. Sketch a circuit that translates signals from individual keys into ASCII.

12.13. The processor can process thousands of instructions in the time required for a single output statement. Yet it is often difficult to witness this phenomenon. Try writing a program that produces a steady stream of output, requiring new computations for each line. A good example is an amortization table. The amortization formula

$$\text{payment} = \frac{\text{principal} * i}{1 - (1 + i)^{-n}}$$

is used to calculate a monthly mortgage payment, where principal is the amount of the mortgage, i is the monthly interest rate, and n is the number of payments.

Humans generally measure the latter two values using years rather than months. A table of interest rates is useful to someone who wants to purchase a home. Write a program that generates a table of payments for various principals ($40–200,000), interest rates (8–15%/year), and durations (15–20 years). The algorithm should calculate the results between output statements. Compare the output time with a trivial program, say, one that prints nothing but zeros.

12.14. Suppose a machine has eight bits to describe a pixel. Then, each pixel can be one of 256 colors. Describe how those 256 colors can be selected from a larger pallet. Does this imply that you can represent more than 256 values with eight bits?

12.15. On a machine with a mouse, find the format of the mouse input. Write an interrupt-driven routine to receive input from the mouse and place an "x" at the location where the mouse was clicked.

12.16. The ASCII character 07_{16} is the bell. Write a program that rings the bell on your terminal. Put it into a loop to ring it several times in succession.

12.17. Find the ASCII codes for deleting the last character and for deleting the entire screen. Write a program to test them.

12.18. Write a program that writes to a disk, one character at a time. Write a second program that reads the data back in. Modify the program so that it writes until the disk is full. Compare the amount of data written to the advertised capacity of the disk.

PART VI

EXTENSIONS

Some topics traditionally associated with computer organization courses do not fit precisely into any of the five models of computation discussed in the previous sections. The topics included in Section VI are extensions that take ideas presented in earlier chapters and push them further. Some of the topics, such as parallel computation, cannot truly be described within those models. Others, such as real arithmetic, may not be appropriate within a given context of machine and curriculum (if your machine does not support hardware floating point operations, real arithmetic might be better discussed in another course, such as numeric methods). These topics have been pulled out of the mainstream of the text and collected here. Each may be covered or not covered without affecting the remaining chapters.

The first two chapters address aspects of computer organization that may not be directly applicable for a particular environment. The material is nonetheless important in environments that support the specific tools.

CHAPTER 13: DEBUGGERS, DEBUGGING, AND ANTIBUGGING. The debugger is the most important tool available to the assembly language programmer, who often feels "thrown to the wolves" with little protection. Careful programming and use of tools reduces the anxiety level. (Chapter 13 assumes some knowledge of material from the first four chapters.)

CHAPTER 14: REAL ARITHMETIC. Throughout the text, all numeric operations have been integer. Many machines also support real arithmetic, but real numbers must necessarily use a distinct internal representation. (Chapter 14 assumes knowledge of material through Chapter 4.)

The final two chapters explore variations on and alternatives to the general models. Although the material may be beyond the general scope of most courses using this text, it serves as an important introduction to advanced courses in architecture.

CHAPTER 15: VARIATIONS ON THE VON NEUMANN MODEL: MICROPROGRAMMED AND RISC MACHINES. Classically, most machines have been microcoded (CISC). Recently, the RISC model has challenged many basic assumptions. The two concepts provide additional models of computation, which interact with the machine language and digital logic views. (Chapter 15 assumes knowledge of material through Chapter 10.)

CHAPTER 16: ALTERNATIVES TO THE VON NEUMANN MODEL: PARALLEL MACHINES. Many computer scientists now believe that the best approach to improving machine performance is using two or more processors in parallel. (Chapter 16 assumes knowledge of material through Chapter 12).

CHAPTER 13

DEBUGGERS, DEBUGGING, AND ANTIBUGGING[1]

One of the most important services provided by the higher-level language compiler is protection from errors. Compilers and interpreters detect large classes of errors, providing appropriate error messages to the programmer. But protection is not the same as prevention. On detecting an error or problem, these systems provide a message that hopefully contains enough information to enable the programmer to fix the problem. Errors detected include everything from improperly declared variables to arithmetic type mismatches to incorrect array references. Many interpreters also protect the programmer by interpreting run-time anomalies. Assemblers provide very little of this protection. In addition, assembly programs invariably are significantly longer (measured in lines of code) than the corresponding higher-level language program. By now, you have explored assembly language briefly, but enough so that you may be wondering how on earth you will ever keep track

[1] The material in this chapter assumes completion of Chapters 1 through 4. Parts of the chapter can be understood earlier, but the references to hexadecimal arithmetic in particular need Chapter 4. A small amount of material (e.g., pointers) is related to Chapter 5. Much of the material is closely related to Chapter 3.

of a working program—never mind one that is not working. Partial solutions to this quandary can be found in the following guidelines. There are two groups of suggestions. The first are applicable to any language and may even sound rather repetitious at this point. The second group is specific techniques for dealing with assembly language problems.

GENERAL GUIDELINES

Preparation

As described in Chapter 3, good programmers prepare for debugging at the time that they write their code. Some of the important advance preparation techniques discussed there included the following.

CHECK POINTS. Use invariants to determine points in your program at which the results are predictable. These points are your first line of defense against errors. Identify them *before* attempting to run your program and include a statement of the relation as a comment. Provide output statements so that you can see the values. (Data will normally be in an internal format.)

ASSUME THAT YOUR PROGRAM IS IN ERROR. Be prepared for errors. You will have them, so anticipate as many as possible. Include information that will help detect and correct the problems.

PLANS. Always have a testing plan. Decide in advance how to tell if the program is correct at a given point. Again, the time to build a plan is when you write the code—not later.

Assembly Error Correction Tools

Error messages in assembly can not only be especially sparse, but can also seem catastrophic: the machine just seems to die. At first, it seems unbearably difficult to get any feedback information. For example, consider the difficulties of outputting simple decimal values in a human-readable form. Use of the available tools will aid the task.

DEBUGGERS. Most assembly language systems provide a very powerful tool called a *debugger.* Use it! It is essential for assembly language programming. Most of this chapter will deal with the use of debuggers for understanding the workings of assembly language programs. (The debugger will allow you to explore a running program—but the representations will be the internal form).

POSITIVE FEATURES OF ASSEMBLY LANGUAGE. Unlike hlls, assembly language is very closely related to the machine. Therefore, it should be possible to follow execution precisely, on an instruction-by-instruction basis. There are few surprises, no unknowns. Because the syntax is simple, problems due to complex expressions (e.g., operator-precedence problems) are almost nonexistent. Using the debugger, you will be able to identify every line of your code as it appears in the machine. But obtaining output from a program is tricky, so you will need to think like the computer "thinks." Because the syntax is simple, you can always interpret an instruction precisely.

Computer and Assembler Error Messages

In hlls, error messages are generally stated in terms of the higher-level language itself. Messages are usually relatively detailed, providing specific information about the item causing the problem. One fact that surprises most novice assembly language programmers is the small number of possible errors. Higher-level languages contain traps that detect many errors and describe the problem to the programmer, hopefully in a helpful and constructive message. But assembly language deals with the machine on its own terms. These terms generally mean that as long as the computer can do something—anything—with the instructions that you have provided, it will do so. The results of the actions do not have to be meaningful, just so long as the operation can be performed. For example, most hlls can detect execution errors such as arithmetic overflow (integer value would not fit in the storage location), or an array subscript that is out of bounds. The computer itself does not care that the value overflowed or the subscript was too large, so it usually provides no error interrupt.

It is important to realize that however aggravating error messages may seem, they are important messages informing the programmer of dangerous conditions—either current and real, or potential. Whenever you encounter an error message, note what it says. Do this even if you do not understand the message. Someone from whom you seek help with your problem may be able to help you more quickly if you can relate the message (and other information). Additionally, since there are actually relatively few distinct error messages to be found in AL, you will eventually start to recognize them. Even if you do not understand the message itself, you will begin to associate it with particular circumstances. Thus, when you encounter the message in the future, you may be able to use that association for understanding the error.

Classes of Error

Recall that the vast majority of errors can be classified as falling into one of three groups:

1. *syntax or assembly errors.* These are detected by the assembler and are the result of a statement that has no legal interpretation in the assembly language.
2. *run-time errors.* These produce an error message when the machine attempts to execute your code.
3. *logic errors.* These produce no error message even though the program produces incorrect results.

Thinking about Errors

Combine your previous knowledge of programming and debugging with your knowledge of internal representation to determine what is wrong with your program. For example, suppose that a program contained the line

```
compare    'A'⇒ reg0
```

and although you were sure that `reg0` contained the character "A", the test returns a "not-equal" result. Create a set of hypotheses about the problem:

- `reg0` was being compared to the number A_{16}, not the character "A";
- `compare` has a default length other than one byte (one character)
- the contents of `reg0` had somehow been destroyed, etc.

One possibility is that the incorrect items were being compared. In fact, without the immediate sign (e.g., "#" in GAL) in front of the operand, it likely is interpreted as an address: $A_{16} = 10_{10}$. The contents of address 10 are probably being used. If you could somehow get inside the computer and examine the contents of both the RAM address and the register, examine the exact structure of the internal command (to see if it contains the "A"), and check the results one step at a time, etc., you could narrow the possibilities significantly. Fortunately, there is a tool to do exactly that: the debugger. Each machine or run-time error causes an interruption in the flow of your program. Control may then be transferred—either automatically or at the programmer's request—to the debugger. The programmer may then use the debugger to attempt to find the cause of the error, fix the error, continue the program, or get out to re-edit the source code.

DEBUGGERS

A debugger is a service program capable of examining the state of your program and reporting the results to you. It can expose the content of registers or main memory, display the current instruction, allow you to step through a program slowly, and even help you modify a program without returning to the editor. Many higher-level languages have some form of debugger. Assembler debuggers are not unlike those debugging tools. In keeping with the generic spirit of this text, the following sections describe general properties of debuggers, illustrating them using GAD, the Generic Assembly Debugger. The debuggers provided with other assembly languages will vary in the specifics but will provide most of the same basic support mechanisms.

Entering the Debugger

There are two primary ways in which a program may enter a debugger: error entries and user-request entries. In the former case, the computer detects a run-time error, but it does not simply stop execution of your program with an error message, as happens in a hll. In assembly language, your program will be temporarily interrupted or suspended, and control will be transferred to the debugger. A very brief error message is provided, together with summary information describing the state of the machine at the time of the error. At that point, the programmer may use the debugger to determine the exact nature of the error.

The second means of entering the debugger—user request—may occur at any point the programmer requests. This provides an excellent antibugging technique, in which the programmer can follow the progress of a program prior to the occurrence of an error, keeping track of potential problems. When an error does occur, the programmer has a body of contextual knowledge to bring to bear on the solution. Once a program is working, the forced entries can be removed. The programmer will often need to gain access to the debugger to check the progress of a program, either because it is not working correctly or because the programmer is being cautious. There are two primary ways to accomplish this.

THE DEBUGGER COMMAND. The programmer can place a debugger `trap` instruction at any point in an assembly program, causing the program to pause and transfer control to the debugger. In GAL, the command is

```
trap    debugger
```

A prudent programmer will place several of these in the program at the time of writing. The program probably has an error, so why not provide the search tools up front? If the program happens to work the first time, enjoy the pleasant experience.

PHYSICAL INTERRUPT. The second means of forced entry is especially useful in the case of infinite loops. At any time, the programmer can force entry into the debugger by pushing the interrupt button on the machine. This is not quite as satisfactory as the debugger command because you cannot easily identify the exact location of entry. Since you cannot time your own actions to the clock speed of a computer, an undetermined number of instructions will have executed. Fortunately, infinite loops often involve very few statements, so they can be identified relatively quickly in the debugger. The interrupt button does have the advantage that you do not need to specify the entry point in advance. The button for a specific machine may be a keystroke combination or a switch provided specifically for the purpose.

Basic Debugger Display

The debugger provides a rich world of tools for examining the contents of an assembly program, including display of important default information, requests for specific information, alteration of memory, tracing capabilities, or simply choices of how you return to your program. The debugger may display all important information continually, or it may require the user to ask for certain items explicitly. Among the most important information available are the following.

REGISTERS. The contents of each register can be displayed, usually in hexadecimal. It may seem annoying that interpretation is usually shown as hex digits (typically eight digits for a 32-bit register), no matter what data the registers represent: binary number, ASCII character, Boolean value, etc. Also, there are values in the registers, even if you have not used them, since a previous program may have used them. And there may be data in all bytes, even though you only used one byte or one word of a register.

REASON FOR ENTRY. This should either be a run-time error (e.g., illegal instruction), or `user-request` if the programmer explicitly requested entry to the debugger.

NEXT INSTRUCTION. This appears as a *disassembly* of the instruction. The command will appear structurally identical to the source code, but the original mnemonic names of operands are no longer available. All operands are displayed as internal addresses (in hex). Note that the instruction displayed is not the offending instruction, but the instruction that is to be executed *next*. Thus, the error message may say "divide by zero", but the instruction displayed might be a `copy`. You will need to look in your own listing to determine the culprit instruction that is immediately prior to one shown.

There will be additional information, most of which appears confusing to the novice programmer. You should immediately familiarize yourself with the display until you can identify the preceding items among the items on the screen.

Examining Memory Content

The most direct and frequently used tools in the debugger are ones for examining the content of various storage locations: registers or main memory, a single byte or a block. Examination of the data is the primary tool for determining the state of your program:

- By examining variables and registers, you can check to see if all intermediate results are as expected. You can tell if input has been successfully received.
- By examining counters you can determine how many times a loop has been executed.
- By examining constants you can detect stray data changes.

REGISTERS. Examine a single data register using the

```
display-register  <n>
```

command. Thus,

```
display-register  0
```

will display the content of register 0,

```
display-register  7
```

will display register 7. Most debuggers allow you to specify multiple registers:

```
display-register  0-7
```

Many debuggers display the register content automatically, so this instruction may not be needed very often.

MEMORY. You can also examine main memory. The display memory command

```
display-Memory    <address>
```

will display a block of memory starting at the address specified. Typically, the block is 16 bytes long, and the display contains both hex and ASCII interpretations. It is often possible to request larger blocks:

```
display-Memory    1000 - 1100
```

will display all memory cells between 1000 and 1100_{16}. A common variation is the Display Byte command:

```
display-Byte      <address>
```

which will display the contents of the single byte at the specified memory address. You may not know yet where the RAM data that you need is located, so this instruction seems very cumbersome at first. You will see, below, that you can always find the needed location.

CONVERSION OF DATA. Most debuggers display all information in the internal form: hexadecimal. But when you wrote your program you probably specified many values in decimal, or as ASCII characters, so you will often want to convert the displayed hex value to see if it is the decimal value you expect. Obviously, you could easily perform the calculation yourself, but the debugger will do it for you. The convert instruction looks like

```
convert           <value-specification>
```

The most direct way to specify the value is simply by typing the value itself. In response, the debugger will display the value in several forms, perhaps unsigned hex number, signed hex number, decimal, binary, and ASCII. Thus,

```
convert           41
```

might produce

```
41 = 41₁₆, +41₁₆, 65₁₀, 0100 0001₂, "A"ASCII
```

The multiple forms are especially useful if you are not quite sure what sort of data the location contains. Since the character or the decimal are both shown, you can make an educated guess at the correct interpretation.

When you have an error or anticipate a problem, the preceding commands may be used in combination to examine most aspects of the current state of the program. For example, if you have passed a character to a subroutine, you may look in the appropriate register to see if it is there. If you do not recognize the representation, use the convert command to see if it is the correct character.

SPECIFYING NUMBERS. By default, debuggers also expect input values to be hexadecimal numbers, which makes sense since the debugger is dealing primarily with internal representations. However, this may be annoying to the human. Numbers other than hex values may be specified by including an indication of the intended base whenever you use a number. For example, the GAD debugger allows several possible input representations (other debuggers have similar choices):

Format	syntax	example
Hex number	just the number	C3 or 123
Decimal number	precede with a "D:"	D:10 (that's one more that D:9)
Binary number	precede with a "B:"	B:1010
Characters	place in quotes.	'A' or '2'

Thus, the specifications 41, D65, B1000001, and 'A' would all be used to specify the same value. For example,

```
display-byte        100
```

and

```
display-byte        D:256
```

have the same interpretation. Beware of problems related to the hex symbols for the values 10 to 15. For example, the colon serves to distinguish D:9 = 9_{10} from $D9_{16} = 217_{10}$.

REFERENCING MEMORY VALUES. If `reg2` contains the value 23423475, one could use the instruction

```
convert             23423475
```

to check the decimal equivalent. Typing the command is cumbersome at best, and error-prone at worst. A shortcut allows you to request the debugger to convert the "contents of register 2":

```
convert             contents(reg2)
```

Any register can be specified in this way. Similarly indirect references (see Chapter 5) can be followed using the contents command. If `reg3` serves as a pointer to an array in RAM, the command

```
display-memory      contents(reg3)
```

will display the contents of the array whose address is contained in `reg3`.

Finally, convert can act as a mini-calculator by specifying an expression rather than a simple number:

```
convert             3+4
```

will behave exactly the same as

```
convert             7
```

Again, combinations of these commands provide flexibility. The command

```
display-byte        contents(reg3) + 10
```

could be used to examine the sixteenth byte of the above array. The command

```
display-memory      contents(PC)
```

could be used to examine the next instruction.

Tracing

It is often useful to step or trace through a program. By executing one instruction at a time, pausing after each, you can verify that control is at the expected statement and examine any relevant memory locations. Once in the debugger, you can ask the machine to execute a single assembly language instruction with the `trace` command:

```
trace
```

After executing a single instruction, the display of such items as register content and next command is updated.

Trace is especially useful when you know approximately, but not exactly, where the program went wrong. Once in the debugger, note any relevant information and step through a few instructions until you can match the executed instructions with a location in your program code. Note that there is no way to "undo" the trace. Therefore, execution may be well past the error before you locate it in your code. But do note that in most cases repeating execution of the program with the same input will generate the same error at the same point. Reassemble your code with a debugger trap inserted prior to the error location. Since you now know where the error occurred, reexecute the code and examine the state when the error occurs.

Even better use of trace can be made if you force entry into the debugger. For example, you can force entry at a point in the program prior to the known erroneous code. Check to see that all values are as you expect. Then trace through the program, checking all important values after each step, until you find one that is incorrect. Note that the instruction displayed in the debugger output is the one that you will next execute using trace. Each time you trace a step, the new next instruction is displayed. Thus, you can follow your code as you trace, to determine not only the values that you compute, but whether or not a jump was taken. If the PC changes suddenly, there was a jump.

As you trace, always think ahead to determine what result you *expect* the next instruction to have. This is very important. By thinking ahead, surprises will make themselves obvious. Remember: you know what you intended better than you know what the program actually did. It is the discrepancies that will help you debug. It may be necessary to repeat the process, not in the vain hope that it will work the next time, but because you may think of a value that you should check at a given point. Do not hesitate to restart the program and reenter the debugger.

The assembly process removes reference to symbolic names in your program. Thus, the debugger will display all references to operands as numeric addresses. These will be very hard to interpret at first (but see below). The instruction itself and its form—size of operand, registers involved and so on—can be seen. What you cannot tell is which "`copy : byte` from memory to `reg1`" is involved. Therefore, it is necessary to be able to isolate the problem into some small section of your program by careful use of `output` and checkpoints.

Many debuggers allow a variation on the trace command:

```
trace n
```

which traces through *n* steps of the program. Some allow a variation that skips over subroutine calls, which is very useful if you are confident that the subroutine works correctly, or if the subroutine involves input. (If trace executes only a single instruction and then returns to the debugger, any input will be treated as input to the debugger—*not to your program*. Thus, tracing through a section of your program that attempts to receive input will act as if the input has not yet been received.)

The command

```
display-Instruction <address>
```

can be used to display or view any command, without executing it. This is useful both to help pinpoint the location in the program and to predict the results as you trace.

EXITING THE DEBUGGER. After you have investigated the contents of your program, you will want to leave the debugger and (hopefully) return to your program. There are several options, ranging from returning to a specific point in your program to restarting the entire machine. The commands are listed here in order of increasing time required to get back into your program.

Return to program at current location. You can request that control of your program continue with the next instruction (the one displayed), using the command

```
go
```

If you have not performed any trace steps, `go` will continue your program from the statement *after* the command that forced entry into the debugger. If you have traced, control will not repeat any statements that you have executed using trace but will continue with the next unexecuted instruction. Unfortunately, the `go` command may not accomplish what you wish because the error may have further repercussions. For example, if the error was an illegal address due to an improperly aligned instruction, the next instruction will also be improperly aligned. Also, since the "bad" instruction does not complete execution successfully, future instructions, which depend upon that instruction, may have bad data.

Restart the program. You can restart your program from the beginning with the command

```
restart
```

Note that this does not reload a clean copy of your program. If the program has changed some values that do not get reinitialized, reexecution will not duplicate the original. The option is useful if you realize that you have traced past an error without determining its cause and you now wish to reexamine the code.

Abort the program. This command halts all aspects of your program and returns control to the system level:

```
abort
```

You can then use the editor to make corrections in the source code and repeat the assembly process. You may also simply reexecute the program without change if you wish to examine it further. This combined action may be preferable to a `restart`, because all values will be correctly reinitialized.

Restart the entire machine. On occasion, things may "really be messed up." In such a case you may need to completely restart the machine. The command

```
reboot
```

accomplishes this goal. The machine may also have a hardware switch or keystroke combination to accomplish the same result. In either case, because there is a chance that you may damage an open file, rebooting should be the last resort means of restarting.

Using the Debugger Advantageously

How does one make use of these tools in a constructive manner? Much time can be wasted asking meaningless questions of the debugger. It is important to use it wisely. There are two situations: (1) accidental entry into the debugger and (2) deliberate entry. In the former case, you must determine what error caused you to be in the debugger, what caused that error, and what corrective action to take. The latter case involves strategic planning, either based on the assumption that there will be an error or as a deliberate attack to examine a specific expected error. In all cases, you will want to have a listing of your program available.

ACCIDENTAL ENTRY. The first thing you must do is determine from *what point in your program* the debugger was entered. You have two immediate tools:

- the error message
- the next statement

Using a listing of your program, attempt to determine the location within your code at which the error occurred. Additional information useful for isolating the error point includes

- *output:* any output produced prior to entry into the debugger isolates the point of error between the last output produced and the first output statement not yet executed.
- *registers:* the contents of the registers can be very useful. For example, a register being used as a counter can help identify the point in the listing corresponding to the error line displayed. Loop counters can reveal how many times a loop was executed before the error; registers holding arguments to subroutines may indicate which statement called the subroutine; etc.

Next, you must determine *why* the program entered the debugger. At one level, you know the answer to this question: the reason for entry is specified in the debugger output. But you did not intend to cause this error. The real question is "Why did your program do other than what you intended?" Look first for a logic error of the types described earlier associated with the particular error message that you have encountered. Sometimes stepping through the next few statements can shed additional light on the problem. For example, if you have a counter that is off by one, you might notice the error the next time it is incremented.

Tools that can prove useful in determining the cause of the error include the values stored in any memory location relevant to the current code, RAM or register. Reconstruction of the erroneous statement can also be useful. When you reconstruct it, do you get what you really intended or do you get a different location or size?

STRATEGIC PLANNING. Eventually you will discover that you enter the debugger deliberately more often than accidentally. The debugger is your most important tool. Plan ahead to use it as your primary tool for all debugging problems, both machine-detected errors and logical errors.

Expect errors. Programs seldom run the first time, so plan accordingly. Start by including several debugger directives in your source code, perhaps one at the end of each logical segment of your code. The first time your program runs, you will be interrupted by each of these debugger commands. At that point, check that all values are what you expect. For example, at entry into a subroutine, all of the argument values should be in the appropriate registers. Don't forget that you can trace a few steps at each entry before continuing with a `go` command. Include lots of "trace" information in the form of extra output.

Recheck values. When you discover an accidental entry into the debugger, you may need to reexamine some of the values that you thought were right earlier in the program. Remember that it is not necessary to reassemble the program—you can re-execute the previously assembled program as many times as you wish.

Loop entry. A debugger directive within a loop body will cause the program to break into the debugger *each pass through* the loop. Thus a loop-structured segment of code could be examined several times with a single debugger statement. You can watch the values change until the error appears. Similarly, a call at the beginning of a subroutine will break into the debugger each time that subroutine is entered.

Examining conditionals. By placing a debugger directive immediately before a `compare`, you can check the values of the items to be compared. Then, by stepping through the program, you can verify that the `compare` produces the expected results by checking to see if the `jump` is taken. You can also examine the condition codes directly, which will help determine the difference between an "equal" or a "greater than" for a jump that allowed both.

Expected status. Comments about expected status of registers help greatly. If two registers should have the same value at some point, indicate that fact in the comments. This will remind you to compare the registers when you are in the debugger. The content of registers on entry and exit from subroutines is an especially valuable piece of information.

Error evaluation. Often you will discover an error but be unable to determine the precise problem while in the debugger. Or you may discover an incorrect result but not enter the debugger. These situations call for "creative debugging." You should always form one or more hypotheses as to the nature of the error and create a situation to test your theory. Place your own call for a debugger entry prior to the expected error. Approach the expected error point using trace, checking all relevant values at each point.

Some Additional Powers

Many debuggers can be used in even more powerful ways. For example, you can

- determine the results of a comparison operation *before* the jump,
- alter control by branching to a new location,
- alter the contents of registers or main memory,
- alter the commands that will be executed in the future,
- trace multiple steps at a time, etc.

One very important power is the ability to examine specific memory locations. For example, if you are using an address register as a pointer, you might want to see the value in the location to which it points. The mechanism involved is a simple (but confusing) extension of concepts covered earlier, with respect to commands such as DispMemory or DisplayByte. The possibilities can best be seen by use of an extended example. Suppose that register 4 has been used as a pointer and now contains the value 00123456. That is, `reg4` is a pointer to memory location 123456. Suppose that that location holds the character "A", and that the subsequent locations (123457, 123458, ...) contain the characters "B", "C", and so on.

```
display-memory   123456
display-memory   00123456
display-memory   contents(reg4)
```

will all display the "A". The location following 123456 is 1+123456, or 1+ (the contents of `reg4`). This can be specified as

```
display-byte     1+content(reg4)
```

The location before 123456 is 123455, which might be indicated by

```
display-byte     -1+content(reg4)
```

The notation that the debugger normally uses to specify the operands of the (next) command, e.g.,

```
<command name>    123(reg5),222(reg4)
```

is quite confusing and does not seem to explain what the operands actually are. In the case of register operands, there is no problem; the syntax specifies the register and you need only look at the display to see its contents. But operands in main memory are not so easy. Recall that the symbolic name that you used in your assembly code is no longer available at execution time. In the normal mechanism for accessing storage locations, the address is composed of a register and a displacement (distance from where the register points). The numbers in the display represent this register value and a displacement. In the example, the first operand is located at the spot 123 bytes past the location to which register 5 points, the second is 222 bytes past where register 4 points. To see what is at these locations, use the `content` operator:

```
display-memory  content(reg5)+123 and
display-memory  content(reg4)+222.
```

Finally, note that if the computer attempts to execute data as an instruction, there is a very real possibility that it will be interpreted as a valid instruction. All that is required is that the bit pattern of the data be the same as that of some instruction (for example, the first byte of the M68000 instruction ORI is all zeros, a very common pattern.) This is a very difficult case because the program would be executing complete nonsense, creating instructions and performing them seemingly at random. It will almost certainly find an illegal instruction very soon, but perhaps not until it has executed one or two erroneous ones. The debugger will inform you what it believes the next instruction to be, but it may look like no instruction you have ever used.

Common Causes of Error

The following short list of errors includes most of the sources of run-time or logic errors in assembly language programs. There are really very few classes of errors. Get used to checking all the possibilities. They are listed in approximately decreasing order of likelihood for a beginning assembly language programmer:

- incorrect operand size
- missing immediate symbol when an immediate operand is intended
- confusion between types (e.g., using character digit as a number)
- register values changed by a subroutine
- other mode inconsistencies (e.g., failure to specify PC relative when it is used)
- confusion between a pointer and the item to which it points
- incorrectly used stack (incorrect increment, wrong number of parameters passed)

REAL DEBUGGERS

As with the GAL language and the GAM machine, it is important to note that whatever real debugger you use will differ somewhat from the GAD debugger.

One distinction that you will certainly note is that the commands are usually especially terse—even more so than the assembly language mnemonics. Often the commands may be only one or two characters. However, you should be able to recognize operations equivalent to almost all of the GAD operations. The terse commands may generate ambiguities with hex numbers: Perhaps "A" means "address," "B" "binary," etc. Check the syntax carefully for these problems.

▷ *Why would debugger mnemonics be so terse?*

Variations, such as default display of registers, are common. Additional powers are also common. Do not be intimidated. You do not need to understand all options to use those that you do understand.

SUMMARY

A debugger is the most important tool available to the assembly language programmer. It is not a universal solution, but when used in conjunction with good programming practices and antibugging techniques, it can help provide rapid solutions for error situations. Typically, debuggers allow you to examine any register or memory location and see the next instruction that will be executed. They may even allow you to modify the current program interactively.

EXERCISES

13.1. Add the debugger trap to any program you have written and step through the program in the debugger. Convince yourself that the program behaves the same as it would without the debugger.

13.2. Find the debugger manual for your machine. Look up the following:
(*a*) display the contents of a register
(*b*) display the contents of a RAM location
(*c*) step through a program
(*d*) get out of the debugger elegantly

13.3. Does your debugger allow you to step over subroutines?

13.4. Create an infinite loop. Enter the debugger while your program is in the loop by pressing the hardware interrupt switch. Verify that you are in the loop by stepping through it for a few steps. Exit using the `go` command. Reenter the debugger. This time exit by using the `abort` command. Try it two more times, exiting with the `restart` and `reboot` commands.

13.5. The `go` command was not very satisfactory with the infinite loop. Create a loop that executes many times. Attempt to stop the program by pressing the interrupt button while it is in the loop. (The loop may need to execute a very large number of times.) Use the `go` command and the program should exit normally.

13.6. Create several experiments to force each of the logical errors mentioned at the end of the chapter. Observe the error messages provided by the debugger.

13.7. Find a complete list of machine errors generated on your computer. Create experiments to cause as many of the machine errors as you can. For which errors could you successfully restart the program from the debugger?

13.8. Write a program that uses immediate values. Use the debugger to find the representation for the immediate value within the instruction.

13.9. Convert the following values to hex:

123456789
987654321
135792468

(Use the `convert` command.)

13.10. Fill an array with unique values. Use the display memory command to see how they are related to each other in memory. Place a debug trap so that you can easily find an instruction accessing the first position of the array.

13.11. Find out if your debugger allows you to alter the values in registers or RAM. Write a program that has a loop. Enter the debugger. Change the values and restart the program. Reenter the debugger and see if the values are changed.

13.12. Does your debugger allow you to alter the PC? Write code that includes a copy to register, and place a debugger trap prior to the instruction. Attempt to step over the instruction by altering the PC.

13.13. Find or write a program that uses indirect addressing. Use the debugger to find the content of the pointer register. Use that value to find the value pointed at in RAM. Use both the two-step method and the single-command method.

13.14. Are the RAM operands of your instructions displayed as simple addresses? Or do they appear to be some form of indirect address? Either way, find the operands in memory.

13.15. Using the debugger, find a `compare` instruction. Predict the result of the comparison. Execute the `compare` and find the answer in the condition code or status register. Ask yourself: what bits changed? Try this with several values so that you can determine the meanings of the individual status bits.

CHAPTER 14

REAL ARITHMETIC[1]

Chapter 4 examined the internal representation of integer numbers. The astute reader may have noted at that time that *real* or *floating-point* numbers were ignored. There were several reasons for separating the treatment of real numbers:

- Many microcomputers do not actually have machine instructions for manipulating real numbers, in which case the programmer must create procedures for performing even the most common of arithmetic operations (or use a prewritten subroutine).
- The representations are considerably more complex than the integer representations.
- Most other examples in the text can be performed without real arithmetic.

The essential features of real arithmetic are included here as a reference section.

THE NATURE OF REAL NUMBERS

In higher-level languages, the programmer may define a numeric variable to be either an integer or a real number. The language then protects the programmer by requiring that numeric expressions contain compatible types. For example, there may be distinct division operations for manipulating integer and real values.

---

[1]This chapter assumes that the reader has an understanding of binary arithmetic and integer representation equivalent to that presented in Chapter 4.

There may be restrictions against adding integer and real values together. The programmer must explicitly convert the type of one to that of the other, for example,

```
assign a⇐float(b) + c
```

might be the proper way to add integer `b` and real number `c`. The primary reason that hlls maintain this requirement is that real numbers have an internal representation distinct from that of integers.

Computer scientists and mathematicians use the term *real number* differently. The latter point out that there are infinitely many real numbers between any two integers. This fact is easy to demonstrate:

> Assume that it were not true. Then there must exist two numbers a and b, such that $a<b$, for which there are no intermediate values. But the average of any two numbers $(a + b)/2$ must necessarily fall between a and b, which contradicts the assumption. qed.

Mathematicians note that this observation is also true for all *rational* numbers (numbers that can be expressed as the ratio of two integers), and the proof is essentially the same. However, mathematicians further distinguish between the *cardinality* of the two sets of numbers—the quantity of possible real numbers and the quantity of rationals are different. Both are infinite, but there are *countably infinite* integers (theoretically, one could enumerate the integers given an infinite amount of time: just start at one and count upwards), and there are *uncountably* many reals. Any attempt to count the reals is doomed to failure. There are so many real numbers that any attempt to enumerate them or list them in order is useless.[2] Computer scientists do not concern themselves with the problem of uncountably infinite numbers—for the simple reason that no machine could possibly list them all. But they do need to worry about the fact that there are a great many numbers between any two integers. The noninteger numbers that can be represented in a machine are what computer scientists call *real numbers*. The computer science definition includes only a very small fraction of the real numbers recognized by mathematicians.

Each of the integers 2, 20, 200, 2,000, and 20,000 can be represented in a 16-bit cell, but 200,000 cannot because 16 bits can only represent $2^{16} = 64K$ distinct items. In a 32-bit computer, the series could be extended to 2,000,000,000. Fractions, such as 0.2, 0.02 and so on, could be added, but only by removing

[2]This apparent contradiction was first shown by the nineteenth-century German mathematician Georg Cantor by use of a now famous *diagonalization* proof, in which he showed that given any purported listing of all real numbers, he could find one not in the list. The distinction is not of particular significance in this chapter, but proofs based on the diagonalization technique are important in theoretical computer science.

some of the representable integers. Unfortunately, there are substantial needs for representations of both the fractions between integers, and the numbers larger than 2^{32}. To represent the large variety of real numbers, we need a new representation scheme, which turns out to be conceptually identical to scientific notation—a representation with which many of you are already familiar.

Scientific Notation

Any positive number can be represented as the product of a fractional number (called the *mantissa*) between one and 10, and 10 raised to some power (called the *characteristic*). Thus,

$$\begin{aligned} 2 &= 2 * 10^0 \text{ (by definition, any number raised to the zero power is 1)} \\ 20 &= 2 * 10^1 \\ 200 &= 2 * 10^2 \\ 2000 &= 2 * 10^3 \\ 20000 &= 2 * 10^4 \end{aligned}$$

and

$$\begin{aligned} .2 &= 2 * 10^{-1} \\ .02 &= 2 * 10^{-2} \\ .002 &= 2 * 10^{-3} \\ .0002 &= 2 * 10^{-4} \end{aligned}$$

Alternatively stated, any single value can have many different representations, each composed of a base number and an exponent representing a power of ten. Thus, (an approximation of) *pi* can be expressed as:

$$\begin{aligned} \pi = 3.14159265 * 10^0 &= \\ 31.4159265 * 10^{-1} &= \\ 314.159265 * 10^{-2} &= \\ 3141.59265 * 10^{-3} &= \\ 31415.9265 * 10^{-4} &= \\ 314159.265 * 10^{-5} &= \ldots \\ 314159265. * 10^{-8} &= \ldots \end{aligned}$$

If the base is known, a computer representation for real numbers need only supply an ordered pair: the mantissa and the characteristic. The multiplication sign and the base of characteristic (10 in the previous examples) may be assumed and need not be explicitly included in the internal representation. The examples would become

[2,0], [2,1], . . .
[2,-1], [2,-2], . . .
[3.14159265, 0], [31.4159265, -1], . . .

If the number has a finite representation, it is possible to find a representation in which the two elements of the ordered pair will both be integers. To see this, note that if the characteristic (which is always an integer) is sufficiently negative, the corresponding mantissa will be an integer (in the example for π above, a characteristic of -8 corresponds to an integer mantissa).[3] Note that each of the previous examples included fractions. We could, therefore, establish a standard representation, built from the existing integer representation by forcing both elements of the ordered pair to be integers.

How large an integer field is needed for each of the two elements of the representation? Is it possible to represent an entire real number in eight bits? Sixteen? Thirty-two? The answer may not be the same for the characteristic and the mantissa. The answer for the characteristic depends upon how large a number is needed; for the mantissa, it depends upon how precise a number is needed. Consider some very large numbers:

the average salary of Computer Science Master's degree graduates in 1988:

$$\$3.47 \times 10^4 = \$34,700$$

the population of the world:

$$5 \times 10^9 = 5,000,000,000 \text{ people}$$

the distance to the sun:

$$1.46 \times 10^8 = 146,000,000 \text{ km}$$

the U.S. national debt (as of 7/16/90):

$$\$3.14483 \times 10^{12} = \$3,144,830,000,000$$

one light year:

$$9.13 \times 10^{12} = 9,130,000,000,000 \text{ km}$$

the distance to the edge of the visible universe:

$$1.05 \times 10^{23} = 105,000,000,000,000,000,000,000 \text{ km}$$

Avogadro's number:

$$6.0238 \times 10^{23} = 602,380,000,000,000,000,000,000 \text{ molecules per mole}$$

[3] Of course, any finite representation of π is only an approximation. It would be more accurate to say that π, represented with nine digits of precision, has a representation in which the mantissa is an integer.

the mass of the sun:

$$2 \times 10^{30} = 2{,}000{,}000{,}000{,}000{,}000{,}000{,}000{,}000{,}000{,}000 \text{ kg}$$

Consider some very small numbers:

the diameter of an electron:

$$\text{less than } 10^{-20} = .000{,}000{,}000{,}000{,}000{,}000{,}01 \text{ m}$$

a barn:

$$10^{-28} = .000{,}000{,}000{,}000{,}000{,}000{,}000{,}000{,}000{,}1 \text{ m}^2$$

the mass of an electron:

$$9 \times 10^{-31} = .000{,}000{,}000{,}000{,}000{,}000{,}000{,}000{,}000{,}000{,}9 \text{ Kg}$$

smallest measurable amount of time:

$$10^{-43} = .000{,}000{,}000{,}000{,}000{,}000{,}000{,}000{,}000{,}000{,}000{,}000{,}000{,}000{,}1 \text{ sec}$$

one Planc unit (the distance light travels in the above time):

$$3 \times 10^{-35} = .000{,}000{,}000{,}000{,}000{,}000{,}000{,}000{,}000{,}000{,}000{,}03 \text{ m}$$

Finally, consider some very precisely specified numbers:

π:

3.14159265

a fairly wealthy person's income computed for income tax purposes:

\$1,234,567.89

the population of the United States (1990 census) was an exact integer around:

249,600,000

e (base for natural logarithms):

2.71828183

(Again, note that e, like pi, has no finite representation. It would be possible to represent them even more precisely than in the examples included here. However, the precision used is sufficient to require careful investigation of the internal representations.)

COMPUTER REPRESENTATIONS

It is fairly easy to see that eight bits (which allows only 256 distinct values) or even 16 bits (64,000 values) are insufficient for the mantissa. But how many more bits are needed? For humans, it is usually easier to think in terms of the number of decimal digits of accuracy needed. The most precise of the preceding examples needed nine decimal digits, but notice that both the large and the small examples, as presented, have far fewer significant figures (digits between the first and last nonzero digit, inclusive). So, perhaps not so many digits of accuracy are usually needed. From the number of decimal digits required, it is easy to determine the number of binary digits needed. Recall that the log of a value is roughly the number of digits needed to represent that value (in a given base). The relationship between base 2 and base 10 logs is easy to determine:

let

$$L_{10} = \log_{10}(N)$$

then

$$\begin{aligned} 10^{L_{10}} &= 10^{\log_{10}(N)} &&= N \\ \log_2(10^{L_{10}}) &= \log_2(10^{\log_{10}(N)}) &&= \log_2(N) \\ & L_{10} * \log_2(10) &&= \log_2(N) \end{aligned}$$

so

$$\log_{10}(N) * \log_2(10) = \log_2(N)$$

But $\log_2(10)$ is a constant. Since log (8) = 3, $\log_2(10)$ must be a little more than 3—or with a little more accuracy, 3.322. Therefore, the number of bits needed to represent a number of a given precision in a computer is a constant, 3.322, times the number of decimal digits needed to represent the number. A nine-digit decimal number requires $\lceil 9 * 3.322 \rceil = \lceil 29.9 \rceil$, or 30 binary digits; seven decimal digits would require $\lceil 23.254 \rceil$, or 24 binary digits.

Similarly, the magnitude of the largest example, 10^{30}, required about two decimal digits for the characteristic. The $\log_{10}(30)$ is about 1.5. This requires five bits. The smallest examples had an exponent of about -43, requiring about six binary digits (plus a sign).

As a first attempt, try a 32-bit representation organized as follows:

- eight bits for the characteristic, and
- 24 bits for the mantissa.

For now, assume that the mantissa is an integer and the characteristic represents a power of 10. This allows mantissa values between 0 and $2^{24} \approx 10^7$. That is, it allows up to seven decimal digits, which is almost as precise as the most precise example above, and therefore seems ample for now. The characteristic can represent values up to 10^{255}—or more likely 10^{127}, if negative values are also allowed. This seems more than ample.

Thus a possible internal representation for real numbers might be

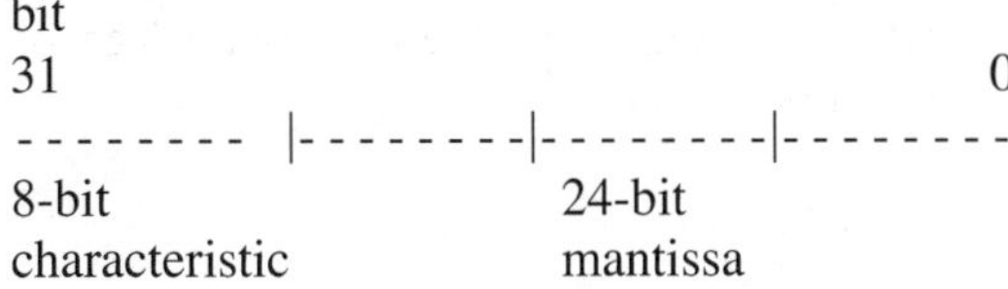

The mantissa may be either a positive or negative number and thus should have a sign bit (note that the sign of the mantissa is actually the sign of the entire number). Additionally, the characteristic can have a sign (positive signs would connote large numbers; negative signs, small numbers). An improved format might be

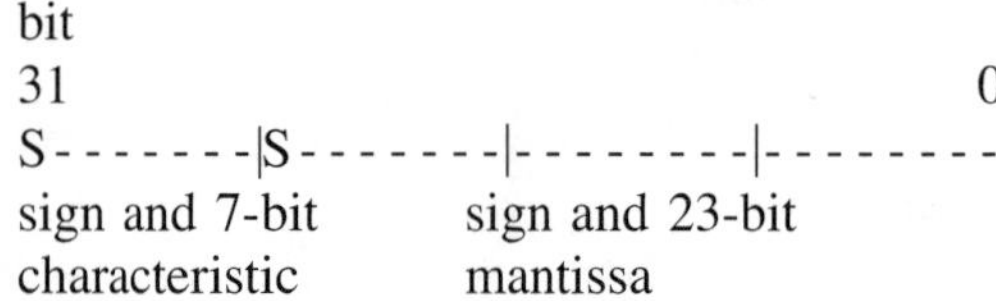

The first problem with this representation is that the sign of the mantissa is actually the sign of entire real number. The sign is thus buried in the middle. It would be convenient for comparison purposes if the sign bit could be located at the left as with integers. In that case, the logic to set the negative bit would not depend on the representation. The common solution to this problem is to move the mantissa's sign to the left-most bit:

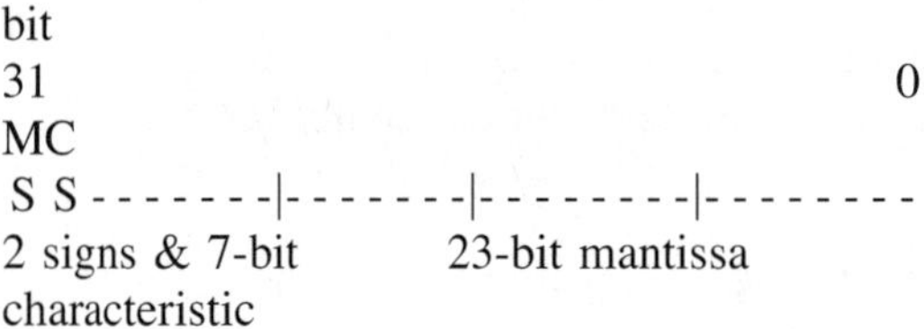

Finally, note that since the internal representations themselves are binary, the underlying operations must also be binary. A shift in the mantissa of one bit to the left is equivalent to multiplying it by 2. Multiplication can also be achieved by adding to the characteristic. Therefore, if the characteristic is interpreted as representing a power of 2 rather than 10, multiplication by 2 can be accomplished either by addition of 1 to the characteristic or by shifting the mantissa one place to the left. Similarly, division by 2 can be accomplished by either subtraction of 1 from the characteristic or shifting the mantissa one position to the right. For purposes of arithmetic manipulation of real numbers, it will often be useful to alter a representation while maintaining the same value. A shift left of one position in the mantissa can be compensated for by reducing the exponent by one; a shift to the right could be balanced by increasing the exponent by one. Thus, interpretation of the characteristic as a power of 2 will result in simpler algebraic manipulation. However, interpreting the characteristic as powers of 2 rather than 10 reduces the range of possible magnitudes by $\log_2(10) = 3.32$. Thus, the effective range of legal values for the magnitudes of real numbers becomes

$$2^{-128} \text{ to } 2^{127} \approx 10^{-38} \text{ to } 10^{38}$$

Although a few more refinements are needed in the representation, these observations provide a basis for the investigation of algorithms for real arithmetic in computers.[4]

Real Arithmetic Operations

MULTIPLICATION AND DIVISION. Not surprisingly, the manipulation of real values is performed in an entirely different manner from integer values. Surprisingly, real multiplication is simpler to describe than real addition and subtraction. To understand real multiplication, consider the equivalent problem in scientific notation. Consider the problem of multiplying two numbers N_1 and N_2. Representing the numbers in scientific notation, the problem becomes

$$\begin{aligned} N_1 * N_2 &= (M_1 * 10^{C_1}) * (M_2 * 10^{C_2}) \\ &= (M_1 * M_2) * (10^{C_1} * 10^{C_2}) \\ &= (M_1 * M_2) * (10^{C_1 + C_2}) \end{aligned}$$

That is, calculation of the product of the numbers requires the product of the mantissas but the sum of the characteristics. A simple algorithm to accomplish this:

Obtain the mantissa of N_1 (by masking out all other bits).
Obtain the mantissa of N_2 (by masking).
Multiply the two mantissas.
Store as mantissa of result.

Obtain the characteristic of N_1 (by masking).
Obtain the characteristic of N_2 (by masking).
Add the the characteristics.
Store as characteristic of result.

Several complications are possible. The resulting mantissa could be too large to store in 23 bits (2^{20} clearly fits in 23 bits, but $2^{20} * 2^{20}$ does not). In that case, an equivalent result can be found by shifting the mantissa to the right (divided by a power of two). This must be compensated for by adding one to the characteristic (multiplying by 2) for each position shifted. Thus, the following step must be added to the algorithm before storing the result:

```
while (mantissa of result is too large)
   shift mantissa right one position
   add one to characteristic
```

[4]We see now why some computer languages use the term *floating point* for real arithmetic. The term reflects the fact that with a given number of digits representable, the binary point (and therefore the decimal point also) can be made to "float" from one position to the next by altering the characteristic. For example, the difference between 1.23 and 12.3 is that the decimal point has floated one position to the right. The internal representation of the mantissa remains the same for either number.

This modification creates a further problem: digits are lost as they shift off the right end of the mantissa. If any nonzero digits are shifted off the right end, some accuracy will be lost. This is a form of *round-off error.* Such errors are a necessary byproduct of real arithmetic. They are the price that must be paid for the flexibility provided by real representations. Although they can never be completely eliminated, they can be minimized through careful planning.

Division is similar to multiplication, but with an added complication in the normalization step: simple integer division does not yield fractional results. That is, `1 div 3` yields 0, and no amount of simple shifting can make that into 0.3333. (An example is included in the Exercises.)

ADDITION AND SUBTRACTION. Real addition poses an "apples and oranges" problem. Numbers with different characteristics cannot be added simply by adding the mantissas. The sum

$$3.14159 * 10^4 + 2.718 * 10^2$$

is not a pure addition problem. The numbers must first be normalized so that they have identical mantissas. There are two possible approaches:

reduce the larger characteristic (divide by 2) and
shift the corresponding mantissa to the left (multiply by 2)

or

increase the smaller characteristic and
shift the corresponding mantissa to the right.

For example, the addition above could be performed by the steps

$$3.14159 * 10^4 = 314.159 * 10^2$$

$$314.159 * 10^2 + 2.718 * 10^2 = 316.877 * 10^2$$

Bits shifted out of the mantissa are lost. Therefore, the latter method seems preferable since any bits shifted out of the mantissa would be the least significant bits, whereas in the former case, the most significant bits would be lost. Thus, the algorithm for addition might be

{extract subparts}
obtain the mantissa of N_1 (by masking).
obtain the mantissa of N_2 (by masking).
obtain the characteristic of N_1.
obtain the characteristic of N_2.

```
{normalize}
  while (characteristics are not identical)
    add one to the smaller characteristic
    shift the correspond mantissa right one position
{perform the addition}
  add the two mantissas.
  store as mantissa of result.
{assure that the answer is representable}
  while (mantissa of result is too large)
    shift mantissa right one position
    add one to characteristic
  store characteristic
```

Subtraction can be performed similarly. (The details are left as an exercise.)

Normal Forms and Standard Representations

Most machines that include real arithmetic operations conform to a standard known as the IEEE Standard 754, which specifies exactly what form is to be used for real numbers: how many and which bits are used for characteristic and mantissa; how to interpret that characteristic and mantissa, etc. By accepting a single standard, data can be recorded using one machine with assurances that the representation will be useful on another machine. More generally, it helps ensure that the result of a calculation will not vary from machine to machine. The standard specifies the representation as

bit 31	sign of mantissa (entire number)
bit 30	sign of characteristic
bit 29–23	remainder of characteristic
bit 22-0	remainder of mantissa.

So far, this is identical to the above format. However, there are some lower-level representational distinctions. The exponent is represented in *excess 127* notation (in excess 127 representation a signed number, N, is represented as the sum of (N+127)). This unusual form simplifies the comparison needed while performing arithmetic operations, since it maps all possible exponents onto the range 0 to 255. The resulting number is always positive. Notice that the sign (left-most) bit of the characteristic is 1 for positive and 0 for negative exponents—the opposite of two's complement.

The standard also specifies a *canonical* or *normalized* form for any value. That is, of the many mantissa-characteristic combinations that can be used to represent a specific value, one representation is selected as the standard or normal form. After completion of any operation, the result will be normalized prior to saving—even if no normalization is required to obtain a result that fits in the space provided. Surprisingly (at first), the normalized form is neither of the two discussed thus far. The mantissa is always represented as a value between one and two. Before you object that not all numbers can be represented as 1.ddd times something, recall that all values are binary. The assumption, therefore, only states that the mantissa is between 1.000 . . . 00 and 1.111 . . . 11. Thus, 5 can be represented as $1.01_2 * 2^2$.

This representation helps prevent excessive round-off errors by reducing shift operations required when manipulating values that are numerically close to each other. The mantissa is always shifted as far to the left as possible. In that case, one additional left-shift would result in a loss of the most significant digit. The binary point does not need to be explicitly represented. It may be assumed to be immediately to the left of the number. There is one further refinement: with the single exception of zero, every number contains at least one 1 bit. Since this digit is shifted as far as possible to the left, the first bit of the mantissa must always be a 1. Since it is always a 1, it is apparently redundant; it can be omitted and simply assumed to exist implicitly at that position. This assumption provides one extra bit of accuracy for the number. The mantissa effectively has 24 bits. The normalization algorithm can be specified as:

```
if mantissa is not zero
   then while (left-most digit is not 1)
      shift mantissa left
      decrease exponent by 1
```

One apparent remaining problem is that of the representation of zero. Since the implicit bit is assumed to be immediately to the left of the binary point, a number with all zeros in the mantissa field is actually a one $= 1.000\ldots0_2$. A number with all ones must be very close to $2_{10} \approx 1.111\ldots1_2$. Numbers between one and zero have negative characteristics. Those greater than two have positive characteristics. It turns out that zero can simply be represented as

$$0 = 1 * 2^{-(127)}$$

It is simply assumed to be very small, indistinguishable from any other value smaller than 2^{-127}. But note that this representation turns out to be

bit 32 (sign)	0
bits 31–23 (characteristic)	0 (= 127 + 127)
bits 23–0	0 (= 1.000 . . . 0)

It is exactly the same as the integer zero. Most hardware has the ability to check for this representation explicitly.

ROUND-OFF ERROR

It is clear that real arithmetic can yield a number of special problems, which are collectively called *round-off error.* This term is technically incorrect since the problems are not really errors. The results are known and predictable. In fact, not all of the problems have anything to do with round-off.

Numbers with Significantly Different Magnitudes

If a large number is added to a small number, one or the other will be shifted during normalization. If the difference is large, for example $4*10^{20} + 4*10^{-20}$, accurate representation of the result would require more digits than are available. If the characteristics differ by more than 23, the addition will force the mantissa of the smaller number to be shifted all of the way out of the space provided. The addition example just cited would require that the mantissa of the second addend be shifted 40 places to the right:

$$4 * 10^{-20} = .4 * 10^{-19} = \ldots = .00000000000000000004 * 10^{0}$$

When the digits fall off the right-hand end, they are lost. Even smaller shifts may cause problems. Any shift large enough to remove several bits will cause the number to be added incorrectly, or with less accuracy than there appears to be.

> ▷ *An experiment: mathematicians know that the sum of a series of numbers will be the same independent of the order in which they are summed. What happens if you attempt to add a series of numbers, such as*
>
> $$\sum_{n=1}^{n} \frac{1}{2^n}$$
>
> *for some large n, on a computer twice, once from largest to smallest, and once from smallest to largest?*

Fortunately, hardware implementation of real arithmetic has an additional advantage. Although the normalized form has a limited number of bits, and communication between registers and RAM is limited by the bus size, there is no restriction about registers that exist entirely within a single ALU. On many machines, the registers for performing real arithmetic are larger than the operands or the result. In such machines, the shifts needed to perform the normalization usually will not result in loss of precision unless the answer itself cannot be represented.

Decimal-to-Binary Conversion (and Back)

If the number $\frac{1}{10}$ is input as a decimal number, the binary representation of the mantissa is 0.000110011001100110011001100, a number that seems very precise but in reality is not exactly one tenth. Just as there is no finite exact representation for $\frac{1}{3}$ as a decimal fraction, there is no finite exact binary representation for $\frac{1}{10}$. Simply entering the decimal value and printing it back out may result in a small round-off error.

Underflow

Underflow is often a confusing problem—how could a number be too small to add? Such errors can occur in at least two ways. Recall the problems of the addition of two numbers of very different magnitude. To add two such numbers:

$$4 * 10^{20} + 4 * 10^{-20}$$

the mantissa of the smaller is shifted to the right, while its characteristic is incremented. Eventually, the interesting digits disappear off the right-hand end of the register. The resulting addition appears as if zero were added to the first addend.

Consider the case of multiplication between two very small numbers:

$$10^{-25} * 10^{-25} = 10^{-50}$$

The result is an even smaller number—so small that it cannot be represented in the allowable number of bits (recall that the limit is approximately 10^{-38}). The result is apparently zero. As with overflow, some machines will trap this error and others will simply set a flag so that the user can trap the error.

Related Problems

"EXCESSIVE" ACCURACY. All floating-point numbers on a given computer have the same internal organization. In particular, there are always 23 bits for the mantissa, independent of how accurate a number was input into the system. The 23-bit representation of the number $\frac{1}{10}$ in the preceding example is no more accurate than the original input. No matter how a number is obtained or calculated, it is only as accurate as the measuring instrument. The fact that the internal computer representation will always provide binary digits equivalent to seven decimal digits in no way implies that the number is really that accurate. Any attempt to use the number in an arithmetic operation will treat it as if it really is that accurate.

OVERFLOW. The result of an operation performed on two numbers may not be representable because the exponent is larger than 127. This results in a condition called *overflow*. Note that any real operation has the potential for overflow. For example, division of a large number by a very small number can cause overflow. As with integers, some machines (or languages) will generate an error condition on overflow; others will set a flag in the status register but not generate an error. Either way, no correct answer results. Overflow can also occur in integer addition when the sum of two numbers cannot be represented in the number of bits allotted for the operands.

INCREASED PRECISION

For some applications, even real representations as described are insufficient. Such applications are indeed the exception but they exist in such fields as high-energy physics and astronomy. For example, large and small numbers such as

the mass of the Milky Way $= 6 * 10^{41}$ kilograms, or
the time for light to traverse one Planc length $= 10^{-43}$ seconds

cannot be represented in the given format. Equally important, precision is limited. The nine-decimal-digit representation of π:

$$\pi \approx 3.14159265$$

cannot be expressed in 23 bits. More accurate representations must also be impossible.

The principles of real representations can be extended to systems with larger mantissas and/or larger characteristics. There is relatively little need to expand the characteristic field significantly. Every increase of one bit in the characteristic doubles the size of possible exponents, which squares the magnitude of the number. On the other hand, an additional three bits in the mantissa are required to increase the accuracy by an amount equivalent to one extra decimal digit. Most extended precision representations therefore add bits almost exclusively to the mantissa. The IEEE standard specifies that *double-precision* numbers will contain 64 bits, distributed as

sign: 1 bit
characteristic: 11 bits
mantissa: 52 bits

Thus, double precision actually slightly more than doubles the precision: the 23 bits in a single-precision mantissa provide approximately seven decimal digits of precision; 52 bits provide almost 16 decimal digits of accuracy. It is "double precision" only in that it uses "double" the storage.

Some machines even provide extended precision beyond double. The Vax computer, for example, provides quadruple-precision arithmetic. Others maintain a larger precision for internal purposes only. In such cases, calculations are performed using a high precision, and the result rounded to fit in single or double precision format. This reduces problems such as round-off error.

CO-PROCESSORS

The complexity of the above procedures for real arithmetic reveals the importance of built-in arithmetic hardware. A hardware floating-point processor may be only three or four times slower than its integer equivalent. But it is clear that executing an entire addition procedure at the machine language level could easily be 30 to

40, or more, times slower. For example, the algorithms given earlier must loop during the normalization process. Each pass through the loop requires three steps and as many as 24 iterations are possible. Some microcomputer manufacturers provide optional co-processors for performing real arithmetic. Typically, the primary machine has a `trap` instruction, which, if there is no co-processor present, simply invokes a procedure to perform the real arithmetic operation. If there is a co-processor present, however, the arguments are passed to the co-processor and that co-processor will perform the task in hardware. The main processor simply waits for the result to be returned.

SUMMARY

There are many more real values than integer values. Therefore, an alternative representation which can represent large, small, and precise numbers is needed. The usual representation, often called floating-point, is based on scientific notation. It has two fields, the characteristic and mantissa, which combined, provide the needed flexibility. If the basic representation does not provide sufficient accuracy, extended precision representations can be used instead. Arithmetic operations are considerably more complex because the two parts of each number must be handled separately. Every value has a normalized or canonical form. Many small computers do not have explicit hardware to perform the operations. Floating-point co-processors can often be added to such machines.

EXERCISES

"We usually need *only* 10 to 15 significant digits. We leave things like the exact measurement of *pi* or *e* to the mathematicians."

Dave Meisel, astronomer

14.1. Write a short program to add the numbers in the series

$$1, 1/(2^1), 1/(2^2), \ldots, 1/(2^N)$$

for N at least 20. Perform the addition from right to left and from left to right. Compare the results and explain any differences. Try it with a larger N. What should the answer be?

14.2. Represent the following numbers in scientific notation:

1.234567890
1234567890.0
0.0000000000123456789

14.3. Perform the following additions, maintaining scientific notation throughout:

$$4.5 * 10^5 + 4.5 * 10^{-5}$$

$$6.7 * 10^5 + 4.5 * 10^7$$

$$2.7 * 10^0 + 7.3 * 10^{-4}$$

14.4. Convert the following base 2 numbers to binary scientific notation:

101010101
1100000000
.0001
.000000000001

14.5. Convert the following numbers from decimal to binary:

0.1
0.01
0.125
0.0625

14.6. Write an algorithm for floating-point subtraction.

14.7. Write an algorithm for floating-point division.

14.8. Describe a series of normalizations needed to perform division within a fixed number of bits.

14.9. Assume you have a machine with no real arithmetic operations. Assume an internal representation for reals formed from ordered pairs on integers. Write a program that can perform real addition.

14.10. Using the same assumptions as in Exercise 14.9, write a program for multiplication.

14.11. Time your program for Exercise 14.9 or 14.10. Run 1000 iterations of a calculation. Compare the result to 1000 iterations of a floating-point co-processor.

14.12. Contrast the internal representations for

a floating-point number with a zero characteristic, and
an integer.

Use your comparison to design algorithms to convert real to integer and vice versa.

14.13. How many bits would be available in quadruple-precision? Of those, how many would you expect to be used for the characteristic, and how many for the mantissa?

14.14. Based on your assumptions in Exercise 14.13, approximately how many decimal digits of accuracy will quadruple-precision provide?

14.15. Write a program that prints out real numbers. You may assume no more than seven digits should be printed.

14.16. Is floating-point arithmetic appropriate for dollar calculations? What potential problems exist?

14.17. Suppose that for some reason, you wanted 16-bit floating-point numbers. Describe the representation. Calculate the largest and smallest numbers that you could represent. How many decimal digits of accuracy does it provide?

14.18. Check if your machine generates real-overflow errors. Write code that doubles a real number until there is a problem. How many iterations should it require? If no error is generated, what indication does it provide in the status register?

14.19. Does the machine generate underflow messages? Proceed as in Exercise 14.18, but divide by two at each iteration. How many iterations should be required? What were the symptoms?

CHAPTER 15

VARIATIONS ON THE VON NEUMANN MODEL: MICROPROGRAMMED AND RISC MACHINES[1]

As the various levels of abstraction have evolved, a problem—or at least a controversy—has evolved with them. The first four models presented in earlier chapters were presented at progressively lower levels. Chronologically, however, the models were developed in roughly the reverse order. As each model developed, it enabled computer scientists to address issues at higher levels of abstraction, building more advanced tools using the existing lower-level models. In general, humans want to envision computers at the higher levels. Figure 15-1a represents the relative levels of abstraction for the various models as presented. A general shift in the development occurred after the introduction of higher-level languages and system-command languages. Further development has taken the form of refinement and improvement in the higher-level languages rather than the creation of new layers.[2] The increased level of hlls has resulted in an increased distance,

[1]Chapter 15 assumes an understanding of the material presented in Chapters 1 through 10.

[2]Some have argued recently that off-the-shelf user applications represent an additional layer in the hierarchy. For example, for many users spreadsheets and databases have replaced hlls as the user view of computation.

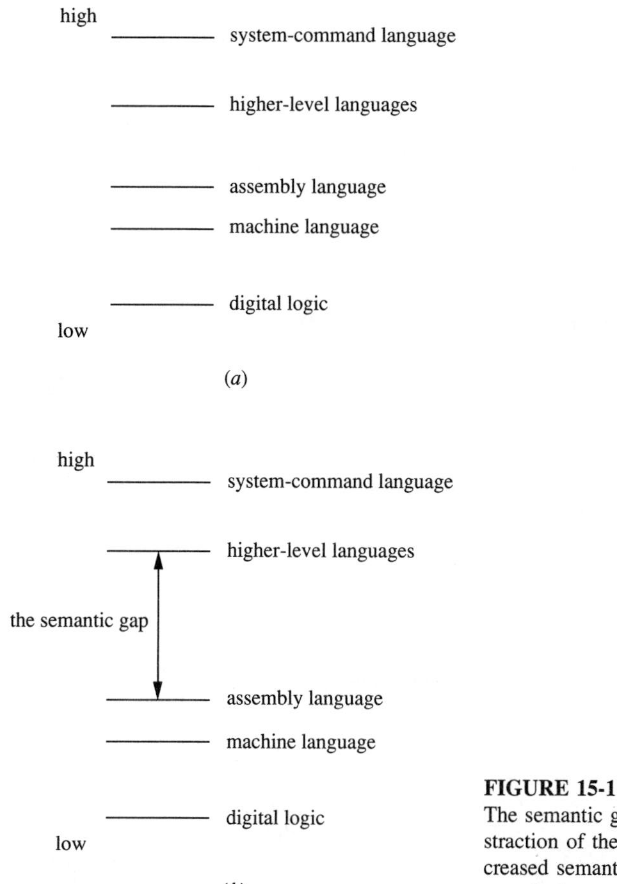

FIGURE 15-1
The semantic gap. (*a*) The relative level of abstraction of the models of computation. (*b*) Increased semantic gap as hll model increases in complexity.

known as the *semantic gap,* between the hll model and the machine language model, as suggested in Figure 15-1b. Bridging the gap has become correspondingly difficult. The endpoints cannot really be changed; the bottom level cannot be raised, and human users certainly do not want to return to lower-level languages.

There are two possible approaches to bridging the gap. The first is the creation of an additional level, as shown in Figure 15-1c. In the microprogrammed model, the machine language, as seen by the programmer, is distinct from the hardware machine built of digital circuits. The other approach, the reduced instruction set computer or RISC model is suggested by Figure 15-1d. It redefines the intermediate level to better reflect the hll model. Since the machine and assembly language models were developed before the higher-level language model, there was no way the creators of those models could have predicted the needs of future models. If the intermediate stepping stones were replaced with models on a more direct path between the high and low levels, the semantic gap could be reduced without creating an extra intermediate model.

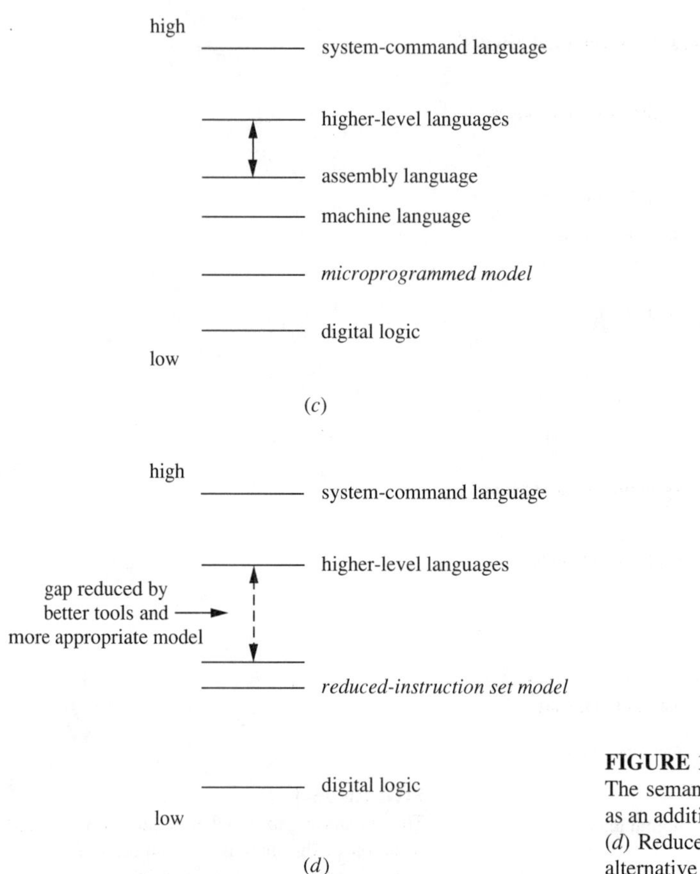

FIGURE 15-1
The semantic gap. (*c*) Microcode as an additional intermediate level. (*d*) Reduced instruction set as an alternative intermediate model.

While both of these models address the same underlying problem, they take very different approaches. Although the microprogrammed model is by far the older approach, the RISC model seems to require fewer modifications of the machine language model. Interestingly, the more complicated microprogrammed model is necessary to understand the impact of the simpler RISC model. The history of the microprogrammed model helps explain why the newer RISC model required so long to develop as a realistic model.

THE MICROPROGRAMMED MODEL

The first approach to narrowing the semantic gap raised the level of the machine language. Unfortunately, this step by itself increases the gap between the machine language and digital logic levels. To reduce this new gap, the *microcode* or *microprogrammed* machine model was inserted between the machine code and digital logic models. The microprogrammed model, first proposed in 1951 by

British engineer Maurice Wilkes, forms a bridge between these two models. The machine language model views the steps of the fetch/execute cycle as primitive actions. The digital logic model views each of those steps as a digital circuit described in terms of primitive logical actions. The microprogrammed model provides an alternate description of the fetch/execute cycle. In this model, the steps of the fetch/execute cycle are described as instructions of a (micro) computer program. This microprogram accepts a "machine language" program as input. For each machine language instruction, the microprogram implements all the steps of the fetch/execute cycle and produces the appropriate changes to the registers of the original machine language computer. The microprogram copies a machine language instruction from memory to the IR, increments the PC, interprets the instruction, fetches the operands, performs the appropriate operation, and leaves the result in the appropriate destination. In the microprogrammed model, the language usually referred to as "machine language" is not actually the language of the hardware machine, just a language interpreted by the microprogram.

Justification

DISCREPANCY BETWEEN MACHINE LANGUAGE AND DIGITAL LOGIC MODELS. In the machine language model as described in Chapter 6, the fetch/execute cycle consists of a series of discrete steps, each step responsible for a segment of the cycle. Each complete cycle interprets a single machine language instruction. In a very real sense, the language used for describing the fetch/execute steps reflects the image of higher-level models. Each step moved, manipulated, or compared data. Each step accessed its operands from source locations and left results in destination locations. As with the higher models, the steps of the fetch/execute cycle create an implicit notion of time in terms of a sequence of steps.

The digital logic view, as described in Chapter 9, however, accomplishes the same results in a very different manner. That view has no specific representation of a step. Rather, the concept of time (and therefore, order) is represented as a sequence of clock pulses. The individual components are aggregates of gates, which may work in parallel. The components perform their tasks under control of the clock. The two models may seem almost incompatible: one is driven by an external force—the clock—and the other generates its own sense of time. In the microprogrammed machine model, these views are not only compatible, but the boundary between them can be moved arbitrarily.

COMPLEXITY OF INSTRUCTION SETS. As hlls became more complex, machine and assembly languages followed suit in an attempt to provide the support needed by the progressively higher-level user languages. The GAL and GEM machines—generic representatives of their respective models—have relatively simple instruction sets: 16 instructions, four addressing modes, eight registers, and 64K of memory. As recently as the late 1970s, such simple instruction sets were realistic for microcomputers (15 to 20 years earlier they were realistic for larger machines). Most modern machines, however, are much more complex, with 100 to 200 or even more distinct instructions, 8 to 16 addressing modes (for each operand; 64 or more total modes for a two-operand instruction), 16 to 32 or more registers, and several million bytes of addressable RAM memory.

The digital logic required to implement the added complexity became a major obstacle. An increased number of instructions means longer opcodes as well as more ALUs. More registers and more RAM mean longer addresses. Decoders for selecting each register operand must be larger; the internal bus must be wider and more complex; the MAR must be larger, etc. An increased number of addressing modes increases the complexity of the operand-fetch step of the cycle, which in turn makes the timing more variable and the timing mechanism more complex. The problems of increased complexity are not solved simply by adding more complex circuitry. Modern computers may need millions of transistors. More transistors means more connections and creates a corresponding increase in the number of circuit crossovers, which in turn greatly increase the complexity of the design of VLSI chips. The number of transistors that can physically fit on a single chip is limited (about 10^6 at the current time).

The increased complexities are balanced by similarities between any two machine code instructions. Many of the individual steps of the fetch/execute cycle—for example, those steps up through the decode step—are identical for any instruction. Many instructions permit the same legal addressing modes. For a given addressing mode, every instruction requires the same substeps to fetch its operands. In a machine with 200 operations, there are necessarily many operations that perform very similar tasks. For example, a machine may have instructions for signed and unsigned multiplication; for both logical and arithmetic negation; for both exclusive and inclusive ors; for packed decimal addition as well as binary addition, etc.

EVOLUTIONARY NEED FOR AN INTERMEDIATE MODEL. Increased complexity may also increase the need for evolution. It may be necessary or desirable to create small variations in the design of a machine. The variations may provide special needs for a specific design, logical improvements or extensions, and even the correction of errors in design. The need for such variations increases with the complexity of the machine architecture. Unlike software, the internal design of a machine cannot be changed by rewriting and resubmitting. Changes in a machine description require redesigning and remanufacturing the circuitry of the VLSI chips. Even very small changes could force a complete redesign of the chip layout.

Background, Review, and Observations

Several additional observations are useful before describing the microprogrammed model.

TRANSITIONS BETWEEN MODELS. The higher-level language, assembly language, and machine language models of computation were bridged by software: compilers and assemblers, which mapped one model onto another. No similar tool provides a similar bridge between the machine language and digital logic models. The machine language model, on the other hand, was apparently constructed from the digital logic model by brute force. An intermediate model might make it easier to map one model onto the other.

RELATIVE "POWER." The statement that one machine is more powerful than another does not mean that it can actually perform operations or solve problems that the "less powerful" machine could not solve. A more powerful machine may be faster or provide mechanisms that are simpler from the programmer's point of view. For example, a machine that has built-in multiplication and division operations cannot solve any problems that are unsolvable on a machine without those operations. One machine will certainly be faster, because it can accomplish in a single step an action for which the simpler machine requires an entire subroutine. One machine is much easier to program because many more details are handled by hardware. A machine that supports the auto-increment addressing mode saves the user the effort when address pointers must be incremented systematically. It is mathematically demonstrable that any result that can be computed on any machine—no matter how complex—can be computed on a machine of very simple complexity.[3]

COMPILERS, DATA, AND PROGRAMS. Recall that data and program are internally identical: a sequence of bits. The code for one program can be data for another. In particular, the data—both input and output—for an assembler is itself a program. This ability to treat a program as data is fundamental to many aspects of computer science. The von Neumann machine is also called the *stored-program* computer because the program can be stored as data.

THE FETCH/EXECUTE CYCLE AS A PROGRAM. The description provided for the fetch/execute cycle closely resembles an assembly language program. Many of the steps of the cycle could even have had the same mnemonic names as GAL commands: `copy` for `fetch`; `add` for `increment`, etc. For example, the

[3]The model for proving claims about machine equivalence is the *Turing Machine,* named for the twentieth century British mathematician Allan Turing, who invented the model and proved the result in 1936—well before the creation of any real (i.e., working) computer. A Turing machine program is represented by a set of 5-tuples: (`oldstate`, `input`, `direction`, `output`, `newstate`). The interpretation of each 5-tuple is that, if the machine reads `input` from a tape while in state `oldstate`, the machine responds by writing `output` to the tape, moving the tape one position toward `direction`, and changing its state to `newstate`. The Turing machine is a popular model for the analysis of computational complexity because of its mathematical simplicity.

first three steps of the fetch/execute cycle could be described using a GAL-like language as

```
(1) copy          PC⇒MAR
    jump:sub      →read                   ;fetch the
                                          ;instruction
    copy          MBR⇒IR                  ;(disregard
                                          ;memory time)
(2) copy          PC⇒source_1
    copy          #4⇒source_2
    add           source_1⇒source_2       ;increment the PC
    copy          result⇒PC

(3) compare       IR⇒ . . .               ;decode the
                                          ;instruction
```

Most of the individual steps of the fetch/execute cycle are directly analogous to assembly language instructions. The microprogrammed model of computation takes advantage of this similarity to describe the action of a relatively complicated virtual hardware on a simpler actual machine.

▷ *Recall that in Chapter 6, it was necessary to point out explicitly that the substeps, such as* `copy`, *of the fetch/execute cycle were distinct from the machine language instructions. Was that a coincidence?*

A Machine Language Interpreter

An assembler can accept assembly language commands for which there are no direct machine language equivalents. Macros are one example of this. The assembly language programmer may not even realize that a particular instruction is actually a macro expanded into several machine language instructions (a machine language debugger would certainly recognize the expansion). Such expansion gives the appearance that the machine is more powerful than it really is. As a simple example, consider a machine that has no `subtract` instruction. An assembler could translate a subtraction instruction into equivalent addition and negation instructions:

```
copy      subtrahend⇒temp
negate    temp                  ;generate two's complement
add       1⇒temp                ;of subtrahend in temp
add       temp⇒minuend          ;minuend + (-subtrahend)
```

Recall that an interpreter is a program that executes source code directly, without first translating it to a lower-level model. Unlike a compiler or assembler, which translates the entire source code to object code before executing any of it, an interpreter executes the source code one line at a time, translating as it executes. The microprogrammed model resembles an interpreter for machine language. An interpreter running on the simple machine that had no subtraction instruction would read each instruction, performing the steps necessary to accomplish the specified action. When it encounters a `subtract` command, it must jump to a routine that performs the steps of the subtraction.

EMULATION. An *emulator* is a program that simulates the behavior of another machine at a fine level of detail. An emulator should not only produce the same final result but should perform all the intermediate actions of the program or machine it emulates. The model should reflect the internal processes as well as the results. Each important aspect of the emulated machine should be identifiable within the emulation. Emulation of a machine language program should simulate each step of the fetch/execute cycle, maintaining the correct values in intermediate registers, etc. It should accurately imitate the original—even in new situations. The only way to assure this is to imitate every (potentially) important substep. Consider the emulation, below, of a (relatively) complicated machine language machine using a (relatively) simpler machine. For clarity, the following models all refer to the original or emulated machine as the machine language model machine. The emulator program is called a μ-machine.[4]

The emulator exploits the similarities between the steps of the fetch/execute cycle and an assembly language to mimic a complicated machine on a simpler machine. Assuming that the emulated machine has instructions similar to GEM instructions, the μ-program might look something like:

```
copy next ml instruction⇒IR
mask opcode_field⇒IR
if opcode = 'add'
   then add the operands
if opcode = 'copy'
   then copy source⇒destination
. . .
```

Such a simple emulation is relatively uninteresting. However, even this simple model reveals a number of problems: How can it find the "next" operation? How can it determine if the opcode represents an `add`? The decode process seems impossibly inefficient. In general, the emulator must perform every step reflected in the fetch/execute cycle.

For each individual instruction of the ml machine, there must exist a series of steps in the μ-machine that accomplish the same task. Remember that this does not imply that the language of the μ-machine must be as rich as that of the ml machine. For each addressable object in the ml machine, the emulator program has a corresponding storage location of its own for representing the contents of

[4]The Greek letter μ—pronounced "mu"—is used to represent the English prefix "micro." It will be used throughout the chapter to help distinguish between the emulator, or microprogrammed machine, and the emulated, or machine language machine.

the ml storage location. Thus, the emulation program contains storage locations representing the `MAR`, `MBR`, `IR`, `PC`, `reg0`, etc. This creates an obvious naming conflict, since the emulator also must have its own `MAR`, `MBR`, etc. In the following discussion, the original terminology will always refer to constructs of the original machine language machine. To distinguish between the registers, storage locations, and other elements of the two machines, the emulator machine's constructs will be prefixed with μ to indicate that they are part of the micro emulator: μ-`mar`, μ-`mbr`, μ-`ir`, μ-`pc`, μ-`reg0`, etc. Presumably, the ml registers must be represented using μ-ram addresses in the emulator.

Each step of the ml machine's fetch/execute cycle must have a corresponding code segment in the emulator. There are segments that move data from the PC to the MAR, increment the PC, etc. Several emulator steps will certainly be required to simulate one of the machine language machine's steps. A significant portion of the microcode will be devoted to syntactic operations, such as decoding the original ml instruction. Therefore, it is reasonable to expect that the microprogrammed machine will be very slow.

> ▷ *At the higher-level language model, interpreted code is typically 10 times slower than compiled code. Is a similar ratio likely for this emulator?*

Consider the simplistic view of an emulation of the first three steps of the fetch/execute cycle, shown in Figure 15-2. In steps 1 and 2, data is moved between the MAR and the PC and between the MBR and the IR by μ-`copy` instructions. Addition is performed by simply using the μ-`add` instruction. This code does indeed look much like a simple description of the steps of the fetch/execute cycle. At step 3, the first interesting interaction occurs. The opcode is isolated from the rest of the ml IR by means of a mask. Successive compares then determine which ml instruction is specified. What was described at the machine language level simply as "decode", and at the digital logic level as a decoder, requires a relatively long series of discrete steps. This code certainly will not be very efficient, but it illustrates the feasibility of constructing a simple machine emulator.

Any attempt to describe the process in terms of the emulator's μ-fetch/execute cycle will be very confusing. However, a brief description of the interaction will help disentangle the process. Consider the first several steps of the μ-fetch/execute cycle as it emulates a ml `add` instruction:

(emulating `fetch` instruction)
μ-1 The emulator fetches its own first instruction by:
    copying the μ-pc into the μ-mar, and
    signalling a μ-memory fetch.
μ-2 The μ-pc is then incremented.
μ-3 When the first μ-instruction arrives at the μ-ir,
    the instruction is decoded and recognized as a μ-copy instruction
μ-4 the PC (of the ml machine) is copied to `source_1`.
μ-6 the value of the PC is finally copied to the MAR.

```
;all operands refer to machine language locations
;all instructions are instructions of the emulator machine

 (1)copy          PC⇒MAR
    jump:sub      →memory_fetch           ;fetch the instruction
    copy          MBR⇒IR                  ;ignores time display

 (2)copy          PC⇒source_1
    copy          #4⇒source_2             ;increment the PC
    add           source_1⇒source_2       ;by 4
    copy          source_2⇒PC

 (3)copy          IR⇒temp                 ;Create working copy
    shift:right   #28⇒temp                ;with opcode in low
    and           #0F⇒temp                ;order nibble. Look only
    compare       #8⇒temp                 ;at opcode. Is it an
    jump:equal    →perform_add            ;ADD instruction? If
    compare       #4⇒temp                 ;not skip to next
    ...
perform_add
    copy          IR⇒temp_op
    and           #FFFF⇒temp_op           ;obtain operand address
address
    copy          temp_op↑⇒source_1       ;fetch operand itself
    ...<fetch second source operand>
    add           source_1⇒source_2
    jump:always   →save_results
perform_subt
    ...
```

FIGURE 15-2
A simple emulator fragment.

When the μ-f/e repeats, it will fetch the μ-jump-to-subroutine instruction to request a memory fetch (to fetch the first GEM instruction). The μ-f/e must execute one full μ-cycle for each μ-instruction. In the given example, at least 14 μ-instructions will be executed by the time the ml `add` instruction is fully emulated. Each of those steps requires one full six-step μ-cycle.

> ▷ *Fortunately, this is the sort of thing from which abstraction normally protects us. Is the emphasis throughout computer science on abstraction worth the effort?*

A Microprogrammed Computer

The primary distinction between the emulator described earlier and a true microprogrammed computer is that the hardware of the latter is designed specifically for the task of emulating machine language. The machine will, therefore, perform some tasks often and some not at all. The μ-cpu, while essentially congruent with previous models, can be tailored to perform well on its specific tasks.

REGISTERS. The μ-machine clearly needs access to all machine language constructs. In particular, it needs access to all of the ml registers. Therefore, it apparently must have two full register sets—its own μ-pc, μ-ir, etc., as well as the ml machine's PC, IR, etc. It also needs access to every ml main memory location. For the moment, assume there are subroutines `fetch` and `store` that perform the tasks.

RAM STORAGE. The μ-machine needs very little temporary storage for its own data. With the exception of the machine language memory fetch and store operations, the operands of most of the μ-operations are ml objects. Since very little storage is needed, μ-registers can be used exclusively. Call the additional registers μ-`temp0,...,` μ-`temp3`. Restricting the operands to registers eliminates the relatively slow memory access needed for RAM operands. Normally, each μ-cycle will require a single μ-memory fetch for the instruction, but none for operands. In addition, the restriction reduces the number of addressing modes required, reducing the complexity of a μ-instruction.

DUAL-USE REGISTERS. Since there are no μ-ram operands, addresses passed to the μ-mar must originate at the μ-pc—never at the address field of the μ-ir. Thus, a single μ-register can fill the roles of both the μ-mar and the μ-pc. This assumption not only saves a register but also eliminates the need to copy the μ-pc to the μ-mar at the beginning of the μ-instruction fetch. Similarly, the contents of the μ-mbr will always represent μ-instructions—never operands. Thus, a single μ-register can serve as both μ-mbr and μ-ir. Once fetched, an instruction is immediately available in the μ-ir, with no need to copy it from the μ-mbr. The beginning steps of the fetch/execute cycle are simplified to

1. signal memory fetch (no copy needed)
   start μ-pc increment
2. complete μ-pc increment
3. decode ...(no copy needed)

The full set of registers addressable by μ-machine instructions:

The original GEM registers:
`Reg0...Reg7`, PC, IR, MAR, MBR, `status`, `source_1`, `source_2`
the μ-machine registers:
μ-pc (= μ-mar), μ-ir (= μ-mbr), . . .
and the working storage registers:
μ-`temp0`, μ-`temp1`, μ-`temp2`, μ-`temp3`,...

For example, an emulator for GEM would need about 32 registers, each of which could be specified in five bits.

THE MICROCODE. As presented thus far, the microprogrammed machine seems hopelessly slow. It requires several micro-instructions to process each macro-instruction. Even with the extra registers, the micro-instructions themselves must each be fetched. As pointed out in Chapter 10, memory fetches are the most significant bottleneck of the fetch/execute cycle. The μ-code appears to be both complex and repetitive. For example, the majority of ml instructions require identical checks for address mode. Although it is true that a microprogrammed machine is not as fast as the corresponding hard-wired machine would be, we will see that the difference is not nearly as great as it may appear.

The emulation program itself could be shortened in many ways, some as straightforward as careful programming. For example, if the set of possible ml addressing modes is both short and consistent across instructions, the μ-machine could use a μ-subprogram to fetch the addressing mode and the operands. Use of subroutines would create a shorter emulation program. Unfortunately, the length of the program is not as great a problem as is the number of steps (and therefore the time) required to emulate each ml instruction.

CONTROL STORE. The μ-program can be surprisingly small. The total number of instructions may be as low as 10 μ-instructions per machine language instruction. The μ-program can therefore be stored in a very high-speed ROM memory known as a *control store*. Since memory fetches are the biggest obstacle to speed, improving memory speed for the μ-machine can dramatically shorten the μ-cycle time. Since every μ-instruction requires a μ-memory fetch, the total emulation time can be reduced in proportion to the speed of the control store.

SINGLE FETCH PER CYCLE. Since there are no μ-ram operands, no μ-instruction ever requires more than one μ-memory fetch. There will never be two waits in any μ-cycle. Machine language memory fetches remain the slowest single step in the fetch/execute cycle. The digital logic model overlapped the "dead time" while waiting for memory with the increment PC step. The microcode itself can be similarly structured. The ml memory fetches can overlap other steps of the ml fetch/execute cycle. The μ-memory fetch can overlap other steps of the μ-cycle.

DECODE. The decoding of machine language instructions can be improved using a binary search. A linear search for a ml opcode may require 15 comparisons. If instead the μ-machine examined the ml opcode one bit at a time—bit 31 then 30, 29, and 28—only four comparisons would be needed to decode the ml instruction (the μ-code will still have as many statements, but fewer steps are executed for each decode step). Potentially, this tree search can yield additional improvement if the ml instructions are grouped so that instructions with similar internal characteristics all have the same leading bits in their opcode. For example, `add`, `subtract`, `and`, etc., all have the same number of operands and the same set of legal operand modes. The fetch/execute cycle for these machines is therefore identical through step 5: perform the operation. If similar instructions had similar opcodes, the μ-program could begin to identify the logical group of the instructions as it searches for the opcode. This results in a shorter length for the μ-program, since much of the duplicated code will be removed.

▷ *Does it also say anything about the required μ-instruction set?*

Alternatively, the μ-machine could use a jump table similar to the ones described in Chapter 11. This would be faster than any search, at the price of a more complex μ-machine, permitting indirect branches.

CODE REPRESENTATION. Finally, since the microcode itself is simpler, the μ-machine can be simpler in general. Each μ-instruction should be somewhat faster.

The Interpretation of the Machine Language Code: The μ-machine

If N micro-instructions are needed for the emulation of each machine language instruction, each μ-instruction would have to be N times faster than the corresponding ml instruction to break even. Fortunately, slight variations in the underlying machine model can provide significant improvements in the speed of the μ-code. The microcode as described thus far was designed to appear as much as possible like the assembler or machine languages. But this is a very specialized machine, one whose only task is to interpret machine language code. The μ-machine and its μ-instruction set should be tailored to its specific task.

INCREMENTING THE μ-pc. The μ-pc and μ-ir are distinct from their machine language counterparts. There need be no interaction between those two μ-registers and any of the ml registers. Therefore, the bus used for incrementing the μ-pc is distinct from that used for moving the ml register data. The μ-pc can be incremented at the same time a ml operation is emulated, shortening the μ-f/e cycle further.

DUAL BUS. Most of the GEM computational instructions require two operands and have a single result. Thus with great regularity, emulation of the last three steps of the fetch/execute cycle for any given GEM instruction will contain four specific steps:

fetch one operand
fetch the other operand
perform the action
store the results.

This regularity suggests a design improvement for a faster internal architecture. Although the two fetches must not interfere with each other, each does have a unique source and a unique destination. The only bottleneck is the common bus. If there were two internal buses, as suggested by Figure 15-3, the two operands could

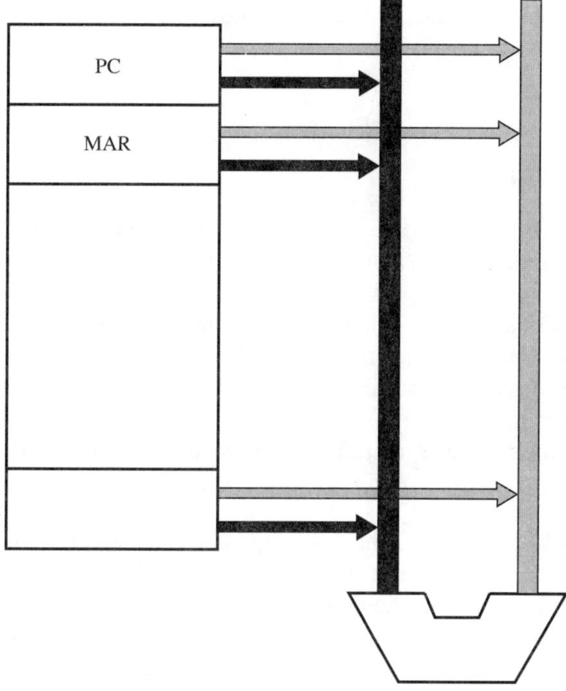

FIGURE 15-3
Two parallel buses for moving data from two registers to the ALU.

be loaded simultaneously. The μ-`copy` instruction could specify two operands. Both are "sources": one to be copied to each of the two registers, `source_1` and `source_2`. The actual instruction could be represented as

```
copy      item1, item2⇒sources
```

There is no conflict between the two items to be copied since they are moved through separate buses. This reduces by one the number of steps required for the emulation of the typical GEM instruction. Further, it does so without creating an elongated instruction. All the μ-operands are registers. Therefore, each operand can be specified in about five bits. Thus, the two operands together are specified in fewer bits than would be required for a single RAM operand. In addition, for this new instruction, the destination registers—the GEM registers `source_1` and `source_2`—can be assumed. They need not be specified at all.

▷ *What happens if the two operands are identical, as in* `add reg2⇒reg2`*?*

IMPLICIT OPERANDS. The operands of the perform step of a ml instruction are fixed: the two source registers. The μ-instructions that emulate the perform step, therefore, will not need to specify any operands at all. By default, the operands are the contents of the source registers. Thus, these commands will be very short, just an opcode, e.g.:

```
add
```

Vertical versus Horizontal Microcode

The μ-machine described above is often called a *vertical microcode* machine because a listing of its code would appear as a vertically oriented block: many instructions in length, but with very short instructions. Some additional variations will complicate the individual instructions but reduce the number needed. Added complications would obviously require that each instruction contain more information—and therefore more bits. A resulting μ-program would therefore be shorter in terms of the number of lines of instructions, but wider in terms of the size of each instruction. Such code is therefore referred to as a *horizontal microcode*.

CONSOLIDATED STATEMENTS. Normally, the last step of each machine language instruction stores the result. The perform step left a value in the result register. In the last step, the value is copied to the destination. Since the store-result step always follows the perform step, the actual destination could be included in the μ-instruction format, thus eliminating one μ-copy instruction. Again, note that the destination will always be a ml register: if the ml command has a RAM destination, the μ-instruction places the result in the MBR.

```
add          ⇒result_location    ;operands are in
                                 ;source regs
```

Placing the two improvements together yields a two-step rather than four-step process:

```
copy         item1,item2⇒
add          ⇒result_location    ;operands are in
                                 ;source regs
```

WIDER INSTRUCTIONS. The two-step operation can be further combined into a single μ-instruction. The two source registers and result register are consistent operands for most operations and can therefore be specified implicitly. Each μ-instruction can specify two input operand registers, an operation and a destination register:

```
operation      source1, source2⇒destination
```

For example, if `temp0` held the value 4,

```
add          PC,temp0⇒PC
```

could be used to increment the PC. This instruction has three operands but requires only 15 bits for the three addresses. More important than size is the dramatic reduction in the number of distinct μ-instructions needed for one ml fetch/execute cycle. Figure 15-4 shows the modified machine. A basic μ-copy instruction (which would be needed to move data from the ml MAR to a ml data register) simply passes a single value through with no ALU intervention:

```
copy      MAR⇒IR
```

▷ *Is there any way to take advantage of the unused second source field?*

BUFFERS. The last μ-code refinement requires an additional refinement of the architecture. Typically, the destination register will be the same as one of the sources. The result must not be returned to a source register too soon. If it were returned before the source to ALU connection was broken, the source would change while the operation was still being performed by the ALU. This would result in unpredictable output. Therefore, the input values are first copied into buffer registers. On the next μ-clock pulse, the values are copied the remainder

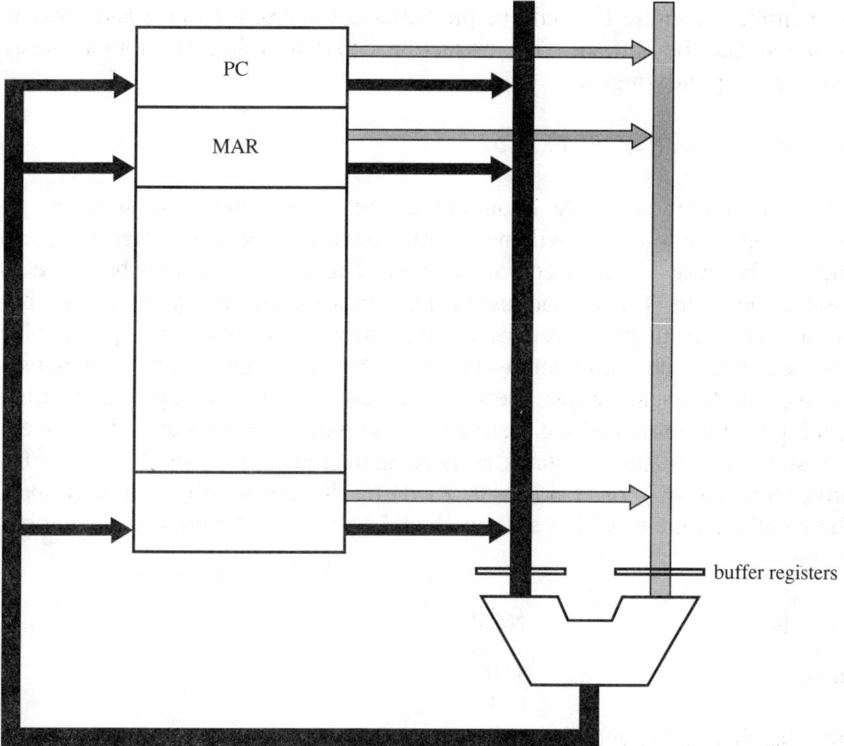

FIGURE 15-4
Two parallel buses for moving two registers to the ALU.

of the way into the ALU. The extra μ-clock-pulse is a small price to pay compared to the saved μ-instructions.

STATUS REGISTER. Since the results of all operations pass through the result register, the μ-status register can be connected to the μ-result register, automatically setting or clearing the negative and zero bits each time any action is performed.

INSTRUCTION DECODING. The binary search for the opcode suggests an additional μ-hardware simplification: only very simple comparisons are needed. The μ-status register always reflects the result of the most recent operation. Since a negative number is identified by a 1 in the left-most bit, any operation (including a `copy`) will set the μ-negative bit if the result of the operation has a 1 in that bit. In particular, loading a machine language instruction into the IR sets the μ-status bit. Therefore, no comparison is needed at all to distinguish those instructions with a 1 in the left-most bit from those with a 0. A simple `jump` on negative separates the instructions. To test the remaining bits of the opcode, the IR can be shifted left one position, leaving a new bit in the left-most position—and in the status register. Thus, if the instructions are carefully coded, a search through 16 possible instructions will require no more than three conditional jumps and three shifts. Shifting the entire IR could be problematic because the mode and operand fields would also be shifted. The instruction could be (almost) simultaneously copied to a temporary register:

```
copy      MAR⇒IR,temp0
```

JUMPS. Jumps are especially important in the μ-machine. Although the μ-program should be short, it will necessarily have a large percentage of `jump` instructions because of the decoding process. These jumps should be made as efficient as possible. The μ-machine design can also take advantage of this observation. As with all previous models, the order of execution in a μ-machine will be sequential, unless directed otherwise. However, the control mechanism will reflect the frequent jumps: every instruction will include a potential jump. Depending on the results of the instruction, the jump may or may not be taken. Each instruction updates the status register, indicating a positive (N=0, Z=0), negative (N=1, Z=0), or zero (N=0, Z=1) result. Every instruction may specify the conditions under which a jump should be taken. The possible conditions might be

`result` **is**	**N&Z**
negative	1 0
zero	0 1
positive (neither of the above)	0 0
never jump	1 1

Thus the final instruction format has six fields:

operation   sources1 & 2⇒destination;jump condition→jump_destination

and is interpreted as "perform the indicated operation using the two operands specified and leaving the result in the destination specified. After completing the specified operation, perform a conditional jump based on the test to the jump-location." No additional steps are required for the jumping operations.

Although a five-operand instruction seems quite complex, it need not be particularly large. Since the total μ-program is still expected to be small, an instruction store of no more than 1000 locations should suffice. Thus, a complete horizontal μ-instruction may fit in the same 32 bits required for a GEM instruction:

field	number of fields	size (bits)	total
opcode	1	5	5
operands	3	5	15
displacement	1	10	10
condition	1	2	2
			32

The full μ-fetch/execute cycle can now be described. Concurrent operations are listed as single steps.

1. a. fetch μ-instruction from μ-ram
   b. calculate (but do not store) incremented μ-pc
2. a. decode μ-instruction
   b. copy operands from registers
3. a. perform operation
   b. set status bits
4. a. store results
   b. compare status register to jump condition
      if matching,
         then set μ-pc to new address
         else set μ-pc to incremented address

Figure 15-5 shows the major logical connections.

The common instructions result in very straightforward μ-code. For example, the body of the μ-code for

```
add      reg2⇒reg3
```

is

```
add      reg2,reg3⇒reg3, (no jump)
```

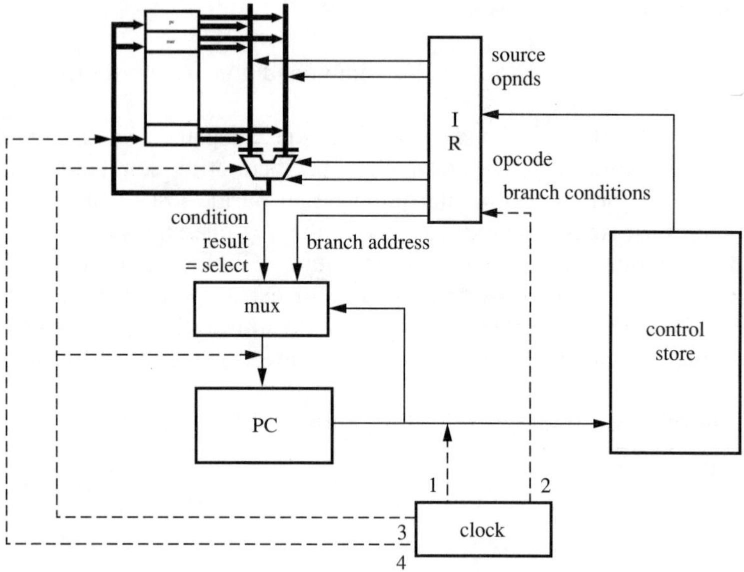

FIGURE 15-5
Logic paths through the microprocess control.

The control steps of the μ-code may be more complicated

```
shift     IR⇒temp, jump on zero→test_for_second_op
```

A Simple Example

Figure 15-6 shows a μ-code segment representing a simplified GEM-like machine. The machine has only four instructions:

mnemonic	opcoded (left-most two bits)
`add`	00
`subtract`	01
`load`	10
`store`	11

Each instruction (except store) assumes that the destination is in a single register (called accumulator) and the source operand is in RAM.

In general, horizontal μ-code runs faster than vertical because fewer instructions are needed. On the other hand, the flexibility and consequent complexity of horizontal instructions requires more memory. Since μ-code is stored in high-speed memory on the same chip as the processor, horizontal code is more expensive. Once again, speed costs money.

```
;Temp registers:
;temp_1 holds the constants 1 for calc two's complement.
;temp_4 holds a 4 for incrementing the pc
top
   copy      PC⇒MAR,source
   signal    read
   add       PC,temp0⇒PC                 ;instr arrives at
                                         ;MBR about here.
                                         ;Bit 31 indicates
                                         ;an add or subt.
   copy      MBR⇒IR,temp;jump neg→not_arith
   copy      IR⇒MAR                      ;MAR is small;
   signal    read                        ;only address fits.
                                         ;All arith ops need oprand
                                         ;- get it. Next bit
                                         ;distinguishes those 2.
   shift     temp;jump neg⇒must_be_subtract
   add       MBR,accumulator⇒accumulator;jump→top

must_be_subtract                                 ;No actual subtract
                                                 ;on this machine.
   negate    accumulator⇒accumulator
   add       templ,accumulator⇒accumulator   ;so use an add
   add       MBR,accumulator⇒accumulator;jump→top

not_arith
   shift     temp;jump neg⇒must_be_store
   copy      IR⇒MAR                         ;Load will need
                                            ;operand
   signal    read
   copy      MBR⇒accumulator;jump→top

must_be_store
   copy      IR⇒MAR
   copy      accumulator⇒MBR
   signal    write;jump→top
```

FIGURE 15-6
A segment of microcode.

REDUCED INSTRUCTION SET COMPUTERS

The *reduced instruction set computer* (*RISC*) model of computation was developed in reaction to the microprogrammed model, which has come to be called the *CISC* (*complex instruction set computer*) model. Like the microprogrammed model, RISC represents a response to the problems created by the semantic gap. But rather than create an added conceptual level, the RISC solution involved simplification. Proponents of the RISC model suggest that a well-designed, simple computer can outperform a complicated machine requiring an interpretation step for each instruction. The essential concept can be stated as "do those things that you do often well."

The RISC model does not simply throw away the microcode model, which would leave a major gap between the machine language and digital logic models. Rather, it pushes the machine language model back down to a much simpler model. But it is not exactly the same simple model as the original machine language model. It is improved in key areas. The proponents look to the significant amount of time that goes into interpretation in a microprogrammed machine, the very skewed distribution of statements in actual production programs, and improved technology in both hardware and software.

Potential Problems with the Microprogrammed Model

RISC architectures are not so much an explicit improvement on the traditional von Neumann design as they are a return to that concept from the microprogrammed machine. The extra level represented by the microprogrammed model does reduce the semantic gap, but at a price of extra complexity in the form of an added level of computation.

INTERPRETED CODE. In a microprogrammed computer, the machine language—as visible to the programmer—is actually interpreted by a simpler microprogram. The μ-machine has its own instruction store, its own fetch/execute cycle, registers, etc. Interpretation of each machine language instruction requires multiple μ-machine instructions. A single interpreted cycle of the machine language model is necessarily several times slower than one μ-machine cycle. In particular, microcode emulation requires two distinct phases for each instruction. The first phase fetches the ml instruction and decodes it; the second executes the instruction. If the μ-code represented a direct implementation of the original source program, rather than an interpretation of machine code instructions, the interpretation portion could be skipped, resulting in significantly faster execution.

PRE-SPECIFIED COMPLEX OPERATIONS. Sequential execution is a characteristic of digital computers. The μ-code machine provides a specific set of machine language instructions that the programmer may access. Since each of these instructions is interpreted by a series of μ-instructions, it is clear that other combinations must be possible in the μ-code—but not available to the user at the machine language level. For example, redundant steps cannot be removed. Consider the two machine language instructions:

```
copy      reg0⇒loc1
copy      reg0⇒loc2
```

A straightforward emulation would copy `reg0` to the MBR twice, once in each instruction. That should not be necessary since the value is in the register after the first `copy`. It seems that lower-level operations might provide more opportunities for optimization.

WASTED MOTION. At the machine language level, the basic fetch/execute cycle of many instructions involves much wasted motion. The model has two principal inefficiencies:

- many instructions do not need every step, and
- specific sequences of steps occur very frequently.

For example, the machine language model predicts that the `copy` instruction requires a complete (six-step) fetch/execute cycle to perform. Within that cycle, the operand value is copied several times:

the actual source operand is copied to `source_1` register,
`source_1` is copied to `result`, and
`result` is copied to the destination (either the destination itself or to the MBR).

The microprogrammed model eliminates the wasted substeps for a machine language copy instruction. But the μ-machine must still emulate every step of the macro f/e cycle including incrementing the macro PC. It must do this for every instruction—even though the increment step is completely predictable.

MEMORY SPEED. Microprogrammed machines rely on very fast ROM memory for the microcode. The speed differential between the μ-control store and the macro-machine RAM is essential for μ-machine practicality. If N μ-instructions are needed for the interpretation of each macro-instruction, the μ-store must be about N times faster to maintain its advantage. Clearly, compiled user programs cannot be placed in ROM, nor will they even fit in a typical cache memory. Fortunately, the speed of conventional memory has increased considerably while its price has fallen almost as much. As regular memory speed improved, the relative advantage of high-speed control store was diminished. Today, 80-nanosecond memory is readily and inexpensively available for most personal computers. Such memory can provide some 12.5 million memory fetches per second. This suggests that if the number of two-fetch instructions can be kept very low, such memory can yield a speed of almost 12.5 million instructions per second (12.5 mips). For the μ-machine interpreter to outperform such macro machines, the micro-engine must be capable of over 100 mips.

Empirical Studies of the Nature of Computation

The concept of a digital computer necessarily preceded the first running program. Similarly the conceptual design of any specific machine (or improvement on a machine) precedes its use. The relative importance of individual features must really be conjecture. But hindsight does provide an important tool for designing new machines. Studies of the use of existing machines reveal much about how people actually use the tools that are provided. In particular, experience with

CISC machines and higher-level languages reveals somewhat of a mismatch. This is surprising, since CISC machines explicitly represent attempts to match the machine language to the expected needs of hlls. Some features or capabilities of any system are used frequently, others seldom. This is particularly true of compiled code. Studies of production programs produced in higher-level languages reveal a consistent pattern of use of machine language features.

ASSIGNMENTS. Roughly half of all hll instructions are assignment statements, compiled to `copy` instructions. Not only is this an extraordinary proportion of execution to be devoted to a single instruction, that instruction is one that seems inefficient at the machine language level.

COMPLICATED ARITHMETIC EXPRESSIONS. The vast majority of arithmetic expressions involve a single operation. Complicated arithmetic operations are relatively rare. In particular, assignment statements seldom involve more than one operator on the right.

CONDITIONAL JUMPS. Conditional statements form the next most common group of instructions.

PROCEDURE CALLS. Calls to procedures and functions are also very frequent, but the nature of the calls contains some surprises. Most procedure calls involve relatively few parameters. Deep nesting of procedures with little intermediate work is rare. The majority of variable references within called procedures are to local scalar variables.

ADDRESSING MODES. In practice, most instructions employ the simpler addressing modes, such as direct address or register operands, rather than complex modes such as indirect with auto-increment.

Observations of the relative frequency of use of features should be relevant in hardware design. In particular, the frequently used instructions and options should be highly optimized. On the other hand, optimization of infrequently used instructions will have little impact on performance. These observations cast doubt on the philosophy of increasingly complex machine languages. The CISC machines contain operations and addressing modes designed to support structures that were introduced for higher-level languages. But if the structures are not used often, there is little reason to optimize that support.

▷ *Does this approach seem reminiscent of the 10%–90% use of the principle of locality?*

Exploitable Properties of the Higher Models

After the adoption of the microprogrammed model, developments continued in both hardware and software design. These advances altered the relative desirability of approaches to selection of a model.

COMPILATION. Direct programming in simple assembly languages like GAL would be exceedingly difficult for the human programmer. The trends toward more complex machine languages and higher-level languages illustrates the desirability of reducing the human overhead. Today, humans do not even want to program in a complex assembly language; it is not likely that they would relish programming in low-level ones. The μ-machine model was proposed before the first compiler. Actual implementation of μ-coded machines started when compilation was still a primitive art. The more complex machine languages made compilation easier. Subsequent advances have reversed the picture. Most notably, improved compiler design enables the production of very efficient and highly optimized machine code. This suggests that compilers and assemblers might create lower-level code rather than complex machine code. That is, compilers could probably generate RISC code from a high-level language. Using C or some other high-level language, a programmer can write code that, when compiled, will run very efficiently.

MEMORY AND REGISTERS. As noted earlier the increased speed of RAM has made longer programs more practical. Similarly, technology that supports increased numbers of registers reduces the impact of any reduction in addressing modes.

Principles of RISC Architecture

In essence, RISC computing skips the microcode interpretation step. Programs are compiled to a very simple machine language—perhaps as simple as microcode. The driving spirit behind RISC computers is the creation of a machine language that is optimized for the way machines are actually used. The major improvements include

- elimination of the interpretation phase of the emulated fetch/execute cycle
- optimization of frequently used commands
- reduction in RAM accesses and increased register usage

The RISC model represents a return to the machine code model—in a highly optimized version. The instruction set is designed to perform the common actions well. It takes advantage of the relatively small number of common instruction types and operand modes, providing a shorter decoding process. The essential differences between the architecture of RISC machines and that of traditional machines are relatively few. In RISC machines,

- The number of distinct instructions is kept to a minimum (if special instructions are needed, subroutines should be used).
- Those that are used are very simple and are highly optimized.
- Addressing modes are essentially nonexistent: the operands for most instructions are assumed to be in registers. Thus, few instructions will fetch their operands from memory.

- Most instructions have the same format to reduce decoding time.
- RISC machines have large numbers of registers. Essentially all operands are kept in registers. Parameters are always passed using registers, and most variables are held in registers.
- Instruction processing is pipelined.

REDUCED INSTRUCTION SET. The greater the number of instructions, the more complicated the hardware. Decoders, addresses, bus connections, and ALUs can all be reduced in size or number with smaller instruction sets. Leaner circuitry means faster execution of individual instructions.

OPTIMIZING THE COMMON OPERATIONS. The RISC design optimizes those machine operations that it does support, which are the most common operations. Since each of the common actions is very efficient, overall performance is also efficient. Some of the mechanisms are surprisingly simple.

DIRECT IMPLEMENTATION. Much of the μ-code was devoted to decoding an instruction. The greater the number of instructions, the more complicated the decoding process. Elimination of the decoding phase reduces the total time for one operation by half or more.

COMPILED CODE. The RISC philosophy assumes that the user will be writing in a higher-level language and that the code will therefore be compiled. In particular, it assumes that software exists to optimize code to match the structures needed by the RISC machine. Not only does simpler code require more statements, but the optimization of RISC machines sometimes requires seemingly unnatural statement orderings.

VARIABLE STORAGE. RISC machines have large numbers of registers, which can be used for local variables and parameters. Since references to global variables are relatively infrequent, this means that most operands of most instructions will be register operands. Thus, RAM memory access will be relatively infrequent. In fact, RISC design demands that, on average, one instruction is executed every memory cycle.

Implementation of RISC Instructions

The small number of instructions, coupled with their simplicity makes it possible to implement each one efficiently. Some of the highlights include the following.

SINGLE-CYCLE INSTRUCTIONS. Perhaps the single most important characteristic of RISC machines is that the fetch/execute cycle for virtually all instructions requires a single fetch: the instruction itself. The operands are always in registers. The only two exceptions are

```
load     RAM_location⇒register
```

and

```
store     register⇒RAM_location
```

Since the RAM access is the most expensive part of each cycle, this creates a minimal execution time per instruction. Execution can proceed as fast as the instructions can be fetched. This also reduces the complexity of the control unit: there is only one addressing mode; instructions are physically shorter; all instructions execute in the same amount of time. The restriction of operands to registers may appear to be problematic. The machine must have a large number of registers. When a RAM operand must be used, it is simply loaded in one step and the operation performed in a second step:

```
load      some_item⇒reg10
add       reg10⇒reg20
```

The `load` instruction cannot be completed in a fetch cycle, but we will see that that does not create as significant a problem as it may seem.

PARAMETER PASSING. RISC machines can take advantage of the observed characteristics of typical subroutine calls—few deep nestings, few parameters, few global variables—using procedure call protocols that would have appeared extravagant on other machines. Parameters and local variables are two important motivators for built-in stacks and indirect addressing. Addressing modes such as indirect with auto-increment exist primarily for manipulating stacks and queues. An obvious reduction in complexity results from the removal of complicated modes.

RISC machines use a large number of registers for procedure calls. In effect, every procedure gets its own register set. Register addressing is not absolute but is relative to a *register set pointer*. Figure 15-7 shows the pointer and the registers assigned to procedure `A`. The registers are divided into three groups: parameters,

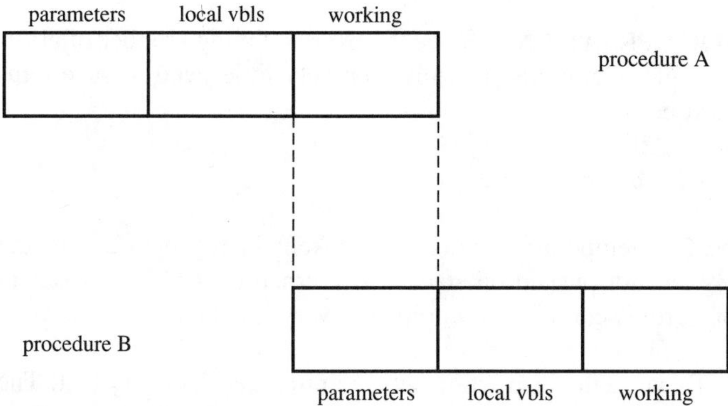

FIGURE 15-7
Overlapped registers for local variables and parameters.

local variables, and working storage. Each group is used for the purpose implied by its name. While `A` is the active procedure, the register set pointer points to the bottom of `A`'s register set. `A` addresses all of its parameters, local variables, and working storage relative to the pointer. When `A` calls procedure `B`, `A` copies the necessary parameters to its own working area before calling `B`. The subroutine jump updates the register set pointer to point to `A`'s working area, which the figure shows overlapping `B`'s parameter area. This creates a sort of automatic context switching. `B` assumes that the pointer designates its own parameter area. That is, the parameters were passed from `A` to `B` by updating the register set pointer. Notice the improvements. Simple register-to-register operations were used to pass the parameters. Values can be returned by the same process. If `A` needs to call `B` (or perhaps some other procedure) again, it can leave the values in the working area. `B` can call another procedure with no need to save the registers passed from `A`.

LOCAL VARIABLES. The same register set pointer provides for easy handling of local variables. When `B` is called, its new register area includes locations for all of `B`'s local variables. Each variable is held at a fixed displacement from the register set pointer. When `B` terminates, the pointer is reset to point to `A`'s register set. `A` can thus call many other procedures (even recursively) without interfering with its own register storage locations. No stack is needed.

COPY. The most common instruction in most programs is the `copy` instruction, yet this is the simplest instruction to optimize. In the machine language model, every instruction involved one or more copy steps. In particular, one description of the `copy` command contained four internal copies. In the microprogrammed model, each macro-instruction including a `copy` required two phases. The `copy` required essentially as long to execute as any other instruction. Virtually all RISC `copy`s are single-step direct copies from one register to another. Consider how this might be optimized. If both operands are registers, the source can be copied directly to the destination through the bus. Nothing needs to be fetched. No ALU or intermediate steps are needed. No explicit store step is needed. A copy can be made in a single clock pulse after decoding.

SIMPLE ARITHMETIC OPERATIONS. Since the overwhelming number of arithmetic operations are single operations, there is relatively little need to save temporary results as would be needed for

```
assign     a⇐(b* c) + (d* e)
```

This implies that the few temporary results can be kept in registers as are the scalar variables. They are not pushed on stacks or returned to RAM. Register to register arithmetic operations can also be completed very quickly.

OPTIMIZED CODE. Because the instruction set is minimal, each is very fast. The decoding step is quick. There is no need to determine the length of the instruction: they are all equal. There is no need to determine the addressing modes: there is only one. Little time is spent decoding the opcode: there are very few. Operand fetches are fast because the operands are normally in registers. The relatively few complex operations are slower, but fewer. Suppose `subtract` were used relatively infrequently, and a machine had no hardware `subtract` command. The total machine architecture would be simpler. The compiler could generate the equivalent negation and addition instructions; little added cost is incurred. More likely candidates for such constructive processes would be rarer variations on basic commands, such as `add-decimal` or `add-with-carry`.

Pipelined Instructions

A water pipe or an oil pipe conducts a product from one end to the other. It is not necessary for the first drop of water to travel all the way through the pipe before the second drop enters the pipe. The pipe conducts a continuous stream of fluid. In previous models, the flow of instructions behaved in exactly the opposite manner. Each instruction or f/e step was executed in its entirety before the next one commenced. RISC machines speed up their cycle by mimicking the behavior of a pipe.

Consider three observations about the fetch/execute cycle as it must work in a RISC machine:

1. The fetch-phase or first three steps of the cycle (fetch instruction, increment PC, decode instruction) are identical for all instructions. Only the execute phase differs, and much of that is the same for many instructions.
2. A memory fetch is the slowest individual operation. Every instruction has at least one RAM memory fetch—the instruction fetch. Only the explicit instructions, `load` and `store`, allow more than one memory fetch.
3. With the exception of jump instructions, the location of the next instruction is known prior to the execution phase of the current instruction.

Pipelined processing takes advantage of these observations to speed up processing. As soon as the first half of the cycle is completed for one instruction, the corresponding step of the next instruction is initiated. For example, the steps for two instructions might be outlined as:

instruction 1		**instruction 2**	
phase		**phase**	
f	`fetch instruction_1`		
f	`increment PC_1`		
f	`decode instruction_1`	f	`fetch instruction_2`
e	`fetch operands_1`	f	`increment PC_2`
e	`perform operation_1`	f	`decode instruction_2`
e	`store results_1`	e	`fetch operands_2`
		e	`perform operation_2`
		e	`store results_2`

During the execute phase of the first cycle, the fetch phase of the next cycle can begin. Consider the synchronization a little more carefully. As soon as instruction 1 has been fetched and the PC has been incremented, there is no reason to wait before fetching the second instruction. Since the memory fetch is the slowest step, it will be advantageous to get a head start. The only restriction on the second instruction fetch is that it must not place a new instruction into the IR until the previous instruction has been fully decoded (which might include operand addresses). Multiple IRs would relieve that problem. Most RISC instructions have no RAM operands, guaranteeing that the perform half of the cycle can complete its task in less time than required by the instruction-fetch portion. In fact, it might be possible to begin a third instruction after instruction 2 has incremented its PC, but before instruction 1 has completed. Figure 15-8 provides an abstract representation of the process over several instructions. The pipelined instructions result in instruction execution at the rate that they can be fetched from memory, with no additional time needed for the execution phase.

Delayed Instructions

There are two potential problems with the pipelined instructions. Generally the results of one operation are complete by the time the next instruction needs them.

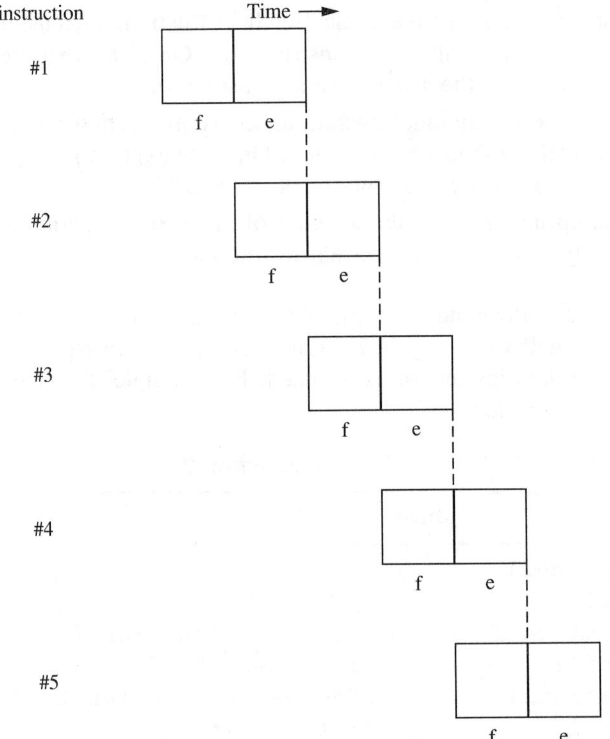

FIGURE 15-8
Pipelined instructions.

In particular, the store of one instruction is complete by the operand fetch of the next instruction. But a `load` instruction requires an extra fetch. Its result will not be ready in time. Apparently, a `load` will not only require more time because of the extra fetch, but it will prevent pipelining of the next instruction. `Jumps` also sound problematic. Apparently, the instruction following a branch will begin execution before the branch is complete.

LOADS. The problematic situations for `loads` are well defined. There is a conflict whenever the register being loaded is needed as an operand by the next operation. The primary solution is a software solution. The compiler detects any conflict. It then attempts to reorder the code to avoid the conflict. For example, suppose the compiler generated the code sequence

```
add       reg1⇒reg2
load      some_loc⇒reg3
add       reg3⇒reg2
```

Clearly the second `add` must wait for the load. The compiler could reshuffle the instructions:

```
load      some_loc⇒reg3
add       reg1⇒reg2
add       reg3⇒reg2
```

The code is equivalent, but the loaded value will not cause a delay. In effect, the `add` is delayed, but the technique is called a *delayed load* nonetheless. Occasionally, the technique creates code that appears incorrect but actually works because of the delay. For example, suppose both `adds` involved the same registers:

```
add       reg1⇒reg2
load      some_loc⇒reg1
add       reg1⇒reg2
```

The reshuffling will create

```
load      some_loc⇒reg1
add       reg1⇒reg2
add       reg1⇒reg2
```

which appears to `load` a value into `reg1` and then add it to `reg2`—twice. However, if the new value does not arrive at `reg1` until after the first `add` has fetched its operands, the code is correct.

If the compiler cannot find any statement that it can move after the `load`, it must insert a `no-op`. In that case, there will be a loss of efficiency. Fortunately, this need not happen often. The large number of registers reduces the number of `loads` required, and intelligent compilers can usually reshuffle when one is needed. In the case of a `store`, there is normally no delay. Execution may continue as soon as the value has been placed in the MBR.

> ▷ *The following instruction need never depend on the value just stored. Why not?*

JUMPS. The second potential problem for pipelined instructions is the `jump` instruction. Following any form of `jump` instruction, the syntactically next instruction may not be executed. If the instructions are pipelined, however, the next will have started (the instruction will be fetched) before the `jump` instruction finishes. The PC does not change until after the unwanted instruction has been fetched. No catastrophic harm has been accomplished yet—no results have been stored; no values have been altered. In the case of an absolute `jump` instruction, the second instruction is simply terminated and any partial results thrown away. If jumps were rare, there would be no harm at all; no significant time would be lost. Unfortunately, we saw earlier that `jumps` (including subroutine calls) form the second largest group of instructions. If every instruction (or even most instructions) were a `jump` instruction, the wasted instructions would defeat the advantages of pipelining.

Efficient compilation can also relieve this problem. A simple optimizing compiler can reduce convoluted code somewhat. But nonremovable `jumps` do occur relatively frequently. As with the delayed loads, the real improvement is created by reversing two instructions and using a *delayed jump*.

```
copy            a⇒b
jump:always     →place
```

is replaced with

```
jump:always     →place
copy            a⇒b
```

On the surface, it appears that the `copy` statement will never be executed, but, follow the details of the overlapped instruction:

jump instruction	**copy instruction**
`fetch the jump`	
`increment the PC (to the copy)`	
`decode the jump`	`fetch the copy`
`fetch the target`	`increment the PC (past the jump)`
`store in PC`	`decode the copy`
	`fetch A`
	`store in B`

The `jump` does not finish changing the PC until after the `copy` has been fetched. Execution of the `copy` completes before the PC is accessed again. Thus, both instructions are executed with no wasted steps. Conditional jumps sound more problematic, but the same mechanism will work—assuming the conditional jump does not depend on the result of the `copy`. It is the compiler's job to optimize code to avoid such situations. Again, `no-ops` are used when no reordering can be found.

RAM ACCESS. Some access to RAM will be necessary no matter how well variables are allocated to registers and no matter how efficient the compiler is. Only `load` and `store` may do so. Note, however, that this potentially could result in three concurrent instructions:

- one in the fetch phase,
- one in the execute phase, and
- one in a memory store cycle.

To maintain the one instruction per memory-fetch rate, memory must be improved to allow two memory accesses per stage. To see how this might be possible, recall that programs can be assembled into two forks: program and data. In the preceding case, one access represents a fetch of the instruction, the other a store of data. The two are in separate forks. If RAM memory is divided into two portions, with separate buses, simultaneous stores present no problem. `Load` instructions create a similar problem: three instructions must execute simultaneously. For example, consider the following sequence of instructions:

```
load
add
subtract
```

At cycle 1, the `load` command is fetched. At cycle 2, the `add` command is fetched and execution of the `load` begins. Since the `load` cannot be completed within the cycle, it must continue into the next. At cycle 3, the `load` is completed, the `add` executed, and the `subtract` is fetched. The steps do not interfere as long as the `add` instruction does not involve the object fetched by the `load` instruction. Again, it is the compiler's job to "anticipate" the needed `loads`, placing them earlier in the code than they might normally appear.

Comparison

Although it is perhaps too early to state definitively that RISC machines are the direction of the future, the outlook is very promising. In the workstation world, RISC machines such as the Sun SparcStation outperform 80386 machines by somewhere between 2 and 5 to one (depending on which model machines are compared and which performance benchmark is used). Clearly many factors other than the RISC-CISC question are involved when one compares machines from multiple vendors, but no matter how one looks at it, the results suggest a significant future for RISC machines.

SUMMARY

The microprogrammed model fits logically between the machine language and digital logic models. In effect, a microprogrammed machine is a very simple machine that runs a program emulating the language known as the machine language. The simple machine differs from other models, in that it provides a more complex data path, allowing simultaneous transfer of information between registers and multi-part instructions. Each instruction can designate multiple operands, distinct destinations, and an automatic jump after the instruction. The multiple parts are designed to take advantage of the repetitive nature of the fetch/execute cycle. The entire microprogram control is kept in a very high-speed cache memory, and no instructions have RAM operands.

The RISC (reduced instruction set computer) model rejects the interpreted machine model and reverts to the original machine code model—using a simplified machine code. The price paid is that the instruction set is minimal. Only the most common instructions exist at the machine level. All others must be built up from the single set. RISC machines place all effort into making individual instructions run efficiently. Three of the major tools used to achieve this reduction are the elimination of RAM operands, increased number of registers, and pipelined code.

SUGGESTED READING

The following texts can provide a more in-depth investigation of CISC or RISC architectures and the relationships between the two.

Hayes, J. *Computer architecture and organization*. New York: McGraw-Hill, 1988.

Hennessy, J., and D. Patterson. *Computer architecture: a quantitative approach*. San Mateo, Calif.: Morgan Kaufman, 1990.

Mano, M. *Computer engineering*. Englewood Cliffs, N.J.: Prentice Hall, 1988.

Patterson, D. Reduced instruction set computers. *Communications of the ACM* (V-28-1) 1985.

Stallings, W. *Computer organization and architecture*. New York: Macmillan, 1990.

Tannenbaum, A. *Structured computer organization*. Englewood Cliffs, N.J.: Prentice Hall, 1990.

Ward, S., and R. Halstead. *Computation structures*. New York: McGraw-Hill, 1990.

Wilkes, M. The best way to design an automatic calculating machine. *The proceedings of the Manchester University computer inaugural conference*. Manchester, England, 1951.

EXERCISES

15.1. Assume GAL is microcoded. Define a microcode language suitable for implementing GAL.

15.2. Complete Project III of Appendix 2.

15.3. Find and read the original paper on microprogramming by Wilkes, cited in the Suggested Reading.

15.4. Describe the changes from the microprogrammed model described in this chapter that would be needed to use a jump table in the decoding process.

15.5. If you were designing a new machine today, would it be microprogramed or RISC? Why?

15.6. Compare and contrast the microcode language of a microprogrammed machine and the reduced instruction set of a RISC machine.

15.7. Create a code segment for which a `no-op` is needed to make a delayed instruction work properly.

15.8. Suppose that (*a*) procedure calls typically had no more than three parameters and five local scalar variables, (*b*) procedures were seldom nested more than five deep, and (*c*) each needed fewer than three temporary storage locations. How many general-purpose registers would a RISC machine need to handle the normal situations efficiently?

15.9. Suppose you were asked to define a language Thin-GAL, which is a RISC version of GAL. What instructions would you remove altogether? What instructions would you add? What operand modes would you eliminate? What impact would an increased register set have on the commands? What impact would the prohibition on RAM operands have on the instruction format?

15.10. Actually define the language for Exercise 15.9. Rewrite any three code segments from Chapter 2 in this language.

15.11. The chapter did not address the issue of I/O for either microprogrammed or RISC machines. What impact would I/O have on each of these models?

CHAPTER 16

ALTERNATIVES TO THE VON NEUMANN MODEL: PARALLEL MACHINES[1]

INTRODUCTION

Each of the models used in this text describes a classic von Neumann machine: binary, single sequentially-addressed (primary) memory, stored program, controller (fetch/execute), sequential instructions. Chapter 11 suggested that the concept of a virtual machine could be used to improve overall performance. It did not change the hardware—just the correlation between user model and physical machine. The microprogrammed model outlined in Chapter 15 is a variation on the original theme, yet it is possible to view it as a basic von Neumann machine running an emulation program. Similarly, interrupts provided a variation on the original model, but those too could be described in terms of the classic fetch/execute cycle. Today, many such variations on the hardware itself are being explored in research laboratories and even in applications settings. Improvements such as miniaturization and very large scale integration speed up existing processes, but they do not change the basic model.

[1] Chapter 16 assumes completion of the material in Chapter 12.

It is also possible to improve performance by creating new forms of computers, ones with alternative underlying assumptions. Although in-depth discussion of such alternatives is beyond the scope of the text, it is possible to provide a very brief overview of one of the more promising of these: parallel machines. The parallel computation model rejects one basic assumption of the von Neumann model: sequential execution. Parallel execution represents only one small change in the model, but it opens up a great many possibilities.

The traditional technique for improving program performance has been to use a faster computer. The primary approach in making faster computers over the years has been to construct logically equivalent machines from smaller components. Smaller machines mean shorter distances for signals to travel, and hence shorter delays between actions. Unfortunately, this approach becomes more difficult with each success. An alternative is to use more than one processor. It seems that twice as many processors should be able to solve a problem in half the time. In a sense, the development of personal computers represented the first example of this principle. Since today's microcomputers are—by almost any definition—more powerful than yesterday's mainframes, placing an entire computer on each worker's desk theoretically increases the total computational power by the number of machines placed in use. Each worker can compute simultaneously. Thus, if N users needed T minutes of computer time on a mainframe, each user with an individual computer should be able to accomplish the task in T/N minutes. Chapter 12 showed that this is not quite true, since from the computer's perspective much time is wasted waiting for the human. On the other hand, added savings may be possible because less overhead is required without the virtual time-sharing machine. In this case, a transition from one computer for N users, to N computers for N users will, hopefully, yield a computational *speedup* of N times the original rate.

> ▷ *This situation is one of several in which the state of the art has come full circle: originally, one machine served one user at a time. Then time-sharing allowed one machine to serve several users at a time and that was an improvement. Later, personal computers served one person at a time. How can that also be an improvement?*

The same principle can be applied to a single user working on a single machine. If that user could be provided with N machines, the work should only take $1/N$ times as long. For example, suppose the user had a program in which the major structure consisted of a block of code of the form:

```
for count ⇐ 1 to N do
    <some computation involving only the Nth element of an array>;
```

Since the computation involves only the Nth element, every computation should be independent of each of the others. The tasks could be performed in parallel, by sending each subtask to a separate processor. Each processor would perform the calculation for a single array element, and the entire task would be complete in the time required by one processor to compute a single element.

Similarly, consider a program in which the primary structure is composed of independent steps:

```
process_1
process_2
...
process_n
```

in which no process depends on the results of any other process. Again, the program could be divided into the *n* separate processes, and each process performed on a separate processor. The total time should be no worse than the time for the longest subprocess.

Semi-parallel Constructs

Simple forms of parallelism are not new and can be found even within the von Neumann model. The RISC machine described in Chapter 15 includes a primitive form of parallelism: pipelined code. In one sense, such code is executed in parallel: one instruction is executed while the next is fetched. Such pipelining can produce very significant speedups. However, it does not represent true parallelism. There is really only one complete processor. It works on only one set of data at a time. It can execute only one operation at a time on that data. True parallel machines have more than one processor.

Other models also included some minor forms of parallelism:

- At the digital electronics level, one higher-level step could be started before the completion of the previous step (e.g., memory-fetch and PC-increment steps).
- All ALUs can simultaneously process a given pair of operands—as long as only a single ALU attempts to store the results.
- Interrupts enabled two blocks of code—either related, as in the case of a debugger interrupt, or unrelated, as in the case of a multi-user operating system—to appear to be performed *concurrently* (logically at the same time), although in reality one CPU still processed only one instruction at a time.
- Input/output peripherals can be viewed as machines running in parallel with the processor and communicating through the I/O channels.

Within a single step, portions of the fetch/execute cycle may be parallel; two steps might be overlapped, or external devices may run in parallel. But *the* main processor is sequential. Is it possible to construct a machine that actually performs multiple instructions in parallel? The answer is certainly "yes!"—but with great complication. A related question is "Would it be desirable to have actual parallel processors?" Again, the answer is "yes!"

How much of the computation process can be parallelized? Perhaps a more fundamental question to ask is, What aspects of the von Neumann machine can be parallelized? If there are two CPUs, are there two control units, or just two sets of ALUs? Are there one or two clocks? One or two sets of memory? How does each processor view the other, as an external device or as an extension of itself? Is one processor in charge, or are they competitive?

Communication between Processes

Many of these questions can be restated in terms of communication: How do two processes communicate with each other? Suppose a single machine is created with two separate CPUs and two separate memories. It is a single machine in the sense that the two subunits together make up a single logical whole. If the programs on the two CPUs make no reference to each other, they might as well be two separate machines (e.g., two personal computers). Parallelism becomes important when the two programs can interact in some manner. The simplest form of communication is synchronization; each processor must have a means of signalling to the other that it should wait or proceed. For example, one processor may need to indicate that it has not completed a result needed by the other. Such communication can be accomplished by one program sending a signal, called a *semaphore,* to the other stating "do not proceed until I tell you to." On receiving the message, the receiver should enter a wait state until a second message, "you may now proceed," is received. Such a simple communication technique might be useful if the two processors shared an external device. Perhaps they both write to the same printer, in which case the semaphore could be used to coordinate the order in which the two processors write on the printed page. For example, one might have responsibility for creating all the headers, and the other for filling in the data. The two processors may work in parallel but their output must be sequential. If one processor writes to a disk drive and a second reads the data from that drive, a semaphore could be used to signal that data had been written. Such a system could be used to preprocess batch input for the second machine.

▷ *Is this related to pipelining?*

Neither of the previous examples is actually a likely candidate for wide use for coordinating parallel processes. The link between the two machines was an external device, which must be considerably slower than either processor. Unless the calculations were quite complex, it would hardly be necessary for two processors to drive a single printer. Indeed, one printer may be insufficient for one processor.

Parallel machines usually have more tightly integrated configurations, sharing more than just an external device. The two primary methods for communicating parallel processors, *shared memory* and *message passing,* each require altering the model of the hardware. In a shared-memory configuration, each processor has access to the same RAM (perhaps in addition to privately accessible RAM). As soon as one processor has saved data into the shared memory, it would be accessible to the other processor. Some semaphore mechanism may still be needed to indicate the status of data, so each machine knows that it is updated. In addition, there needs to be a mechanism for resolving contention for memory. That is, if two processors attempt to write to the same memory location at the same time, there must be a mechanism to resolve the question: "Whose value gets placed in the location?" Similarly, if both attempt to read simultaneously but from two different locations, there must be a mechanism for preventing the two addresses from being merged into some sort of hodgepodge of meaningless information.

In a message-passing configuration, no memory is shared. Each machine may communicate with the other by sending a message. The mechanism is essentially the same as if the processors were input and output devices. One processor places a value in a buffer and issues a send command. The second receives an interrupt indicating that data has arrived. The message may be more complex than the simple yes/no of the semaphore. There are no problems of memory or bus contention, but each processor must be prepared to deal with the interrupts as they arrive. Any delay in responding may slow down the other processor.

TOPOLOGIES AND ALGORITHMS

In order to select a configuration for the processor, one first needs to envision how it will be used. Processors can be connected in many ways. Perhaps the most important aspect of the configuration is the *topology:* the description of the machines in terms of the communication links that connect them. Logically, it would seem best if every processor could talk with every other processor. Unfortunately, distinct paths between any two of N processors require $N^2/2$ data paths. (Yes, this should sound strangely similar to the problems of communications between registers within a single processor.) Alternatively, some form of global bus could be used, but such a system would require synchronization. With a single processor, the internal bus is controlled by the CPU, but a full multiple-processor configuration lacks a central controller. A bus would also require some message labeling, so that each processor could determine which messages it should read from the bus, and even the source of any message that was received (with a single processor, the source of data never mattered to a register).

Normally, a much more restricted topology is used—one in which each processor can talk only with specified neighbors. If two non-neighbors need to communicate, the assistance of intermediate processors must be invoked. For many applications such communication is quite sufficient. In general, the algorithm and the topology are intimately related. Each topology has a class of algorithms that it can perform well. Some algorithms can make excellent use of simple topologies such as a pipeline, while others require much more complicated configurations. Following are several of the more common topologies, each with an example of an algorithm that takes advantage of the particular configuration.

Vector Processing

An easy-to-envision use of parallel processors is vector processing. For example, suppose that you wish to square every element of a linear array. The operation on any cell is the same and independent of the others. The parallel process could be described as

For every processor_i
  compute: array[i] ⇐ array[i] * array[i]

Unfortunately, this description does not address one of the most central issues: communication. How do the values get into the array? How does each processor access elements of the same array, etc. These questions can better be addressed in the context of pipelines.

Pipelines

A pipeline is a series of processors connected as a linear array. In the typical pipelined process, each processor performs a portion of a process and passes the partial result on to the next processor. The analogy to RISC pipelined code is quite valid. The important characteristic of pipelined processors is that when each processor has completed its single step of the program, it can start over using new data—it need not wait until all processors have completed their tasks. While the second processor is processing the first set of data, the first processor can start to process the next set of data. For example, consider first a machine designed to add $N+1$ numbers. If N processors are arranged as in Figure 16-1, a simple algorithm could be run on each processor K:

add values from above (input) and from left (processor k−1)
  pass the sum to processor at right (k+1)

The first processor receives both of its two inputs from the outside world, adds them, and passes the sum on to the second, which receives an additional input and adds it in, and so on. When the running total leaves the last processor, it is equal to the sum of all the inputs. By itself, this algorithm saves nothing since no addition may start until the previous sum has been completed. Consider a situation in which a large number, M, of such summations is needed. The algorithm for each processor can be modified slightly:

while more numbers arrive
  add input to result from processor k−1
  pass the sum to processor k+1

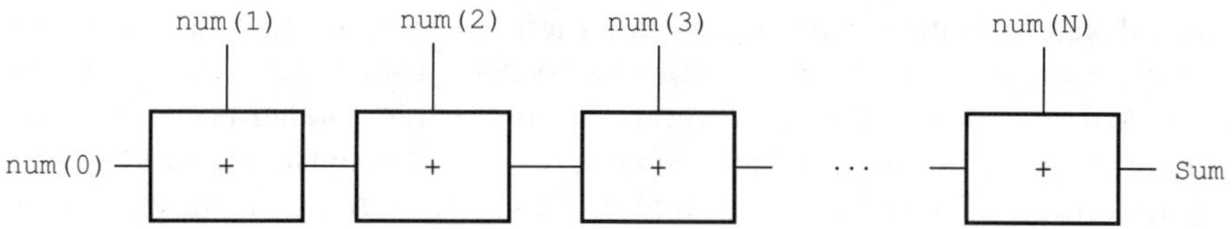

FIGURE 16-1
A pipelined adder.

Each processor may start on a new computation as soon as it has completed its role in the previous one. The output from the last processor is thus the series of summations. Once started, the N processors complete a new summation of N numbers as fast as each single processor can complete its simple addition. The total time is proportional to the number of summations M, not $M*N$. The partial sums flow through the processors like water through a pipeline.

Algorithms such as the preceding are said to be *systolic*. The word systolic means "pumping" (the same term used to refer to the larger of the two numbers comprising your blood pressure). A typical systolic algorithm works as a pipeline: each processor completes a portion of the task, passes its results on to the next processor, and repeats the same calculation of the next data item. Generally, very good efficiencies can be obtained by systolic processes. The primary constraint is that the task must be sufficiently modular so that it can be broken into N pieces for the N processors. Message passing in examples such as this is relatively light: each machine passes one value per computational cycle. (The next section includes an example of a two-dimensional systolic process.)

Unfortunately, the preceding example may not be practical for large N because it assumes that each processor has a unique input channel—a situation that is seldom economical. More often, a single processor is designated as the input processor, and a single processor (not necessarily distinct from the previous) as the output processor. For example, a parallel system might be given as input a series of function definitions $f_1 \ldots f_n$ and be expected to create as output the series of integrals of the input functions:

$$\int f_1 \, dx \ldots \int f_n \, dx \qquad \text{on the interval } [0\text{–}1]$$

For each processor$_i$ in the machine, an identical program

```
for i-1 functions
   receive function from processor_{i+1} (from right)
   pass to processor_{i-1} (to the left)
calculate ∫ f_i dx
pass the answer to processor_{i-1}
while more answers arrive
   forward any answers from processor_{i+1} to processor_{i-1}
```

provides the needed computation. This algorithm numbers the processors from left to right like the previous algorithm. However, input passes from right to left, enabling clearer numbering of tasks. The rightmost processor, N, receives the input, and the leftmost processor, 1, is the output register. Each processor first passes i-1 values to the i-1 processors to its left (by passing the values first, the other processors can get started on their task sooner). Then the processor does its primary task: calculating the ith integral (this is the true parallel portion). Each processor passes its result to the left. Finally, it passes the remaining results from its right to its left. By passing its own result before forwarding the answers from the right, it assumes that its own answer will be output before the later values, and therefore that the results will appear in the same order as the original input.

Not all pipelined programs represent algorithms that are essentially identical to single processor algorithms. Suppose that you want to use the same N processors to sort N data elements. One algorithm allows each processor to find the largest element that it receives and pass the rest on to the next. After each has found its maximum, the processors contain the sorted data.

```
read (max) from left                      ;first value is largest so far
while more input do
  read (new)
  if (new > max)                          ;is the new one largest of all
     then swap (new, max)                 ;send the smaller
  send (new) to right
```

All that remains is for each processor to send its local max out to the right:

```
send max to right
while values arrive from the left
  pass value to the right.
```

The values will exit the pipeline in increasing order. Note that this algorithm sorts in time proportional to N, which seems to contradict the general guideline that sorts require N*log(N) steps—but that rule assumes only one processor.

Grid or Matrix Problems

Picture a two-dimensional matrix, as in Figure 16-2, in which each cell contains a processor. Each processor can communicate with its four physical neighbors. There are at least two broad classes of problems for which this configuration is useful: two-dimensional systolic or pipeline problems, and physical modeling problems in which each processor can model a physically distinct subset of the data.

When an engineer or physicist needs to model physical phenomena such as weather or temperature conduction through a solid, it is often useful to make the simplifying assumption that the entire object being modeled can be approximated by dividing it into subpieces and modeling each subpiece. At any instant in time, each subpiece is assumed to be influenced only by its immediate neighbors. A grid array of processors can be used for such a problem by assigning the responsibility for each physical segment to a single processor. Each processor runs an iterative process:

```
for time ⇐ 1 to T
  value(segment(i,j),time+1) =
     f(segment(i,j), segment (i+1,j), segment (i,j+1),
        segment (i–1,j), segment (i,j–1), time)
```

In each time interval, the value for each segment is calculated based on its own previous value and the previous values of each of that segment's four neighbors.

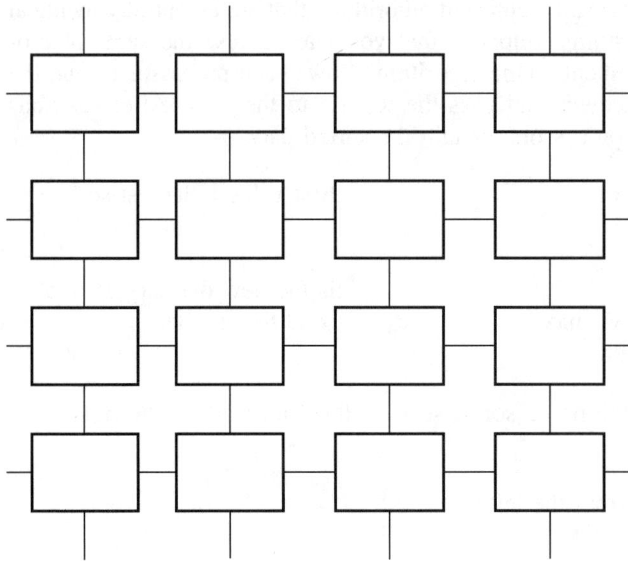

FIGURE 16-2
A two-dimensional grid of processors.

For example, the temperature of a segment on a sheet of metal at a given time is dependent on its own previous temperature as well as the temperature of its neighboring segments in the previous time interval. Each processor sends its own description to its neighbors and likewise receives the description of its neighbors. It then calculates its new values based on those descriptions. Each segment can be calculated in parallel since the values for time, t, depend only on the values for time t-1. Note, however, that it is necessary to assure that no processor gets more than one time slice ahead of the others. This is generally assured by the structure of the full algorithm:

```
for time ⇐ 1 to T
    transmit current values to all neighbors
    receive values from four neighbors
    value(segment(i,j), time+1) ⇐ function of neighbors' values
```

The process can never perform its calculation until it has received the current values from its neighbors, assuring that the processors stay in step with each other.

Matrix multiplication provides another obvious use for a two-dimensional pipeline. Recall that the product C of two $n*n$ matrices A and B is defined by

$$c_{ij} = \sum_{k=1}^{n} a_{ik} * b_{kj}$$

Each of the n^2 individual cells requires a series of n multiplications and n-1 additions, or a total of n^3 multiplications (and as many additions). Using a matrix of processors, the problem can be solved with N multiplications per processor. The general idea is that two streams of values are passed across each processor, one consisting of a row from the first matrix (passed horizontally) and the other of a column of the second matrix (passed vertically). For such applications, it is often useful to treat the edge processors as if they are logically connected to the opposite edge, as in Figure 16-3.

Each pipeline is thus converted to a ring. Such a topology is called a *torus* or a *toroidal* matrix. To calculate the matrix product, assume that each processor$_{i,j}$ starts with the values of $a_{i,j}$ and $b_{i,j}$ (the values could originally have been passed from a common input processor). Processor$_{0,0}$ could calculate its value immediately, but the others must shift their values so that each contains a and b values that participate in their product.

```
for count ⇐ 1 to i
   processor_{i,j} passes its a value to the right
for count ⇐ 1 to j
   processor_{i,j} passes its b value down
```

Each processor$_{i,j}$ will then calculate $c_{i,j}$ using the algorithm:

```
pass own values to neighbor processors:
   pass a_{i,j} right to processor_{i,j+1} {actually j+1 mod n}
   pass b_{i,j} down to processor_{i+1,j} {actually i+1 mod n}
set sum ⇐ 0
```

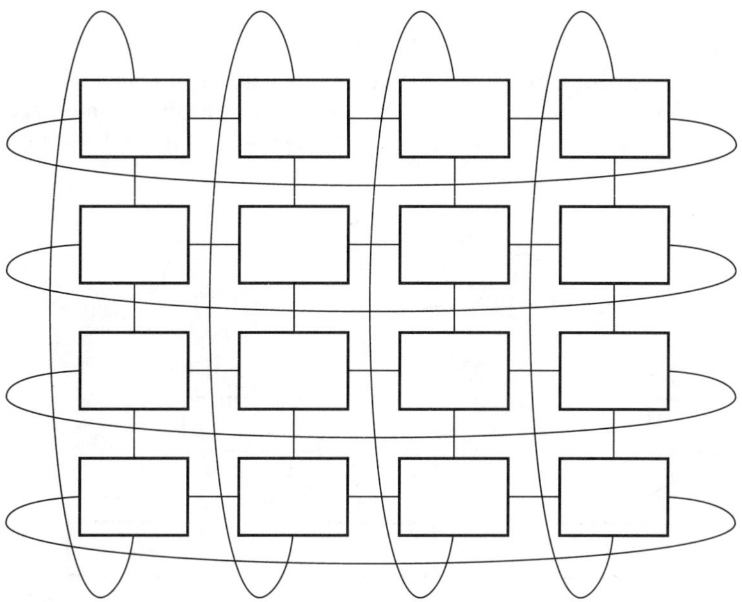

FIGURE 16-3
Toroidal arrangement of processors.

```
for count ⇐ 1 to n do
  receive a_{i,j-count} from above {assume modular counters}
    hold and pass on the value
  receive b_{j-count,i} from left
    hold and pass on the value
  set sum ⇐ sum + ( a_{i,j-1} * b_{j-1,i})
```

For example, $\text{processor}_{1,1}$ will first pass its values to $\text{processor}_{2,1}$ and $\text{processor}_{1,2}$. Since the connections wrap around, the first values that processor will receive will be

$$a_{n,1} \text{ and } b_{1,n}$$

followed by the pairs $a_{n-1,1}$ and $b_{1,n-1,}$ then $a_{n-2,1}$ and $b_{1,n-2,}$ until it finally receives the last values $a_{1,1}$ and $b_{1,1}$.

It is also possible to configure a three-dimensional matrix. Whereas each processor in the two-dimensional matrix has four neighbors, processors in the three-dimensional matrix would each have six neighbors. Note the increased number of neighbors not only increases the physical complexity of the system but also increases the complexity of the programs that run on the system. In the pure pipeline model, all input came from a single direction. Therefore, the program always knew the source of the input. As the number of possible sources of input increases, so too does the complexity of the program that must deal with the input.

Trees

The processors in the previous examples all seemed to work as a team, without any specific leader. Some problems seem to demand that one process be in charge and delegate authority. A processor could be configured as in Figure 16-4 with

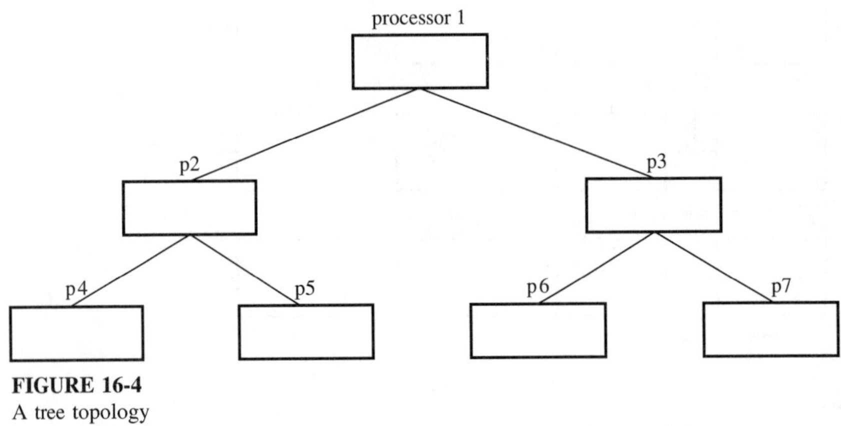

FIGURE 16-4
A tree topology

subordinate slaves, to which it hands out portions of the task and then collects the answer when complete.

The obvious task for such a system is a calculator. Each node receives an expression to be calculated. The processor notes the primary operator and passes the two operands to subordinate processors:

```
accept expression: operand1 operator operand2
for each operand 1 & 2
   if operand is atomic, i.e., contains no operator
   then
      use operand as is
   else
      pass operand expression to a subordinate processor
      use the result when returned as operand
apply operator to the two operands
return result.
```

For example, in processing the expression

$$(((7 + 4) * (9 / 3)) - ((1 * 6)\text{-}(4 / 2)))$$

processor 1 would accept the entire expression and start a series:

$$(((7 + 4) * (9/3))\text{-}((1 * 6)\text{-}(4/2))) \rightarrow P1$$

$$((7 + 4) * (9/3)) \rightarrow P2 \qquad ((1 * 6)\text{-}(4/2)) \rightarrow P3$$

$$(7 + 4) \rightarrow P4; \qquad (9/3) \rightarrow P5; \qquad (1 * 6) \rightarrow P6; \qquad (4/2) \rightarrow P7$$

Then processors 4 through 7 each calculate a value and pass the result back up the tree:

$$P4 \rightarrow 11; \qquad P5 \rightarrow 3; \qquad P6 \rightarrow 6; \qquad P7 \rightarrow 2$$

$$P2 \rightarrow 33 \qquad P3 \rightarrow 4$$

$$P1 \rightarrow 29$$

After processors 2 and 3 perform their calculations, P1 can produce the final result. Of course, this example would probably generate more overhead, due to the communication requirements, than it saved. However if the "atomic" operands were themselves quite complicated (e.g., each atomic operator was a function call such as square root), significant savings would result. Note that the parent node is necessarily idle while it awaits the results from its two child processors. Most algorithms using such a topology take advantage of the idle process by using the parent to perform the calculations of one of the child nodes: P1 passes to itself and P2; P2 to itself and P3, etc. For this example, only four nodes would be needed.

Hypercubes

In all the previous examples, the processors were always conveniently situated next to the processors with which they needed to communicate. With more complex algorithms, each processor may need to communicate with a greater number of other processors—in the worst case, with all other processors. Since it is not practical to connect each processor to every other processor directly, the processors can pass messages in relay fashion:

```
for a given processor
receive a message
examine the address
if the address = processor ID
   then accept the message
   otherwise passes it on toward the intended recipient.
```

The problem with this approach is that, in an application with many processors, a processor could spend a significant fraction of its time passing messages. In the limiting case it could even deadlock, being unable to process any data at all.

The *hypercube* configuration helps reduce message passing by reducing the length of the paths between nodes. The term hypercube is used because hypercubes may have more (or less) than three dimensions. The concept of a four-dimensional cube is often confusing at first but is easily understood by looking at the relationship between a 3D hypercube (a conventional cube) and a 2D hypercube (a square). The 3D cube is composed of two 2D cubes, connected so that every vertex of one 2D cube is connected to the corresponding vertex of the second 2D cube. For example, assume that the two squares form the top and bottom of a cube. Each corner of the top square is connected to the corresponding corner of the bottom one by a side edge. A one-dimensional cube is a line. A two-dimensional cube is constructed by connecting the end points of two lines. Similarly, to construct a 4D hypercube from two 3D cubes, connect each of the eight vertices of one cube to the corresponding vertex of the other. Figure 16-5 shows several hypercubes.

Picture a cube with a processor at each vertex. A three-dimensional cube would have eight processors. The advantage of a hypercube is that the path length from any given processor to any other processor is kept small and easy to calculate. The path length is the same as the dimensionality of the cube: the log of the number of processors. To see this, consider any two vertices on a cube. The vertices can be connected by a path along the edges of the cube. There is never any reason for a path to traverse two edges within any one dimension because such a path would simply return to the side from which it started. Each vertex differs from the other in three dimensions, so the maximum path length is 3. A four-dimensional hypercube has 16 vertices and a maximum path length of 4.

The calculation of an address for a hypercube is also easy. Consider each node to have an address represented as a binary number between 0 and $2^n - 1$, where n is the dimensionality of the cube. Let each bit position of the address represent a dimension (e.g., left, right, or vertical) and choose the connections so

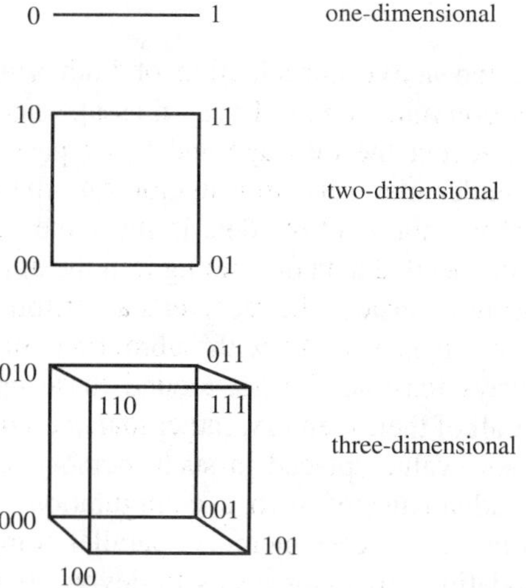

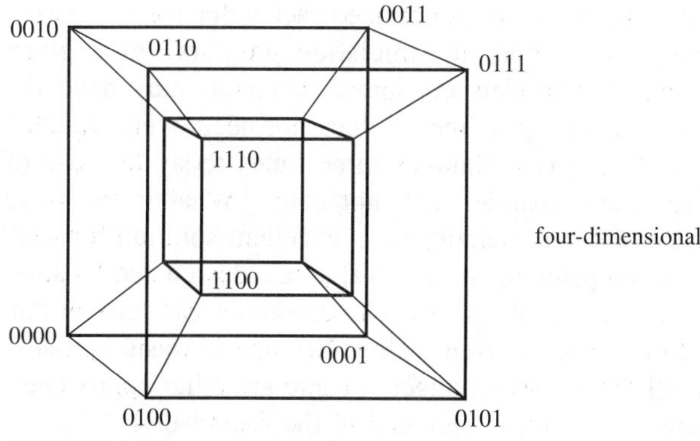

FIGURE 16-5
Hypercubes in one to four dimensions.

that all nodes in a given plane share a common bit. When a message is received, it can be processed by

```
if address = node_number
   then keep and process message
   otherwise
      determine first bit at which they differ
      send message in corresponding direction
```

More complicated topologies are possible, each additional complication bringing some new capability at some additional overhead.

MEMORY ORGANIZATION

Each processor of a parallel machine may have its own memory, or a single memory may be shared between the processors. There are advantages and disadvantages to each approach.

Shared Memory

Message-passing topologies require the active participation of both sender and receiver processors for interprocess communication. Every message necessarily interrupts the receiving processor to accept the message and either pass it on or process it. In some situations, the sender may send information that the receiver does not care about, or the receiver may not want the data in the same order that the sender delivers it. Sending only the needed data or sending it in the appropriate order requires that the sending algorithm consider the receiver's algorithm, or that the receiver explicitly request the data it needs. As with subroutines on single-processor machines, this is not always feasible. To get around these problems, parallel machines could share part or all of their memory, rather than pass messages explicitly from processor to processor. Values placed in such memory would be available to other processors. The advantage of such a configuration, called a *shared-memory,* or *PRAM* (parallel random access memory) parallel computer, is that as data is updated, only the updating processor needs to devote its resource to that action.

In some situations, a given processor does not need each value for a variable, simply the latest one. Consider an economic simulation program. At a given instant, one processor, say one that models consumer behavior, may need the current price of some product, perhaps gasoline. It does not need every updated price, only the current price. If the price changes three times today because of hostilities in the Middle East, the consumer may not care. "What is the price now?" is the important question. Shared memory is an excellent solution for such problems. The price-calculator can place the current value in a designated location within shared memory whenever it has an update. The consumer can look at that location only when it needs to know the current value. No time is wasted passing messages back and forth for all the unused changes. (There are other approaches: an alternative message-passing algorithm is included in the Exercises.)

Of course, shared memory introduces a new set of problems—problems intimately related to the problems introduced by direct memory access forms of I/O (described in Chapter 12). Clearly, if two processors attempt to write to memory at the same time, some mechanism is needed to prevent the result from being gibberish. A simultaneous read and write also cause a problem: is the value read equal to the value before or after the write (or worse, some combination)? Even simultaneous reads can cause a problem if the addresses become merged on the bus. Bus arbitration mechanisms may be more difficult because of the number of processors involved, but more importantly because of the need for clock synchronization between all processors. Although it is not necessary to exclude all concurrent access, most shared-memory systems place restrictions on the nature of the allowable shared access. The common taxonomy of allowable read/write control mechanisms includes the following:

EREW (exclusive read, exclusive write). The easiest to understand strategy is EREW. Each processor must have complete or exclusive control of the bus long enough to complete a read or write operation.

CREW (concurrent read/exclusive write). In the CREW model, a cell is allowed to be read by multiple processors simultaneously, since such concurrency will not alter the answer. As with EREW, simultaneous writes are forbidden, since that could create unreliable values.

CRCW (concurrent read/concurrent write). CRCW is exactly the opposite of EREW: each processor may simultaneously read from, or write to, a given address. This requires that the two processors have separate memory busses. It also raises the question "What does it mean for two processors to write to the same location?" There are usually strict conditions on the legal forms of such writes. One interpretation is that a write operation is only completed if all processors write exactly the same value. Amazingly enough, this interpretation enables some surprisingly fast algorithms. A concurrent write has the logical result equivalent to "if the value from processor 1 equals the value from processor 2 (equals the value from processor 3 . . .), then store the result," but with no explicit conditionals in the code.

A COMPROMISE: BUTTERFLY OR SWITCHING NETWORKS

Greater numbers of processors with access to a given memory location and greater quantities of shared memory both increase the complexity of the processor interconnections. A configuration that may combine the best of both the message-passing and shared-memory worlds is a *butterfly network* (also called a *shuffle network*). Suppose that you have n processors and n memories. Further suppose that there are n*log(n) switches that connect the processors to the memory, as in Figure 16-6. That is, each processor is connected to two switches, and each switch is connected in turn to two more switches (or to memory at the last step). Each switch corresponds to one bit of the memory segment address. In log(n) steps, any processor can reach any one of the n memories. The processors are not inhibited by message passing; memory access is controlled, yet every processor can reach the data in every memory.

ARCHITECTURES: INSTRUCTION AND DATA CONFIGURATIONS

A final classification of parallel machines specifies how closely related the individual CPUs are. Two processors are said to be *tightly coupled* if both run the same code at the same time. The processors share a control unit but have separate ALUs. Many of the preceding examples for pipelines and grid machines used the same (or very similar) code on each processor. All processors need not run the same code. For example, the tree-configuration example seems to run distinct code on each processor. In fact, several variations exist, which are classified along a standard taxonomy. One way to describe the classic von Neumann machine would be as a single-instruction stream, single-data stream (or *SISD*)

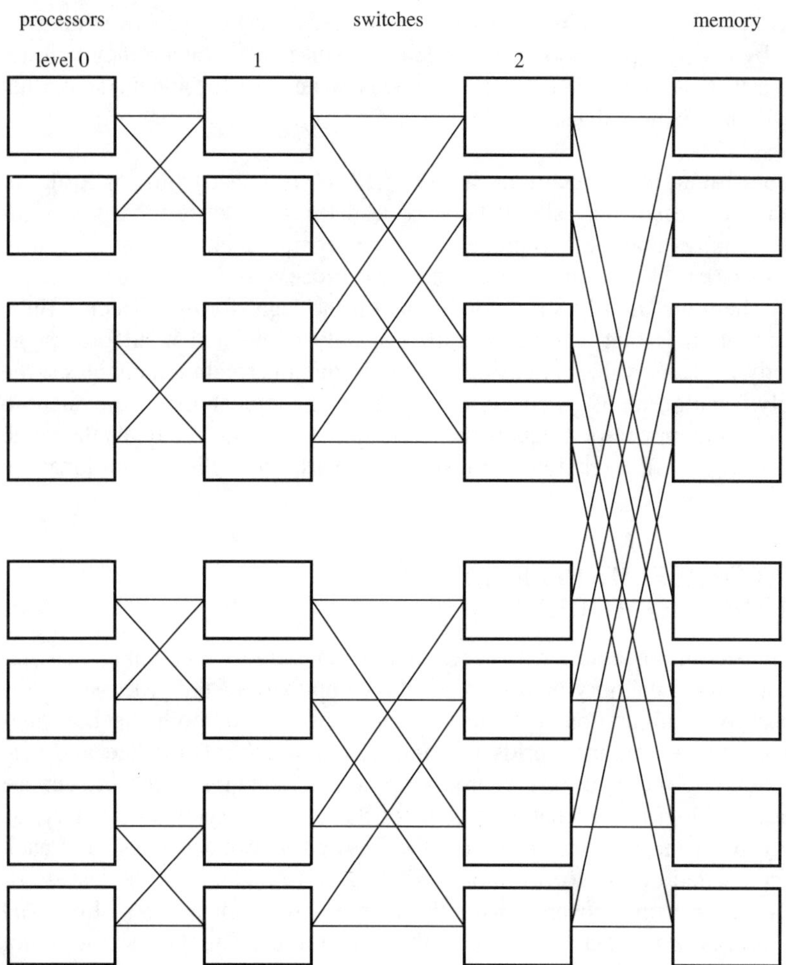

FIGURE 16-6
A butterfly or shuffle-exchange network.

computer. The machine executes a single instruction at a time on a single stream of data. Parallelization could be achieved either by manipulating multiple data items in parallel or executing multiple instructions in parallel, or both. The two most common categories of parallel machine are MIMD and SIMD.

MIMD (multiple instruction, multiple data) (pronounced "mimdy"). Each processor runs its own code on its own data. Each processor is relatively autonomous, although there may be shared-memory mechanisms. MIMD is the least tightly coupled of the parallel configurations. Although the processors described in most of the examples of this chapter ran very similar code, they were described as if each was fully autonomous. The tree and hypercube models may provide the best MIMD examples.

SIMD (single instruction, multiple data) (pronounced "simdy"). Picture one program running on several processors all in "lock step." At any instant, each processor is processing the same instruction, but on a different set of data. This is particularly useful for array processing in which exactly the same logical operations must be applied to each cell of the matrix. The configuration is even much more powerful than it may appear at first. In some SIMD machines, each instruction may really be of the form:

```
if (some logical condition)
   then perform the step
```

where the logical condition may involve the value of the operand and/or the address of the processor. Thus, at a given instant each of the various processors may or may not be performing the current action. Very complicated programs can thus be written in which the steps for each process are a subset of the entire set of instructions. It may sound inefficient to have instructions that are not performed. But with a sufficiently large number of processors, very impressive results are possible. SIMD machines have been built with as many as 64,000 processors (the Connection Machine, built by Thinking Machines Corp.). In such a machine, even if only half of the processors execute each instruction, 32,000 operations are executed concurrently.

Very Large Scale Parallelism

With very large numbers of parallel processors, truly distinct approaches to computation are possible. The models may appear truly distinct from any von Neumann based model. It is possible to think in terms of many processors working together in some very loose configuration. The parts on an automobile work together in a very precise manner, but traffic flows (or doesn't) on the basis of a much looser interconnection. The "market" that controls the price of commodities is the interaction of many forces. Similarly, a parallel computation system may involve many loosely connected machines. Three such approaches are introduced briefly.

ASSOCIATIVE MEMORY MACHINES. Searching is a common and time-consuming task in many computer applications. Consider a database system in which the data record for Jane Doe must be accessible by either name or account number. Many schemes exist to reduce the time needed to search through a large number of records to find the appropriate record. Most such schemes involve continual updates of the database (alphabetized list for binary search), empty space (hash coding), or redundant data. One approach uses an alternative model of memory, called *associative memory* (a related concept appeared in the context of cache memory). Functionally, traditional memory could be described as a black box into which data could be stored and retrieved. For retrieval, a program sends memory an address, A. Memory returns the content, V, of the location A. In associative memory, the function can be thought of as exactly the reverse. The processor sends a value, V, to memory. Memory returns the address, A, where the value is stored.

To see how this could be useful, think of an associative memory as organized into records of two parts: key and data. A program can pass a candidate key value to memory, and the memory returns the location of the key. Since the key and data are stored as a record, the address of the key provides address of the data. For example, when "Jane Doe" is passed to the memory, the entire associative memory is searched in parallel and the address of the string "Jane Doe" is returned. Since the additional information about her account is stored next to her name, it can easily be retrieved once the address of the key is known. In reality, a pointer to the rest of the record is all that is normally saved with the key, enabling more records to be kept in associative memory and processed in parallel.

DATA FLOW COMPUTERS. The *data flow* model of computation (not to be confused with data flow diagrams—a technique used in systems analysis) assumes that there are many small processors. Each processor performs an operation not when it is instructed to do so, as in conventional machines, but when it has data on which to perform the operation. For example, a data flow machine that proved De Morgan's law might be configured as in Figure 16-7.

> ▷ *Does the data flow look strangely like a circuit to perform the same calculation?*

No commercial data flow machines are yet available. The significant problem inhibiting the development of data flow computers is that of delivering the data to the desired location. The illustrations in the figure seem to imply that the data flow machine is somehow hardwired, which would be fine if the computer would be used for one and only one (unchanging) purpose. For practical situations, an additional feature called a distribution network must be added. The distribution network must deliver the results to the desired location. Since the destination

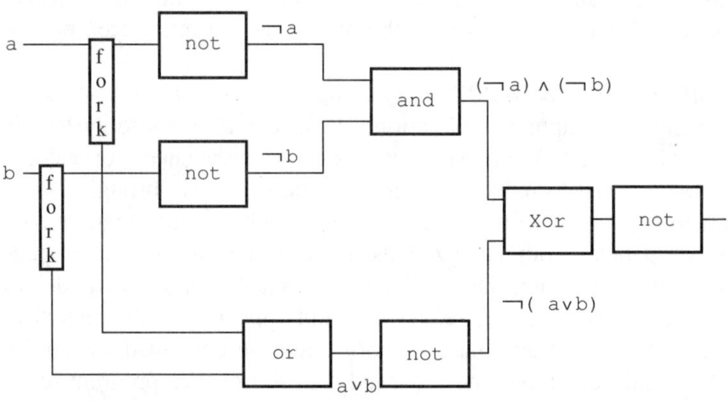

FIGURE 16-7
A data flow program to demonstrate De Morgan's law.

could be anywhere in the system, some delivery mechanism is needed. Some set of processors is used to deliver intermediate data (make it "flow") from the point where it is calculated to the point where it is needed. Perhaps they are arranged in a configuration reminiscent of the butterfly machine. It is obvious that programming data flow machines will require languages very distinct from the imperative languages that most of us are used to.

NEURAL NETS. A second radical departure from von Neumann architectures is inspired by models of the neural interconnections within an animate brain. Not only do the interconnections seem to be more important than the calculations of any one node, but the machines seem to be able to "learn"—an ability normally thought of as human, or at least animate. Neural nets require very large numbers of simple processors, although most work to date simulates the full network on relatively few processors. Communication between processors consists of simple activations or inhibitions, rather than more complex symbols used in most systems. Programs in a neural net are characterized by the interconnections between processors, rather than by the steps each process executes.

EFFICIENCY

Unfortunately, life is not quite as simple as all of these good ideas might suggest. In reality it is very hard to realize the ideal speedup. Using N processors may not produce results N times as fast (in fact, *Amdahl's law* states, in essence, that there is always a point beyond which it is useless to add additional processors). The best improvement that one could hope for with N processors would be a speedup of N times. That is, if it takes T seconds with one processor, the ideal time using N processors is

$$T_n = T/N$$

Generally, there are portions of a program that cannot be speeded up. If only a portion of the program involved parallelizable loops, there will be times when some of the processors are idle, waiting for a chance to perform a calculation. The *efficiency* of the program is the ratio of the actual speedup realized to the ideal speedup possible with N processors. An efficiency of 1 means that the added processors were fully utilized. There are at least two factors—other than simply the nature of the algorithm—why efficiencies will often be less than 1. First, not all programs—or parts of programs—lend themselves to parallelization. For example, consider the code

```
input     (a);
assign    b⇐a²;
assign    c⇐2* b;
```

Clearly the second step cannot be started until the first step is complete, and the third must await the second. This sequence of steps is said to be inherently sequential—it cannot be parallelized. In such a case, the theoretical optimum is less than 1. Second, the overhead of communication or coordination between the processors requires additional steps not present in sequential processes. These physical and logical constraints will drive many of the design choices for parallel architectures.

It is not a trivial task to recognize situations in which computations can be parallelized. There are at least three general approaches to parallelizing the code:

- programmer-controlled parallel processes. The programmer explicitly indicates which parts of the program can be run in parallel and which cannot. Such programming can be written in specialized languages designed explicitly for parallel programming (e.g., Occam, Linda) or using parallel variations of existing sequential languages (Parallel C, Concurrent Pascal). Either way, this nontrivial task is left to the programmer.
- Parallelizing compilers can detect situations in which code segments can be run in parallel. Such compilers are necessarily very conservative: it is better to miss a chance for parallelization than to incorrectly parallelize a segment that cannot be correctly parallelized. To envision the problem, consider two expressions involving array elements A[i] and A[j]. There is no way to determine in advance if these two expressions might ever refer to the same data item.
- Some computer scientists advocate totally new approaches to programming that will facilitate parallel computation. Typically, these approaches involve non-imperative language paradigms such as logic, functional, object-oriented, or constraint-based approaches.

SUMMARY

Multiple processors can be connected together to run in parallel. Several topologies exist for connecting the machines, including pipelines, arrays or grids, tree structures, and hypercubes. Communication between machines can be accomplished either through shared memory or message passing. In the case of shared memory, access can be concurrent or exclusive. Processors may share the control unit, in which case they are said to be tightly coupled (SIMD) or they may have fully independent processors (MIMD). Leading-edge concepts include associate memory, neural nets, and data flow machines.

SUGGESTED READING

Akl, S. *The design and analysis of parallel algorithms*. Englewood Cliffs, N. J.: Prentice Hall, 1989.

Almasi, G., & A. Gottlieb. *Highly parallel computing*. Redwood City, Calif.: Benjamin/Cummings, 1989.

DeCegana, A. *Parallel processing architectures and VLSI hardware,* volume 1. Englewood Cliffs, N. J.: Prentice Hall, 1989.

Hoare, C. *Communicating sequential processes*. Englewood Cliffs, N. J.: Prentice Hall, 1980.

Hockney, R. and C. Jesshope, *Parallel computers 2*. Philadelphia: Adam Hilgar, 1988.

EXERCISES

16.1. Describe how a tree organization might be useful (a) in a language such as Prolog or (b) in theorem proving.

16.2. Consider the gasoline price/consumer model used as an introduction to shared memory. The message-passing algorithms discussed included mostly unsolicited messages. An alternative to either shared memory or frequent unneeded message passing would be requested information only. The price-calculator processor keeps its own updated gas price. When the consumer needs to know the value, it asks the price calculator for the latest value by sending it a request message. The calculator responds to the request by sending back the price. Discuss the pros and cons of such a system.

16.3. Discuss the impact of the use of global variables upon a compiler that must detect situations in which the code can be parallelized.

16.4. Systolic algorithms on single-input pipeline topologies are very common (the only example given in the text of a one-dimensional systolic process had multiple-input processors). Describe a systolic algorithm to calculate

sqrt (log ((n^2) * (e^n)))

for a series of values of n, using a four-processor pipeline.

16.5. What new problems will the programmer face on parallel machines?

16.6. Write an algorithm for N processors that calculates all of the primes less than N^2. *Hint:* if it's prime, it is not divisible by n for any $n < N$.

16.7. Suppose you have a tree-structured set of processors. What is the maximum distance a message would have to travel from one processor to another?

16.8. Suppose you have a linear array of processors, numbered 1 to N. Suppose every message includes a destination address. Write an algorithm that runs on processor i. It should receive messages, check to see where they are addressed, and either keep them or pass them on.

16.9. Write an algorithm similar to that in Exercise 16.8, but for a four-dimensional hypercube.

16.10. How many nodes in a five-dimensional hypercube?

16.11. Suppose you were building an optimizing compiler that accepted a typical (sequential) hll and produced parallel code for the language. What are some of the techniques that you could use to recognize sections of code that could be parallelized?

16.12. Suppose you were redefining Hill to create Par-Hill-el, a language that allowed the user to specify parallel processes. What structures would you add to the language?

16.13. Suppose you were designing a debugger for parallel programs. What extra features would you want to add? What extra problems would you face? What new errors could occur?

16.14. What impact would parallel computation have on the assembly or machine language? Would the type of parallelism make a difference?

APPENDIX 1

ASSEMBLY LANGUAGE STRUCTURE AND STYLE GUIDE

Your best protection against errors starts with the development of a very careful programming style. You should begin now to develop habits that lead to programs that are both easy to read and easy to debug. While the physical appearance of a program does not necessarily mean that you are approaching the problem correctly, carefully structured and documented programs are easier both to read and to debug. Additionally, you will find that attention to style actually reduces the number of errors that you make. Although many of the rules provided here may appear to be dogmatic and to require extra time, it is time well spent. The *total time* spent creating a program that runs correctly will actually be shorter if you follow these rules diligently. The time to follow these guidelines is *while you are writing the program:* Never write a sloppy program, intending to "clean it up later." The intent of demanding programs that look good is that paying attention to detail forces you to get both the general algorithm and the "little" points correct. This is especially important in assembly language programming since the language does little to help protect you. The rules are not designed simply to produce pretty code; they will help you get the program written easily and quickly.

These structure and style guidelines were prepared in the dogmatic style of the early chapters of the text. The guidelines are intended to provide a solid basis for starting to program in assembly language. The rules are all typical of those used in computer science courses at colleges and universities. They are similar to many that you will find in industry. You will seldom go wrong by following these rules in your initial explorations of assembly language. Later, as you explore more exotic aspects of assembly language, you will discover situations in which you will want to vary the structure.

Some rules will not be comprehensible at early points in the course, and some will not even be relevant at first. As you progress through the book, more and more of the guidelines will make sense. It is a good idea to review them periodically.

Comments

Comments are essential—all programs should be well-documented. Remember that assembly language programs are harder to understand than higher-level language programs; therefore, documentation is even more critical.

1. HEADING. Begin all programs with a block comment, which should include the following:

A brief title for the program;

The author's name;

The date written and last revised;

A brief description of the problem and what the program does, giving information about complex algorithms and outside references;

A description of the input required by the program and the output that it produces;

A description of important data structures (e.g., tables, lists, stacks, queues, etc.) used in the program.

Other important information such as registers used, global variables, etc.

Similar but less extensive documentation should be given at the beginning of *each module, procedure, or function*. The author's name need not be given if it is the same as for the main program. Procedure and function documentation should describe *what* the routine does, and *how* it does it (if it is not clear from the body of the routine). Additionally it should indicate the expected parameters, how they are to be passed and the role of each parameter. Pre- and post-conditions make excellent documentation for procedures.

2. PROCEDURES AND FUNCTIONS. Subprograms with good documentation in the heading should require relatively few comments within their bodies. Comments within program segments should be used sparingly to describe what is being done, *why* particular actions are taken, or what *conditions* are true at that point in the program. The "how" should be apparent from the program or the description at the beginning of the procedure, function, or program. *If you find that you need many comments within program segments, take that to be a sign that your program is probably not well-organized.* Start by creating smaller procedures or modules.

3. DECLARATIONS. In the variable and constant declaration section of your program, procedure, or function, use comments to *describe all variables* individually, e.g.,

```
sum  variable:integer    ;running sum of all input values
done variable:character ;indicates if last item has been
                        ;read
```

4. ORGANIZATION. Arrange your comments *neatly.* When comments occupy several lines, each line should start in the same column. Note that assembly language comments come in two "flavors": full line and annotation (right end only).

Full line comments are easier to read. Use them to describe *blocks* of code. Precede each block of code with a block of comments describing the general function of the section. Use the right-hand annotation only to explain minor details about individual lines, such as reminders of the role of a variable. Never simply repeat what the code says. If the statement is "`Add  a ⇒ b`", do not annotate it by writing "add a to b." This is obvious to any reader. Instead write "B now contains the total income."

Place an emphasis on *why* a statement or block of statements is there rather than precisely what it does. What a statement does can be seen by inspection; why the programmer wanted to cannot!

5. PROGRAM STRUCTURE. "Mark" the "end" statement for each "compound statement" with a comment or label.

```
    jump:greater    →else_part
then_part
    <statement>
    <statement>
    jump:always     →next_statement
else_part
    <statement>
    <statement>
                 ;end of conditional
next_statement ...
```

Variables and Constants

6. NAMES. Use descriptive names for all variables and constants. One or two letter names will almost never accomplish this. Make your program readable (as much like English as possible)!

7. CONSTANTS. Declare constants when the meaning is not absolutely obvious.

```
add     #80→reg0
```

is not nearly as clear as

```
add     line_length⇒reg0
```

Generally, programs should contain few numeric literals other than 0 or 1 outside of the definition section. Constants and equates make your program more readable by making the purpose of statements involving the constant clearer. Also, changes and corrections often are easier if the constant has been declared because a single change can correct every usage of that value.

8. LOCAL VARIABLES. Global variables should always be avoided in procedures or functions. The only storage locations that should be used in procedures or functions are the formal parameters, local variables, and special-purpose structures (e.g., the chess board in a chess program).

Organization and Readability

9. WHITESPACE. Use blank lines to break a program into logical segments (much like paragraphs). For example, separate each block of code from its data section by a blank line. A blank line should also be used to set off a section of a program unit (main program, procedure, or function) from the preceding portion. Liberal use of white space improves readability. In general, include blank lines to separate

- logically separate portions
- data manipulation segments from control segments
- program from data
- blocks of comments from blocks of code

Some programmers like to separate procedures or collections of procedures with a line of stars, for example,

```
*********** stack procedures and functions***********
```

You may also find is clearer to use blank lines to set off "`begin-end`" blocks and other logically self-contained sections, such as separating control structures from loop bodies.

10. LENGTH. Keep the program units (functions and procedures) short. The average length should be equivalent to no more than 10 to 15 Pascal lines, excluding the declarations, comments, etc. Program bodies (from the `begin` statement to the `end` statement) that exceed what can be seen on the screen at one time are often too complex to be easily understood. If your routines are consistently longer, they are too long. Some procedure and function bodies may be quite short when used to hide the implementation of a data structure.

Input/Output

11. ECHO-INPUT. If there is any possibility that the value of keyboard input data may not be read correctly, it should be displayed (echoed) immediately upon input.

12. INTERMEDIATE VALUES. Output intermediate checkpoints if there is any doubt as to the accuracy of the answers.

13. OUTPUT. Make sure that all output is clear, labeled, well-organized, and readable. Tables and lists of values should be well-structured (e.g., in neat columns).

14. USER INSTRUCTIONS. Interactive programs should provide the user with complete information (in the output) about what the program does and how to use it. When input is called for, useful messages should be printed to tell the user what values are being requested and in what form. Remember, the user may not be able to see the actual code!

Miscellaneous

15. CONTROL STRUCTURE. Use only control structures that have higher-level language equivalents—unless there is a compelling reason to do otherwise.

16. TRICKS. Given the choice of being tricky or clear, *always be clear.* The millisecond you save will never be noticed; the extra hour of confusion will be. If your program is to be run thousands of times, you can easily optimize it later if the original code is well-written.

17. INDENTATION. Always indent loops, conditional structures, procedures, etc. Take control of the appearance of structure by selecting a format that reflects your intent.

18. SYMBOLS. Use EQUates, macros, subroutines, standard structures, and any other tools you can find to improve structure and increase readability.

19. ERRORS. Anticipate errors. Provide trace information in your program at the time that you write it.

20. VIOLATIONS. Violation of these rules should reflect a deliberate and conscious action. There are valid reasons for violating the rules, but you should be *very* aware that your action may cause confusion. You should weigh the pros and cons before violating these rules. That's what guidelines are for, after all: to provide a generally safe path.

APPENDIX 2

TERM PROJECTS

Learn by experience—preferably other people's
found in fortune cookie

I hear; I forget
I see; I remember
I do; I understand
Chinese proverb

The approach of this text assumes that the primary reason for computer scientists to learn assembly language is as a tool for the exploration of the inner workings of a machine. Implicit in that assumption is a second assumption: learning requires doing. Most students learn more during the laboratory phase than during the textbook phase of a course. Therefore, the organization of the text provides most or all of the essential knowledge of assembler language in the first half, allowing the later chapters to explore lower-level details with the aid of the language. Two common approaches for student exploration are

- a term project
- a coordinated semester-long series of projects.

The first of these projects, the emulator, has been tested at three colleges, using three different machines and four different assemblers; the second at two colleges.

PROJECT I. BUILD AN EMULATOR FOR THE GEM MACHINE

Write a program in the real assembly language for your machine (referred to here as the *host* machine) that emulates the GEM CPU at the clock-pulse level. That is, your program should simulate the fetch/execute cycle for the entire GEM machine (or an appropriate subset; see "variations"). Each substep should be simulated in the appropriate order; each movement of data between the registers and the bus; each ALU action; etc. Building the emulation requires three major steps.

a. Build a clock-pulse level description

Write a description of the fetch/execute cycle for the GEM language. For each instruction, describe all substeps required. The steps should accurately reflect the fetch/execute cycle and memory restrictions. For example, it should use the wait time during the instruction fetch to update the PC. The level should be such that any two events occurring at a single clock pulse will not interfere. You may assume either that the number of clock pulses is constant for all instructions or that a clock pulse represents a single event. Be sure to distinguish between any two events that cannot occur simultaneously. (Note that the goal of this section is to create a description of everything that the first step must be able to do. Care at this point will save grief later.)

b. Build a "box"

You need a box to house your processor. It will serve two purposes:

> it is the interface between your emulated processor and the human user, and it provides the system-level support tools.

The reason for building the box first is that it becomes your tool for debugging the "hardware" as you build it. The visible box includes the following physical display items:

REGISTERS. It should contain feedback to the human user in the form of register displays. For each GEM register, the display should indicate the current content of the register. Ideally, the display is a row of "lights," each light corresponding to one bit of the register. (An alternative, which will be better for some host machines: display the hex values contained in the registers.) Display the general purpose registers, the IR, PC, and status registers.

CONTROL BUTTONS. The user must be able to control the GEM machine. The box contains "buttons" for this control. Ideally, the user pushes the button by using a mouse. For machines without a mouse, use short commands:

Start: starts the fetch/execute cycle running.

Trace: like start but only allows one f/e cycle.

Stop: terminates execution of the cycle (results are identical to the `halt` command).

Power: Turns the power off (ends the emulation program).

Reboot: "restarts" the emulation program by resetting the PC and starting.

Display memory: acts like the fetch instruction cycle, but does not execute.

SCREEN. Any output from the program should be displayed on GEM's screen—a subsection of your host machine's screen.

INPUT/OUTPUT SUPPORT. Your program should provide the system-level I/O interface. Use the I/O port method. If the host keyboard is pressed, deliver the character to the GEM input port; if the GEM user program places data in the GEM output port, display it on the GEM screen. Your box program has the responsibility of communicating with external devices according to the commands of programs written in GEML. Use the I/O ports as follows:

0–1: keyboard input (even byte is status, odd the data)

2–3: screen output

4–5: boot device

KEYBOARD. Use your real keyboard as an input device to GEM.

BOOT DEVICE. (Optional) You should pick a default external file (device and file name) from which your boot program loads a systemless program to run. The box routine should open the host file on the boot device. Place your boot program in simulated ROM, starting at GEM memory location 10. The box program should initialize the GEM PC to point to location 10. The user and the boot program should both assume that the user program will begin at location 100_{16}.

Test each of the individual components of the box. For at least one register, display the value held in the corresponding internal location. Make sure you can detect the buttons when they are pressed. Write a short string to the GEM screen. Accept a keyboard input and deliver it to the GEM input port.

c. Build the internal GEM machine

Your program must represent the component parts of the GEM machine and the processes manipulating those parts. For example, each GEM storage location such as the PC should be represented by a host storage location (probably called `gem_pc` to keep it distinct from the PC of your machine). Each of the ALU's can be represented by a short procedure that finds its arguments in the locations `source_1` and `source_2` and leaves its output in result. Each clock pulse can be designated by a labeled statement. Your program should perform each of the f/e substeps determined in step a. For example, at clock pulse 1, it should send (copy) the contents of the PC onto the bus and load (copy) the value from the bus to the MAR (it could simultaneously send it to `source_1` to be incremented). Steps like "decode" are sometimes confusing. A hardware decoder selects the operation in a single step. The closest analogy in a program is a jump table. You may prefer to use a case structure.

GENERAL OUTLINE. The following general outline of the overall program structure will help get you started:

```
while (power on) do
  update box
    (update registers)
    (check I/O)
  in any button has been pressed
    respond to the button
  if in run state
    run one f/e cycle
```

Notes and simplifying assumptions

Operands set. You may simplify the GEM instruction set without sacrificing any general principles. Suggestions: (1) eliminate the addressing modes by eliminating the direction bit for all instructions other than `copy`. Assume the destination is always the register operand. Most other mode options can also be eliminated: indirect, immediate, number of RAM operands (although you may again wish to allow several modes for `copy`. (The test data provided assumes unidirectional commands, and no immediate, but does allow indirect addressing.)

Instruction set. You could also reduce the instruction set to eight instructions and a trap:

```
1   0001   Copy
2   0010   Load_address
3   0011   Trap
4   0100   jump (allow indirect; assume all ops set CCR)
6   0110   jump to Subroutine
8   1000   Add (build all other arith ops from add & not)
C   1100   And
E   1110   Not
F   1111   Rotate
```

This instruction set is sufficient for writing minimal programs but is very inconvenient (for example, notice that the return from subroutine will require an indirect branch). You may wish to simply ignore the `trap` instruction, implementing all others.

Memory. The CPU does not control memory. Emulation of memory is problematic for many students. There is no way to represent the fact that a memory fetch occurs concurrently with other CPU actions. Nor does the CPU have any control over when a requested value actually arrives in the CPU. Your program should place a value in the MAR and call a memory-fetch routine—but not use the value from the MBR until it can realistically be expected to be available. Assume that a memory fetch requires three clock pulses.

Registers. You may wish to reduce the number of registers, more to reduce screen clutter than any program logic that may be saved. Also, you may assume that the stack pointer is one of the numbered registers (since GEM instructions do not include SP as an addressable register).

Status register. Preferably, the zero and negative bits should be set by any command that alters register content. You may restrict this action to the compare command. However, there is no compare in the restricted instruction set, so you will have to set the bits for all commands if you use that set. The status register should also contain a run bit that indicates whether or not the machine is running. The trace, start, and run buttons, as well as the halt instruction, should all set this bit.

Stack. The boot program should set the system stack pointer before handing control to the user.

Trace, halt, and stop. The trace button is your greatest debugging tool—use it. Note that the trace button, the halt command, and the stop button all turn the run bit of the status register off.

Display memory button. You can use this button for stepping through memory to observe the results of your running program. If you also create a "load PC button", you can gain additional flexibility.

Variation: `trap`. The trap instruction could be used to provide I/O services, `trap 0` meaning input and `trap 1` meaning output. In this case, the system housekeep should take care of all aspects of the I/O. The user program would not be expected to check the status byte.

PROJECT II. CALCULATOR: A MULTI-STEP PROJECT

This project is a series of individual projects. Each project builds on the previous one. Each successive project requires a slightly better understanding of computer organization. As such, the mini-projects can be written successively as a course progresses. (Each mini-project includes an indication of the chapter material assumed.)

Mini-Project 0: Pascal Calculator (Optional Starting Point, Chapter 1)

Write a higher-level language program that functions as a calculator. It prompts the user for two numbers separated by an operation, performs the operation, and prints out the result. It should continue performing calculations as long as the user requests them. This project can serve as a guideline for the following ones.

Mini-Project 1: Single-digit Calculator (Chapter 2)

Read in two small single-digit numbers, echo the numbers to the screen with a "+" between them, and write the sum. Note that "small" as used here means such that the sum of the two numbers is a single digit (i.e., less than 10). The only "trick" required here uses the fact that the character representations of digits are in numerical order, as expressed in Hill by the relationships:

```
numeric_value(digit) = ord(digit) - ord('0')
```

and

```
character_rep(small_num) = char(ord('0') + small_num)
```

Mini-Project 2: Controlled Calculator (Chapter 3)

Modify the adder to detect illegal digits and to allow the user to enter multiple pairs of numbers to be added. If an input character is not a digit, the program should print 'x' rather than echoing the value, and should skip the answer. It should terminate when both input values are zero.

Mini-Project 3: Multiple Digits (Chapter 4)

Allow multiple-digit input and output values. Convert the input stream to binary using the multiplicative method. Assume that all numbers (input and output) are less than 32K. Convert the result to a string of output digits using a modified subtraction method: start with the assumption that the sum requires no more than five digits; divide the sum by 10^4 to find the first digit. You may include the leading zeros in your answer. Don't forget that input and output are characters, but arithmetic is binary.

Mini-Project 4: More Control (Chapter 5)

Allow larger numbers without leading zeros and provide prompting messages to the user. You can use the division algorithm to allow arbitrarily large numbers (up to a limit imposed by your machine) for output by using a stack (recall that the division algorithm generated the output digits in reverse order, so you will need a stack). Printing messages requires a subroutine that accepts a pointer to an array containing the message. Your program should produce multiple messages, such as 'welcome instructions,' 'continue questions,' and 'thank you closings.'

Mini-Project 5: Multiple Operations (Chapter 5)

Allow multiple operations on input. Add exponentiation, a^b (input as $a\,\hat{}\,b$) as a legal operation. A simple case statement can enable multiple operations. The exponentiation requires a subroutine rather than a single-step operation.

Variation. Use a recursive subroutine to calculate the exponential value.

Mini-Project 6: Large Numbers (Chapter 8)

Some machines restrict the operands of multiplication or the quotient of division. These restrictions may limit the straightforward application of the conversion algorithms. For example, the 68000 restricts the operands of multiplication to 16 bits, even though legal products can be very large (32 bits). Since the multiplicative algorithm multiplies by 10 (for conversion from decimal), the largest number that you can input by straightforward application of the algorithm is about 650,000. Output runs into the analogous problem with division. You can get around the problem by using the observation that you can break a number into two parts: high-order and low-order. For example, if a number is broken into two 16-bit chunks `num_lo` and `num_hi`, you can multiply the number by 10 using the relationship:

$$num * 10 = (10 * num\_lo) + (10 * num\_hi * 2^{16})$$

The only problem is the multiplication by 2^{16}, since that number will not quite fit into 16 bits. This problem is solved using the observation that shifting 16 bits to the left is equivalent to multiplying by 2^{16}. So the product

$$(10 * num\_hi * 2^{16})$$

becomes

$$\textit{Shift } (10 * num\_hi) 16 \textit{ bit positions}$$

It may also be solved by very careful placement of operands in memory. The output depends on the observation that a large number, say 123456789 can be broken into two segments

12345 and 6789

by dividing and "`moding`" by 10,000.

Mini-Project 7: Digital Logic (Chapter 9)

Replace the (single-step) `add` operation of the calculator with an emulation a digital adder. Your emulation should reflect the logic of the cascading adder described in Chapter 9. That is, it should accept two numbers and add them together bit by bit, calling a half adder (also an emulation) twice for each bit position. Neither the adder routine nor the half-adder routine should contain any additions. The control algorithm for the adder is

for each bit position i (right to left)
  half-add a_i and b_i
  half-add sum_i and $carry_{i-1}$

Optional. Set the negative, zero, and overflow bits of the condition-code register according to the results of the addition.

Mini-Project 8: Floating Point (Chapter 14)

Modify the program to accept floating-point numbers. You will assume that all input will be of the form: `ddd.ddd`. That is, there will always be an integer and a fractional part. Your program should convert the input to standard real format. If your machine has either built-in floating-point hardware or a co-processor, you may use that, or you may call a library floating-point arithmetic routine. After performing the arithmetic, you should convert it to a suitable form for output. *Warning:* this problem is much harder than it may appear at first.

Optional variations. (*a*) Allow scientific notation forms of input (e.g., 1.23E+5) and output. (*b*) Build the subroutines to perform the arithmetic.

PROJECT III. A MICROCODE EMULATION (A VARIATION ON PROJECT I)

Perform an emulation as described in Project I, but as an emulation of a microcoded machine rather than a machine constructed from digital logic. Use a modified top-down approach. Create a series of logical steps that should interpret a sequence of GEM statements. The steps should resemble horizontal microcode instructions: specifying sources and destinations, micro-operations, branch targets, and conditions. Build subroutines or macros corresponding to each of the needed micro-operators. Your program should interpret the microcode program and call the appropriate subroutines.

Ideally, your microcode emulation will be written as a series of macros or subroutine calls. Unfortunately, the branch associated with each micro-instruction creates nasty complication for subroutines: subroutines always expect to have a single return address. One way around the problem is to pass the (address of the) alternative destination as an argument to the subroutine. The subroutine can "return" by branching to the address specified in the destination argument if it first removes the regular return address from the stack. Macros may provide a straightforward emulation technique, depending on the allowable forms on your machine. As in Project I, each part of the machine—registers, ALUs, etc.—should be emulated. You should create the same "box," etc. The only distinction is the mechanism by which you accomplish the substeps of each GEM instruction.

Note that this project has three parts: (*a*) definition of a suitable microcode, (*b*) construction of the microcode machine, and (*c*) the microcode emulation of the GAL machine.

Variation. Attempt a Thin-GAL emulation (see Exercise 15.9).

PROJECT IV. AN ASSEMBLER OR DISASSEMBLER

The correspondence between machine language and assembly language is straightforward. Write a program to perform the conversion.

Assembler

Write your program in the "real" assembly language available for your machine. Your assembler should be able to read an arbitrary program written in the generic assembly language and create the corresponding generic object code. Assume that only single-module programs will be used (i.e., there is no linker).

Note that the purpose of the project is to explore the relationships between the abstract models at the assembly and machine language levels; it is not to create the world's most efficient assembler.

Hints:

1. Agree to some simplifying assumptions, such as

Maximum length for an identifier: eight characters

Syntax: every field terminates with a blank or a comma

Modes are specified by leading markers (e.g., ^ in *front* of the operand name for indirect)

Reduce the complexity of GEM (fewer registers, fewer modes, max program length)

Specify a limited number of directives (variable, constant, end)

Produce only very limited assembler error messages

2. Start by building a collection of input and helper routines, such as

get_string (reads in a series of characters, until some terminator is encountered. It should return a pointer to the string) skip_white_space (skips all white space up to the next "interesting piece of input")

identify (finds a given identifier in a list of identifiers)

3. Note that GAL and GEM are very regular in format: all GEM instructions are the same length; GAL syntax is uniform (differing only in the number of legal operands).
4. The two passes are relatively easy to create because all instructions are the same size.

Disassembler

It should take a GEM program and build the corresponding GAL program. Clearly, there is no way to generate the original variable names—nor the comments. But GAL statements logically equivalent to the GEM statements should be possible.

Hints:

1. Generating variable names is somewhat of a problem. Two possible solutions: (*a*) Pre-generate a list of dummy names, such as `var1`, `var2`, and so on. Assign the first name to the first address encountered, the second to the next, and so on. (*b*) Create a function, Generate_symbol, which returns a new symbol every time it is called. The names it generates could be the same as above: `var1`, `var2`, etc. Again, you might find it helpful to establish an upper limit—say, 99 variables.
2. Recall that GEM uses absolute addresses, so each GEM address corresponds to a unique GAL identifier or statement.
3. You may assume that all instructions are legal. That is, once you have verified that the source is in a register, you can ignore the immediate bit.

PAIRED PROJECTS

In a paired project, two students each complete a project that, when complete, must interact with the other. Such paired projects help create a sense of real-world compatibility problems.

The assembler and disassembler projects could work together as a paired project. One student's program must disassemble the output of an assembler created by the other. The final output should be equivalent to the input originally given to the assembler (modulo variable names and comments, of course).

Similarly the assembler project could be used to create input for the emulator project. The microprogrammed project could be divided into two subprojects: microengine and microprogram.

INDEX